Shared Stages

SUNY series in Modern Jewish Literature and Culture
Sarah Blacher Cohen, editor

Shared Stages

Ten American Dramas of Blacks and Jews

Edited and with an Introduction by

Sarah Blacher Cohen

and

Joanne B. Koch

STATE UNIVERSITY OF NEW YORK PRESS

Cover image: CMCD

Published by
State University of New York Press, Albany

© 2007 State University of New York

All rights reserved

Printed in the United States of America

For information, contact State University of New York Press, Albany, NY
www.sunypress.edu

Production by Judith Block
Marketing by Fran Keneston

Library of Congress Cataloging-in-Publication Data

Shared stages : ten American dramas of Blacks and Jews / edited and with
    an introduction by Sarah Blacher Cohen and Joanne B. Koch.
        p. cm. — (SUNY series in modern Jewish literature and culture)
    Includes bibliographical references.
    ISBN 978-0-7914-7281-1 (alk. paper)
    ISBN 978-0-7914-7282-8 (pbk. : alk. paper)
    1. American drama—African American authors. 2. American drama—
Jewish authors. 3. African Americans—Drama. 4. Jews—Drama.
5. American drama—20th century. 6. American drama—21st century.
I. Cohen, Sarah Blacher. II. Koch, Joanne B.

PS628.N4S53 2007
812'.54080896073   2007005606

10 9 8 7 6 5 4 3 2 1

Contents

Acknowledgments

The idea for an anthology of plays about African Americans and Jews began with our observations of classroom inter-group tensions, unmistakable beneath the mask of twenty-first century political correctness. In our work at two universities, Sarah at the University at Albany, State University of New York, and Joanne at National-Louis University in Chicago and Evanston, we noticed two conflicting trends. On the one hand, many groups on campus had developed enough sense of separate identity to reach out to others in significant multicultural activities. On the other hand, there was a suspicion of "the other," a resistance to dialogue. This negativity undermined the kind of empathy that had, in the sixties, been more prevalent on university campuses and was trying to emerge once more. So we really have our students to thank initially, particularly those who were forthright about their concerns, who tried to develop greater respect for diversity in the classroom and beyond.

James Peltz, Acting Director of the State University of New York Press, immediately welcomed the idea of an anthology of plays about Blacks and Jews. With his keen editorial eye, he recognized the intrinsic merit of the project and marshaled his staff to give it the attention he thought it deserved. The Lucius N. Littauer Foundation and William Lee Frost, its president, provided a generous grant to assist in the production of the book. Not only have they helped us but they have been especially important in developing the critical canon of Jewish American literature.

We were motivated by the inspiring works of the playwrights who eventually became part of this collection. Each work was another argument for the effort to bring shared experiences to theater audiences, and through this book to readers everywhere.

The willingness of Anna Deavere Smith to take on the personae of African Americans and Jews in the Crown Heights conflict of 1991 motivated us to select plays that would show a wide spectrum of relationships. Alfred Uhry was the first of the playwrights to allow his outstanding play to be part of our collection. He liked the idea and encouraged us to seek out other plays that would deal with Black-Jewish relations. John Henry Redwood, while presenting the plight of a Jewish man confronting rabid anti-Semitism so believably, demonstrated enormous sensitivity in his depiction of African American women. Knowing that he died with so many other plays unwritten, we regard his contribution as particularly precious. The late Herb Gardner generously consented to give our collection the benefit of his priceless comedy. Michael Henry Brown provided us with a work that toughly confronts and undercuts Black and Jewish stereotypes. OyamO contributed a play that is unique in depicting the ordinary Black man's struggle for dignity in the days surrounding the assassination of Dr. Martin Luther King, Jr., and the ways in which Jews shared in that struggle. Barbara Lebow forced us to look at the peace-loving sixties, with Black and Jew marching arm in arm, through the lens of the disillusioned nineties. Tom Cole dramatized the gulf that separates the Jewish person in the helping professions from the Black veteran raised in an urban ghetto, and Lewis John Carlino demonstrated that race, gender, age and economic differences might be overcome by the simple human need for companionship.

Informing our choices of these plays were the individuals who had shaped our view that stages could be shared in ways that would entertain, disturb, uplift and electrify theater audiences. Among these are African American playwright Steve Carter, Chicago artist and author of children's books Jan Spivey Gilchrist, illustrator of the six books in Koch's *Families in Touch Series,* child psychiatrist Linda Nancy Freeman, who collaborated with Koch on the book *Good Parents for Hard Times* in 1992 and shared emotional stories of growing up Black in Boston, and helping to integrate her all white grammar school. Chuck Smith, so significant in bringing the works of Black playwrights to Chicago theaters, provided useful comments on authenticity in portraying Black characters. The late novelist and Professor of African American Studies at Northwestern University, Leon Forrest, psychiatrist Dr. F. Theodore Reid and late family friend Alice Turner all contributed their hopes and insights concerning the future of Black-Jewish relationships.

Our colleagues were instrumental in moving this anthology forward. The development of *Soul Sisters,* our own musical dealing with the drama of Blacks and Jews, proceeded in tandem with our vision for this anthology. Thanks to Faculty Development and Performance Grants which Sarah received from the SUNY Research Foundation, *Soul Sisters* had its first full-scale production at the University at Albany. President Karen Hitchcock; William Kennedy and the New York State Writers Institute; Leonard Slade, co-chair of Africana Studies; professor and novelist Alan Ballard; Judith Baskin, chair of Judaic Studies; and Warren Ginsberg, chair of the English Department, gave us their enthusiastic support. The play's many benefactors, such as philanthropists Neil Golub and Edward Swyer, also helped sponsor an awards ceremony honoring Blacks and Jews who had contributed to improving relations in the New York Capitol area and the country at large. As the anthology developed, the late President of the University at Albany Kermit L. Hall, Dean of Arts and Sciences Joan Wick-Pelletier, and Associate Vice President for Academic Affairs William Hedberg provided their continued support.

When *Soul Sisters* was presented at National-Louis University in Evanston, then President Curt McCray, Professors Ed Risinger, Amy Ressler, Lee Ramsey, Joyce Markle, Steven Masello, Bruce Boyer, Rene Roy, Vice Provost George Litman, and Dean Martha Casazza, were incredibly supportive, bringing in university students and high school students representing the multicultural makeup of the Chicago area to see this play and discuss its implications. Current President Richard Pappas and Provost Kathryn Tooredman have supported the writing of *Shared Stages* with professional development grants as the anthology moved into its completion phase.

A number of people made a joint contribution, to the anthology and to the evolving musical, *Soul Sisters*. Paul Graubard, producer of the Jewish Theatre of the Berkshires, helped us develop our new script about a Black singer and a Jewish singer searching for their roots. Composer Mark Elliott wrote the title song for our show and other original music. Actor-Playwright Charlayne Woodard and Composer-Cantor Jeff Klepper were incredibly helpful in the earliest stages of our work, advising us on African American and Jewish music and mores. Composers Debbie Friedman, Doug Mishkin, Linda Hirschhorn, Rosalie Gerut, and Stuart Rosenberg were among the first to allow us to use their songs for our show. Julian Bond, distinguished for his life-long activism on behalf of civil rights, and for his leadership of the NAACP, gave us some of the first encouraging words about our new musical and some valuable suggestions.

The Chicago Writers' Bloc, bolstered by grants from the Dramatists Guild Fund, Inc., and later the Richard H. Driehaus Foundation, gave playwrights Joanne Koch and Sarah Blacher Cohen a chance to enhance their new work in critique sessions and staged readings. An equally important infusion of talent, interpretation and insight was provided by the actors, directors and musicians who participated in the many presentations of *Soul Sisters* at 28 universities, synagogues and community centers around the country. Jacque Tara Washington, Vikki True, Lee Rausch, Peter Schneider, Mari Andreyco and Ericka Wilcox were the original team that brought the show to life, but when the play was taken to the Midwest and other venues, Carole Bellini-Sharp, Lynne M. House, Jenna Jackson, Laurie Holton Nash, Marlo Stroud, Nikki Rich, Diana Basmajian, Diane Dorsey, Gerald Rizzer, Liz Zoller and

Doug McDade—all had a hand in shaping the evolving musical. They also offered insights about the way Blacks and Jews related and came into conflict in the second half of the 20th century. Most gratifying to us has been the way *Soul Sisters* has brought together Jewish and African American communities, such as the joint sponsorship by the Chicago Urban League and the Anti-Defamation League of the show at a Young Leaders United Benefit in 2001 or the 2006 presentation by the Sarasota Jewish Theater and the West Coast Black Theatre Troupe. We can't begin to name all those whose comments in post-play discussions enhanced our own play and this anthology.

Sarah's husband, Gary Cohen, and Joanne's husband, Lewis Z. Koch, provided much more than moral support. In addition to being Sarah's partner for over four decades, Gary has been an astute critic of Sarah's many books and plays and of her collaborative musicals. A philosopher in his own right, he has brought profound insights to Sarah's writing. He has welcomed into their home through the years Sarah's students, some of them studying the drama of Blacks and Jews as a formal class.

Sarah's nieces and nephews have been like children to her and were particularly helpful in responding to the play *Soul Sisters* in the Berkshires, Albany and Milwaukee: most notably Steve and Monique Pommier Blacher, Lisa Blacher, Bruce Blacher, Sheryl and Claudio Pelc and their daughter Rabbi Julie Pelc, Lynn and Bill Hurwitz, Perry and Roberta Rosen, Nancy and Howard Shimon, Sandy Bernstein and Steve Borenstein, and Stuart and Dianne Blacher.

Lewis Z. Koch, an investigative reporter and television news producer during the sixties and seventies, brought home direct accounts of Malcolm X, Dr. King, Fred Hampton, and many other key figures. Later he co-authored books, articles and a syndicated newspaper column with Joanne and produced one of her first plays. In their long, loving partnership Lewis has been instrumental in Joanne's writing—and everything else. The Koch children—Rachel, Joshua and wife, Jane, Lisa and husband, Michael Kornick—have kept Joanne's education going, and now, grandchildren Zachary, Sophie and Samantha are helping her to see the world with fresh eyes.

Sarah and Joanne also wish to remember their mothers and fathers who set them on a course of judging people as Dr. King would have wished, not by the color of their skin but by the content of their character. So thank you to Sarah's remembered parents Louis and Mary Kaminsky Blacher, her sister Bess Rosen Lichterman and brother Ben Blacher, and her late sister Dorothy Seidelman and her late brother David Blacher. Joanne owes her legacy to her beloved late parents Dr. Isadore and Ceil Schapiro, and is indebted to the late Noreen Schapiro, and to brother Sheldon and Mona Schapiro, Michael Koch and Marilyn Bizar.

We were lucky enough to have a network of colleagues and friends who shared in the creation of this anthology. They supplied useful comments and moral support. For Sarah these include literary mentors Cynthia Ozick and William Kennedy; authors Norma Rosen, Steve Stern, Thane Rosenbaum, Melvin Bukiet, and Jonathan Rosen; composer/historian Jack Gottlieb; devoted editor Robert Mandel; professors Alan Berger, Gila Naveh, Ezra Cappell, Charlotte Goodman, Elaine Safer, and Ellen Schiff; English Department Chairs Warren Ginsberg, Tom Cohen, Steve North, and Mike Hill; Director of the Disability Resource Center Nancy Belowich-Negron; SUNY professors Judy Baskin, Sarah Freifeld, Helen Elam, and Judy Barlow; former dean Francine Frank; Chats Director Mary Valentis; longtime friends Evelyn and Neil Aronson, Helen and John Moshak, Rhoda and Sid Feldman, Jean Schaefle, Bill Sommer, Nancy Schiff, and Leslie and Michael Diamond; and benefactors Sarah Harris, Hank Linnett, Bob and Bea Herman, and the late Abe Sherer.

Sarah would also like to thank those expert rescuers enabling her to remain a productive writer: Doctors Tom Smith, Jonathan Rosen, Gavin Setzen, Andrew Dubin, Gary Bakst, Neil Lava, and Joel Valentini; physical therapists Chrissy Bailie and Louanne Kuntz; hand therapist Celeste Freeman; speech therapist Brenda Nixon; and devoted caregivers Miriam Skansi, Dawne Larkin, Cathleen Chludzinski, Kimbria Edmunds, Colleen Petrie, Laura Tschantret, and Aesook Oliver.

Sarah is indebted to a few individuals who helped her with the manuscript in its final stages: angels Isabelle and Ricardo Nirenberg; miracle worker Marla Frazer; and selfless amanuensis Jesse Greenberg for enabling her to retain her creative voice.

Joanne extends thanks for friends, especially the late Lynn Jacob, Scott and Jill Jacobs, Barbara Volin, Phyllis and Louis Butterman, Inez Levy, Bonnie Koch, Brad and Terry Landis, Hope Landis, Karyn Meyers, Roberta Temes, Michael and Deb Scher, playwrights June Finfer, Barbara Georgans, Chloe Bolan, Zan Skolnick, Tom Weber, Joseph Urbinato, Lisa Holmes, Grace Fishman, Joe Savit, Charles Grippo, Kenan Heise, Jan Johnson, Gillian Gibson, Les White, Jill Elaine Hughes, directors Herb Isaacs, Peter Loewy, Lara Tibble, Sandy Shinner, Guy Barile, Carole Provonsha, John Sparks, Allan Chambers, Joan Mazzonelli, producer Elayne LeTraunik, as well as producer/choreographer Judith Rose.

Sarah's Rabbis Dan Orenstein and Rena Kieval, Rabbi Paul and Faye Silton, and Chaplain Janie Garnett, Joanne's Rabbis Peter Knobel and Rabbi Andrea London and members of the Beth Emet Chug— Freeds, Kelbers, Tatars, Granats, Rubenstein/Padawers, Denlows, Newbergers, Taubers/Rosens, Friedmans, Whiteleys, Garfields, Teshers, Huberts, Kayes, Feldmans, Axelrods and Levins—keep the spirit of the struggle for civil rights and genuine friendship alive in us.

Thanks go to excellent typist Lori Saba, outstanding copyeditor Janet Peltz, innovative cover designer Jackie Merri Meyer, and resourceful marketing director, Fran Keneston. We're especially grateful to senior production editor, Judy Block, for her meticulous attention to detail and for her artistic eye in creating a most handsome book. Above all, we extend our appreciation to James Peltz, who brought our anthology to fruition with his usual expertise and unusual dedication. Through the years, James has been not only a valued editor-in-chief, but a kind and considerate friend.

Introduction

Interwoven Destinies: The Drama of Blacks and Jews

You cannot have a friendship unless everybody is tall and everybody is looking one another in the eye.

—Roger Wilkins

Maybe Jews and Blacks lock horns more than other groups because we are the only ones who take each other seriously, the only minority groups who still seem to believe that our destinies are interwoven.

—Letty Cottin Pogrebin

We could have called this collection of plays "divided stages" as well as "shared stages," since the interaction of the characters within them is not always positive. The unusual relationship of Blacks and Jews, the two minority groups in twentieth-century America which have been the most inextricably linked to one another, has given rise to a variety of plays which depict that "interwoven" connection. Some reflect idealistic, even romanticized notions of how close the two groups are; others demonstrate actual coalitions and real hostilities between them. From the best dramatic literature on this subject produced in the United States in the past forty years, we have chosen ten plays that dramatize Black-Jewish relationships, some by Black playwrights, some by Jewish playwrights, and some by others. Set in urban and rural, northern and southern locales at various time periods in post-World War II to present day America, they concern characters of different ages, genders and life experiences. Through these dramas, the playwrights express various perspectives, illuminating the alliances and conflicts that have marked the dialogue of diversity on stage and off.

We have selected these plays not only to insure equality of representation, but to display the unique talents of these individual dramatists,

1

some established, some emerging, who create powerful, even unforget-
table moments on the stages of our imaginations. Although these plays
have had productions and, in some cases, individual publication, they
have never before been included in the same collection. By placing them
all in the same room to keep company with each other, we are inviting
readers to test the truths of their own experience against the truths
expressed in these plays. We hope readers will derive heightened meaning
from their intimate association with this lively assemblage of characters,
this resounding clash of symbols, this authentic forum of ideas.

Drama is a highly collaborative art. Taking up a play in a book
presses the reader into creative service as director, set designer and actor
performing all the roles. For the drama of Blacks and Jews, that means
walking in the shoes of the markedly "other," occupying the emotional
space of say a Black woman who has been raped by a white man, of an
eighty-year-old Jew who lies and laughs to survive, of a Black Vietnam
veteran who sees his buddies destroyed in Asia and returns to find his
family disintegrating in the Detroit urban ghetto. Making such psychic
leaps transforms the reader. This identification with the often unfamiliar
characters of minority drama may be demanding, yet it can set the stage
for significant new dialogue in the real world.

American drama is best understood with some sense of its historical
background, its connection to the real world of its time. We cannot, for
example, appreciate one of the first successful American plays, the adaptation of Harriet Beecher Stowe's *Uncle Tom's Cabin*, without recognizing the struggle for emancipation and the Civil War which preceded it.
Nor can we grasp the impact of *A Raisin in the Sun* without recognizing
that housing integration in 1959 had not been achieved in the United
States in the North or the South. Though great plays endure in spite of
changing circumstances, the plays in this collection, crucially influenced
by the shifting alliances between minority groups, require special understanding of their protean settings, their varying contexts.

Black-Jewish dialogue has changed throughout the twentieth century. From 1910 to 1964, "genuine empathy and principled alliances
[existed] between Jews and Blacks."[1] It was the period when W. E. B.
Du Bois, editor of *The Crisis*, and Abraham Cahan, editor of the *Jewish
Daily Forward*, could advocate for Black and Jewish rights in their respective publications, a time when Rabbi Abraham Joshua Heschel and
Reverend Martin Luther King, Jr., marched arm in arm to Selma, followed by an army of united Blacks, Jews and white Christians, all determined to achieve integration. This halcyon era of mutual appreciation
and sympathy did not, however, prevail.[2]

After 1964, this period of Black-Jewish cooperation was not even
remembered in the same light by both groups. According to Cornel

West, the image of Blacks and Jews united against racism is often "downplayed by Blacks and romanticized by Jews." He claims that Blacks downplay this cooperation because they focus on the widening economic gap between the two. They see the rapid entree of most Jews into the middle and upper middle class as spawning "both an intense conflict with the more slowly growing black middle class and a social resentment from a quickly growing black impoverished class." Jews, West finds, "tend to romanticize this period because their present status as upper middle dogs and some top dogs in American society unsettles their historic self-image as progressives with a compassion for the underdog."[3]

Some Jewish playwrights tend to glorify the good old days when the two groups were united in a common cause, projecting a future when bigotry would not exist between them. In their generous treatment of Blacks and Jews on stage, it is as if these playwrights were allying themselves with those Jews who, in fact, supplied three-fourths of the money for Dr. King and constituted two-thirds of the white volunteers who went to the South to register Black voters. The playwrights we have chosen, however, offset exclusively positive sentiments with negative ones by including glimpses of the real inequities that have existed. They introduce dramatic moments of conflict, fear and anguish that have gone hand in hand with gestures of caring and mutual concern. In so doing, they provide a more authentic portrayal of the kind of sharing that has taken place between the two groups.

Some Black playwrights have used their Jewish characters as the target of their bitterness, resentment and even anti-Semitism. They scorn whites, including Jews who presume to understand Blacks, when these whites are the very source of their simmering rage. The Black playwrights we have chosen do not focus exclusively on rage. They show a spectrum of feelings on the part of Blacks and Jews. They depict not only hostility, but also compassion, warmth and genuine friendship.

Even in the best of times, shared stages of theater and American life have not always been equally shared. These ten plays reveal initially unequal relationships between master and servant, doctor and patient, lawyer and client. The Jew may start out with some social or economic advantage, but the Black may possess the basic wisdom to alter that situation. In many cases, as in *Driving Miss Daisy*, the relationship is transformed and redeemed by the end of the play. In *Sarah and The Sax* and *I'm Not Rappaport*, there is a ruefully comic sharing of contrasting life stories which transform misery into mirth. There is a compassionate union among victims of southern bigotry in *No Niggers, No Jews, No Dogs* and a strained partnership between the common man and the professionals in *I Am a Man*. There is an exchange of healing music when racism and anti-Semitism injure innocent lives in *Soul Sisters*. In

The Day the Bronx Died, there is the joint suffering of the trauma of urban wars, and in *Medal of Honor Rag*, there is the shared torment of the Vietnam War, crippling the psyche on the home front. In *The Left Hand Singing*, there is the jubilant idealism of youth paired with the wrenching disillusionment of embittered elders. In *Fires in the Mirror*, there is the juxtaposition of hostile and friendly voices, cynical and idealistic ones, alternating on stage in monologue rather than dialogue. Through the complex sharing in all these plays, new stories with unforeseen dimensions emerge about who these characters have become, how they relate to each other and what the future might hold for them—and for us.

The capitalization of B in Black(s) varies from playwright to playwright. The editors of this volume have chosen to capitalize it in their introduction, but elsewhere in the anthology it varies according to the choice of the playwright. The same is true of stage directions and other stylistic choices made in different ways by different playwrights. We have tried to remain consistent within each play, but these may vary from play to play.

Common Ground

Focusing on the common ground, rather than the battleground, Julius Lester, in his essay, "The Lives People Live," delineates six areas of common history and common suffering which unite African Americans and Jews:

(1) Both groups begin their histories in slavery.

(2) Both groups have been demonized by the white majority; both have been compared to the devil, complete with horns and tails; both have been denigrated as "sexually licentious."

(3) Segregation and ghettoization have been the fate of Jews and Blacks, with the word "ghetto" first used to refer to the section of Venice near the iron foundry (in Italian, *ghetto*) where Jews were forced to live. Later the urban enclaves in northern and southern segregated cities became the ghettos of the Blacks, with Blacks in the North sometimes moving into the same areas once tacitly designated for Jews.

(4) Both Blacks and Jews were expelled from their original homelands, dispersed throughout the world and compelled to live in a Diaspora. Blacks, however, were enslaved from all parts of Africa and were unable to maintain a "common language" and "common memories," while Jews, through the Hebrew language and a shared religion, were able to keep Israel alive for 2000 years. As Lester says, "For Blacks the Diaspora is permanent."[4]

(5) Political oppression marks both groups. Blacks and Jews have been restricted by law, prevented from moving about freely, denied both a free choice of occupation and freedom of "social relationships."

(6) Violent attacks, torture and deadly policies threatened both groups with genocide. For Jews, pogroms in Eastern Europe murdered and maimed hundreds of thousands. For Blacks, race riots, lynchings and casual neglect marked life in the Jim Crow South. Anti-Semitism, a useful political tool for centuries, became in the hands of Hitler's Third Reich a program for extermination that led to the murder of six million Jews, the majority of the Jews of Europe. How many Africans died during the centuries of the slave trade? Though some have reckoned the toll as 100 million, Lester's admittedly "conservative" estimate is 15 million.

But Blacks and Jews have fought back through oral and written literature and, when possible, through armed resistance. As Lester recognizes, "Blacks and Jews share much in how they resist and fight back against an oppressive value structure and preserve a sense of self and people-hood independent of the pariah status."[5] This resistance runs through all the plays in this collection, sometimes through the use of forceful arguments of social protest, sometimes through the shocking, fact-based dialogue of urban naturalism, sometimes through the wise parables of quasi-preachers and sometimes through the powerful weapons of self-defense: folklore, humor and music.

African American playwright John Henry Redwood resists and fights the oppression of racism and anti-Semitism through his social protest play, the very title of which—*No Niggers, No Jews, No Dogs*—expresses an old derogatory connection between the two minority groups, particularly in the South. What startles us with a seeming exaggeration at the outset turns out to be a literal report of one way Jews and Blacks were yoked together in mutual dehumanization.

In the *No* Play, as Redwood abbreviates it, the Jewish Yaveni Ahronson, "disguised" as the gentile Jack Arnold, encounters this sign when he arrives at his new home in Mississippi:

YAVENI: "WELCOME TO THE TOWN OF HOLMAN IN THE GREAT MAGNOLIA STATE OF MISSISSIPPI." A little further down the road, a larger sign read, "NO NIGGERS, NO JEWS, NO DOGS." There it was in writing, Negroes and Jew, together, relegated to the same level as dogs. But I convinced myself that it didn't refer to me, because I was a goy, and I was in a car with the most beautiful woman in the world whom I loved very much . . . and that was all that mattered.

Years later, in 1949, Yaveni, rejected by his Christian wife, makes his way to a small town in North Carolina, determined to reclaim his Jewish identity and his empathy for oppressed minorities. He befriends a Black family headed by Rawl and Mattie Cheeks with whom he feels an immediate kinship, recognizing their shared persecution as the hated outsider.

Redwood's Yaveni cannot stand idly by while whites torture Blacks, any more than he could dissociate himself from his own people at the time of *Kristallnacht*, the beginning of the Holocaust. In Yaveni's mind, Blacks and Jews must take action to change their lot. He realizes now that they must join together to eradicate such overt bigotry and prevent further victimization. The African American women in this play, who seem forced to accept their fate, cannot simply follow Yaveni's advice to destroy the "no" signs and reveal their violations by the white man.

> MATTIE: You've been down here and known my family all of two months and you got the nerve to tell me how to keep my family going? You get your research done and you go back to Cleveland. But we'll still be Negroes down here in Halifax, North Carolina, trying to do the best we can while you go back to being white.

One of Redwood's great contributions to American drama is that he depicts African American women as strong and persevering, believing as he does that Black women are largely responsible for the survival of his people in America. They are the true heroes in this play. Patient and resilient, Redwood's African American women find their own way to gain retribution and prevent further humiliation. While sensitively capturing the anguish of the persecuted Jew, Redwood unflinchingly recognizes that Jews can sometimes escape violation and destruction when African Americans cannot. At least this is the case in America. Redwood's frank admission of inequalities between Jews and Blacks makes the moments of genuine caring in this play compelling. Redwood dramatizes conflict but illuminates the compassion each has for the other's plight—Jew for African American, male for female.

Verbal Weapons

In the arsenal of the oppressed, humor, satire and imaginative tales are the most potent weapons. Overtly laughing in private and covertly laughing in public at bosses, bigots, bullies and dictators have helped both groups to maintain their dignity and a sense of control in a world where they have been controlled and ridiculed.

Their unique humor is the best antidote to counteract the poisonous despair within them. As playwright Thomas W. Jones II explains in his Preface to the anthology *Black Comedy: 9 Plays*, and demonstrates in his own play *Wizard of Hip*, "African-American humor functions to heal, to clarify, to assert . . . using comic linguistic based art to bridge reality with mythic possibility. And this work is the work of generations healing the wounds. To laugh is to diffuse the powerful rage burning beneath the soul."[6] This laughter is not just a pale alternative to murder and violent retaliation. It is a major enhancement of life. With its therapeutic properties, its restorative powers, it is a boundless source of vitality and endurance.

Wry verbal mastery of intolerable reality takes the sting out of adversity in the riffs of the homeless Black character, The Sax, in Lewis John Carlino's one-act, *Sarah and the Sax*. His makeshift lyrics, foreshadowing rap, disturb the silence of his solitude and amuse mainly himself.

> THE SAX: (*Mumbling to himself as he crosses to the bench.*) Tom Mix, pick up sticks, get my licks, sweat my fix, watch the dicks—Tracy.

His unexpected audience of one sitting next to him on a bench in Central Park is his comic direct opposite: Sarah Nodelman, a plump, Jewish lady of about fifty-five. Every inch of her is an embodiment of the middle class. The Sax, who seems to have been expelled from the class system altogether, is a thirty-year-old, barefoot Black man wearing sunglasses; "his tattered old sweatshirt and denims are encrusted with grime of almost geologic age." He carries an old saxophone on a string around his neck and plays it periodically.

A caricature of the overfeeding Jewish mother, Sarah Nodelman invites The Sax over for home-cooked meals. She promises to make all the kosher delicacies she has made for her son, Herbie. She assures The Sax her food and her company will be good for him, will make him less lonely. She effusively makes all the overtures to strike up a friendship, while he sullenly rebuffs her efforts.

The anger of The Sax escalates until Sarah is forced either to give up or confess that she has been lying, presenting a fabrication of herself. She has used a lie about her son as The Sax uses his music—to express unutterable grief and frustration, to ease his pain.

> SARAH: I'm a phony. (*THE SAX turns towards her.*) I can't help it. Listen. My Herbie don't live on Long Island in a nice home with a nice family. And I can't take his temperature and buy him sneakers. You see, my Herbie don't live at all. He died in Korea in 1951. (*A long silence. THE SAX lets out a*

stream of air, not quite a whistle.) . . . I'm sorry I lied to you.
(There is a long silence . . . Slowly THE SAX *picks up his saxophone
and begins to play. The music is a sad jazz and into it is woven
"Home on the Range," along with old Hebraic melodies. These
are notes of compassion and sorrow, not anger now. . . .)*

The comic juxtaposition of two wildly different people becomes a
poignant connection of two suffering souls, shifting ever so gradually
with each gesture Sarah makes to have friendship with The Sax. Her
willingness to expose her painful secret transcends the barriers of age,
gender and race. The Sax now responds not to the stereotyped Jewish
mother as over-zealous nurturer. With his "notes of sorrow and compassion," he seeks to comfort the more universal mother, still grieving over
the loss of her son. By commiserating with her, he not only gains release
from his alienated self; he is also able to accept her maternal solace.

Lying, fabrication, inventing identities is a form of the humor of
verbal retrieval, the word triumphant over the situation, for both Blacks
and Jews. What happens to them is far from funny, but what they say
about it can transform disaster into drollery, woe into whimsy. In the
case of Herb Gardner's play, *I'm Not Rappaport*, 80-year-old Nat
Rappaport explains to his 80-year-old Black benchmate, Midge Carter,
the necessity of lying for survival:

> NAT: Not lies—(*Sits upright on bench.*) Alterations! I make
> certain alterations. Sometimes the truth don't fit; I take in
> here, I let out there, till it fits. The truth? What's true is a
> triple By-Pass last year at Lenox Hill, what's true is Grade Z
> cuts of meat from the A. and P., a Social Security check that
> wouldn't pay the rent for a chipmunk; what's true is going to
> the back door of the Plaza Hotel every morning for yesterday's
> club-rolls. I tell them it's for the pigeons. I'm the pigeon. Six
> minutes dead is true—(*Takes bunch of pages from briefcase.*)
> here, Dr. Reissman's bills; here's the phone number, call him.
> A fact. And that was my last fact. Since then, alterations. Since
> I died, a new policy!

Nat's new policy is not merely to complain but to make comedy out of
complaints, to amuse himself and Midge. In so doing he becomes one
of those Jews and Blacks on stage able to laugh together at life and to
laugh at the funny performances of the other.

In Gardner's *I'm Not Rappaport*, the comedy is bittersweet by the
time both characters are laughing. This play is, in some ways, a variation
on the vaudeville routines pairing two ethnics. However, Midge and Nat

are not just comic stereotypes of Blacks and Jews with exaggerated tell-tale physical features, predictable behavior and stock verbal responses. Gardner does not mechanically make them the butt of each other's jokes but allows them to be the originators of them in the most difficult circumstances. This time they are fleshed out humans, recognizable as Jew and Black facing the indignities of old age together in a predatory urban setting. At first, the voluble Jew's humorous fabrications keep the Black man entertained, making him the straight man in his senior citizen vaudeville routine. Through his interaction with Nat, the near-blind, taciturn Midge becomes more assertive, even taking on the bully of Central Park who is attacking the two old men. Though he's not entirely victorious, he holds on to a piece of the scoundrel's buckskin jacket and a powerful "chunk of satisfaction." He has the last laugh, a laugh shared by the two, now as equal friends. Gardner's vaudevillians thus join the ranks of the other suffering creatures on earth who invented laughter, who employ the comic to endure the painful conditions of their life.

"Is it an accident," asks Julius Lester, "that many of the most original and creative comedians in America are either Jewish or Black? Lenny Bruce and Richard Pryor could have been brothers. Without Jews and Blacks, I wonder if there would be laughter in America."[7] From minstrels to vaudeville comics to today's popular comedians: Woody Allen and Bill Cosby, Chris Rock and Jackie Mason, Bernie Mac and Gary Seinfeld, Jews and Blacks have used humor as a form of camouflaged hostility against the forces of oppression. Vacillating between the sneer and the smile, the grimace and the grin, they have belittled the towering strength of the giant majority and elevated their own status in the process.

Battlegrounds

Jews and Blacks have not always been jesting friends, despite their frequently shared status as outcasts and pariahs. Centuries of white Christian and later Islamic anti-Semitism shaped Black attitudes towards Jews, as racism, slavery and *realpolitik* influenced many Jews alternately to fear and denigrate Blacks. The nature of the sharing among Blacks and Jews, on stage and off, has frequently been ambivalent.

If Blacks drew inspiration from Exodus and used the enslavement and liberation of the ancient Hebrews as the basis for spirituals, escape and uprisings, they also picked up the stereotypes projected by Christians of the Jew as the betrayer and exploiter. Ralph Ellison has remarked on "the preference of the slaves in re-creating themselves, in good part, out of the images and myths of the Old Testament Jews,"[8] but other writers have pointed to the tendency of Blacks to absorb the anti-Semitism embedded in Christian culture. Richard Wright noted in *Black Boy* that "we had been taught at home and in Sunday school that Jews were Christ killers."[9] Both strands—identification with the ancient Hebrews and identification with white Christian hatred of Jews as the archetypal betrayers—became part of Black cultural heritage.

This ambivalence within the complex of relations between Blacks and Jews has found expression in the writing of both—but it has been expressed differently in different periods. Louis Harap, in his book, *Dramatic Encounters*, finds the shifting forms of the civil rights movement a major influence on the way writers have depicted Blacks and Jews. "In the proletarian 1930's and 1940's and the radical 1960's, Jewish and Black writers were generally positively oriented toward each other and sensed their common goals."[10] The culmination of this union was the Mississippi "Freedom Summer" of 1964 when over half the young people participating in the movement for Black voter registration were Jewish, when Andrew Goodman, Michael Schwerner—part of this Jewish movement to work with Blacks—and James Chaney, a young Black man from Mississippi working with them, were murdered.

Jewish involvement in progress for Blacks has not always been completely altruistic. At times the coalition was motivated by self-interest, recognition that policies securing minority rights would benefit Jews as well as Blacks. Relationships were often skewed or paternalistic, satisfying egos rather than sufficiently recognizing Blacks' needs to control their own lives. When it came to the Civil Rights Movement, as Andrew Hacker observes, "Blacks were always the junior partners, who were expected to accept not only the pace and goals deemed suitable by whites, but also to assume a demeanor which made whites feel at ease."[11]

In the musical *Soul Sisters*, Joanne Koch and Sarah Blacher Cohen dramatize a rocky friendship between Sandra, a Jewish established singer of Black music, and Cleo, a Black woman who displaces her as a singing star. Cleo becomes fed up with junior partnership and deference. When Sandra is asked to bow out of singing at a civil rights benefit and Cleo is invited to take her place, Sandra turns on Cleo and fires her. When Cleo's star has risen and Sandra has retreated to drink and self-pity, Cleo finally vents her frustration and anger, insisting she has earned the right to move up: "We've been beaten because we're Black, raped because we're Black, lynched because we're Black—why not a little pay back because we're Black?"

Later, when the two women are together for the first time in years, preparing for an anti-apartheid concert, they still have crucial disagreements.

SANDRA: There's a guy outside with a loudspeaker and a sign: "Stop Whites and Jews from eliminating Blacks. Stop the

Genocide." Since when did Jews destroy Blacks? And where do they get off using words like genocide?

CLEO: What would you call the systematic killing and enslavement of millions of Blacks?

SANDRA: But Cleo, this guy is saying 200 million were killed in the "Black Holocaust." Where does he get a number like that?

CLEO: If you count all those since the beginning of slavery then . . .

SANDRA: Well, if we counted all the Jews who were killed since Roman times, we'd be getting way past the six million of the real Holocaust.

CLEO: Jews can usually hide. We can't. Don't get me wrong— we don't want to. Anti-Semitism is bad, but how do you compare that to the hatred against Blacks?

SANDRA: Jews were hated way before America was discovered.

CLEO: You think Americans are the only ones who hate Blacks? Look at how the Europeans carved up Africa.

SANDRA: And then they decided to carve up the Jews—(*A beat of strained silence.*) Warring holocausts . . .

Warring holocausts will come up again and again in these plays. Each minority group thinks it was the most persecuted, endured the most indignities, withstood the most atrocities, suffered the most fatalities.

Music offers a way to temper the animus of warring holocausts. In a collection by and about Blacks and Jews, we could not omit the importance of music. Its unifying effects appear in the actions of Carlino's The Sax, with poignant melodies replacing strident words. OyamO tells us that his character of the Bluesman is the source "from whom the entire story of *I Am a Man* emanates." In *Soul Sisters*, music facilitates the journey into the world of the other and serves for its two principal characters as the only path to self-discovery. Sandra's immersion in Black music draws her to the Civil Rights Movement. Her singing of Yiddish and Hebrew songs allows her to reclaim her own roots in Eastern Europe and the Holocaust. For Cleo, music is her ticket to success, her means of grasping the African in her African American identity, her source of comfort when tragedy strikes. The inequality of her relationship with

Sandra—first as her secretary, then her replacement, then her rival and superior—is finally negotiated through music. As Mark Elliot's lyrics in the song "Soul Sisters" express it: "If we'd look beyond the pain inside us, we'd see there's so very much that binds me to you."

Soul Sisters is a musical drama of Black-Jewish sisterhood. Bound together with ties of pain and exhilaration, the women protagonists are ultimately energized by each other, strengthened by each other's resolve. They take risks to go on the front line of their battle against racism. They initiate the healing concert. They make the impassioned plea for unity.

Unequal Roles

Jews and Blacks in literature and life have often shared a teacher and student relationship, based on the fact that Jews were, at certain key moments, in a position of having the educational wherewithal to counsel and defend Blacks, as well as having the shared suffering to understand their plight. Arthur Spingarn, fighting the legal battles for the NAACP, Samuel Leibowitz defending the Scottsboro boys in the 1930s, Jack Greenberg bailing out Rosa Parks and thousands of other Blacks from Southern jails during the Civil Rights Movement[12]—these are just a few of the advocates who provide actual models for such characters in plays, novels and films.

In Richard Wright's novel, *Native Son*, when protagonist Bigger Thomas refuses to reenact events for police because they "hate black folks," his Jewish lawyer, Boris Max, replies,

> They hate others too . . . they hate trade unions. They hate folks
> who try to organize . . . They hate me because I'm trying to help
> you. They're writing me letters calling me a "dirty Jew."[13]

In literature, as in the pre-wartime devastation of the forties, failure to see is a prelude to destruction. This is the case in Arthur Miller's novel, *Focus*, as it is unforgettably in Ralph Ellison's *Invisible Man*. The racist is incapable of seeing the Black person or the Jewish person as an individual human being. As Louis Harap has pointed out, bigotry is blind. "Just as the racist doesn't see the individual Black (the 'invisible man') but only his stereotyped notion of one, so the anti-Semite—frequently also the same person—does not see any given Jew but only 'Jews' as conceived by the stereotype."[14]

The Mayor of Memphis, as depicted by OyamO in his play, *I Am a Man*, illustrates the blindness of the hater. The hero of this play, O.T. Jones, is head of the local garbage workers' union, a union comprised of

Blacks. He boldly stands up to the Mayor, even before help arrives from union headquarters in New York.

JONES: I'm in control here!

MAYOR: *(Derisive chortle.)*: In control, is it? I'll tell you what. I'll go over to that meeting and personally explain what I've been trying . . .

JONES: You will do no such a thing. Dem mens won't hear a word you say lessen I authorize you ta speak.

MAYOR: Unless you what me?

JONES: I believe you heard me.

MAYOR: *(Out of control.)*: I don't need some nigger to authorize me to do anything!

(JONES slaps the MAYOR's face resoundingly which literally knocks the MAYOR on his ass. The MAYOR is both emotionally and physically stunned and then a bit fearful as JONES hovers over him.)

JONES: I ain't no nigga! I am a man. You hear what I say? <u>I AM A MAN</u>!

Jones is clearly the protagonist of this drama, one who has many antagonists—not just the obvious ones, including the Mayor, but also the people who have come to Memphis, Tennessee, to advise him on the alien art of negotiating with the white establishment. OyamO's Jewish character, Joshua Solomon, is genuinely concerned and engaging. He's a tough Jewish labor negotiator from New York who knows how to confront rednecks and how to unmask the Mayor of Memphis, whom he reveals to be a Jewish convert to Episcopalianism. He charges the Mayor with resisting the minimal demands of the garbage workers union as part of his sell-out to the white power structure.

Here OyamO dramatizes one of the underlying themes of plays about Blacks and Jews. Integration for Blacks and assimilation for Jews may be necessary, expedient, politic, but they often have at their root an element of self-hatred. Integration is regarded as an insult by those Blacks who lack the means to rise into positions of power; assimilation is an affront to those Jews who risk discrimination by keeping their names and their religion and even making a conspicuous show of it.

Solomon is a well-intentioned negotiator, as is the Black and brilliant Willins who "calls the shots" on union strategy. But Willins insists and Solomon agrees that having Martin Luther King Jr., in Memphis, speaking and leading marches, is the way to achieve a raise for the local garbage workers. The uneducated, impecunious Jones wants to leave the famous Dr. King out of the fight and handle the battle with his own people. The national advisors, the middle-class Black Willins and the Jewish Solomon, and, by implication, the northern-based national officials, prevail. King is assassinated. The garbage workers wind up with an 8-cent-an-hour raise. Jones feels he's lost everything and indirectly caused the death of his people's leader, but he reluctantly leads his men back to work, recognizing that this is the first time in the history of the entire South that the city has made an agreement with a public employees' union. Jones can no longer afford to be the "student" to either the Jewish teacher or the better-educated middle-class advisor. In an existential moment, in full awareness that the boulder must be rolled up the mountain once more, alone and unaided by middle-class Blacks and well-meaning Jews, this ordinary man chooses faith and joy over despair and bitterness.

In this play, Jones finally acquires one of the most valued virtues in drama: self-knowledge. He recognizes the failures of his advisors and his own foolishness for allowing the "other" to dictate his destiny. From OyamO's perspective, Jews, educated Blacks and radical Blacks can only go so far in helping to uplift the common Black man. The playwright stands close to his protagonist, supporting him with the music of The Bluesman. OyamO emphasizes the need for the ordinary man to improvise with his own instruments, rather than follow the formal beat of some established score.

In *Medal of Honor Rag*, playwright Thomas Cole cares about his hero, but is forced to view his situation from the perspective of the outsider, the white man confronted with this question: How does a Medal of Honor winner wind up dead in an attempted armed robbery? Cole's answer is: He returns from the Vietnam War to the ghetto wars of the U.S.A. Cole's drama is based on the true story of Dale Jackson, a decorated Black Vietnam veteran from Detroit who is suffering from many social and psychological ills, some of them identifiable, such as post-traumatic-stress syndrome. Others have something to do with being given national recognition for bravery, while the nation refuses to recognize his immediate need to pay his wife's hospital bill. Cole's play is a stark therapy session, unrelieved by intermission or humor, during which Doc, a Jewish therapist, tries to reach D.J. He reads from D.J.'s file, finding one source of D.J.'s psychological damage in the mission America sent him to carry out.

Doc: This man was sent by his country to fight in a war. A war unlike any war he might have imagined. Brutal, without glory, without meaning, without good wishes for those who were sent to fight and without gratitude for those who returned. He was trained to kill people of another world in their own homes, in order to help them. How this would help them we do not really know.

Unable to get Dale to open up to him, Doc tries to relate his own suffering to the fate of this African American devastated by the meaningless carnage of the Vietnam War. Doc's parents perished in Auschwitz while he, sent to America, survived. He tells D.J., "I had my own case of survivor guilt."

Why can't Doc help Dale recover his honor? Why can't the old tradition of Jewish professionals coming to the aid of beleaguered Blacks work in this situation? What happened to the common ground? The doctor, whether perceived as Jewish or as representative of concerned middle-class whites, is rendered helpless in the face of forces working against the Black veteran. During the late sixties and early seventies, Blacks were fighting and dying in Vietnam in record numbers. (Blacks comprised 14% of the 58,000 deaths in the Vietnam War, though they were 11% of the young male population nationwide.)[15] This play stands as a symbol of the maltreatment of Blacks during and after their service in America's wars.[16]

The enormous sacrifice of Blacks in Vietnam came at a time when conditions were worsening in Black urban enclaves. The looting and fires in Chicago, Detroit, New York and other cities after the 1968 murder of Dr. King devastated these communities. In the case of Dale Jackson, the sheer frustration of being unable to raise the money to take care of his wife, of no hope of economic progress after being paraded around the country as the poster-boy for recruitment to Vietnam, triggered an attempt at robbing a grocery store that may actually have been a form of suicide.

Doc: He took out a pistol, but never fired a shot, while the manager empties his own gun, at point-blank range, into D.J.'s body. . . . His body went on a last unexpected jet airplane ride to Arlington National Cemetery, where he was given a hero's burial with an eight-man Army Honor Guard.

Playwright Cole makes no attempt to soften or sentimentalize the outcome for D.J., just as he doesn't allow Doc to make any meaningful connection to the beleaguered veteran, forced to fight for economic survival on the urban home front after barely surviving combat in Vietnam.

Doc is unable to cure D.J., though other similar post-war dramas, such as Arthur Laurents' play *Home of the Brave*, have more optimistic conclusions.[17] Cole's theme is alienation and disconnection. The conversation doesn't flow freely, as it does between Gardner's Nat and Midge. Nor are there arguments that produce greater understanding, like those between Redwood's Yaveni and Mattie, or ultimately between Koch and Cohen's Sandra and Cleo. Doc's tortured communication with D.J. gives him a glimpse of the torment of the war abroad. Doc can only guess at the torment of the war at home by D.J.'s obituary. When he reports the tragic outcome for D.J., Doc does so with a sense of inevitability, recognizing that diseases bred of despair and poverty can be fatal.

Northern and Southern Exposures

Looking back at *Medal of Honor Rag* and forward to *The Day the Bronx Died*, we confront a kind of poverty which worsens among many urban and rural Blacks after World War II, even as the Black middle class and other minority groups are prospering. As Julius Lester wisely points out: "To speak of Black-Jewish relations without addressing the concrete despair of Blacks is to indulge in nostalgia for a time that never was. Poverty does not ennoble; it embitters. It embitters until people are left with no power except that of hatred and destruction."[18] Statistics of poverty, such as, "Death or incarceration claims one third of Black men before the age of 30,"[19] may be greeted with indifference. Yet when that translates into the real fate of an individual, such as Dale Jackson, and when that fate is dramatized by a skilled playwright, the statistic takes on tragic significance.

Cole's Jewish doctor and Michael Henry Brown's Bronx-born Manhattan condo resident represent those Americans who have moved up and away from a core of Black people whose lives are virtually hopeless. The fact that most Jews once lived in the dire poverty of Eastern European restricted communities or *shtetlach*, and also faced poverty when they first arrived in this country, no longer provides common ground with Black residents of contemporary urban ghettos. In the sixties and seventies, those *shtetls* were seen by many American Jews through the rose-colored glasses of nostalgia, in musicals like *Fiddler on the Roof*. Meanwhile, many Jews and other whites were moving out of mixed neighborhoods, like the Bronx, to more affluent all-white areas. This "white flight," as it's been called, is not merely a product of Jews and others running from their onetime neighbors.

According to playwright Michael Henry Brown, the transition from livable neighborhoods to blighted Black ghettos was not entirely the fault of fleeing, indifferent whites. Indifference and destructive rampages on the part of Blacks were equally to blame for the death of shared communities. In Brown's play, *The Day the Bronx Died*, the African American man Mickey looks back on his youth in a Bronx neighborhood just beginning to suffer from urban blight. His vantage point now is middle class, a nice building in Manhattan, and a good job, but his 13-year-old son has been hospitalized, struggling to survive a brutal subway mugging. Back in 1968, when Mickey was young, he was friendly with Billy Kornblum, both boys sharing a passion for baseball. Mickey's mother condoned the friendship because a Jew, according to her, was not like other whites.

> MOTHER: Now a Jew, he be a different kind of white animal . . . Fact, he not like white people at all. . . . No, no, the Jew be a different breed all together . . . more . . . human . . . almost . . . colored . . . Yes, Sir, the Jew, he be alright.

In Brown's play, Alexander, the toughest kid in their mixed Black and Jewish Bronx neighborhood, conveys the negative stereotypes of Blacks who saw the Jew as just another oppressive boss. While white Christians dominated corporate entities which supplied the energy and goods to Black urban areas, Jews were frequently the white bosses or storeowners whom Blacks encountered in the Bronx or Harlem. In Harlem, for example, even though more than 50% of the stores were owned by Blacks and other non-whites, Jews owned about 40% of the stores.[20]

> ALEXANDER: They're all cheap. My Moms says they're like squirrels . . . they store away every penny like a squirrel do nuts. It's all a plot, man. That's why they don't believe in Christmas . . . so they don't have to buy presents."

Yet Alexander is the one who dies preventing a gang thug from killing Billy Kornblum, the Jewish friend of Mickey who threatens "to blow the whistle" on the gang guy's killing of a white cop. The Bronx dies when Alexander is killed, because even though Alexander flirted with violence and was ambivalent about Jews, he had a sense of decency, a sense of justice that seems to be gone forever. The Jewish boy, Billy, moves to Larchmont at the end of the play. Big Mickey, though living with his own family in fashionable Manhattan, high above the fray, faces their vulnerability. His own son, injured by the same kind of gang thug who killed Alexander, may not survive the death of decency.

Michael Henry Brown is a playwright who holds the mirror up to his own people and is not afraid to comment on the blemishes he sees. This honesty is rare in political rhetoric, but a requirement for authenticity in enduring drama and literature. Initially, Sandra in *Soul Sisters* is a self-centered woman who disavows Jewish causes. She is a flawed individual rather than an exemplary representative of her people. Willins in *I Am a Man*, though an educated and successful Black man, provides advice that turns out to be disastrous. In a climate of political correctness, writers might be tempted to put forth characters in their ethnic dramas who are washed of all impurities, the perfect African American, the perfect Jew. It is natural that contemporary dramatists would want to avoid any implication of racism or anti-Semitism, but they can't produce believable characters unless they create them with all their imperfections.

> BIG MICKEY: . . . You see . . . a disciple of peace dies in Memphis and it leads to rage in the Bronx. Come 3 o'clock, if you were white, your ass was grass. Nobody black stood up when Spectre Gestapo'd the neighborhood supermarket. They destroyed it. Nobody black said a damn thing when Milton Friedman got the shit beat out of him as he opened his bakery one morning. No one black, of good conscience, said a fucking word.

When speaking of decency, Michael Henry Brown demands as much of his Black characters as he does of his Jewish characters. Brown takes the unpopular view that the decimation of Black neighborhoods, such as the Bronx, is caused in part by Blacks venting indiscriminate anger, albeit at intolerable conditions. Then, when nothing is left but a shambles, there's what Brown calls the "blame-everybody-but-your-fuckin'-self" attitude. Young Mickey and Billy could be good friends in a Bronx which had decency. In such a place, they were equals.

Genuine friendship between Jews and Blacks of the type author Roger Wilkins described where "everybody is tall and everybody is looking one another in the eye"[21] rarely occurs in plays by Blacks, plays by Jews or plays by other white writers, because it has rarely occurred in life. But some playwrights and some plays hold out a promise of such equally shared lives. Whether this promise is a mirage or a vision of the future is for the reader or the audience to decide.

Alfred Uhry's *Driving Miss Daisy*, winner of the 1988 Pulitzer Prize for Drama, is such a play which portrays this miraculous sharing. In it Hoke Coleburn is the Black chauffeur foisted on the 72-year-old Daisy Werthan by her son, Boolie. They go through twenty-five years together in the course of the play, moving from a servant-mistress relationship in the beginning to something very different at the end. Each scene brings the relationship to a new point of understanding until finally Hoke is not just a friend. He's the only true friend Miss Daisy has.

Trust grows gradually between the two, but not without suspicion, anger, false starts and wry comedy. Tending the grave of her husband at the cemetery, Daisy, the feisty realist, recognizes she is aging and cannot depend on her son, Boolie, to care for her in life or at her burial plot in death. With bristling humor, she acknowledges that Boolie will take care of her out of obligation, not out of love. Hoke, the steadfast man of feeling, thinks the family, not a stranger, should be the caretaker. Ironically, Hoke, the stranger, will prove to be the most attentive to Daisy's needs.

> DAISY: Boolie's always pestering me to let the staff out here tend to this plot. Perpetual care they call it.
>
> HOKE: Doan' you do it. It right to have somebody from the family lookin' after you.
>
> DAISY: I'll certainly never have that. Boolie will have me in perpetual care before I'm cold.

Daisy is the grateful receiver of Hoke's services but repays him in many ways. Boolie may pay him with money for his chauffeuring, but Daisy, a former teacher still mentally alert in her late seventies, teaches Hoke how to read. Teacher and student are both enriched by the experience. Daisy discovers she still has something of value to offer another human being, and Hoke gains access to books and the expanded world they provide.

Despite the growing appreciation they develop for one another, the two don't glide smoothly toward comfortable sharing. When Hoke has been driving from Atlanta to Mobile and needs to stop to relieve himself, Daisy urges him to wait. Hoke explains that being colored he couldn't use the toilet at the Standard Oil Station, but Miss Daisy, still imbued with Atlanta's longstanding prejudice towards Blacks, orders him to wait. She can't fathom the indignities he faces. Hoke loses his temper.

> HOKE: I ain' no dog and I ain' no chile and I ain' jes' a back of the neck you look at while you goin' wherever you want to go. I a man nearly seventy-two years old and I know when my bladder full and I gettin' out dis car and goin' off down de road like I got to do. And I'm takin' de car key dis time. And that's de end of it.

Years later, when an ice storm hits and the power goes out, Hoke surprises Daisy by showing up just to bring her coffee and keep her company. Daisy

is genuinely touched and pleased to be able to tell Boolie she doesn't
need him. But what Daisy does realize ultimately, as she declines into old
age, is that she does need Hoke, that his tenderness is just as vital to her
as the compassionate music of The Sax was to Sarah.

Driving Miss Daisy is also representative of the plays in this collection which are influenced by the region of the playwrights' upbringing,
as well as their ethnicity. Southern Jews tended, like Daisy's son, Boolie,
to follow the pattern of southern culture, even though they were de-
spised as a group by many southern whites. Before emancipation some
owned slaves. During the Civil War some Jews held office in the Confederate government and fought on that side. After the war, those who
were more affluent had Blacks as servants. Those who were merchants
had Blacks as customers because they would allow them to try on mer-
chandise, whereas other whites wouldn't permit that. Thus, Boolie and
Daisy, despite a gloss of liberalism, relate to Hoke at first as a servant,
not as a man. It can be argued that Uhry's view of Hoke and Daisy is
a product of his perspective as a southern Jewish man growing up in
Atlanta during the forties and fifties. Does the tenderness of the relationship which finally emerges show that Blacks and Jews can overcome the
southern legacy of racism, or is it a romantic view of what remains a
master-servant relationship, with the servant simply enduring his suffering more stoically than the white? Is Hoke really driving Miss Daisy in
new directions, or is he being driven by the forces of southern prejudice
to stay in his place?

Advocates of Peace, Fomenters of War

Driving Miss Daisy, despite a few references to racial unrest and anti-
Semitism in the twenty-five years spanned by the friendship, doesn't
focus on political issues which came to a head in 1964. At this time the
ideal of Blacks and Jews together reached its zenith and began to decline.
In that critical year, the first African American woman to have her play
done on Broadway wrote her last play, which expressed an eloquent plea
for intergroup understanding.

Lorraine Hansberry was a pivotal figure for African Americans, for
women and for Jews. In her plays and other writings, Hansberry expresses a guarded hopefulness about the future for Blacks and women
and a solidarity with Jewish aspirations and Jewish pride. Hansberry was
not only the first Black woman to receive a Broadway production with
her play *A Raisin in the Sun*; she also won the Drama Critics Circle
award for best play. *Raisin*, as Sydne Mahone points out, "introduced
the Black experience as subject matter worthy of dramatic treatment and

mainstream attention [and] now stands as a classic within the African-American canon."[22] At the time of its premiere, Hansberry was "a pioneer who took up a pen and, as Zora Neale Hurston wrote, 'threw up a highway through the wilderness' for the passage of the many writers who would follow.' "[23]

Less well known are Hansberry's views on the bonds between Blacks and Jews. Married to a Jewish man, Robert Nemiroff, and having worked with a Jewish producer, Philip Rose, who helped catapult her to fame with the Broadway and film version of *A Raisin in the Sun*, she spoke out in plays and public statements to express solidarity with Jews. She insisted, for example, that it was correct to try Adolph Eichmann in Israel and important for Black men and women to stop thinking racially when it comes to the oppression of people.[24]

Before her untimely death Hansberry wrote a last play of social significance, *The Sign in Sidney Brustein's Window* (1964), with a Jewish protagonist, Sidney Brustein, surrounded by disillusioned radicals in the Greenwich Village of the late 1950s. *Brustein* opts finally for active resistance to the ills of society—many of which are represented in microcosm in this play. He sees his decision to start a newspaper as a means of fighting for all the wronged people, regardless of race or religion: "One does not smite evil any more: one holds one's gut, thus—one takes a pill. Oh, but to take up the sword of the Maccabeans again!"[25]

As these words were being spoken on a New York stage, two New York Jewish boys, Andrew Goodman and Michael Schwerner, were making their way to Mississippi to meet with a Black civil rights worker, James Chaney. Goodman and Schwerner were representative of thousands of Jews who had joined forces with African Americans to defeat together the forces of oppression. These Jews battling against segregation comprised the majority of the whites who went down South to help with voter registration and were the chief contributors to Dr. Martin Luther King, Jr. These modern Maccabeans would have made Sidney Brustein and Lorraine Hansberry proud. But alas, Lorraine Hansberry died on January 1, 1965, and with her passing seemed to go the spirit of a shared struggle that imbued many Blacks and Jews of her lifetime.

Barbara Lebow's play, *The Left Hand Singing*, begins on a note of high idealism in that so-called Freedom Summer of 1964, with three college students: Linda Winnick, a Jewish young woman from New York City; Wesley Partridge, a white Methodist Christian young man from Charlotte, North Carolina; and Honey Johnson, an African American young woman from the small town of Opelika, Alabama—all heading to register voters in Mississippi. The Jewish woman and the Christian man convince the reluctant Honey, who wants to teach in her home town, to join them in their worthy quest. They go down and are murdered by bigots, parallel to the actual Goodman, Schwerner, Chaney murders of August, but their bodies aren't discovered until four years later. In the years following the gruesome discovery, their parents try to remain friends, but there is a rift between them and a period of great disillusionment. By the 1990s, John, Wesley's minister father, feels the hopeful coalition of Christians, Jews and Blacks, once cemented by idealism, is no longer holding together.

> JOHN: I've been feeling like everything has broken down. What our children were trying to do. "Black power," "white supremacy," riots, people like you and Maddy, who were working together, turning on each other. Nothing holding together, nothing working anymore.

Later in the play, Bea, the Jewish mother of Linda, is mugged by a Black man in New York City. Though she had been regularly going down to Opelika, Alabama, to help Honey's mother, Maddy, distribute food and books to the Black children, she now decides not to go. She doesn't tell Maddy why she's changed her plans, because she's ashamed of her racist response to the attack. Yet Maddy sees right through her. A shrewd detector of hypocrisy, she employs caustic satire to undercut the politically correct attempts whites make to "do good." She dismisses them as latter-day Eleanor Roosevelts, gallivanting all over, "sticking their noses in other people's business." In her eyes, the white Jewish Bea is a dilettante activist, flitting off to Argentina to help find the disappeared when her efforts as savior of the Blacks are not appreciated. The Black Maddy is committed to helping the most desperate of her people, while the white Jewish Bea, embittered by having lost a daughter to the civil rights cause, wants nothing more to do with Blacks.

> MADDY: You want him to say he's sorry he needs your money and sorry he tore up the streets in Watts and Detroit and sorry he doesn't appreciate all you've been trying to do for him?

> BEA: This is just why I didn't tell you! (*Headed out.*) Forget it! It's none of your damn business anyway!

Like a tangled skein of yarn, the lives of Lebow's characters are composed of complicated interconnections with each other and with the strands of history. Altered attitudes about womanhood, for example, intertwine with other cultural threads to produce the special texture of the characters' lives in Lebow's play. Responding to the growing equality of men and women, Lebow does not create male reincarnations of Chaney,

Schwerner and Goodman. In her play she makes two of the three young idealists who sacrifice their lives for freedom female and endows them with as much grit and determination as the original young men. The bonding of Honey and Linda suggests the type of bold cooperation that in 1972 brought Bella Abzug and Betty Friedan to advance Shirley Chisholm as both the first woman and the first African American to campaign for President.[26] The respect and warm friendship Linda and Honey have for each other as they prepare to fight for Black voting rights remind us of Gloria Steinem, teaming up with Black activist Flo Kennedy to fight for women's rights[27] or marching arm-in-arm with author Alice Walker and feeling an even more intimate relationship with Walker's Black fictional characters.[28]

The older generation of women, the surviving mothers of Honey and Linda, don't experience the sisterhood that motivated their daughters. They are bound, after all, by tragedy. Lebow wisely shows disputes between Maddy and Bea during the nineties which threaten to destroy their bitter bond.

The coalition of Black women and white women, including those who were Jewish, who fought for women's rights starting in the late sixties and through the seventies, was always threatened by differences in their economic agendas and life experiences. The Women's Movement of that period, despite efforts to embrace all women, tended to have a white, middle-class hue, with its focus on freeing women from domestic servitude to get jobs in a workplace that would offer them equal pay with men. Yet for Black women of all economic levels, getting out of the house to work was nothing new. As Toni Morrison, the only Black woman to win the Nobel Prize for Literature, explained in discussing the difference in the writing of Black women and white women:

> Aggression is not as new to black women as it is to white women. Black women seem able to combine the nest and the adventure. They don't see conflicts in certain areas as do white women . . . We, black women, do both.[29]

Lebow underscores this type of difference, making Bea the less daring individual thrown by her encounter with urban crime and Maddie the one who wades into the thick of the poverty quagmire threatening her people. There are overtones here of suspicion of the white humanitarian who might harbor racism and the aggressively separatist Black person who might be anti-Semitic, feelings which undermined the earlier interracial, ecumenical spirit of feminism.[30]

The Left Hand Singing ends, not with the acrimonious fight of the surviving mothers, but on a different note. We're transported back to the

beginning of the young people's journey, just as they are embarking on
the great adventure.

HONEY: Now do we sing We Shall Overcome?

LINDA and WES laugh, drop hands.

LINDA: How can you make fun of that song?

HONEY: How can you be such a knee-jerk?

LINDA: How can you be such a—

WES: How 'bout us making a toast. *(He grabs a coffee cup, as
do the others.)*

HONEY: All right. *(Starting big, a joke.)* Here's to—*(Suddenly
quiet.)* . . . to the summer of '64.

LINDA: *(Quietly.)* To changing the future. *(Pause. They look at
each other happily.)*

ALL THREE: The future! *(They raise their arms in a toast as
lights fade to black.)*

In light of what we know will happen to these three idealistic young
people, to end with their hopefulness is just to underscore Lebow's sense
of the gap between the dream of Black, Jew and white Christian allied
together to achieve equality and the grim reality of alienated cultures and
unspoken but ubiquitous racism. Lebow's coda reminds us how complex
the network is that connects cultures. She shows how fragile the web is,
always threatened by generational and historical forces, simmering ha-
treds and suspicions that only require some angry rhetoric and a few
violent acts to destroy the alliance.

The Deepening Divide

How does that 1964 idealism look from the vantage point of the early
twenty-first century: tragic, hopeful, foolish, quaint? Certainly things
changed. The mood of Lebow's play is similar to that of Michael Henry
Brown's bitter recollection of the Bronx, Tom Cole's anguished exami-
nation of the return of a Medal of Honor winner, and even the pain
beneath the comic surface of Herb Gardner's dialogue. The hindsight of

the nineties gives us an "after the Fall" feeling. Gardner's Central Park is no Garden of Eden. The place is riddled with dope dealers, pimps, thugs and fake cowboys who assault and steal from enfeebled old men. The world changed during the post-sixties decades. And this change was reflected in novels, plays and poetry that began to reveal a deepening divide between Blacks and Jews, if not an outright hostility.

In Bernard Malamud's 1971 novel, *The Tenants*, a Black writer and a Jewish writer fight it out almost to the death. Though Malamud had written earlier stories including "Angel Levine" and "Black Is My Favorite Color," depicting more benign relationships between the two groups, he is far less hopeful here. Despite his claim that his novel was actually "a prophetic warning against fanaticism" and an argument for the "invention of choices to outwit tragedy," *The Tenants*, as Louis Harap points out, seems to offer no choice but "mutual destruction."[31]

Equal fury was expressed by some Black playwrights and poets, especially as the promise of the late fifties and early sixties failed to produce substantive change. This more militant, separatist posture had, in the early sixties, run parallel to integrationist views. Even as Hansberry was affirming her belief in Blacks and Jews united for social justice, other Black writers and activists were anxious to seize control of their own movement, expel whites, including Jews, who had been so prominent in the struggle. Whereas Black playwright Ed Bullins, more concerned with giving birth to an authentic Black theater, made only a few uncomplimentary references to Jews, LeRoi Jones (later Amiri Baraka), in his 1964 play *Dutchman*, explodes with fury.

Jones is contemptuous of whites, especially Jewish self-proclaimed esthetes, who presume to understand Black music. He resents their professed familiarity with this music when they don't comprehend the principal component of it: the underlying rage directed toward them as oppressors. Nor do they realize that Blacks need to sublimate their rage to create this unique music admired by whites. Without this sublimation, Jones warns us, Blacks would resort to murder to preserve their sanity.

> If Bessie Smith had killed some white people she wouldn't have needed that music. She could have talked very straight and plain about the world. No metaphors. No grunts. No wiggles in the dark of her soul. Just straight two and two are four. Money. Power. Luxury. Like that. All of them. Crazy niggers turning their backs on sanity. When all it needs is that simple act. Murder. Just murder! Would make us all sane.[32]

Nikki Giovanni, in her poem "The True Import of Present Dialogue, Black vs. Negro," part of her 1970 collection, *Black Feeling, Black*

Talk/Black Judgment, echoes Jones' hostility. Giovanni speaks of having Blacks "poison" and "stab" Jews. Railing against Blacks' dependence upon Jews, she warns them in her "Poem (No Name No. 3), "Anne Frank didn't put cheese and bread away for you/ Because she knew it would be different this time." Giovanni, therefore, claims in her "Love Poem" it is "impossible to love/ a Jew."[33]

Hovering in the background of this growing loveless relationship between Blacks and Jews were the motherlands: Africa and Israel, whose interests came into conflict on the global stage. The escalating struggle against apartheid in South Africa and the clash of Islamic and Arab interests with Judaism and Israel increased tensions in America between Blacks and Jews. After the 1967 victory of the Israelis and the resulting acquisition of additional land, they were no longer regarded as the underdog. The allegiance of Blacks to the Third World and to Arab Muslims, in particular, thus flourished from the late sixties through the eighties and led to unqualified endorsement of Arab hostility to Israel.[34] This Black affinity for the Arabs coincided with the change in mood and leadership of the Civil Rights Movement, with its pressures on whites, including Jews, to leave their significant positions at NAACP, CORE and SNCC. Black leaders, such as Stokely Carmichael, were contemptuous of Jews trying to tell Blacks how to run their movement. They not only attacked American Jews for paternalism toward Blacks, but they blamed them for support of "Zionist imperialism" and Israeli cooperation with the oppressive government of South Africa.

Cornel West sees the two groups as vying for the moral high ground, at best, attacking the other's morality, at worst. "Blacks often perceive the Jewish defense of the State of Israel as [an] instance of naked group interest, and . . . an abandonment of substantive moral deliberation. At the same time, Jews tend to view Black critiques of Israel as Black rejection of the Jewish right to group survival and hence as a betrayal of the precondition for a Black-Jewish alliance. What is at stake here is not simply Black-Jewish relations, but, more importantly, the moral content of Jewish and Black identities and of their political consequences."[35]

In the seventies and eighties, the most compelling dramas about Blacks and Jews were the ones enacted in the public arena, with heated battles over principle and practice ferociously waged between real life protagonists and antagonists. With these life embroilments seeming so irreconcilable and with a growing awareness of separate group identity, Jewish and African American playwrights shifted their focus from dramatizing these hopelessly tangled relationships to creating plays about their own people.

Arthur Miller, for example, whose *Death of a Salesman* had given us a Loman family without a defined ethnic background, wrote *Incident at Vichy* in 1964, depicting French Jews waiting for interrogation during the Holocaust. During that same year, Miller wrote his autobiographical confessional play, *After the Fall*, in which the protagonist attempts to expiate his own Holocaust survival guilt. His 1968 play, *The Price*, involves a conflict between two brothers whose deceased family's valuables are assessed by an elderly Jewish appraiser, a rich source of Jewish humor and wisdom. In 1972, Miller created his comic version of Genesis, *The Creation of the World and Other Business*. In 1980, Miller wrote *Playing for Time*, his television adaptation of Fanya Fenelon's Holocaust diary, depicting the Jewish women in Auschwitz who played music for the Nazis to save their lives, while their fellow Jews were being sent to the crematoria.[36] A delegate to the Democratic National Convention of 1972 after serving as President of P.E.N. and later representing writers in the struggle to reduce their persecution in the former Soviet Union, Arthur Miller hardly divorced himself from secular politics and international issues. Yet one can see a stronger sense of his Jewish identity and a greater preoccupation with Jewish concerns in his plays of 1964–1980.

This was also the case with a number of lesser known playwrights writing on Jewish themes whose works were performed at theaters, some of which were devoted exclusively to performing Jewish works. Significant in this theater network were New York's Jewish Repertory Theater founded by Ron Avni and the American Jewish Theater founded by Stanley Brechner.

This same time period was one of tremendous creativity for Black playwrights who wrote dramas focusing on the salient issues confronting Blacks themselves. Though African Americans were the largest minority group in the United States in the twentieth century, only a handful of their plays had been produced. The Negro Ensemble Company brought the works of African American playwrights to fruition by creating a theater dedicated to plays written by Blacks and produced, directed and performed by Blacks for primarily Black audiences. Established by playwright and co-founder Douglas Turner Ward, NEC became the place where such eminent Black playwrights as Lonnie Elder, *Ceremonies in Dark Old Men* (1969), Joe Walker, *The River Niger* (1972), Steve Carter, *Eden* (1975), and Charles Fuller, *A Soldier's Play* (1981) launched their work. Producing more than two hundred new plays and providing a showcase for the work of more than four thousand cast and crew members, the NEC not only encouraged the founding of African American theaters but also influenced regional theaters across the country to present works by Black playwrights as part of their regular season.[37] The Tony Award–winning Victory Gardens Theater of Chicago, for example, discovered playwright Steve Carter through his productions at NEC, made him a resident playwright in 1981 and produced every one of his plays as they emerged over the years.[38] Also in 1981, journalist and novelist John A. Williams wrote the play *Last Flight to Ambo Ber*,[39] which tackled the complicated situation of Ethiopian Jews, 17,000 of whom were airlifted to Israel during the 1980s. With its combination of African Americans, Black African Jews and white Jews, this drama is a rare expression of the confluence of Black and Jewish interests during these decades.

In 1984, August Wilson, later the best known and most respected African American playwright of our time, committed himself to writing a ten-play cycle chronicling each decade of the Black experience in the twentieth century. In 1987 he received a Pulitzer Prize for his second play, *Fences*, and in 1990 for his fourth play, *The Piano Lesson*. For these and many other of his plays which received great acclaim, he was hailed by *New York Times* theater critic Frank Rich as a "major writer, combining a poet's ear for vernacular with a robust sense of humor (political and sexual), a sure instinct for crackling dramatic incident and passionate commitment to a great subject."[40]

As many Jewish and Black playwrights were regaining a sense of connection to their own people, players on the political stage were engaging in debates that threatened to flare into hate fests. Grim realities in the outside world eclipsed the aesthetic realities of the plays themselves. The death of Black communities such as the Bronx and Detroit was an immediate type of conflagration that Jews in the 1970s could not extinguish, and it left noxious clouds of hostility in its wake. The help of Jewish professionals, so welcome and crucial in the first sixty years of the century, was neither wanted nor accepted. In some circles, Jews began to be blamed for Black "genocide" and every other manner of Black suffering and disadvantage. The bond between Jews and Blacks, strengthened by formerly shared interests, was weakened and some would say broken. Jews retreated from their support of affirmative action which would reduce their ranks at universities and prevent them from being hired for choice jobs. They went on the offensive to combat the onslaught of Black anti-Semitism and anti-Zionism. *New Republic* editor-in-chief Martin Peretz and other writers expressed a new brand of what Peretz called "muscular Judaism," taking the offensive on Israel and lambasting the incendiary rhetoric of Louis Farrakhan, the emerging leader of the more militant Black Muslims.[41]

Especially in the course of the eighties, there was a corresponding separatism on the part of Black politicians, punctuated in 1984 by Democrat presidential candidate Jesse Jackson referring to New York City as "hymietown."[42] The alliance, however, wasn't utterly destroyed, as evidenced by many coalitions of Blacks and Jews who worked together to elect the first Black mayors in Chicago, Philadelphia and New York. But these advances occurred as poverty, crime, drugs, and an epidemic called AIDS disproportionately affected Blacks, giving political victories a sense of tokenism.

By 1991 the righteous anger of disenfranchised Blacks and increasingly conservative Jews would boil up into the Crown Heights riots, dramatized by Anna Deavere Smith in her play, *Fires in the Mirror*. The drama is entirely comprised of the words of the participants, culled from interviews but without the use of a narrator, fictional characters or interpolated material from the playwright. As originally conceived and presented, Ms. Smith "embodied" the various characters in a tour de force, one-person performance. A television broadcast and video made from the play also features Ms. Smith playing all the characters herself, though her play was subsequently performed around the country by mixed casts assuming multiple roles which crossed gender and color lines. The video and various stage performances have made use of appropriate music— black soul music, rap rhythms, Hasidic melodies or *niggunim*—to provide a context for the words. The actual script of the play relies entirely on words, leaving the reader to produce the music, recognize the discord and perceive the possibility of harmony. Anna Deavere Smith sees it as her job to put forth a stark juxtaposition of conflicting characters without offering a resolution. She documents the clash of identities, symbols, human lives, creating greater clarity without compromising differences or diminishing the intensity of the event.

The basic facts of the conflict, as established in the background information provided for the broadcast of the play, are these: On August 19, 1991, in the Crown Heights section of Brooklyn, New York, one of the cars in a three-car procession carrying the spiritual leader of the Orthodox Jewish community, the Lubavitcher Hasidic *Rebbe*, ran a red light, hit another car, and swerved onto the sidewalk, killing Gavin Cato, a seven-year-old Black boy from Guyana and seriously injuring his cousin Angela. That evening, amid rumors that a Hasidic-run ambulance helped the Jewish driver and passengers and left the children to die, a group of young Black men fatally stabbed Yankel Rosenbaum, a 29-year-old Hasidic scholar from Australia. "For three days, Black people fought police, attacked Lubavitcher headquarters, and torched businesses while Hasidic patrols responded with their own violence."[43]

As one reads the voices of Jews and African Americans in Smith's play, the term "warring holocausts" comes to mind again, for each group has suffered and each individual feels that the suffering of his or her group is the most extensive, profound and deserving of redress. Here is Minister, for the Honorable Louis Farrakhan, Conrad Mohammed who states that the Holocaust which exterminated six million Jews in Europe

did not equal the crime of enslaving Africans, packing them onto ships
for months in the middle passage, depriving them through rape and the
depredations of slavery of their very identity.

> MINISTER CONRAD MOHAMMED:
> That, uh, crime also stinks
> in the nostrils of God,
> But it in no way compares with the slavery of our people
> because we lost over a hundred
> and some say two hundred and fifty,
> million
> in the middle passage
> coming from Africa
> to America.

Minister Mohammed and his Black Muslim brothers are further incensed
over the Jews' usurpation of the role of the chosen people, a role he
thinks rightfully belongs to Blacks.

> The Honorable Louis Farrakhan
> teaches us
> that we are the chosen of God
> We are those people
> that almighty God Allah
> has selected as his chosen,
> and they are masquerading in our garment—
> the Jews.

This quantification of suffering, or vying for chosen-ness, is part of a
dangerous and ultimately dehumanizing competition. This play shows
what a moral quagmire we sink into when Americans compete for the
dubious distinction of most-victimized minority.

Letty Cottin Pogrebin, feminist author and eloquent foe of anti-
Semitism, whose family story precedes Minister Muhammed's words in
this play, is reluctant to tell about her Uncle Isaac, not wanting to "make
hay with the Holocaust," but she ultimately reads from her own account
of the man who was chosen by the Jewish council of his town to survive
and bear witness. This included the unspeakable horror of guiding his own
wife and children into the gas chamber and later being obligated to tell the
tale again and again until his own death. The Black residents of Crown
Heights who speak to and through playwright Anna Deavere Smith fail to
recognize the Holocaust in Europe as a common ground of misery for

Blacks and Jews. The lashing out at Jews and the cold-blooded murder of Yankel Rosenbaum seemed to Blacks a justified reaction to what they perceived as Jewish privilege and indifference to their suffering.

Yet to Jews who had survived the Holocaust or experienced deadly rioting in the form of Russian pogroms, Crown Heights might have been Kishinev, Russia, or Berlin, Germany. Without warning, oppressors unleash their fury against innocent victims. Those who lost their loved ones wanted to die themselves. In a section of Smith's play called "Pogroms," Reuven Ostrov, a Russian Jewish chaplain at Kings County Hospital, describes an anguished son's account of his old Russian Jewish mother who committed suicide shortly after she heard of the stabbing of Yankel Rosenbaum. She had left Russia eleven years ago (1980) because of the persecution there, but when this same persecution started to happen to Crown Heights, she felt like it was Russia all over again.

> REUVEN OSTROV. It became painful
> And it felt like, like there was no place to go.
> It's like you're trapped,
> everywhere you go there's Jew haters
> And then he told me she commit suicide . . .
> The window was open
> which is never open
> because she was afraid of the cold,
> even in the summertime.
> And he saw his mother
> with blood all over her
> landed head first
> on the concrete side of the apartment building.
> After that we already knew this was getting serious
> because we had,
> we had Sonny Carson come down
> and we had, um,
> Reverend Al Sharpton come down
> start making pogroms.

The Jewish voices in Smith's arresting play express, as Ethan Goffman notes in *Imagining Each Other*, "an ingrained fear of anti-Semitism, of words leading to mob action,"[44] rather than a deep hatred of Blacks. It is the Jew's anguished memory of past afflictions which exacerbates their torment in the present. It is their recall of former grim betrayals which heightens their current fear of ubiquitous Jew-baiters. Jews can't hear a mob shouting "Hitler didn't finish the job" without placing the words and speakers within "a brutal historical awareness, for it is this history,"

Goffman claims, "which spurs the taunts, words calculated for maximum effect. Black hatred of Jews, the rioting that erupted in Crown Heights, and the death of Yankel Rosenbaum—in this version of events, all are merely continuations of a great historical pattern of Jew hatred, tacitly backed by authority, that transcends time and place. Rosenbaum's parents were Holocaust survivors; in a context quite different from Nazi Germany, their son suffers the same fate."[45]

Yet from the Black perspective, the death of Gavin Cato and the perceived callousness of the Jews toward the accident which killed him is part of *their* larger historical patterns of enslavement, lynching and indifference to Black humanity. Reverend Al Sharpton accuses the Jews of killing a child and "walking away like [they] just stepped on a roach!" Some of the Blacks perceive the Jews as the ones who are the makers of pogroms. The common historical suffering which once drew Blacks and Jews together had also given both groups a learned suspicion, a heightened sensitivity to slights, an acquired instinct for self-defense. In this instance the lessons of racism and anti-Semitism caused them to suspect each other, to react with hostility and even violence to behavior they perceived as threatening their very survival. This irony of shared suffering turning into a cause of conflict, of mutual compassion reversing to mutual hatred, is a startling if grim insight in Smith's polyphonic drama.

Black and Jewish perceptions of what actually happened in Crown Heights are so contradictory that only their juxtaposition in such separate monologues, faithfully rendered by the playwright, seem to fairly dramatize the event. "Perhaps the only answer to these extremes of misunderstanding, Goffman suggests, is *Fires in the Mirror* itself; its remarkable human spectrum creates a kind of dialogue composed of overlapping monologues in which the participants refuse to listen to each other. In Anna Deavere Smith the clash of ethnic heritages that make up America is at once ugly, vivid, beautiful, and terrifying."[46] The playwright's inclusion of these often conflicting voices is yet another reminder that Jews and Blacks may be the only minority groups, as Pogrebin put it, "who still seem to believe that our destinies are interwoven."[47]

As a dramatist Smith is admirably impartial, but deceptively skillful in the way she arranges the monologues not only for purposes of contrast with one another but for maximum revelation of individual complexity. She places Minister Mohammed's official declaration of Black chosen-ness and African American victimization after Pogrebin's personal account of a family member who suffered the ravages of the Holocaust. In some cases, we see the private side of public figures revealing their vulnerabilities. Instead of Reverend Al Sharpton's usual media flamboyance, he gives a tender tribute to the troubled soul singer James Brown, who served as his father. Smith juxtaposes Sharpton's resolve to do his "own cultural thing," to wear the same stylized hairdo of father figure James Brown, with Orthodox Rivkah Siegal's ambivalence about concealing her hair beneath ritually prescribed wigs which she regards as inauthentic head coverings that reinforce her insularity.

The variety of voices Smith provides brooks no stereotypes. Leading African American intellectual Angela Davis admits she's always thought of herself as a "race woman," a person profoundly connected to her people. But in this rare disclosure, she is not the expected race woman. She offers the metaphor of "the rope attached to that anchor" of race which "should be long enough to allow us to move into other communities to understand and learn."

Never disrespectful, never so respectful that she eliminates verbal tics or grammatical errors, the playwright captures the comic surfaces and the tragic depths of her characters. With each group she depicts the accents and outlook of individuals with such attention to idiosyncrasy that we are moved to laughter and tears in quick succession. Because she can tolerate ambiguity without positing inflexibly right answers, she encourages us to resist easy conclusions. She's like a female Solomon who gives no fixed final judgment, but shows us what happens when the child—in this case the community—is cut in two. Her play is healing in the sense that it gives us the pieces of what once was a community and makes us ask, Could this community be put together? She resists the traditional resolution that we find in more conventional drama. She brings theater back to the real world, challenging us to identify and embrace the contradictions without judging the outcome. The vividness of the community she presents, in what seems like its entirety, can't help but remind us what it might be if it were united. By holding the mirror up to these intensely different individuals, Anna Deavere Smith allows us to experience fires that do not destroy. Rather, they illuminate.

Looking to the Future

On August 20, 2002, on the eleventh anniversary of the accident and rioting, the Associated Press reported the public meeting and embrace of two men linked by the loss of their loved ones during the Crown Heights rioting. Carmel Cato, the father of Gavin Cato, the boy who died when hit by a Jewish driver, said he hoped love and understanding would be a legacy of the riots. Norman Rosenbaum, the brother of the rabbinical student, Yankel Rosenbaum, slain by Black youths, said the symbolism of their meeting should not be lost on anyone. Rosenbaum said the two should stay in contact regularly, "but when it came to today, we felt that it was very important that this day above all other days that we do get together." Cato said, "We are strong, we are loving, and we will keep that loving going."[48]

Here are ten plays representing the drama of Blacks and Jews. They may make us angry, may cause us to laugh, may challenge us intellectually, may move us to see people with fresh eyes. They may compel us to see the characters as individuals beyond stereotypes, beyond the cosmetically altered, beyond politically correct representatives. We hope these plays instill respect for the differences that make the human drama authentic. In Cato's words, these plays may even inspire us "to keep that loving going."

Notes

1. Cornel West, "Black-Jewish Relations," in *Blacks and Jews*, ed. Paul Berman (New York: Delacorte Press, 1994), p. 146.

2. The ties that have bound these groups together are largely woven of mutual suffering, of sharing the position as the hated outsider. Jonathan Kaufman, in his book, *Broken Alliance: The Turbulent Times Between Blacks and Jews in America* (New York: Touchstone/Simon & Schuster, 1995), shows how the alliance was strengthened in the early part of the century. For example, between 1889 and 1919, an average of 100 Black men were lynched every year in the South. These brutal murders were sometimes celebrated by whites with picnics, picture postcards and a carnival atmosphere. Between 1880 and 1920, oppression and government-sponsored anti-Semitism in Europe, including violent attacks called "pogroms," propelled more than two million Jews to come to America. In 1909 Blacks and Jews, working with others, established the National Association for the Advancement of Colored People. Two Jewish brothers, Joel and Arthur Spingarn, served as the NAACP's first leaders, with Joel presiding on and off from 1914 to 1939 and Arthur heading its legal battles. In 1913 Leo Frank, a Jewish owner of a pencil factory, was accused of murdering a white employee. He was pardoned by the Governor of Georgia but then lynched by white men after his release from prison, marking a resurgence of the Ku Klux Klan and a grim statement that the Klan would be after Jews as well as Blacks (Kaufman, pp. 23–32).

3. Cornel West, *Blacks and Jews*, pp. 146–147.

4. Julius Lester, "The Lives People Live," in *Blacks and Jews*, ed. Paul Berman (New York: Delacorte Press, 1994), p. 166.

5. Ibid., p. 167.

6. Thomas W. Jones II, "Preface," in *Black Comedy: 9 Plays*, eds. Pamela Faith Jackson and Karimah (New York: Applause, 1997), p. ix.

7. Julius Lester, op. cit., p. 167.

8. Ralph Ellison, "The World and the Jug," in *Shadow and Act* (New York, 1964), p. 117, quoted in Louis Harap, *Dramatic Encounters* (New York: Greenwood Press, 1987), p. 3.

9. Richard Wright, *Black Boy*, (New York, 1945), pp. 53–54, quoted in Louis Harap, op. cit., p. 5.

10. Louis Harap, *Dramatic Encounters*, p. 4.

11. Andrew Hacker, "Jewish Racism, Black Anti-Semitism," in *Blacks and Jews*, p. 162.

12. Jonathan Kaufman, *Broken Alliance*, p. 5.

13. Richard Wright, "How Bigger Was Born," *Native Son* (New York, 1966 [c 1940]), p. 364, quoted in Louis Harap, *Dramatic Encounters*, p. 5.

14. Louis Harap, *Dramatic Encounters*, p. 5.

15. "Of all enlisted men who died in Vietnam, Blacks made up 14.1% of the total. This came at a time when they made up 11% of the young male population nationwide." "Vietnam War Casualties by Race, Ethnicity and National Origin," The American War Library Homepage, http://members.aol.com/warlibrary/vwc10.htm.

16. Jonathan Kaufman, *Broken Alliance*, pp. 41–43. Kaufman's overview shows that previous wars raised hopes for Black veterans, hopes which were then dashed, as when they returned from World War I to a spate of riots which killed Blacks and some whites in Chicago and other cities. After World War II, Blacks expected greater equality, but instead there was the fifties in which change, such as the mandated integration of schools, was put on paper but resisted in practice. Going back to the Civil War, Kaufman illustrates how hopes were raised by Reconstruction and the opening of state and federal legislatures to Black representation. Then came the Great Compromise of 1877, when northern troops were pulled out of the South in exchange for southern support of Rutherford B. Hayes, leaving Blacks to the "mercy" of southern whites who removed them from office and established Jim Crow laws of segregation throughout the South. Thus the Vietnam experience for Black veterans wasn't a departure from an attitude of welcoming Black veterans home after serving gallantly in foreign wars. It was another example of using Blacks for military service, yet failing to reward them with any meaningful gains if they survived their tour of duty.

17. Arthur Laurents, *Home of the Brave*, in Ellen Schiff, ed., *Awake and Singing: 7 Classic Plays from the American Jewish Repertoire* (New York: Penguin, 1995), pp. 371–449.

In Arthur Laurents' play, *Home of the Brave*, first produced in 1945, the veteran paralyzed by survivor guilt is Jewish, and it is his belief that he was glad his friend was killed by the Japanese because the friend harbored anti-Semitic feelings. This belief is complicating his recovery. But recover he does, because the doctor in this case recognizes that the Jewish soldier, Peter Coen, simply experienced what every surviving soldier experiences momentarily when a buddy is shot—joy and relief that he has survived. The outcome of the play is more optimistic than Cole's *Medal of Honor Rag*. If we focus on the United States, a Jew had a better chance of recovering from the World War II experience and prospering than did a Black veteran.

18. Julius Lester, "The Lives People Live," p. 175.

19. Ibid., p. 171. Lester also invites us to consider the following bleak statistics gathered in the early 1990s: "Seventy-five percent of all Black infants are born to unwed mothers, half of whom are teenagers" (p. 171). Blacks comprise 12% of the population but account for 45% of all deaths by fire. Forty-seven percent of all Black seventeen-year-olds are functionally illiterate (p. 173). Henry

Louis Gates, Jr., referring to the recalcitrant social problems that lie at the roots of Black rage, also lists these facts: "One Black man graduates from college for every hundred who go to jail. Almost half of black children live in poverty." Henry Louis Gates, Jr., "The Charmer," *The New Yorker*, May 6, 1996, p. 131, quoted in Ethan Goffman, *Imagining Each Other* (Albany, NY: State University of New York Press, 2000), p. 224.

20. Louis Harap, op. cit., p. 14. "The sociologist, Herbert J. Gans, reports results of a survey by a 1968 Mayor's Task Force on the ethnicity of business owners in Harlem. It showed that Jews owned about 40 percent of all stores in Harlem. All white-owned stores added up to about 47 percent. Thus, 53 percent were owned by Blacks or other non-whites. But the actual capital invested by non-whites was only 10 percent of the total."

21. Roger Wilkins, quoted in Ethan Goffman, *Imagining Each Other: Blacks and Jews in Contemporary American Literature* (Albany NY: State University of New York Press, 2000), p. 207, is a Pulitzer Prize–winning author, columnist and distinguished professor.

22. Sydne Mahone, *Moon Marked & Touched by the Sun: Plays by African-American Women* (New York: Theatre Communications Group, 1994), p. xxv.

23. Ibid.

24. Lorraine Hansberry, *To Be Young, Gifted and Black: Lorraine Hansberry on Her Own Work*, adapted by Robert Nemiroff, with an introduction by James Baldwin (Englewood Cliffs, NJ, 1969) p. 177, cited by Louis Harap, op. cit., p. 7. Hansberry wanted her people to be as outraged at Eichmann as they were at the murderers of Emmet Till and Medgar Evers. She wanted them to be as insistent that Eichmann be tried in Israel as they were for Black judges to rule on civil rights legislation and capital punishment:

> For me there is a strong and powerful current of Justice in the fact: a representative figure of Nazism tried on Jewish soil. Under Jewish justice. By Jewish judges. I am moved by the thought of it. It is about time.

25. Lorraine Hansberry, *The Sign in Sidney Brustein's Window* (New York: Samuel French, 1993), pp. 82–83.

Hansberry's plays were never doctrinaire, but they did reflect her view that "there are no plays which are not social and no plays that do not have a thesis." Hansberry, however, insists that the playwright have talents equal to the task of dramatizing the message. "The problem is that there are great plays and lousy plays and reasonably good plays; when the artist achieves a force of art which is commensurate with his message—he hooks us. When he doesn't, we are bored or offended about being lectured to, and confused because we think it must be the 'Message' which is out of place—or uninteresting or trivial or ridiculous because of the clumsy way he has hurled it at us." Lorraine Hansberry, *To Be Young, Gifted and Black*, adapted by Robert Nemiroff (New York: New American Library, 1970), p. 119, cited in Steven R. Carter, *Hansberry's Drama* (Champaign, Ill.: University of Illinois Press, 1991), p. 89.

26. Sheila Rowabotham, *A Century of Women* (New York: Viking, 1997), p. 437.

27. Carolyn G. Heilbrun, *The Education of a Woman: The Life of Gloria Steinem* (New York: Dial Press, 1995), pp. 204–205. Always trying to prove that feminism was not a movement limited to upper-middle-class white women, Gloria Steinem made it a point to speak out on women's issues in the early seventies with African American women, including day care pioneer Dorothy Pitman, lawyer and activist Flo Kennedy and sister *Ms.* Editor, Margaret Sloan. There is every indication that these political partnerships became lasting friendships.

28. Gloria Steinem, *Outrageous Acts and Everyday Rebellions* (New York: Holt, Rinehart and Winston, 1983), pp. 267–268.

29. Toni Morrison, Interview with Claudia Tate in *Black Women Writers at Work*, edited by Claudia Tate (New York: Continuum, 1983), pp. 117–31, quoted in Carolyn G. Heilbrun, *Writing a Woman's Life* (New York: Ballantine Books, 1988), p. 61.

30. Elly Bulkin, Minnie Bruce Platt, Barbara Smith, *Yours in Struggle* (Brooklyn, New York: Long Haul Press, 1984).

31. Louis Harap, *Dramatic Encounters*, p. 25.

32. LeRoi Jones, *Dutchman and The Slave* (New York: Morrow, 1964), p. 35.

33. Ethan Goffman, *Imagining Each Other*, p. 218. Goffman's contention that it is not hatred of Blacks but fear of mob action against Jews that colors Jewish reactions to angry rhetoric is helpful in understanding the way Jews recoil at the incendiary speeches of a Louis Farrakhan or the hostile attitude towards Jews expressed in some of the poems of Nikki Giovanni. In *Imagining Each Other*, Goffman says that references to Anne Frank disregarding Blacks (p. 105) and lines like "it's impossible to love a Jew" (p. 106) set off alarm bells with echoes of past pogroms and annihilations. Goffman quotes from Nikki Giovanni, "The True Import of Present Dialogue, Black vs. Negro," *Black Feeling, Black Talk, Black Judgment* (New York: Morrow, 1970).

34. Louis Harap, op. cit., p. 17. Since its recognition in 1948 by the United Nations, Israel had been regarded as a struggling democracy of gritty pioneers, many of them Holocaust survivors, barely holding their own amidst a sea of hostile Arabs led by menacing dictators. Israel's victory in the 1967 Six-Day War left the country in control of land previously occupied by Arabs. From this time to the present day, that land would be disputed, though part of it was returned in 1978 as an outcome of the Camp David Accords. Yet growing military might and administrations leaning more and more to the right, caused Israel to be seen by many as the occupying nation denying the underdog Palestinians their right to statehood.

35. Cornel West, op. cit., p. 148.

36. http://www.ibiblio.org/miller/life.html. "A Brief Chronology of Arthur Miller's Life and Works," based in part on "Literary Chronology" and appendices printed in Robert A. Martin and Steven R. Centola, ed., *The Theater Essays of Arthur Miller* (New York: Viking, 1978); Arthur Miller, *Arthur Miller's Collected Plays: 1957–1981* (New York: Viking, 1981); Joanne Koch, "How Can I Call Him Arthur? An Interview with Arthur Miller," *Chicago Tribune Sunday Magazine*, January 31, 1971, pp. 42–43.

37. http://www.pbs.org/wnet/americanmasters/print/negro_ensemble_ co.html, "American Masters," material accompanying PBS broadcast on WNET New York of program in series on Negro Ensemble Company, 2003, Educational Broadcasting Corporation.

38. Steve Carter, *Eden*, in *Black Thunder: An Anthology of Contemporary African-American Drama*, William B. Branch, ed. (New York: Mentor, 1992). This collection also includes *The Taking of Miss Janie* by Ed Bullins, *The Colored Museum* by George C. Wolfe and *Ma Rainey's Black Bottom* by August Wilson. For Steve Carter's commentary on writers of color, see "New Traditions Compendium Forums & Commentaries: 1992–96," http://www.ntcp. org/compendium/artists/STEVE.html.

39. John A. Williams, *Last Flight to Ambo Ber,* unpublished manuscript of the 1981 production in Boston; listing of Williams' publications and productions at "The Mississippi Writers Page," John Alfred Williams. http://www.olemiss.edu/ mwp/dir/williams_john_a/.

40. http://www.dartmouth.edu/~awilson/bio.html, a website established by Dartmouth College in response to Wilson's teaching there, includes an August Wilson chronology and the Frank Rich assessment. August Wilson's plays have been published individually, in anthologies and in small collections, though his complete collected works have not yet been published in one volume. August Wilson, *Fences* (New York: New American Library, 1986); *The Piano Lesson* (New York: Plume, 1990).

41. Jonathan Kaufman, *Broken Alliance*, pp. 8–10.

42. Ibid., p. 256. At the time Jesse Jackson made the "hymietown" remark, Blacks constituted one fourth of the Democratic voters in America, but Jews were the largest group of contributors to the Democrat Party.

43. Anna Deavere Smith, *Fires in the Mirror* (New York: Anchor/Doubleday, 1993), p. xiii.

44. Ethan Goffman, *Imagining Each Other*, p. 218.

45. Ibid., p. 218.

46. Ibid., pp. 207–208.

47. Letty Cottin Pogrebin quoted in Henry Louis Gates Jr., "The Uses of Anti-Semitism," in *Blacks and Jews*, ed. Paul Berman (New York: Delacorte Press, 1994), p. 228.

48. The 2002 meeting was the second public meeting for Carmel Cato and Norman Rosenbaum. The first meeting took place at City Hall with Mayor Giuliani, who had defeated previous mayor, David Dinkins, partly as a result of the Crown Heights fallout.

At that meeting Mr. Rosenbaum had this to say to the people of Crown Heights: "Violence can never be justified, nor ought it to be condoned." Jennifer Steinhauer, "10 Years Later, A First Meeting of 2 Symbols of Crown Hts." August 21, 2002. *The New York Times,* pp. A15 & B2.

Selected Bibliography

Berman, Paul, ed. 1994. *Blacks and Jews: Alliances and Arguments.* New York: Delacorte.

Bulkin, Elly, Minnie Bruce Pratt, and Barbara Smith. 1984. *Yours in Struggle.* Brooklyn. New York: Long Haul Press.

Bullins, Ed. 1992. *The Taking of Miss Janie.* In *Black Thunder: An Anthology of Contemporary African-American Drama*, William B. Branch, ed. New York: Mentor.

Branch, Taylor. 1988. *Parting the Waters: America in the King Years 1954–63.* New York: Touchstone.

———. 1998. *Pillar of Fire: America in the King Years 1963–65.* New York: Touchstone.

Branch, William B., ed. 1992. *Black Thunder: An Anthology of Contemporary African-American Drama.* New York: Mentor.

Budick, Emily Miller. 1998. *Blacks and Jews in Literary Conversation.* Cambridge UK: Cambridge University Press.

Carmichael, Stokely. 1968. "Toward a Black Liberation." In *Black Fire: An Anthology of Afro-American Writing*, LeRoi Jones and Larry Neal, eds. 119–32. New York: Morrow.

Carter, Steve. 1992. *Eden.* In *Black Thunder: An Anthology of Contemporary African-American Drama*, William B. Branch, ed. New York: Mentor.

Carter, Steven R. 1991. *Hansberry's Drama.* Champaign, Illinois: University of Illinois Press.

Cohen, Sarah Blacher, ed. 1997. *Making a Scene: The Contemporary Drama of Jewish-American Women.* Syracuse, New York: Syracuse University Press.

Cole, Johnnetta Betsch, and Beverly Guy-Sheftall. 2003. *Gender Talk: The Struggle for Women's Equality in African American Communities.* New York: Ballantine Books.

Crouch, Stanley. 1995. *The All-American Skin Game, or the Decoy of Race.* New York: Pantheon.

Ellison, Ralph. 1966. "The World and the Jug." In *Shadow and Act*, 115–47. New York: Signet.

———. 1972. *Invisible Man.* 1947. Reprint. New York: Vintage.

Gates, Henry Louis, Jr. 1996. "The Charmer." *The New Yorker*, April 29 and May 6, 116–31.

———. 1994. "The Uses of Anti-Semitism." In *Blacks and Jews*, ed. Paul Berman. New York: Delacorte Press.

Giovanni, Nikki. 1970. *Black Feeling, Black Talk, Black Judgment.* New York: Morrow.

Goffman, Ethan. 2000. *Imagining Each Other: Blacks and Jews in Contemporary American Literature.* Albany, New York: State University of New York Press.

Hansberry, Lorraine. 1969. *To Be Young, Gifted and Black: Lorraine Hansberry on Her Own Work*, adapted by Robert Nemiroff, with an introduction by James Baldwin. Englewood Cliffs, New Jersey: Prentice Hall.

———. 1993. *The Sign in Sidney Brustein's Window.* New York: Samuel French.

Harap, Louis. 1987. *Dramatic Encounters: The Jewish Presence in Twentieth-Century American Drama, Poetry, and Humor and the Black-Jewish Literary Relationship.* Westport, Connecticut: Greenwood.

Heilbrun, Carolyn G., 1988. *Writing a Woman's Life.* New York: Ballantine Books.

———. 1995. *The Education of a Woman: The Life of Gloria Steinem.* New York: Dial Press.

Hentoff, Nat. 1972. *Black Anti-Semitism and Jewish Racism*. New York: Schocken Books.

Jackson, Pamela Faith, and Karimah, eds. 1997. *Black Comedy: 9 Plays*. New York: Applause.

Jones, LeRoi. 1964. *Dutchman and The Slave*. New York: Morrow.

Kaufman, Jonathan. 1995. *Broken Alliance: The Turbulent Times Between Blacks and Jews in America*. New York: Touchstone.

Koch, Joanne. 1971. "How Can I Call Him Arthur? An Interview with Arthur Miller." *Chicago Tribune Sunday Magazine*, January 31, 42–43.

Laurents, Arthur. 1995. *Home of the Brave*. In Ellen Schiff, ed., *Awake and Singing: 7 Classic Plays from The American Jewish Repertoire*. New York: Penguin, pp. 371–449.

Lester, Julius. 1994. "The Lives People Live." In *Blacks and Jews*, ed. Paul Berman. New York: Delacorte Press.

Mahone, Sydne. 1994. *Moon Marked & Touched by the Sun: Plays by African-American Women*. New York: Theatre Communications Group.

Malamud, Bernard. 1971. *The Tenants*. New York: Farrar, Straus & Giroux.

Martin, Robert A., and Steven R. Centola, eds. 1978. *The Theater Essays of Arthur Miller*. New York: Viking.

Miller, Arthur. 1981. *Arthur Miller's Collected Plays: 1957–1981*. New York: Viking.

Podhoretz, Norman. 1966. "My Negro Problem—and Ours." In *The Commentary Reader*, ed. Norman Podhoretz. New York: Atheneum.

Rowabotham, Sheila. 1997. *A Century of Women*. New York: Viking.

Tate, Claudia, ed. 1983. *Black Women Writers at Work*. New York: Continuum.

West, Cornel. 1993. Introduction to *Fires in the Mirror*, by Anna Deavere Smith. New York: Anchor.

———. 1994. "Black-Jewish Relations." In *Blacks and Jews*, ed. Paul Berman. New York: Delacorte Press.

Williams, John A. 1970. *The King God Didn't Save: Reflections on the Life and Death of Martin Luther King, Jr.* New York: Coward-McCann.

———. 1981. *Last Flight to Ambo Ber*, unpublished manuscript of the 1981 production in Boston.

Wilson, August. 1986. *Fences*. New York: New American Library.

———. 1990. *The Piano Lesson*. New York: Plume.

———. 1992. *Ma Rainey's Black Bottom*. In *Black Thunder: An Anthology of Contemporary African-American Drama*, ed. William B. Branch. New York: Mentor.

Wilson, Midge, and Kathy Russell. 1996. *Divided Sisters: Bridging the Gap Between Black Women and White Women*, New York: Anchor Books.

Wolfe, George C. 1992. *The Colored Museum*. In *Black Thunder: An Anthology of Contemporary African-American Drama*, ed. William B. Branch. New York: Mentor.

Wright, Richard. 1966. *Native Son*. 1940. Reprint, New York: Perennial.

———. 1989. *Black Boy*. 1937. Reprint. New York: Perennial.

No Niggers, No Jews, No Dogs

John Henry Redwood

John Henry Redwood

A woman is like a tea bag. You never know how strong she is until she gets into hot water.

—Eleanor Roosevelt

Though John Henry Redwood started writing so he would have something to perform, everything he's written so far features a woman as the major character. His most frequently performed play, *The Old Settler,* is about the reconciliation of two sisters who have been estranged. The drama opened in 1994 in a co-production at the McCarter Theatre and the Long Wharf Theatre, then went on to many productions internationally and in the United States, where it won an American Theater Critics Award.

No Niggers, No Jews, No Dogs, developed at the Cleveland Playhouse in 2000, then produced Off-Broadway in 2002 at Primary Stages and at the Philadelphia Theatre Company, depicts two related African American women raped by the same white man. These women must choke back their own rage and grief to protect their loved ones. "I believe African-Americans have survived on this continent because of the strength and perseverance of the Black woman," says Redwood. "If her history isn't told, we are remiss in telling our history in general."[1]

Redwood attended the University of Kansas on an athletic scholarship in the early sixties and also served in the Marines. He began acting, establishing a career on Broadway and in regional theaters, and then developed an equal passion for writing plays.

"I'd like to start my own theater, because I would want one that is playwright-friendly," the actor and playwright had told *The Philadelphia Inquirer*. He was rehearsing for a theater appearance in his Philadelphia hometown, when he died on June 17, 2003, of heart disease.[2] He was only 60 years old, in his prime as playwright and actor.

He had appeared in all of August Wilson's plays, especially in the lead role of Troy Maxson in *Fences*, which he portrayed ten times. He was acclaimed for his performance in the one-man *Paul Robeson* by Philip Hayes Dean, and for his performance in the one-man play by James Still, *Looking Over the President's Shoulder*, about Alonzo Fields, the chief butler at the White House under four presidents.

When portraying Fields, the role he was about to reprise when he died, Redwood always carried a little piece of the man's life with him, a small container of dirt from the black cemetery behind a church built in 1854 in Lyle Station, Indiana. "There's dirt from the site of his father's general store . . . and all this dirt is mixed into this little tin and it sits in my suitcase. It's on stage with me at all times."[3]

Redwood's plays—including his first one, *Mark VIII:XXXVI*, and *A Sunbeam, Acted Within Proper Departmental Procedure, An Ole Soul a Young Spirit*, and a number of commissioned works for young audiences— are rooted in the earth of his people. Especially through their women characters, these plays communicate a sense of dignity, intelligence, devotion to family and faith in the face of struggle, frustration and tragedy. Whether he was depicting real individuals or creating them, Redwood felt a responsibility to focus on authentic Black people. "Black people are not really going to come to the theater unless they're invited, and how do you invite them without putting some of their stories up on the stage?"[4]

Notes

1. Nathaniel Graham Nesmith, "A Discussion with African-American Playwrights," *The Dramatist*, January/February, 2002, page 6.

2. http://www.philly.com/mld/philly/news/obituaries/6162576.htm, *The Philadelphia Inquirer* Regional Home Page, Obituary Posted Wednesday, June 25, 2003, "John Henry Redwood, actor, playwright," by Desmond Ryan, Inquirer Theater Critic.

3. http:www.ahtkc.com/shows/reviews/rev0203.shtml, Robert Trussell, "One man's life: Actor and playwright feel connected to White House butler's story," *Kansas City Star,* September 7, 2002.
4. Ibid.

No Niggers, No Jews, No Dogs

Cast of Characters

MATOKA (TOKE) CHEEKS, black girl. Typical talkative, high-energy 11 year old. Must be able to carry a tune and remember melodies.

AUNT CORA,** black woman. Mid-twenties/early-sixties. Mattie's Aunt. She is always humming, "near the cross." We only see the face of Aunt Cora as a young woman in her mid-twenties.

MATTIE CHEEKS, black woman. Mid-forties. Very feminine and emotional. While on occasions she may outwardly appear stern, inside she is soft and loving. She exhibits a strong sense of family and inner strength.

RAWL CHEEKS, black man. Mid-forties, Mattie's husband. Volatile and quick tempered. A strong family man who loves his wife and adores his daughters.

YAVENI AARONSOHN, Jewish man. Sixties, scholar and friend of the Cheeks family. Emotional. Uses humor, on occasions, to camouflage pain and guilt.

JOYCE CHEEKS, black girl. 17 years old, Mattie's oldest daughter. Very smart and sharp. Takes after her father in temperament. A teen on the threshold of womanhood. Events in the play make her sullen and rebellious.

**It is suggested that the same actress play the role of Aunt Cora, young and old, since the face of the older Aunt Cora should never be seen.*

Act 1

Scene 1

Time: *Summer, 1949, Saturday evening at dusk.*

Place: *All scenes take place in Halifax, North Carolina; the house exterior and yard of the CHEEKS household.*

At Rise: *We see a wooden house which stands on cinder block/brick stilts located at the corners, middles and sides of the house. We can see under the house. The roof is made of tin with a crude chimney protruding from it. Windows and a screen door can be seen in the exterior (the screen door should have a spring which will enable it to slam). There are steps which lead up to the porch of the house from the yard. There is a porch swing*

45

hanging from the ceiling at one end of the porch. In the yard a tree stump can be seen, as well as a huge, black, cast-iron kettle, which sits on the ground with large rocks circling its bottom. There is a pump with a tin run-off board from which the CHEEKS family draw their water. On the run-off board sits a bucket, containing drinking water, covered with a burlap cloth. Another bucket sits on the ground at the end of the run-off board. A dip-cup hangs off the side of the pump. Also in the yard, around the side of the house, chopped wood is stacked. The screen door opens slowly and a Black girl, MATOKA CHEEKS, peers out. She cautiously looks around.

MATTIE (*Offstage.*) Matoka Cheeks? You go on and put that food in that basket, girl. Ain't nobody paying you no never mind.

MATOKA hurriedly enters from the house and crosses to the far edge of the porch, opposite the porch swing. She is carrying a plate covered with a cloth and a covered mason jar with liquid in it. MATOKA puts the plate and jar in a straw lunch basket, which sits at the edge of the porch, and closes it. Unknowing to MATOKA, a Black woman, AUNT CORA ALLEN, has quietly entered. She is dressed entirely in black. Her attire is from another time, i.e., long dress, gloves and hat with the veil pulled down over her face. She is carrying a kerosene lamp to light her way. Looking up, MATOKA sees AUNT CORA and freezes for a beat.

MATOKA: (*Screaming.*) Mama!

MATOKA turns and exits into the house running. AUNT CORA begins to hum the spiritual, "Near the Cross," as she crosses to the porch. She is always humming this spiritual. She takes the basket, then turns to leave. Another Black woman, MATTIE CHEEKS, comes to the screen door. Seeing AUNT CORA, she enters onto the porch from the house.

MATTIE: Aunt Cora?

AUNT CORA stops humming and stands still. She does not turn to face MATTIE.

MATTIE (*Cont'd.*): Joyce said a white man down at the feed store said something out of the way to her this morning. Talked all under her clothes. She's a full grown woman in the body now, Aunt Cora.

AUNT CORA begins humming again, then exits.

(*Calling after her.*) We love you, Aunt Cora.

Lights go to black.

Scene 2

Time: *The next day, Sunday afternoon.*

At Rise: *We see a Black man,* RAWL CHEEKS, *sitting at the edge of the porch, hunched over a chessboard, studying the chess pieces. Opposite him, also at the edge of the porch, sits a white man,* YAVENI AARONSOHN. *He too is studying the chess pieces.* YAVENI *wears a yarmulke on his head. The two men sit in silence for a beat with their eyes affixed to the board.* RAWL *finally moves one of the pieces, taking one of* YAVENI's *pieces off the board in the process.*

RAWL: Check!

YAVENI: Very good! Very good! But you did not pay attention to my Knight.

YAVENI moves his Knight, taking the chess piece that RAWL *had just moved.*

Checkmate.

RAWL again studies the board for a beat, then picks up the King looking for a move to get out of checkmate.

It's no use. There is no place to move. Your King is captured.

RAWL angrily slams the King down on the board, then gets up and paces.

There's no reason to be upset with yourself . . . or my chess piece. You're doing remarkably well having just learned to play only three days ago.

RAWL: I don't know how I missed that!

YAVENI: Remember, I told you, the Knight is the only piece on the board that can jump over other pieces. That's why I enjoy using it so much. You must make sure you know why your opponent makes a move. Always assume that there is a good reason for every move your opponent makes, even if it does not seem logical. We both know that some things aren't always what they appear to be. So, once you understand his move . . .

From offstage the screams of a girl can be heard.

MATOKA: (*Offstage.*) Daddy! . . . Daddy! . . .

MATOKA enters running. She runs directly into RAWL's *arms. She is simultaneously screaming and laughing. She is dressed in her "Sunday Best."*

Daddy, tell Joyce to leave me alone!

Almost immediately behind MATOKA, *another Black girl,* JOYCE CHEEKS, *seventeen, enters, also running. She too is dressed in her "Sunday Best." She runs around* RAWL *trying to get to* MATOKA.

Daddy, make her stop!

JOYCE: You think you're funny, Matoka!

MATOKA: Daddy!

RAWL: Okay! Okay! What are you two fussing about now?

MATOKA: Joyce is always bothering me!

JOYCE is still trying to get to MATOKA.

JOYCE: Matoka thinks she's smart. She know I always wear those green socks to match my dress and she got up this morning and hid them so she could wear them . . .

MATOKA: I did it last night . . .

JOYCE: Then she lied . . .

RAWL: Don't you let your Mama hear that word coming out of your mouth.

JOYCE: Then she told a story and said she didn't know where they were.

MATTIE enters carrying a pocketbook and Bible. She too is dressed in her "Sunday Best."

    Then I get to Sunday school and see them on her big, old, rusty feet.

MATOKA: You just mad because you wanted to wear them so old long head Sammy Hunter could see you in them.

MATTIE: Now you two just hush all that fuss. (*Coldly.*) Hello, Yaveni.

YAVENI: Good afternoon, Mattie.

MATTIE: Did you girls say hello to Mr. Aaronsohn or did you just run in here fussing?

MATOKA: Hello, Mr. Aaronsohn.

JOYCE: (*Coldly.*) Hello, Mr. Aaronsohn.

YAVENI: Good afternoon, Ladies.

RAWL: (*To MATOKA.*) So, did you sing those folks up on their feet this morning . . . make them shout?

MATOKA: Sister Bell, but she always shouting, no matter what.

RAWL: *Laughs.*

MATTIE: You hush up all that talk! Doing all that fussing after church.

MATOKA: Joyce started it.

JOYCE: You just leave my things alone.

MATOKA: They ain't none of your things, you old do do head.

MATTIE: What did you call your sister?

MATOKA: (*Scared.*) Nothing.

MATTIE: You talking like that on a Sunday? You know I don't stand for that kind of language . . . and in front of company too. Excuse yourself to Mr. Aaronsohn.

YAVENI: There's no need . . .

MATTIE: (*Directly to YAVENI.*) I said beg Mr. Aaronsohn's pardon.

MATOKA: I'm sorry, Mr. Aaronsohn.

YAVENI: Apology gladly accepted, Matoka.

MATTIE: Now you go on back to one of them trees and get me a switch and wait inside.

MATOKA: Mama, I only said . . .

MATTIE: What did I tell you?

MATOKA: (*Pleading.*) I said I was sorry, Mama.

MATTIE: Are you back-talking me, girl?

MATOKA: No, Ma'am.

MATTIE: Then you go on and do what I told you.

MATOKA: (*Defeated.*) Yes, Ma'am.

MATOKA exits.

MATTIE: (*Calling after her.*) And don't get me no small switch either.

There is an awkward silence.

JOYCE: Mama, she wasn't being fresh. I was just teasing her about the socks. I called her a name first. She didn't mean it.

MATTIE: You want some too?

JOYCE: No, Ma'am.

MATTIE: Alright then. (*To RAWL.*) You all . . .

JOYCE: But she didn't mean it.

MATTIE: You go in there and wait for me too.

JOYCE exists into the house.

(*Calling after JOYCE.*) And both of you change out of them clothes. I ain't going to be whipping no clothes. (*To YAVENI.*) Mr. Aaronsohn, I don't mean to be rude, but for however long you're going to be here doing your research, . . . no signs, or whatever it is you're doing, I would appreciate it if you don't get all up in between me and my family.

YAVENI: I understand and I apologize.

MATTIE: Thank you. (*To RAWL.*) You all packed?

RAWL: I ain't taking that much because I ain't got that much to take.

MATTIE: What time is Earl coming to pick you up?

RAWL: He'll be here along about six o'clock.

MATTIE: Well, let me go in here and change and take care of this business so I can start warming up the food. You planning on having supper with us, Mr. Aaronsohn?

YAVENI: I think I'm going to let the Cheeks family have this afternoon together alone.

MATTIE: That's right thoughtful of you.

MATTIE begins to exit.

RAWL: Really something the way Joyce took up for Toke . . . ain't it?

MATTIE stops and looks at RAWL, then exits.

YAVENI: Mattie called me Mr. Aaronsohn. I guess that means I'm also in trouble.

RAWL: I think you're about right there.

YAVENI: Maybe I should have followed the example of one who has been married to her for eighteen years and, how do you say, kept my trap shut.

RAWL: I think you're about right there too. You see, I know Mattie. She ain't going to do nothing to Joyce and Matoka. Both of them girls will jump on Mattie with their mouths and Mattie ain't going to whip nobody. You know why? Because she don't really want to whip them in the first place. You mark my word. Don't let Mattie's tough talk fool you. And, maybe she didn't show it, but she loves the way Joyce took up for her sister.

YAVENI begins putting the chess pieces in a cloth bag.

YAVENI: I think you should take the chess set with you so you can practice. Then let's see how much better you've gotten when you return.

RAWL: With all that digging, I think I'll be too tired to have my mind on any chess.

YAVENI: How long are you going to be gone?

RAWL: A month or two. Maybe three. It depends on how many graves have to be dug up and how many men they have to do it with.

YAVENI: That doesn't sound like a job I would like to do.

RAWL: Even my brother James will be there.

YAVENI: Will he?

RAWL: Sure enough. He heard how good they was paying for digging up them dead white folks and decided to come on down from Cleveland and get some of that money.

YAVENI: When you see him, tell him thanks for putting in a good word with you and Mattie for me. I didn't know where to start to find a family like yours for my research.

RAWL: How's that coming?

YAVENI: I'm just beginning work on a chapter about the negative psychological effects of signs.

RAWL: Signs?

YAVENI: Yes. "No Colored Allowed," "No Jews."

RAWL: I've seen them all my life, but I ain't never seen nothing against no Jews.

YAVENI: They're there.

RAWL: So there are other people besides us colored these crackers don't like.

YAVENI: Oh, yes, my friend, there are.

RAWL: Yeah, well anyway, I'm going to thank him for all the money you're paying us for that research. I plan to add that to the money I'll be getting for digging up those graves and see if we can get some running water in this house . . . if they ever get the water line out this far . . . to us colored folks. What they pay me for those three months would take me a year to make on this place, and I'll still be back in time to bring in the peanuts and corn. Then we want to see if we can send Joyce over to Elizabeth City State to get at least one year of college.

YAVENI: She's a very smart young lady.

RAWL: Yeah, smart, stubborn, prideful and feisty with a very bad temper. Mattie says she takes after me . . . not the smart part though.

YAVENI: I can believe that . . . about the temper I mean. I've seen how you manhandled my chess piece when you lost the game.

JOYCE and MATOKA enter from the house. They have changed clothes but wear no shoes. JOYCE is carrying an empty water bucket.

Nonetheless, it seems to me, maybe it is not the best thing digging up people from their resting place.

JOYCE: White people do it all the time. They call it Archeology.

YAVENI: Yes, but that's for scientific and educational purposes.

JOYCE: And that makes it right?

RAWL: Joyce, you know better than to interrupt grown folks when they talking, don't you?

JOYCE: Yes, Sir.

RAWL: Now don't you go thinking you're grown and all because you've turned seventeen. You're not thinking like that I hope?

JOYCE: No, Sir.

RAWL: I thought your Mama had some business to take care of with you two.

MATOKA: Mama said she didn't feel like whipping nobody on Sunday . . .

RAWL: (*To YAVENI.*) What I tell you?

MATOKA: She said with you going away, it will be sad enough around here.

RAWL: Then what are you two suppose to be doing?

JOYCE: Getting some water.

MATOKA: Getting the wood for the stove.

RAWL: Well, go on then.

JOYCE and MATOKA turn to leave.

RAWL (*Cont'd.*): But first, I want some sugar.

MATOKA runs into RAWL's arms giving him a kiss and hug.

(*To JOYCE.*) Oh, I see! So you think you too grown. No more running into Daddy's arms and giving him hugs and kisses. I guess you want Daddy to come to you. Alright.

RAWL playfully approaches JOYCE who begins to back up laughing. RAWL grabs JOYCE and begins to tickle her. JOYCE screams with delight.

You going to come to me when I ask for a kiss? . . . Huh?

JOYCE: Yes, Daddy! . . . Yes! . . . Yes . . .

MATOKA jumps on RAWL to help her sister.

RAWL: You promise?

JOYCE: Yes! . . . Please, Daddy . . . I promise . . . Stop! . . . You're going to make something happen! . . .

RAWL stops tickling JOYCE. MATOKA climbs off RAWL.

RAWL: Now, I can use a hug and kiss.

JOYCE crosses to RAWL giving him a hug and kiss. MATOKA joins them.

RAWL *(Cont'd.)*: Now go on and do what your Mama told you to do.

JOYCE and MATOKA go down the steps into the yard. JOYCE crosses to the pump and starts priming it by pouring water from the tin can down the throat of the pump while pumping the handle. MATOKA crosses around the side of the house and begins collecting firewood.

YAVENI: I see what you mean about Joyce being feisty and smart.

RAWL: Yeah. I don't know where she gets it from, but Joyce is the smart one in the family . . . reading all the time . . . anything and everything. Matoka's the singer. I don't know where she gets it from either.

YAVENI: *(Laugh.)* I think I'll be going. Are you sure you won't have time to practice your chess game?

RAWL: No, I won't be able.

YAVENI: Very good. *(Calling into the house.)* Good-bye, Mattie.

JOYCE and MATOKA, having completed their respective tasks, pass RAWL and YAVENI on their way into the house.

MATOKA: Goody-bye, Mr. Aaronsohn.

JOYCE: Good-bye.

YAVENI: Good-bye, Ladies.

JOYCE and MATOKA exit into the house as MATTIE comes to the screen door.

MATTIE: You sure you don't want to sit down and take a plate of supper with us, Yaveni?

YAVENI: No. Thank you very much, Mattie, but I have some typing to do.

MATTIE: You be careful driving them roads. And make sure you get back to Miss Osgood's before it gets dark.

YAVENI: I most certainly will. Thank you.

MATTIE exits back into the house.

Mattie called me Yaveni again. I must be forgiven.

RAWL: Mattie can't stay cross long.

YAVENI extends his hand to RAWL. They shake.

YAVENI: Good luck, my friend. I'll see you in a couple of months, maybe sooner I hope.

RAWL: And you do like Mattie say and be careful. You know what I mean.

YAVENI: Yes, I do and I thank you. But you be careful also.

YAVENI exits. After a beat, MATTIE enters from the house.

MATTIE: You come on and get washed up so you can sit down and eat without rushing.

RAWL: Why are you so put out today?

MATTIE: Am I?

RAWL: You sure are.

MATTIE: It's Sunday, Rawl! What's Yaveni doing here on Sunday? You know it ain't right with me having no white man always hanging around my house . . . and especially on Sunday.

RAWL: James has spoken for him. He ain't going to be living here. He's just going to be coming around and asking questions for that book of his.

MATTIE: Well, he can't be coming around whenever he wants. I'm going to tell him no Sundays. That's the Lord's day even if you and Yaveni won't give it to Him.

RAWL puts his arms around MATTIE.

RAWL: (*Lovingly.*) Aw, come on now. Why you getting like this?

MATTIE: Maybe it has something to do with having to sleep in our bed all by myself for two or three months.

RAWL: You know why I'm going.

MATTIE: We can make do without my daughters' father going off to dig up some dead white folks. We got trouble enough with these living ones running around up here now without you digging up those that have already been gotten rid of.

RAWL: Make do? Me farming somebody else's land. You washing white folks' clothes.

MATTIE: And we make do.

RAWL: Is that what we're going to tell Joyce when we don't have the money for her to go to Elizabeth City State? And what happens when it's Toke's turn to go to college? How many of Joe Flood's white shirts will you have to wash and iron to send her? Or are they supposed to stand over that pot and stir Joe Flood's son's shirts? Don't nobody, colored or white, like that old, poor buckrah no ways. (*Pause.*) If you would let us move up to Cleveland, you wouldn't have to be washing no shirts and I wouldn't have to be farming and plowing and the girls wouldn't have to be missing school so they could pick cotton and pull tobacco. James will help us get started. He's doing right nice . . .

MATTIE: How "right nice" can James be doing if he's going to go all the way down to Alabama to help you dig up some dead white folks?

RAWL: Him and me can start working on our plans to start fixing cars together and you won't have to be washing no white man's shirts.

MATTIE: What's the matter, white men don't wear shirts in Cleveland?

RAWL: While I'm away I want you to think about Cleveland.

MATTIE: Rawl, we've gone into this, Lord knows, I don't know how many times and I keep saying I don't want to leave Halifax.

RAWL: What will you be leaving? What?

MATTIE: This is where I was born. I can walk less than a mile and see my people.

RAWL: You can see their graves that's all you see.

MATTIE: And that's enough for me. Who's going to take care of Aunt Cora? I can't leave her. Who's going to feed her?

RAWL: We don't have to live up there until we die. Maybe just until the girls get grown. There are more chances for them up there. We can always come back to Halifax. Look at Miss Elizabeth and Miss Quilly, they lived up there in Harlem for almost thirty-five years then they moved back here.

MATTIE: Moved back here to die.

RAWL: (*Screaming.*) I'm dying here, Mattie. I don't know if I can stay here much longer . . . cow-towing to these crackers . . .

MATOKA enters from the house.

MATOKA: Mama, Joyce said the cornbread is almost done. She's setting the table.

MATTIE: We're coming, Baby. You go on and pour some hot water in the pan so Daddy can wash up.

MATOKA: Yes, Ma'am.

MATOKA exits into the house.

MATTIE: (*Lovingly.*) You go on and get washed up for supper while we put the food on the table. I'm going to fix you a bag so you can have something to eat on the trip. I guess I better put a little something in there for Earl too.

RAWL: Sally will probably make him a bag.

MATTIE: If Sally can get out of her bottle long enough.

RAWL: (*Grabbing at MATTIE.*) Now that's not nice.

MATTIE: (*Pulling away.*) Go on now and get ready . . .

RAWL: I am ready.

MATTIE: You better go on now. The girls will hear.

RAWL: That ain't what you be saying . . . It's, "Oooo . . . Oooo . . . Okay, (*Louder*) Okay, (*Louder*) Okay!"

MATTIE: Rawl! Hush up!

Laughing, RAWL puts his arms around MATTIE again, hugging her.

RAWL: I'm sure going to miss the sight of you . . . the smell of you . . .

JOYCE and MATOKA enter from the house.

JOYCE: The food is ready, Mama, and the table is set.

MATOKA: And I'm hungry.

MATTIE pushes RAWL towards the back of the house, slapping him on the rear end. MATOKA laughs.

MATTIE: We'll eat just as soon as Daddy gets washed up.

Laughing, RAWL exits around the side of the house to the back porch. He begins to take off his shirt as he exits.

RAWL: (*Mimicking.*) Oooo . . . Oooo. Okay . . . Okay . . . Okay . . .

MATOKA: What's that mean?

MATTIE: Never mind. (*Quickly to JOYCE.*) Don't you open your mouth.

MATTIE goes up the steps, to the door.

JOYCE: Mama, . . . you ain't worried none I hope.

MATTIE: (*Pause.*) No, I ain't worried none. Why'd you ask that?

JOYCE: It's just with Daddy going away . . .

MATTIE: No, I ain't worried. Let's go eat. After supper, when Daddy is gone, we're going to wash the dishes and get dressed and go on back to church.

MATOKA: Aw, Mama!

MATTIE: Don't you be complaining about going to church, child.

MATOKA: Reverend Fentress preaches too long, Mama. And no matter where I sit, Sister Bell always sits next to me. Then the spirit hits her and she hits me . . . (*Demonstrating*) throwing her arms and hands all over and I have to keep trying to get out of her way.

MATTIE: (*Suppressing laughter.*) Don't be making fun of a saint being touch by the Holy Spirit, girl.

MATOKA: I'm worrying about her touching me.

MATTIE: You don't hear Joyce complaining.

MATOKA: That's because Joyce thinks she's going to see old pigeon-toed Sammy Hunter.

JOYCE: Oh, hush, Miss Know-it-all.

MATOKA: Why don't Daddy . . .

JOYCE: Why "doesn't" Daddy.

JOYCE exits into the house.

MATOKA: (*Calling after her.*) So what? (*To MATTIE*) Why doesn't Daddy have to go to church?

MATTIE: Because Daddy is a heathen.

MATOKA: When I grow up I'm going to be a heathen too.

MATTIE: You get your behind in this house, girl, and shut up all that talk.

MATTIE takes a harmless swipe at MATOKA's rear end as they exit into the house.

Scene 3

Time: *Six weeks later.*

At Rise: *Matoka is sitting on the porch steps singing, "Way Down Yonder in the White Man's Field," to a Black, home-made doll.*

MATOKA: (*Singing.*) Way down yonder in the white man's field,
  Way down yonder in the white man's field,
  Never made enough to pay my bills,
  Way down yonder in the white man's field,
  Three at the foot and three at the head,
  A pallet on the floor for my bed,
  All we had to eat was a guinea knot,
  And a glass of water was all we got.

JOYCE enters from the house carrying a book.

  Way down yonder in the white man's field,

JOYCE: You better empty those slop buckets like Mama told you before she gets home.

MATOKA: I ain't.

JOYCE: It's your turn to empty them, Matoka!

MATOKA: I didn't do nothing in them. You did.

JOYCE: I did not!

MATOKA: I heard you. You make so much noise it wakes me up. That's how I heard you. Psssss (*Laugh*).

JOYCE: You so nasty.

MATOKA: (*Mimicking.*) "You so nasty."

JOYCE: You watch. I ain't going to take up for your butt this time. When Mama gets ready to whip your behind I'm going to come out here with my book and sit down and read.

MATOKA: I ain't studying you.

YAVENI enters.

YAVENI: Good morning, Ladies.

MATOKA: Hello, Mr. Aaronsohn.

JOYCE: Hello.

There is an awkward silence.

YAVENI: Well, . . . how are you ladies today?

MATOKA: Fine. Mama went over to Mr. Joe Flood's to take his white shirts she washed.

YAVENI: I thought about something I needed to ask her before going to the courthouse. Do you think she'll return soon?

JOYCE: She should be back in a piece.

YAVENI: Yes. Well, do you mind if I wait a while?

JOYCE: Suit yourself. But you have to wait outside.

YAVENI: That's fine.

There is another awkward silence. YAVENI sits on the edge of the porch. JOYCE crosses to the porch swing and sits. She opens her book and begins to read.

MATOKA: We ain't allowed to let anybody in the house when Mama and Daddy ain't home. And even Mama won't let a man in the house when Daddy ain't home . . . it's her doing. Daddy didn't ask her to be like that. She says that's the way you respect your husband as the man of the house. And no man can sit down at the table and eat before Daddy . . . not even the preacher.

YAVENI has taken out a pocket notebook and is writing down what MATOKA is saying.

MATOKA: You know that some women will let the preacher come to their house and sit down and eat before the man of the house and children . . . even sit at the head of the table. But Mama says ain't no man, don't matter none if it is the preacher, ain't no man going to sit down and eat before her husband and children. I'll get you a chair so you won't have to be sitting in the sun.

YAVENI: That's quite alright, Matoka. I'm perfectly comfortable right here. (*To JOYCE.*) What are you reading?

JOYCE: I'm reading the fourth book of the twenty-four books of Homer's *Iliad*.

YAVENI: (*Incredulous.*) Really?

Another awkward silence.

YAVENI (*Cont'd.*): Do you think I might have some water?

MATOKA begins to go up the stairs.

MATOKA: I'll get a glass for you.

YAVENI: There's no need. I can drink out of the . . .

MATOKA: Dip-cup?

YAVENI: Yes.

MATOKA: Mama always gives company water in a glass.

YAVENI: The dip-cup will be just fine.

MATOKA: Okay. I'll get it for you.

MATOKA runs down off the porch to the pump. She removes the dip-cup from its hanging place. She then removes the burlap cloth that covers the water bucket and puts the dip-cup in the bucket and withdraws it filled with water.

JOYCE: What are you researching?

YAVENI: What?

JOYCE: You want to know what I'm reading, I want to know what you're writing.

YAVENI: Fair enough. I'm writing a book . . . an independent comparative study of the similarities in racial suffering between Negroes and Jews. That's what I was researching in Raleigh for the last month.

JOYCE: I read where Jews owned slaves. You going to put that in your book?

YAVENI: (*Pause.*) Uh, yes. I'm going to put that in the chapter after the one about Negroes who owned slaves.

MATOKA crosses to YAVENI, handing him the dip-cup.

MATOKA: Here's your water!

YAVENI: Thank you.

YAVENI takes the dip-cup from MATOKA and drinks.

YAVENI: (*Finishing.*) *Taiem* (Hebrew).

MATOKA: What's that mean?

YAVENI: That means "delicious" in Hebrew.

MATOKA: Oh. (*Pause.*) Why do you always wear that beanie on your head? It's too little to keep your head warm. My Uncle James sometimes sends me comic books from Cleveland and there's a little boy in one of them that always wears a beanie except he has a propeller on the top of his and when the wind blows, the propeller goes round and round.

YAVENI: (*Laughing.*) It's not a beanie, Matoka. It's called a yarmulke and observing Jewish men wear them because we're supposed to keep our heads covered in the presence of YUD HAY VAV HAY . . . God, because of the *shechinah* . . . God's radiance. So since God is everywhere, we must always wear our yarmulkes.

MATOKA: Oh, . . . Even in church?

YAVENI: Especially in church. Except, we don't call them churches. We call them temples or synagogues.

MATOKA: Oh . . . Well, when we go in our churches the men take their hats off, but the ladies have to have something on their heads. Not the little girls though. Sometimes it ain't got to be nothing but a handkerchief held down with a hairpin.

YAVENI is writing in his notebook again.

And you know how we say excuse me in church?

YAVENI: No.

MATOKA: When the preacher is preaching and you have to go to the outhouse . . .

JOYCE: Matoka! You shouldn't be talking like that to company . . . especially to men folk! You can say go get some water or something!

MATOKA: I ain't studying you. (*To YAVENI.*) When Reverend Fentress preaches, everybody has to go to the outhouse . . .

JOYCE: Alright, you just wait until I tell Mama how you been talking.

MATOKA: And you just wait until I tell Mama you said BUTT . . . and BEHIND. Now. (*To YAVENI.*) Everybody has to go to the outhouse because Reverend Fentress preaches so long. But when you have to go, you point this finger in the air, and bow your head and tip-toe out of the church. Like this.

MATOKA demonstrates the "excuse me" movement.

YAVENI: Like this?

YAVENI attempts the "excuse me" movement but does not tip-toe.

MATOKA: Yeah, except you have to tip-toe out.

YAVENI: Like this?

YAVENI tries again as best he can.

MATOKA: (*Laughs.*) Well, I guess that will have to do.

YAVENI: Thank you, Matoka.

YAVENI pulls out a pocket watch and looks at it.

I think I'll have to come back later. I want to make the Post Office before it closes.

JOYCE: Sorry, Mr. Aaronsohn, Mama should have been back by now.

YAVENI: That's alright, Joyce. I'll come back. Thank you for the water . . . and the lesson, Matoka.

MATOKA: Welcome.

YAVENI exits attempting to use the "excuse me" method MATOKA "taught" him. MATOKA laughs.

JOYCE: Matoka, you talk too much.

MATOKA: I do not.

JOYCE: Mr. Aaronsohn don't want to know nothing about saying "excuse me" in no colored church and people going to the outhouse.

MATOKA: There ain't nothing wrong with talking about that. Everybody has to go to the outhouse. Even Mr. Aaronsohn has to go to the outhouse when he goes to church on Sunday. That's what's wrong with you. You think you never have to go, even if it ain't Sunday.

JOYCE: See, you run your mouth so much you don't even listen. He told you they don't call them churches. And they don't go to the synagogues on Sunday, they go on Saturdays.

MATOKA: You storying. Don't nobody go to church on Saturday.

MATTIE enters, unsteadily, dragging a large laundry basket behind her. Her clothes are in disarray, but we know that she has done her best to straighten them out. Although she struggles to appear normal, we detect something amiss.

JOYCE: I told you, they don't call them churches.

MATOKA: I ain't studying you.

JOYCE: I know you better be studying them slop-buckets before . . .

JOYCE, seeing MATTIE first, crosses to her, taking the basket from her.

JOYCE: . . . Mama? . . . Are you alright?

MATTIE: I'm fine. Just a little tired.

MATOKA: Mr. Aaronsohn was here. He said . . .

JOYCE: What happened to your clothes? Why did you come through the woods?

MATTIE crosses to the porch laboriously.

MATTIE: Let me just sit here a piece.

MATTIE sits on the edge of the porch.

JOYCE: Do you want to go inside and lay down?

MATTIE: I don't feel like climbing them steps right now. Just let me sit here. Matoka, Baby, go start a fire in the stove and boil up some water for me please.

MATOKA: Mr. Aaronsohn said he'll be back.

JOYCE: Go on and do what Mama told you.

MATOKA: You ain't nobody's Mama . . .

MATTIE: You go on now, Baby. Please.

MATOKA goes around the side of the house and begins to collect firewood. MATTIE is still in a great deal of discomfort.

JOYCE: You want me to go to Mr. Sessoms' long store and try and call Daddy, Mama?

MATTIE: (*Desperate.*) No! . . . Don't do that. (*Calmer.*) Everything is alright. (*Calling.*) Toke?

MATOKA: Ma'am?

MATTIE: I need Aunt Cora. I want you to go get her for me.

MATOKA: (*Scared.*) Mama . . . it's been a long time since I been out there . . . I ain't never been out there by myself.

JOYCE: I'll go, Mama. Toke's always been scared of Aunt Cora.

MATOKA: Who you talking about is scared?

MATTIE: Ain't no need in you being scared of your Aunt Cora, child. She ain't going to hurt you none. She love you.

JOYCE: I'll go after you lay down. Go on now, Toke, and heat up the water.

MATOKA: I'm going!

MATOKA exits into the house. JOYCE crosses to the pump and uncovers the water bucket. She puts the dip-cup in the bucket and takes it out filled with water. She crosses back to MATTIE and gives her the water. MATTIE drinks.

JOYCE: Why won't you let me call Daddy, Mama?

MATTIE: Because there ain't nothing your Daddy can do here.

JOYCE: Something ain't right. (*Pause*) I ain't no child, Mama.

MATTIE makes sure MATOKA is out of hearing range.

MATTIE: (*Pause.*) Toke can't hear this . . . not right now. (*Pause.*) Mr. Joe Flood . . . done invaded . . . my privacy.

JOYCE: (*Pause.*) What you mean, Mama?

MATTIE: (*Pause.*) He done forced himself on me.

JOYCE: Oh, Mama, no. (*Pause.*) What we going to do?

MATTIE: Don't you worry none now. I'm going to be alright.

JOYCE: (*Angered*) Damn him to hell!

MATTIE: Joyce! Don't you ever let me hear words like that coming out of your mouth. You hear me?

JOYCE: I hear you . . . but I mean it.

MATTIE: You don't say that about another human being, no matter what.

JOYCE: Joe Flood ain't no human being and I hope he burns in hell.

MATTIE: Don't do that, Baby. Sometimes when you wish something bad on someone, you wish it on yourself. Vengeance is mine sayeth the Lord. God will take care of Mr. Joe Flood.

JOYCE: Daddy will take care of Mr. Joe Flood.

MATTIE: (*Pause.*) Your Daddy ain't got to know.

JOYCE: What?

MATTIE: (*Pause.*) We ain't going to tell him.

JOYCE: Why not? Look at what Joe Flood did to you!

MATTIE and JOYCE are unaware that YAVENI has come back and is listening.

MATTIE: I don't care. We ain't going to tell your Daddy about this.

JOYCE: You mean to tell me you're going to let Joe Flood force himself on you . . . have his way with you, and get away with it?

MATTIE does not answer.

JOYCE (*Cont'd.*): You're going to go into town and tell Sheriff Morrissey, ain't you?

MATTIE: And just what do you think Sheriff Morrissey is going to do? I'll tell you what. Laugh. That's right, laugh.

JOYCE: Then what are you going to do?

MATTIE: (*Pause.*) Nothing.

JOYCE: That ain't right, Mama.

MATTIE: Right? We're colored folks living in North Carolina. It ain't right that we got to drink from a colored water fountain. Right don't count for us, Joyce.

JOYCE: Not being able to drink behind some old stinky cracker at a water fountain ain't the same thing, Mama! That white man took his way with you!

MATTIE: Like I said, there ain't nothing we can do about it.

JOYCE: Daddy would do something.

MATTIE: What, Joyce? What do you think your Daddy will do?

JOYCE does not answer.

You're just like him. Flying off the handle without thinking. Just like I keep telling you, your temper will get you in trouble and your Daddy's temper will get him killed if he finds out. Is that what you want for your Daddy?

JOYCE does not answer.

MATTIE (*Cont'd.*): (*Louder.*) Is it?

JOYCE: No. Ma'am.

MATTIE: Well, I don't want it either and I ain't going to have it. I ain't going to be talking to my husband through six feet of dirt. I ain't going to spend the remainder of my nights reaching for the warm body that used to lay next to me in the bed, feeling nothing but the emptiness of a cold sheet. That's why I ain't telling him. Because I know what will happen. You understand me?

JOYCE: Yes, Ma'am.

MATTIE: But you ain't sure I'm right.

JOYCE does not answer.

I've seen it, Joyce. (*Pause.*) I know you love your Daddy and you think I'm betraying him, and that I'm asking you to betray him too if we don't tell him, but I'm asking you to do just that and not say nothing. If it has to be told, let me do it, Baby . . . in my own time . . . in my own way. (*Pause.*) Please. (*Pause.*) And we ain't going to tell Matoka either. She's too young to know about all of this. Besides, she talks too much. (*Rising.*) Now help me into the house.

JOYCE: Mama . . .

MATTIE: We ain't going to speak on it no more, Joyce. You're a girl now, but when you become a grown woman . . . a wife and mother, you'll understand that there are just some things a colored woman will do . . . has to do . . . to keep her family going.

JOYCE: How old do I have to be, Mama? If Joe Flood isn't stopped, how long before I look old enough for him to look that way at me . . . at Matoka?

MATTIE: That ain't never going to happen.

JOYCE: I sure wish I could believe that, Mama.

MATTIE: (*Calling.*) How's the water coming, Toke?

MATOKA: (*Offstage.*) It's almost boiling, Mama.

MATTIE and JOYCE begin to climb the steps. YAVENI enters from where he stood listening.

YAVENI: Mattie?

JOYCE: (*Angered.*) What do you want?

MATTIE: Joyce! You mind your mouth, young lady. How long you been here, Yaveni?

YAVENI: I went to my car . . .

MATTIE: How long?

YAVENI: (*Pause.*) I heard.

MATTIE: Did you hear or were you listening?

YAVENI: (*Pause.*) I was listening.

JOYCE: You didn't go to your car. You stood there being nosey . . . seeing what you could find to put in your notebook.

YAVENI: That's not true. I went to my car. I got in and started the engine. I was about to drive off, when I looked up and saw this woman standing in front of the car. I don't know where she came from, but she wasn't there when I got in the car. She was dressed in black from head to toe . . . with a black hat and veil covering her face. I called to her to get out of the way, but she wouldn't move. She just stood there . . . humming. I was scared, but I got out of the car and started walking toward her. I asked who she was and she just walked right past me in this direction . . . only, she didn't walk along the path. She walked in the thickets. I followed her at a distance because I wanted to see where she would go. Then she disappeared. I must be honest with you, I came here because I was scared to walk back to my car. Then I heard you talking . . . and yes, I listened.

MATTIE: How much did you hear?

YAVENI: Everything. Mattie you've got to tell the authorities . . .

MATTIE: Joyce, I want you to go down by the creek and see if you can find Aunt Cora.

JOYCE: Mama you need to lay down.

MATTIE: I will just as soon as I finish with Mr. Aaronsohn. Now you go in. And take Matoka with you so I can do what I need to do.

JOYCE: I don't want to leave you by yourself.

MATTIE: Go on now, Joyce.

JOYCE: (*Calling.*) Toke!

MATOKA comes to the screen door.

Come on, we're going out to Aunt Cora's.

MATOKA: I ain't.

JOYCE: Come on, Matoka. Mama said so.

MATOKA: (*Pleading.*) No, Mama . . . please.

MATTIE: Alright. Let her stay.

MATOKA: And don't mention my name.

JOYCE exits.

MATTIE: Matoka, did you empty them slop-buckets?

MATOKA: No, Ma'am. I was fixing to clean them when Mr. Aaronsohn came and he wanted some water and . . .

MATTIE: Girl, if you don't clean them buckets, you better.

MATOKA: Yes, Ma'am.

MATOKA exits into the house. MATTIE makes sure she is out of hearing range.

MATTIE: Having you here, "observing" my family for your research is Rawl and his brother's idea. I didn't want any part of it. So, I'm going to tell you right now, Mr. Aaronsohn, I don't care how much you're paying us, I ain't going to have you getting all up in between me and my family.

YAVENI: You've already told me that. But you have to tell the authorities what that man did to you.

MATTIE: Whatever authorities you think is down here, ain't going to do nothing. They don't care.

YAVENI: I don't believe that. I have to agree with Joyce, you've got to try. If they know they can do that to you with impunity, they will continue to do it.

MATTIE: You think this is the first time something like this has happened to a colored woman? You think I'm the only Negro woman this has been done to? We live with this down here all of our lives.

YAVENI: That's exactly the point. Because it has been done for so long, it should be stopped.

MATTIE: Not at the cost of me losing my husband.

YAVENI: If you do not let him exert himself as a man you lose him anyway. If you do not tell Rawl and he finds out, you too will have killed him . . . his spirit. You've got to give him that chance, Mattie.

MATTIE: You've been down here and known my family all of two months and you got the nerve to tell me how to keep my family going? You get your research done and you go back to Cleveland. But we'll still be Negroes down here in Halifax, North Carolina, trying to do the best we can while you go back to being white.

YAVENI: I'm not white, Mattie. I'm Jewish.

MATTIE: (*Pause.*) When you go to that courthouse today and you get thirsty, what water fountain are you going to drink out of, Mr. Aaronsohn?

YAVENI: (*Pause.*) That's not the point.

MATTIE: What water fountain?

YAVENI does not answer.

MATTIE (*Cont'd.*): You ever call a colored person a nigger, Mr. Aaronsohn?

Again, YAVENI does not answer. MATTIE rises to go into the house.

I'm feeling a little worn right now. I need to go lay down.

YAVENI: Mattie . . . you do know if Rawl finds it out from anyone other than you, you will have a greater problem.

MATTIE: Until you can answer those questions I just asked you, until I can know the real reason you came all the way down here to North Carolina to write about some Negro folks you don't even know, I'm going to tell you for the third time, don't be getting all up between me and my family.

YAVENI: I don't know what you mean.

MATTIE: I think you're researching more than you say you are. That's what I mean.

MATTIE crosses up to the screen door.

YAVENI: If you tell one lie, then you must tell another to cover the first lie. (*Reflective.*) Then your whole life becomes a lie.

MATTIE: I ain't told no lie, Mr. Aaronsohn!

YAVENI: I beg your pardon, Mattie, but there is the lie of omission . . . just as deceitful.

MATTIE: Good-bye, Mr. Aaronsohn. I ain't feeling too friendly towards white folks right now.

MATTIE opens the screen door to go into the house.

YAVENI: Uh . . . Mattie?

MATTIE: (*Annoyed.*) What?

YAVENI: Uh . . . well . . . What about the woman at my car?

MATTIE: What about her?

YAVENI: Well . . . Who is she?

MATTIE: My Aunt Cora.

YAVENI: Why is she dressed like that . . . in this weather . . . wearing a veil?

MATTIE: You ain't got no count to worry, Mr. Aaronsohn. She ain't studying you.

YAVENI: That's exactly what I think she was doing, studying me.

MATTIE exits into the house.

YAVENI: (*Calling after her.*) Can you call me Yaveni again, Mattie?

After a beat, MATOKA *enters from the house.*

MATOKA: Mama told me to walk you to your car because you're scared of Aunt Cora. (*Laughing.*) Come on. Aunt Cora ain't nobody to be scared of. She ain't paying you no never mind.

MATOKA exits running. YAVENI *quickly exits behind her. Lights go to black.*

Scene 4

Time: *Later the same day at dusk.*

At Rise: MATTIE *enters from the house carrying the food basket. She crosses to the edge of the porch and sets the basket down in its usual spot. She stands for a beat looking for* AUNT CORA, *then turns and crosses to the screen door to go into the house. At this time,* MATTIE *hears the humming of, "Near the Cross," coming from offstage. After a beat,* AUNT CORA *enters. She crosses to the porch and picks up the food basket. She then turns to leave.*

MATTIE: Hello, Aunt Cora.

AUNT CORA *stops but, again, does not turn to face* MATTIE. *She also stops humming.*

Why did you bother that white man this morning? You know you ought not to be doing that. Scared him half to death. (*Pause.*) I ain't never known you to do nothing like that before. You do that for any particular reason, Aunt Cora?

AUNT CORA *begins to exit, humming the same spiritual. After a beat . . .*

(*Calling after* AUNT CORA.) It . . . happened to me, Aunt Cora.

AUNT CORA *stops again, and stops humming, but still does not turn to face* MATTIE.

(*Pause.*) Mr. Joe Flood done put his hands on me. The black cloud of what white men do to us colored women hangs over me now. God knows, I don't want that cloud hanging over my babies.

After a beat of silence, AUNT CORA *exits humming.*

MATTIE (*Cont'd.*): (*Calling after* AUNT CORA.) We love you, Aunt Cora.

Lights go to black.

Scene 5

Time: *Three months later.*

At Rise: *MATTIE enters slowly from offstage carrying a pail filled with vegetables picked from her garden. She wears a straw hat to protect her head from the sun. She crosses to the pump. Setting the pail on the ground, she leans against the pump. It is evident that MATTIE is uncomfortable. She takes the priming cup and primes the pump. She takes her handkerchief from around her neck and puts it under the running water. She then pats the back of her neck and forehead with the wet handkerchief.*

MATOKA: (*Offstage.*) Mama! . . . Mama! . . .

MATTIE attempts to regain her composure as MATOKA enters running.

Daddy's coming home! . . . Daddy's coming home Sunday!

JOYCE enters carrying a brown paper bag.

MATTIE: How do you know?

MATOKA: When we went into Mr. Sessom's long store to buy the molasses, Mr. Sessoms said Daddy called and asked him to get a message out to you that he was coming home Sunday. I can't wait.

JOYCE: (*Accusing.*) Me either.

MATTIE and JOYCE stare at one another.

MATOKA: Ain't you happy that Daddy's coming home, Mama?

MATTIE: (*Worried.*) I sure am, Honey. (*To JOYCE.*) I hear Brother Owens is going to slaughter that mean old hog he got some time tomorrow . . .

MATOKA: Oooooo! Mama, can we go watch?

MATTIE: Ain't no enjoyment in watching one of God's creatures die, Matoka!

MATOKA: But there sure is enjoyment in eating it.

MATTIE: Don't you sass me, girl.

MATOKA: Yes, Ma'am.

MATTIE: (*To JOYCE.*) Now, I'm going to give you a piece of money to go over and see if Brother Owens is willing to sell us a couple of pieces of ham or some chops from that hog. I want to have something special for your Daddy when he comes home.

JOYCE: (*Accusing.*) You got something special, ain't you, Mama?

MATTIE and JOYCE stare at one another again.

MATOKA: Can I go too, Mama?

MATTIE: I need you to go out to Aunt Cora's and get those baskets. I don't have any more to put her food in.

MATOKA: Mama, please, I don't want to go . . .

MATTIE: Now you stop all that foolishness. Aunt Cora ain't never done nothing to you and she ain't going to do nothing to you. It's time you stop being scared of your own blood. You're eleven years old.

MATOKA: Can we wait until I get twelve?

JOYCE: Me and Toke can go out to Aunt Cora's from Brother Owens place and get the baskets.

MATOKA: That's a good idea, Mama!

MATTIE: I guess that will be all right. Maybe I'll ask Mr. Aaronsohn if he would like to have a meal with us.

JOYCE: Mr. Aaronsohn a Jew, Mama. He don't eat pork.

MATTIE: (*Annoyed.*) I'm going to make chicken and dumplings too, Joyce.

MATOKA: Mr. Aaronsohn got in trouble.

MATTIE: Got in trouble? How?

JOYCE: We saw Mr. Joe Flood, Mr. Cole Gordon and two other white men, I ain't never seen before, go up to Mr. Aaronsohn when he was coming out of the telegraph office . . .

MATOKA: They took his beanie off his . . .

MATTIE: It's a yarmulke, Matoka. Now you remember that and stop calling it a beanie. That ain't no respect.

JOYCE: They cut it up and threw it on the ground and spit and stomped on it. Then they told Mr. Aaronsohn that they would do the same thing to his Jew ass . . .

MATOKA: Ooooooooo!

MATTIE: Joyce!

JOYCE: I'm just telling you what they said, Mama.

MATTIE: I don't care what they said there, you ain't got to let that word come out of your mouth here. You can say, "so and so" or something.

JOYCE: They didn't say "so and so," Mama. You wanted to know what happened and I'm telling you the truth of it . . . the way it happened. They told Mr. Aaronsohn they would do the same thing to his Jew ass . . .

MATTIE slaps JOYCE.

MATTIE: Don't you try talking around me, girl. Your tongue is like a shovel and it's going to dig your own grave.

JOYCE: I was just telling the truth, Mama. The truth!

JOYCE turns to walk away.

MATTIE: Don't you walk away from me when I'm talking to you.

JOYCE stops.

   I ain't talking to no back, Joyce.

JOYCE turns facing MATTIE.

MATOKA: We learned us a new . . .

MATTIE: Not now, Matoka! (*To JOYCE.*) Ever since your Daddy's been gone you've been walking around here like you never have to go to the outhouse. You think you're grown? You think because your Daddy ain't here, you're in charge? (*Pause.*) Do you?

JOYCE: (*Sullenly.*) No.

MATTIE: You ain't talking to Matoka.

JOYCE: (*Deliberately.*) No . . . Ma'am.

MATTIE: That's more like it.

JOYCE: Can I go now?

MATTIE: Not until we get things back to the way they was before your Daddy left.

JOYCE: Things will never be the way they were before Daddy left.

MATTIE: I told you before, I ain't talking about that.

JOYCE: You trying to pretend it didn't happen?

MATTIE: I know it happened because it happened to me. You got some nerve walking around here with your lip dragging the ground. It happened to me!

JOYCE: It happened to all of us . . . including Daddy. What are you going to do when it happens to you again, Mama? . . . When it happens to me? When it happens to Matoka?

MATTIE: I don't want to talk about it in front of Matoka.

JOYCE: Why not? She's already heard it, Mama. I've heard it. You want to hear what it sounds like coming from Mr. Joe Flood? You want to hear what Daddy will hear when he's in town . . . what somebody at the church might hear?

MATTIE: I don't want to hear.

JOYCE: I didn't want to hear either, but I heard it . . . and Matoka heard it too. After they told Mr. Aaronsohn what they would do to his "so and so," Mr. Joe Flood asked him if they were both getting their chocolate milk from the same black cow . . .

MATOKA: We learned us a new song at choir practice today, Mama!

JOYCE: He called you a cow, Mama! . . .

MATOKA (*Singing.*)

> I will sing, Alleluia
> I will sing, O'Lord
> I will sing, Alleluia, O'Lord
> You are the source of my supply
> Lord, I pray you will lift me high
> I will sing, Alleluia, O'Lord.

MATOKA puts her hands over her ears and continues singing as MATTIE and JOYCE continue talking.

JOYCE: That's what Daddy will hear another man call his wife . . . a black cow. And he'll know that you let Mr. Joe Flood . . .

MATTIE: (*Screaming.*) I didn't let him!

JOYCE: You didn't do anything about it. It's been three months and you ain't said nothing to Daddy. Daddy would make sure that it didn't happen to me and Matoka. He would protect us with his life.

MATTIE: Is that what you want, Joyce? . . . for your Daddy to give up his life.

JOYCE does not answer.

I fought that white man with all my might . . . I fought him until I had no more strength left in me. I fought him.

MATTIE takes MATOKA's hands from over her ears.

I fought, Matoka. You hear me?

MATOKA stops singing.

Both of you got to believe, I fought. And as I was fighting I was thinking, "I can't let this happen to me," and I kept fighting and fighting and fighting . . . until all the fight was gone.

JOYCE: But you gave up. All that fighting you did didn't mean nothing because after it was over you did nothing.

MATTIE: I'm doing something. I'm making sure that you girls grow up with a mother . . . and a father. I'm making sure your Daddy stays alive.

JOYCE: Why are you so sure Daddy won't be able to take care of himself . . . and Mr. Joe Flood?

MATTIE: Because I've seen what can happen, Joyce. You think I'm talking off the top of my head? You young people think life started when your life started. No! A whole lot of people were here before you were even a dream. And they had things happen to them that made them the way they are when you first meet them . . . things you know nothing about. You see your Aunt Cora? (*To MATOKA.*) You see that woman you been running around being afraid of?

JOYCE: She can't help if she scared of Aunt Cora, Mama. Most people would be. And we're not talking about Aunt Cora.

MATTIE: Joyce, you're a smart girl, but you've got to listen to learn, but first you've got to learn to listen. Aunt Cora wasn't always the way she is.

A special comes up on AUNT CORA, as a young woman in her mid to late twenties. She is wearing a cheerfully colored dress of the nineteen-teens.

She was full of life. There was two things she loved to do more than anything else . . . laugh and sing. She used to laugh so big and hard that the tears would just be rolling down her cheeks.

The young AUNT CORA laughs.

And she could really sing.

AUNT CORA begins to sing, "Jesus, I'll Never Forget." For a beat MATTIE, JOYCE and MATOKA, are silent as if they can hear her singing.

I think that's where Toke got her singing from. She sang in the church choir . . . just like Matoka. That's right. Right there at the First Baptist Church of Halifax. She was closer to me in age than she was to her own brother and sisters. She took to me like I was her little sister. She took me everywhere and I loved being around her. We were always laughing and kidding. Then she met Charlie Scott from up in Roanoke Rapids and they came together with a powerful love. He had just come home from overseas fighting in the First World War and they just tried to be with each other all the time. But she never forgot me. A short time after being together they decided to get married. They wanted it to be real legal with a marriage certificate and all . . .

AUNT CORA: Uh, uh! No jumping no broom for me.

MATTIE: So they went down to Raleigh and got married by the Justice-of-the-Peace. They took me with them. That was the first time I had ever been out of Halifax. Now Aunt Cora had her marriage certificate, but she said that she really wasn't married until she was married in her church with a preacher and all . . . in the sight of the Lord. So they came back to Halifax and got married again in front of family and friends . . . and God. I think that was Reverend Fentress' very first wedding . . .

MATOKA: Uoo! I'm surprised they ain't still standing there.

JOYCE punches MATOKA.

MATTIE: Charlie Scott and his brother and some of their friends built this house out here and they moved in. That's right, this was . . . is your Aunt Cora's house . . .

AUNT CORA: The first things I brought into my new house was a Bible, a box of salt, a broom and that pretty marriage certificate. I put that certificate in a frame and I hung it on the wall where everybody could see it and know that I was married and not just living common law . . .

MATTIE: . . . And you see where I hung your Daddy's and mine right next to it. Now before Aunt Cora met Charlie Scott, there was this white man who was after her. He had a wife and children, but that didn't make him no never mind. He wanted him some Cora Allen . . .

AUNT CORA: Every time he'd see me, he would be talking all under my clothes . . . and making all kinds of nasty gestures with his hands and such . . .

MATTIE: When Aunt Cora married Charlie Scott, that white man got as mad as a wet hen. He wanted to be her first man. One night after choir practice, when Charlie Scott was up in Weldon visiting his Mama who had taken sick, Aunt Cora walked part of the way home with a few of the other choir members. But she still had to walk a good little piece by herself. Charlie Scott usually met her and walked home with her but this night, for some reason, he didn't get back from Weldon in time. Anyway, as the story was told by Aunt Cora . . .

AUNT CORA: As I was walking down the road, a car full of white men and boys passed me. They turned the car around and started following me down the road . . . making all kinds of foul suggestions to me. The white man that was after me was in the car too. I got scared and left the road and started running through the wood toward home. But them men jumped out of the car and ran me down . . . (*Pause.*) and took their way with me. I don't rightly know how many of them took part because I just closed my eyes and laid there. But I do know the white man that wanted me was first . . . as if to say, "since I couldn't be your first man, I'm going to be your first white man." Then, as if violating me that way wasn't enough, one of the men said that he had never seen a woman pee before. So they made me stand up in front of them naked and told me to pee . . .

AUNT CORA *breaks down.*

MATTIE: She said when she couldn't, one of the men slapped her on the behind like he was slapping a mule until the poor thing started relieving herself. And they watched . . . and laughed. After they had finished having their fun, they just left her there crying. She said she didn't know where she got the strength from, but she stumbled her way through the woods to this house. She worked hard to clean the smell of them men off of herself before Charlie Scott got home. But, she couldn't clean off all the scratches from men and bushes and sticks and rocks on the ground. She even had a bite mark on the top of her bosom . . . where one of them men had bit her. When Charlie Scott got home and saw all of them scratches and bruises, . . .

AUNT CORA: I had to tell him what happened . . .

MATTIE: Now as I said, Charlie Scott had fought in the war. So I guess he was so mad that he didn't see them white men as any different than those Germans he had just finished fighting against . . .

MATTIE/AUNT CORA: I guess he forgot he was in America . . . in the South . . .

MATTIE: Because Charlie Scott loaded his shotgun and filled his pockets with buckshot and all by his lonesome commenced to walk down the main street to town until he got to Mr. Gerard's Dry Goods store, where some white men used to sit in front of. I don't think Charlie Scott knew if any of them white men were the ones that was in the woods, he just started shooting . . .

MATTIE/AUNT CORA: Those white men were ducking and running and shouting.

MATTIE: I hear tell, one of them "brave" white men was screaming, "Don't shoot me . . ."

AUNT CORA: "Please don't shoot me . . ."

MATTIE: Charlie Scott then reloaded his shotgun and walked down to Webster's filling station where he opened fire again. He didn't kill nobody, but he shot a white man in the leg and later the leg had to be taken off. While Charlie Scott was loading his shotgun for the third time, a bunch of white men jumped him and dragged him away. (*Pause.*) When next a colored person saw Charlie Scott, he was hanging from a limb down by the creek.

AUNT CORA begins to rock and hum.

At the funeral, Aunt Cora just sat there rocking and humming. That's when Charlie Scott's Mama started screaming at her, in front of everybody, "Why did you tell him? You think you the only colored woman this has happened to? He would be walking around today if you didn't tell him. You killed him just as much as they did!"

The special goes down on AUNT CORA.

(*Pause.*) Ever since that day, Aunt Cora has been wearing black . . . and humming.

There is silence.

MATOKA: If this was her house, how did she end up living way out there in the woods?

MATTIE: Aunt Cora never set foot in this house again. She went to live with her brother, Uncle Walter. That was his house out there. He never married, so when he died Aunt Cora just stayed on.

MATOKA: Poor Aunt Cora.

MATTIE goes up the steps and crosses to the screen door.

JOYCE: Why are you telling us this now?

MATTIE: I guess it's time you both knew. Maybe it's because your Daddy's coming home and I don't know what's going to happen . . . when I tell him what I got to tell him.

JOYCE: What's that?

MATTIE: (*Pause.*) That I'm pregnant.

JOYCE: Oh, Mama . . . No!

Lights go to black.

Act 2

Scene 1

Time: *The next Saturday afternoon.*

In dark we hear the voice of MATOKA *singing, "Way Down Yonder in the White Man's Field."*

MATOKA: (*Singing.*) Way down yonder in the white man's field,
Way down yonder in the white man's field,
Never made enough to pay my bills,
Way down yonder in the white man's field,

At Rise: *We see* MATOKA *jumping rope in the yard to the cadence of the song.*

Three at the foot and three at the head,
A pallet on the floor for my bed,
All we had to eat was a guinea knot,
And a glass of water was all we got.

RAWL *enters from the house. He runs off the porch and attempts, unsuccessfully, to join in on the rope jumping and singing.*

MATOKA: Daddy! You're messing me up.

RAWL, *still singing, takes* MATOKA's *hand and they dance a dance that is unique to this family.* MATTIE *and* YAVENI *enter from the house.* YAVENI *is wearing a torn yarmulke he has attempted, in vain, to repair.*

MATTIE: Toke, don't you go getting all sweaty now. You got to go to choir practice.

RAWL *and* MATOKA *continue to dance and sing.* RAWL *runs up on the porch and pulls* MATTIE *down to dance with them.*

RAWL: Come on here, woman! What you looking all mopey for?

MATOKA *laughs.* MATTIE *refuses to dance.*

You act like you're sorry your man is home.
MATTIE: You know I don't like Matoka singing that song . . . and you out here helping her.
RAWL: It's only a song!
MATTIE: What if some white man came by and heard her singing that "song?"

JOYCE *enters from the house.*

RAWL: To hear anything back up here in these woods, you can't be just "coming by." You have to be "digging" your way back up in here. And ain't Yaveni white?
JOYCE: Mr. Aaronsohn said he ain't white, he's Jewish.

A beat of silence.

JOYCE (*Cont'd.*): Come on, Toke. I don't want to be late for choir practice.
MATOKA: You just want to get there early so you can see old cock-eyed Sammy Hunter.

JOYCE: Daddy, tell Matoka to come on.

MATTIE: You better get yourself going, girl.

JOYCE and MATOKA begin to exit.

RAWL: Ain't you girls forgetting something?

MATOKA: (*Teasing.*) Oh, . . . Good-bye, Mr. Aaronsohn.

RAWL: I got your "good-bye, Mr. Aaronsohn." You better get your pretty self over here and give me some sugar.

MATOKA runs to RAWL and kisses him as he hugs her.

(*To JOYCE.*) Well? I thought you and me set things straight before I went away. Now, I know you don't want for me to have to come over there.

JOYCE sullenly crosses to RAWL and hugs him.

(*To MATTIE.*) Now, what's wrong with you?

MATTIE crosses to RAWL and all four embrace.

RAWL (*Cont'd.*): My ladies. I missed all of you.

JOYCE pulls away.

JOYCE: I missed you too, Daddy. Come on, Toke.

RAWL: (*To JOYCE.*) What's the matter, Baby?

JOYCE: Nothing. Come on, Toke.

JOYCE exits.

MATOKA: Bye everybody. (*To RAWL.*) She'll be alright soon as she sees old liver-lips Sammy Hunter.

JOYCE: (*Offstage.*) Come on, Matoka!

MATOKA: Sammy Hunter.

MATOKA exits running.

YAVENI: I would say Mr. Sammy Hunter possesses an over-abundance of abnormal physical attributes, many of which I have never heard. There is "long-head," . . . "cock-eyed," . . . "liver-lips," . . .

RAWL: That boy ain't that bad. Toke's just making all that stuff up.

MATTIE: Before you leave, Yaveni, I got something for you.

MATTIE exits into the house.

RAWL: Something ain't right with my ladies. Toke seems to be the only one acting normal.

YAVENI: It has been three months. They're just getting used to you being home again. Tomorrow it will be just like you never went away.

RAWL: I know my ladies, Yaveni. Something ain't right.

YAVENI: As I said with chess, sometimes things aren't always what they appear to be. And speaking of chess, how's your chess game?

RAWL: I ain't had no time for no chess with all that grave digging.

YAVENI: Well, we must take to the battlefield again very soon.

MATTIE enters from the house carrying a yarmulke. She hands it to YAVENI.

MATTIE: I made this for you. Now you can throw that thing you have on your head to the pigs.

YAVENI: What do you mean? I repaired this myself.

MATTIE: That's just what I mean.

YAVENI: (*Moved.*) I thank you so very much, Mattie.

YAVENI removes the repaired yarmulke from his head and puts it in his pocket. He then puts the new one on his head.

YAVENI (*Cont'd.*): Perfect fit. Thank you.

RAWL: You want me to throw that other one away.

YAVENI: No thank you. Once a yarmulke is used, you never throw them away. Beside, this one has a very special meaning.

There is a moment of silence.

RAWL: Talking about pigs. What happened to them pork chops?

YAVENI: I don't understand.

RAWL: Joyce said Jews don't eat pig. What do you think pork chops are? Man sat there and ate him a whole belly full of pork chops . . . talking about he don't eat no pig. No you gobble it.

YAVENI: I think I'm going to leave now.

RAWL: That's right. Go on and leave. But, I'm going to warn all the pigs in Halifax County about the man that's walking around here talking about he don't eat no pig . . . but eats pork. Now you get your pig-eating self off my dirt.

Laughing, RAWL crosses to the pump and takes a drink of water from the water bucket.

YAVENI: I can take a subtle hint. Good-bye, Mattie, and thank you for dinner . . . and for the yarmulke. (*Cryptically to MATTIE.*) Are you going to be alright?

MATTIE: Yes.

YAVENI: Are you sure?

MATTIE does not answer.

I know. I know. I learn very quickly. Don't be getting all up between you and your family. You take care. (*To RAWL.*) You! You are *meshuggeneh*!

YAVENI exits.

RAWL: (*Calling after him.*) I don't know what that means, but you're another one. It don't matter if it's a sow, a hog or a little baby pig, old "Mr. Don't Eat No Pork" will eat it. Ate half my pork chops . . . just like he birth that hog. (*Laughing.*)

YAVENI: (*Offstage.*) *Meshuggeneh!*

RAWL: I got your *Meshig* . . . (*To* MATTIE.) I bet he ain't had a meal like that since he's been down here. What all that you and him was talking about?

MATTIE: I was feeling poorly for a while. I'm better now.

RAWL: What happened to his yar . . . ?

MATTIE: Yarmulke. While you were gone, some white men in town took it and spit on it and ripped it up.

RAWL: Why didn't he just get in touch with his people up in Cleveland and have them send him another one?

MATTIE: I don't think Yaveni got any people.

RAWL: Why do you think that?

MATTIE: I don't know. There something wrong . . . a sadness. I always get a troubled feeling coming from him.

RAWL takes MATTIE *by the hand and begins to cross towards the house.*

RAWL: Yeah, well, I've been having a feeling for three months and it's causing me some trouble.

MATTIE pulls her hand away.

MATTIE: Rawl . . . I need to talk to you before the girls get back.

RAWL reaches for MATTIE *again.*

RAWL: Yes, Lord . . . I need to talk to you too before the girls get back.

MATTIE pulls away again.

MATTIE: I'm serious, Rawl.

RAWL: And I'm three months full of serious. So you just come on now and . . .

MATTIE: I'm pregnant.

RAWL is stunned for a couple of beats, then he again grabs MATTIE'*s hand and starts pulling her towards the house.*

RAWL: Well, the bread is already baking in the oven and there ain't nothing we can do about it until it's done. So come on.

MATTIE: It . . . It ain't your bread, Rawl.

RAWL stops. There is a silence. He then drops MATTIE'*s hand.*

RAWL: (*Pause.*) Come again?

MATTIE: (*Pause.*) It ain't your baby.

RAWL: (*Chuckle.*) You kidding . . . right?

MATTIE: (*Pause.*) I wish I was, Rawl. God knows I wish I was.

RAWL backs away from MATTIE.

RAWL: Whose is it?

MATTIE: I don't know . . .

RAWL: You don't what?

MATTIE: I mean you don't know him.

RAWL: Where is he?

MATTIE: I don't know.

RAWL: Is his damn name "I don't know" too? (*Screaming.*) Who the hell is he?

MATTIE: I don't have a name.

RAWL: Why? Was it just somebody passing through?

MATTIE: You don't know him.

RAWL: (*Screaming.*) Don't keep telling me that! How do you know I don't know him if you don't have a name? (*Pause.*) Where did you do it? Or are you going to tell me you don't know?

MATTIE: What does it . . . ?

RAWL: (*Screaming.*) Where? . . . Where my daughters sleep?

MATTIE: No, I . . .

RAWL: . . . in our bed?

MATTIE: No.

RAWL: Where then?

MATTIE: Why does it matter? . . .

RAWL: I ain't going to ask you again. Where?

MATTIE: (*Searching.*) Where . . . Where . . . he stayed.

RAWL: (*As if to himself.*) And then you let yourself go and get knocked-up by him to boot. I was all the time asking you to give me a son before we got too old . . . and you wouldn't do that. Now you . . . (*To MATTIE.*) Was it somebody at that church? All them men running around down there with their zippers down. Deacon This and Trustee That and Reverend . . . Reverend Fentress! You love you some Reverend Fentress. Can't nobody say a word against him. Like he was God instead of God.

MATTIE: Reverend Fentress wouldn't do that. He's married.

RAWL: Well that didn't make a big hell of a difference to you when your draws caught fire and you got yourself knocked-up.

MATTIE: Rawl, please don't talk like that.

RAWL: Don't tell me how the hell to talk.

RAWL charges at MATTIE with his fist raised to hit her. MATTIE closes her eyes and lifts her face to accept the blow which never comes. RAWL, catching himself, freezes for a beat with his fist in the air. He slowly lowers it and sits. After a beat, humming can be heard. Shortly thereafter, AUNT CORA enters and stands at the edge of the yard looking at them. She stops humming. RAWL, seeing AUNT CORA, gets up and exits in the opposite direction. AUNT CORA continues to look at MATTIE for a beat. She then begins to hum again as she crosses to the edge of the porch and picks up the lunch basket. She turns and exits the same way she came. Lights go to black.

Scene 2

Time: *Sunday, the next morning.*

At Rise: *We see* RAWL *sitting on the steps of the porch. He is deep in thought.*

MATOKA *enters from the house. She is dressed in her "Sunday Best" for church. She crosses to* RAWL *and kisses him on the cheek.*

MATOKA: Morning, Daddy.
RAWL: Hmmmm?
MATOKA: I just said, good morning.
RAWL: Oh, good morning, Sugar.

Not detecting any playfulness in her father, MATOKA *crosses to the porch swing and sits. She begins swinging.*

MATOKA: I can't sit next to you because I have my church clothes on and they'll get dirty. (*Pause.*) I'm going to sing the song we practiced yesterday in church. (*Pause.*) You going to come hear me? (*Pause.*) Mama said she's glad when I'm singing because that's the only time you come to church.
RAWL: No, Baby. I can't come today. I ain't feeling in too good a way to go into no church.
MATOKA: You think maybe that's the best time to go?

RAWL *smiles at* MATOKA, *but does not answer.*

MATOKA (*Cont'd.*): You want to hear me sing the song now since you won't hear me sing it in church.
RAWL: Sure, Baby.
MATOKA: (*Singing.*) I will sing, Alleluia
     I will sing, O'Lord
     I will sing, Alleluia, O'Lord
     You are the source of my supply
     Lord, I pray, you will lift me high
     I will sing, Alleluia, O'Lord
     I will sing . . .

JOYCE *enters from the house. She too is wearing her "Sunday Best," except, she is carrying her shoes and socks.*

JOYCE: Come on, Matoka, we're going to be late for Sunday School.
MATOKA: And old buck-tooth Sammy Hunter. I was ready before you, right, Daddy?

RAWL does not respond.

JOYCE: You know better than to put your shoes on before we get out to the black-top.

MATTIE enters from the house. She is carrying a woman's hat.

MATOKA: I'd rather have my shoes dirty than my feet. That's what shoes are for . . . to keep your feet clean. Now we walk out there and get our feet all dirty, then put our clean socks and shoes on our dirty feet. Right, Daddy?

MATTIE: You better get those shoes off, girl.

MATOKA begins removing her shoes and socks.

MATOKA: (*To JOYCE.*) You all the time think you somebody's Mama.

JOYCE: I sure wouldn't want to be yours.

MATTIE: Joyce? You're a young lady now. I reckon it's about time you start wearing a hat to church.

MATTIE crosses to JOYCE and places the hat on her head as if performing a "Rite of Passage."

MATOKA: Oh, Lord . . .

MATTIE: Don't you be using the Lord's name in vain.

MATOKA: I just said . . .

MATTIE: Don't you be giving me no mouth, girl.

JOYCE crosses to RAWL giving him a hug and kiss.

JOYCE: Good morning, Daddy.

RAWL: Good morning, Sweety. That hat looks real nice on you.

JOYCE: Thank you. I'm glad you're home.

MATTIE: You girls go on so you don't be late.

MATOKA hugs RAWL.

MATOKA: Bye, Daddy.

RAWL: You sing your little heart out for me, alright? Heaven is still asleep, so you wake all those angels up.

MATOKA: I will.

MATOKA crosses to MATTIE and hugs her.

  Bye, Mama.

JOYCE: Bye, Daddy.

MATTIE: (*To MATOKA.*) Don't you go running all over that church cutting the fool. You know I'll find out and your little hind-parts will be mine.

MATOKA: Yes, Ma'am.

MATTIE: And you mind your manners . . . and Joyce.

MATOKA: Yes, Ma'am.

MATTIE: Don't keep "yes ma'aming" me. I know you, Matoka.

MATOKA giggles. The girls turn to leave.

RAWL: Joyce.

JOYCE: Yes?

RAWL: You ain't said bye to your Mama.

JOYCE crosses close to MATTIE.

JOYCE: Good-bye.

MATTIE hugs JOYCE tightly. JOYCE does not hug her back. Then, with a mother's loving touch MATTIE straightens the hat on JOYCE's head.

MATTIE: Good-bye, Joyce.

The girls turn to leave.

RAWL: Wait a minute.

RAWL crosses to the girls and hugs them together.

My ladies know that I love them with all my heart, don't they?

JOYCE: Yes.

MATOKA: Yes, Daddy.

RAWL: Never forget that . . . no matter what. Now, go on.

MATOKA: See you next year, Daddy. Reverend Fentress is preaching today.

The girls exit. There is a beat of silence.

MATTIE: I left a plate on the table for you last night. (*Pause.*) You didn't touch it. (*Pause.*) You want me to fix you something now. You must be hungry.

RAWL: I ain't.

Silence.

MATTIE: You didn't come to bed last night. Where did you sleep?

RAWL: How come you think I slept?

MATTIE: What did you do?

RAWL: I just walked around.

MATTIE: All night?

RAWL: I walked some . . . sat some . . . and walked around some more until I found myself back here. I don't know where I walked or how far. I just found myself back here.

MATTIE: What was you doing?

RAWL: Thinking.

MATTIE: Thinking about what?

RAWL: (*Explodes.*) Will Uncle Remus sing, "Zippa Dee Doo Da," at church today. What do you think I was thinking about, Mattie?

MATTIE: I'm sorry.

MATTIE starts to exit back into the house.

RAWL: Did it happen because I went away to Alabama to work?

MATTIE: (*Pause.*) No.

RAWL: Was it happening before I went away?

MATTIE: No, Rawl!

RAWL: Well, what then? I walked around all night trying to figure out all those question words in Matoka's school book . . . Why? . . . Who? . . . Where? I already know "When" and "How." Why couldn't you have talked to me if something was wrong?

MATTIE: Nothing is wrong.

RAWL: (*Screaming.*) Then why?

MATTIE does not respond.

RAWL (*Cont'd.*): Did I ever hit you?

MATTIE: No.

RAWL: Disrespect you? . . . Curse at you? . . . At my girls?

MATTIE: No.

RAWL: Well, dammit to hell, talk to me! Why did you let yourself go and get knocked-up?

MATTIE: I didn't let myself. It just happened.

RAWL: "Just happened?" You're walking down the road and here comes some guy walking down the road from the other direction. You trip on a rock and fall down. Your dress blows up and your draws come down, if you have any on at all, and your legs spread open. He trips on a stick, his fly flies open, and he falls between your legs and you get knocked-up. THAT'S what you call "just happened!"

MATTIE: Rawl, please don't talk vulgar. You never did that before.

RAWL: I never thought my wife was as vulgar as I'm talking. (*Pause.*) What about my girls? What you going to tell them?

MATTIE: They already know. (*Pause.*) Joyce knows it ain't yours. Toke just knows I'm pregnant.

RAWL: Matoka's not stupid, Mattie. She can count. She knows I've been away for three and a half months. What does she think you're going to have, a elephant? Who else knows?

MATTIE: (*Pause.*) Yaveni.

RAWL: Yaveni? (*Pause.*) Was it him?

MATTIE: Rawl, you shouldn't be talking no foolishness like that.

RAWL: Why not? You're always worrying about him. You told him to come here to eat, then let him almost eat up all of my pork chops. You spend all that time making him a yar . . . Why does he know?

MATTIE: He seen me get sick a couple of times. He could figure it out.

RAWL: What you letting him come around for?

MATTIE: I wasn't letting him, Rawl. You let him! I didn't want no part of it, but you wanted him to know things about us for money.

RAWL: Did he have to know you got knocked-up before I? . . .

MATTIE: Will you please stop saying that? Can't you say pregnant?

RAWL: You're pregnant when you're going to have a baby by a man you love or been with for some time. You're pregnant when someone asks you who the father is and you can say more than "I don't know." Other than that, you're knocked up. Understand?

MATTIE: (*Emotionally beaten.*) Yes, I understand. I'm not feeling too well. I think I need to go in and lay down a while.

MATTIE starts to cross to the steps.

RAWL: What is it you expect from me, Mattie?

MATTIE: (*Emotionally beaten.*) I would like for you to look into your heart and the memories of our mind and draw on all the beauty that has been in our lives. Then do for me the best your heart will allow. I would like for you to know how much I truly love you.

RAWL: I never raised my hand to you in the eighteen years we've been married . . . and yesterday . . . yesterday I almost hit you. I never thought I'd come close to hitting you or any other woman. I've never even spanked my girls. So, I walked around all night thinking about how much I loved you. Thinking about what I did to make you find your way to another man. This way maybe I could work it out in my mind . . . in my heart. Maybe I could do better if only I knew where I went off the road. (*Pause.*) I reckon, I'm saying, I can try and work with this, but the only way I can do that is if you get rid of that baby.

MATTIE: Rawl, please don't ask me to do that.

RAWL: You want me to stay here and look at what you and another man did every day until I die?

MATTIE: It ain't the baby's fault, Rawl. I can't kill my baby. Don't make me choose between you or it. Please don't . . .

RAWL: You want me to sit across the table looking at some other man's bastard eating my food?

MATTIE does not respond.

You love him and you want the baby around to remind you of the Daddy.

MATTIE: No!

RAWL: Then why can't you?

MATTIE: The baby is God's will!

RAWL: (*Explodes.*) Don't give me that crap! I ain't Joseph and you damn sure ain't no Virgin Mary. At least a angel came to Joseph in his sleep and told him Mary was goin to have a baby by another man ahead of time. But ain't no angel come to me in my sleep and told me squat.

MATTIE: I didn't say it was God's baby. I said it was God's will.

RAWL: Well, Rawl's will say I will leave your behind if you're planning on birthing that baby. What's going to happen when them nosey "Sisters" and "Brothers" down there at that church find out?

MATTIE: They ain't got to know nothing.

RAWL: Now, that all depends on what the baby comes out looking like, wouldn't you say, Mattie? When that baby is born, you don't think that one of your "Sister So-and-sos" and "Brother What's-His-Name," down there at that church ain't going to count back nine months? Earl knows where I was two or three months ago. He was with me digging up them dead white folks. And if Earl knows, then Sally knows. And when Sally gets into her bottle, then the whole town will know. This is a small town, Mattie. A flea could break wind at one end of town and a mule will smell it at the other end. You going to be walking around that church looking like a ant that swallowed a watermelon, talking about it's "God's will?" Them women down there will figure out when the bull's eye was hit and when you're supposed to drop the load. And they'll have your behind on the mourner's bench so fast, it'll make your head swim.

MATTIE: (*Screaming.*) Shut up!

Silence.

(*Fiery.*) For better or for worse. That's what we said eighteen years ago, and I meant it. I knew that there was going to be times when things would be bad . . . when each of us would be tested by God and man . . . when our marriage would have to face forces as powerful as a tornado sweeping across a cotton field. But, I believed that if we just held hands and stood facing that tornado together, that we might bend . . . bend all the way down until our foreheads were almost touching the ground, but as long as we kept holding on to each other hands, we would not break. And I knew there would be times when each of us would have to face that world out there alone, but that we could stand up to anything . . . anybody, because the spirit of the other was with us. And when you came in here mad and whipped by that world out there, I stood there and said, "Give me your rage. Bring it home to me. That's what I'm here for." Because I knew that if you tried to let that rage out outside of this house, out there in that world, those white folks would kill you. Every colored woman knows she has to be strong to be able to take on the rage her man can't let loose anywhere else. And I was strong. And I absorbed it . . . head on . . . point blank. (*Softly*) And then I put my arms around you and pulled your head to my breast and told you that it was alright; that I knew you were the man that world out there was afraid to let you be; that I never asked you to be a Superman, just my man. Then I cried for you . . . cried the tears that you were too much of a man to cry. And I did it with all the love I could muster up from the very bottom of my being. Now I'm asking you to hold my hand and face this tornado with me . . .

Mattie puts her hand out to Rawl.

. . . to have faith in my love for you; to help me care for and accept the responsibility that the Lord has given to grow inside me.

Rawl does not take Mattie's hand.

Rawl: (*Pause.*) I can't, Mattie.

Rawl exits into the house. Mattie sits on the edge of the porch. After a beat, Yaveni enters. Seeing Mattie, he knows things did not go so well.

Yaveni: Are you alright?

Mattie shakes her head indicating "Yes."

I came over to see if everything was alright. I wanted to come back yesterday, but thought better of it.

Mattie: I think that was a good idea.

Yaveni crosses to the pump and removes the burlap cover from over the water bucket. He takes the dip-cup and draws water from the bucket. After replacing the burlap, Yaveni crosses to Mattie, handing her the cup. Mattie drinks.

Yaveni: He didn't hit you did he?

Mattie: He would never hit me.

Yaveni: I'm sorry. It's just that I've seen his temper . . .

Mattie: I'm fine, Yaveni. Thank you.

Yaveni: Does he know?

Mattie: Yes, I told him yesterday.

Yaveni: How did he take it?

Mattie: Not too good.

Yaveni: I know this must be killing him.

Mattie: It's killing me too!

Yaveni: Then why don't you just tell him your pregnancy is the result of a rape? That's not the same as him thinking you were willingly with another man.

Mattie: You think that going to stop him from trying to find out who did it? . . . From going around town asking both colored and white folks if they know who did it. And then there'll be that one white man who's never even seen me before, but who wants to see what this "uppity nigger" is going to do about it if he was the one who raped me, who will say, "Yeah, I did it. So what?" . . . and my husband will be gone.

YAVENI: I've seen someone hurting like him before. Mattie, if you don't tell him, I will.

MATTIE: And so help me God, I'll make sure that you cut him down from that limb all by yourself. And I'll pray for that sight to be with you for the rest of your life. You think you can take that?

RAWL enters from the house. He is carrying a suitcase and a frame.

YAVENI: Good morning, Rawl. I thought I'd stop by and see if you were interested in a game of chess. There's not too many people down here who play . . . or at least, are willing to play with me.

RAWL comes down the stairs into the yard. He throws the frame out into the field (offstage).

Well, I guess there will be no chess today.

RAWL: I left money on the table. I'll send more from Cleveland. (*To* YAVENI.) Do you know who it was?

YAVENI: Rawl . . .

RAWL: (*Screaming.*) Do you know who it was?

MATTIE is pleading with her eyes for YAVENI to say "No."

YAVENI: (*Reluctantly.*) No. No, I don't.

RAWL: Was it you?

YAVENI: That's an insult, Rawl. I think you owe both Mattie and me an apology.

RAWL turns to leave.

MATTIE: Rawl, I love you. At least take that with you.

RAWL: I love you too, Mattie.

RAWL exits. MATTIE just stands crying. YAVENI stands uncomfortably. After a beat, MATTIE slowly crosses the yard and exits. After a couple of more beats, she re-enters carrying the frame. She crosses to the steps of the house.

YAVENI: What's that, Mattie?

MATTIE: Our marriage certificate.

MATTIE goes up the steps and exits into the house holding the frame against her breast. Lights go to black.

Scene 3

Time: *Three months later, at dusk.*

At Rise: *MATTIE enters from the house with the food basket. Her pregnancy is visibly evident. She crosses and sets the food basket at the edge of the porch, but this time near the porch swing. She waits a beat, looking round, then crosses to the porch swing and sits. After a beat, we hear the humming. Shortly thereafter,* AUNT CORA *enters. She notices* MATTIE *and the location of the food basket. She hesitates, then crosses to the basket, picks it up and turns to leave.*

MATTIE: Aunt Cora?

AUNT CORA *stops but does not turn around. She has stopped humming as well.*

(*Rising.*) Please give me time.

After a beat, AUNT CORA *turns, and for the first time faces* MATTIE.

(*Pause.*) You know everything that goes on around here, don't you, Aunt Cora? That's why you scared Yaveni a while back when he was leaving and led him back to the house so he could hear what Joe Flood did to me. (*Pause.*) Joe Flood was one of them white boys that took his way with you . . . who wanted you so badly, wasn't he, Aunt Cora? Because of that one white man, you lost your husband, I lost my husband . . . and I lost you. You lost your man because you told and I lost my man because I didn't tell. Charlie Scott is gone for eternity and that's a long time. But, even though my bed is empty and my sheets are cold, I know that the blood is still running warm in Rawl's veins. And that's all that matters right now. Did I do right, Aunt Cora? Did you do right? Or maybe there ain't no right. I miss Rawl so much, just as I know you miss Charlie Scott. I would go to Cleveland and get my man, but I would never leave you, Aunt Cora. I guess the one thing that keeps me from being like you is my three children. Now, my womb-opener don't like me and is talking about leaving and the man I love wants to kill the one growing in me before it starts breathing. (*Pause.*) All because of that one white man.

There is a beat of silence. AUNT CORA *then begins to hum as she exits.*

Thank you for listening to me. (*Calling after* AUNT CORA.) We love you, Aunt Cora!

Lights go to black.

Scene 4

Time: *A week later.*

At Rise: MATTIE *is sitting on the porch swing with a large bowl in her lap, snapping string beans.*

MATTIE: (*Calling.*) Toke?

MATOKA: (*Offstage.*) Yes, Ma'am?

MATTIE: (*Calling.*) You make sure you put them jars in that pot before the water starts boiling. I don't want that hot water splashing up on you.

MATOKA: (*Offstage.*) Yes, Ma'am.

MATOKA enters from the house carrying a Mason "canning jar."

Mama, this top is too tight. Can you open it?

MATTIE takes the jar and attempts to open it with no success.

I told you it was too tight. If Daddy was here, he'd pop it right open.

MATTIE: Just sit it on the side, Matoka. Maybe Joyce can open it when she gets back with those other jars. What's taking her so long anyway? I want to put these string beans up before it gets too dark.

MATOKA: And you're going to put up some blackberries with dumplings too, ain't you, Mama?

MATTIE: I reckon. But you and Joyce will have to go pick them. I ain't up to picking no berries.

MATOKA: I can pick them by myself.

MATTIE: Now you know I ain't letting you go back there in them woods by yourself, Matoka. I told you I don't want you going off by yourself.

MATOKA: You let Joyce go by herself.

MATTIE: And I still worry about her, but Joyce knows a little bit more about what to do.

JOYCE enters.

What took you so long? Where are the jars?

JOYCE: Mr. Aaronsohn has them in his car. Since you don't want us riding in no white man's car, I walked back and he said he would bring them out here so I wouldn't have to carry them. I didn't want to ride with him no ways.

MATTIE: When I said about the car, I didn't mean Mr. Aaronsohn.

JOYCE: He's a white man, ain't he? Oh, that's right, he ain't white, he's Jewish.

MATTIE: Where is he, Joyce?

JOYCE: He was talking to some "real live white men" in town when I last saw him. Those white folks were all excited about something. He told me to go on home and he would be along shortly . . . like he's somebody's daddy.

MATTIE: Ain't no need you blaming him for what happened to me, Joyce.

MATTIE jumps from the baby kicking inside of her.

MATOKA: Oooo! Was that it? Can I feel it, Mama? You promised.

MATTIE: Alright, come on.

MATOKA crosses to MATTIE and puts her hand on the swell of her mother's abdomen.

MATOKA: It stopped!

MATTIE: It ain't going to move when you want it to, Matoka. It's going to move when it gets ready.

MATOKA: Oooo! Oooo! I feel it. It moved! Come on, Joyce, and feel our new brother or sister!

JOYCE: It ain't no brother or sister of mine.

MATTIE: It only a baby, Joyce. None of us have any choice as to who our Mamas and Daddies are.

JOYCE: I have a choice. That's why I'm going up to Cleveland to be with my Daddy.

MATOKA: I ain't going because I don't like Daddy no more.

MATTIE: Don't you be talking like that about your father. This is still his house and you're still his daughter. And if he walks in here in the next twenty minutes, he will still sit at the head of my table and you will still do what he tells you to and like it.

MATOKA: But, he left us and now we're all the time fussing.

MATTIE: I don't care, Matoka. You ain't saying you don't like him when you're filling your mouth full of the food we buy with the money he sends every week.

JOYCE: She didn't mean nothing, Mama.

MATTIE: And I don't want to hear no disrespect out of your mouth either, Joyce.

MATTIE gets up and storms into the house.

MATOKA: See? We're all the time fussing.

JOYCE: When I get up to Cleveland and start working. I'll be able to help Daddy send money back for your train fare.

MATOKA: I ain't going to leave Mama! Who's going to help her with the baby? Daddy leaves and now you want to go!

JOYCE: Why are you blaming Daddy? Didn't you understand? It ain't Daddy's baby. That's Mr. Joe Flood's baby! Mama don't have to have that baby.

MATOKA runs at JOYCE screaming and swinging her fist at JOYCE.

MATOKA: You shut up . . . It ain't . . . You're lying . . .

YAVENI enters carrying a carton of Mason "canning jars." MATTIE enters from the house.

MATTIE: What are you two doing out . . .

MATOKA keeps trying to hit JOYCE.

MATOKA: You shut up . . .

MATTIE: Stop it, Matoka! You hear me?

YAVENI *puts the carton down on the ground and pulls* MATOKA *away from* JOYCE. MATOKA *breaks away and exits running.* MATTIE *runs behind her, calling after her.*

Matoka! Matoka! Where are you going? (*To* JOYCE.) What did you do to her?

JOYCE: Told the truth.

MATTIE: And what truth did you tell, Joyce?

JOYCE: That it's not Daddy's baby. That it's Mr. Joe Flood's baby.

MATTIE: She knows all of that, Joyce. She just ain't ready to face up to it, but she knows that. There was no call for you to be so mean to her. Getting back at me is one thing, but she loves you. She's a little girl and she's just scared. Her father's gone and her sister and best friend is talking about leaving.

JOYCE: I ain't talking about it, Mama. I'm going.

MATTIE: You're starting to smell yourself, Joyce. I ain't going to be taking too much more of it. I'll still send you for a switch . . . big belly and all.

There is a silence.

YAVENI: I'm going to have to be going also, Mattie.

MATTIE: (*Stunned.*) What? . . . Why? . . . I mean . . . I never thought about you leaving.

YAVENI: (*Accented.*) Come on, already! There are no Jews here to sit *Shiva* for me in case one of these *paskunyak* down here hangs me. (*Laugh.*)

MATTIE: Why are you leaving, Yaveni?

YAVENI: Let's just say, I was told that I've worn out my welcome in this town. I was confronted by some men in town and they informed me that it might be advantageous to my health if I chose another geographic location to complete my research. Their description of what they would do to me brought to mind images of Sammy Hunter (*Chuckle.*) So after accepting a deadline of two days to leave, I returned to my car to find "nigger-lover" written in paint on the driver's side and a *swastika* painted on the passenger's side. (*Pause.*) I just stopped by to bring you those jars. Now I have to go and try and get that art work off my car. I can't drive from North Carolina to Cleveland with my car looking like an advertisement for the Ku Klux Klan.

MATTIE: I'm so sorry, Yaveni.

YAVENI: So am I. I'll say my good-byes now because I don't think it's a good idea for me to come back here. I don't want to cause you any more trouble than I may have already. You've been very good friends to me these last seven months.

MATTIE: You come back here when you're ready to leave and I'll have some pork chops ready for you to take on your trip.

YAVENI: You're a wonderful cook, Mattie, but what those men in town did to me reminded me that if I'm going to be what I'm supposed to be . . . well, maybe my eating pork chops is not a very good thing. I hope you understand.

MATTIE: I understand, Yaveni. (*Pause.*) But you bring yourself on back here and say good-bye. I ain't studying these white folks.

YAVENI: Yes, Ma'am.

YAVENI turns to leave, then turns back.

Mattie, if you would allow me, this one time, to get all up between you and your family, I would like to say a few words to Joyce.

MATTIE: You go right ahead, Yaveni.

YAVENI: Joyce. I know you're angry with me because of what a white man did to your mother . . . because you see me as white. You make fun of me when I say I'm not white, I'm Jewish. Well, you're right. At one time I declared myself white, not Jewish. I didn't want to be Jewish because where I came from Jews caught hell . . .

MATTIE: Caught the devil, Yaveni.

YAVENI: Sorry. I was born in a *shtetl* . . . a small village near the city of Kostroma, Russia. One day when I was in my early teens, our village was destroyed by the Russians for no other reason than it was a Jewish village. After that, my family decided to leave Russia. We moved to Munich in Germany. (*Chuckle.*) We didn't know at the time that we were moving right out of the proverbial "frying pan into the fire." Eventually, I was sent on to America, to Cleveland, to live with my aunt and uncle. They had a printing shop and had changed their names from Aaronsohn to Arnold to sound more American, but more importantly, less Jewish. They strongly encouraged me to work very hard at losing my accent . . . and I did. Then I met Mildred. To me there was none more beautiful . . . more pleasing to the eye. One day Mildred told me she was going back to Mississippi to attend college, in her hometown. I couldn't imagine the pain of life without her. That's when I became Jack Arnold . . . the *goy* . . . the gentile. I followed Mildred to Mississippi to attend college, . . . but truthfully, to be near her. Mildred and her older brother picked me up from the train station and drove me the rest of the way to their hometown. As we approached the town limits, there was this big sign that read, "WELCOME TO THE TOWN OF HOLMAN IN THE GREAT MAGNOLIA STATE OF MISSISSIPPI." A little further down the road, a larger sign read, "NO NIGGERS, NO JEWS, NO DOGS." There it was in writing, Negroes and Jew, together, relegated to the same level as dogs. But I convinced myself that it didn't refer to me, because I was a *goy*, and I was in a car with the most beautiful woman in the world whom I loved very much . . . and that was all that mattered. One day Mildred's brother invited me to go for a ride with him and some of his friends. It wasn't until I was in the car that I heard for the very first time the expression, "nigger-knocking." I didn't know what it meant, but my sense of it told me that it wasn't a good thing for the intended Negro. What I failed to realize was that there was no "intended Negro," because any Negro would do. We came upon a colored man walking down the road carrying a bushel of corn. That's when I saw the bats come out from under the car seat. As we drove up next to the man, two of the fellows leaned out of the car window and hit him with the bats. The man lunged forward . . . face first, into a tree, then slid down to the ground. Corn was everywhere. As he lay on the ground groaning and squirming, they laughed. The man was hurt real bad and all we did was laugh and call him names. (*To* MATTIE.) You once asked me if I ever called a colored person a "nigger." (*Pause.*) The answer is . . . yes. That day I did. (*Pause.*) The guys were laughing so hard that they didn't notice that I was actually crying for the man. They thought I had laughed until I cried, but I was just crying because I had seen this done to other human beings in Russia. Mildred and I got married in 1917. We had no children. The one child we had was still-born and Mildred never got pregnant again. I had no contact with my family in Munich for fear that Mildred would find out about my heritage. My aunt in Cleveland had died and my uncle had returned to Germany heartbroken. So, I had no one but Mildred. After almost twenty years, my uncle began writing me from Germany to let me know about my family and the problems the Jews were faced with in Germany. Then one day a large envelope arrived which contained only a yarmulke, the same yarmulke the men in town destroyed, and a very simple note which read, "Come back to your people, Uncle Moishe Aaronsohn." He had changed his name back to Aaronsohn. That was the last time I heard from anyone in Germany. I began to take notice of what was happening there in the newspapers. I overheard comments in stores and on the streets about what a good job the Germans were doing to solve their "Jew Problem." (*Pause.*) Then it happened. (*Pause.*) *Kristallnacht.*

MATTIE: What's that?

JOYCE attempts to answer but MATTIE signals for her to keep quiet.

YAVENI: (*Angered.*) *Kristallnacht!* "Night of broken glass." (*Pause.*) November 9, 1938, Nazis wearing swastika armbands began breaking the windows out of synagogues and temples, burning Torahs and killing Jews. Over ninety Jews were murdered that one night.

All of this was happening while I . . . the *goy*, was having a dinner party at his home. At the party I was treated to the usual jokes. (*Mimicking*.) "You know how to get rid of all the niggers and kikes at the same time? Round up all the niggers and tie a dollar bill around their necks and put them on a boat back to Africa. Then the Jews will follow and stay there until they get every one of those dollar bills." I was the only one not laughing. I could still see that colored man squirming and groaning on the ground. (*Pause*.) And I could still hear my voice scream "nigger." Mildred wanted to know what was the matter. (*Reflective*.) I got up and climbed the stairs to our bedroom. I reached way in the back of my closet and pulled out the large envelope containing the yarmulke Uncle Moishe had sent me. I put it on my head and went down stairs and sat at the table. While every eye in the house was on me, I cradled a piece of bread in my hand, and from the deep recesses of my being, I said the *Motzi*, the blessing for bread (*recites in Hebrew*). *Baruch ata Adonai Elohainu melech ha'olam hamotzi lechem min ha'aretz*. Then I began to eat. After they recovered from being stunned, the guests began to excuse themselves, leaving shocked and confused. Mildred's brother came over to me and said, "If I had my shotgun, I'd blow your damned head off, you lying Jew son-of-a-bitch." Mildred slowly went upstairs and came down with two suitcases. She stopped in front of me and quietly said, "I'm glad that Jew baby you put in me died. Then she walked out. That was the last time I saw the woman I loved . . . the woman I became a *goy* for.

YAVENI breaks down. Silence.

MATTIE: What happened then?
YAVENI: Nothing. I sat around the house for another day . . . waiting for my own personal *Kristallnacht*. But it never came. So, I decided to push the issue. (*Angered*.) I took an ax and saw and drove out to the "NO NIGGERS, NO JEWS, NO DOGS" sign, and in broad daylight, chopped it down. People were standing around watching, but again, they did nothing. I went back to the house and waited another night, but still nothing happened. So, I packed some things in a bag and drove out of Mississippi. But as I was leaving Holman, in the "Great Magnolia State of Mississippi," I looked in the rear view mirror and saw the sign, "NO NIGGERS, NO JEWS, NO DOGS," standing again.

Silence.

MATTIE: You've never told that story before, have you, Yaveni?
YAVENI: (*Pause*.) No.

MATTIE: You've been traveling the country ever since looking for forgiveness. All this research and writing and such to make up for what
you did. Maybe it's time for you to forgive yourself, Yaveni. I'm sure
God has.

YAVENI: I wish I could be sure. (*Pause.*) Joyce, I hope my story is helpful
to you. Please don't let the actions of that one man destroy your love
for your family. It only takes one hateful act. Don't let it destroy who
you are.

*AUNT CORA enters stumbling. She is not humming. Her clothes are covered
with dried blood and in complete disarray. MATTIE and JOYCE run to AUNT
CORA.*

MATTIE: Aunt Cora! . . . What happened? . . . Did you fall? . . . Joyce, get
some water!

YAVENI steps in to help.

YAVENI: Let's sit her down.

MATTIE and YAVENI help AUNT CORA to the edge of the porch where she sits.

MATTIE: Where are you hurt?

*JOYCE returns with the dip-cup of water. MATTIE takes it and holds it up for
AUNT CORA to drink.*

Joyce, go inside and get me a towel.

*JOYCE exits into the house. YAVENI attempts to inspect AUNT CORA for the
source of the blood. AUNT CORA looks up at YAVENI, who jumps back.*

MATTIE (*Cont'd.*): It's alright, Yaveni. She's just making sure who you
are. She likes you.

YAVENI: Thank you. That's nice to know.

MATTIE: I can't see where she's hurt.

JOYCE re-enters with a towel.

Wet it, Joyce!

*JOYCE crosses to the pump and lays the towel on the run-off tin. She then
pours water on the towel from the drinking bucket. MATTIE is still examining AUNT CORA.*

YAVENI: All the blood is smeared on the outside of her clothes.

*AUNT CORA looks up at YAVENI again, and again YAVENI moves back, this
time knowingly.*

MATTIE: (*To YAVENI.*) What's the matter with you?

YAVENI: (*Pause.*) I don't think this is Aunt Cora's blood, Mattie.

MATTIE: Then where did it come from?

MATOKA: (*Offstage.*) Mama! . . . Joyce! . . .

MATOKA enters running and out of breath.

MATTIE: What's the matter? Are you alright?

MATOKA: Yeah!

MATTIE: Don't be scaring me like that! Didn't I tell you I didn't want you going off by your lonesome?

MATOKA: Mama . . . Mr. Joe Flood is dead!

MATTIE: (*Pause.*) What?

MATOKA: Somebody killed Mr. Joe Flood!

MATTIE: Where did you get that from?

MATOKA: I was in Mr. Sessoms' long store to buy some candy with the nickel Daddy sent me and everybody was talking about it. Say they found him this morning in his bed all cut to pieces.

JOYCE: Remember, Mama, I told you about all them white folks being all excited in town. That's what it was.

Silence, MATOKA crosses to JOYCE and whispers in her ear.

Mama . . . Toke's afraid to tell you the rest.

MATTIE: What is it, Joyce?

JOYCE: Well . . . Toke heard tell . . . Well . . . Mr. Joe Flood's . . . uh . . . manhood . . . had been cut off . . . and put in his mouth.

AUNT CORA begins to hum, but this time louder than usual, as she continues to stare at YAVENI. After a beat, YAVENI and MATTIE knowingly stare at one another.

MATTIE: Oh, God . . . Oh, Lord Jesus . . . No.

MATOKA: What's the matter, Mama?

MATTIE: Uh . . . Nothing, Baby . . . Uh, Matoka, I told you not to go off by yourself. Now you go on in the bedroom and stand in the corner.

MATOKA: Mama, I'm sorry!

JOYCE: Mama, she didn't . . .

MATTIE: You hush, Joyce! Go on and do what I told you, Matoka!

MATOKA: Yes, Ma'am.

All wait quietly until MATOKA exits into the house.

MATTIE: I don't want Matoka out here, Joyce! It's alright, Aunt Cora. It's alright. Joyce I want you to go inside and find something to put around Aunt Cora . . . something long. Hurry!

JOYCE quickly exits.

MATTIE (*Cont'd.*): (*To YAVENI.*) You knew about Joe Flood being dead when you came here.

YAVENI: I knew something had happened. I didn't know exactly what. That's why they were so angry and wanted me to leave.

JOYCE re-enters with an old coat.

JOYCE: Will this do?

MATTIE: Yeah, that'll do just fine. Now, I want you to take Aunt Cora home. And take her the back way through the woods. And stay with her. Don't let her go nowhere. Me and Toke will be along as soon as I get some food together for her . . . I know the poor thing ain't had nothing to eat. We got to change her out of them bloody clothes before she goes wandering off again.

YAVENI: Anything I can do?

MATTIE: (*Almost pleading.*) You can stay from getting all up in between me and my family.

YAVENI: (*Knowingly.*) I understand, Mattie.

MATTIE: Thank you.

YAVENI: No, thank you.

MATTIE: I got to go talk to the Lord.

JOYCE: Mama, you ain't going to be doing no praying for Joe Flood?

MATTIE: No, Baby. I'm going to ask God for forgiveness and guidance because when Toke brought the news about Mr. Joe Flood being dead, I was thinking, "I hope it's so. Oh, God, please let it be so." Then I'm going to get ready because I'm going up to Cleveland and get my man.

Lights go to black.

Scene 5

Time: *Two days later, at dusk.*

At Rise: *YAVENI is pacing in the yard. He crosses up to the edge of the porch.*

YAVENI: (*Calling.*) Come on, Mattie!

MATTIE and JOYCE enter from the house. JOYCE is carrying a suitcase which she sets at the edge of the porch. MATTIE places a small carrying bag next to the suitcase.

MATTIE: I'm moving as fast as I can, Yaveni.

YAVENI: They gave me two days, but they didn't say what time on the second day. So, I want to leave as soon as possible.

MATTIE: You're the one who wanted to wait until it got dark, now you're fussing.

YAVENI: I know. I just think it would be better if we left at night, then we wouldn't be so noticeable.

JOYCE: If these white folks were going to do something, they would have done it by now. Most of them are as glad to see Mr. Joe Flood gone as the colored people, otherwise there would be a whole peck of trouble.

MATTIE: White folks don't think a colored woman would have the nerve to do something like that anyway. All Sheriff Morrissey did was ask about colored men. Not one word about these colored woman down here.

YAVENI: What about this Jew?

MATTIE: You said Sheriff Morrissey already asked you questions. He wouldn't let you leave here if he thought you did it.

YAVENI rushes around picking up suitcases as he speaks.

YAVENI: I'm not just talking about Sheriff Morrissey. Leo Frank, a Jew in Atlanta, who was accused of murdering an Irish girl who worked in a pencil factory, was tried and found guilty... not proven guilty. While he was waiting for a new trial, a mob of white men, took him from the prison and hanged him. They lynch Jews too, Mattie! I'm going to take these bags to the car. Please hurry, Mattie!

YAVENI exits with the bags.

JOYCE: I told you he acts like he's somebody's daddy. Now he's acting like he's somebody's husband.

MATTIE: The man has a right to be scared, Joyce. He didn't ask for all of this. (*Calling.*) Them eggs boiling yet, Toke?

MATOKA: (*From off stage.*) Almost!

MATTIE: Alright, Joyce, you get to be the woman you say you are.

JOYCE: How am I suppose to be a woman when you're sending me over to stay with Sister Bell while you're gone, like I'm a child?

MATTIE: I don't care how much woman you think you are, I ain't going to leave you and Matoka to stay here by yourselves. Now you spend the nights at Sister Bell's and then you and Matoka ... both ... can come back and feed the chickens, collect the eggs, water the garden and make sure things are alright around here while I'm gone. Sister Bell is going to fix the food for Aunt Cora, and you and Toke bring the baskets over here when you come. I would tell Aunt Cora to go over there, but Sister Bell's scared of her. I want both of you back at Sister Bell's before it gets dark. You hear me?

JOYCE: Yes Ma'am.

MATTIE: And don't you mention nothing ... not a word, Joyce, to Sister Bell or anybody, about Aunt Cora and the blood. Nothing!

JOYCE: Don't you think I know that, Mama?

MATTIE: I'm just saying ... And don't say anything to Toke either. She talks too much.

JOYCE: Yes, Ma'am.

MATTIE: And if Sheriff Morrisey comes around again to ask any more questions ... I don't think he will, but just in case, you answer just like you did before.

JOYCE: Mama, I know what to do. Don't worry.

MATTIE: Earl will be coming around to check on things too.

JOYCE: Mama, please . . .

MATTIE: (*Loud.*) This is serious, Joyce . . .

MATTIE grabs JOYCE and hugs her.

   I'm sorry, Baby.

JOYCE: (*Pause.*) You think Daddy is going to come back home with you?

MATTIE: (*Jokingly.*) If he don't want to, I'll drag him (*Laugh*) . . . (*Serious*) I don't know, Sugar.

JOYCE: Why don't you call him first at Uncle James'?

MATTIE: I don't want to talk to him through no machine. I would write a letter before I did that. I want him to be able to see me . . . look in my eyes and see what's in my soul and know that I did nothing wrong and I ain't doing nothing wrong.

YAVENI enters.

YAVENI: Mattie, we've got to hurry.

MATTIE: Alright, Yaveni. Alright. (*Calling.*) You about finished packing the food, Toke?

MATOKA: (*Offstage.*) Almost! Mama, what's kosher?

MATTIE: (*To YAVENI.*) You trying to convert my babies?

JOYCE: Kosher pork chops is a contradiction.

MATTIE: Let me go in here and help this child along. She's slower than molasses running up a hill in the winter time.

MATTIE and JOYCE exit into the house. After a couple of beats, AUNT CORA enters. YAVENI and AUNT CORA stare at one another for a beat. AUNT CORA begins to approach YAVENI.

YAVENI: (*Apprehensive.*) Mattie? . . . Come on . . . (*Louder.*) Aunt Cora's here. (*To AUNT CORA.*) It's alright if I call you, Aunt Cora?

AUNT CORA is now standing very close to YAVENI. MATTIE, JOYCE and MATOKA enter from the house. MATOKA is carrying a suitcase.

MATTIE: It's alright, Yaveni. I told you before, she likes you. That's the closest she's been to a white man . . . any man since . . .

YAVENI: Maybe three nights ago?

MATTIE: She's saying thank you.

YAVENI: Yeah? In what language?

MATTIE: Okay, girls . . . Ladies, I'm going to get your Daddy. Give me kisses and hugs.

JOYCE and MATOKA cross to MATTIE, giving her hugs and kisses.

JOYCE: Bye, Mama.

MATOKA: Why can't we all go, Mama?

MATTIE: Because there ain't enough money for all of us to go. If Mr. Aaronsohn wasn't taking me with him, there wouldn't even be enough money for me to go.

MATOKA: (*Feigning sulking.*) Bye.

MATTIE: Bye, yourself. I'll be back in a few days. Now don't you go showing your hind-parts because I ain't here. I'll hear about it. You mind Sister Bell . . . and Joyce. And you help them watch out for Aunt Cora.

MATOKA: Mama, do we have to stay at Sister Bell's? She says grace so long the food gets cold.

MATTIE: Yes, you got to stay at Sister Bell's? And I don't want you going off by yourself. You hear me?

MATOKA: Yes, Ma'am.

MATTIE: (*Pause.*) You all go on now and help Mr. Aaronsohn pack the car.

YAVENI: (*Pleading.*) Okay, Mattie?

YAVENI, JOYCE and MATOKA exit. MATTIE crosses to AUNT CORA.

MATTIE: I'm going up to Cleveland to get my man, Aunt Cora. I've prayed and prayed for everything to be alright between Rawl and me. Now I just got to leave it in the hands of the Lord. I wish I could bring Charlie Scott back to you, Aunt Cora. I want to ask you to watch over my babies. I've never been away from them before. Please don't let no harm come to them. (*Pause.*) But you do that anyway, don't you, Aunt Cora. Just like you watched over me when I was little. (*Pause.*) I got to tell you this, Aunt Cora. I think . . . maybe I'm going to have to move to Cleveland like Rawl wants. If I'm going to ask him to accept another man's baby, it's only right that I do that . . . that I put it right in some way. Besides, these folks down here in Halifax wouldn't let him lift his head up. You know that. They'd be talking all behind his back about this baby not being his, and I don't want that for him. And depending on what the baby comes out looking like, it won't have any peace either. I feel my girls will be safer up there too. Maybe we won't have to worry too much about what happened to you and me happening to them. I guess what I'm saying is, Aunt Cora, I'm going to have to leave Halifax. I don't want to, but I feel I got to. You can always come with us. I don't know how folks will take you up there, but you're welcome to come with us. I wish you would. I can promise for all of us that you will be buried with Charlie Scott no matter what . . . no matter where you're at. Will you think about it Aunt Cora . . . Please?

JOYCE and MATOKA enter.

MATTIE (*Cont'd.*): What are you two doing back here?

JOYCE: Matoka forgot the eggs.

MATOKA: I ain't forgot nothing. You forgot them.

A car horn is heard blowing.

JOYCE: Mama, if you don't go on, Mr. Aaronsohn is going to have to go to the outhouse.

All eyes turn to AUNT CORA as she crosses to the steps. She stops and looks down at the steps for a beat, then up at the house. MATOKA slowly crosses to AUNT CORA and takes her hand.

MATOKA: Want me to help you, Aunt Cora?

Together, they slowly ascend the steps. They stop at the screen door. After a beat, MATOKA opens the door. AUNT CORA hesitates, then slowly exits into the house. MATOKA continues to hold the screen door open. After another few beats, AUNT CORA re-enters from the house carrying her framed marriage certificate. She descends the steps, then turns to look at the house again. She begins to hum MATOKA's newest gospel song, "I Will Sing, Alleluia."

MATOKA: Mama, you hear Aunt Cora? She knows my song!

MATTIE: Aunt Cora knows a whole lot of things, Baby.

AUNT CORA turns and looks at Mattie, still humming.

JOYCE: It ain't your song. You think just because you sing it, it's your song?

MATOKA: And you think just because Sammy Hunter's head is shaped like a banana, he one of the bunch.

JOYCE goes up the steps to enter the house.

Where you going?

JOYCE: I'm going to help your slow poke self get the eggs before Mr. Aaronsohn has a fit.

MATOKA: Ooooooo.

JOYCE: Oh, hush up!

JOYCE exits into the house.

MATOKA: (*Following JOYCE.*) Always thinking you somebody's Mama.

MATTIE and AUNT CORA are left alone, facing one another. AUNT CORA holds the frame tightly to her breast. After a beat we hear MATOKA singing along with AUNT CORA's humming.

MATOKA: (*Singing offstage.*) I will sing, Alleluia
   I will sing, O'Lord
   I will sing, Alleluia, O'Lord . . .

MATTIE: I'm real scared, Aunt Cora . . . Please pray for me.

MATOKA: (*Singing offstage.*) You are the source of my supply

Lord, I pray, you will lift me high
I will sing, Alleluia, O'Lord
I will sing . . .

MATTIE hugs AUNT CORA. We can hear MATOKA singing. We can hear AUNT CORA humming. We can hear the car horn in the distance. Lights go to black.

END OF PLAY

Sarah and The Sax

Lewis John Carlino

Lewis John Carlino

W hen the short plays of Lewis John Carlino, *Snowangel and Epiphany,* were first produced under the title *Cages* in the early sixties, starring Shelley Winters and Jack Warden, the playwright was compared to Tennessee Williams and Jean Genet. "A worthy launching of what could be a career of consequence in the theater for Mr. Carlino," wrote Howard Taubman in *The New York Times,* praising Carlino for using shock effect, not for the end of sensationalism, but to arrive at "illumination and compassion." "Off-Broadway has not produced a more wildly inventive mind this season," wrote Norman Nadel in *The New York World Telegram and Sun.*[1]

In the one-act *Sarah and The Sax,* the wildly inventive mind of Carlino is most evident in the character of "The Sax," an alienated Black bard who speaks in just barely intelligible yet eerily poetic jazz riffs. The miracle of illumination and compassion comes when Sarah Nodelman, an overly friendly Jewish mother, manages to make contact with the misanthropic Sax. No longer offering him hackneyed psychology to clear his mind and home-cooked dinners to fill his belly, she tells him the absolute truth of a devastating loss that has traumatically changed her life. No stranger to grief, The Sax consoles her with his healing music.

In addition to this small gem, Carlino wrote *Telemachus Clay* and *Doubletalk,* all produced in the '63-'64 season, earning him the Vernon Rice Award for his contribution to the off-Broadway theater, and the Drama Desk Award, naming him best playwright of the season. Carlino, who had earned his graduate degree in playwriting at the University of Southern California, returned to Hollywood in 1966 to adapt a David Ely science fiction novel for film, titled *Seconds.* He adapted his own novels, *The Mechanic* and *The Brotherhood,* into films, the latter becoming a popular pre-Godfather Mafia movie starring Kirk Douglas. He launched his directing career with his screenplay adaptation of *The Sailor Who Fell from Grace with the Sea,* starring Kris Kristopherson and Sarah Miles. His work in television includes his adaptation of the Gay Talese novel *Honor Thy Father* and a television series, *Doc Elliot.*

He was nominated for an Academy Award© for his film adaptation of Hannah Green's novel *I Never Promised You a Rose Garden,* but he is best known for adapting and directing Pat Conroy's novel *The Great Santini,* about a Marine fight pilot unable to express love to his son except through discipline.[2] With Robert Duvall in the lead role, and Carlino's ability to make disaffected and alienated characters strangely sympathetic, *The Great Santini* reaches for tragedy as the commander of this dysfunctional family battalion, unable to find glory in army combat, makes one last noble gesture in his capacity as a pilot.

Carlino is a master of what is now called the "character-driven" film but what used to be called just good dramatic writing. Whether he is writing plays or screenplays, he seems to appreciate that the most difficult contemporary struggle of our times is for one human being to connect on an honest level with another human being—be that in one's own family or with a stranger on a park bench.

Notes

1. Lewis John Carlino, *Cages,* New York: Random House, 1963, quoted on the jacket.
2. Lewis John Carlino, personal communication, April 10, 2003.

Sarah and The Sax

Cast of Characters

SARAH, *plump woman of about fifty-five.*

THE SAX, *Black man of about thirty.*

Scene: *A park bench, the morning of a summer day, the present. There is a tree behind the bench and shrubbery to the left of it. A waste can is downstage right.*

At Rise: *Sarah is seated, crocheting a doily. She is a plump, Jewish woman of about fifty-five. There is a shopping bag to one side of her feet. Birds chirp, unseen, high in the secret green of trees. Sarah looks up, savoring the sound. She smiles. An ambulance siren wails by. Her look changes to one of concern and worry. The sound of the siren fades. Sarah goes back to her crocheting. Her attention then turns toward the sound of someone mumbling, offstage right. The mumbling becomes louder until finally The Sax enters. He is a Negro, about thirty, with a few scraggly hairs of chin beard. He wears a fedora, the brim of which has been cut off. Fastened to the fedora is an assortment of Willkie-Roosevelt-Dewey type buttons. A less illustrious category includes numbers of the local unions. The Sax wears sunglasses and is barefoot. His tattered, old sweatshirt and denims are encrusted with grime of almost geologic age. The Sax carries an old saxophone on a string, fastened around his neck.*

THE SAX: *(Mumbling to himself as he crosses to the bench.)* Tom Mix, pick up sticks, get my licks, sweat my fix, watch the dicks—Tracy. Con the hicks. *(He sits. He is completely oblivious of Sarah who watches him with unmasked curiosity. The Sax is in his Elysium. He is away, gone, floating in a world of his own making.)* How's tricks, Dorothy Dix?

SARAH: *(Thinking he is talking to her.)* The name is Sarah Nodelman and if I should tell you the truth, I'm not so good. I got a leg, *(She taps her knee.)* it hurts so much with the humidity, it's talking to me since nine o'clock.

THE SAX: *(Looks at her with surprise, then turns away, blotting her from his consciousness. He speaks to himself.)* Crash, into the circle of golden silence comes this yapper makin' like the aspirin commercials on telaversion. Man, they're droppin' off the telephone wires! *(He takes out an immaculately clean rag and carefully unfolds it. He begins to polish his saxophone.)*

SARAH: *(Putting down the doily.)* I'm not looking at the television for two days, now. Something is wrong with the tube. Everybody's got only a half a head. Two days now I'm waiting for the man to come fix. You know what's the trouble? Nobody is caring. They all make too much money. You think the man who fixes is worrying because I got to sit lookin' at everybody with a half a head? Believe me, he don't. Oh, but last week it was beautiful. I was looking until sometimes one o'clock. I saw. . . .

THE SAX: Saw! Saw! Hack saw, band saw, back saw, bone saw, hand saw, jig saw, crosscut, rip saw, wood saw, buzz saw, see *saw*! Et tu, Brute? *(He punctuates with one short honk on his saxophone. A silence. Sarah smiles.)*

SARAH: That's a very nice poem. I heard that one before.

THE SAX: *(To her, without looking at her.)* Dig, baby, am I telepathizn' with you? I mean, you a yapper and you makin' with sounds that are hangin' up my tympanic membrane. Cool it. You know what I mean? 'Cause the jazz you comin' off with it buggin' me. I'm tellin' you, I am *bugged*!

SARAH: *(Looking up into the tree.)* Yeah, a couple fell on me. They're eating the leaves. It's a shame. Maybe you should move this way a little so you won't be disturbed. *(The Sax moves to the opposite side of the bench, away from her.)* Yeah, that's a very nice poem. Et tu, you brute. That's from Jakespeare. I know. Sometimes they're playing also him on the television. One time even with Marlon Branden.

THE SAX: *(To some unseen listener.)* Ooo, daddy, this ananda killer is too much. *(To Sarah.)* Wee oo, baby you a rectangle. Get yourelf a Guru. *(He finishes wiping his saxophone, then plays a short passage, pointing the saxophone up into the tree behind the bench. The music is clean, highly complex, virtuosic.) (Music No. 1)* Hey, you little chickadees, you dig that? My answer to Buxtehude! *(A short honk.)* Yeah, an that's for Honegger, Hindemith, Schoenberg, shoo-fly, and all them cats!

SARAH: It's nice you can play music. You should be thankful for such a talent.

THE SAX: *(Turned away from her, his hand cupped to his ear.)* Where is that sound comin' from?

SARAH: My son, Herbie, when he was in high school, he used to play the ocarina.

THE SAX: I don't care if the cat blew piccolo.

SARAH: A piccolo, that's right! Only smaller and wider. Oh, it was nice. He used to play for me "Home on the Range." An you wanna know something? He never learned music. All with the numbers. All day long, up and down the house. *(To the tune of "Home on the Range.")* Three three, four, five, six. Four, three, five, six, seven . . . A very gifted boy. All with the numbers, I'm telling you.

THE SAX: Drag . . . drag. Who gonna give you a gig with a ocarina?

SARAH: Can you play "Home on the Range" on that saxingphone?

THE SAX: Wee ooo, it's a break from Bellevue, and this one's the *leader*! Head for the BMT! *(One short honk on his saxophone.)*

SARAH: Maybe you don't like that kind of music. You look like one of those jazzy musicians. Are you one of those bee boppers?

THE SAX: Yeah, well, you know, baby. You gotta blow. You wail, swing, hurry on back, screech through a few C's till ya got pimples on your back.

SARAH: My Herbie had pimples on his face till he was eighteen. It made him so bashful, he wouldn't go to none of the dances. But they went away as soon as he went in with the Army. Just like medicine.

THE SAX: Drag . . . drag, mamala. Army's a drag. They don't got no pizza.

SARAH: What a happy letter I got from him when they went away. He was like a new person.

THE SAX: Yeah, man. How you gonna swing without pizza? What a wig. Suck all that mozzarella down your gut. Yeah, baby. Pizza! Greasy, easy, slidy, sloppy, sticky, pizza! Gimmi, gimmi, man. I dunk it in my Bosco! *(A high school cheer.)* Yea, pizza! *(A short honk on his saxophone. A silence.)* Viva Zapata, and pizza!

SARAH: You like pizza?

THE SAX: *(Shouting to his unseen listener.)* Never mind the BMT! Head for the Empire State! It's our only chance!

SARAH: With Herbie, knish. I make them very light. Some people, let me tell you, like rubber they come out. You know something, it's funny by the store I see now they got frozen knish. What a world.

THE SAX: *(Shouting.)* Pizza! Pizza! I like it! Greasy, cheesy, slimy, suck the mozzarella off, pizza! I want it! I love it! Gimmi, gimmi! It's cool. *(Music No. 2.)* *(He plays a passage projecting pizza. It is music that slides. It is woven with old Italian themes.)* Yeah!

SARAH: *(Impressed with the music.)* That's very nice. But you shouldn't eat it cool. It makes a heavy ball in your stomach and what happens? You should pardon the expression, constipation.

THE SAX: *(Picks up an imaginary telephone and dials. Then, secretly into the phone.)* Hello, FBI? This is the blob. I wanna report an enemy agent. *(Sarah looks around.)* That's right. She carryin' a bomb. A mouth bomb. It keeps goin' off and I can't stop it. The populus is dyin' in the streets. *(Sarah is confused by his antics.)* Ok. Check. Sub rosa. Entrez nous. Got it. Swing, daddy. *(He hangs up, then turns to Sarah and says with gravity.)* Ok, baby, your cop-out days are over. They're sendin' down their best man with an electric chair. *(Music No. 3.)* *(He sticks his tongue out at her, then plays a fanfare. Then, in a March of Time voice:)* And so Jack Sterling brings still another enemy to justice in his never-ending fight for God and country! The blob strikes again! *(A short honk.)*

SARAH: *(Shaking her head.)* I give him good advice and he calls the FBI on me!

THE SAX: Advice! Advice! Add the vise. The vice of adding the vise, twice vice. Unwise to squeeze the vise. A bad vice of lice and mice playing dice with people, like the cloud daddy with no face. *(Sharply, to Sarah.)* Who asked you? I mean, who really *asked* you, baby?

SARAH: *(Hurt.)* So what is it against the law to give a little suggestion how you should eat?

THE SAX: *(Mumbling into the opening of his saxophone.)* Hey, man, you dig what this chick is puttin' down? They the dangerous ones. You hep? On guard, dig? Or like the French say, "E pluribus unum."

SARAH: Listen, from the way you look, a few suggestions you could stand.

THE SAX: *(To his saxophone.)* Make out she's not here.

SARAH: For example what's the matter you can't afford a pair of shoes? You know you could get lock jaw walking like that besides it being unsanitary? And what is it a new style with the dirty clothes? Fifteen cents in the launderette and you could look like a human person.

THE SAX: *(Closing his eyes.)* She ain't here. She ain't here.

SARAH: The beard, that's all right. I know all the jazzy musicians have them.

THE SAX: *(Sarcastically.)* Thank you.

SARAH: You're welcome, I'm sure. Believe me, you would do yourself a favor if you looked a little better. You should see my Herbie, now. Socks and shirt changed every day. Spotless. Even on the week-end, when he don't work. His wife and children, the same thing. Clean like a pin. Neat. Nice. You know he got his last promotion because of that? What should your mother say if she saw you looking like this; like a bum? A nice talented boy.

THE SAX: *(Looks at her. Then into his saxophone.)* Hey, man, I gotta talk to you. *(He talks into the opening, secretively. We cannot hear his words, only a mumble. He waits a moment, then sticks the mouthpiece into his ear and listens. He nods affirmation.)* Uh huh. I'm hep. *(He smiles.)* Wail, man. *(His face goes serious. He speaks into the opening once more, this time with a British accent.)* Squadron leader Wembly to command. *(He gets up and moves away from Sarah, then turns, pointing the saxophone at her.)* Approaching target. Target in sight! *(The mouthpiece goes to his ear. He nods.)* Rodger and out. *(Music No. 4)* *(He approaches Sarah and annihilates her with short, machine gun blasts on the saxophone. Sarah stares at him, shaking her head at this strange behavior. The Sax finishes his attack and sits on the bench once more. He speaks into the opening of the saxophone.)* Mission accomplished. *(Music No. 5) (He lets Sarah have one last shot, then shakes hands with the mouthpiece.)* Good show, old man. Well done.

SARAH: What's that supposed to mean?

THE SAX: *(Shouting.)* Quiet! Silence! You can't speak! You're dead!

SARAH: So I'll be a talking ghost if you don't mind. You should be ashamed. Listen, there's enough people in the world being killed without you should make a joke. At your age such games are not so funny.

THE SAX: *(A preacher's voice.)* And I say to you, brethren, judgment is at hand. Retribution lies in your liverwurst. Dig? "For that which is born, death is certain, and for the dead birth is certain. Therefore grieve not over that which is unavoidable." Chapter two, verse twenty-seven, Upanishads.

SARAH: What's that?

THE SAX: Zen.

SARAH: Ten?

THE SAX: Zen! Zen!

SARAH: Oh, sen-sen. I never use it. A little parsley, it's enough.

THE SAX: *(Screaming.)* Bwana! Bwana! Boys, they go! All 'fraid! Me 'fraid! *(He points to Sarah, speaking excitedly to some unseen companion.)* White witch doctor. Bad ju ju. No! No, me go! Me 'fraid! She make bad devils. Even kill simba. Me go! Me *'fraid (His tone changes. His is The Sax once more.)* 'Course, man, if you was to lay a double saw buck on me, I'd stick around. Yeah, baby, an for an extra five, I'd get them cats back to carry all this jazz. Oh no! No Diner's Card! The cash. *(He pantomimes taking the money.)* Ok. Great, man. Oh, one more thing. From now on you carry your own rifle, dig? *(He jumps up and down and hollers some made-up African jibberish to an unseen group.)* I don't know what it means, either, but it sounds good. *(A short honk on the saxophone. He sits. Sarah, who has been watching all this, shakes her head.)*

SARAH: Listen, making fun of me, I don't mind. But if the police see you doing such crazy things, they'll take you away for sure, believe me. In five minutes you're in the FBI, you're in the Air Force, and then all of a sudden you're Jungle Jim. What kind of a thing is that for your age?

THE SAX: Age, smage. There is no age. Dig, baby. I am the embryo of the universe. I am the foetus shrinking into pre-natal reality. I am the amoeba, and before that, water. And before that, the idea. I am ananda. I am aksa! *(Angrily.)* So will you quit *buggin'* me? I don't want to talk to you, dig? Keep your helpful hints to yourself. You hip? Just take your straight jackets and blast off! Quite *buggin'* me! *(Sarah is hurt, but she does not move. The Sax continues to clean his saxophone, ignoring her. He moves his bare feet back and forth, on their heels, as he works.* SARAH *looks at his feet, then at him, then back at his feet. She reaches for her purse and extracts three one dollar bills. She straightens them out and holds them out to The Sax.)*

SARAH: It's not much, but at least a pair of sneakers you'll be able to buy. *(The Sax looks at the money, then at Sarah, then turns away. Sarah shrugs and puts the money into the opening of the saxophone.)* So don't be ashamed somebody should want to help you a little. *(The Sax turns and sees the bills. He extracts them, gets up, takes a few steps forward, and places them on the ground. He walks back to the bench in silence, sits, and turns away from her. He wipes the inside of his saxophone as if it had been contaminated. Sarah looks at The Sax, then at the money on the ground. There is a long silence. Finally, she gets up, goes to the money, picks it up, returns to the bench and sits. She puts the money back into her purse. A long moment passes. She looks at The Sax.)* I'm sorry. I didn't mean to offend you, believe me. *(The Sax remains turned away.)* I truly am. *(She shakes her head.)* Sometimes we do things and we don't think about the other person's feelings; only ours and what we wanna do. If you feel insulted, you got a right. What a world. You think you know how to do things, you don't. Everything is changing. Just now I don't know if I offered you the three dollars for your good or for mine. You got a right to be insulted. What a world. *(She shakes her head.)*

THE SAX: *(Quietly, still turned away from her.)* Can it, baby. Father Confessor is out to lunch. *(Sarah smiles, then goes back to her crocheting. Another siren wails by. She shakes her head, sadly.)*

SARAH: What a life. Every minute, somebody's got a tragedy. *(The chirping of the birds fades in as the sound of the siren diminishes. Sarah smiles again.)* This is such a nice park. Little? Yes. But so nice. Especially in the morning, like now. Eleven years I'm coming here on Thursday after my shopping before going home. I don't live here. Uptown, 92nd Street and West End. You know where that is? *(The Sax does not respond.)* They got a park up there, too. Along Riverside Drive. But what kind of a place is it? You walk across the street and you're in the Catskills. It's the country. Who wants to be in the Catskills and in New York at the same time? For me, one thing or the other. Here it's nice. You got all the buildings and not so much grass like a forest. You know you're still in the city. I do my shopping on Houston Street. Such a wonderful butcher he's there. Listen, if it seems like a long way to come for meat, I'll tell you something. I wouldn't spend a nickel on those crooks uptown. You know something? Listen, I'll tell you something save you a lot of grief. Every butcher between 29th Street and 102nd is high. *(The Sax turns and stares at her.)*

THE SAX: *(His eyes wide with shock.)* Hey, baby, you puttin' me on?

SARAH: I'm not putting you on or off. It's the truth.

THE SAX: *(A spirit of conspiracy.)* Are you sure?

SARAH: Certainly I'm sure. It's like a club. One week I went to a whole bunch of them. And you know what? High! Every one of them. But not just a little.

THE SAX: *(Incredulous.)* *All* of them?

SARAH: All!

THE SAX: Man, there must be a shipment come in on a cattle boat.

SARAH: I don't know how they can do it.

THE SAX: Well, they can afford it. They must be makin' a lot of bread.

SARAH: What's the matter you don't listen! I said *butchers*, not bakers.

THE SAX: Yeah! Yeah!

SARAH: Oh, don't worry. Wait a while, we'll have the same condition with the bakers, too.

THE SAX: I'm hep, baby. Yeah, and if it keeps comin' in like this, the candlestick makers, too. *(Gleefully.)* Everybody will be high!

SARAH: Candles I'm not worried. Once a year, on Chanukah, I can afford it.

THE SAX: Wail, mamala. All of 'em; Doctors, lawyers, Indian Chiefs, rich men, poor men, beggar men, thieves! Uptown! Downtown. All around the high town. *(He sings.)* We'll have Manhattan, the Bronx, and Staten Island, too. *(A short blast on his saxophone. Sarah smiles.)*

SARAH: That's right. Once it begins, it's like the measles. But not my butcher on Houston. Now there's a real human person. A profit he makes, but a robber he's not. Such a nice man. Eleven years, he never disappointed me. Special he orders a pullet for me every week. Friday I make chicken paprikash. You ever try it?

THE SAX: No.

SARAH: Oh, it's very good. Next to knish, Herbie's favorite. A little chopped onion with wine just right. Mushrooms and bouillon and a lot of sour cream. Then the paprika. You got to brown the onions just right, though. And you got to be careful to get a good pullet. That's the main thing. One with a fat breast. *(She fishes in her shopping bag.)* Look, let me show you. *(She takes out a chicken wrapped in brown wax paper, and unwraps it. The Sax seems hypnotized by her. She holds the chicken up to him, feeling the breast.)* Look. Look at that. That's a chicken for paprikash. Meat all over. *(She holds up one of the legs.)* Look at that. Did you ever see something like that? Go ahead, feel it. *(The Sax hesitates.)* Go on. It won't bite you. *(The Sax takes the chicken's head and opens and closes the beak, just to make sure. Convinced, but not completely, he touches the breast, tentatively. Then he wipes his fingers on his trousers, with a sickly smile.)* Did you ever feel something like that?

THE SAX: *(Shaking his head.)* Uh uh.

SARAH: Such a nice man. Eleven years and he never forgets to order for me special. *(The chicken lies in her lap.)* Oh, boy, you should see my Herbie eat. Every Friday night at least two hours at the table, with laughing and joking and yelling at me because I never had enough sour cream. Oh, that was a long time ago. Now he lives on Long Island in a fancy house with his wife and two children and I hardly ever see him any more. Aw, it's all right. It's good he should have a life of his own. So I'll eat alone Friday night. You got to let them go. That's right. He's a good boy. He deserves a life of his own. So proud of him. A regular big shot with an office on Madison Avenue and a secretary and a little Italian car what looks like a perculator. So it won't kill me to eat alone. It's funny, I got the habit so long, I can't stop. Friday night; paprikash. I guess it makes me feel he's there. Yes, you gotta let them go. *(She stares for a moment, absently, into space, then checks herself and wistfully wraps the chicken up once more and replaces it in her shopping bag. She looks up and sees The Sax watching her.)* Are you still living at home?

THE SAX: *(Shaking his head.)* Uh uh.

SARAH: Oh, then your mama feels the same thing, believe me. Do her a favor, will you? See her as much as you can. Don't be a stay-away son.

THE SAX: *(Laughing.)* Oh, oh, baby, you too much. You know that? You the cream of the crop, the pick of the pack, the best of the brood. Wail, mamala!

SARAH: So what did I say that was so funny?

THE SAX: Ize a motherless child.

SARAH: *(Shocked.)* You got no mother?

THE SAX: Daz right, honey chile.

SARAH: And no family?

THE SAX: 'Course I got family. Man, you should see all the kin I got in New York State Orphanage, and the monkey ward in Bellevue. And, man, have I got family in Lexington! They all *love* me. 'Course we don't have no chicken paprikashala on Friday night, but we make out. Man, have I got family! I told ya! I am the embryo of the universe. I am the amoeba and before that, water and before that, the idea. I am ananda. I am aksa. Family? I got 'em on 126th Street and Lex. I got 'em on Mulberry and Mott. I got 'em on 82nd, and Amsterdam, Canal, Avenue C and Third, Coney, 184th, the Bronx, 20th and 8th, 42nd. I got 'em on the 3rd Avenue El., on the A, the D, the E train, the Canarsie Line. I got 'em on Fulton St., Broom, Church, De Kalb Avenue. *(A short honk on his saxophone.)* I got 'em!

SARAH: But you really don't have any relatives of your own?

THE SAX: *(Defiantly.)* Sure! Sure I do!

SARAH: Who?

THE SAX: *(Thinks a moment, then grins.)* Well, I got a few Uncle Toms.

SARAH: Yeah? You see them often?

THE SAX: Not much. They mostly stay down south.

SARAH: Oh, that's a shame.

THE SAX: That's what I say. You see . . . *(He catches himself.)* Hey, baby, look, are you puttin' me on?

SARAH: I'm not putting nothing on you. It's nice you have some uncles. How come they all have the same name?

THE SAX: *(Agitated.)* Er . . . look, mamala, what say we drop it, huh? I was just jazzin' ya.

SARAH: Jazzing?

THE SAX: Yeah, you know. Like jokin' . . . kiddin'.

SARAH: Kidding?

THE SAX: Uh huh.

SARAH: There's no uncles?

THE SAX: Uh uh.

SARAH: You got nobody? Really? Not even a cousin someplace? Even one you don't like?

THE SAX: Uh, uh.

SARAH: *(Shaking her head.)* He's got nobody, and he kids. Some joke. Pardon me if I shouldn't laugh.

THE SAX: I don't need anybody, see? I swing. I mean like you got barnacles hangin' on ya, how ya gonna make it to Yucatan on a peyote pilgrimage, when you get the twitch. I mean, how you gonna make the happenin's, dig?

SARAH: That's what people are to you; barnacles?

THE SAX: Me and Nelson Eddy, baby, we the vagabond kings. I don't need anybody. I don't need diddly. *(He caresses his saxophone.)* I got my man here, and we wail. *(Speaks into the opening.)* Right? *(A honk in response to his question.)* See? He understands me. I mean, when I get my hot breath goin' through his guts, there's nothin', nothin' else. Up, down, and around and around the sound. And it's me and him and we's blowin' drifts off Everest. We's looking down at the stars. *(Music No. 6.)* We's out Gabin' Gabriel. We *swing*!

SARAH: You swing, ha?

THE SAX: Yeah, baby.

SARAH: So can it take your temperature when you're sick?

THE SAX: Oh, man . . .

SARAH: Well can it? Does it know how to make a mustard plaster or chicken soup or call on the telephone for some medicine in case, God forbid, you should need some medicine? So what's the matter with people?

THE SAX: *(Turning away from her.)* People, steeple people, lethal people, creeple people, feeple, deeple, neeple, gleeple, seeple, people. The phonies, the baloneys, the salamis and the knockwurst people. Drags . . . drags! Phoney . . . phoney . . . phoney! *(His British accent.)* Extremely distasteful.

SARAH: Who else you got?

THE SAX: Me. Me and my man! And sound, baby. You dig? You know what that is, mama? It's mama. It's cool and sweet and clean. It's mine and my man's. It's happy and sad and it don't need nobody but me and him to make it that way. Nobody! And it don't make pain for nobody. And the fuzz can't take it. And the Bible slappers can't take it. We make it, and nobody can take it. And my man's always there when it's cold and there's no horse, when it's night and rainy and there's no junk. He's always there and he's straight and true and he's enough. He's orgone, baby. You understand?

SARAH: No.

THE SAX: *(Disgusted.)* Yeah, well it figures.

SARAH: Listen, I know what you're talking about, but it doesn't mean I have to understand.

THE SAX: Man, she's putting me on again.

SARAH: You're a grown man and you don't even know a little about living.

THE SAX: *(Laughs.)* I don't know. *(Laughs.)* Oh, man, you too much. *(He speaks into the opening of the saxophone.)* Wembly to flight leader. Wembly to . . .

SARAH: No, you don't. And don't play another game on me. It won't help you.

THE SAX: I don't need help. You deaf or somethin'?

SARAH: I'm not deaf and you're wrong. First you say you got family all over in Coney Island and Canarsie and the Bronx, and then you say you don't need anybody. People are barnacles? Listen, everybody should be so lucky and have a few. You think they're not important, you're crazy. You think a saxingphone is enough, you're crazy. Nothing takes the place. Heartbreak it can give you, believe me. I know. When Herbie was young, popular he wasn't. He was naturally shy and the pimples didn't help him, neither. So he didn't go around much with the other kids. Movies and the library. That was my Herbie. He was an old man at fifteen. And I couldn't do anything. Heartbreak, believe me. I know. Then, he went in with the Army. Everything changed. He was with people all the time. You should read some of the letters I got from him. What a change. You don't even know a little about living if you think that thing *(Indicates the saxophone.)* can take the place of a human person.

THE SAX: Cut out, baby. Try the ASPCA.

SARAH: He makes wise cracks, yet. He thinks it's funny.

THE SAX: *(Picks up his imaginary phone and dials.)* Hello, Frankenstein laboratories? Lemme talk to Frank. Hello, Frankie, baby? Say, man, I want you to send over one of them human persons you been turnin' out there. I don't care. Any shape. Any color. You pick it out. Surprise me. Yeah. *(Then, looking directly at Sarah as he speaks into the phone.)* Oh, say, Frankie, baby, one thing. Would you check it out and make sure it doesn't have any greed? That's right. Also, deceit, and hate, and paranoia, and violence and ignorance. Would you? You don't *have* any without them things? Oh, that's a drag. Yeah, I understand. Ok. Say hello to all the boys in the lab. Keep in touch, hear? *(He hangs up, then grins at Sarah.)* He don't have none without. How about that?

SARAH: *(Smiling. She gets the point.)* That's not a person you're asking for. It's a saint. There's none around here, believe me. They live some other place. Are you digging?

THE SAX: *(Angrily.)* Well I don't!

SARAH: I don't either. Take what you got and make the best of it. You think you're a privileged character or something? There's no privileged characters. So how come everybody's got to be a saint for you to like them?

THE SAX: They don't have to be *nothin'!* I just want them to leave me alone! I want *you* to leave me alone. Is you diggin' *me?*

SARAH: All right. I'll leave you alone. Don't get nervous. Two people say a few words to each other, nobody should have to get nervous.

THE SAX: *Grand!*

SARAH: But a little quiet argument never hurt anybody. You want I should change benches?

THE SAX: *(His eyeballs rolled back in his forehead.)* It don't matter. Ize just yogaed you out of my fore-consciousness. My Karma body has gobbled your identity and the Bodhisattvas are dancin' ring around the rosey all fall down around your ghost. You have been osmotized into my Nirvana?

SARAH: Is that good?

THE SAX: It's better than pizza!

SARAH: *(Smiles.)* That's nice. *(The Sax puts his head on the back of the bench. We see only his neck. Sarah tries to go back to her crocheting, but somehow the sunshine, the sound of the birds, prevent her. She looks around.)* Such a nice park. Such nice birds. It reminds me sometimes on Sundays, before my husband, Jules, . . . God rest his sweet soul . . . before he went to rest, he would take me and Herbie down to the Battery, to the old Aquarium. Such a nice park there. And the river. And such fishes you could see there. So many colors. And sharks and octopuses. You know, with a hundred arms? Such a fish that one is. They say the Italians eat them. Well, you live and learn.

THE SAX: *(His head still out of sight.)* Aquarium, solarium, planetarium, vegetarium, librarium, sanitarium. All around the mulberry bush, pop goes the needle. *(Imitating various voices. The first, a New York bus driver.)* I tole ya, lady, this bus only goes to a hunnret an' twenty fifth street. *(His television voice.)* Are you bothered by falling hair, falling teeth, falling gamma particles? *(His female tourist voice.)* Are you really a beatnik? *(His ward attendant voice.)* It's all regulation. We just wrap you up in this wet sheet for two weeks, and you'll be well again. Now just relax. *(His analyst voice.)* Of course those giant insects you're seeing are part of the illusionary visio-psychic side effects caused by the reduction of dosages during your withdrawal.

SARAH: *(Still in her reminiscence.)* There was a little delicatessen near the park. I remember it had kosher frankfurters. So wonderful. So crispy, outside on the skin, they snap when you bite them.

THE SAX: *(His congressman's voice.)* It is my contention that the dangers of residual radio activity after the bomb dropping are greatly exaggerated.

SARAH: Between them, they could eat half a dozen.

THE SAX: *(His welfare voice.)* Now tell me, do you consider yourself in the below average income bracket?

SARAH: Not to mention a couple'a cream sodas apiece.

THE SAX: *(His dilettante voice.)* But really? Do you really believe jazz constitutes a major cultural trend?

SARAH: Once, even, we took the ferry to the Statue of Liberty.

THE SAX: *(His pushcart vendor's voice.)* Lady, a whatsa matta you? Please no toucha da figs. Nonchu see they soft? Pleasa no touch.

SARAH: Jules was very proud. A very patriotic man, he was. He cried. We went up inside the torch and he cried.

THE SAX: *(Himself.)* Like, man, we gonna blow. We gonna wail. And everybody's gonna get high and juiced out'a his gourd! And we gonna blast all the phonies! And we gonna shake *up* some cement! There's gonna be happenins, baby, *happenins!*

SARAH: That was a day I'll never forget. And Herbie, he wasn't ashamed to see his father cry. He was proud. Proud like him.

THE SAX: It's wide, man, wide. And nobody's closin' any doors. We's goin' out on the rooftops to watch the mushroom grow.

SARAH: And then, that night, cocoa and a strudel before bed and nobody could talk. All sitting in the kitchen and nobody talking.

THE SAX: *(Quietly.)* Yeah, man, happenins like you never dug before. We'll all get high and juiced to watch.

SARAH: Such a day that was.

THE SAX: And . . . and we'll all have cocoa and strudel . . .

SARAH: Such a day.

THE SAX: Yeah.

SARAH: *(A long moment of silence as they move back into their respective thoughts. Sarah shakes her head, wistfully.)* It seems like everything happens yesterday, last week, last year. Such a thief is time, you know? A regular robber.

THE SAX: *(Not looking at her, touched by the note of quiet sadness they have both created.)* Yeah, well it's like when you take a clock, dig? And you turn it. And then you got ... well ... you know ... like it's turning backwards like. And that means like ... oh, man, you know. Like that.

SARAH: *(Nodding.)* That's so true. *(There is another moment of silence. The Sax unfolds a small, three-sided suntan reflector of the type that is held under the chin. He holds it under his chin. Sarah stares, incredulously, then begins laughing, softly.)*

THE SAX: Wazza matter? Wazza matter with you?

SARAH: *(Trying to control her laughter.)* Pardon ... pardon my laughing, but it seems a little ridiculous you should be wanting a tan.

THE SAX: That's how much you know. It happens I've become rather pale with too much indoor living. If them office cats in Rockefeller Center can do this, so can I. You got any objections?

SARAH: No, no. Why should I object? *(Giggling.)* You do what you want. You wanna look crazy, go ahead. It's your life. *(Her giggle gets away from her. The Sax does not respond. He sits defiantly, his face in the reflector. The sound of Sarah's infectious laughter begins to reach him, though. He knows she's onto his ruse. His face begins to break into a smirk. He tries to control it. He has to turn away from her to hide it. Then, as Sarah's laughter continues, The Sax begins to giggle as well. His giggle builds until he is laughing along with her. Sarah is laughing so much, there are tears in her eyes. The Sax, unable to hold it any longer, surrenders himself to his laughter, joining with her.)*

THE SAX: *(Throwing the reflector into the air.)* Wee oo, baby, you too much. Wail, chick, *wail!* *(Their laughter joins again and finally subsides.)*

SARAH: *(Wiping her eyes and blowing her nose.)* Excuse, excuse me. Oh, my goodness such laughing and with a corset like this. Oh, you're a bad boy to do such a thing to me. *(The Sax grins.)*

THE SAX: *(Innocently.)* Who me? I didn't do nothin'. *(He takes a maple seedling from the bench, splits it, licks it, and pastes it on his nose. He turns to Sarah. Sarah, just about controlling her laughter, sees The Sax with his double nose and bursts out once more. The Sax joins her. He stamps his feet. He jumps up and down on the bench. He honks his saxophone. He makes it laugh.)* Wail baby! *(He flicks the seedling off. Their laughter subsides once more.)*

SARAH: *(Catching her breath.)* Oh, you're such a bad boy.

THE SAX: *(Shaking his finger at her.)* And you is such a bad girl. *(He chuckles, then all quiets to silence. Both become lost in their own thoughts. There is no sound except for the birds in the trees above them.)*

SARAH: *(Blows her nose again, then looks at The Sax who has resumed shining his saxophone. She seems to be sizing him up for something.)* Listen, tomorrow night, you got a big date or something?

THE SAX: Uh, uh.

SARAH: Well, it's only a suggestion and you shouldn't feel insulted and if you say no I won't be insulted either and believe me, it has nothing to do with no shoes.

THE SAX: What's on your mind, mamala?

SARAH: Well, as I said, you shouldn't be insulted. It's not charity. It's an invitation. An invitation between two people. *(The Sax looks at her, curiously.)* You wanna come to my house tomorrow night for chicken paprikash?

THE SAX: Send that one again?

SARAH: You wanna come eat chicken with me tomorrow night?

THE SAX: *(Suddenly feeling betrayed.)* Are you kiddin'?

SARAH: What's to kid? It's a simple question.

THE SAX: Look, when I need soup I'll go to welfare.

SARAH: What's the matter you didn't hear I said an invitation, not charity?

THE SAX: Yeah, how's come you're invitin' *me*?

SARAH: Well . . . I just . . . thought maybe . . . *(She is at a loss to explain.)*

THE SAX: *(Angrier.)* How come?

SARAH: I just thought you would like to have a home meal, that's all. So what is it a crime?

THE SAX: Listen, baby. I don't want your three bucks. And I don't want your chicken. Man, you comin' off with some bad jazz. I don't *want* it, hear?

SARAH: All right! So call the police and have me arrested for asking!

THE SAX: Don't come off with that jive to me.

SARAH: All *right*! Finish it, would you? *(A silence.)* I don't know what's the matter. Everytime I open my mouth I gotta make an apology?

THE SAX: You is goin' back in my Karma body. I should'a never left you out.

SARAH: So I'm back.

THE SAX: *(Concentrating, his eyes closed.)* Yeah, yeah. That's it. Swingin'. Now! Now, you know what you are?

SARAH: What?

THE SAX: Obliterated!

SARAH: Wonderful. I hope you'll be very happy. *(A silence.)* I never saw such a touchy person. You can't say a word without becoming an enemy. *(She leans toward him.)* Listen, I'm *no* enemy. Sometimes I make mistakes, like with the three dollars, but an enemy, I'm not.

THE SAX: *(Ignoring her.)* You is air, chick. Less than that; a vacuum totalis!

SARAH: I know what's the matter. You think I don't understand? What a foolish boy. You think I raised a boy your age without understanding even a little? You wanna be independent because it's a crazy world and it scares you. And it's a dragging.

THE SAX: *(Still turned away from her.)* Yeah, baby, you got all the answers.

SARAH: Not all. Maybe a few. Who's got all of them? Only those saints you're asking for. Take a little advice, don't be afraid.

THE SAX: Afraid? Me? Do I look afraid?

SARAH: You should pardon my honesty, yes.

THE SAX: Oh, man . . .

SARAH: Well you do. What's the matter with some friendliness? You act like a victim. So what are you a victim of, a little kindness? What a world when you have to apologize for trying to be kind. You know what? I think you got some kind of syndrome.

THE SAX: *(Sarcastically, a saccharine smile.)* You don't say?

SARAH: That's right. The health section of the paper it says people that act like you, they got syndromes. I don't know exactly what it means, but I think you got one.

THE SAX: Thanks for the info.

SARAH: You're welcome, I'm sure. I think that's what Herbie had before he went in with the Army. And you know what's the cure?

THE SAX: *(His Freud accent.)* Tell me, Doctor Noodleneck.

SARAH: Nodelman.

THE SAX: Oh, ja.

SARAH: People.

THE SAX: Oh, ja?

SARAH: That's right. Talking and laughing and working with them.

THE SAX: Vorking?

SARAH: What's the matter, that's not part of living? I'm sure you could get a good job playing your saxingphone somewhere.

THE SAX: A good job, like Herbie?

SARAH: That's right.

THE SAX: Maybe even get a pair of shoes?

SARAH: Why not? And a suit maybe.

THE SAX: And a house on Long Island?

SARAH: Sure. And then a wife and children and you got somebody.

THE SAX: And a little Italian car. *(Imitates her accent.)* Vat looks like a perculator? *(He is angry. There is a sharp, unfriendly edge to his sarcasm now.)*

SARAH: It's possible. You could have anything you wanted if you wasn't afraid to take a chance. You see, there it comes back to being afraid.

THE SAX: *(His anger mounting.)* What else could I have, mamala?

SARAH: Anything. Maybe a little bungalow on the beach.

THE SAX: Yeah?

SARAH: And a rowboat to go fishing.

THE SAX: Uh huh.

SARAH: And Book of the Month Club.

THE SAX: Oh, my, *that's* a good one.

SARAH: One of those credit cards. Wouldn't that be nice?

THE SAX: Lovely.

SARAH: Listen, what am I talking about? Those are all just *things*. Most of all is, you could have a family and that would be somebody.

THE SAX: *(Screams. He can no longer stand it.)* Aggggh! And how about an ocarina? Could I have one of them, too?

SARAH: *(Surprised at his anger.)* What's the matter?

THE SAX: I don't *want*! *That's* what's the matter. I hate them things you been rattlin' your trap about. I don't want clean shirts, or a house, or a car, or a bungalow on the beach. I don't want no family! I don't want to belong to nobody and nothin'. You dig? Is that plain? I hate them. And I hate the cats that got 'em. And I hates the cats that talk about 'em. 'Cause you know what it means! Nothin'! Minus zero! We gonna break, break it all up and it don't matter who's got what and who's got who. We gonna have a helluva time when it goes, mamala! An' that's why I hate it. I can't wait. I wanna start right now. I wanna start breakin' it up right now! Yeah! Burn it up, break it up, shake it up! Yeah! *(Music No. 7.)* *(He picks up his saxophone and begins to play. The music is unlike any we have heard before. It is wild, destructive, cacophonic, dissonant. It has the scream of revolt, destruction, chaos in it. It breaks all the rules of harmony and melody. Yet, in its wildness, there is a frightening beauty about it. It expresses the rhythm of the age. It is formless, yet with a form and validity of its own. It is relentless, clear in its meaning, uncompromising in its message. Sarah watches, spellbound and frightened by it. The Sax sweats. He circles Sarah, blasting her with the sounds of his protest. The notes are like hammer blows against her. The piece ends in a final, maddening shout chorus, a crescendo of dissonance. The Sax, sweating, breathless, continues where the saxophone left off.)* You get on the train and go out to Long Island and take *Herbie's* temperature! Herbie, with his office and his car. You take him home for paprikashala, buy *him* a pair of sneakers. Take *him* to the Statue of Liberty! You lonely? Go to your Herbie, but for Chris' sakes leave me alone! *(Music No. 8.)* *(He goes back to the saxophone. This time the music is even more awesome than before. It is the ultimate in his expression of anger and fear. He ends his statement by blowing the last note in Sarah's face. He sits back on the bench, turned away from her, breathing*

I'm Not Rappaport

Cast of Characters

NAT, white man about eighty.
MIDGE, black man about eighty.
DANFORTH, jogger, forties.
LAURIE, pretty girl about twenty-five.
THE COWBOY, tall man about thirty-five.
GILLEY, Irish kid about sixteen.
CLARA, Nat's daughter, early forties.

Act 1

Scene: *A battered bench on an isolated path at the edge of Central Park Lake, early October 1982, about three in the afternoon. To the left of this center bench is a smaller, even more battered one with several of its slats missing. Behind these benches is the Gothic arch of an old stone tunnel, framed above by an ornate Romanesque bridge which spans the width of the stage. Before the curtain rises we hear the sound of a carousel band-organ playing "The Queen City March."*

At Rise: *Two men, MIDGE and NAT, both about eighty years old, are seated at either end of the center bench; they sit several feet apart, an old briefcase between them. MIDGE is black and NAT is white. MIDGE wears very thick bifocals and an old soft hat; he is reading* The Sporting News. *NAT wears a beret and has a finely trimmed beard, a cane with an elegant ivory handle rests next to him against the bench. The two men do not look at each other. A JOGGER runs by on the bridge above, exits at right. An autumn leaf or two drifts down through the late afternoon light. Silence for a few moments; only the now distant sound of the Carousel music.*

NAT: O.K., where was I? *(No response. He smacks himself on the forehead.)* Where the hell was I? What were we talking about? I was just about to make a very important point here. *(to MIDGE)* What were we taking about?

MIDGE: *(No response. He continues to read his newspaper for a moment.)* We wasn't talking. *You* was talking. *(turns page)* I wasn't talking.

NAT: O.K., so what was I saying?

MIDGE: I wasn't listening either. You was doing the whole thing by yourself.

129

NAT: Why weren't you listening?

MIDGE: Because you're a Goddamn liar. I'm not listening to you any-more. Two days now I ain't been listening.

NAT: Stop pretending to read. You can't see anything.

MIDGE: Hey, how 'bout you go sit with them old dudes in fronta the Welfare Hotel, them old butter brains—*(pointing about the lake)* the babies at the Carousel, them kids in the boat—or some o' them junkie-folk yonder, whyn't you go mess with them? 'Cause I'm not talking to you anymore, Mister. Puttin' you on notice of that. You may's well be talking to that tree over there.

NAT: It's a lamp-post.

MIDGE: Sittin' here a week now, ain't heard a worda truth outa you. Shuckin' me every which way till the sun go down.

NAT: *(slapping the bench)* I demand an explanation of that statement!

MIDGE: O.K., wise-ass; for example, are you or are you not an escaped Cuban terrorist?

NAT: *(slapping the bench)* I am not!

MIDGE: O.K., and your name ain't Hernando—

NAT: Absolutely not!

MIDGE: So it's a lie—

NAT: It's a cover-story! *(pause)* My line of work, they give you a cover-story.

MIDGE: Are you sayin'—?

NAT: All I'm saying, and that's *all* I'm saying, is that in my particular field you gotta have a cover-story. More than that I can't divulge at the present time.

MIDGE: Honey-bun, you sayin' you're a spy?

NAT: I'm saying my name is Hernando and I'm an escaped Cuban terrorist.

MIDGE: But what kinda weirdo, bullshit cover-story is—?

NAT: You don't think I *said* that to them? That's what *I* said to them. I said to them, an eighty-one year old Lithuanian is a Cuban Hernando? That's right, they said, tough luck, sweetheart; yours is not to reason why. That's how they talk. Of *course* you don't believe it! You think *I* believe it? Such dopes. But it's a living. I beg you not to inquire further.

MIDGE: But why'd they pick an old—

NAT: Do *I* know? You tell *me*. A year ago I'm standing in line at the Medicaid, a fellah comes up to me—boom, I'm an Undercover.

MIDGE: *(impressed)* Lord . . .

NAT: Who knows, maybe they got something. They figure an old man, nobody'll pay attention. Could wander through the world like a ghost, pick up some tidbits.

MIDGE: *(nodding, thoughtfully)* Yeah . . .

NAT: So maybe they got something, even though, I grant you, they screwed up on the cover-story. All I know is, every month, a thousand bingos is added to my Social Security check.

MIDGE: Bingos?

NAT: Bingos. Dollars. Cash. It's a word we use in the business. Please don't inquire further. *(silence)* Please, I'm not at liberty. *(longer silence)* O.K.; they also gave me a code name. "Harry."

MIDGE: Harry?

NAT: Harry Schwartzman.

MIDGE: What's your real name?

NAT: Sam Schwartzman. *(outraged)* Can you believe it? Can you *believe* it? That's some imaginative *group* they got up there, right? That's some bunch of geniuses! *(then, shrugging)* What the hell, a thousand bananas on your Social Security every month you don't ask fancy questions.

MIDGE: Best not, best not. *(leaning closer)* So, do ya . . . do ya ever pick up any information for them?

NAT: Are you kidding? Sitting on a bench all day with a man who can't tell a tree from a lamp-post? Not a shred. *(glances about, leans closer)* Fact is, I think they got me in what they call "deep cover." See, they keep you in this "deep cover" for years; like five, maybe ten years they keep you there, till you're just like this regular person in the neighborhood . . . and then, boom, they pick you out for the big one. Considering my age and general health, they're not too bright. *(reaches into briefcase)* O.K., snack-time.

MIDGE: *(nodding)* Yeah. Deep cover. I hearda that . . .

NAT: *(taking foil-wrapped sandwich from briefcase)* Here. Tuna salad with lettuce and tomato on whole wheat toast. Take half.

MIDGE: *(accepting sandwich)* Thank ya, Sam; thank ya.

NAT: Yeah, comes three o'clock, there's nothing like a nice, fresh tuna salad sandwich.

MIDGE: *(chewing)* Uh-huh.

NAT: *(chewing)* Crisp.

(Silence for several moments as their old jaws work on the sandwiches.)

MIDGE: *(suddenly)* Bullshit! *(sits upright)* Bullshit! Lord, you done it to me *again*! You done it! *(throws the sandwich fiercely to the ground)* Promised myself I wouldn't let ya, and ya done it again! Deep cover! Harry Schwartzman! Bingos! You done it again!

NAT: *(smiling to himself as he continues eating)* That was nice . . . a nice long story, lasted a long time . . .

MIDGE: *(shouting, poking NAT sharply)* That's *it*! That's it, no more conversin'! Conversin' is *over* now, Mister! No more, ain't riffin' *me* no more!

NAT: Please control yourself—

MIDGE: *Move* it, boy; *away* with ya! This here's *my* spot!

NAT: Sir, I was—

MIDGE: This is *my* spot, I come here first!

NAT: I was merely—

MIDGE: Get offa my spot 'fore I lay you out!

NAT: *Your* spot? Who made it *your* spot? Show me the plaque. Where does it say that?

MIDGE: Says right here . . . *(remains seated, slowly circling his fists in the air like a boxer)* You read them hands? Study them hands, boy. Them hands wore Golden Gloves, summer of Nineteen and Twenty-Four. This here's *my* spot, *been* my spot six months now, my good and peaceful spot till you show up a week ago start playin' Three Card Monte with my head. Want you *gone*, Sonny! *(continues circling his fists)* Givin' ya three t'make dust; comin' out on the count o'three. *One*—*(rises, moving to his corner of the "ring")*

NAT: Wait, a brief discussion—

MIDGE: Sound of the bell I'm comin' out. *You* won't hear it but I *will*. *Two*—

NAT: How you gonna hit me if you can't *see* me?

MIDGE: Dropped Bill D'Amato in the sixth round with both eyes swollen shut. I just keep punchin' till I hear crunchin's. *Three!*

NAT: *(rising, with dignity)* Please, sir—this is an embarrassing demonstration—

MIDGE: *(moving in NAT's general direction, a bit of remembered footwork, jabbing)* O.K., comin' out, comin' out; comin' at ya, boy, comin' at ya—

NAT: *(moving behind bench for protection)* Sir, you . . . you have a depressing personality and a terrible attitude!

MIDGE: *Prepare* yourself, Mister, prepare yourself, get your—*(MIDGE suddenly lunges, bumping against the bench, stumbling—he struggles to keep his balance, grabbing desperately at the air—then falls flat on his back in the path. He lies there silently for several moments. Quietly, frightened:)* Oh, shit . . .

NAT: *(aware that MIDGE is in danger, whispering)* Mister . . . ? *(No response. He leans forward; urgently.)* Mister, Mister . . . ? *(Silence. He moves towards MIDGE as quickly as possible.)* Don't move, don't move . . .

MIDGE: *(trembling)* I know . . .

NAT: Could be you broke something . . .

MIDGE: *(softly)* I know. Oh, shit. Never fall down, *never* fall down . . .

NAT: *(kneeling next to him, trying to calm him)* It's nothing; I fall down every morning. I get up, I have a cup of coffee, I fall down. That's the system; two years old you stand up and then, boom, seventy years later you fall down again. *(gently, firmly)* O.K., first thing; can you lift your head? *(MIDGE hesitates, frightened, then raises his head a bit.)*

Good sign. Put your head back. *(as MIDGE carefully rests his head back)*
Good, good, good . . . *(carefully, knowledgeably, touching MIDGE, checking for damage)* O.K., feeling for breaks, checking the pelvic
area . . . feeling the hip now . . . If you like this we're engaged. *(MIDGE
moans softly, frightened.)* Don't worry; breaks is also nothing. Everybody breaks. Me, I got a hip like a tea-cup. Twice last year; I just got
rid of my walker. *(Continues checking MIDGE's left leg, MIDGE winces.)*
I was also dead once for a while. Six minutes. Also nothing; don't
worry. They're doing a By-Pass, everything stops; they had to jump-
start me like a Chevrolet. *(starts checking MIDGE's right leg; MIDGE
apprehensive)* Six minutes dead, the doctor said. You know what it's
like? Boring. First thing you float up and stick to the ceiling like a
kid's balloon, you look around. Down below on the bed there's a
body you wouldn't give a nickel for. It's you. Meanwhile you're up
on the ceiling, nobody sees you. Not bad for a while, nice; you meet
some other dead guys, everybody smiles, you hear a little music; but
mostly boring. *(He has finished checking MIDGE's legs.)* O.K.; can you
move your arms? *(MIDGE demonstrates a few, short, boxing jabs.)* Excellent. O.K., good news: each item functional. Now, from experience,
lie there and relax five minutes before you get up. *(MIDGE murmurs
obediently.)* O.K., best thing for relaxing is jokes—*(rising to center
bench near him)* Willy Howard, you hearda him? The best. O.K., years
ago he had this great routine, see—
MIDGE: That was another lie, wasn't it?
NAT: What?
MIDGE: 'Bout you bein' dead.
NAT: A *fact*, that was an absolute—
MIDGE: Man, you ain't even *friendly* with the truth! *Lies.* Goddamn *lies.*
(slaps the ground) It's your Goddamn lies put me on the canvas here!
Got me fightin', fallin' down—
NAT: *Not* lies—*(sits upright on bench)* Alterations! I make certain alter-
ations. Sometimes the truth don't fit; I take in here, I let out there,
till it fits. The *truth*? What's true is a triple By-Pass last year at Lenox
Hill, what's true is Grade Z cuts of meat from the A. and P., a Social
Security check that wouldn't pay the rent for a chipmunk; what's true
is going to the back door of the Plaza Hotel every morning for
yesterday's club-rolls, I tell them it's for the pigeons. I'm the pigeon.
Six minutes dead is *true*—*(takes bunch of pages from briefcase)* here,
Dr. Reissman's bills; here's the phone number, call him. A fact. And
that was my *last* fact. Since then, alterations. Since I died, a new
policy! This morning I tell the counterman at Nedick's I'm an American Indian. An Iroquois. He listens; next thing I know I'm remem-
bering the old days on the plains, the broken treaties, my Grandpa

fighting the Cavalry. Not important *he's* convinced; *I* am, and I love it. I was one person for eighty-one years, why not a hundred for the next five?!

MIDGE: *(after a moment, resting on his elbows, thoughtfully)* Them club-rolls; how early you figure a fellah oughta show up down there to—

NAT: *Rolls, rolls;* you missed the whole *point*—

MIDGE: *(rising carefully to small bench)* The *point*? I *got* the *point*; the point is you're crazy, the point is you ain't never seein' your marbles again!

NAT: Ah, how fortunate, an expert on mental health. My daughter Clara, she's another expert—*(holds up one of the pages)* here, wants to put me in a home for the ridiculous. "No sense of reality," she writes, "in need of supervision," she writes. This she writes to my therapist, Dr. Engels. Trouble is I don't have a therapist and I'm Dr. Engels. I give her the address of the Young Socialist's Club on Eighty-Sixth, I'm listed there as Dr. Friedrich Engels. *(leans closer to him)* Crazy, you say? Listen to me, listen to Dr. Engels. You're a wreck. Look at you; is this who you want to be? Is this what you had in mind for old, this guy here? A man who obviously passed away some time ago? Whatta you got left, five minutes, five months? Is this how you want to spend it? Sitting and staring, once in a while for a thrill falling down? *(urgently)* No, *wrong*, you gotta shake things *up*, fellah; you gotta make things *happen*—

MIDGE: *(truly outraged)* Hold it now! Hold that mouth right there! You tellin' *me* how to live? *You* tellin' *me*? You talkin' to an *em*-ployed person here, Mister! *(retrieving his newspaper from NAT's bench, returning with great dignity to his own)* Midge Carter; you talkin' to Midge Carter here, boy—Super-in-tendent in charge of Three Twenty-One Central Park West; *run* the place, *been* runnin' it forty-two years, July. They got a furnace been there long as *I* have—an ol' Erie City Special, fourteen *tonner*, known to *kill* a man don't show he's boss. Buildin' don't move without that bull and that bull don't move without *me*. Don't have to make up nobody to be when I *am* somebody! *(settling himself proudly on small bench)* Shake things up, huh? Don't shake *nothin'* up. How you figure I keep my job? Near fifteen years past retirement, how you figure I'm still Super there? I ain't mentioned a raise in fifteen years, and they ain't neither. Moved to the night-shift three years ago, outa the public eye. Daytime a buncha A-rab Supers has come and gone, not Midge. Dozen Spic Doormen dressed up like five-star generals, come and gone, not Midge. Mister, you lookin' at the wise old invisible man.

NAT: No, I'm looking at a dead man! *(points cane at him)* Fifteen years, no raise; it's a dead person, a ghost! You let them rob you!

MIDGE: They don't rob me; *nobody* robs me, got a system. You see that boy come every day, five o'clock? That's Gilley; give him three bucks, nobody robs me. Ten blocks from here to my place, walks me there, protects me.

NAT: From who?

MIDGE: Him, for one. Fifteen a week, he don't rob me—but nobody *else* neither, see; now *that's* Social Security—

NAT: *(laughing)* Oh, God—

MIDGE: Keep chucklin', sugar; ain't nobody dyin' of old age in *this* neighborhood.

NAT: Job! I see what your *job* is. Groveling! You're a licensed groveler!

MIDGE: *(rises from bench, shouting)* Super at Three Twenty-One, still got a *callin'*—only thing people got to call *you* is "hey, old man!"

NAT: What do *you* know? What does a *ghost* know? *(rising proudly)* People *see* me; they *see* me! I *make* them see me! *(his cane in the air)* The night they rushed me to Lenox Hill for the By-Pass, as they carried me out on the *stretcher*, six tenants called the Landlord to see if my apartment was available. Now, every *day*, every day at dawn I ring their bells, all six of them—the door opens, I holler "Good morning, Vulture; Four B is still unavailable!" I hum the first two bars of "The Internationale" and walk away.

MIDGE: *(moving towards him)* Old *fool*, crazy old fool; they can't see *you*. They can hear ya, but they sure can't *see* ya. Don't want to *look* at your old face; mine neither—I just help 'em out. Don't you get it, baby?— *both* of us ghosts only *you* ain't noticed. We old and not rich and done the sin of leavin' slow. No use to fight it, you go with it or you break, boy; 'specially bones like *we* got.

NAT: *(shouting)* Traitor! Traitor in the ranks! It's people like you give old a bad name—

DANFORTH'S VOICE: *(shouting)* Carter—

NAT: It's *your* type that—

DANFORTH'S VOICE: Carter—*(PETER DANFORTH enters on the Bridge, Up left, jogging; he is the same man who ran by earlier. DANFORTH is in his early forties and wears a newly purchased jogging outfit.)* Carter . . . ah, good, *there* you are, Carter . . .

MIDGE: *(glancing about, not sure who it is or where the voice is coming from)* Midge Carter, here I am.

DANFORTH: *(slowing his pace)* Here, up here . . . on the bridge . . . *(jogging in place, cordially)* Danforth . . . Peter Danforth, Twelve H . . .

MIDGE: *(squinting up)* Danforth, right . . .

DANFORTH: *(breathlessly)* Been looking for you—several days now—they told me you might be in this area—our meeting, remember?

MIDGE: Our meetin', yeah . . .

DANFORTH: How about right here, soon as I finish my run?

MIDGE: Right here, you got it.

DANFORTH: Be right with you . . . *(quickening his pace again)* Three more miles, be right with you, Carter; looking forward to it . . .

MIDGE: *(shouting up, as DANFORTH exits right)* Lookin' forward to the meetin', yessir; been on my schedule . . . *(suddenly whispering, terrified)* Oh shit, the Man, the Man, he found me—

NAT: What man?

MIDGE: *The* Man, *the* Man, been duckin' him, he *found* me.

NAT: *What* man? What is it, Carter?

MIDGE: *(sits on center bench, trembling, brushing off clothes, adjusting hat, trying to pull himself together)* Mr. Danforth, Twelve H, Head o' the Tenants' Committee. Place is goin' co-op, he says they got some reorganizin' to do, says he wants to see me private . . .

NAT: *(softly, nodding)* Ah, yes . . .

MIDGE: Last fella wanted to see me private was when they found my wife Daisy under the Seventy-Ninth Street Crosstown. *(buttoning sweater, trying for a bit of dignity)* See, problem is, it's been gettin' around the buildin' that I'm kinda nearsighted—

NAT: *(sitting next to him)* Nearsighted? Helen *Keller* was *near*sighted.

MIDGE: Got the place memorized, see. But last week I'm in the basement, lady from Two A sees me walk right smack into the elevator door. Mrs. Carsten, Two A, she's standin' in the laundry-room watchin' me. Figured I'd fake her out, so I do it *again*, like I was *meanin'* to do it, like it's this *plan* I got to walk into the elevator door—dumb, dumb, *knowed* it was a dumb move while I was *doin'* it. Just kept slammin' into that elevator door till she went away. I'm shoutin', "gonna have this thing fixed in a jiffy, Mrs. Carsten!" Next thing I know Danforth wants to see me private. *(hits himself on the head)* Panicked on the *ropes* is what I did; that's what blew it for me in the ring too . . .

(Silence for a moment.)

NAT: *(quietly)* Are the cataracts in both eyes?

MIDGE: *(after a moment; quietly)* Yeah.

NAT: How many times removed?

MIDGE: Left twice, the right once. But they come back.

NAT: That's what they do. They're dependable. And how bad is the glaucoma?

MIDGE: Drops an' pills keep it down. 'Cept night-times. Night-times—

NAT: Night-times it's like you're trying to close your lid over a basketball.

MIDGE: No lie. No *lie*. When'd it start with you? Start with me four, five years back; nothin' on the sides. No p'ripheral vision, doc says. Five years back—*(He waves.)* So long, p'ripheral vision. Then one mornin' there's this spot in the middle . . .

NAT: Ah, the spot, the spot . . .

MIDGE: Like the moon, this dead pearly spot . . .

NAT: The moon exactly . . .

MIDGE: And it gets to growin' . . .

NAT: Oh, yes . . .

MIDGE: Then, thank the Lord, it stops. Then what you got is the pearly moon spot, no p'ripherals, and this ring between 'em where folks come in and out.

NAT: Exactly; like birds. *(leans close to him)* You get color or black and white?

MIDGE: Mostly blue. Blue shadows like. Weird thing is, all my dreams is still in full color, see everything real sharp and clear like when I was young—then I wake up and it's real life looks like a dream.

NAT: Exactly! Same with me *exactly*! I hadn't thought about it till this minute! *(his arm around MIDGE)* Carter, we're connected. Why? Because we both got vision. Who needs sight when we got vision! Connected! Yes, even with your cowardly personality and your chicken-shit attitude. Yes, I'm sure now. Our meeting with Danforth will go well, I'm convinced.

MIDGE: *Our* meetin'? What—

NAT: Yes, I have decided to handle this Danforth matter for you. Don't worry, the Exploiters, the Land Owners, the Capitalist Fat Cats, I eat them for lunch.

MIDGE: *(alarmed)* Hold on now, boy, I never asked—

NAT: Don't thank me. I ask for nothing in return, only to see justice. Don't thank *me;* thank Karl Marx, thank Lenin, thank Gorky, thank Olgin—

MIDGE: Hey, don't need *none* o' you guys—

NAT: But mostly thank Ben Gold; in Nineteen-Nineteen I join the Communist Party and the human race and meet Ben Gold. *He's* the one, *that* was vision—*(as MIDGE starts to edge away from him on the bench).* Ben Gold who organized the Fur Workers and gave them a heart and a center and for a voice! What a voice, you thought it was yours. I'm watching skins at Supreme Furs, he makes me Assistant Shop Chairman; I'm at his side when we win. A ten percent wage increase and the first forty-hour week in the city! We win! *(bangs his cane on the ground)* Where is he? Where is Danforth? Bring him to me. Bring me the Fascist four-flusher!

MIDGE: *(softly, covering his face)* Oh my God . . .

NAT: *(turns to answer MIDGE)* O.K., O.K., the Soviet Union, throw it up to me; everybody does. They screwed up, I'm the first one to admit it. I promise you, Carter, they lost me, *finished*. I gave up on them . . . but I never gave up on the ideas. The triumph of the pro-letariat, a workers' democracy, the ideas are still fine and beautiful, the ideas go on, they are better than the people who had them. Ben Gold, they hit him with the Taft-Hartley and the fire goes out, but the voice goes on; the conflict goes on like the turning of the stars and we will crush Danforth before supper-time. *(He taps his cane with finality; sits back, crosses his legs, waiting for his adversary.* MIDGE *is silent for a moment. Then he turns to* NAT, *quietly, calmly.)*

MIDGE: You done now? You finished talkin'? *(*NAT *nods, not looking at him.)* O.K., listen to me; Danforth comes, don't want you speakin'. Not a word. Not one word. Don't even want you here. Got it? You open your face once I'm gonna give Gilley ten bucks to nail you permanent. Got that? Am I comin' through clear?

NAT: *(turns to* MIDGE, *smiling graciously)* Too late. I have no choice. I'm obligated. The conflict between me and Danforth is inevitable. I am obligated to get you off your knees and into the sunlight.

MIDGE: No you ain't. Lettin' you outta that obligation right now. *(leans towards* NAT, *urgently) Please*, it's O.K., I got it all worked out what to say to him. Just gotta hang in till I get my Christmas tips, see—they only got to keep me three more months till Christmas and I'll be—

NAT: Christmas! Compromises! How do you think we lost Poland? Danforth has no right! The man has no right to dismiss you before your time—

MIDGE: Man, I'm eighty-*one*—

NAT: And when we finish with *him*, at five o'clock we'll take care of the hoodlum, Gilley; the one that walks you home. Together we'll teach *that* punk a lesson!

MIDGE: *(looks up at the sky, desperately)* Why, Lord? Why are you doing this to me? Lord, I asked you for help and you sent me a weird Commie blind man . . .

NAT: What Lord? Who is the Lord you're talking to? Oh *boy*, I can see I've got a lot of work to do here . . .

MIDGE: *(turning sharply u.r.)* Shit, here he comes, the Man comin' now . . .

NAT: *(turning u.r.)* Ah, good, I'm ready . . .

MIDGE: *(grips* NAT'S *arm)* Please, baby; I'm askin' ya, please be quiet—

NAT: Calm down, Carter—

MIDGE: Never done you no harm—

NAT: It's not him anyway. *(learns to right, peering up at Bridge)* No, definitely not him. It's a pretty girl.

MIDGE: How do you know?

NAT: Because of the glow. When I could see, all pretty girls had a glow. Now what's left is the glow. That's how you can tell.

NAT: Also she was married. Yeah, went to work so her greenhorn husband could go to Law School, become an American Somebody. Comes June, Arnold Pearlman graduates, suddenly finds out he's an attorney with a Yiddish-speaking wife who finishes yachting-caps. Boom; he leaves her for a smooth-fingered Yankee Doodle he met at school. Four months later Hannah took the gas; a popular expression at that time for putting her head in an oven . . .

MIDGE: Poor Ella Mae cryin', me hearin' my new mouth say goodbye. She was near seventy then but when my mind moves to her she is fresh peach prime . . .

NAT: September, a month before she took the gas, I see her in the Grand Street Library, second floor reading-room. A special place, quiet, not even a clock; I'm at the main table with *Macbeth*, I look up, there's Hannah Pearlman. She doesn't see me, her head is buried in a grammar book for a ten-year old. She looks up, she knows me, she smiles. My heart goes directly into my ears, bang, bang, bang, I'm deaf. I don't speak. I can't speak. I'm there in the house of words, I can't speak. She puts her hands under the table, goes back to her book. After a while she leaves. I didn't *speak* . . .

MIDGE: *(bangs his fist on the bench)* Goddamn smile got me two more wives and nothin' but trouble! Damn these teeth and damn my wanderin' ways . . . *(Takes out huge handkerchief; the Carousel music fades.)*

NAT: I didn't *speak*, I didn't *speak* . . .

MIDGE: *(blowing his nose)* There's dope makes you laugh and dope makes you cry. I think this here's cryin' dope.

NAT: *(bangs his cane on the ground)* Stop, stop! Nostalgia, I hate it! The dread disease of old people! Kills more of us than heart failure!

MIDGE: *(drying his eyes)* When's the last time you made love to a woman?

NAT: Listen to him, more nostalgia! My poor shmeckle, talk about nostalgia! It comes up once a year, like Ground Hog Day. The last time I made love was July Tenth, Nineteen Seventy-One.

MIDGE: Was your wife still alive?

NAT: I certainly hope so.

MIDGE: No, I meant—

NAT: I know what you meant. With Ethel it wasn't always easy to tell. *(smacks his forehead)* *Shame* on me! A good woman, a fine woman, was it *her* fault I would always be in love with Hannah Pearlman?

MIDGE: See, last time for me I was bein' unfaithful. Damn my fickle soul, I cheated on them all. Daisy, I was seventy-six, still had somethin' on the side; somethin' new.

NAT: Carter, this is the most courageous thing I ever heard about you.

MIDGE: No courage to it, it's a curse. "Don't do it, Midge; don't *do* it," I kept sayin' while I did it. *Damn* my cheatin' soul.

NAT: No, no, you were *right*! You dared and did, I yearned and regretted. I *envy* you. You were always what I have only recently become.

MIDGE: A dirty old man.

NAT: A *romanticist*! A man of hope! Listen to me, I was dead once so I know things—it's not the sex, it's the romance. It's all in the head. Now, finally, I know this. The shmeckle is out of business, but still the romance remains, the adventure. That's all there *ever* was. The body came along for the ride. Do you understand me, Carter?

MIDGE: I'm thinkin' about it . . .

NAT: Because, frankly, right now I'm in love with this girl here.

MIDGE: *(after a moment)* Well, fact is, so am I. I got to admit. *(peers up at LAURIE for a few seconds)* Son-of-a-gun . . . First time I ever fell in love with a white woman.

NAT: The first? Why the first?

MIDGE: Worked out that way.

NAT: All the others were black? Only black women?

MIDGE: Listen, you ran with a wild, Commie crowd; where *I* come from you stuck with your own. Bein' a black man, I—

NAT: A what?

MIDGE: A black man. Y'see, in *my* day—

NAT: Wait. Stop. Excuse me . . . *(A beat; then NAT takes his bifocals out of his jacket-pocket, puts them on, leans very close to MIDGE. He studies him for a few moments; then, quietly:)* My God, you're right. You *are* a black man.

(Silence for a moment. Then NAT bursts into laughter, pointing to MIDGE.)

MIDGE: *(after a moment, catching on to the joke, a burst of laughter)* Sly devil, you sly ol' *devil* . . .

NAT: *(laughing happily, pointing at MIDGE)* Hey, had ya goin', had ya goin' there for a minute, didn't I . . . ?

MIDGE: *(claps his hands, delighted laughter building)* Had me goin', had me goin', yeah . . . Lord, Lord . . .

NAT: *(hitting his knees, roaring)* I love it, I love it, I love it—*(Fresh gales of stoned laughter, they rock on the bench.)*

MIDGE: Stop, stop, I'm gonna die . . .

NAT: I'm gonna drop dead right here . . . *(suddenly stops laughing)* Wait a minute, Carter; is it *this* funny?

MIDGE: *(stops laughing, considers it, bursts into laughter again)* Yes, it is. It is, definitely . . . *(They point at each other, laughing at each other's laughter, laughing now at the fact that they are laughing; they fall on each other, shaking with mirth, threatening to roll off the bench. MIDGE suddenly leans back on the bench and abruptly falls asleep, snoring loudly.)*

NAT: Carter, what are you doing? We're right in the middle . . . *(MIDGE keeps snoring.)* How do you like that? One joint, look at this.

(MIDGE *suddenly wakes up and, as if by request, bursts into song.*)

MIDGE: *(singing)* "I'm Alabamy bound,
  There'll be no heebie'-jeebies hangin' 'round . . .

(rises to this feet, singing, strutting, gradually working in a small soft-shoe)

  Just gave the meanest ticket-man on earth
  All I'm worth
  To put my tootsies in an upper berth.
  Just hear that choo choo sound,
  I know that soon we're gonna cover ground . . ."

(NAT *rises to his feet, inspired, joining in the soft-shoe, finishing the song with him*)

MIDGE and NAT: *(harmonizing)*
  "And then I'll holler so the world will know,
  here I go,
  I'm Alabamy Boooouuund!"

(LAURIE, *who has been listening to* MIDGE *and* NAT *sing their song from her ledge on the Bridge, far above them, smiles at them now, nods her approval, holds her hands up in a brief moment of applause, then returns to her sketching*).

MIDGE: I think the woman's crazy about us.

NAT: Please, I knew it when she first showed up.

MIDGE: You got any more of that dope?

NAT: Now we're gonna do a Willy Howard routine. You think you were laughing *before*, wait'll you hear—

MIDGE: How about I do a Joe Turner song first, and *then* we do Willy Howard?

NAT: You just sang.

MIDGE: *(sitting* NAT *on the bench)* That was half an hour ago.

NAT: Really?

MIDGE: *(looking up, announcing this for* LAURIE*)* "So long, Goodbye Blues," by Big Joe Turner, Boss of the Blues—*(singing soulfully; a slow steady rhythm, snapping his fingers, performing for* LAURIE*)* "Well now, so long, goodbye baby
  Yeah, well, soon now I'm gonna be gone
  And that's why I'm sayin', baby—"

NAT: *(a burst of applause, rising)* That was exquisite. Now here's Willy Howard—*(glancing up at* LAURIE, *performing this for her)* O.K., Carter, I'm Willy Howard, you're the Straight Man. Whatever I say to you, you say to me "I'm not Rappaport." You got that?

MIDGE: Yeah.

NAT: O.K., picture we just met.

MIDGE: O.K.

NAT: Hello, Rappaport!

MIDGE: I'm not Rappaport.

NAT: Hey, Rappaport, what happened to you? You used to be a tall, fat guy; now you're a short, skinny guy.

MIDGE: I'm not Rappaport.

NAT: You used to be a young fellah with a beard, now you're an old guy without a beard! What happened to you?

MIDGE: I'm not Rappaport.

NAT: What happened, Rappaport? You used to dress up nice, now you got old dirty clothes!

MIDGE: I'm not Rappaport.

NAT: And you changed your *name* too!

(A beat—then NAT *bursts into laughter; even if he wasn't stoned, this routine would leave him helpless.* MIDGE *regards him solemnly, thinking it over—then suddenly gets it, joining* NAT's *laughter, pounding* NAT's *shoulder.)*

MIDGE: *(through his laughter)* "And you changed your name *too* . . ." Lord, Lord . . . *(shouting up at* LAURIE *to make sure she got the punch-line)* "And you changed your *name* too!"

DANFORTH'S VOICE: *(shouting)* Right with you, Carter . . . *(*DANFORTH *enters on bridge, at left, jogging.)*

MIDGE: *(still laughing)* Oh, shit; he's here . . .

DANFORTH: Right with you . . .

NAT: *(laughing)* He's here! Good!

MIDGE: *(trying to control his laughter)* He's here, gotta shape up, boy . . . *(scurries to bench to get* NAT's *briefcase)*

NAT: *(delighted)* Don't worry, we'll take care of him—

MIDGE: No, no, there's no "we"; there's no "we" here—*(grips* NAT's *arm urgently, tries to stop himself from laughing)* You don't say *nothin'*, Mister, you don't open your *mouth* . . . *(a fresh burst of laughter)* You'll ruin me, boy; I'll be out on the street *tomorrow* . . .

*(*DANFORTH *stops on Bridge, winding down from his run, jogging in place, controlling his breaths, stretching himself against the Bridge lamp-post at right.)*

NAT: A piece of cake. The little I can see, the man is a wreck.

MIDGE: *(still chuckling softly)* Please, *please*, baby . . . are you my friend?

NAT: Of course.

MIDGE: Then go over there, friend. *(points to stone ledge, far left, at edge of lake)* Sit over there and don't open your mouth. Not a word.

NAT: *(after a moment)* You'll call me when you need me?

MIDGE: *(hands* NAT *his briefcase)* Soon's I need you. Please, move it.

NAT: *(He has stopped chuckling.)* O.K., O.K. . . . *(Reluctantly, he starts down left.)* Remember, I'm ready.

MIDGE: I know that.

(DANFORTH, having completed his winding-down ritual on the Bridge, starts down towards MIDGE at the bench, entering through the Tunnel Archway, mopping himself with a towel. NAT settles himself with some dignity on the far left ledge, some distance from them, crossing his legs, his briefcase and his cane at his side. LAURIE has stretched out on the Bridge ledge above, her eyes closed, a "Walk-man" plugged into her ears, her shoulder-bag under her head.)

DANFORTH: Carter, hi.

MIDGE: Hi.

DANFORTH: Don't think we've really been formally introduced. I'm Pete Danforth. *(They shake hands.)*

MIDGE: Hi, Pete. They call me "Midge."

DANFORTH: Hi, Midge. Glad we decided to meet here. Chance to stay outside; y'know, after my run. Truth is, I hate running. Being immortal takes too much time.

(He chuckles.)

MIDGE: *(sitting on bench)* "Midge" for midget. My third wife, Ella Mae, give me the name; near two and three-quarter inches taller'n me so she called me "Midge." Name stuck with me fifty years.

DANFORTH: Tell ya one thing, it's good to be reminded of what a great park this is. Goddamn oasis in the middle of the jungle.

MIDGE: Next two wives was normal-sized women, so it didn't make much sense. Name stuck with me anyway.

DANFORTH: Luckily my teaching schedule gives me two free afternoons this semester. Chance to really use this park. It's been years. I teach Communication Arts, over at the Manhattan Institute on Sixtieth. No air in the place. Dreary. Been thinking about holding one of my classes out here in the—

MIDGE: What kinda arts?

DANFORTH: Communication. Communication of all kinds. Personal, interpersonal, and public; pretty much the whole range of—

MIDGE: You teach talkin'.

DANFORTH: *(He smiles.)* More or less; yes.

MIDGE: So you must know we 'bout at the end of the chit-chat section now; right?

DANFORTH: Right, right . . . *(sits next to MIDGE on bench, carefully folding his towel)* Funny thing, by the way, I really didn't know—that is, I wasn't aware until just a few days ago—that you actually worked in the building; that you were employed there.

MIDGE: Keep to myself. Do my job.

DANFORTH: Of course. I just wanted you to know that the problem we've got here had not come to my attention sooner simply because you, personally, had not come to my attention. Frankly, I've been living there three years and I've never run into you.

MIDGE: I'm mostly down in the boiler-room; don't get a lot of drop-ins.

DANFORTH: Of course. *(silence for a moment)*

MIDGE: Keep movin', boy, you on a roll now.

DANFORTH: Yes, well, as you know, Three Twenty-One will be going Co-op in November. We'll be closing on that in November. We've got Brachman and Rader as our Managing Agent; I think they're doing an excellent job. As President of the Tenants' Committee I'm pretty much dependent, the whole Committee is really, on their advice; we've basically got to place our faith in the recommendations of our Managing Agency.

MIDGE: And they're recommendin' you dump me.

DANFORTH: Midge, we've got some real problems about your remaining with the building staff.

MIDGE: Ain't that the same as dumpin' me?

DANFORTH: *(after a moment)* Midge, it's not for four weeks, it's not till November, but, yes, we will have to let you go. There are various benefits, Union Pension Plan, six weeks Severance Pay; that's a check for six weeks salary the day you leave, that's . . . Midge, I'm sorry . . . *(sadly; shaking his head)* God, I hate this; I really hate this, Midge . . .

MIDGE: How 'bout *I* hate it first, then you get your turn.

DANFORTH: *(quietly)* Midge, think about it, isn't this the best thing for *every*body? The pressure on you, tenants' complaints, trying to keep up. *(his hand on MIDGE's arm)* Time, Midge—we're not dealing with an evil Tenants' Committee or a heartless Managing Agent—the only villain here is time. We're *all* fighting it. Jesus, man, have you seen me *run*? It's a joke. I can't do what *I* did a few years ago either.

MIDGE: Hey, don't sweat it, son. See, Brachman and Rader, all due respect, is full of shit. Fact is, you need me. *(leans back calmly)* Got an ol' Erie City boiler down there; heart of the buildin'. Things about that weird machine no livin' man knows, 'cept Midge Carter. Christmas. Take me till Christmas to train a new man how to handle the devil. *(pats DANFORTH's knee)* You got it, have the new man set up for ya by Christmas.

DANFORTH: Midge, we're replacing the Erie City. We're installing a fully automatic Rockmill Five Hundred; it requires no maintenance. *(Silence for a moment; MIDGE does not respond.)* You see, the Rockmill's just one of many steps in an extensive modernization plan; new electrical system, plumbing arteries, lobby renovation—

MIDGE: Well, *now* you're *really* gonna need me. Pipes, wires, you got forty years of temporary stuff in there, no blueprints gonna tell you where. Got it all in my head; know what's behind every wall, every stretch of tar. *(clamps his hand on DANFORTH's shoulder)* O.K., here's the deal. My place in the basement, *I* stay on there free like I been, *you* get all my consultin' free. No *salary*, beauty deal for ya—

DANFORTH: Midge, to begin with, your unit in the basement is being placed on the Co-op market as a garden apartment—

MIDGE: Don't you get it, baby? Blueprints, blueprints, I'm a walkin' treasure-map—

DANFORTH: Please understand, we've had a highly qualified team of building engineers doing a survey for months now—

MIDGE: *(suddenly)* Hey, forget it.

DANFORTH: You see, they—

MIDGE: I said forget it. Ain't interested in the job no more. Don't *want* the job. Withdrawin' my offer. *(turns away; opens his newspaper)*

DANFORTH: *(moving closer)* Midge, listen to me . . .

MIDGE: Shit, all these years I been livin' in a garden apartment. Wished I knew sooner, woulda had a lot more parties.

DANFORTH: I have some news that I think will please you . . . *(his hand on MIDGE's arm)* Two of the older tenants on the Committee, Mrs. Carpenter, Mr. Lehman, have solved your relocation problem. Midge, there's an apartment for you at the Amsterdam. No waiting-list for *you*, Mr. Lehman seems to know the right people. Caters especially to low-income senior adults and it's right here in the neighborhood you've grown used to—

MIDGE: Amsterdam's ninety percent foolish people. Ever been in the lobby there? Ever seen them sittin' there? Only way you can tell the live ones from the dead ones is how old their newspapers are.

DANFORTH: As I understood it from Mr. Lehman—

MIDGE: Amsterdam's the end of the line, boy.

DANFORTH: I'm sorry, I thought—

MIDGE: You ask Mr. Lehman *he* wants to go sit in that lobby; you ask Mrs. Carpenter *she* ready to leave the world. You tell 'em both "no thanks" from Midge, he's lookin' for a garden apartment.

DANFORTH: See, the problem is—

MIDGE: Problem is you givin' me bad guy news, tryin' to look like a good guy doin' it.

DANFORTH: *(after a moment)* You're right, Midge. You're right. You're dead right. *(bows his head, genuinely upset)* I've handled this whole thing badly, *stupidly*, I'm sorry, this whole thing . . . this is terrible . . .

MIDGE: *(patting DANFORTH's hand)* Don't worry, Pete, you're gonna get through it.

DANFORTH: *(rises, pacing in front of bench)* Damn it, I tell you what I can do—what I will do—I'm getting you *ten* weeks Severance, Midge. *Forget* six, a check for ten weeks salary the day you go, I'm gonna hand it to you *personally*. And if the Committee doesn't agree, the hell with them; I'll shove it through, that's all. Least I can do. Ten weeks Severance; how does that sound to ya?

MIDGE: Well, better than six, I guess . . . *(nods thoughtfully)* Sounds better, but I—

DANFORTH: *(shaking MIDGE's hand with both of his)* That's a promise, Midge. Shove it down their throats if I have to. *(moving briskly towards the stone steps at right to exit)* I'm sure we'll have no problem with—

NAT: Unacceptable. *(calmly, rising from ledge at far left)* We find that unacceptable. *(DANFORTH stops, NAT moves slowly towards him.)* Mr. Danforth . . . Mr. Danforth, I'll speak frankly, you're in a lot of trouble. *(brisk handshake)* Ben Reissman; Reissman, Rothman, Rifkin and Grady. Forgive me for not announcing myself sooner but I couldn't resist listening to you bury yourself. Our firm represents Mr. Carter, but, more to the point, we act as legal advisors to the HURTSFOE unit of Mr. Carter's union. HURTSFOE; I refer to the Human Rights Strike Force, a newly-formed automatic-action unit who, I'm sorry to say, you're going to be hearing a lot from in the next few weeks. *(sits next to MIDGE on bench, DANFORTH standing before them)* Personally, I find their methods too extreme; but I report and advise, that's all I can do. The ball is rolling here, Mr. Danforth.

MIDGE: Go away.

NAT: Mr. Carter keeps saying to us "go away"; we were arguing this very point as you ran by earlier. But, of course, as he knows, we are an automatic function of his union for the protection of all members. I have no choice.

MIDGE: *(grips NAT's arm)* Man wants to give me ten weeks severance—

NAT: A joke. The fellow is obviously a jokester.

DANFORTH: Mr. Reissman—

NAT: Speak to me.

DANFORTH: I'm not sure that I understand the—

NAT: Of course not. How could you? *(crosses his legs, continuing calmly)* I will educate you. The situation is simple, I will make it simpler. We don't accept ten weeks severance, we don't accept twenty. What we accept is that Mr. Carter be retained in the capacity of advisor during your reconstruction period, which I assume will take a year, maybe two. At this point, we'll talk further.

MIDGE: *(to DANFORTH)* I don't know him; I don't *know* this man.

NAT: Quite so; Mr. Carter is more familiar with Rifkin and Grady, the gentler gentlemen in our firm. It was thought best to send "The Cobra" in on this one. An affectionate term for me at the office.

DANFORTH: *(sharply)* Look, Riessman—

NAT: Speak to me.

DANFORTH: *(steps towards him, firmly)* I don't know what your game is, fellah, and I don't know your organization; but I *do* know Local Thirty-Two of the Service Employees Union—

NAT: And do *they* know you're planning to fire Mr. Carter?

DANFORTH: Not yet, but we—

NAT: And do *you* know that there's no mandatory retirement age in Mr. Carter's union? And do *you* know, further, that this means Carter has the right to call an arbitration hearing where he can defend his competence? And that you will have to get a minimum of four tenants to *testify* against him? Oh, that will be interesting. *Find* them. I want to *see* this, Danforth. Four tenants who want to be responsible—*publicly* responsible—for putting this old man out of his home and profession of forty-two years. *(his hands on MIDGE's shoulder)* A man who was named "Super of the Year" by the *New York Post* in Nineteen Sixty-Eight; a man who fought in World War Two, a man who served with the now legendary Black Battalion of Bastogne at the Battle of the Bulge. The clippings will be xeroxed and circulated, the worms you find to testify will be informed. *(rises from bench, pointing cane at DANFORTH)* And—*and* are you aware that for as long as you insist on pursuing this matter, for as long as this hearing lasts—and I promise you we will make it a *long* one—you can *make* no contract with Local Thirty-Two? That without a union contract you can *have* no Co-op sale, no building corporation? Time, my friend, time will be *your* villain now. My firm will go *beyond* this hearing if justice fails us there. I'm talking *months*, cookie; I'm talking litigation, appeals, the full weight and guile of Rothman, Rifkin, Grady and The Cobra. *(He lowers his cane to his side, moves slowly towards DANFORTH; quietly.)* Sir, I urge you to consider, win or lose, the massive and draining legal fees you will incur in pursuing this matter. I urge you to compare this time, cost, and embarrassment to the tiny sum it will take to keep Mr. Carter on salary. I urge you for *all* our sakes. *(DANFORTH stands there in silence for a few moments, clearly confused. MIDGE has remained on the bench, listening with fascination.)*

DANFORTH: Reissman . . .

NAT: Speak to me.

DANFORTH: I'm, frankly, a little thrown by this. I . . . I mean, you're asking me to just accept—

NAT: Accept or don't accept; I'm obligated to report this to HURTSFOE immediately.

DANFORTH: I knew about the right to arbitration—Midge, I just didn't think you'd really want—

NAT: He wants. Meanwhile HURTSFOE goes after you tomorrow anyway—

DANFORTH: Me?

NAT: They'll make an example of you, you're perfect for them—

DANFORTH: But what have I—?

NAT: Idiot, you've hit every Human Rights nerve there is. I'm talking old, I'm talking black, I'm talking racial imbalance—

DANFORTH: Racial *imbalance*? The man was walking into *walls*. For God's sake, the man's an easy *eighty*.

NAT: There's nothing, I promise you, easy about eighty. Damn it, why am I even bothering to *warn* you. *(picks up his briefcase)* Tomorrow you'll see it all. Time to let HURTSFOE out of its cage—*(turns sharply, starts walking towards stone steps at right, to exit)*

DANFORTH: *(moves towards him, angrily)* Now look, Reissman, I find it hard to believe that I would be held personally responsible for—

NAT: *(starting briskly up steps)* You'll believe it tomorrow when they picket in front of your school. What was the name of that place, the Manhattan Institute? They'll believe it too. And then the demonstrations in front of your apartment building—*(stops half-way up steps, pointing cane down at DANFORTH)* The name Danforth will start to *mean* something—you'll become an *adjective*, my friend, a symbol, a new word for the persecution of the old and disabled, the black and the blind!

DANFORTH: Wait a minute—

NAT: Do it, Danforth, *fire* him, it's your one shot at immortality! *Do it . . . (MIDGE holds his hand up in alarm.)* Yes, Carter, forgive me, I *want* it to happen . . . I want to see HURTSFOE in action again . . . *(tenderly, looking away)* Those crazy wildcats, it's hard not to love them. Those mad, inspired men. I want to hear the old words, alive again and pure . . . "Strike for a humane existence" . . . "Strike for universal justice"—*(His cane in the air, shouting.) Strike, strike—*

DANFORTH: *(shouting)* Hold it! Wait a minute! This . . . this whole Goddamn mess has gotten out of hand . . . *(continuing firmly)* Reissman, believe me, this was never my own, personal thing; I represent a Committee, the joint wishes of a—

NAT: I'm sorry, the spotlight falls on you because it must. Because you are so extraordinarily ordinary, because there are so many of you now. *(starts down steps towards him)* You collect old furniture, old cars, old pictures, everything old but old people. Bad souvenirs, they talk too much. Even quiet, they tell you too much, they look like the future and you don't want to know. Who *are* these people, these oldies, this strange race, they're not my type, put them with their own *kind*, a building, a town, *put* them someplace. *(leans towards him)* You idiots, don't you know? One day you *too* will join this weird tribe. Yes, Mr. Chairman, you *will* get old; I hate to break the news. And if you're frightened now, you'll be terrified then. The problem's *not* that life is short but that it's very long; so you better have a policy. Here we are. Look at us. We're the coming attractions. And as long as you're afraid of *it* you'll be afraid of *us*, you will want to hide us or make us hide from you. You're dangerous. *(grips his arm urgently)* You foolish bastards, don't you understand? The old people, they're the *survivors*, they *know* something, they haven't just stayed late to ruin your party. The very old, they are miracles like the just born; close to the end is precious like close to the beginning. What you'd like is for Carter to be nice and cute and quiet and go away. But he won't. I won't let him. Tell him he's slow or stupid—O.K.—but you tell him that he is unnecessary, and that is a sin, that is a sin against life, that is abortion at the other end. *(Silence; NAT studies him for a moment.)* HURTSFOE waits. The arena is booked, the lions are hungry . . .

DANFORTH: *(quietly, earnestly)* Ben, I'm glad you shared these thoughts with me. I'd never really—

NAT: I'm through communicating with you, I'm communicating with Carter now. *(sits next to MIDGE on bench)* Carter, what shall we do with him? I leave it to you.

MIDGE: I think . . . I think we should give him a break.

DANFORTH: Ben, I'm sure that I can persuade the members of the Committee to re-evaluate Midge's—

NAT: Carter, what are you *saying*? What happens to the Cause? Are you saying you just want to keep your job and forget about the Cause?

MIDGE: Frankly, yes; that's what I'm sayin'. Forget the Cause, keep the job.

DANFORTH: *(perches opposite them on small bench)* I think it's essential that we avoid any extreme—

NAT: Carter, are you asking The Cobra *not* to strike?

MIDGE: Don't want that Cobra to strike, no.

DANFORTH: Next Committee meeting's in two weeks, I'll explain the—

NAT: Mr. Danforth, my client has instructed me to save your ass. Quickly, the bomb is tickingly . . . *(DANFORTH leans towards him intently.)* Two weeks is too late. Tonight. Jog home to your phone, call the members of your committee. Don't persuade, don't explain; announce. Tell them there's a job for Carter. Guide. Counselor. How about Superintendent Emeritus? Has a nice sound to it. Meanwhile, speak to *no* one; the union, your managing agent, *no* one. HURTSFOE gets wind of this, we're *all* in trouble. *(hands him business-card from briefcase)* When you're finished with the Committee, call here. Before ten tomorrow if you want to stop HURTSFOE. Speak only to the lady on the card, Mrs. Clara Gelber; tell her to reach a man called "Pop"—he's one of HURTSFOE's top people—tell her to inform him that the Carter matter has been resolved, this "Pop" fellow will take it from there.

DANFORTH: *(reading from card)* "Park East Real Estate Agency..."

NAT: HURTSFOE's advisory group; smart people, good hearts, they negotiate with Management. *(hands him another card)* Here; if there's trouble tonight, call me—*(They both rise.)* That's my club on Eighty-Sixth, ask for Dr. Engels, he'll contact me. *(pats DANFORTH's cheek)* Goodbye and good luck.

(DANFORTH moves briskly towards the stone steps; stops, turns to them.)

DANFORTH: *(quietly)* Midge ... Ben ... I want you to know that this has been a very important conversation for me, for *many* reasons ... a lot of primary thought ...

NAT: I think it's been an important conversation for all of us. Goodbye.

DANFORTH: An important exchange of ideas, a ... a sudden awareness of certain generational values that I—

NAT: I warn you, one more word and there'll be a citizen's arrest for crimes against the language.

DANFORTH: *(He smiles; shakes his head.)* Fact is, certain areas, I *do* have trouble talking ...

NAT: Also leaving. Go now, the phone! *(DANFORTH races briskly up the steps.)* Quickly. Let me see those sneakers flash!

(DANFORTH exits. NAT turns triumphantly towards MIDGE, his cane held high in the air like a sword of victory.)

MIDGE: *(He slumps forward on the bench.)* Never; we ain't never gettin' away with this ...

NAT: *(to himself, smiling)* Truth is, I always *did* want to be a lawyer ... but years ago there were so many choices ...

MIDGE: Black Batallion of *Bastogne*? ... We ain't never gettin' away with this ... Gonna catch *on* to us, only a matter of *time* now; find out you ain't no lawyer, find out there ain't no HURTSFOE—

NAT: You're better off than you were twenty minutes ago, right? You still have your job, don't you? A week, a month, by then I'll have a *better* idea, another plan. What's wrong with you? Why aren't you awed by this triumph? Why aren't you embracing me?

MIDGE: *(rising, angrily)* Was playin' that boy just *right* 'fore you opened your mouth. Had him goin' for extra severance—catches on now, I lose it *all*. What I do to deserve you? What I *do*, Reissman—

NAT: I'm not Reissman. Reissman is the name of my pick-pocket surgeon.

MIDGE: O.K., *Schwartzman*, you're Sam Schwartzman—

NAT: Not him either.

MIDGE: Then who the hell *are* you, Mister? Shit, if you ain't Hernando and you ain't Schwartzman, and you ain't Rappaport, then—

NAT: *(softly, looking away)* Just now I was Ben Gold. I was Ben for a while . . . You use who you need for the occasion. An occasion arises and one chooses a suitable person to—

(During these last few lines GILLEY has stepped forward from the shadows on the Bridge above, at left, near the ledge where LAURIE has drifted off to sleep—a sudden sense of his presence has awakened her; frightened, she has swept up her bag and art supplies, raced across the Bridge and exited at right. GILLEY is an Irish kid, about sixteen; an impassive, experienced, and almost unreadable face. The faded color of his jeans and jean-jacket and his careful, economical movements make him inconspicuous and, in a sense, part of the park; for all we know he may have been standing there in the shadows for an hour. He has a constant awareness of everything around him, the precision of a pro and the instincts of a street creature. We hear the distant sound of the Carousel band-organ playing "Queen City March," the last melody of the fading day. During the last fifteen minutes or so the pretty colors of the autumn afternoon have gradually given way to the dark shadows of early evening, the faint chatter of crickets and the lonely lights of the two lampposts on the Bridge, reminding us of the isolated and near-empty section of the park we are in. GILLEY stands quite still now on the Bridge, a silhouette beneath the lamplight, looking off at what must be the other benches along the lakeside, studying the few remaining people on them and their possessions, considering the possibilities. NAT has suddenly interrupted his last speech to look up at the Bridge.)

NAT: *(cont'd.)* Who's that? There's no glow, the girl is gone. *(MIDGE knows the all too familiar figure on the Bridge and that it is the appointed "collection" time; he turns away, trying to look unconcerned.)*

MIDGE: Nobody. That's nobody.

NAT: That's *him*, right? The punk.

MIDGE: Ain't *the* punk; just some punk.

NAT: That's our punk, isn't it?

MIDGE: Not *our* punk, not *our* punk; just *my* punk.

NAT: Excuse me, I have something to discuss with him—*(He starts towards the Bridge—MIDGE grabs both of NAT's arms and quite forcefully pulls him back—GILLEY starts slowly, casually down the back stairs to the Tunnel, towards MIDGE and NAT.)*

MIDGE: *(a strong grip on NAT, whispering urgently)* Now you listen here to me, No-Name. This kid, you run your mouth on *him* he finish you, then finish me sure. Sit down—*(shoves NAT down on bench, sits next to him)* These kids is crazy; beat up old folks for *exercise*, boy. Sass this kid he stomp us *good—(pointing to the offstage benches)* and these folks here, while he's doin' it they gonna keep *score*, gonna watch like it's happenin' on the T.V. *(GILLEY appears in the darkened Tunnel, some distance behind them. He remains quite still, deep in the Tunnel, waiting.)* Toll on this bridge is three dollars and that bridge gonna take me home. *(rises, taking his newspaper)* Call it a *day*, boy. See you sometime. *(MIDGE starts into the Tunnel towards the waiting GILLEY. Silence for a moment.)*

GILLEY: *(flatly)* Who's that?

MIDGE: Friend of mine.

GILLEY: Where's he live?

MIDGE: Dunno. Hangs out here; he—

GILLEY: *(moves down behind NAT's bench, leans towards him; quietly)* Where you live?

NAT: First I'll tell you where I work. I work at the Nineteenth Precinct— *(turns, holds out his hand)* Danforth; Captain Pete Danforth, Special Projects, I—

GILLEY: *(takes his hand; not shaking it, just holding it, tightly)* Where you live?

NAT: Not far, but I'm—

GILLEY: Walk you home, y'know.

NAT: That won't be necessary, it's—

GILLEY: Cost you three.

NAT: Listen, son, I don't need—

GILLEY: Cost you four. Just went up to four, y'know. *(to both)* Saw this lady this morning. Dog-walker, y'know. Five, six dogs at a time. Give me an idea. Walk you both home. Terrific idea, huh? *(to NAT)* Terrific idea, right? *(Silence for a moment. GILLEY tightens his grip on NAT's hand. NAT nods in agreement. GILLEY lets go of his hand; pats NAT gently on the head.)* Right. Walk you both; four each.

MIDGE: But our deal was—

GILLEY: Four.

MIDGE: O.K.

GILLEY: Right. *(starts into Tunnel)* O.K., boys; everybody walkin'; convoy movin' out. *(MIDGE walks dutifully behind him. NAT remains seated. A moment; GILLEY moves slowly back to NAT's bench, stands behind him.)* Hey, that's everybody, right? *(Silence for a moment. NAT hesitates; then picks up his briefcase and slowly, obediently rises, his head bowed. GILLEY nods his approval, turns, starts walking into the Tunnel; MIDGE following.)* O.K.; nice and slow; movin' out, headin' home, boys ... *(NAT remains standing at the bench. This immobility is not a conscious decision on NAT's part; he just finds himself, quite simply, unable to move.)*

MIDGE: *(stops, turns to* NAT; *a frightened whisper)* Come on, *please,* move . . . *move,* Mister . . . (GILLEY *stops in the Tunnel, aware that he is not being followed. He turns to* NAT; *starts quickly to the bench, shoving* MIDGE *out of his way as he moves towards* NAT. NAT *holds his hand up urgently,* GILLEY *stops just in front of him.)*

NAT: *(quickly)* Take it easy, I don't fight with Irish kids. I know the same thing now that I knew sixty-five years ago: don't fight with an Irish kid. *(points to him)* How did I know Irish? I hear; I know all the sounds. But better, I know the feelings. This is because sixty-five years ago I was you. Irish kids, Italian, Russian, we *all* stole. Then, like now, the city lives by Darwin; this means everybody's on somebody's menu— *(passionately, moving closer to him)* Trouble is, you got the wrong supper here. Me and Midge, you're noshing on your own. We live in the streets and the parks, we're dead if we stay home; just like you, Gilley. You're angry. You should be. So am I. But the trouble's at the Top, like always—the Big Boys, the Fat Cats, the String-Pullers, the *Top*—we're down here with you, kid. You, me, Midge, we have the same enemy, we have to stick together or we're finished. It's the only chance we got.

(Silence for a moment.)

GILLEY: Five. Went up to five. Y'mouth just cost ya a dollar. (NAT *does not respond.* GILLEY *holds out his hand, calmly.)* O.K., that's five; in advance, y'know.

NAT: *(softly)* No. I can't do that. I won't do that. Gilley, please understand; we mustn't do this. *(touching his jacket-pocket)* I have twenty-two dollars; I would share it with you, gladly share. But not like *this,* not us . . .

GILLEY: Great. Gimme the twenty-two. *(shaking his head)* Y'mouth, I'm tellin' ya. It's costin', y'know.

NAT: *(quietly, sadly)* I'm . . . I'm very disappointed . . .

MIDGE: *(whispering)* Give it to him.

NAT: I can't do that, kid; not *all;* that's unreasonable. (GILLEY *reaches for* NAT's *pocket,* NAT *shoves his hand sharply away.)* I have limited funds. I can't do that.

GILLEY: *(calmly takes hunting knife in fancy leather sheath from his belt; unsheathes the knife, holding it down at his side)* Ask you once more.

MIDGE: *(from Tunnel, trembling)* Please, *give* it to him, Mister . . . please . . .

NAT: Gilley, this is a mistake. Don't do this. (GILLEY *glances quickly about the area to see if he is being observed, then holds up his knife; a demonstration.)* No, no knives, not for us. Not between us. We're together—

(NAT *makes a sharp underhand move with his cane, hitting* GILLEY's *wrist;* GILLEY *drops the knife, holding his wrist in pain and surprise;* GILLEY *looks at* MIDGE *as though to ask for aid with a misbehaving child, then kneels down quickly to pick up his knife.* NAT, *more in fear and frustration than courage, raises his cane in the air with both hands, shouting—an angry, gutteral, old battle cry—and strikes a sharp blow on the back of the kneeling* GILLEY. GILLEY *cries out in pain, rising, outraged, leaving his knife, slapping the cane out of* NAT's *hand—*NAT *steps back, helpless now;* GILLEY *grabs him by both shoulders and swings him around fiercely, flinging him backwards with a powerful throw,* NAT *falling back against the stone ledge at the edge of the lake, hitting the ledge sharply and then rolling off onto the path where he lies quite still, face down, away from us.* GILLEY *glances about, grabs up the wallet from* NAT's *coat, then moves quickly towards the Tunnel, shouting over his shoulder at* MIDGE.)

GILLEY: Tell you friend the rules! You better tell your friend the rules, man—(GILLEY *stops—looks back for a moment at the very still form of* NAT—*then races quickly off into the darkened Tunnel, forgetting his knife, disappearing into the shadows of the park.* MIDGE *moves down towards* NAT *as quickly as possible, kneels next to him.*)

MIDGE: (*quietly*) Hey . . . hey, Mister . . . ? (*Silence, he touches* NAT, *gently.*) Come on now, wake up . . . wake up . . . (NAT *remains quite still. Silence again.* MIDGE *rises to his feet, shouting out at the lake.*) Help! . . . Over here!. (*No response.* MIDGE *looks out across the lake, a near-blind old man staring into the darkness around him.*) Look what we got here! (*Silence again; only the sound of the early evening crickets. The park grows darker,* MIDGE's *face barely visible now in the lamplight, as*)

THE CURTAIN FALLS

Act 2

Scene: *The same; three in the afternoon, the next day. Before the curtain rises we hear the Carousel band-organ playing "We All Scream For Ice Cream."*

At Rise: MIDGE *is alone on the path; he is seated at the far left end of the center bench, his newspaper unopened on his lap, looking straight ahead, unable to relax in the pleasant sunlight that shines on the bench. The Carousel music continues distantly now; the melody drifts in and out with the gentle autumn breeze.* LAURIE *is in her usual position on the Bridge, far above* MIDGE, *sketching dreamily.* MIDGE *continues looking solemnly out at the lake. A full minute passes.*

We begin to hear NAT's *voice, off left, singing "Puttin' on the Ritz," approaching slowly.* MIDGE *looks left, then immediately opens his newspaper, holds it up to his bifocals, "reading."* NAT *enters u.l. moving slowly down the path with an aluminum walker. The walker is a three-sided four-legged device with three metal braces holding the sides together; his briefcase and cane are hooked over two of the braces; there is a three-inch gauze bandage above his right eye. Although NAT moves very slowly he manages to incorporate the walker into his natural elegance, using the walker rhythmically rather than haltingly, a steady ambulatory tempo to the bouncy beat of his song, as he approaches the bench. MIDGE is turned away with his newspaper, ignoring him completely. NAT continues towards the bench, singing the song with great gusto, pausing momentarily to tap his walker on the path for rhythmic emphasis, then continuing to the bench, parking the walker next to it as he finishes the last line of the song. NAT sits carefully on the bench. MIDGE continues to read his newspaper, making no acknowledgement of NAT's arrival.*

NAT: *(rubbing his hands together)* Well, that punk, we got him on the run now. *(He leans back comfortably.)* Yessir, got him where we want him now. *(jabbing the air)* Boom, on the arm I got him; boom on the back. Boom, boom, boom—

MIDGE: *(not looking up from paper)* Tell me somethin', Rocky; you plannin' to sit here on this bench? 'Cause if you *are* I got to move to another spot.

NAT: I'm sure you were about to inquire about my health. *(taps his hip)* Only a slight sprain, no breaks, no dislocations. I am an expert at falling down. I have a gift for it. The emergency room at Roosevelt was twenty dollars. Not a bad price for keeping the bandit at bay.

MIDGE: *(folding newspaper)* *You* movin' or am *I* movin'? Answer me.

NAT: I guarantee he will not return today. He wants the easy money, he doesn't want trouble—

MIDGE: *(puts on his hat)* O.K., leavin' now . . .

NAT: And if by some odd chance he *does* return, I feel we were close to an understanding. We must realize, you and I, that this boy is caught like us in the same dog eat dog trap—

MIDGE: *(He rises.)* Goodbye; gonna leave you two dogs to talk it over. Movin' on now.

NAT: Wait, Carter—

MIDGE: *(leans close to him)* Can't see your face too good; what I *can* see got Cemetery written all over it. So long for *good*, baby.

NAT: Sir, a friendship like ours is a rare—

MIDGE: Ain't no friendship. Never *was* no friendship. Don't even know your Goddamn *name*.

NAT: Yesterday you helped a fallen comrade—

MIDGE: You was out *cold*, Mister. Waited for the ambulance to come, done my duty same's I would for *any* lame dog. Said to myself, that ain't gonna be *me* lyin' there. *(takes GILLEY's leather-sheathed hunting-*

knife from his pocket) See this item here? Kid run off without his weapon, see. He comin' back for it today sure. I come here to give it back to him, stay on that boy's *good* side. *(Starts down path towards stone ledge at far left)* O.K., waitin' over here so he sees you and me is no longer *associated*; which we *ain't*, got that? He comes, don't want you *talkin'* to me, *lookin'* at me, contactin' me any way whatever.

NAT: So; the Cossack leaves his sword and you return it.

MIDGE: You bet. *(settles down on ledge)*

NAT: *(leans towards him)* You have had a taste of revolution and will not be able to return to subjection, to living in an occupied country!

MIDGE: Watch me.

(He closes his eyes, puts his huge handkerchief over his face, curls up on ledge. CLARA enters on the stone steps at right; attractive, early forties, stylishly bohemian clothes; she is walking quickly, purposefully down the steps towards NAT's bench. NAT rises, using the bench for support, unaware of the approaching CLARA, pointing his cane at MIDGE.)

NAT: No, *no*, you must not pay this punk for your existence, to live in your own land!

MIDGE: *(from under the handkerchief)* Nap-time now. You're talkin' to nobody.

NAT: Exactly! No one! Surrender to the oppressors and you are no one! *(MIDGE begins to snore quietly.)* Sure, sleep! Sleep then, like any bum in the park—

CLARA: *(stopping on steps)* Excuse me . . .

NAT: *(still to MIDGE)* A *napper* . . .

CLARA: Excuse me, I hate to interrupt you when you're driving somebody crazy . . .

NAT: A napper and a groveler! Why did I waste my time!?

CLARA: *(seeing the walker, the bandage; concerned, frightened, moving towards bench)* God, what happened? . . . Are you all right?

NAT: Everything's fine; don't worry, don't worry . . .

CLARA: Stitches this time?

NAT: A scratch.

CLARA: Your hip?

NAT: A sprain, a sprain . . .

CLARA: Dad, what happened? Why didn't you *call* me? Another fight, right? You got into another fight, didn't you?

NAT: *(sits on small bench)* What fights? I don't fight.

CLARA: How about four weeks ago? How about attacking that poor butcher at Gristede's? What was that?

NAT: I didn't attack the butcher. I attacked the meat. That was because of the prices.

CLARA: He said you shoved all the meat off his display-counter with your cane—

NAT: It was a demonstration—there were thirty people in the store, I was trying to rally them, the meat-shoving was an illustration—

CLARA: The meat hit the butcher and you threw out your hip. Also the chances of starting a commune on Seventy-Second and Broadway are very slim. What happened this time, Dad?

NAT: Well, a young boy—confused, disadvantaged, a victim of Society—

CLARA: A mugger. *(She nods.)* You fought with a mugger. *(pacing anxiously behind center bench)* Of course, of course, it was the next step; my God . . .

NAT: We were talking, we reached an impasse—

CLARA: That's it. No more. I can't let this happen anymore. I let it go, I've been irresponsible. You have to be watched. I'm not letting you out of my sight, Dad.

NAT: Stop this, you're frightening me . . .

CLARA: Oh, *I'm* frightening *you*, huh? I live in terror—the phone will ring, the police, the hospital. My God. It was quiet for a month, but I should have known. This guy Danforth calls this morning and I know you're on the loose again—

NAT: Ah, good, he called—

CLARA: Oh, he *called* all right—*(takes out message; reads)* "Tell HURTSFOE that the Carter matter is settled, I reached the Committee; Reissman said to call." . . . Jesus, HURTSFOE again; HURTSFOE's on the march again. I take it you're Reissman.

NAT: That was yesterday—

CLARA: And tomorrow who? And tomorrow *what*? I came to tell you it's the last *time*! No more calls—

NAT: You *covered*, didn't you?

CLARA: Yes, yes. Once again, once again. Christ, in one year I've been the Headquarters for the Eighth Congressional District, C.B.S. News, the Institute for Freudian Studies, and the United Consumers Protection Agency . . .

NAT: *(fondly)* Ah, yes, UCPA . . .

CLARA: *(sighs, nodding)* UCPA, UCPA. Look, Dad—

NAT: What's *happened* to you? My own daughter has forgotten what a principle is!

CLARA: *What* principle! There's no *principle* here. It's fraud. Personal, daily fraud. A one-man reign of terror and I'm the one who gets terrorized. Never knowing who the hell I'm supposed to be every time some poor sucker calls my office. A *principle*? You mean when that panic-stricken Manager of the Fine Arts Theatre called thinking there was going to be a Congressional Investigation because he showed

German movies? I *still* don't understand how you convinced him you
were a Congressman—

NAT: What, you never saw an Elder Statesman before?

CLARA: But there's no such *thing* as a Floating Congressional District—

NAT: It's *because* he didn't know that he deserved it! That and showing
movies by ex-Nazis. These people think that nobody *notices*, Clara—

CLARA: No *more*! It's over! Today was my last cover, that's what I came
to tell you. Little did I know you were also back in combat again. *(sits
on center bench, opposite him)* Searched this damn park for two hours—
(pointing u.r.) What happened? You're not giving speeches at the
Bethesda Fountain anymore?

NAT: Why should I? So you can find me there? Shut me up, embarrass
me?

CLARA: It's *me*, huh? It's me who embarrasses *you*—

NAT: Exactly; hushing me like I was a babbling child, a—

CLARA: Embarrassment, let's talk about embarrassment, O.K.? Three weeks
ago I come back to my office after lunch, they tell me my Parole
Officer was looking for me.

NAT: *(bangs his cane on the ground)* Necessary retaliation! It was important that you see what it's like to be pursued, watched, guarded . . .
(turns to her, quietly) You *do* frighten me, Mrs. Gelber. You do frighten
me, you know. I'm afraid of what you'll do out of what you think is
love. Coming to the Fountain once a week—it's not stopping me
from talking; that's not so bad. It's the test questions.

CLARA: I don't—

NAT: The test questions to see if I'm too old. *(taps his head)* Checking
on the arteries. "Do you remember what you did yesterday, Dad?"
"Tell me what you had for lunch today, Dad?" One wrong answer
you'll wrap me in a deck-chair and mail me to Florida; *two* mistakes
you'll put me in a home for the forgettable. I know this. My greatest
fear is that someday soon I will wake up silly, that time will take my
brain and you will take me. That you will put me in a place, a home—
or worse, *your* house. Siberia in Great Neck. Very little frightens me,
as you know; just that. Only what you will do.

CLARA: Dad . . .

NAT: I don't answer the door when you come. That's why. I watch
through the hole in the door and wait for you to go away. That's why
I moved from the Fountain, Clara. And why next week you won't find
me *here* either.

CLARA: *(after a moment)* You don't understand; I . . . I care . . . Someone
has to watch out for you. Jack doesn't care, or Ben or Carole. They
don't even speak to you anymore.

NAT: Good, God bless them; lovely children; lovely, distant children.

CLARA: This isn't fair, Dad; I don't deserve this . . .

NAT: Dad. Who is this "Dad" you refer to? When did *that* start? I'm a "Pop," a Pop or a Papa, like I always was. You say "Dad" I keep looking around for a gentleman with a pipe.

CLARA: O.K., why don't I just call you "Dr. Engels" then? *(Silence for a moment; NAT turns to her.)* Did you really think you fooled me? Dr. Engels the therapist? Dr. Fred Engels from the Socialists' Club? Really now.

NAT: But why did you keep writing all those letters to him—?

CLARA: Normal conversation with you is hopeless. Seemed like the best way to reach you. I sent "Dr. Engels" twelve letters in two months, I said everything I felt.

NAT: Smart. Smart girl. Well, at least you're still smart . . . even though the passions are gone, even though the ideals have evaporated . . .

CLARA: Stop . . .

NAT: I remember when you believed that the world did *not* belong to the highest bidder . . .

CLARA: The old song, stop . . .

NAT: This, of course, was before you went into Park East Real Estate, before you gave up Marx and Lenin for Bergdorf and Goodman . . .

CLARA: Jesus, at least get a new set of words—

NAT: Look at you! Look what you've become! Queen of the Condominiums, peasant skirts for two hundred dollars, betrayer of your namesake—

CLARA: Goddamn *name*—

NAT: Clara Lemlich, who stood for something—

CLARA: You *gave* me the name, I had no *choice*—

NAT: Clara Lemlich, who stood for something and stood up for it . . .

CLARA: *(leans back on bench)* Ah, you're rolling now . . .

NAT: Cooper Union; November, Nineteen-Nine . . .

CLARA: You're only eight . . . .

NAT: *(looking away)* I'm only eight, the Shirtwaist Makers are there, thousands of them . . .

CLARA: *(whispering)* You're standing in back with your father . . .

NAT: I'm standing in the back with my father, he holds me up so I can see. A meeting has been called to protest conditions. Gompers speaks, and Mary Drier, Panken and Myer London. All speak well and with passion, but none with the courage to call a general strike. All speak of the Bosses who value property above life and profits above people, but all speak with caution.

CLARA: *(whispering)* Until suddenly . . .

NAT: Until suddenly from the back of the hall, just near us, rises a skinny girl, a teen-ager; she races up onto the platform, this little girl, she races up unafraid among the great ones; she shouts in Yiddish to the thousands, this girl, with the power of inspiration . . . this girl is Clara Lemlich. "I am a working girl, one of those striking against intolerable conditions. I am *tired* of listening to speakers! I offer a resolution that a general strike be called—*now!*" *(softly)* A moment of shock . . . and then the crowd screams, feet pound the floor! The Chairman, Feigenbaum, calls for a second; the thousands cry "second!" in one voice. Feigenbaum trembles, he shouts to the hall, "Do you mean this in good faith? Will you take the Jewish oath?" Three thousand hands are raised—my father is holding me up, his hands are not free, "Raise your hand, boy, raise your hand for us and I will say the oath"—my hand goes up, I feel his heart beating at my back as my father with the thousands chants the solemn oath: "If I turn traitor to the Cause I now pledge, may this hand wither from the arm I raise!" Again there is silence in the hall . . .

CLARA: *(softly; caught up in the story again, as always)* And then Feigenbaum shouts . . .

NAT: And Feigenbaum shouts—*(He raises his fist in the air.)* a general strike has been called! *(A moment; then he lowers his fist.)* Thirty-two years later, December, Forty-One, Roosevelt vows vengeance upon the Fascists and the next day *you* are born with a powerful scream at Kings County Hospital—I say to your mother, "Ethel, sounds to me like Clara Lemlich." This is the name . . .

CLARA and NAT: *(together)* and this is the passion you were born with.

CLARA: *Finis.*

NAT: *(turns to her)* And only forty-one years later you have turned into my own, personal K.G.B.

CLARA: Go to hell.

NAT: I can't; you'll follow me.

(She turns to him, sharply.)

CLARA: Clara, Clara—it's not a name, it's a curse. The Cause, the Goddamn *Cause*—everybody else gets a two-wheeler when they're ten, I got *Das Kapital* in paperback. Sundays you sent me out for bagels and lox and the *Weekend Daily Worker*, I hide it in the bag so half of Flatbush Avenue doesn't point at me. Fights at school, kids avoiding me, daughter of the Reds. My friend Sally—my *only* friend—we're down in the street on a Saturday morning, she tells me she believes in God. I'm confused, I run upstairs to the Central Committee; "Pop, Sally Marcus says she believes in God, what should I tell her?" "Tell her she'll get over it," you say. I tell her, she tells her mother and the next day I got *nobody* on the block to play with; *alone again, alone*—

NAT: *(leans towards her)* Unfair! This isn't *fair.* Later you believed in your *own* things and I loved you for it. You gave up on the Party, I respected you. The Civil Rights, the Anti-War; you marched, you demonstrated, you *spoke*—that was you, nobody *made* you, you loved it—

CLARA: I *did* love it—

NAT: You *changed*—

CLARA: No, I just noticed that the world didn't.

NAT: Ah, first it was me, then it was the world. It's nice to know who to blame. Ten *years*, what have you done?

CLARA: What have I *done*? I got married and had two children and lived a life. I got smarter and fought in battles I figured I could win. That's what I've done.

NAT: Lovely. And now, at last, everybody on the block plays with you, don't they? Yes, all the kids play with you now. You married Ricky the smiling Radiologist; he overcharged his way into a house in Great Neck where your children, as far as I can see, believe firmly in Cable Television. They'll fight to the death for it! And all the kids play with *them* too. It's the new Utopia: everybody plays with everybody! My enemies, I keep up! My enemies, I don't forget; I cherish them like my friends, so I know what to *do*—

CLARA: And what's that? What the hell do you do? Lead raids on lambchops at Gristede's? Oh, God, it's all so easy for you, I almost envy you. You always know what side to be on because you fight old wars; old, old wars . . . *(at bench, leaning towards him)* The battle is *over*, Comrade; didn't you notice? Nothing's *happened*, nothing's changed! And the Masses, have you checked out your beloved Masses lately? They don't *give* a crap. *(He turns away.)* Are you listening! *(grips his arm urgently)* Are you *listening* to me? I have received your invitation to the Revolution and I send regrets. I'm busy. I've given up on the Twentieth Century in favor of getting through the week. I have decided to feel things where I can get to feel something *back*; got it?

NAT: I was wrong; you're not even smart anymore. So not much changed. So what? You think I don't know this? The proper response to the outrages is still to be outraged.

CLARA: *(her arms outstretched in mock supplication)* Forgive me, Father; I'm not on the barricades anymore! I haven't been arrested for ten years, I'm obviously worthless! If you were talking to me in jail right now you'd be overjoyed—

NAT: Not overjoyed. *Pleased* maybe . . .

CLARA: Christ, I was the only kid at the Columbia riots whose father showed up to coach! I *still* don't believe it! There you are on the steps of the Administration Building, shouting at the cops, pointing at me—*(imitating NAT)* Hey Cossacks, look at this one! You can't stop her! *Four* of you—it'll take *four* of you to put her in the wagon!

NAT: It took *six*!

CLARA: *(She suddenly starts to laugh.)* My father, my riot manager; God, I still don't believe it . . . a night in the slammer, and you waiting for me in the street when I got out . . . champagne, you had *champagne* . . .

NAT: *(laughing with her)* It was a graduation, what parent doesn't show up for a graduation?

CLARA: Why the hell am I laughing?

NAT: Because it was funny.

CLARA: *(shaking her head)* Jesus, what am I going to do with you?

NAT: *(quietly)* Hello, Rappaport . . . *(No response; he raises his voice.)* Hello, Rappaport!

CLARA: I'm not playing.

NAT: Come on, we'll do the "don't slap me on the back" one. You remember.

CLARA: *(turns away)* I don't.

NAT: Hello, Rappaport!

CLARA: Stop . . .

NAT: Hello, Rappaport; how's the family?

CLARA: *(after a moment, softly)* I'm not Rappaport.

NAT: Hello, Rappaport; how's the shoe business?

CLARA: *(smiling)* I'm not Rappaport.

NAT: *(leans towards her, slaps her on the back)* Hello, Rappaport; how the hell are ya?

CLARA: *(doing the routine)* I'm not Rappaport, and don't slap me on the back!

NAT: Who are *you* to tell me how to say hello to Rappaport!?

(They both laugh. Silence for a moment.)

CLARA: *(turns to him; quietly)* Pop, I have to do something about you.

NAT: No, you don't.

CLARA: Pop—

NAT: At least I'm "Pop" again—

CLARA: You'll get killed. The next time you'll get killed. I dream about it.

NAT: In general, you need better dreams—

CLARA: I want you out of this neighborhood, I want you off the street. I want you safe. I'm determined.

NAT: *(reaching for walker)* I have an appointment—

CLARA: *(holds his arm, firmly)* O.K., we have three possibilities, three solutions. You'll have to accept one of them. First, there's living with me in Great Neck; you'll have your own room, your own separate—

NAT: Rejected.

CLARA: Second; Ricky has found a place, not far from us, Maple Hills Senior Residence. I've checked it out; it's the *best* of them—*(taking Maple Hills book from hand-bag, showing pages)* really attractive grounds, Pop; this open, sunny recreation area—

NAT: Rejected.

CLARA: O.K . . . O.K., there's one more possibility; I'm not crazy about it but I'm willing to try it for one month. You stay at your place, you do not hide from me, you make yourself available for visits by me or some member of the family once a week. You don't wander the streets, you don't hang around the park; you go out every afternoon to *this* place . . . *(more gently, taking brochure from hand-bag)* West End Senior Center; I was there this morning, Pop; this is a great place. Hot lunch at noon and then a full afternoon of activities . . .

NAT: *(puts on bifocals, holds brochure up to his eyes, reading)* "One o'clock; Dr. Gerald Spitzer will present a slide presentation and informative program on home health services; refreshments will be served. Two o'clock; Beginners Bridge with Rose Hagler. Three-fifteen; Arts and Crafts Corner supervised by Ginger Friedman . . ." *(He studies the brochure for a moment.)* O.K. . . . we got these possibilities; we got exile in Great Neck, we got Devil's Island, and we got Kindergarten. All rejected. *(hands her back the brochure; rises from bench, opening the walker)* And now, if you'll excuse me . . . *(He starts moving down the path to the right with the walker. We begin to hear the distant sound of the Carousel as he continues down the path.)*

CLARA: All right, here it is: I'm taking legal action, Pop, I'm going to Court. *(NAT stops on the path, his back to her. She remains on the bench.)* I saw a lawyer a month ago after the Gristede Uprising; I'm prepared. Article Seventy-Eight of the Mental Hygiene Law, judicial declaration of incompetency, I'll get Ricky and me authorized as custodians. According to the lawyer I've got more than enough evidence to prove that you are both mentally and physically incapable of managing your-self or your affairs. In addition to a proven history of harassment, impersonation and assault. *(She turns away; quietly, firmly.)* I look at that bandage, I . . . You can hardly see, and with that walker you're a sitting duck. I don't want you hurt, I don't want you dead. Please, don't force me to go to Court. If you fight me, you'll lose. If you run away, I'll find you. I'm prepared to let you hate me for this.

(Silence for a moment.)

NAT: You're not kidding.

CLARA: I'm not.

(Silence again; only the sound of the distant, gentle Carousel music. He moves back to the bench, sits next to her.)

NAT: *(quietly)* Clara, I've got to tell you something. I put it in my papers, a letter for you when I died, you would have known then . . . *(hesitates a moment, then proceeds gently)* Your mother and I, it was not the liveliest association, but there was a great fondness between us. Whatever I tell you now you must know that. August, Nineteen Thirty-Nine, I'm at the Young Worker's Club on Houston Street; you talked about dialectical materialism and you met girls. It's a Friday night, the day of the Hitler-Stalin Pact; Ribbentrop shakes hands with Molotov on the front page of the *Journal-American* and this woman bursts into tears. Everyone's arguing, discussing, but this woman sits there with her tears falling on the newspaper. This was Ethel, your mother. My heart was hers. Soon we are married; two years later you are born—and during the next ten years those other people. Fine. All is well. Then . . . then comes October, Fifty-Six . . . October Third . . . *(He lapses into silence, turns away.)*

CLARA: Tell me. What is it?

NAT: I met a girl. I fell in love.

CLARA: You're human, Pop, it happens. There's no need to feel—

NAT: I mean in *love*, Clara. For the first and only time in my life; boom.

CLARA: Don't worry, it's not—

NAT: Clara, she *was* a *girl*. Twenty-four; I was fifty-five.

CLARA: *(riveted)* What happened? Where did you meet her?

NAT: It was in the Grand Street Library, second floor reading room. I'm at the main table, I look up, I see this lovely girl, Hannah, Hannah Pearlman; she's studying a grammar-book. She looks up, she *smiles* at me. I can't speak. She goes back to her book. She has a sad look, someone alone. I see a girl, troubled, lost, marks on her hands from the needle-trades. She rises to leave. Someone should speak to her. Can it be me? Can I have the courage . . . ? *(softly, with love)* I speak. I *speak* to her; and for hours our words come out, and for hours and days after that in her little room on Ludlow Street. It was the most perfect time. She tells me I have saved her from killing herself . . . I saved her just in time . . . just in time, Clara . . . she did not die, she did not die . . . *(Silence for a moment. Then he speaks briskly, as though awakening from a dream.)* Well, I'm married to Ethel, nothing can come of it. Four months, it's over. She goes to live in Israel, a new life. Six months later, a letter . . . there is a child . . .

CLARA: My God . . .

NAT: A girl . . . And then, every year or two a letter. Times goes by, I think often of the library and Ludlow Street. Then silence; there are no letters, never another. Three months ago there's a message for me at the Socialists' Club: Sergeant Pearlman will be here at five. Five o'clock, at the door, Sergeant Pearlman is a girl. In Israel, women, everybody's in the Army for a year. Well, Sergeant Pearlman . . .

CLARA: Yes . . .

NAT: Sergeant Pearlman is my daughter. Twenty-six, a face like her mother; a fine face, like a painting. She herself is an artist; she comes to this country to study at the Art Student's League and to find me. *(Silence for a moment.)* Here's the point. She has decided to take care of me; to live with me. That's why I've told you all this, so you'll know. In December, we leave for Israel. This is where I will end my days. You see, there is nothing for you to worry about.

(Silence for a few moments.)

CLARA: *(quietly)* This is . . . this is a lot for me to take in, all at once. A lot of information . . .

NAT: Not easy, but I'm glad I told you. Better you know now.

CLARA: I want to meet her.

NAT: You shall.

CLARA: When?

NAT: In two days, Friday. At the Socialists' Club, in the dining-room, Friday at lunchtime. I'll bring sandwiches.

CLARA: Good. *(after a moment; softly)* She'll . . . she'll take care of you.

NAT: That's the point.

CLARA: *(letting it all sink in)* Israel . . .

NAT: Yes, Clara. *(She turns away, trying to cover her emotion. He touches her arm; gently.)* Clara, don't be upset. I'll be fine. It's for the best, Clara . . . *(She rises briskly from the bench.)*

CLARA: Well, at last you've got a daughter who's a soldier.

NAT: Sit. Where are you going?

CLARA: *(checks watch)* My train. You know, the Siberian Express.

NAT: *(He holds out his hand to her.)* They got them every half-hour. Sit a minute.

CLARA: Got to go. See you Friday. *(She moves quickly towards the stone steps at right; near tears.)*

NAT: Wait a minute—*(She goes quickly up the steps.)* Hey, Rappaport! Hello, Rappaport! *(She exits.)* Rappaport, what happened to you? You used to be a tall, fat guy, now you're a—*(She is gone. He shouts.)* Rappaport! *(Silence for a moment. He speaks quietly.)* Hey, Rappaport . . . *(Silence again. NAT remains quite still on the bench; he strokes his beard nervously, sadly. He suddenly winces, as though aware for the first time of the pain in his hip; shifts position on the bench. MIDGE, still lying on the stone ledge at far left, lifts the handkerchief off his face.)*

MIDGE: You made it up.

NAT: *(softly)* Of course.

MIDGE: You made it all up . . .

NAT: Go back to sleep.

MIDGE: Conned your own kid, that's a sin.

NAT: I did it to save a life. Mine.

MIDGE: *(sitting up on ledge)* You ain't a nice person. 'Shamed I even sung a song with you.

NAT: You don't understand. Nursing homes danced in her head; desperate measures were required. *(grips walker, rising forcefully from bench)* *You*, you would just go toddling off to Maple Hills.

MIDGE: Wouldn't hustle my own child to save my ass.

NAT: She's not mine anymore. She has become unfamiliar. *(starts moving u.l. on path, in walker, as though to exit past MIDGE at ledge)*

MIDGE: Won't get away with it anyway. In two days, she'll—

NAT: *(continuing forcefully up path)* In two days I'll be in Seattle . . . Hong Kong, Vladivostok, Newark; I'll be where she can't get me.

MIDGE: Seattle; shit, you can't get *downtown*, boy.

NAT: I'll be *gone*, somewhere, when she comes to the Club, I'll be *gone*—

MIDGE: *(angrily, blocking his path)* And what *she* do? Wait there all day, thinkin' you're dead? *(NAT stops, MIDGE pointing at him.)* What kinda man *are* you? Smart talk and fancy notions, you don't *give* a damn!

NAT: A *letter*, I'll . . . I'll leave a letter for her . . . *(Silence for a moment; he sits on the small bench, upset, confused.)* I'll send her a letter, I'll explain the necessity for . . . my behavior . . . *(He trails off into silence, exhausted, at a loss for words; he stares thoughtfully out at the lake.)*

MIDGE: *(suddenly looks up at Bridge, whispering)* Gilley—

(We have seen THE COWBOY enter u.r. on the Bridge a few moments earlier, strolling halfway across the Bridge before MIDGE notices him; a tall, genial-looking tourist, about thirty-five, he wears an immaculate white Stetson, finely tailored buckskin jacket and polished boots. He moves politely towards LAURIE, stopping a respectful distance from her, peering at the sketch she's been working on; LAURIE apparently unaware of him. NAT lost in his own thoughts, continues to look out at the lake, unaware of MIDGE and the scene above him.)

THE COWBOY: *(cordially, tipping his Stetson)* Afternoon, M'am. *(She does not respond.)*

MIDGE: *(softly, squinting up at them)* No, ain't Gilley; too big . . .

THE COWBOY: *(pleasantly, indicating sketch, a well-mannered Western voice)* Well now, M'am, you sure got that lake just right. Fine work, I'd say. Looks just like—

LAURIE: *(not looking at him)* Fuck off, Cowboy.

THE COWBOY: *(cordially, tipping his Stetson, as though returning her greeting)* Afternoon, M'am.

LAURIE: How did you find me?

THE COWBOY: Natural born hunter, Miss Laurie. 'Specially rabbits.

LAURIE: Ever tell you how much I hate that bullshit drawl? *(turns to him)* What is this, Halloween? You haven't been west of Jersey City.

THE COWBOY: Pure accident of birth, M'am. My soul's in Montana where the air is better.

LAURIE: *(abruptly hands him bank-envelope)* See ya later, Cowboy. *(She starts briskly, calmly, across Bridge to right.)*

THE COWBOY: Well, thank-you, M'am. *(opens envelope, starts counting bills inside)*

MIDGE: Sure don't *sound* like Ella Mae . . .

THE COWBOY: *(quietly)* Three hundred and twenty . . . ? *(LAURIE quickens her pace across the Bridge, almost running.)* Three hundred and twenty outa two *thousand—(LAURIE races towards the stone steps at right, THE COWBOY darts U.L., disappearing. MIDGE quickly grabs NAT, breaking into his reverie, pulling him to his feet.)*

MIDGE: Come on now—*(moving NAT into the safety of the shadows at the left of the bridge, whispering)* Bad business . . . bad park business here.

(LAURIE races breathlessly down the stone steps towards the Tunnel, an escape—but THE COWBOY suddenly emerges from the Tunnel, blocking her path.)

THE COWBOY: *(calmly, evenly)* See the rabbit run. Dirty little rabbit. *(He grips her arms, thrusts her forward towards the bench; she bumps against the bench, dropping her sketch pad. He remains a few steps away; continuing quietly, evenly.)* I live in a bad city. What's *happenin'* to this city? City fulla dirty little rabbits. Park fulla junkies; *un*reliable, *dis*honorable junkies . . .

LAURIE: That's all I could—

THE COWBOY: *(holding up the envelope)* Kept your nose filled and your head happy for a year and a half and look what you do. Look what you do.

LAURIE: *(moving towards him)* Sorry, right now that's the best I—*(He slaps her hard across the face with the bank-envelope, jerking her head back; then he throws the envelope full of bills to the ground.)*

NAT: *(from shadows at far left)* What? What happened . . . ?

MIDGE: *(holding NAT's arm, whispering)* Shhhh . . . stay now.

THE COWBOY: *(calmly again)* You . . . you got to take me serious. 'Cause you don't take me serious I don't get my money and you don't get older. *(A moment; then he moves past her at the bench, starting towards the Tunnel.)* My cash. Tomorrow. Here. Six o'clock.

LAURIE: Need more time . . . not enough time, I can't—*(In one, quick, almost mechanical movement, he turns and hits her sharply in the face, as though correcting an error. She blinks, dizzy from the blow, sits down on the bench, trembling; there is blood on her lip. NAT takes a step forward in his walker, but MIDGE holds him firmly in the shadows.)*

THE COWBOY: *(kneels next to her at the bench; quietly)* Mustn't say "can't," Miss Laurie. Don't say that. You are the little engine that can. I believe in you. *(takes out his handkerchief, starts quite delicately, carefully, to dab the blood off her lip, speaking gently)* This gets around, folks'll start thinkin' The Cowboy's got no teeth. Law and order ain't reached these parts; fellah like me got to protect himself, right? *(She nods.)* My cash. Tomorrow. Here. Six o'clock. And don't try to hide from me, little rabbit. Don't do that. That would be a mistake. *(She nods. He rises, puts his handkerchief back in his pocket; shakes his head sadly.)* Damn town. Damn town's turnin' us all to shit, ain't it? *(turns, walks briskly into the darkened Tunnel, tipping his hat cordially as he exits)* 'Afternoon, M'am.

(LAURIE kneels down on the ground, sobbing, retrieving the envelope and the scattered bills. MIDGE moves out of the shadows and quickly towards her, NAT moves slowly towards her in his walker. MIDGE reaches his hand out tentatively, tenderly touches her shoulder.)

MIDGE: You O.K., lady?

LAURIE: *(tears streaming down her face)* Great. Just great. *(She looks up at them.)* Fellahs . . . how ya doin', fellahs?

MIDGE: Here . . . take this. *(He gently hands her his handkerchief; she accepts it, rising to sit on bench. MIDGE points in the direction of THE COWBOY's exit.)* That boy; he a dealer, or a shark?

LAURIE: Dealer. But he gave me credit.

MIDGE: Can you get the money? *(She shakes her head hopelessly. He nods.)* Uh-huh. What I heard, lady, you best get outa town; fast and far.

LAURIE: I was just gettin' it together . . . straightening out, Mister . . . *(shaking with sobs, opening sketch pad, showing him the pages)* Art School, I started Art School, see . . .

MIDGE: *(softly, touching her shoulder)* Outa town, chil'; fast and far.

LAURIE: These guys, you don't get away; they got branch offices, man, they got chain stores . . .

NAT: She's right. *(parks his walker next to the bench)* Other measures are called for. *(He sits next to her.)* Tell me, Miss; two days from now, Friday, what are you doing for lunch on Friday?

LAURIE: *(quietly, trembling)* Friday . . . ? Jesus, looks like Friday I'll be in the hospital. Or dead maybe . . . or dead . . .

NAT: *(his arm round her; gently, firmly)* No, you won't be in the hospital. I promise you. And you will not die . . . you will not die.

(BLACKOUT. In the darkness we hear the sound of the Carousel band-organ playing "The Sidewalks of New York"; the music building gradually louder in the darkness, reaching a peak and then slowly fading as the lights come up.)

It is six o'clock, the evening of the next day. MIDGE and NAT are alone onstage, seated on the center bench. NAT wears dark sunglasses, a white silk scarf and an old but stylish Homburg, his cane at his side, his walker folded and hidden behind the bench. He looks serious and elegant. MIDGE wears an old suit-jacket instead of his usual sweater, and a hat that he had once considered fashionable. The Bridge lampposts are lit above; the dark shadows of early evening gather in the Tunnel and along the path. MIDGE glances anxiously up and down the path. He lights a cigarette, inhales, coughs. Silence for a few moments.

NAT: Time, please.

MIDGE: *(takes out pocket-watch, holds it up against his bifocals)* Ten to six.

NAT: Good. Say my name again.

MIDGE: I got it, I got it; you keep—

NAT: Say the name.

MIDGE: Donatto.

NAT: The whole name.

MIDGE: Anthony Donatto.

NAT: Better known as?

MIDGE: *(impatiently)* Tony The Cane. O.K.? Now will ya—

NAT: Tony the Cane Donatto. Good. O.K., *your* name.

MIDGE: I—

NAT: Your name.

MIDGE: *(with a sigh of resignation)* Kansas City Jack.

NAT: *Missouri* Jack, *Missouri* Jack. *See,* it's lucky I asked.

MIDGE: Missouri Jack, Kansas City Jack, what the hell's the *difference?* He ain't even gonna ask me.

NAT: It could come *up.* In these matters details are very important. Details is the whole game, believe me. What time is it?

MIDGE: I just told—

NAT: Missouri Jack is better than Kansas City Jack. Has a sound to it. Music. I know these things. Details is everything. You should introduce yourself to him.

MIDGE: Nossir, *nossir;* do what I *said* I'd do and that's *it.* Don't even like doin' *that* much. Dicey deal here, say the least—*(starts to cough, indicates cigarette)* Looka me, ain't had a cigarette thirty-two years, July; you got me smokin' again. *(pointing at him)* O.K., promised that po' girl I'd help her out, but I ain't hangin' around here a second longer'n I have to. You a time-bomb, Mister, I hear you tickin'.

NAT: I ask you to look at the record, sir! I ask you to look at the *harm* I've done you! Gilley did not return yesterday as I predicted and he did not come today. No more pay-offs; correct?

MIDGE: O.K., so far he—

NAT: And your job—has anybody there *mentioned* firing you since I dealt with Danforth? Do you still have your home?

MIDGE: Yeah, well, O.K., so far they—

NAT: And today a few minutes of your time to help the victim of Gene Autry; the woman requires our aid. He comes here, you go up to him, you say, "Excuse me, my boss wants to see you," you send him over to me and you're *done*; finished.

MIDGE: You bet; then I *split*, that's *it*. Go home, hear about it on the T.V. *(shaking his head mournfully)* Still don't see why you even need me to—

NAT: *Details, details;* gives him the feeling I've got a staff, an organization. It fills in the picture. Details are crucial. I know my business. What time is it? *(MIDGE sighs, takes out his pocket-watch. NAT turns, squinting into the Tunnel.)* Nevermind; he's here. On the button.

(MIDGE turns sharply as THE COWBOY emerges from the darkened Tunnel. NAT adjusts his Homburg, crosses his legs, leans back on the bench. THE COWBOY walks down to the ledge at far left, glances about, then looks solemnly up at the Bridge. After a few moments he sits down at the edge of the ledge, takes off his Stetson, starts cleaning it carefully with a small brush, waiting. MIDGE remains quite still on the bench, looking out at the lake. Silence for a few moments.)

NAT: *(whispering)* Now. *(MIDGE continues to look out at the lake. NAT whispers again.)* Now, Carter. *(MIDGE rises, buttons his jacket, straightens his hat, preparing himself; then crosses to within six feet of THE COWBOY. THE COWBOY is looking away from him, watching the path at left.)*

MIDGE: *(barely audible)* Excuse me, my boss wants to see you. *(No response; he speaks a bit louder.)* Excuse me, Mister . . . my boss wants to see you.

THE COWBOY: *(turns to MIDGE)* You talkin' to *me*, partner?

MIDGE: Yeah. *(points behind him)* My boss over there, he wants to see you.

THE COWBOY: Your boss?

MIDGE: Yeah, I'm on his staff? He wants to see you.

THE COWBOY: Who the hell're you?

MIDGE: Me? I'm nobody. I'm on the staff.

THE COWBOY: *(leans towards him)* What do you want with me? Who are you?

MIDGE: I'm . . . I'm Missouri Jack.

THE COWBOY: Missouri Jack. Sounds familiar. You ever—

MIDGE: You don't know me. I'm nobody.

THE COWBOY: Nobody?

MIDGE: Yeah, definitely. Nobody at all; believe me. *(THE COWBOY shrugs, turns away.)* Him, over there, he's somebody. He wants to see you.

THE COWBOY: I'm busy.

MIDGE: He's the boss. Donatto. Tony Donatto.

THE COWBOY: *(sharply)* Great. I'm *busy*.

MIDGE: *(turns instantly, starts walking briskly towards the stone steps at far right)* O.K. then, guess I'll be on my way. Yeah, gotta be getting' along now. Nice meetin' you, pleasure talkin' to you . . . *(THE COWBOY has turned away, ignoring MIDGE, watching the path.)*

NAT: *(to COWBOY, loudly)* Hey, Tom Mix. *(THE COWBOY turns; NAT pats the bench.)* You, Roy Rogers; over here.

THE COWBOY: What do *you* want?

NAT: I want not to shout. Come here. *(No response. MIDGE quickens his pace up the steps.)* Laurie Douglas, two thousand dollars.

THE COWBOY: What—

NAT: You know the name? You know the sum? *(pats bench)* Here. We'll talk.

THE COWBOY: *(THE COWBOY starts towards him. MIDGE stops in the shadows half-way up the steps, turns, curious, watching them at a safe distance. NAT will remain aloof behind his sunglasses, seldom facing THE COWBOY, never raising his voice.)*

THE COWBOY: *(approaching bench)* What *about* Laurie Douglas? Who are you?

NAT: I am Donatto. Sit.

THE COWBOY: Look, if that junkie bimbo thinks she can—

NAT: The junkie bimbo is my daughter. Sit.

THE COWBOY: She's got a father, huh? *(sits)* Thought things like her just accumulated.

NAT: *(taking old silver case from jacket, removing small cigar)* Not that kind of father. Another kind of father. I have many daughters, many sons. In my family there are many children. I am Donatto. *(He lights the cigar. THE COWBOY studies him.)*

THE COWBOY: I never heard of—

NAT: On your level, probably not. *(patting THE COWBOY's knee)* A lot of you new boys don't know. I fill you in. My people, we work out of Phoenix. We take commands from Nazzaro, Los Angeles; Capetti, New Orleans . . . *(No response; NAT leans towards him.)* Capetti, New Orleans . . . *(turns to MIDGE)* Jack, he doesn't know Capetti, New Orleans . . . *(NAT chuckles heartily, MIDGE stares blankly back at him; NAT turns to THE COWBOY again.)* Capetti will be amused by you. I am not. Capetti, many years ago, he gives us our name—I talk of the old days now, the good days—he calls us, me and Jack, "The Travel Agents." This is because we arrange for trips to the place of no return. You understand?

THE COWBOY: *(sharply, snapping his fingers)* Let's get *to* it, pal, there's some *bucks* owed me—

NAT: *(covers THE COWBOY's snapping fingers with his hand, gently)* Please don't do that, it upsets me. We will speak of your problem now. The girl, Laurie; I am not pleased with her. A two grand marker for drugs, she brings shame on my house. She says she is slapped, threatened. I am unhappy with this. It is not for you to deal with her. She is of my family. Forget the girl, you never met her. Forget, Cowboy, or you yourself become a memory.

THE COWBOY: *(smiles, leans back on bench)* You tryin' t'tell me that two old guys like you—

NAT: Of course not. We don't touch people like you; we have *people* who touch people like you. I pick up a phone, you disappear. I make a call, they find you floating. Yes, we are old now, the Travel Agents; many years since we did our own work. In Fifty-Four, our last active year . . . *(turns to MIDGE)* how many floating, Jack? *(MIDGE stares blankly back at him for several moments, then NAT turns to THE COWBOY again.)* He doesn't remember either.

THE COWBOY: *(leaning very close to him)* Don't like the sound of this, hoss; it does not ring right in the ear.

NAT: Don't you understand? Missouri and me, we fly here personally from Phoenix last night to speak to you—

THE COWBOY: If you just came in from Phoenix what were you doing here yesterday?

NAT: Yesterday? What're you—

THE COWBOY: And the day before that. Seen you here two days runnin'.

NAT: You . . . you are mistaken—*(MIDGE starts to retreat up the steps towards the exit.)*

THE COWBOY: *(lifts walker up from behind bench)* Had this with you yesterday. I got an antenna picks up all channels, Dad; helps me not to wake up dead.

NAT: I advise you to call your people, check the name—

THE COWBOY: Game's over, stop it—

NAT: Call them now—

THE COWBOY: Please don't continue this. I'm gettin' depressed—

NAT: You are making a serious mistake, a very serious—

THE COWBOY: *Please* don't do this—*(He throws the walker clattering to the ground.)* *Hate* bein' played foolish; *hate* it. First she cons me, then she gets two old creeps to front for her. Don't *like* it. *(pacing behind bench)* City gone rotten, shills like you, this Big Apple's just rottin' away . . . *(NAT starts to rise, he pulls him sharply back down onto the bench.)* This is hurtin' me. Makin' me *feel* bad. *(pulls off NAT's sunglasses)* Who *are* you, man? *(yanks off his Homburg)* What's the deal? Where is she?

NAT: *(quietly)* A . . . a note was left with my attorney this morning. If I do not return by seven they will send people here. His card—*(hands him business card)*

THE COWBOY: *(crushing the card in his hand)* You're out of aces, friend. Where's she hidin'? Where's she at?

NAT: I am not at liberty to—

THE COWBOY: *(grips NAT's scarf, pulls him close)* Run a street business. Lookin' bad on the street, girl's makin' me look like shit on the street. Got folks *laughin'* at me. *(gives him one fierce shake)* You got to take me *serious* now. You got to tell me where she's at.

NAT: *(quietly, unable to make his mind work)* Allow me to introduce myself; I . . . I'm . . . *(THE COWBOY pulls the scarf tighter around NAT's neck, like a kind of noose, shaking him violently now, shouting.)*

THE COWBOY: You in harm's way, Dad, you in harm's *way* now! Got to *tell* me, got to *tell* me! Gonna rock you till the words come out— *(shaking him fiercely, continuously, rhythmically, NAT half-way off the bench now, almost falling to the ground)* Rock you, rock you, rock you—

MIDGE: *(taking a step down the stairs)* Leave him be! Leave him *be* now!

THE COWBOY: *(continues shaking NAT)* Rock you, *rock* you—

MIDGE: Leave the man be! Leave him go else I get a cop!

THE COWBOY: *(turns, still holding NAT)* Well now, it's Mr. Nobody . . .

MIDGE: *(retreating a step)* You . . . you go away, you leave him be else I get a cop. *(pointing up the stairs, trembling)* Cop right near—cop-car at the boathouse this hour, right near.

THE COWBOY: That case you don't *move*, little man, you stay right there . . . *(MIDGE hesitates; then starts up the stairs.)* I ask you not to go, little man . . . *(MIDGE continues up the stairs as quickly as he can; THE COWBOY lets go of NAT, letting him fall to the ground, starts towards the stairs.)* Askin' you to *stop*, buddy; stop right *there*—*(MIDGE stops on the stairs, his back to THE COWBOY. THE COWBOY continues towards the base of the stairs; MIDGE turns, holding GILLEY's unsheathed hunting-knife high in the air; the large blade glistens. THE COWBOY stops; backs up a bit towards the Tunnel. The knife is shaking, MIDGE grips the handle with both hands to steady it. THE COWBOY tips back his Stetson.)* Well now, well now . . . what do we got here?

MIDGE: We got a crazy old man with a knife.

THE COWBOY: Crazy ol' man, you can't even see me.

MIDGE: *(still trembling)* See a blue shadow with a hat on it. Come close enough I stick you. *(a step forward, thrusting knife)* I swear I stick you, boy. *(THE COWBOY starts retreating back towards the Tunnel; smiles, tips his hat, as though gracefully admitting defeat.)*

THE COWBOY: 'Afternoon, Jack. 'Bye now . . . *(He turns as though exiting into the Tunnel; it would appear to* MIDGE *that* THE COWBOY *is leaving, but we can see that he was merely ducked into the shadows within the Tunnel, at right, where he waits for* MIDGE. MIDGE *continues towards the Tunnel, his courage and pride building, his knife raised high.)*

NAT: *(from the ground, whispering)* Get away, Carter . . . get away . . .

MIDGE: *(moving into Tunnel, shouting)* Now *you* the one goes away, *you* the one does the leavin', Cowboy; this here's *my* spot . . . *(continuing into Tunnel, unaware that* THE COWBOY *is hidden just behind him in the shadows of the Tunnel Archway)* Mess with me, I peel you like an apple! Sliced Cowboy comin' up! Cowboy Salad to go—*(THE COWBOY moves suddenly out of the shadows behind* MIDGE—*We see the sharp, violent thrust of* THE COWBOY's *hand as he grabs* MIDGE's *shoulder—*

BLACKOUT; *the sudden loud, pulsing rhythm of the Carousel band-organ playing "Springtime in the Rockies." The powerful sound of the band-organ continues in the darkness for a few moments and then the red-orange colors of autumn gradually light up the sky behind the Bridge, leaving the d.s. area in darkness and the Bridge and the Archway in stark silhouette. Leaves fall against the red-orange sky; the Carousel music continuing powerfully for several moments and then slowly fading into the distant, more delicate, melody of "The Queen City March" as the rest of the lights come up.)*

It is twelve days later, a cloudy autumn morning, eleven o'clock. NAT *is alone onstage, seated at the far left end of the bench. He wears his bifocals, a thick woolen scarf, and a faded winter coat; his walker folded at his side, his briefcase nowhere in sight. He remains quite still, staring rather listlessly out at the lake; from time to time he shivers slightly in the October breeze, holds the scarf up closer about his neck. He seems fragile, older—or rather he seems to be his own age, very much like any old man whiling away his morning on the park bench. Several moments pass. A few autumn leaves drift lazily down on the path. Silence except for the now quite distant and gentle sound of the Carousel music. After a while* NAT *reaches into his jacket-pocket, takes out the West End Senior Center brochure, holds it up to his bifocals, studying it. Several more moments pass.*

We see MIDGE *appear in the darkened Tunnel; he is moving slowly and carefully through the Tunnel with the aid of a "quad-cane"—a cane with four aluminum rubber-tipped legs at its base. It takes him several moments to reach the bench; he crosses in front of* NAT, *pointedly ignoring him, sits at the far right end of the bench, opens his copy of* The Sporting News, *starts to read. The Carousel music fades out. Silence for a few moments.* NAT *turns, leans towards* MIDGE.

MIDGE: *(quietly)* Don't say a word.

NAT: *(after a moment)* I was only—

MIDGE: Not a word, please. *(Silence again.* MIDGE *continues to read his newspaper.)*

NAT: I was only going to say that, quite frankly, I have missed you, Carter.

MIDGE: O.K., now you said it.

NAT: *(after a moment)* I would also like to express my delight at your safe return from the hospital. I only regret that you did not allow me into your room to visit you.

MIDGE: Ain't lettin' *you* in there—shit, tell 'em you're a doctor, start loppin' off pieces of my foot. Had twelve beautiful days an' nights without you.

NAT: Quite right. I don't blame you.

MIDGE: Told 'em, don't let him in *whatever* he says—he tell you he the head of the hospital, tell you he invented *novocaine,* you don't let him in.

NAT: I certainly don't blame you. The fact is I've stopped doing that.

MIDGE: Yeah, *sure—*

NAT: It's true. Since the Cowboy—an episode during which, may I say, you behaved magnificently, not since General Custer has there been such behavior—since that time I have been only myself. That Friday, Clara comes lunchtime to the Socialists' Club, I tell her the truth. She comes, there are tears in her eyes, I decide to tell her the truth. I will admit I was helped in this decision by the fact that the girl, Laurie, did not show up. *(He turns away, quietly.)* I could have covered, another story, my heart wasn't in it. My mouth, a dangerous mouth; it makes you Missouri Jack and almost kills you, makes an Israeli family and breaks my daughter's heart. I have retired my mouth.

MIDGE: *(still looking away, bitterly)* Yeah, well, long's we talkin' *mouth* damage, boy-lawyer for the Tenants' Committee found out there ain't no HURTSFOE; I'm outa my *job* now. Yeah, movin' me and the Erie City out in four weeks. No extra severance neither. Danforth come to the hospital to tell me personal; bring me a basket of fruit. Now 'stead of my Christmas cash I got six fancy pears wrapped in silver-paper.

NAT: I . . . I deeply regret—

MIDGE: 'Sides which, look what you done to Laurie. How you expect her to show up? Said you'd help her with that Cowboy; now she's in worse trouble then ever. *(bangs his quad-cane on the ground)* 'Sides which, there ain't one good hip left on this bench now. And long's we keepin' score here, what happened to Gilley? Tell me the truth; Gilley's *back,* ain't he?

NAT: *(after a moment)* Yes. *(quietly)* He charges six dollars now.

MIDGE: So seems to me you pretty much come up O for Five on the whole series here.

NAT: Please, I assure you, my wounds require no further salt . . .

MIDGE: 'Nother thing—I ain't no General Custer. Way I heard it, the General got wiped out. Well, not *this* boy. Shit, wasn't for a lucky left jab I near blew that Cowboy away. *(takes a small piece of buckskin-fringe from his pocket)* See this? Small-piece of that Cowboy is what it is. His jacket, anyways. Near took a good slice outa that boy, 'fore he dropped me. *(leans back on bench, smiling)* Know what I seen in the hospital every night, fronta my bed? I seen that Cowboy's eyes, them scared eyes, them big chicken eyes when my weapon come out. That was one surprised, frozen-solid, near-shitless Cowboy. Dude didn't know *what* happened. Dude figured he had me on the ropes, out come my weapon and he turn *stone*. Lord, even eyes like mine I seen *his* eyes, they got *that* big lookin' at me. Yeah, yeah, he seen *me*, all right, he *seen* me; gonna be a while 'fore he mess with *this* alley-cat again. *(studying the piece of buckskin)* Must be a way to frame a thing like this . . .

(Silence; then the distant Carousel band organ starts playing its first song of the day, "Sidewalks of New York"; NAT looks up, realizing what time it must be.)

NAT: *(starts to rise, using bench for support)* Unfortunately, I must leave now . . .

MIDGE: *(turns to him, smiles)* Best news I heard all day.

NAT: I am expected at the Senior Center at noon. The day begins at noon there. I must be prompt; Clara checks up. *(unfolding the walker)* Also weekends in Great Neck. I am seldom in the park anymore.

MIDGE: *(returns to his newspaper)* News is gettin' better and better . . .

NAT: *(steps inside of walker, his hands on the rails)* The hospital said you just got out, I came today on the chance of seeing you. I felt I owed you an apology; also the truth. My name is Nat Moyer; this is my actual name. I was a few years with the Fur Workers' Union, this was true, but when Ben Gold lost power they let me go. I was then for forty-one years a waiter at Deitz's Dairy Restaurant on Houston Street; that's all, a waiter. I was retired at age seventy-three; they said they would have kept me on except I talked too much, annoyed the customers. I presently reside, and have for some time, at the Amsterdam Hotel; here my main occupation is learning more things about tuna fish than God ever intended. In other words, whatever has been said previously, I was, and am now, no one. No one at all. This is the truth. Goodbye and good luck to you and your knife. *(He starts moving slowly up the path with his walker towards the exit at left.)* Better get going to the Center. At Twelve guest speaker Jerome Cooper will lecture on "Timely Issues for the Aging," refreshments will be served to anyone who's alive at the end . . .

MIDGE: *(quietly, shaking his head)* Shit, man, you *still* can't tell the truth.

NAT: *(continues moving away)* That was the truth.

MIDGE: Damn it, tell me the truth.

NAT: I *told* you the truth. That's what I was, that's *all*—

MIDGE: *(angrily, slapping the bench)* No, you wasn't a waiter. What was you really?

NAT: I was a waiter . . .

MIDGE: *(shouting angrily)* You wasn't just a waiter, you was *more* than that! Tell me the truth, damn it—

NAT: *(He stops on the path; shouts.)* I was a *waiter*, that's it! *(Silence for a moment; then he continues up the path. He stops after a few steps; silence for several moments. Then, quietly)* Except, of course, for a brief time in the motion picture industry.

MIDGE: You mean the movies?

NAT: Well, *you* call it the movies; *we* call it the motion picture industry.

MIDGE: What kinda job you have there?

NAT: A job? What I did you couldn't call a job. You see, I was, briefly, a mogul.

MIDGE: Mogul; yeah, I hearda that. Ain't that some kinda Rabbi or somethin'?

NAT: In a manner of speaking, yes. *(moving towards MIDGE at bench)* A sort of motion picture Rabbi, you might say. One who leads, instructs, inspires; that's a mogul. It's the early Fifties, Blacklisting, the Red Scare, terror reigns, the industry is frozen. Nobody can make a move. It's colleague against colleague, brother against brother. I had written a few articles for the papers, some theories on the subject—*(sitting on bench)* suddenly, they call me, they fly me there—boom, I'm a mogul. The industry needs answers. What should I do?

MIDGE: *(leans towards him, intently)* What *did* you do?

NAT: Well, that's a long story . . . a long and complicated story . . . *(He crosses his legs, leans back on the bench, about to launch into his story, the Carousel music building loudly as . . .*

THE CURTAIN FALLS

Soul Sisters

Joanne Koch
and
Sarah Blacher Cohen

Joanne Koch and
Sarah Blacher Cohen

Joanne Koch and Sarah Blacher Cohen had their first collaboration reach off-Broadway in 2000. They began to work together ten years earlier when Joanne had established her career as a playwright, screenwriter and nonfiction writer and Sarah had distinguished herself as a scholar, author and editor, specializing in humor, drama and Jewish American literature.

Koch won recognition individually for her plays *Haymarket: Footnote to a Bombing* (First Prize Piscator Foundation/Southern Illinois University International Playwriting Award), *Nesting Dolls* (Chicago Foundation for Women Grant, Midwest tour, local PBS broadcast), *A Leading Woman* (Richard H. Driehaus Foundation Grant), *Teeth* (Illinois Arts Council and Dramatists Guild Fund grants), *Hearts in the Wood* (Illinois Arts Council Fellowship for book of the musical composed by James Lucas). *Safe Harbor,* the drama based on a family trying to survive the Nazi occupation of Salonika, Greece, was first produced at the Organic Theatre in Chicago by Red Hen, and annually since then in the Chicago

182

area and Los Angeles. *High Top Tower,* the television series Koch wrote, received an Emmy Award, while her other teleplays, including *The Price of Daffodils; Flying Feathers; Baby, You're Okay; The Thirty-Six* and *Today I Am a Person* were broadcast and honored. Koch is also the author of ten nonfiction books, including *Good Parents for Hard Times,* with Dr. Linda Nancy Freeman, and the *Families in Touch Series.*

Cohen received accolades for the off-Broadway play, *Shlemiel the First,* written with Isaac Bashevis Singer, and for a cross-country tour of her play with music, *Molly Picon's Return Engagement. The Ladies' Locker Room,* Cohen's prize-winning comedy about disability, was widely produced and published in her acclaimed anthology of contemporary plays by Jewish American women, *Making a Scene.* She continued to write praiseworthy scholarly books, including *Cynthia Ozick's Comic Art: From Levity to Liturgy* and *Saul Bellow's Enigmatic Laughter.* She edited and contributed to such highly respected books as *Comic Relief, Jewish Wry,* and *From Hester Street to Hollywood.* She continues to serve as general editor of the SUNY Press Series on Modern Jewish Literature and Culture and the Wayne State Press Series on Humor in Life and Letters.

In terms of theater, Joanne and Sarah have realized their greatest success with projects they wrote together. The musical *Sophie, Totie & Belle,* about a fictional meeting of the late, great entertainers Sophie Tucker, Totie Fields and Belle Barth, has had more than a dozen productions, including off-Broadway, Philadelphia, Miami Beach, Boca Raton, Sarasota and Tampa, Florida. Adaptations with Saul Bellow's approval of his classic short stories "The Old System" and "A Silver Dish" premiered in 1995 as *Saul Bellow's Stories on Stage* in Albany and Boston and were performed for the San Diego Barbra Streisand Festival with Harold Gould in the lead roles. The Cohen and Koch drama about the person Ben Gurion called "the most remarkable Jewish woman of the twentieth century," *Henrietta Szold: Woman of Valor,* has toured widely from New York to Florida and in the Midwest. Cohen and Koch received a grant from the Hadassah International Research Institute on Jewish Women at Brandeis University to contribute to a documentary on Henrietta Szold. The newest products of the Koch-Cohen collaboration are the musicals *Danny Kaye: Supreme Court Jester,* with many original songs by Mark Elliott, and *American Klezmer,* with music by Ilya Levinson and lyrics by Owen Kalt. Developed at Theatre Building Chicago's Stages '04 Festival and produced in 2006 by West Coast Jewish Theatre in Hollywood, California, *American Klezmer* is currently touring the country.

Soul Sisters, their musical about an African American singer and a Jewish American singer trying to sustain sixties idealism, was launched in 1997 with workshops at the Jewish Theater Group of the Berkshires, where Julian Bond, instrumental in the civil rights struggle, provided positive feedback, encouraging the playwrights to take what he considered an important musical drama to universities around the country. Koch and Cohen eventually brought *Soul Sisters* to twenty-eight universities and communities.

Both playwrights are also teachers of writing and literature. Joanne Koch is Professor of English and director of the graduate writing program at National-Louis University as well as a frequent lecturer in Screenwriting at Columbia College Chicago. Sarah Blacher Cohen has been Professor of English at the University at Albany, State University of New York, for thirty-two years. Koch and Cohen discussed *Soul Sisters* with African American students and Jewish students in their classes who argued about which Holocaust was worse—the genocide of European Jews or the genocide of Africans and African Americans through slavery and ongoing racism. The playwrights were old enough to know about an earlier period when Jews and Blacks had marched arm in arm, yet young enough to believe music and theater might be a way to open a dialogue again. In the words of their *Soul Sisters'* characters, "We would be fools to think we could quickly change bad feelings existing for many years. But music . . . music gives us a second chance at life."

Music Permissions for Soul Sisters

"Them There Eyes," by Maceo Pinkar, William Tracy, and Doris Taub, © 1930 by Bourne Co. Copyright renewed. All rights reserved. International Copyright Secured.

"God Bless the Child," by Billie Holiday and Arthur Herzog, Jr., © 1941 by Edward B. Marks Music Company. Copyright renewed. Used by permission. All rights reserved.

"Miss Otis Regrets," by Cole Porter, © 1934 Warner Brothers Inc. (Renewed). All Rights Reserved. Used by permission. Warner Bros. Publications U.S. Inc., Miami, Florida 33014.

"Strange Fruit," words and music by Lewis Allan, © 1939 (Renewed) by Music Sales Corporation. (ASCAP) International Copyright Secured. All rights reserved. Reprinted by permission.

"Joy to the World," words and music by Hoyt Axton, © 1970 by Irving Music, Inc. (BMI) International Copyright Secured. All rights reserved. Reprinted by permission.

"Talk Is Cheap," words and music by Mark Elliott, © 1997 by Mark Elliott. Written for the play *Soul Sisters* by Joanne Koch and Sarah Blacher Cohen. Used by permission.

Soul Sisters

Cast of Characters

SANDRA LANGLEY, a popular young Jewish American singer, twenty-seven, specializing in African American songs.

CLEO WILLIAMS, a newcomer to Chicago, twenty-four, African American, working as a waitress to support herself and her son, Robbie.

STANLEY KLEIN, Sandra Langley's Manager, forty.

EMCEES, NEWSCASTER, male offstage or recorded voices.

Slides, period music and a few simple props are used to convey the change of time and place. Music of the late sixties underscores slides of the Civil Rights struggle to include a Black girl in a Birmingham hospital after the church bombing, March on Selma, Dr. Martin Luther King Jr., and Abraham Heschel marching arm in arm, King's speech at the Lincoln Memorial, President Kennedy, then President Johnson, relating to other scenes of mid-sixties Civil Rights protests.

Act 1

Scene 1: *A Jazz club in Chicago, August, 1967. SANDRA LANGLEY, in spangled evening gown, sits ringside. CLEO WILLIAMS, in a short cocktail waitress uniform, sets down an empty tray and is about to pull up a chair. Piano music in the background.*

SANDRA: Psst. Honey.

CLEO: Me?

SANDRA: I am starving. Is there any way I can get some food when the set is over?

CLEO: Actually, I'm through, but I heard Sandra Langley was going to sing.

SANDRA: If you can have two eggs over easy and some buttered toast ready for me after she sings, I'll have fifty dollars ready for you.

CLEO: For fifty dollars, I'd make it myself, but the kitchen's closed. I can find you a ham sandwich.

SANDRA: Fine, only don't tell my mother about the ham. *(Knocking back a drink.)* And don't tell my manager about the double scotch.

EMCEE VOICE: Ladies and Gentlemen—Tonight—Chicago's Club Alabam has a special treat. Direct from her late show at the Blue Note, the singer whose jazz hits are causing a sensation!—Miss Sandra Langley!

186

SANDRA: I'm on.

CLEO: You're Sandra? *(SANDRA nods yes. CLEO goes off to get the order.)*

SANDRA: *(sings "Them There Eyes" by Maceo Pinkar, William Tracy and Doris Taub)*

> I fell in love with you
> First time I looked into
> Them there eyes.
> You got a certain little
> Cute way of flirtin' with
> Them there eyes.
> They make me feel happy
> They make me feel blue
> No stallin', I'm fallin'
> Going in a big way for sweet little you
> My heart is jumpin'
> You sure started somethin'
> With them eyes.
> You'd better look out
> Watch them if you're wise
> They sparkle
> They bubble
> They're gonna get you in a whole lot of trouble
> Them there eyes.

CLEO: *(spoken as she watches from the sidelines.)* Sandra Langley!

SANDRA: Thank you. Thank you very much. Billie Holiday was not just a great song stylist, but also a composer. Tonight I'd like to do a song she wrote herself—"God Bless the Child." While I sing this, think of all God's children now trying to go to school together—from Boston to Birmingham. *(SANDRA sings "God Bless the Child," by Billie Holiday and Arthur Herzog Jr.)*

> Them that's got shall get.
> Them that's not shall lose.
> So the Bible says
> And it still is news.
> Mama may have
> Papa may have
> But God bless the child
> That's got his own
> That's got his own.
> Yes the strong gets more
> While the weak ones pay.
> Empty pockets don't
> Ever make the grade.

Mama may have
Papa may have
But God bless the child
That's got his own
That's got his own.
Money—you've got lots of friends
Crowding round the door.
When your gold and spending ends
They don't come no more.
Rich relations give crusts of bread and such.
You can have yourself
But don't take too much.
Mama may have
Papa may have
But God bless the child
That's got his own.
That's got his own.

SANDRA: Thank you. To help all our children, please, come to the benefit at the amphitheater next month. I'll be there with Harry Belafonte on one side, Sidney Poitier on the other, and Dr. Martin Luther King Jr., leading the way. See you there. (*SANDRA waves to audience, goes to her table.*)

EMCEE VOICE: Sandra Langley everyone. Goodnight—or rather, good morning. (*Applause.*)

CLEO: (*Rushing in with her plate of food and bottle of scotch.*) One ham, (*Dropping her voice to a whisper.*) ham sandwich, one bottle of scotch.

SANDRA: (*Pulls out a hundred dollar bill.*) You earned this.

CLEO: A hundred dollars.

SANDRA: (*Eating.*) Did you like the songs?

CLEO: I've heard you on the radio, but I thought you were . . . Are you sure there's no African blood running through your veins?

SANDRA: (*Draining the drink.*) I feel a lot more connection to Billie Holiday than I ever did to Golda Meir.

CLEO: Billie was always my idol. Billie and Mahalia. (*Singing.*) "He's got the whole world in his hands. He's got the whole, wide world . . ."

SANDRA & CLEO: (*Singing.*) "in His hands. He's got the whole world in his hands. He's got the whole world in his hands."

SANDRA: How would you like a job—uh . . . ?

CLEO: Cleo, Cleo Williams. What kind of a job?

SANDRA: I need a personal assistant.

CLEO: That's not a maid is it? When I left South Carolina I swore I'd take any work I could get—except for that.

SANDRA: I need a secretary, someone who likes music, who could maybe go over lyrics with me, set up recording dates, keep the calendar straight. I'll pay twice what you get here.

CLEO: I like music, but I didn't go to college.

SANDRA: That's OK—I didn't finish. Left in my sophomore year. My mother had a fit.

CLEO: I left in my junior year of high school. I had Robby. My baby's eight now.

SANDRA: Then you better get home. Here's our office number and address—and my home number. Stanley gets there early, but I don't have to be there until noon—lunch with some record mogul. Call if I'm not there by quarter to.

CLEO: You mean you want me to start tomorrow?

SANDRA: Why not?

CLEO: Well, doesn't your manager have to interview me? What if he doesn't like me?

SANDRA: Stanley—oh he'll like you, especially when I tell him I'm paying your salary. Now the first thing we've got to do is to get Stanley to cough up a few more bucks for a new back up group. The piano is fine, but I want a different sound for the next recording session—not that old 50's stuff—something post-Beatles, post-Stones, but still mellow. And I want a mixed group—at least one Black man in the bunch.

CLEO: I'll let *you* tell him about that.

SANDRA: Now Cleo—if you're going to represent me, you've got to learn from your soul sisters. You gotta demand that good ole RESPECT. *R-E-S-P-E-C-T. That's what I'm gonna get for me.* Come on, Cleo. *R-E-S-P-E-C-T. That's what I'm gonna get for me.* (CLEO *joins reluctantly.*) Shout out Cleo!

CLEO: *R-E-S-P-E-C-T. That's what I'm gonna get for me.*

SANDRA: A little louder, now...

SANDRA & CLEO: *R-E-S-P-E-C-T. That's what I'm gonna get for me.*

SANDRA: Now you're talking. *(Gulping down her scotch.)* You come to work for me, I'm gonna make you a stand up lady.

CLEO: *(Closing the top of the scotch bottle.)* Remember to be there by noon.

SANDRA: *(Unscrewing the bottle and pouring herself another)* It's Stanley I want you to stand up to—not me.

CLEO: Well it's 3 A.M. already.

SANDRA: That's when the guys come to jam at the old Club Alabam.

CLEO: *(Closing the top of the scotch bottle.)* I just don't want you to have too much of that nasty stuff.

SANDRA: Go home and fuss over Bobby—
CLEO: Robby.
SANDRA: Robby.
SANDRA: Go on. I'm gonna sing with the guys for awhile. (*SANDRA downs another drink, as CLEO looks disapprovingly.*)
SANDRA: Go on now. See you tomorrow. (*Jazz music in the background.*)
CLEO: Thank you, Sandra. I just can't believe it.

(*SANDRA goes off scat singing. CLEO, clutching her money, walks downstage, as if talking to her young son, ROBBY, in amazement.*)

CLEO: Robby. I'm gonna start a new job—a new life. We got lucky, honey—a white woman who loves Black folks, even more than her own. You just dream on, my big boy, while I sing Grandmother's Lullaby. (*CLEO sings a bit of the folk song, "All the pretty horses.*) "Hushabye. Don't you cry. Go to sleep my little baby. When you wake, we shall take, all the pretty little horses. Dappled and grey, we'll ride away, all the pretty horses.*"

Scene 2: *One month later, a recording studio in Chicago. STANLEY, a balding man in his forties, paces while CLEO takes notes.*

STANLEY: Cleo, we gotta help Sandra decide which numbers to do for the Civil Rights Benefit. She's been *hocking me a chainik* for days now. "Which would Dr. King like? Which would Stokely like? I tell her, "Don't make such a *tzimmes* about it. We'll find the poifect songs."
CLEO: I hope her *hocking* won't turn into a bad cough . . .
STANLEY: No, it just means she's been hitting my tea kettle and making a carrot stew.
CLEO: (*Puzzled.*) Oh . . . as long as it's nothing serious.
STANLEY: No, no, everything will be copascetic, especially with you on board. Belafonte's going to do "We Shall Overcome" and "Jamaica Farewell." (*STANLEY imitates Belafonte with a calypso refrain and dance step.*) "Down the way where the nights are gay and the sun shines brightly on the mountain tops." Then I figure Sandra could do one from the "Old Spirituals in New Clothes" album. (*Singing in Paul Robeson style.*) "Go down, Moses, way down in Egypt's land—*"
CLEO: Stanley, who's performing in this concert—you or Sandra?
STANLEY: You're right. You're right. Always wanted to be a singer. Tried out for *South Pacific.* (*Singing in an exaggerated manner.*) "Some enchanted evening . . ." But they gave the part to Ezio Pinza. Go figure. They had a thing for Italians.
CLEO: (*Flipping the page of her notebook.*) Sandra has asked a new guy in on the recording session—Kelvin.
STANLEY: Yeah, I noticed. What's wrong with Harry? He toots his own horn pretty good.

CLEO: He's great. He just needs a little help. She wanted a more, you know, happening sound—more sixties going into seventies.

STANLEY: A happening sound—that's a good one. Why can't she be on time? Now that would be a happening! Harry and the guys have been here for hours. Before you know it, we'll be going into overtime and she—

CLEO: You know how it is. She has to unwind after a show—she's got to—what we call—cool out.

STANLEY: Unwind, cool out . . . That's what I call a nice way of saying she's going to be hung over again. She gets so fogged up she can't tell the difference between a bagel and a bialy.

CLEO: Well . . . I have a pretty good idea of what she wants. Say she's doing "Miss Otis Regrets." I noticed Harry plays a bunch of runs during the bridge. Well, she'd like a little drum and maybe electric guitar with the piano.

STANLEY: That's gonna cost a fortune.

CLEO: No, Stan—Kelvin can handle it. I heard him on the South Side. Kelvin plays electric guitar as good as Jimi Hendrix. Thanks for giving him a chance. See it works like this . . . .

CLEO: *(Singing "Miss Otis Regrets" by Cole Porter.) "Miss Otis regrets she's unable to lunch today, madame. (Speaking.)* Guitar riff in there, maybe. *(Singing.) Oh Miss Otis regrets she's unable to lunch today. (Speaking.)* Repeat the riff . . . .*(Singing.) She is sorry to be delayed, but last night down in lover's lane she strayed, Madame. Miss Otis regrets she's unable to lunch today." (Speaking.)* Then maybe a nice soft drum brush comin' in on the last line . . .

STANLEY: Where'd you learn to sing like that?

CLEO: Come on, Stanley.

STANLEY: I mean it. You've got a helluva voice.

CLEO: Oh, it's nothing. Been singing in Bethany Baptist since I was five. But now, with Robby and moving to Chicago, I can't even find time for praying. Forget choir practice.

(SANDRA appears, hung over, irritable, wearing dark glasses, an unbuttoned coat, a sixties tunic and pants with an attractive pendant.)

CLEO: Hi Sandra. *(CLEO automatically helps SANDRA off with her coat and rushes to get her coffee.)* I was explaining to Stanley about the back-up idea.

STANLEY: I'll work on it. Maybe we can try it out at the Bonds for Israel benefit.

SANDRA: I didn't agree to that.

STANLEY: I thought for sure you'd say yes. Golda Meir is speaking.

SANDRA: I have a problem with Israel. You know that, Stanley.

STANLEY: How's it going to look if they have Sammy Davis Junior and not you?

SANDRA: I don't care what Sammy does—or Marilyn Monroe or Elizabeth Taylor. They can all wear golden *chais* as big as Miami Beach for all I care. Organized religion is not for me. I do benefits for Civil Rights—that's it. (STANLEY *looks at* CLEO *who shrugs.*)

CLEO: I've been trying to talk her into it, but—

STANLEY: It doesn't have to be an Israeli song. Couldn't you just sing "Go Down Moses"—to plug the new album?

SANDRA: I care about what slavery did to the U.S.—not what happened in Egypt three thousand years ago.

STANLEY: How about what happened a few years ago in Europe? How about the deaths of six million in—

SANDRA: There are 25 million black people in the U.S.—millions of them going through hell while we stand by. That's my cause. Now let's get going. (SANDRA *sips, then spits out her coffee.*) Cleo this coffee is lousy. Make a fresh pot. (CLEO *starts to go.*) No, I want you to be on book. Make sure I don't screw up the lyrics. (*To* STANLEY.) "Down by the Riverside" will come first. And we use the new guy and the new arrangement. I don't want to sound like Pete Seeger for Chrissake. I want to cut a single of "Miss Otis"—maybe "Sweet Georgia Brown" on the flip side.

STANLEY: If we don't get started, there won't be enough money for a single.

(SANDRA *puts on headphones and goes into an area as if going into a soundproof booth.* CLEO *goes to a table with a stack of sheet music. As the music the spiritual, "Down by the Riverside," starts,* CLEO *sways to the familiar tune, her eyes closed. She obviously knows every note by heart.*)

SANDRA: All right, hit it guys. (*Singing.*)
> *I'm gonna lay down my sword and shield*
> *Down by the riverside*
> *Down by the riverside*
> *Down by the riverside*
> *I'm gonna lay down my sword and shield*
> *Down by the riverside*
> *Down by the riverside*

(CLEO *now starts singing along.*)

> *I ain't gonna study war no more*
> *I ain't gonna study war no more*
> *I ain't gonna study war no more*
> *I ain't gonna study war no more*

> *I ain't gonna study war no more*
> *I ain't gonna study war no more.*

(SANDRA sings with headphones as if in soundproof booth and CLEO puts down the music and sings below.)

> *I'm gonna put on my golden shoes*
> *Down by the riverside*
> *Down by the riverside*
> *Down by the riverside*
> *I'm gonna put on my golden shoes*
> *Down by the—*

CLEO: *(Suddenly realizing SANDRA's mistake, signaling to her)* Long white robe.

SANDRA: *(Taking off her headphones.)* What?

CLEO: Long, white robe—not golden shoes.

SANDRA: Well, shit. *(Motioning to stop the accompaniment.)* Why didn't you tell me sooner?

CLEO: I got into it myself.

SANDRA: *I'm* supposed to get into it. You're supposed to stay out there making sure it's right.

CLEO: *(Bristling.)* Yes ma'am.

SANDRA: Let's take that again.

CLEO: Long, white robe, *then* golden shoes.

SANDRA: Damn.

STANLEY: The guys are due to go on lunch break soon, anyway. When we come back, we'll have—

SANDRA: Why not work straight through? I'm on a roll.

STANLEY: We'll be on overtime.

SANDRA: Who cares? "Sandra sings Billie and Ella" is going platinum. We can afford it.

STANLEY: Okay. Just make sure you stick with coffee. *(Phone rings.)*

SANDRA: *(To STANLEY.)* You're sounding more like my mother every day.

CLEO: *(Answering.)* Yes Mrs. Langley, how are you? *(Listening.)* Okay, Rose.

SANDRA: I'm not here.

STANLEY: *(Going off stage and speaking to the musicians.)* We'll pick it up in ten fellas. Sandra wants to keep going.

CLEO: *(Covering phone.)* She called before. This time she says it's urgent.

SANDRA: It's always urgent. *(Picks up the phone.)* Mom, I already told you. I can't go to Israel. It conflicts with the Civil Rights Benefit. Family obligations? Oh Mom, please don't start. My work is my obligation. *(Motioning for CLEO to help her out.)*

CLEO: *(Loudly.)* Miss Langley—we're ready to start recording now!

SANDRA: They're calling me, Mom . . . I know it's hard for you to go alone, but . . . Aunt Esther will be there. *(Shouts at CLEO.)* Coming.

(Returns to phone.) Now Mom, have a good time. Say hello to all the cousins. *(She hangs up with relief.)*

CLEO: I guess your Mom really wants you to go with her.

SANDRA: Ever since Dad died, she wants me to be her full-time companion. She thinks I'm still ten years old.

CLEO: Moms always think you're ten . . . She sounds nice.

SANDRA: Don't let her fool you. She's the guilt queen. That's the one thing I got from religion—Jewish guilt.

CLEO: What about down-home-South-Carolina guilt? Honey, I'm still paying that off—sending money to my mama and grandmother Turnbull.

SANDRA: Lucky you have a grandma. Mine died in Poland—before I was born.

CLEO: You call having Minnie Lou Turnbull running your life "lucky"? Let me tell you, Mother Turnbull has more power at 75 than the whole N DOUBLE A C P put together. She raised me while Mama worked at white people's homes and she figures that gives her the right to order me around for the rest of my life. *(Catching herself.)* Oh, I'm sorry, I mean she worked for southern whites—not folks like you.

SANDRA: Hey Cleo—I'm not white—remember?

CLEO: Yeah, well, Mama worked while Mother Turnbull kept all six of us in line.

SANDRA: Did she work for any Jews there?

CLEO: One I remember, because she took a ham sandwich there once and they got upset.

SANDRA: Were there any poor Jews in Charleston, maybe living in the Black neighborhood?

CLEO: In Charleston Blacks were separate—period. No poor Jews there. I didn't know there were any poor Jews, anywhere.

SANDRA: Stanley used to be poor. His parents had to give him away during the Depression—put him in an orphanage when he was three. That's why he's so worried about money all the time.

STANLEY: *(Returning.)* The boys will work straight through. They love that golden overtime.

CLEO: I can't stay. My son is graduating from third grade. Getting an award for being best speller. You should see him with his little friend David Fine, practicing their words, so cute. He can even spell Mississippi backwards.

SANDRA: Why didn't you tell me?

CLEO: It's just third grade.

SANDRA: It's just your only son. What are you wearing?

CLEO: This.

SANDRA: Take this necklace. *(Gives her the necklace she's wearing.)*
CLEO: Oh no, I couldn't.
SANDRA: Take it. It's an Indian war shield. Supposed to bring luck.
CLEO: Thank you, Sandra.
STANLEY: *(Hands her several bills.)* You tell your son *Mazel Tov* from Uncle Stanley *(CLEO doesn't get it.)* Congratulations. And tell him pastrami spelled backward is I-M-A-R-T-S-A-P. Imartsap. See I'm not so dumb.
CLEO: No, you're not dumb. You're real sweet. You know, I've been worried because the other kids have Dads coming.
STANLEY: My Dad wasn't at my graduation. You tell—
CLEO: Robby.
STANLEY: Robby . . . I'll be there for his next graduation. *(CLEO smiles warmly.)*
SANDRA: Go on. Get out of here. *(CLEO gathers her things.)*
STANLEY: Let's pick it up from—
CLEO: Long white robe. *(Waiting to hear SANDRA get it right.)*
STANLEY: Long white robe. Let's try it again fellas.
SANDRA: *(Puts on headphones.)*

> *I'm gonna put on my long white robe*
> *Down by the riverside*
> *Down by the riverside*
> *Down by the riverside*
> *I'm gonna put on my golden shoes*
> *Down by the riverside*
> *And study war no more. (CLEO nods and leaves.)*

(Lights fade, as if the recording session is continuing.)

Scene 3: *A few days before Labor Day, 1967. STANLEY's office, Chicago. A tape recorder is on the desk, along with SANDRA's purse and coffee cups.*

SANDRA: Why don't we just try it with you weaving in and out in the background?
CLEO: You really mean it?
SANDRA: Sure, just for the hell of it. We'll tape it right here in the office. If we don't like it, we don't have to use it on the album.
CLEO: Okay. Great.
SANDRA: *(Sings the spiritual "Go Down Moses" as CLEO sings counterpoint.)* "Go down, Moses, way down in Egypt's land. Tell ole Pharaoh to let my people go."

(SANDRA and CLEO continue singing in the background as slides and sound bites emerge.)

VOICE OF H. RAP BROWN: *(Slide of H. Rap Brown of Black Panthers.)* All power to the people!

MARTIN LUTHER KING JR.'S VOICE: *(Slide of burning buildings.)* Violence has no place in our movement. Ours is a non-violent struggle for our rights, rights given to every American regardless of the color of his skin.

ANNOUNCER'S VOICE: *(Black people assembling in a meeting room.)* Chicago is hosting two great events this Labor Day weekend: the National Conference for New Politics and the great Civil Rights Benefit at the Amphitheater.

VOICE OF MILITANT BLACK LEADER: *(Slide of Militant Black Leader addressing conference.)* What does Black power mean to Black entertainers? It means we're not going to tolerate white performers doing our music, stealing our songs. It's still white people in blackface. Sandra Langley doesn't belong with Belafonte and Dr. King. Her people are a bunch of Zionists. Let her go and sing for them. Let MY people go. It's our Civil Rights rally. And we want our people singing our songs!

SANDRA & CLEO: *(Finishing with sweet harmony.)* "Go down, Moses, way down in Egypt's land. Tell ole Pharaoh to let my people go." *(SANDRA clicks off the tape recorder.)*

SANDRA: Not bad. We'll play it for Stanley, see what he thinks.

CLEO: You mean that?

SANDRA: Sure. I'd like a backup group on the next album.

CLEO: A Black backup group?

SANDRA: Why not? I'm just doing my bit. Lots of us are helping change things.

CLEO: Why do your people care so much about civil rights, the NAACP and all that?

SANDRA: Plenty of places Jews weren't free, I guess, so they feel they've got to fight stuff like segregation wherever it hits.

CLEO: But what about you?

SANDRA: It started with the music. I'm sitting in the middle of a white suburb, but the Blues . . . mmm . . . I always felt some connection to all that grief. Chubby, white, lonely little Sandra tunes into "Willow Weep for Me." Pretty soon I'm crying like a baby. Next thing ya know, I'm doin' gigs for civil rights.

CLEO: So that's how you wound up singing "Oh, Freedom." *(Collecting tape recorder and her notes.)* That's what I told the Committee you'd be doing for the benefit.

SANDRA: I can't decide if I should do that jazzy version with Kelvin and the guys or—

CLEO: *(Popping out a tape.)* Kelvin's good, but I'd do it simpler—the Bethany Baptist way.

SANDRA: Show me.

CLEO: I haven't sung it for a long—

SANDRA: Go ahead. It'll come to you.

CLEO: *(Singing the spiritual "Oh, Freedom.")* Oh, Freedom. Oh, Freedom. *(STANLEY comes in agitated, then stops for a moment, listens with surprise as CLEO sings.)*
> Oh, Freedom over me.
> And before I be a slave,
> They can lay me in my grave.
> And the Lord will spread that Freedom over me.

STANLEY: Incredible, Cleo.

SANDRA: *(To STANLEY.)* I've been thinking about forming a little backup vocal group—Cleo and maybe one more—

CLEO: Then you're serious about me doing backup?

SANDRA: Let Stanley listen to the tape. But yeah, I think we should try it.

STANLEY: What tape?

SANDRA: Now don't start thinking you're one of those Supremes and become another Diana Ross and leave me without an assistant.

STANLEY: What tape?

CLEO: I wouldn't. Ooo, wait 'till I tell Robby.

STANLEY: What tape?

SANDRA: Cleo and I made a little tape of "Go Down." *(Handing him the tape recorder.)* Give a listen.

STANLEY: Not now. We have a problem. The Benefit Committee wants an all Black roster of entertainers.

SANDRA: So where does that leave me?

STANLEY: They want you to . . . to bow out, gracefully.

SANDRA: Is that what they said?

STANLEY: They didn't say it. They didn't have to.

SANDRA: Oh sure, I suddenly discovered a previous engagement—right— after two months of advance publicity.

STANLEY: They don't want it to look as if they're dropping you, because you're white.

SANDRA: I was Black enough to sing every song Billie Holiday ever recorded. Black enough to raise over a million for the March on Selma. Black enough to bail out protestors from Birmingham jails. What right do they have to throw me out now? *(She pours scotch from a flask in her purse into her coffee cup and takes a drink.)*

STANLEY: *(To CLEO.)* Maybe you can reason with her.

CLEO: Try to understand, Sandra . . . They have to be on their own. We're not ungrateful, but we . . . they have to be . . . you know, independent. It's kind of like in the Bible. We got to find our own leaders to take us into the promised land.

SANDRA: That's bullshit! I'm not trying to keep anyone from the promised land, goddammit. I'm trying to help them get there.

CLEO: They don't want help. They have to do it on their own.

STANLEY: Cleo understands. Listen to her. We could issue a press release.

CLEO: Sure. A conflicting engagement—in . . . L.A. maybe?

SANDRA: *(Sarcastically.)* Why not Watts?

STANLEY: We could still book you at the Fairmont in Frisco. They've been dying to have you there.

SANDRA: Yeah, sure. I'll see you tomorrow—late, very late. *(Grabbing her things.)* I helped with the voter registrations, the funerals for Goodman, Schwerner, Chaney. Christ, we gave our blood. What more do they want! *(CLEO is torn and uncomfortable. SANDRA storms out of the room.)*

CLEO: What are you going to do?

STANLEY: Have you ever sung professionally?

CLEO: I soloed at church, a few weddings, parties. Sang Billie Holiday's songs—nothing like Sandra—but people said it was good. Listen to the tape we made. I do the back up.

STANLEY: Why don't we make one with just you?

CLEO: Now?

STANLEY: I need to go back to the Committee with a replacement. To tell you the truth, I don't have a Black performer to give them. Now just sing something into the tape recorder. It's not poifect, but it will give them an idea. What can you do?

CLEO: Maybe one of Billie's early hits—"Body and Soul," "Strange Fruit," "Willow Weep for Me."

STANLEY: "Strange Fruit"—yeah, why not. It's about the only one Sandra hasn't recorded. If you can sing a song about a lynching, it shows you've got guts. The committee might go for that. *(Dropping a new tape in the tape recorder.)* Let's do it.

CLEO: *(Singing "Strange Fruit" by Lewis Allan.)*
> Southern trees bear a strange fruit
> Blood on the leaves and blood at the root
> Black bodies swinging in the southern breeze
> Strange fruit hanging from the poplar trees.
> Pastoral scene of the gallant South
> The bulging eyes and the twisted mouth
> Scent of magnolia sweet and fresh
> Then the sudden smell of burning flesh.
> Here is a fruit for the crows to pluck
> For the rain to gather
> For the wind to suck
> For the sun to rot
> For the tree to drop
> Here is a strange and bitter crop.

(STANLEY stares silently for a beat. He clicks off the tape recorder.)

CLEO: How was it?

STANLEY: You have no idea what you've got, do you? I'm going to the Committee with this tape. I'll tell them Sandra was needed in San Francisco—and slip you in as a replacement.

CLEO: I feel like Judas . . . Oh my God, I'm sorry.

STANLEY: I don't worry too much about words. I look for heart. And you've got it.

CLEO: But Sandra gave me my only chance. I was just a waitress at Club Alabam.

STANLEY: That doesn't mean you were supposed to stay a waitress.

CLEO: She wanted to be there with Belafonte and Dr. King. She's done more for my own people than I have—much more. It's her spot.

STANLEY: Not any more. Someone's got to take her place—why not you? You won't get star billing, but it would be a great debut. This could launch your career.

CLEO: That's why I feel so awful. I want it so bad. And I don't want to want it.

STANLEY: Sandra would do it, if the tables were turned.

CLEO: What if the Benefit Committee doesn't like my voice?

STANLEY: That's impossible. Besides, they know they're putting Sandra in a terrible spot. They want to say yes to me.

CLEO: It seems so unfair. She works to give Black women a chance and it's her chance I wind up taking.

STANLEY: There's an old saying I've adapted from a very wise man named Hillel. "If I am only for myself, who am I? But if I am not for myself, who will be for me—and if not now—when?"

Scene 4: *The day before the Civil Rights Benefit.* STANLEY'*s office.* SANDRA *storms in carrying a copy of* Variety.

SANDRA: Cleo! . . . Cleo!

CLEO: *(Offstage.)* I'm bringing the coffee. Hold on! *(She comes in with coffee.)*

SANDRA: *(Adding scotch to coffee from a flask.)* Have you seen the trades this morning?

CLEO: Not yet. I—

SANDRA: *(Reading from the gossip column.)* "Sandra Langley has suddenly pulled out of the Chicago Civil Rights Gala. She will be replaced by a Black newcomer—Miss Langley's own secretary with no singing experience, a Miss Cleo Williams. Sandra's bad fortune could be Cleo's lucky break." *(*SANDRA *slaps the paper down.)*

CLEO: I told Stanley—

SANDRA: Oh sure, you begged him not to give you the break.

CLEO: I didn't want to take your spot.

SANDRA: *(Using an exaggerated Black accent.)* I'm just a church singer, a little colored girl from the choir. "I don't know nothin' 'bout birthin' babies" *(Dropping accent.)*—or knifing someone in the back.

CLEO: Ever since you took me out of Club Alabam, I've been kissing the ground you walk on. And you've been going on about freedom, civil rights—talking about Billie and Ella—and me—as soul sisters—claiming you want to . . . you want to help us—help me—to give me a leg up.

SANDRA: Not when you're stepping on my back to get to the top. *(SANDRA sips the coffee, spits it back in the cup.)* This coffee stinks.

CLEO: Is that why you had to put so much gin in it?

SANDRA: You're fired!

CLEO: Sandra don't do this. You'll regret it tomorrow. I want to go on working for you. This little gig won't change anything. You'll still be the star.

SANDRA: Not for long. Once you're in the spotlight—it's like a fix. First a little, then more and more. Pretty soon, you'll want it all the time— all for yourself.

CLEO: All I want is enough money to support my Robby. If people like my singing, that's a bonus.

SANDRA: Don't give me your fake modesty.

CLEO: Sure, I'm flattered they asked me for the gala. But I know galas don't happen very often. I need a secure job with you. Things will be the same as before.

SANDRA: Everything has changed already. You worked it, honey, so I'm out and you're in. Go ahead, goddammit. Get out. Before you take my accompanist and my arrangements. Get out!

(CLEO gathers her things in disbelief and flees.)

Scene 5: *1967. Civil Rights Benefit*

VOICE OF ANNOUNCER: And now . . . to close our incredible gala . . . a brand new singer, Cleo Williams, to give us a song that's been lifting our spirits since they took us from Africa, singing the way she sang it at the Bethany Baptist Church in her home town of Charleston, South Carolina.

CLEO: *(Appears in a spotlight in a plain white dress. She's uneasy at first, as she sings.)*
  Oh, Freedom, Oh, Freedom
  Oh Freedom over me
  And before I be a slave
  They can lay me in my grave
  And the Lord will spread freedom over me.

CLEO: *(Speaking to the audience.)* I'm really not accustomed to singing by myself. I used to sing in a church choir. So please join me now for one more chorus. *(Singing.)*

Oh, Freedom, Oh, Freedom
Oh, Freedom over me
And before I be a slave
They can lay me in my grave
And the Lord will spread Freedom over me.

(Ending with an incredible drawn out gospel riff on the word Freedom)

Freedom. Freedom. I said Freeeeeeeeeeeeeeeedom. (Thunderous applause.)

(Crossfade to opposite side of the stage where SANDRA *is alone, drinking and listening to* CLEO's *performance on the radio.)*

SANDRA: *(Talking to the radio, after applause.)* You're good. *(Softly.)* Did you have to be so damn good? *(Louder, to radio.)* I said, "Did you have to be so good?"

Scene 6: *1972. A swanky New York nightclub. The backstage area. Underscore "Joy to the World," as if it is just concluding.*

VOICE OF PLAZA EMCEE: Let's give a big hand to the new recording sensation, Miss Cleo Williams, in her final appearance at the Plaza. She'll be back after Mort Sahl reads his newspaper version of the Watergate break-in.

*(*STANLEY *welcomes* CLEO *as she finishes the set, holding a check out to her.* CLEO *wears a chic 70's miniskirt and elegant boots.)*

STANLEY: Terrific Cleo. The next set will be even better. The later you perform on a Saturday night in New York, the bigger the crowds. They love you.

CLEO: They love Mother Turnbull. That's who they love. I didn't know she was hiding there in me. Was I too . . . I don't know . . . too bold?

STANLEY: *(Handing her the check.)* Welcome to the seventies, Cleo, where men are men and women are men. Anyway, here's something from the management that would make Mother Turnbull proud.

CLEO: *(Staring at the size of the check.)* Stanley . . . oh my Lord.! This must be a mistake.

STANLEY: It's no mistake. You deserve it. "Soul for the Seventies" just went double platinum. I've got concerts booked until 1980. I even have you set up for a date in Central Park. You have arrived!

CLEO: When Robby hits sixteen, I'm gonna get him the biggest, flashiest Cadillac—no, no maybe a Mercedes. That's classier, right. Maybe a red one, a two-seater. Oh yes.

STANLEY: Whoa! Hold on. The boy hasn't even got his license. You just drove him to David's Bar Mitzvah.

CLEO: He even wore one of those little black beanies—so cute.

STANLEY: It's great they're still friends.

CLEO: The best. David and Rob . . . now that they're thirteen, all they talk about is cars. Stanley, don't *hock me a chainik* and don't make a *tzimmis* . . . He'll be a good driver. He's good at everything.

STANLEY: Start him off with a used car, then he can—

CLEO: Now you listen to me. That boy has suffered with me through all the hard times. He's been the latchkey kid, the one who couldn't afford the fancy gym shoes. Now he's gonna enjoy the good times. The day he hits sixteen he's gonna own the coolest, brightest car he could ever dream of. And I'm gonna say, "Happy Birthday, Rob. Happy Birthday."

STANLEY: All right, all right.

CLEO: And you send part of this check to Sandra.

STANLEY: I tried before. You know she won't take it.

CLEO: The trades say she's drinking, big time.

STANLEY: She's lost. Her mother died a few weeks ago. Ever since . . . she's just hangin' on by her fingernails—small clubs and big drinks.

CLEO: I didn't know about her mother.

STANLEY: I've been pulling strings behind the scenes just to get her a few bookings. But once I book her, nobody wants her back again.

CLEO: Where is she singing now?

STANLEY: *(Making a face.)* Milton's Lounge.

CLEO: Ooo. She really has hit bottom.

STANLEY: The only place that would take her. I'm going over there just to give her a little moral support.

CLEO: After I finish this set, I'll come by, try to talk to her. Maybe she'll apologize.

STANLEY: Yeah, like Nixon is goin' to apologize for Watergate.

CLEO: She gave me a start, Stan. I wouldn't have any of this if she hadn't—

STANLEY: That doesn't mean you have to be indebted to her for the rest of your life.

CLEO: Yes it does. She's like Mother Turnbull. She's going to make me pay my dues. But you know something Stanley. I can afford them now.

Scene 7: *Same night, two hours later. A split scene—the Plaza area remains on one side of the stage, while lights come up on the other side of the stage— a tacky makeshift dressing room area of Milton's Lounge where* SANDRA *drinks and tries to recall words for "Joy to the World." This effort is interrupted with glances at a box of mementos left by her mother.*

SANDRA: *"Joy to the world, all the boys and girls . . ."* Why Mom? Why couldn't you tell me before? *"Joy to the fishes in the deep blue see, Joy to you and. . . ."* I knew there was something, something you and Dad were hiding. But I,

ist who IS Soul for the Seventies. Miss Cleo Williams! Let's give her a big New York City welcome!

CLEO: Thank you, thank you everyone. *(Sniffing the air.)* We've got lots of folks on the grass tonight, don't we? Whew. *(She weaves around a bit as if high on pot.)* Some people get high—on grass, on booze, because they're shy. Now, you're not gonna believe this, but I used to be awfully shy... No, it's true, I always got pushed around—especially by men. Honey, I had no respect. But then, I started getting smart. I started rememberin' what my Grandmother Minnie Lou Trumbull used to say. I'd come back from being with my man and she'd say, *(CLEO puts hands on hips, like grandma.)* "Well?"

I'd say, "What do you mean, Grandmother?"

"I mean, did he propose?"

I'd say, "No, we just talked."

And she'd say, "Did he give you a ring?"

I'd say, "No, we just talked." And she'd say, "How many times I have to tell you, girl—Girl, you gotta make that man of yours come across. You gotta lay down the law. Either he delivers or you show him the door!"

(CLEO speaking with music under.) So I listened to my Grandmother Minnie. And the very next time I saw my man, before he sweetened me up with his pretty words and his honey kisses, I told him what grandmother told me.

(CLEO sings "Talk Is Cheap" by Mark Elliott.)

> *You say you want my love and my devotion—*
> *You say you want me to give my heart to you.*
> *You say your love for me is like an ocean,*
> *But baby, how do I know that it's true?*
> *You say you love me.*
> *You say you need me.*
> *You say we'll never be apart.*
> *You say you want me*
> *But you'll say anything*
> *To win this woman's heart.*
> *You say you'd climb the highest mountain.*
> *Well, you just go do that, then we'll see*
> *But 'til then I know talk is cheap—*
> *Yes, I know that talk is cheap.*
> *I learned the hard way, talk is cheap*
> *Until you prove it to me.*
> *You say I'm special.*

You say I'm perfect,
That I'm the only one for you.
You say I'm gorgeous,
But I don't need your words
To tell me that is true.
You say you'd swim the deepest river
Just to spend an hour or two with me
But don't you know that talk is cheap.
Yes, I know that talk is cheap
My Mama told me talk is cheap
Until you prove it to me.
I don't believe a thing I hear, and only half of what I see.
Any man that takes me on ain't gonna find a fool in me.
But if you stand behind the words you say, I'll stand beside you, come
    what may.
Actions speak louder than words, Yeah, Yeah, Yeah.
Actions speak louder than words!
You say you love me
You say you need me
You say you'll always be my man.
You say you need me,
And that you want me to love you
Like you know this woman can
You say you'd cross the burning desert
Just to put your lovin' arms 'round me
Well, let me tell you
Talk is cheap
I know you know that talk is cheap
Grandma told me talk is cheap
Oh I can tell you, talk is cheap
Until you prove it,
Until you prove it,
Until you prove it to me!

(Audience claps wildly as CLEO *bows and blows kisses.)*

Thank you. Thank you.

Scene 2: *Fall of 1978. A room in a rehabilitation clinic. A suitcase is opened on the bed.* SANDRA *puts a few last items in the suitcase. She stops to hold the box of mementos from her mother.* STANLEY *puts a tape in his tape recorder.*

STANLEY: They won't mind if I play a little music here, will they?

SANDRA: It's a rehab clinic, Stanley—not a morgue. *(*STANLEY *starts the tape of Klezmer music.)*

STANLEY: Everyone's suddenly into their roots. A few years ago, I couldn't give this stuff away. Now Klezmer is big. It's kinda Jewish jazz. Makes you want to dance, doesn't it?

(He dances for a minute in Hasidic fashion.)

SANDRA: *(With a wry smile.)* Well, it's a little bouncy for someone just climbing out of her own private hell.

STANLEY: *(He turns the music off.)* The important thing is, you're clean, Sandra. No more booze. No more late night fights with the management. I can book you again.

SANDRA: I want to show you something, Stan. *(SANDRA removes from the memento box a soiled yellow star made from fabric, a crumpled piece of paper and a letter.)* These are the heirlooms. The ones that matter to me now. . . . I thought Mom and Dad were superficial people—with no grasp of what it meant to fight for freedom. When Mom died, I was angry, angry they had kept their lives secret from me. Listen to this. *(She reads the letter.)* "Dear Sandra—We didn't want to burden you with our history. We wanted you to be a happy American girl. That's why we changed our names from Levitsky to Langley, so no one would persecute you. That's why we kept the tattooed numbers hidden, always long sleeves, even in summer. That's why we didn't teach you our beloved Yiddish." *(She sets aside the letter.)* They knew so well who they were, but they never wanted me to suffer from being a Jew. So I never really was one. They gave every penny they had to Israel. And I called them "Zionist imperialists."

STANLEY: At least you understand now.

SANDRA: How do I let them know? *(She smoothes out a crumpled piece of paper.)* . . . This little paper—they kept it all those years—it's a song, in Yiddish. But translated it means, "Never say that you are going your last way."

STANLEY: *"Zog nit keynmol az du geyst dem letstn veg."*

SANDRA: You know it?

STANLEY: The Holocaust resistance song—from the Warsaw Ghetto uprising. We sing it every year to remember the six million.

SANDRA: "We. . . ." I never felt part of that "we." I'm through with self-hatred, Stan. I'm through being the self-hating Jew. I'm not going to be a pale imitation of a Black woman, either. I don't know where that leaves me, but I'm going to find out.

STANLEY: Keep it up and you'll be turning into a real *mensch*.

SANDRA: *(Sings "Hymn of the Partisans" in Yiddish by Hirsh Glick, music Dmitri Pokrass, first with STANLEY's help, then in English on her own.)*
      Zog nit keyn mol az du gest dem letstn veg
      Khotsh himlen blayene farshteln bloye teg.

Kumen vet nokh undzer oysgebenkte sho—
S'vet a pyk ton undzer trot—mir zaynen do!
Never say that you are going your last way,
Though lead-filled skies above blot out the blue of day.
The hour for which we long will certainly appear,
The earth shall thunder 'neath our tread that we are here! (STANLEY
hugs her and takes her suitcase, walking ahead of her offstage. SANDRA
*puts the mementos back, adds in the Klezmer tape, clutches them. She
looks out.)* Mom—we're still here.

SANDRA: (*Alone on stage now, sings "We're Here," music and words by*
Rosalie Gerut.)

We're here. Our seeds are planted in the land
We're here, although they thought we'd die at their command
We're here and no one ever will erase our stand
We're here to love again to live, begin again to give, we're here.
We came, dry branches fallen from the tree
We came, not knowing how this strange new world would be
We came, with all the memories of the ones we left behind
We turned our lives away from death
We took another breath
And sang our songs
Once more we would be heard
We carry tears for many lost lives
We bear the names of those whose cries
Went up like smoke lost in the skies
Yet once more strong we join in song
And once again we will dance
The wedding music will enhance our lives
Our children will once more smile
And we will sing "Am Yisrael Chai!"
Lay di day lay di day di day
Lay di day lay di day di day
Lay di day lay di day di day
Lay di day lay di day di day
And once again we will dance
The wedding music will enhance our lives
Our children will once more smile
And we will sing, "Am Yisrael Chai!"
Lay di day lay di day di day
Lay di day lay di day di day
We are here!

Scene 3: *October, 1980. Reception area of a recording studio.* CLEO *is on
the phone.*

CLEO: Rob Williams—you are not going to tell me how to run my private life. Yes, I care about Wesley, but he doesn't understand my career. I'm seeing other men and he knows it. *(Listening, taking offense.)* Forget what the *National Inquirer* says, I did not—Let's talk about *your* private life. Have you got a date tonight? *(Disturbed by what he says.)* Rob Williams you listen to me. You're not marching against any Nazis. Let David march. That's *his* cause. A Black man has to be crazy to stick his neck out for some junior Hitler to—Don't you sass me now. . . . I do not sound like Grandmother Turnbull. Rob, don't you go—

OFFSTAGE VOICE: Miss Williams, the musicians are waiting . . .

CLEO: Coming . . . Rob—*(realizing Rob is no longer there, hangs up. She picks up some music and goes off.)*

Scene 3A: *October, 1980.* SANDRA'*s place.* SANDRA *wears a simple ethnic tunic and pants. She's rehearsing for* STANLEY *who has his chair turned to face her, as if he's in the audience and she's on stage.*

SANDRA: *(As if to an audience.)* I'm Sandra Levitsky. You may know me as Sandra Langley. I used to keep my own cupboards bare and fill them up with the artistic goods of my Black friends. When they laid claim to their own, my storehouse was empty.

STANLEY: You're actually going with "Levitsky"?

SANDRA: Yeah. That was their name.

STANLEY: I'm not crazy about all that cupboard stuff. Just say it straight.

SANDRA: *(Taking a breath, starting again.)* I'm Sandra Levitsky. I made my records as Sandra Langley. For a long time I didn't know who I was. *(*STANLEY *nods approval.)* I felt lost, utterly alone, like Jacob, sleeping on his pillow of stone . . . *(to* STANLEY*)* Here's my favorite part. . . .

*(*SANDRA *sings part of "Climbing That Ladder: The Dream and the Stone" by Doug Mishkin.)*

> . . . *We all return to the place of the dream and the stone*
> *To the space between life lived together and life lived alone*
> *Well, a dream and stone will do things to your life*
> *Show you your ladder to climb*
> *With your angels around you*
> *Your loved ones surround you*
> *Climbing one step at a time*
> *Climbing that ladder, your angels will wake you*
> *Climbing that ladder, your spirit will shake you*
> *Climbing that ladder, together they'll take you*
> *To a dream that only you can make true*
> *It's a dream that only you can make true.*

STANLEY: I like it. "Climbing That Ladder." "*The space between . . .*"
SANDRA: *"life lived together and life lived alone."*
STANLEY: Nice.
SANDRA: Now here I thought I'd say, "From then on, I was determined to find all kinds of Jewish music—music I didn't even know existed, like this Yiddish song introduced by Martha Schlamme."
STANLEY: Uh-oh.
SANDRA: *"Lo mir alleh fraylech zein."* It means: Let us all be merry, let us all sing for a tomorrow without need. (*SANDRA tries to sing the opening of the Yiddish song by A. Goldfaden.*)
> *Lo mir alleh fraylech zein. Lo mir alleh zingen.*
> *Lo mir alleh fraylech zein. Lo mir alleh zingen.*
> *Zingen far cholem*
> *Zingen far broit—*
STANLEY: That one needs a little work.
SANDRA: Why didn't they teach it me, Stan? Why didn't they tell me? We once got stuck in an elevator. Mom went to pieces. She started crying and calling out . . . I guess it was Yiddish. My father said, "Rose, we're not there anymore." I never knew what "there" was. But I knew "there" was a secret—some horrible secret—some big black hole. My shrink says I drank to fill up the hole. If I knew how it really was in the camps . . . I've been reading about it.
STANLEY: You can understand why they didn't tell you.
SANDRA: Yeah . . . I went to a children of survivors' meeting—they call them survivors now. Lots of kids had problems, mostly trying to find out why we couldn't suffer, why our folks were so damn protective.
STANLEY: At least you had folks . . . (*SANDRA acknowledges this.*) What are you doing to close the act?
SANDRA: A little surprise for you, Stan. (*As if to audience.*) "Lots of us once had to hide who we were to survive. Now, we can hold our heads up anywhere in the world, especially in Jerusalem (*Pronouncing it the Hebrew way*), Y'rushalayim."
STANLEY: Oy, Hebrew *and* Yiddish?
SANDRA: *"Jerusalem of gold, of copper and of light. Behold I am a harp for all your songs."*

(*Singing a few lines from "Jerusalem of Gold" by Naomi Shemer.*)
> *Y'rushalyim shel zahav*
> *V'shel n'choshet vshel or*
> *Halo l'chol shi'rayich ani kinor.*
> *Y'rushalyim shel zahav*
> *V'shel n'choshet vshel or*
> *Halo l'chol shi'rayich ani kinor*

(STANLEY claps slowly, with feeling.)

Scene 4: *1982. In the dressing room of the Apollo Theatre. CLEO is putting on an African headress. STANLEY, wearing a natty jacket and carrying flowers, knocks.*

CLEO: I need a few more minutes. *(Breaking into a smile as STANLEY enters.)* Stanley. *(She hugs him.)* I missed you. Africa was . . . I can't even express it.

STANLEY: Like the first time I went to Israel. I didn't expect to get so emotional, but when I walked up to the wailing wall, I . . . I started wailing.

CLEO: Yeah.

STANLEY: *(Gazing at her lovingly.)* You look fantastic.

CLEO: I have presents. *(She gives him two boxes.)* Genuine teak from Ghana, probably made by my great-great-great-great uncles. And some news—

STANLEY: You could work more African music into the act. The audiences love that Miriam Makeba tune.

CLEO: This is not about "Wimoweh." I found something in Africa. I found out I'm really in love . . .

STANLEY: *(Hopefully.)* Oh?

CLEO: With Wesley.

STANLEY: *(Covering his disappointment.)* Oh.

CLEO: He's just what I need. Something to balance off all the jazz and glitter.

STANLEY: Nothing like a teacher's salary to bring down the bottom line.

CLEO: I don't need money. I've got the rest of Robby's tuition socked away and he's doing great. C'mon. Be happy for me, Stanley. *(Pinching his cheek affectionately.)*

STANLEY: Cleo, are you sure this guy is right for you? You've had other guys. Lots. None of them lasted.

CLEO: Yes I'm sure. Wesley never gave up on me. And Lord knows I gave him cause. He's always been there.

STANLEY: Because if he, in any way, hurts you, I'm gonna punch him in the nose. You don't know this, but when they turned me down for *South Pacific*, I was a trainer for Muhammed Ali. I even sparred with him one night. But they kicked me out cause I was too rough. Gave him the one-two punch.

CLEO: *(Laughing.)* Stanley, you're a man of many talents.

STANLEY: And Cleo, you're a woman of many talents. I have to confess ever since you sang "Miss Otis Regrets" I've been just a little bit in love with you.

CLEO: Stan, how sweet. You know how fond I am of you. Any family would be lucky to have you.

STANLEY: I don't have a family. I was the kid in the orphanage that no one wanted to take home. I was going to write a musical about my life called *Little Orphan Stanley*, but somebody beat me to it.

CLEO: Stanley, you're like a father to me. You've taught me so much.

STANLEY: And I have a lot more to teach you. Like how to make gefilte fish and a potato kugel. And I don't want this Weston mixing in and spoiling things.

CLEO: Wesley, not Weston. He'll like you, too.

STANLEY: Yeah, like a father. Too bad. Beauty's supposed to fall in love with the beast—not make him *mishbukhah*—a relative.

CLEO: Always joking.

STANLEY: Yeah, a barrel of laughs.

CLEO: Stan, I owe everything to you. Those people at the orphanage didn't recognize quality. I would have chosen you for my family in a heartbeat. *(CLEO gives STANLEY a hug.)* I'm sure Sandra feels the same way. I hear she's getting back on her feet.

STANLEY: Yeah, the college circuit. The feminists love her. She dresses as the sister of Moses and sings "Miriam's Song." They go wild.

CLEO: Does she know about my appearance in Central Park? The spot on Johnny Carson? You'd think she'd make one lousy phone call when I was chosen as *Downbeat*'s favorite—

STANLEY: You better get ready. They've renovated the Apollo and the whole place is sold out. *(CLEO turns to fix her hair, put on her African headdress. STANLEY stares at her for a moment, resigned.)*

STANLEY: That Weston—

CLEO: Wesley.

STANLEY: Wesley . . . he's a lucky man. *(CLEO leaves as lights go down. She adds some African jewelry to her outfit.)*

Announcer: And now, just back from her trip to Africa, Cleo Williams.

CLEO: *(Walking into the spotlight.)* How about this get up? Would you believe my great-great-great-great grandmother wore something like this? Growing up, all I knew about Africa was—Tarzan movies, spear chuckers, cannibals . . . So when I find Africans have their own ancient culture—art, music, dance—I'm amazed . . . and proud. Miriam Makeba brought this song over from Africa. *(CLEO sings a portion of the African folk song, "Wimoweh.")*

> *Weeeeeeeee Ohoooh Wim-o-weh*
> *Wim-o-weh, o-wim-o-weh,*
> *Wim-o-weh, o-wim-o-weh,*
> *Wim-o-weh, o-wim-o-weh,*
> *Wim-o-weh, o-wim-o-weh,*

Wim-o-weh, o-wim-o-weh,
Wim-o-weh, o-wim-o-weh,
(Talking as the beat continues.) The people of the village are getting
ready for a lion hunt. For tonight, the lion sleeps. Tomorrow we will
hunt him.)
Wim-o-weh, o-wim-o-weh,
Wim-o-weh, o-wim-o-weh,
Wim-o-weh, o-wim-o-weh,
Wim-o-weh, o-wim-o-weh,
Wim-o-weh, o-wim-o-weh.
Whuh, whuh, whuh, Wimoweh
Weeeeeeee Ohoooo Wim-o-weh

(in high pitched, percussive African style)

Weeeeeeeeeeeeeeeeeeeeeee Ooooh Wimoweh.

CLEO: When I was in South Africa my people were singing this anthem.
In Zulu it means: "Lord save our people. End wars and suffering."
(CLEO sings the South African Anthem.)
Ksosi sikela L'Afrika
Ksosi sikela L'Afrika
Malapaganaso phondo Yo
Yrisa Nemithandopo. Yetka
Ksosi Sikela, Thinna Malapayo.

*(The piano now underscores "Movin' up," adapted from the spirituals "Keep
your hand on the plow" and "Movin' up a little higher," as CLEO speaks and
moves to the rhythm.)*

From Africa, we were taken against our will, thousands and thousands
of us, to America. But even in our chains, unable to stay together as
families, forbidden to read—we looked up to heaven and we said,
we're going to keep on singing, and keep on learning and some day
we'll be . . .
(CLEO sings.) *"Movin' up, up a little higher. Movin' up, up a little higher."*
(Speaking as the beat continues.) Who can recount every African
American hero who kept the spirit and the faith alive? Frederick
Douglass and Harriet Tubman before emancipation. W.E.B. Dubois
and Langston Hughes and Zora Neal Hurston after. All through our
troubles, Black people fought the wars of Americans—from The Revolutionary War to the War against Hitler—and finally they were recognized—as equal and no longer separate. And when the first equal
rights laws were on the books Rosa Parks and Martin Luther King, Jr.,
said—We will demand more laws. And we will put them into action.

We're movin up now, up a little higher
We're movin' up, up a little higher

(CLEO *speaks with beat continuing.*).

So I tell you all tonight—you who are Black and you who are white—
we're not just dreamers—we're doers—we're changing the world and
no one is going to stop us.
    We're movin' up—oh yes we're movin' up
    Higher and higher—Great God we're movin' up.

Scene 4A: *Crossfade to a college auditorium.* SANDRA *dressed as Miriam,
sister of Moses, getting ready to go on stage.*

SANDRA: Did you ask her?

STANLEY: I hinted.

SANDRA: Do you think she still hates me?

STANLEY: She never hated you . . . She was disappointed, but grateful . . .
    always grateful.

SANDRA: That was the trouble. It's like a friend who lends you money.
    You're grateful, but you're no longer friends. I want us to be friends.

SANDRA: Will you ask her?

STANLEY: I'll ask her. Now get out there. Your audience is waiting.

SANDRA: What's her next booking?

STANLEY: An anti-apartheid rally.

SANDRA: I can relate to that. The sixties all over again.

STANLEY: No, the eighties are much more complicated. Lots of water
    under the bridge since then. The Middle East . . . Africans and Israelis,
    African Americans and Jews. . . . Not much of a bridge left.

SANDRA: Then we have to rebuild the bridge.

STANLEY: What if Cleo says no?

SANDRA: Then I'll keep trying until she says yes.

STANLEY: All right. I'll talk to her. Now sing already!

SANDRA: *(As if to a college audience.)* Hello, Vassar. Lots of important
    women came from here. But did you ever notice many important
    women in the Bible turn out to be the bad guys—Delilah, Jezebel,
    Eve. And when Hollywood gets ahold of these stories, the hero women
    are often forgotten. Without Miriam, Moses wouldn't have been
    saved as a baby and he might never have had the guts to cross the Red
    Sea. And where would Charlton Heston be? Could it be true that
    Miriam and the women actually led the way, dancing with their timbrels?
    *(SANDRA, using a tambourine, sings part of "Miriam's Song" by Debbie
    Friedman.)*
        And the women dancing with their timbrels
        Followed Miriam as she sang her song

Sing a song to the one whom we've exalted,
Miriam and the women danced and danced the whole night long.
When Miriam stood upon the shores and gazed across the sea,
The wonder of this miracle she soon came to believe.
Whoever thought the sea would part with an outstretched hand,
And we would pass to freedom and march to the promised land.
And Miriam the prophet took her timbrel in her hand,
All the women followed her just as she had planned.
And Miriam raised her voice in song. She sang with praise and might.
"We've just lived through a miracle. We're going to dance tonight."
And the women dancing with their timbrels
Followed Miriam as she sang her song.
Sing a song to the One whom we've exalted
Miriam and the women danced and danced the whole night long.

SANDRA: Last time I performed here most of the faces in the audience were white. I sang only Black songs then. I owe a lot to Blacks who created jazz. But rhythm and Jews are no strangers. So I owe a lot to the Jewish composer who created the most exciting union of the Black jazz tradition with his own Jewish melodies and rhythms—Mr. George Gershwin. (SANDRA *sings parts of "It Ain't Necessarily So," words by Ira Gershwin, music by George Gershwin.*)

It ain't necessarily so. It ain't necessarily so.
De t'ings dat yo lible to read in de Bible
It ain't necessarily so.

SANDRA: Funny, it doesn't sound Jewish, right? But it's really a Torah blessing adapted by the Gershwins for the wicked character Sportin' Life in *Porgy and Bess* who tries to woo people away from the Bible.

It ain't necessarily so. It ain't necessarily so.
(now with a Hasidic intonation)
Lie die die dee die die, dee die die dee die die
dee die die dee die die dee die.
I'm preachin this sermon to show
It ain't nessa, ain't nessa, ain't nessa, ain't nessa,
Ain't necessarily so.

Scene 4B: *A few weeks later.* STANLEY's *office in Chicago.* STANLEY *and* CLEO *are in the midst of an argument.*

STANLEY: This, this doesn't sound like you.

CLEO: Why? Because I've always been so nice, so subservient, such an Aunt Jemima?

STANLEY: I never thought of you as an Aunt Jemima. Believe me.

CLEO: I'm doing this concert for a good cause.

STANLEY: But look who's sponsoring it? The man's a demagogue—an Anti-Semite. Rob hates him.

CLEO: Don't you go taking Rob's side.

STANLEY: Rob's right. He stayed non-violent. He kept the faith. I'll never forget when he marched against the Nazis in Skokie.

CLEO: That was a crazy thing to do. Rob should be paying attention to his own career. He's not like David. David's father has connections.

STANLEY: Rob's mother has connections. I was thinking of asking Rob to come to work for me when he graduates.

CLEO: Maybe for awhile, but he can go farther than managing two aging divas.

STANLEY: One of those aging divas—the older one—wants to be there at your next concert.

CLEO: Oh sure. Like she cares about apartheid.

STANLEY: She cares about you.

CLEO: Yeah, that's why she stayed away for 10 years.

STANLEY: I'll agree to the anti-apartheid concert—with Mr. Demagogue's sponsorship—if you agree to do a number there with Sandra.

CLEO: She does back up—I do the lead.

STANLEY: I'll tell her.

CLEO: *(Exiting.)* Tell her I'm thinking about it. I'm not jumping the minute she snaps her fingers.

Scene 5: *Fall, 1983, Chicago, backstage of a University auditorium packed to capacity. CLEO, wearing a costume of African design, is on the phone.*

CLEO: Robby, the place is already packed and it's not even time for the concert. *(Listening with disappointment.)* Oh, I thought you'd be here. *(Listening with alarm.)* Forget Olympia Park! That's Klan territory . . . What do you mean mock slave auction? . . . Of course it's wrong but . . . At least wait until . . . Please . . . please be careful. *(Hangs up phone, very worried.)*

STANLEY: *(Entering.)* What a crowd. Feels like they're about to explode. *(Looking at CLEO.)* What's the matter?

CLEO: A fraternity is having a slave auction. Did you ever hear of anything so sick?

STANLEY: A what? Don't those manure-head fraternity boys, those Alpha Falfas, know there are no more massas or plantations? Where are those lamebrains from—the boonies?

CLEO: Olympia Park.

STANLEY: Oh. That's where they had that Klan parade.

CLEO: David really wants Robby to go with him to protest this craziness. They're always there for each other. But it's too dangerous for a Black man in that neighborhood.

STANLEY: You don't think they've burned crosses on Jewish lawns? Klan lovers are equal opportunity haters.

CLEO: The auction is happening tonight. How far from here to Olympia Park?

STANLEY: Don't even think about it.

CLEO: He's no match for those racists. Why does he insist on doing his own thing?

STANLEY: With a mom like you, I wouldn't expect him to do anything else. He'll be all right. Now you got to do your thing. *(Lights dim and come up on a dressing area as* CLEO *sits down at a makeup table, gets busy with her makeup.* SANDRA *quietly joins her.)*

CLEO: Could you hand me that eyeliner?

SANDRA: Sure. *(They put on makeup for a bit.)* How's Rob?

CLEO: He's graduating in May with his M.B.A., but he's still fighting the good fight.

SANDRA: Will he be here tonight?

CLEO: No. Busy. *(Trying to forget Rob's phone call.)* Stanley's threatening to hire him as soon as he finishes.

SANDRA: He could do worse.

CLEO: I didn't know you were involved in fighting apartheid. I was surprised when Stanley asked if you could join me for this benefit.

SANDRA: Once I embraced my own people, it wasn't so difficult to reach out to old friends.

CLEO: It sure took you long enough.

SANDRA: Always too proud for my own good. I kept track of all your triumphs, though. Once I stopped drinking, I actually enjoyed your success.

CLEO: I married Wesley.

SANDRA: Good. He's down to earth. A teacher puts some sandbags on those ankles—otherwise you float up and away on all that applause. I had to come crashing down before I got it right.

CLEO: No more drinking?

SANDRA: Not today, or yesterday, or the last ten years.

CLEO: That's great. Now remember, this is going to be a mixed audience. A lot of militants. Some are angry, very angry.

SANDRA: Tell me about it. There's a guy outside with a loudspeaker and a sign: "Stop Whites and Jews from eliminating Blacks. Stop the Genocide." Since when did Jews destroy Blacks? And where do they get off using words like genocide?

CLEO: What would you call the systematic killing and enslavement of millions of Blacks?

SANDRA: But Cleo, this guy is saying 200 million were killed in the "Black Holocaust." Where does he get a number like that?

CLEO: If you count all those since the beginning of slavery then . . .

SANDRA: Well, if we counted all the Jews who were killed since Roman times, we'd be getting way past the six million of the real Holocaust.

CLEO: Jews can usually hide. We can't. Don't get me wrong—we don't want to. Anti-Semitism is bad, but how do you compare that to the hatred against Blacks?

SANDRA: Jews were hated before America was discovered.

CLEO: You think Americans are the only ones who hate Blacks? Look at how the Europeans carved up Africa.

SANDRA: And then they decided to carve up the Jews—*(A beat of strained silence.)* Warring Holocausts . . .

CLEO: Yeah.

SANDRA: How can we measure who suffered more—your ancestors sold into slavery or my parents deported to Auschwitz? *(They look at each other with new understanding, for the first time, equally tall and looking one another in the eye.)* We have to start somewhere. That's what tonight is about—right?

CLEO: Maybe apartheid will end while we're still young enough to cheer . . . You have another gig tonight?

SANDRA: Why?

CLEO: We could have a date . . . in Olympia Park.

SANDRA: They don't want us in Olympia Park. I've never had the guts to walk there—forget singing there.

CLEO: Rob's protesting there with his friend David. I'm going to march with them. How about you?

SANDRA: *(Hesitantly.)* You and Robby? You've never marched with him before.

CLEO: No, I never did. What about it? *(Seeing her reluctance.)* You don't want to go, do you?

SANDRA: I gave a lot—

CLEO: Of money, but you never put your life on the line—no—neither did I. But what's the point of fighting against apartheid when we've got it in our own backyard? *(She accepts SANDRA's reluctance.)* It's not *your* struggle, is it?

SANDRA: I want to do what I can . . . *(Smiles for a beat.)*

CLEO: Sure. Here's what I'm going to sing. You can tell me what you're going to do.

SANDRA: Thank you, Cleo, for letting me back in—if you're letting me back.

CLEO: Not if you get more applause than I do. *(CLEO and SANDRA walk to the "stage" area. SANDRA stands off to the side, out of the spotlight.)*

CLEO: *(Addressing the audience.)* Thank you for coming. Fighting apartheid is everyone's job. It's a long, hard job. I have a son who was born after one of our leaders was put in prison. My son is grown now and this great man is still behind bars. Let's all sing one of Dr. King's favorite songs for Nelson Mandela.

CLEO: *(Sings spiritual "We Shall Overcome.")*
> We shall overcome
> We shall overcome
> We shall overcome some day.
> Oh oh deep in my heart
> I do believe
> That we shall overcome some day.

SANDRA: *(Coming forward, speaking to the audience.)* I used to think there was only one cause—civil rights for African Americans. Then I discovered that my people had a cause. When my parents were thrown into concentration camps, nobody stood up for them.

CLEO: Anti-Semitism is wrong. When thousands of my people were gunned down in Soweto—the rest of the world was silent.

SANDRA: Apartheid is wrong. How can one group of human beings be free when another is in chains? *(To CLEO.)* Cleo and I found out we have our own Midwestern brand of racism right here in our own south side backyard. And tonight, we're going to join her son and his friend—his Jewish friend—in protesting it. *(CLEO looks at SANDRA, surprised, touched as SANDRA reaches out her hand. CLEO takes it.)*

CLEO & SANDRA: *(Singing in harmony.)*
> We'll walk hand in hand
> We'll walk hand in hand
> We'll walk hand in hand some day.
> Oh oh deep in my heart
> I do believe
> That we'll walk hand in hand some day.
> Oh oh deep in my heart
> I do believe that
> We shall overcome
> Yes we shall overcooooooome. Toooo-Today!

(Applause. Lights go down.)

VOICE OF NEWSCASTER: *(As if over the radio.)* Last night during a march protesting a mock slave auction at an Olympia Park fraternity, Rob Williams, the only son of popular recording artist Cleo Williams, was seriously injured. David Fine, who accompanied young Williams, is also hospitalized. Cleo Williams, who marched arm in arm at the protest with singer Sandra Levitsky, has gone into seclusion.

Scene 6. *CLEO's place, a few days later. CLEO is lost in her grief. SANDRA enters with flowers and a portfolio of music. She tries to comfort CLEO.*

SANDRA: Cleo . . . How is he doing? *(CLEO just shakes her head and cries.)* I tried to see Robby in the hospital, but they said no visitors. Intensive care. I called you and called you but no answer.

CLEO: I've been at the hospital for the last three days. Sleeping at Robby's bedside. Wesley's there now.

SANDRA: David's in terrible condition, too. The *Olympia News* has Robby and him fighting each other. Jews against Blacks.

CLEO: I saw David helping Robby.

SANDRA: And I saw those thugs club both of them, shouting "Kikes and Niggers, get the hell out of here!"

CLEO: My baby. *(She cries.)*

SANDRA: Is there anything I can do for you, for Rob? I don't know why they took him to a different hospital.

CLEO: Like the old days, separate but equal . . . The doctors say I have to be prepared for anything.

SANDRA: *(Squeezing CLEO's shoulders.)* Cleo . . . when I was really down . . . it was music . . . music brought me back.

SANDRA: *(Standing behind CLEO, SANDRA sings a traditional portion of synagogue liturgy in Hebrew, "Oseh shalom," to the melody of "Amazing Grace," slowly at first.)* "Oseh sha-lom, bi-me-ro-mav, Hu-ya-a-seh sha-lom . . ."

CLEO: *(Sings "Amazing Grace" simultaneously.)* SANDRA:

Amazing Grace	*Oseh sha-lom*
How sweet the sound	*bi-me-ro-mav*
That saved a wretch like me.	*Hu-ya-a-seh sha-lom*
I once was lost but now I'm found	*Aleinu ve'al kol Yisrael.*
Was blind but now I see.	*Ve-i-me-ru a-mein.*

STANLEY: *(Knocks at the door.)*

CLEO: *(SANDRA ushers him in.)*

STANLEY: Any change? *(CLEO shakes her head no.)* The telegrams and cards and flowers are pouring into the office. The whole world is pulling for Rob.

STANLEY: I checked on David, I'm afraid he's taken a turn for the worse.

SANDRA: Oh, no.

CLEO: Why? Why the good people? Why not the haters? *(Crying.)*

STANLEY: Yeah. Hate groups in Olympia Park are organizing. They're grinding out pamphlets about their racial superiority, about Blacks and Jews destroying their neighborhood.

SANDRA: Sounds like the beginnings of Nazi Germany.

CLEO: Or the place where I grew up.

STANLEY: They're afraid of Black-Jewish unity.

SANDRA: They even tried to divide us.

STANLEY: I just hate to see them get away with it.

SANDRA: They won't—not without a fight. We could continue the protest Robby and David started.

STANLEY: Not on the streets—I can't believe you two were marching with those kids.

CLEO: I don't have the strength to fight them anymore.

SANDRA: We don't have to use our fists. We can use our voices.

STANLEY: Yes . . . in a concert.

SANDRA: For Robby and David.

STANLEY: And all the victims of this awful prejudice.

SANDRA: And you think you could get an audience, a peaceful audience?

STANLEY: The Mayor would jump at the idea. I know some leaders from the Black and Jewish communities will support it. And their people will come. And many decent white folks will show up too. It will be a solidarity concert and a healing concert. We'll have it early in the evening, so families can come with their children. You'll be safe. You just provide the music.

SANDRA: Cleo, we could sing for Rob . . . for David.

CLEO: I don't know. I just want them to live.

Scene 7: *The "healing concert" one week later. STANLEY comes out, tries to quiet the crowd.*

STANLEY: Will everyone please take their seats. Quiet. Kids, parents, please . . . It's my honor to present two great women whose singing has thrilled people around the world. Cleo Williams and Sandra Levitsky. *(Applause.)*

SANDRA: Cleo and I would like to welcome you to our concert for healing and unity.

CLEO: No one can make it easy—no one can make it bearable—when your child is hanging between life and death. I don't care what religion you are, what race—You're the most miserable soul in the universe. And you finally know what the old spiritual means:

CLEO & SANDRA: *(Sing part of "You Gotta Cross That Lonesome Valley," SANDRA doing harmony.) You got to cross that River Jordan.*
> *You got to cross it for yourself*
> *Nobody else can cross it for you*
> *You got to cross that River Jordan for yourself.*

CLEO: We're here tonight because my son, Rob Williams, and his friend David were seriously injured in a protest against bigotry. They risked their lives to insure equality and dignity for all.

SANDRA: You may have heard they were fighting each other. They weren't. They were fighting racism together, fighting to put an end to people being treated as less than human. We were there. We saw that senseless hatred. We also saw courage, the courage of Rob and David and other good people. We're here tonight to prove that music is more powerful than hate.

CLEO: We would be fools to think we could quickly change bad feelings existing for years and years. But music . . . music gives us a second chance at life. Centuries ago Abraham's wife, Sarah, and her handmaid, Hagar, were divided forever. But think what would happen if they came to understand each other. (CLEO *and* SANDRA *sing "Sarah & Hagar" by* Linda Hirschhorn)

CLEO: *I am calling you Oh Sarah, This is your sister,*
  Hagar.
  Calling through the centuries to reach you from afar.
SANDRA: *It was I who cast you out, in fear and jealousy.*
  Yet your vision survived the wilderness to reach your destiny.
SANDRA & CLEO: *We must speak each other's names, sing each other's songs*
  And share the dream of a homeland for which our peoples long
  We must hear each other's prayers, sing each other's songs,
  And share the dream of a homeland for which our peoples long.
CLEO: *(To audience.)* We can go right on hating each other. Or we can open our hearts. All I know is we each have a soul.
SANDRA: She's my soul sister.
CLEO: And I'm hers. (CLEO *and* SANDRA *sing "Soul Sisters" by Mark Elliot.*)
CLEO: *Down deep in our souls we are connected.*
SANDRA: *Down deep in my heart I know what it's like to be you.*
CLEO: *Raised in different homes, with different families*
SANDRA: *Still we share a lot that is the same*
CLEO & SANDRA: *My sister, soul sister.*
  If we'd look beyond the pain inside us
  We'd see there's so very much that binds me to you.
  All the things that seem to work against us
  Just grow unimportant when I see
  My sister, soul sister.
  We're wandering through the desert, praying for some rain
  We're wandering through our lives, praying the joy outlasts the pain.
  We've both felt so alone that we were unable to see
  There's not just you,
  There's not just me,
  Together it's "we"!
CLEO: *How could we not see the love around us?*
  When all of the hate around us is so easy to see.
SANDRA: *Now at last I've got myself an ally*
  Who was here on my side all along
SANDRA & CLEO: *My sister, soul sister.*
  Your sister needs you.

Your sister needs you.
Your sister needs you.

(STANLEY comes out clapping. As a curtain call, he encourages the audience to sing a song printed in the program, "We Will Be Free" by Jeffrey Klepper and Stuart Rosenberg.)

SANDRA: *This road we're on is a rocky road*
Try to climb so high, brings you down so low
CLEO: *But there's a reason we carry on*
When we're together we are as one.
STANLEY, SANDRA, CLEO: *(Encouraging the audience to join in.)*
We will be free
When there is justice
We will be free
When there is hope
We will be free
When we join together
We will be free
Oh yes, we will be free!

THE END

I Am a Man

OyamO

OyamO

OyamO was born Charles Gordon in Elyria, Ohio, but Africanized his name in the sixties to distinguish himself from another Black playwright, Charles Gordone, author of *No Place to Be Somebody*. OyamO utilized his Miami University of Ohio t-shirt, capitalizing the ending "O" to make his name absolutely unique.[1]

Working with the Black Theatre Workshop in Harlem, an arm of the New Lafayette Theatre, he developed *The Breakout,* published in 1969. In the seventies he joined the Yale University graduate playwriting program, premiering the play *The Resurrection of Lady Lester,* dealing with noted tenor saxophonist Lester Young. Recognition of his playwriting came with a string of prestigious awards, including a Guggenheim Fellowship, a Rockefeller Foundation Fellowship, a McKnight Foundation Fellowship, and three National Endowment for the Arts Fellowships. He distinguished himself as a teacher at Emory University, Princeton University and the University of Iowa Playwrights Workshop. He is currently an Associate Professor of Theatre and English at the University of Michigan.[2]

He was commissioned to write *I Am a Man* by New York City's Working Theatre in 1992, but it soon was produced across the country at the Goodman Theatre in Chicago, the Arena Stage in Washington D.C., the Meadow Brook in Rochester, New York, the San Diego Repertory Theatre and, in 2002, the Trueblood Theatre in Ann Arbor, Michigan. The title, *I Am a Man,* came from the strike placards worn by the 800 striking sanitation workers in Memphis during the1968 labor dispute that brought Dr. Martin Luther King, Jr., to the place where he would be assassinated.

OyamO's choice to focus on T.O. Jones, the union's president, and to use the historically significant figures simply as references, along with his use of the blues weaving in and out of the events, makes this play as bold and distinctive as the playwright's name. OyamO gives us a broad spectrum of the tensions within the African American community, depicting in dialogue and attitude a variety of conflicting views as to how to achieve progress. It is the playwright's dramatic achievement that these conflicting views are realized in dynamic characters, people who are striving for freedom but in the process, tragically, pave the way for the death of their greatest leader.

OyamO has also written a film adaptation of *I Am a Man* for Home Box Office. Other projects include the world premiere of his play *Let Me Live* at the Goodman Theatre and the premiere of *Famous Orpheus* at Geva Theatre. The Seattle Children's Theatre commissioned and produced a stage adaptation of Patricia Polacco's popular children's book, *Pink and Say,* about the friendship of two teenage boys, one Black and one white, during the Civil War. He has participated in the O'Neill Summer Playwrights Conference, a major incubator for new plays.

Notes

1. http://www.theblackmarket.com/ProfilesInBlack/Oyamo.htm.
2. OyamO bio from unpublished script, *I Am a Man,* 2002.

I Am a Man

Cast of Characters

BLUESMAN: experienced blues vocalist and blues guitar player from whom, in a sense, the entire story emanates, but who is an unobtrusive physical character.

JONES: 40, speaks with vocal, gestural and emotional ebullience. Beefy, but average height, very friendly, but also bullheaded about some things. Somewhat vulnerable, a bit fearful and not well educated, quit Memphis Public School in the 8ᵗʰ grade. But he's naturally intelligent—common street sense, a cajoling wit, a generous nature, a lot of heart.

REV. MOORE: Late 30s, educated but also "down home" feeling, thinking and, sometimes, speaking. Understands Jones' world and his intentions, but also is aware of the realities of the world of the "others." Is Pentecostal or Church of God in Christ. Colorful dresser, speaks rapidly with lots of gestures, restless manner.

REV. WEATHERFORD: Late 30s, white man, a Brit from Canada, patrician looking, quite proper, dapper conservative dressing, but very sincere in his loving nature, a devoted Christian who ministers to a Black church. Only slightly naïve. A manner that may appear comical to others. Knows how to enjoy a good laugh at himself.

MAYOR: A sick man with a mission, but not without a certain dignified dedication, even if to misguided principles, and a gracious civility. Intelligent to the point of arrogance, but a bit insecure about his status and social position. A very stubborn, clever manipulator. A good politician from an old, wealthy Southern family.

JOSHUA SOLOMON: White, 50s, tough, N.Y.-based labor negotiator who is not averse to swearing and throwing a fit, but who is the ultimate peacekeeper. He's blunt, but always well meaning. He's thin and full of bantam rooster courage. He knows how to get to a man. He's honest and knows when to stay out of fights. Great agitator and organizer from the old days. Walks with a limp due to childhood polio.

CRAIG WILLINS: Black. A brilliant, hardworking labor union troubleshooter with an often nasty disposition. Impatient, pushy, bullying, but sincerely dedicated to the union.

ALICE MAE JONES: Jones' wife. Somewhat ignored by Jones. A mother of five children, weary, lonely, angry. The love she has for her husband has grown fragile over the years.

MISS SEC'Y: Black. Early 30s, first secretary of the local NAACP, educated, down-to-earth, tries to remain respectful towards people like Jones. Well organized and has good understanding of how to make things happen. Very careful, too careful.

SENIOR NEGRO COUNCILMAN: 40s, caught in the middle, but politically astute enough to stay there for the time being, genuinely confused, but wants to be helpful, rather nervous.

SWAHILI: 20s, enraged, has grand illusions of the "Black Nation," full of rhetoric and style, but dangerous.

BROTHA CINNAMON: Teenager, a camp follower who wants to be correct, follows orders and repeats slogans. Not really dangerous even in looks. His militant rituals are comical but sincerely practiced.

POLICE CHIEF: white, 50s, an efficient police chief, denigrating towards Jones and Co., would like to "crush" the strike but obeys the Mayor.

SOLICITOR: A closet Southern white liberal who is exasperated by the system for which he works, honest, angry, rebellious, fed up, practical, compassionate.

COLLABORATOR: A disguised voice and image always in shadows, an undercover informant—impossible to tell whether Collaborator is man, woman, Black or white, old or young, a complete mystery.

REV. BILLINGS: 30s, and educated bourgeois Black preacher from an affluent church, leader in the community.

TWO COPS: One Black, one white, young.

OFFSTAGE VOICES: MLK, WILSON, LAMPLEY, TUCKER, HENDRICKS, VOICES 1, 2, 3, 4, 5, AND 6 at beginning of script. VOICES 1, 2, 3, 4 at very end of script. VOICE 2 at end of script is that of KING.

Prologue

(Prominent around the playing areas should be white flats or projection screens onto which the various settings will be projected and strategically placed racks of costumes and necessary props. When the lights are at half, we hear the VOICE OF MLK.)

MLK VOICE: "And there is, deep down within all of us, an instinct. It's a kind of drum major instinct—a desire to be out front, a desire to lead the parade, a desire to be first. And it is something that runs a whole gamut of life . . . And the great issue of life is to harness the drum major instinct . . ."

(The BLUESMAN *enters alone playing his guitar while the houselights remain up full. The number is an up-tempo, dancing blues, a life joy blues. [He also can be accompanied by three other musicians, keyboards, bass, traps, if a full combo is desired.] The* BLUESMAN *should be able to play the harmonica well. His music remains instrumental until the house is settled at which time the houselights go to black and the* BLUESMAN *begins singing the lyrics in a single spotlight or in a small lighted area near or in the playing space. The song is Muddy Waters' "Garbageman"—from tape* Muddy Waters, Can't Get No Grindin', *MCA Records, Original Chess Records, 1990, actual recording March, 1972. Note: the music could be James Brown or Aretha Franklin, et al. Projected images are of bars along Beale St. and/or of that kind of neighborhood in a typical Black urban ghetto setting. Projected on one screen is:* JANUARY, 1968. *Lights rise on* JONES *who enters alone, salutes the* BLUESMAN, *rhythmically reacts to the music, gets two drinks.* ALICE MAE *enters.* JONES *gives her a drink and seats her in a corner where she sullenly watches him. The* ENSEMBLE *shortly follows. The full lights slowly rise on a jumping Beale Street Bar where off-duty* SANITATION WORKERS, *dance popular dances to the "Garbageman" song. Two or more of the* MEN *wear jackets with lettering across their backs that say "MEMPHIS SANITATION DEPT."* THEY *are drinking and having a funky ball. There's* ONE OR MORE WOMEN *present who dance with the men. He motions to* ALICE *to come dance with him. She shakes her head negatively. He instantly shrugs it off.* SOME MEN *approach him for small loans which he generously gives. The physical gestures of asking and loaning are large.* ONE OF THE WOMEN *sexily dances with* JONES *who is a bit of a good humored showoff. The* WOMAN *goes too far as does* JONES. ALICE MAE *becomes incensed; she snatches* JONES *away from the* WOMAN, *pushes her, calls her a bitch.* JONES *and* OTHERS *try to keep the women apart. A chair is knocked over.* ALICE MAE *storms out. The lights crossfade with projections as music fades out. Projections become shifting images of hardworking garbage crews, trucks, garbage. Finally an image of an old style garbage truck is projected. It is a barrel-shaped, side loader with a compactor. Images fade to black. In the blackness we hear a thunderstorm raging, the sound of compacting machinery sputtering into motion and the* VOICES OF TWO MEN *screaming for help as they are slowly crushed to death.)*

MAN 1: IT'S GON' HOLD US! IT'S GON' HOLD US!
MAN 2: NO! KEEP PUSHING! PUSH!
BOTH MEN: HELP! HELP! HELP!
MAN 1: IT WON'T STOP!
MAN 2: KNOCK ON THE SIDE! KNOCK!

(For a few moments we hear frantic pounding on metal mixed with screams for help.)

MAN 1: *(sobbing, gasping)* IT AIN'T GON' STOP!
MAN 2: LAWD GOD HAVE MERCY! HELLLLP!
BOTH MEN: HELLLLLP!

(The breath has been crushed from them and all we hear is flesh and bones being smashed, cracked. Then a moment of silence.)

End of Prologue

(As the lights rise slowly, we hear the spiritual hymn "Amazing Grace" being sung by an offstage assemblage of rough male and female voices. They sing it in a "fundamentalist" manner and with great sorrow as if in mourning. Lights rise first on the BLUESMAN accompanying the offstage VOICES. Near him are REV. MOORE AND JONES. Projected over their heads is a portrait of the Last Supper. On the flats are projected images of both the interior and exterior of a rather impoverished storefront church in a run-down neighborhood. On one of the flats is projected the words: STOREFRONT CHURCH, A SUNDAY AFTERNOON, EARLY FEBRUARY, 1968, BEALE STREET, MEMPHIS, TENNESSEE. As REV. MOORE speaks, the OFFSTAGE VOICES/CONGREGATION respond verbally to his remarks as during a Black fundamentalist church sermon. The BLUESMAN speaks the first words of REV. MOORE's following speech.)

BLUESMAN: Praise His Name. We've come here this Sunday afternoon to mourn the passing of two good men who died trying to clean up garbage here in Memphis.

REV. MOORE: No words will bring those men back to their families, but we can remember that Jesus was a garbage collector too. Praise His Name! He went about the world trying to clean up garbage. People's lives were full of garbage, still are, all kinds of garbage: hatred, spite, envy, vanity, violence, despair. They fight and kill each other in wars all over the world for reasons so old they can't even remember them. Jesus tried His best to destroy the garbage, but, like our dearly departed, He also lost His life. But all of us are better off for it. Praise His Name. I bring my words to a close, and at this time I relinquish the pulpit to Deacon T.O. Jones. The widows asked him to speak today. As ya'll know, Deacon Jones is the man who started the union local 1733. Since 1964 he's been the official organizer in Memphis for The American Federation of State, County and Municipal Employees. He worked with our dearly departed and he cried with them; he laughed with them; he starved and suffered with them. And, like them, he never lost his faith or courage. Deacon Jones.

(After JONES has spoken a few lines, LIGHTS crossfade, going to black on MOORE and the rest of the stage, leaving only Jones lighted; PROJECTIONS of the "church" crossfade with those representing the "union hall," interior,

where a large photo of George Meany dominates. When the lighting changes are complete, we are in the "union hall." A Projection says: RETAIL CLERKS UNION HALL, SUNDAY EVENING. BLUESMAN speaks first words of JONES' following speech.)

BLUESMAN: Mah story hard, but it mus' be tole, so everybody straight. Our two union brothas died 'cause day was tryin' to work on a rain day.

JONES: Day come ta work that day, but it was rainin' bad. Thunda and lightnin' storm, and da rain, it look like da whole Mississippi pourin' down on Memphis. Day don't let ya wuck in the rain. Got ta wait 'till the rain finish and maybe you get a few hours wuck. The men gon' wait fah da rain ta stop. So da garage foe'men, he cain't have no cullud peepas sittin' in the garage where da white folks sit. So the two cullud wuckers went to sit in da garbage truck in the yard. Alright. Da truck cab locked up. Can't git in dere. Day go to the foe'men. Foe'man tell 'em day cain't sit in the garage wit da white crew chiefs. Day just hafta wait in the rain. Foe'men, say: "Ya'll sit in the back of da truck. It's dry. Plenty room back dere. Ain't picked up no garbage yet." Alright. So da two men go ta sit in the back of the truck in the bailer where day loads the garbage. Dey sittin' back dere when lightnin' strike da truck and make the bailer machinery start up by itself. Da men strugglin' ta get out foe day gits crushed; day screaming fa help, but da thunda cover day screams. Cain't nobody hear dem. The machinery done crush da men ta deaf 'foe anybody knowed what happen. Machinery was broke in the fust place and the foe'man knowed it. Foe'men knowed dat bailer lahble ta start anytime. But he ain't care; he ain't care about dese two cullud mens. He cain't hear day screams while day dying. So our two union brothas is gone, and da family grievin' 'cause day don't know what da future holin' fa dem. It's winta in Memphis, and fah dese two families it's gon' be winta for a long time. We got to hep dem like as if day was our own family.

(Reaches into pocket and pulls out money and ceremoniously counts it into his hat, passes the hat to SOMEONE who carries it offstage.)

I hole onta half my paycheck from the union. I hole onta half my check, 'cause I knowed the family gon' need our help in dis time of day grief and mornin'. Let's all search our hearts and pocketbooks an' fine even just a few pennies. Let's do it now and spare these families mo' grief. While we doin' dat, let's talk about action.

(We hear RECORDED MURMURING SOUNDS OF HUNDREDS OF MEN at a union meeting. ALL INDIVIDUAL VOICES OF THE MEN we hear, except Jones, can be recordings or live actors who play multiple roles.)

JONES: Dis aftanoon we taken an' buried our brothas. Tanight we meetin' ta end da madness what kilt 'em. We got ta stop da conditions foe two moe die. Testify in yo' name!

JERICHO WILSON: *(recorded voice)* Jericho Wilson. I got 23 years on Sanitation. My oldes' boy in Veet-nam, but when I come home now, I feel like I been in Veet-nam. Totin' and runnin', runnin' and totin'. In New York peepas put day garbage by the curb. Save time and labor. I'm almost 50. It's time for progress.

JONES: We hear dat! We ain't no mules!

CARL LAMPLEY: Carl Lampley. We need new tubs, for one thing. Take fah ninstance, I pour the garbage in my tub and it leakin'. Now, when I put it on my head, the holes in the tubs commence ta oozing. Next thing ya know I got stinkin' garbage runnin' all down my clothes. And all day got to do is git new tubs and tek care of the ones we got. We needs all new equipment, specially new trucks that's safe.

JONES: We 'sposed ta tote garbage, not wear it! And new tubs wit good handles? We want roller carts where we don't hafta tote nothin' a'tall! And, most important, no more mens git eat up by the bailer, like we some kinda sacrifice to a wild beast. Amen! *(A loud "amen" from* VOICES*)*

SAMMY TUCKER: Sammy Tucker. Da rules say when it rainin', you go in an' git two 'r's pot (part) pay if it don't stop. I repo'ted ta wuck dat time T.O. know 'bout. But da foe'man say, say "Go back home, Sammy." Alright, come payday; I'm lookin' fah two hours from rain day. It ain't deah! Foe'man say, say "Git outten mah face!" He done kept all da white ones, give 'em whole pay.

JONES: What day doin' on dis work rules bidness is worser den what the crow did to the buzzard an' da mule. Day got us caught 'tween the mule's ass and his tail.* White folks the mule and we da buzzard. Old Crow sittin' up deah waitin' fah both a us ta drop dead, so he kin feast. *(Laughing and affirmation from* VOICES*.)*

SEAN HENDRICKS: Sean Hendricks. We hears too much abuse from foe'mens. Remine me a slavery when day whupped ya for any little thing. Now day just cusses ya, in front of everybody, like you some ole dog. And den why I got ta be on probation when you first git the job. Probation don't do nothin' but make da foe'mens rich. Day make us pay dem if we want ta keep the job. And I don't make but one dolla and forty cents an hour. Cain't afford ta pay no foe'mens no kinda way.

---

*American Negro Folktales, Richard Dorson, Fawcett, 1958, p. 114.

JONES: Ain't no man deserve ta be cussed like a mule an' dis probation bidness is bad bidness for the Black man. Look like you stay on probation all yo' life while you collectin' otha peepa's garbage. We tryin' ta tell 'em, say, the plantation days done run through. We needs more den a sack a meal and hog jowls. Up in New York City Mayor Lindsay pay his sanitation men good! *(Affirmations from VOICES.)*

JONES: *(tapping his skull)* Alright, I got da grievance mechanics. We must take some kinda action now.

VOICE 1: I say strike!

VOICE 2: Brotha Jones call a strike in '66. Mayor call a injunction; we ain't had no strike yet.

JONES: In '66 da International Union don't want nothin' ta do wit no strike. And so dat injunction stop 'em cold. International order us back ta wuck, not me!

VOICE 3: We talkin' 'bout a strike in Memphis. What we need wit International?

JONES: Support! We gon' need day support! We meeting in the Retail Clerks Union Hall 'cause we can't afford to build our own union hall. We ain't got no independent strike fund in da Memphis local, and das 'cause we ain't payin' dues. I catches nothin' but da devil when I come huntin' dues! I mention dues, cullud peepas turn white and disappear.

VOICE 4: Dues kinda heavy what we gittin' in return.

JONES: Fo' dollas? Fo' dollas a munt! Union git us mo' pay, but union need support. Now, you kin argue dat point or you kin move on. Ya'll cain't have no union lessen da union kin collect dues. Got ta hep ourselves. *(mildly condescending)* Dat's order, propa order. Sometimes ya'll don't' hear me. It break down to dis: You don't do it wit propa order, you cain't do it. I cain't put it more simple. Okay? Look, I put it this way: What ya'll wanna do?

VOICE 1: I say again strike!

JONES: And what about the Mayor's '66 injunction against a strike? It's still in force far as I know.

VOICE 1: What about it? Das yo' job to deal wit dat.

JONES: And what about support? We stop takin' garbage, everybody upset. We ain't got a hunded dollas in the treasury. You cain't even talk to a lawyer on the phone for less than a hunded dollas. We cain't affo'd no kinda bills ta pay.

VOICE 2: Why we got to pay somebody else so we kin strike?

VOICE 3: Cain't we just vote on it. There's 800 men here. Day can speak fah dayself. I move we strike.

VOICE 4: I second da motion.

JONES: It's moved and seconded that we strike. Any moe discussion? *(silence)* Alright, let me say one thing and den we votes. Callin' a strike on 'r own ain't no small thing. If ya want it ta work, ya'll got ta take holt and push together. People can't be fallin' off when it's time ta move. I been here since the beginnin' and ya'll know dat I ain't never stop fighting fah yaw. But now we gon' hafta fight together. Ya'll ready fah da question?

UNISON: Question!

JONES: All those in favor say Aye!

UNISON: AYE!

JONES: All those oppose? *(silence)* Da motion carry; Mayor got him a strike. *(Cheers)*

(BLUESMAN picks up on "Every Buzzard" and sings those words blues fashion as Lights and Images shift to a large meeting room in city hall. PROJECTIONS show a huge replica of the Memphis City Seal. The MAYOR, CHIEF OF POLICE, and TOWN SOLICITOR are present. In the shadows appears the COLLABORATOR whose face and body are blotted out. From the clothes or whatever else may be partially discernible it is impossible to tell whether the COLLABORATOR is a man or a woman, black or white. When the COLLABORATOR speaks, its voice is distorted. The OTHERS speak and refer to the COLLABORATOR. The COLLABORATOR can hear but not see the OTHERS.)

MAYOR: So, essentially we have a wildcat strike.

COLLAB: Yep. That's about it.

BLUESMAN: That Jones is such an ignorant man or maybe he's just forgetful.

MAYOR: Back in '66 we settled all the grievances just by sitting down and talking. This whole thing could be solved if he just came in like a man and talked to me.

COLLAB: That's just what he intends to do.

MAYOR: I see. So, is there anything else the Advisory Board should be made aware of?

COLLAB: There is some gossip about T.O. Jones separating from his wife or such.

MAYOR: Well, that's irrelevant, but good to know. If he can't keep a family together, how does he expect to keep that so-called union together? Chief, you can dismiss your agent, so we can begin our meeting.

CHIEF: I'll contact you in a few days. You are dismissed. *(The monitor goes blank, then off.)*

MAYOR: Gentlemen, let me make clear that I first conferred with the senior Negro councilman before convening this Advisory Board meeting, and for the record let it be noted that I personally solicited his advice and asked him to intercede, which he agreed to do. Have I made myself clear?

UNISON: Quite clear, Mr. Mayor.

SOLICITOR: *(a bit tense)* But he should be informed about our deliberations. He is a member of the Mayor's Advisory Board.

MAYOR: Duly noted. Now, just in case we can't prevent this so-called strike, I've asked you all to come up with contingency plans. Chief?

CHIEF: Well, we've been watching 'em closely. Not too much has changed. They still drink on Beale St. and sing the blues, fight a lot, especially on Saturday night. I expect they'll fuss and fume for a day or two and then go back to work. I should have enough squad cars on hand to escort the garbage trucks and protect the garages if necessary. I don't expect any mass action here like in other cities, but I'm ready for that too.

MAYOR: The Sanitation Commissioner feels he can convince at least 100 sanitation workers to remain at their jobs, and he'll hire another hundred. He plans to have once a week collections within days. Mr. Solicitor?

SOLICITOR: *(weary resignation)* The 1966 Injunction remains in force, but it's irrelevant to any union worth its salt. Strikes by municipal and state employees are illegal in Tennessee, but International AFCSME is out to challenge that law, even if it means jails and fines. A strike is inevitable unless we settle immediately.

MAYOR: *(a bit sharply)* Which is why I look forward to my meeting with Jones.

(Lights and Images shift to a "bar" on Beale St. where T.O. JONES, the SENIOR NEGRO COUNCILMAN and REV. BILLINGS, a Black minister, enter and go to a table. The PROJECTED IMAGES are of Beale St. circa 1968. THE BLUESMAN sings a medium tempo blues and accompanies himself on guitar. T.O. rocks with the beat obviously enjoying himself. We hear the recorded sounds of OTHERS carousing, loudly enjoying the music. A LONE WOMAN dances drunkenly, sadly, but seductively. BILLINGS is quite visibly upset being there. The music shortly fades to silence.

JONES: Bartender, a beer for the Councilman and a coke for the Reverend.

BLUESMAN: Do you have to tell everyone I'm a minister?

JONES: You is a minister.

BILLINGS: I know what I "is." Councilman, you should not have agreed to a meeting in a Beale Street Bar! It's inappropriate, disgraceful, and that woman is being blatantly lewd!

COUNCILMAN: You two . . . ah . . . let's . . .

JONES: Ain't nothin' wrong wit dat woman, 'cept she feel like dancin' out what on her mine. Peepas does dat all the time heah. Somethin' happen, day don't unnastan' it, day come dance, cry, fall down; and den day goes home an' go ta sleep.

BILLINGS: I shouldn't be seen in this kind of place at all. And what is that overpowering odor?

JONES: Sweat! Garbage man's honest sweat. Dis bar is our unofficial meetin' place, Rev. Billings. Dis the kinda place where Jesus preached, accordin' ta da Bible.

BILLINGS: The Bible also says something about dens of iniquity.

COUNCILMAN: Look, gentlemen, we didn't come together to bicker over theology.

(BROTHER KENNY approaches the table and motions for JONES to speak with him privately. Jones steps a short distance with the man.)

JONES: 'Scuse me. Whas hapnin', Brotha Kenny?

KENNY: Fightin' the lizard for leavin's. I knowed you havin' a impo'tant meetin' 'n all. But things tuck a ton fah da worse with da wife. Stroke come back an' I hada put her in the hospital.

JONES: Oh Lawd, how is she?

KENNY: She got ta stay deah, and day axin' fah money. Don't git pay 'till Friday, but hospital wants day payday now. Anything you kin let me have, I 'preciate.

JONES: Heah's twenty. Union ain't got much in the welfare fund, but see Brotha Rock; he chairman of the welfare committee. On Sunday, I ask Rev. Moore do a special collection.

KENNY: Danky, Brotha Jones. I knew if I spoke to you personal, I'd git some hep. May Gawd bless ya. I won't hole ya up no moe.

JONES: Night, Brotha Kenny. I'm prayin' fah ya wife.

(JONES returns to the table where BILLINGS AND THE COUNCILMAN wait impatiently.)

BILLINGS: Look, can we get this over?

JONES: Git what ova?

COUNCILMAN: T.O., the Mayor says you and a few men are going on strike. Is this true?

JONES: The Mayor done plugged into the bush telegraph real good, ain't he?

COUNCILMAN: T.O., if five people get together to do something in Memphis, the whole town knows.

JONES: Why you suddenly concern about a strike?

BLUESMAN: Because I live here too. Those people at City Hall are not going to recognize a union. I know those people!

COUNCILMAN: They smile and invite you over for barbecue, and when you get there, they put the barbecue sauce on you. For them it's 1850. Certain ideas are traditional to them. You know and I know they're not going to give up tradition. You've got to be less confrontational. Forget the strike, sit down and talk to the Mayor.

JONES: I am gon' talk to 'im. I'm gon' tell 'im we gon' strike if conditions don't change. And den he do what he got ta do and I do what I got ta do. Das how life go.

BILLINGS: Are you aware of how much suffering you'll be bringing on those 800 men and their families? I thought you cared about your "union" brothers.

JONES: I do care, das why we strikin'. Will you help feed the strikers and take up a weekly collection for dem in yo' church?

BILLINGS: I should say not!

JONES: Why not?

BILLINGS: I've never seen any of your men in my church.

JONES: What dat got ta do wit grits and gravy for hungry chillens?

COUNCILMAN: If you call off this strike, I'll personally intercede with the Mayor and . . .

JONES: Naw, da Mayor got ta recognize the unioin and deal wit us legal, none of dis personal intercede.

BILLINGS: I think your stubbornness is due to your turbulent personal life.

JONES: Whatchu mean by dat, Rev.?

BILLINGS: The "bush telegraph" says you're so busy with the union and other vices that you ignore your family.

JONES: Sound to me like you been out shaking the bushes like a common, lowlife coon trying ta shake blackberries. (BILLINGS *gets up and stomps out without a word.*)

COUNCILMAN: Jones, in Memphis, you need the churches. That man is with the Ministers' Coalition. He could get some important ministers to negotiate with the Mayor on your behalf. You just insulted him.

JONES: (*sarcastically*) Since he a man of God, maybe he kin fine it in his heart to forgive me. The Ministers' Co'lishon ain't on strike, we is.

COUNCILMAN: Jones, what do you want?

JONES: I already 'splained what da union wan . . .

COUNCILMAN: I'm asking what do you want? You are the union. You founded it; you're the president.

JONES: Oh, I see. Well, let me put it dis way: My great granddaddy was a slave in Alabama. He was trained to be a blacksmith. Got tired a bein' a slave. He runaway to Memphis. Dat's still South, but he ain't wanna leave da South, and he don't want nobody ta know he a runaway slave. What you reckon he do?

COUNCILMAN: Jones, I . . . this is not what I . . .

JONES: What you reckon he do?

COUNCILMAN: I don't know.

JONES: He *pretend* he a slave. He work on blacksmith jobs and git money like he hired out for rent by a master. He pretend he belong to a certain sea captain. Keep his house fa him when he at sea. Great granddaddy make up a whole story 'bout dis sea captain. Say he run a ship dat sail to India and China. Now, dere ain't no sea captain, of course. Never was. But folks don't know it. My great granddaddy knowed how to tell a great story.

COUNCILMAN: Yes, fine, but . . .

JONES: Let me roun' off my remarks. Oncet a year, a white man'd come visit grandaddy. He met great granddaddy in Alabama. Dis white man was living den in Virginia, but he ain't care nothin' 'bout no slavery. He against it. He like my great granddaddy. Become his fren. Da white man *pretend* he da sea captain. He walk aroun' Memphis wit great granddaddy and order him about like a master, and let everybody see. Den the white man go back to Virginia. And great granddaddy keep on pretending he a slave so's he could be free.

COUNCILMAN: I see, but . . .

JONES: Dere's mo'. Well, it turn out dat da white man was really a mulatto who was pretending ta be white in Virginia.

COUNCILMAN: Fine, but what's the point?

JONES: I ain't got to da point yet.

COUNCILMAN: You haven't?

JONES: Now, two generations lata, here come my daddy.

COUNCILMAN: *(resigned)* What happened to your daddy, T.O.?

JONES: My daddy was the youngest chile out of 19 childrens. He become a minister who wuck in a lumbermill. Daddy wucked in the lumbermill 'till about 1935. Dat's Depression. Daddy got let go dat year. Day let him go 'cause da fo'eman got some nephew coming from Europe what need a job. So daddy left dat job and he chop cotton until he die. Now dere's me.

COUNCILMAN: Yes, you at last.

JONES: At last. I come 'long and wucked for Sanitation Department. Times done change. I ain't got ta *pretend* I'm a slave so I can be free. And I'm tired a bein' let go anytime somebody feel like it. Back in '63 day fired me 'cause I start a union. But I'm still here, and so is the union. Dat's what I want. I want a union where you ain't got ta pretend nothin', and you cain't be let go just 'cause somebody else want yo' job. I'm gon' make da Mayor recognize my union.

COUNCILMAN: T.O., I think you better get prepared for a whole lot of trouble.

(Lights and Images crossfade with the previous storefront church where REV. MOORE speaks as JONES approaches and enters the lighted playing space.)

BLUESMAN: *(in bluesmode)*
    WHOLE LOTTA TROUBLE HEADING THIS WAY
    WHOLE LOTTA TROUBLE HEADING THIS WAY
    YEAH, WHOLE LOTTA TROUBLE HEADING THIS WAY

(The VOICE OF REV. MOORE cuts in and interrupts BLUESMAN who fades to silence. Moore holds a few sheets of paper, a manila envelope and a pen. He wears workclothes, his lunch bucket is nearby. JONES has entered by now. It is Tuesday evening.)

REV. MOORE: He telling you right, Brotha Jones. If you go looking for trouble, it's easy to find.

JONES: Rev. Moore, I hears what you saying, but, say fah'ninstance . . .

MOORE: That's another thing right there: You can't be going off tellin' some instance about what happened to yo' uncle's mule in Pulaski, Tennessee. Lawd ha' mercy! Keep it simple!

JONES: But if you coulda heard dem men's explainin' day complaints . . .

JONES: I don't hafta hear their complaints. I got a gang of sanitation workers in my congregation. Just lost two, remember?

MOORE: I know what they feeling and I support them 100%, but the way I got it written out here is your best approach. Get in there, talk straight with the man, state your demands and ask him to respond.

JONES: Seem like he already respond, just like a snake in da back alley.

MOORE: Lawd Ha'mercy! Don't walk up in the snake's office and call him no snake. You asking 'im to bite you. You got to charm a snake, see? We talking sho'nuff politics now. Leave the snake some hole he can crawl out. Don't block all the holes or you can't get out either.

JONES: Well, I do mah bes', but dat Mayor need a good preachin' to.

MOORE: Maybe he do, but the Mayor is Episcopalian, see? And you can't be preaching to no Episcopalian. Soon as you start sweatin' and shoutin', they fall apart. I've seen that with my own eyes! Lawd ha' mercy!

(HE and JONES snicker at that.)

JONES: Rev. Moore, you's a complete mess.

MOORE: I'm gon' be a mess if I don't get to work right now. Got two barges fulla cotton setting at the warehouse dock now. I woulda had 'em unloaded, but I had to take two nights off this week 'cause I had ta bury those two men and do family counseling. *(mimicking)* "Don't let it happen again," my foreman said. Can you imagine? Don't let anybody die because I've got to unload some cotton barges. Told the man I'm a preacher and when the Lord calls me to shepherd His flock, I go.

JONES: Amen. When you gon' quit da crane operator job; you always complainin' 'bout runnin' dat crane.

MOORE: When the Lawd say quit, I quit. I figure the Lawd gon' tell me ta quit soon as I get a big enough congregation. That's according to the Doctrine of secularistic nonsecularism which comes from the School of Multiple Reality Fusion.

JONES: Yeah, well, I unnastan' da confusion part alright.

MOORE: Then you understand more than me. Reality, brotha Jones. Reality is the only order that exists; all you got to do is figure out what reality is, then act accordingly, with moral integrity as your guide. They didn't teach me that at the Seminary; learned it on the street.

JONES: What is you tryin' ta say to me?

MOORE: Dreams cost you more than anything else in the world. I want a big church, you want a union. We both have to stay on top of things, follow reality, and, as Rev. Powell up in New York say: Keep the faith.

JONES: I unnastan' dat.

MOORE: *(pause, hand up to ear)* Right now I hear the Lawd calling me.

JONES: What he say?

MOORE: He say: "Get yo' Negro butt to work." Lawd ham'mercy! *(handing JONES a large brown manila envelope)* Now, you take this paper and study it real good before you speak with the Mayor tomorrow.

JONES: I'm going home right now and study it. And, Rev., me and da mens thank you for yo' precious time.

MOORE: Praise da Lawd for that!

(The Lights and Projection Images shift to the streets where JONES, accompanied by the BLUESMAN, walks home. The BLUESMAN plays a kind of walking blues that is both sad and foreboding. The Projected Images are a collage of the Black Memphis ghetto at night, closed storefronts, junk strewn vacant lots, boarded up windows, dilapidated, jerry built buildings. JONES carries the envelope. Two objects are thrown from the darkness and land at his feet, a cheap suitcase tied with a rope and a tattered U.S. Navy duffle bag. He stops and begins squinting into the surrounding blackness. The BLUESMAN continues playing but very low, occasionally punctuating the ensuing conversation with bluesy guitar sounds, sometimes discordant, atonal flatted fifths.)

JONES: Alice Mae, you ain't had ta do all dis.

ALICE MAE: *(voice from the blackness)* Ollie, I done mo' den dat. I changed all da locks too.

JONES: Woman, couldn't ya wait 'till the mornin'? Where I'm 'sposed ta go dis time a night?

(Dim lights rise momentarily on ALICE MAE, a big boned, sad-looking woman. The lights will periodically rise and dim on her during her lines. It gives the illusion that she appears and disappears and in different locations throughout

the scene. Jones turns and speaks towards her new location each time she momentarily appears. Photo images of her from happier days with T.O. can be used here if necessary. These images can appear and disappear in various locations around the playing space. His life with her is ephemeral; they are married in name only.)

BLUESMAN: I know dat's a lie. You know where you goin' alright.

ALICE: You know just what she look like. Go wallow in the mud wit dat pig you was dancin' with the otha night, whoever she is! Or go to hell, if you want! She look like she comes from hell anyhow!

JONES: Look here, Alice Mae, you been tryin' ta accuse me of. . .

ALICE: *(viciously, on the verge of tears)* Nigga please! Don't even start to shape yo' mouth into a lie. *(JONES is stunned with the truth of what she says, drops his head. ALICE disappears.)*

JONES: Seems you coulda at least talk to me 'foe you do all dis. You gon' put me out my house and not even talk to me!

ALICE: *(from the blackness)* We cain't talk no more. All we do is fight and scream. Cain't do that around the children no moe. Day done suffer enough, and so have I. Go stay in the union hall. *(Dim lights momentarily rise on her in a different location.)*

ALICE: Tell the union to cook yo' dinner and wash yo clothes. See how much the union love you. That union is all you ever care about. We don't count. You ain't da kinda man who care about his wife and childrens. You ain't dat kinda man at all. *(Lights out on her.)*

JONES: Don't you tell no lie neither! Dem childrens ain't never been hungry and day got clothes on day back and a shack over day heads. Don't tell me I don't care about mah childrens. I ain't gon' hear dat!

ALICE MAE: *(from the blackness)* You ain't gon' hear nothin' nobody say now. You think you a big leader or somethin'. Thomas Oliver Jones, President of Local 1733. *(Dim lights rise on her.)*

ALICE: Hmph! I was witchu when you was hustling pool in the pool halls, when you was out on the streets scheming. When day used to call you Ollie da Octapus 'cause you had yo' hands in every hustle on the streets. See, don't talk no stuff to me. I know what happened. I done read you for years. I know plenty 'bout you, especially yo' promises. You done made promises to plenty women. They talkin', see? And them promises you made to me? I'm still waitin' on a decent house wit a yard. I been waiting 15 years. Look like me and yo' childrens go from bad to worse and worser and all you think about is a buncha mens totin' garbage. Give dem half yo' paycheck, nevamine yo' family! Das fine and noble, Ollie, but look at the garbage I been totin' all dese years! Yo' garbage! *(Lights fade on her.)*

BLUESMAN: *(hurled into the blackness)* Alright, you want me tell ya I ain't no saint? I ain't neva met nobody wit two legs dat was. All you saints hiding in the darkness behind yo' doors, all you saints listening to me right now. Come out and show me what a saint look like!

JONES: I done eat dirt too, but I still ain't dirt. I'm just a man. Dem buncha mens totin' garbage stayed by me when day fired me in '63. Rememba? We ain't had two pennies ta rub tagetha. Rememba? Rememba when da mens took up collection every week, branged us groceries, branged us clothes, paid da light bill, an' whatinsoeva we needed? While I'm wuckin' any kinda job I could git, includin' hustlin' when I had ta, dem garbage totin' mens toted you all ova town ta do ya shoppin'. Day come by when da childrens git sick. Day show me day respeck us, loved us. Day remember how hard I fight fah dem. Sho, I love da union. *(Dim lights rise on her.)*

ALICE: Then carry yo' ass to the union and git you some lovin', 'cause you sho ain't gittin' none here.

JONES: Don't talk to me like dat, bitch! Dat's my house and I'm comin' in it. I got wuck ta . . .

ALICE: Nigga, I swear befo'e my God, you try to come in this house tonight, me and you gon' fight like the hounds of hell! Ambalance gon' carry one of us outta here tonight! I swear befo'e my God! *(Lights fade out on HER.)*

JONES: Alice Mae, listen ta reason: Dis union bidness somethin' I hafta do. I ain't no rich man kin buy mah way into history books, an' I ain't no scholar kin talk his way into dem. Da union is what I got. I cain't quit da union! *(Dim lights rise on HER.)*

ALICE MAE: *(in weary tears)* I don't want you ta do nothin', but carry yo bags to somebody else doe. Das all I want. Some peace. Das all I want, Ollie, some womanpeace right now. I'm sorry, Ollie, but it's what I have ta do.

JONES: *(after a pause, pulling out some bills)* Well, I guess day ain't nothin' moe ta say. I ain't got but a few dollas, but you kin . . .

ALICE: I don't want yo last dolla, Ollie, but try to rememba me and da childrens when you git paid, okay? Das all I axe, okay?

JONES: Okay.

(ALICE MAE and HE impulsively hug each other. She is crying. With great emotional effort SHE gently pushes him away and turns her back. HE picks up his bags.)

JONES: Alice Mae?

(SHE turns back to him, hopeful of reconciliation.)

ALICE: Yes, Ollie?

JONES: I'll be stayin' down at the Lorraine Motel in case you need me.

ALICE: *(bitterly disappointed)* Okay, Ollie. The Lorraine Motel.

(HE trudges away, the BLUESMAN leading. HE looks back, shakes his head and walks into the blackness. The BLUESMAN plays a walking blues informed by an immediate sadness and subdued rage. Lights and Images shift to the MAYOR's "office" space, a desk and two chairs. Music fades out. It is early Thursday evening. HE sits busily scribbling. JONES, in a suitjacket and tie and carrying a nearly empty duffle bag, enters. The MAYOR gets up to greet him, hand heartily extended which JONES grasps. The BLUESMAN smiles knowingly and takes a seat in the shadows.)

MAYOR: It's been awhile, Mr. Jones.

JONES: Yeah, reckon so.

MAYOR: Have a seat.

JONES: Thank you, Mr. Mayor.

MAYOR: I don't believe I've seen you since the Sanitation Dept. family picnic back in what? '65 was it?

JONES: Believe it was, Mr. Mayor.

MAYOR: *(recalling)* Yes, it was. You were there with your family I recall. What's that oldest one's name, Bubba or something like that?

JONES: Naw, Bubba da second one. He long about 12 years old now. He smellin' his manhood coming on.

MAYOR: Twelve? Isn't it remarkable how fast children grow?

JONES: Yeah, I 'speck das da truf.

MAYOR: Hard to keep up with them. Expensive raising children nowadays, isn't it?

JONES: I 'speck so. I never did meet yo' family, but I pray da Lawd day doin' fine.

MAYOR: *(perfunctorily)* Oh, the missus is just fine. Thank you. Jones, as you may recall, I'm a frank man. How'd you like to be foreman over the truck drivers in all the colored wards?

JONES: *(confused at first)* Foreman?

MAYOR: Yes, foreman. You'd be making almost $4.00 an hour. With that kind of money a man could make enough to take care of his family pretty well.

JONES: *(understanding the bribe offer, tense.)* I ain't come lookin' fa no job, I got one, and dat job brang me here.

MAYOR: And what job is that?

JONES: *(pulling out the papers)* I come to pree-sent this list of union demands.

MAYOR: "Union demands," indeed! The very words are offensive to some people hereabouts.

JONES: Well, Mr. Mayor, but we feel it is our right ta have better wages and better workin' condition. What I got listed here say: We the Public Works Employees of Memphis, Tennessee, do hereby demand recognition for the American Federation of State, County and Municipal Employees as da legal collective bargainin' agent for the Public Works Department of the City of . . .

MAYOR: You memorized it?

JONES: I study it, sho. I got a copy fah you also.

MAYOR: Well, you don't have to recite it to me. I know how to read, Mr. Jones.

JONES: I was just makin' sho' you ain't miss none of it. It's betta when ya say a thing. Den peepas knows what you meaning, 'cause day see yo face and know dat you mean bidness.

MAYOR: You've convinced me that you mean *(correcting)* "business." So, tell about this business, Mr. Jones.

JONES: We fidden ta strike come Monday 'lessen our demands are met.

MAYOR: Is this what you've decided?

JONES: It's what da union decided.

MAYOR: What union? The city recognizes no labor union and has never officially done so since 1819 when Memphis was founded.

JONES: 1819 gone, and we fidden ta strike.

MAYOR: "Fidden'" or no, as the primary representative of the citizens of this community, I am informing you that a strike by city employees is illegal and anyone who violates the law will be prosecuted and jailed. Do I make myself clear?

JONES: Let me be clear too.

(JONES begins undressing which first perplexes the MAYOR and then amuses him. Jones strips off his outer garments and dons workman clothes. BLUESMAN playfully strums "stripper" music during the undressing. When he's done, he turns to the MAYOR.)

JONES: I'm ready ta go ta jail now.

MAYOR: I beg your pardon?

JONES: I'm ready ta go ta jail now. Monday we gon' strike. And da '66 injunction still running.

MAYOR: Mr. Jones, your striptease was certainly dramatic, though not titillating. But I can assure you that no one need go to jail.

JONES: When the injunction break, somebody got ta go ta jail, and I 'speck it's me, since I'm president.

MAYOR: But why do you want to go to jail?

JONES: I don't wanna go ta jail, but da law is da law.

BLUESMAN: Mr. Jones, when I was Public Works Commissioner in '62, I gave you people due consideration. You and I and a few others sat down and talked.

MAYOR: There was no public fuss, no need to strike. You remember? Such was the case also in 1966. In fact, I personally promoted several colored men to truck driver. Now, I can assure you that I'm the same fair man now as I was then. We can reach an equitable agreement without . . .

JONES: *(interrupting)* Mayor, one man good, anotha man bad. Cain't be waitin' and hopin' we git a good man. We wants it wrote out in 'greement wit the union, so's we kin have good even when it's bad runnin' Public Works Department.

MAYOR: *(impatient, exasperated)* Let me line up the facts for you. One, . . .

JONES: *(interrupting)* Ain't matta how you line up da facts if dat line don't lead to da union.

MAYOR: *(burst of anger)* I will not be subject to anyone's demands. I have the interests of this city to protect and, believe me, Mr. Jones, I will protect them.

JONES: *(angry, but cool)* Mr. Mayor, you lookin' at a impo'tent part of yo' city right now. Me and da mens I represents. You 'sposed ta protect all da peepas. I 'speck sanitation workers need plenty protection, totin' all dat garbage.

MAYOR: Maybe you better consider the options open to me. There are hundreds of men out there who would appreciate an opportunity to be employed by the Public Works Department.

JONES: *(openly angry, standing)* Scabs? You put on scabs?

MAYOR: *(standing and close to shouting)* New sanitation workers is what I'd call them. We can't allow garbage to accumulate. That's endangering public health. I won't stand for that! You understand me, Jones?

JONES: Well, da mens cain't stan' no moe of dese conditions. We shall not be moved! You unnastan' me, Mr. Mayor?

MAYOR: I do speak English.

JONES: I ain't talkin' 'bout whatchu speakin', I'm talkin' 'bout whatchu hearin'! You ain't hearin' me. Da mens meetin' in the Retail Clerk's union hall rat now waitin' fah word from me. If I goes back dere and tell 'em ta withhold service, day gon' sho'nuff do dat. So, you better sit yo ass down and listen ta me. *I'm* in control here!

MAYOR: *(derisive chortle)* In control, is it? I'll tell you what. I'll go over to that meeting and personally explain what I've been trying . . .

JONES: You will do no such a thing. Dem mens won't hear a word you say 'lessen *I* authorizes you ta speak.

MAYOR: Unless you *what* me?

JONES: I believe you heard me.

MAYOR: *(out of control) I* don't need some *nigger* to authorize *me* to do anything!

(JONES slaps the MAYOR's face resoundingly which literally knocks the MAYOR on his ass. The MAYOR is both emotionally and physically stunned and then a bit fearful as JONES hovers over him.)

JONES: I ain't no nigga! I am a man. You hear what I say? *I AM A MAN!*

(The MAYOR scrambles backward to his feet as he tries to recover and regain his composure. JONES glares at him. The BLUESMAN has gotten up and struck an ominous chord.)

MAYOR: You get out of my office now!

(THEY stare at each other for a moment. Then JONES storms out, the BLUESMAN trailing. The MAYOR picks up the phone. On a chord from the BLUESMAN Lights and Projected Images shift to Jones' room at the Lorraine Motel, a space with a chair and a nightstand. WEATHERFORD AND MOORE, in black suits and collars, anxiously follow JONES into the room. The images are of the Lorraine Motel neon sign and the surrounding neighborhood in 1968, dilapidated, weathered, worn, old and bitter. JONES dresses as he and the MINISTERS speak. WEATHERFORD speaks in a precise British accent although he is a naturalized Canadian.)

MOORE: You cain't be going 'round slapping the mayor upside his head! Lawd ha'mercy!

BLUESMAN: You've unwisely increased his intransigence.

WEATHERFORD: Yes, I fear that you've unwisely increased his intransigence.

MOORE: I told you not to get emotional around no Espiscopalian! Lawd ha' mercy! Teach me how to pray! He coulda had you lynched!

JONES: Naw! I knew he wouldn't do dat. The Mayor's a wrong man, but, underneath it all, he ain't a bad one. He was in the wrong and he knew it. I could see it in his eyes.

WEATHERFORD: I suggest the spontaneous physical assault was equally wrong.

MOORE: Amen! Violence won't settle the strike.

JONES: I know that Rev. Moore, Rev. Weatherford. I believe nunviolence, but . . . well, I was peaceful, 'til he called me a nigga to my face. Anyhow, whas done is done. I gotta move on now.

MOORE: Jones, I . . .

WEATHERFORD: Forgive my interruption, Rev. Moore, but his assessment is quite rational. We should be marshalling effective community support now.

JONES: There you go!

WEATHERFORD: And we should start with the Memphis Ministers Coalition.

MOORE: Hmmph! I don't get along with that coalition; they have social status on the brain.

WEATHERFORD: Perhaps, but their influence is seminal in Memphis. They're the most powerful Negro organization in town.

JONES: But they down on the union man.

MOORE: Brother Weatherford, you've only been in Memphis about six months now. London is not like Memphis atall. Let me explain: Lots

of those ministers in the coalition have those big fine church buildings, the ones that good white Christian folks abandoned when Negroes moved into their neighborhoods. And when the Negro ministers
who run the coalition got into those abandoned churches, they started
breathing the same stale air.

JONES: Amen. Back yonda, in '66, one of dem coalition ministers tried
to stop us from striking! Went ta preachin' against us. Asked the Lawd
to evict us from the building we was renting. Even got ta talkin' in
tongues 'n carryin' on!

MOORE: Lawd ha'mercy!

WEATHERFORD: The Lord works in mysterious ways, His wonders to
perform. We mustn't forget Isaiah, Chapter 1, Verse 18: "Come now
let us reason together . . . though your sins be as scarlet, they shall be
white as snow; . . ."

MOORE: Lord, forgive me, but that's the one verse in Isaiah I don't like.

WEATHERFORD: Truly?

MOORE: Truly, but that's another story. He's right, T.O., we gotta get
that coalition on our side. Rev. Weatherford, you take on the coalition; I'll take on the Negro Ministerial Alliance. That way we'll cover
all the Negro ministers in town.

JONES: Fine. Ya'll got da ministers, but rememba, dis is a labor movement, not no prayer meeting. I run things, and I intend to make dat
Mayor accept my union. I'll personally contact my international and
the AFL-CIO peepas. Plus the NAACP. I know whole lotta peepas
on Beale Street come help us. And what about white people in
Memphis? We should git some support from da white folks too.
Rev. Weatherford?

WEATHERFORD: Unfortunately, I can't help you there. I'm the pastor of
an all Negro congregation; I live in an all Negro neighborhood; and
the only organizations I belong to are all Negro. I don't know any
white people in Memphis. I fear you will simply have to find someone
whiter than me to be a knowledgeable liaison. I detest being so anomalous, but such are the present unequivocal circumstances.

MOORE: Do you talk like that when you preach in your all Negro church?

WEATHERFORD: Well, rather . . .

MOORE: Lawd ha'mercy! You wanna keep being a pastor at a all Negro
church, you gon' have to speak a different language. (mimicking)
"Anomalous" and "Unequivocal circumstances" won't bring the Holy
Spirit anywhere near your all Negro church.

WEATHERFORD: (poking fun at himself) I am resolutely striving away from
tedious intellectual discourse toward an effective homiletic permuta-
tion, as it were. (THEY all laugh. JONES is finished dressing and prepared
to depart.)

JONES: It's time to rock and roll.

(As the BLUESMAN *strums an ironic chord, Lights and Images shift to NAACP offices where* MISS SECRETARY *waits. A huge image of W.E.B. Dubois dominates. Other images are of various civil rights protest activities of the '60s.* JONES *merely walks into her space from his previous position. The dialogue should begin before he enters, immediately after* JONES' *previous line. It is now Saturday afternoon.)*

MISS S: The NAACP is a civil rights organization, not a labor advocate group.

JONES: Day violatin' our right to strike 'cause we public works.

MISS S: T.O., it's more complicated than that. *You* said that they treat the workers badly because they are Negro.

JONES: I said that, sho'. Das a problem. But we ain't striking to be Negro, we striking for a union. Put da union in place first and den work out da mechanics 'bout bein' Negro.

MISS S: A good labor lawyer is what you need for that. You should contact your international for that kinda help.

JONES: International ain't got two cents in dis quarta yet.

MISS S: You mean they don't know you're goin' on strike?

JONES: We cain't be waitin' fah peepas sittin' behine desks up North to tell us when we kin strike. We at the battle front, not dem.

MISS S: T.O., I think you have to get the international's approval. I mean, your local is affiliated. You're a paid organizer. You need their support.

JONES: Well, I 'tend ta call dem soon as we get da strike goin'.

MISS S: That's not what I mean.

JONES: Das what we mean.

MISS S: *(sighing heavily in resignation)* Are you planning to picket or anything?

JONES: We havin' a 'mergency meetin' with the Mayor's Advisory Bode tomorrow. If day don't go 'long wit my demands, then we strike.

MISS S: *(laughs somewhat derisively)* Tomorrow! Why, that's utterly ridiculous, there's no time to . . . a few days more would . . .

BLUESMAN AND JONES: *(angrily, sensing condescension)* It's all the time we got! Do da bes' you can.

MISS S: But, T.O., okay. All right . . . I understand all that, honest I really do. My origins are humble too, but I can't get my board of directors together on such short notice.

JONES: *(rising to leave)* We ain't waitin' on nobody.

MISS S: I'm with you, but you have to trust me. This is a complex situation. It'll take some complex maneuvering, you know?

(Lights and Images shift to a City Hall meeting room again. It is Saturday evening. The MAYOR *and* CHIEF OF POLICE *watch and listen to the* COLLABORATOR.*)*

MAYOR: Is there anything else we should know about?

COLL: Well, not much else, Mr. Mayor. 'Cept maybe you might be interested to know that Jones been staying over at the Lorraine Motel ever since his wife threw him out. That's where Martin Luther King stays whenever he comes to Memphis. Could be a coincidence or not. But since Hoover thinks that King is definitely hooked up with the Communists, it's something we feel we should keep an eye on.

MAYOR: Fine, see that you do. Chief?

CHIEF: You're dismissed for now.

MAYOR: I won't be at the meeting with the so-called strikers. I intend to monitor events from my office. The Senior Negro Councilman will preside. I trust you've taken precautions?

CHIEF: Of course. *(handing him a pistol)* And keep this with you. Just a further precaution.

(Lights and images cut to the special meeting. A screen says: FEB. 22, CITY COUNCIL CHAMBERS. JONES, MOORE and the CHIEF wait expectantly. The BLUESMAN plays gospel style riffs on "We Shall Not Be Moved," a traditional spiritual. Flashbulbs go off. We hear sounds of hundreds of grumbling men in a cavernous meeting chamber. A large city seal of Memphis dominates the room. The SENIOR NEGRO COUNCILMAN enters, sits under the seal, and raps his gavel to begin the meeting. A few flashbulbs go off. The music fades to silence.)

COUNCILMAN: Let it be understood that the Advisory Board's purpose here is to get information and make recommendations to the full City Council. No decisions can be made this morning.

JONES: Den watchu call us here for? We need a decision now!

(We hear sounds of applause and cheers of support. The COUNCILMAN is shaken.)

COUNCILMAN: We've heard Mr. Jones. Would anyone else like to contribute?

(JONES looks sternly at the men which apparently intimidates them. He turns back to the COUNCILMAN.)

JONES: We say we wants ta be recognized as a union now!

COUNCILMAN: I just saw a few hands go up. Let the men speak for themselves. We want to hear directly from their mouths!

JONES: We speakin' wit one voice tonight.

COUNCILMAN: *(to the MEN)* Look, you men have the authority of the Board to back you up. Don't be intimidated by this man's rudeness and disrespect for your intelligence.

JONES: Onliest one rude here is you! You has no respeck!

MOORE: He's the elected representative of the union. He speaks for the men.

COUNCILMAN: Unacceptable! The city does not recognize that union and therefore will not entertain the showboat ranting of some so-called representative.

BLUESMAN: Rantin'! You wanna hear some rantin'? Let me tell 'bout that city seal you got hanging over yo' head.

JONES: See dat steamboat? It bring slaves up and downriver for trading. The cotton boll? Dat's what da slaves pick ta make a few peepas rich. That oak leaf is where day tied the slave to beat him or where they hanged him. Used ta whip ya wit dem oak sticks too. Dat piece a machinery? Dat's the wheel of progress dat grine the slave up. Da Civa War ova, but we still fighting against slavery. Chop cotton for three dollas a day or tote garbage for one dolla and sixty cent a hour. Da union come here ta finally stop slavery.

COUNCILMAN: Out of order! Be silent or be held in contempt.

JONES: Since when we in coat and who made you judge?

COUNCILMAN: I'm warning you . . . I

JONES: We don't take order from a flunkey. Where da Mayor hidin'?

COUNCILMAN: This hearing is adjourned! Clear the chambers!

JONES: Yeah, we'll clear the chambers alright. Let's have us a parade! Let's clear outta hear and have us a parade. We'll picket the whole town. Some of ya'll put the word out. Git everybody you can down here now. Let's take our grievance to the world!

(JONES and the MEN break into a spontaneous and spirited reprise of "We Shall Not Be Moved," lyrics appropriately adapted to the immediate circumstances. Led by JONES, the MEN begin filing out. The CHIEF and the COUNCILMAN angrily exit. Lights and Images crossfade. Sounds of street traffic and a public demonstration drift in. It is the afternoon of Feb. 22. JONES leads the men from the "Council Chamber" to the "street." The images are of a street down which JONES, MOORE AND WEATHERFORD enter in single file as if in a parade/demonstration. Images should be photographs of the actual demonstrations and marches that were ongoing during the strike. There especially should be photos of the men carrying signs that all say I AM A MAN. These photos and film clips of same can be obtained from the Mississippi Valley Collection at the Memphis State Library and/or from Europe Withers, the then photographer of the Tri-State Defender. SEVERAL INVADERS march through on the periphery in a doubletime lockstep. The music fades out. Near Jones, Moore and Weatherford walk TWO POLICEMEN, ONE BLACK AND ONE WHITE. THEY wear riot gear and carry gas masks, shields and batons. THEY have a walkie talkie from which we hear occasional static. The images will change appropriately with the ensuing activity. The BLUESMAN strolls by playing improvisationally, receives tips in his cup.)

WEATHERFORD: Seems to be some delay up front.

JONES: Probably traffic. Day should halt traffic for us 'stead of da otha way 'round.

MOORE: Since this march is spontaneous, we have to accept delays because the police are playing it by ear too. We shoulda planned this. Something ain't right. You think there's trouble up there?

WEATHERFORD: *(mischievously)* There's about 12 ministers at the head of the march. Their presence assures a modicum of sobriety.

MOORE: Indubitably! Perhaps!

WEATHERFORD: The ministers up front are well versed in Martin Luther King's tactics of nonviolent resistance.

JONES: Ain't got nothin' ta worry about, Rev. Moore.

MOORE: *(muttering aloud)* Maybe. I dunno.

JONES: Ain't been no trouble yet and we ain't lookin' for none.

MOORE: But I seem some of them Invaders lurking around. I hear they talk a lot of revolutionary stuff.

JONES: Let dem Invaders talk. Day only talkin' and we only walkin'.

WEATHERFORD: What in Heaven's name are Invaders?

MOORE: It's a gang of young hotheads that claims to be revolutionaries. Hmph! They got their name from a tv program called Invaders.

WEATHERFORD: A TV program?

MOORE: As the Lord is my witness. Those people make me nervous hanging around here.

JONES: Don't worry 'bout no Invaders; day ain't got two cents in this quarta. Everything is unda con . . . Wait a minute. Looka dere.

(JONES stares intently at one of the POLICEMEN, calls out to him and approaches him.)

JONES: Peewee Slocum? Is that Peewee, Jasper Slocum's baby brotha?

(The BLACK POLICEMAN pulls off his sunglasses, recognizes and smiles.)

BLK. POL: Thomas Oliver Jones, I'll be damned. Ain't this somethin'! *(THEY laughingly embrace.)*

JONES: Last time I seed you yo' brotha was chasin' you along the river, fidden ta kill you. Said you threw his bike into the Mississippi River.

BLK. POL: I did and he caught me and beat my butt all the way home.

JONES: I ain't never seen no cullud child run dat fast. How is Jasper?

BLK. POL: Aww, he moved over ta a little town in eastern Tennessee, say he don't like western Tennessee. Uh, brotha Jones, if you don't mine me axin', how long ya'll gon' be marchin'? My wife folks comin' over today and she got a barbecue all planned.

JONES: I don't reckon this one today gon' las' too long. It just grew, sudden. Look here, dis is Rev. Weatherford and Rev. Moore. Day supporting us.

BLK. POL: Pleased ta make yo' acquaintance, reverends. I been knowin' T.O. since I was almos' a baby. Him and my big brotha was in the Navy together. *(referring to the other* WHITE POLICEMAN*)* And this is my partner, Jeffrey Cavender.

WEATHERFORD: It's certainly a pleasure to make both your acquaintances.

WHITE POLICEMAN *(removing glasses, shaking hands.)* Likewise, reverends.

MOORE: This weather is perfect, Lawd ha'mercy!

WHITE POL: Supposed to stay this way all day and most of tomorrow.

WEATHERFORD: *(lustily)* Lord have mercy for that as well.

MOORE: Too bad ya'll have to carry all that heavy equipment on a day nice as this.

BLK. POL: It's our job, ain't got no choice.

MOORE: Yeah, duty first, right?

WHITE POL: Yep, that's about it. Gotta put bread on the table like everybody else.

(CROWD SOUNDS AHEAD increase and shortly afterwards so does the walkie-talkie static. Suddenly, A CLEAR VOICE blares out from the walkie-talkie.)

VOICE: CLEAR THE STREETS! CODE 5! REPEAT: CLEAR THE STREETS! CODE 5!

POLICEMEN: MOVE! MOVE! MOVE! MOVE! MOVE! MOVE! MOVE! MOVE! MOVE! MOVE!

(The Lights abruptly reflect an almost surrealistic terrorism. POLICEMEN suddenly don glasses and begin spraying mace into the eyes of everyone. CROWD SOUNDS: PEOPLE yelling, screaming, running. SEVERAL PEOPLE run across the playing space yelling and rubbing their eyes. POLICEMEN spray and club them as they pass. Sirens wail in the distance. Tear gas is released. The Cops put on gas masks. Projected Images change rapidly and reflect what really happened in the actual march of Feb. 22, 1968. The BLUESMAN plays discordantly, wildly as the activity swirls about him. JONES, yelling to the Policeman to stop, tries to fight the POLICEMEN, but is pulled offstage by MOORE who suffers from macing. WEATHERFORD, blinded by the mace, stumbles about, his eyes burning from the mace. He unbuttons his coat and frantically searches for a hankie. The WHITE COP sees this and yells.)

WHITE COP: He's got a gun! Watch out!

(The WHITE COP fires twice, hitting WEATHERFORD in his chest which instantly kills him.)

POLICEMEN: MOVE! MOVE! MOVE! MOVE! MOVE! MOVE! MOVE! MOVE!

(Lights and images crosscut to interior and exterior shots of the Lorraine Motel, JONES' room. The Music has faded to silence. The BLUESMAN sits in a

corner, softly playing a slow, meditative tune. The Sign says: LATE THAT EVENING, LORRAINE HOTEL, JONES' ROOM. JONES is alone, nursing his bruises.)

VOICE OF MLK: ". . . nations are caught up with the drum major instinct. I must be first . . . God didn't call America to engage in a senseless, unjust war, [such] as the war in Vietnam. We are criminals in that war . . . And we won't stop it because of our pride, and our arrogance as a nation . . ."

(The phone rings. The music fades to silence as the lights fade to black on the BLUESMAN.)

JONES: Hello.
TELEPHONE VOICE: Is this *the* T.O. Jones?
JONES: It is. Who dis?
VOICE: T.O. Don't that mean TAKE OUT?
JONES: Who is dis?
VOICE: I'm a messenger.
JONES: From who?
VOICE: From people who uphold morality.
JONES: Why you call?
VOICE: Don't you have two sons?
JONES: What you want?
VOICE: I saw your sons coming home from school. They always come the same way.
JONES: What about my sons?
VOICE: They come from a nigger like you; means they're polluted too. Yore whole line got ta be stopped.
JONES: You want me—come git me, if you a real man. You know where I'm at, otherwise you ain't shit!
VOICE: Well, nigger, in case you don't know it yet, yore dead. And we gon' hack off yore sons balls, just ta make certain yore kind don't propagate. And, speaking of shit, we're gon' cut off yore head and shit in yore mouth. Bye, nigger!

(HE angrily hangs up, thinks a moment, gets scared, searches a piece of luggage, pulls out a pistol. He grabs the phone, nervously dials ALICE MAE. The phone awakens her. Dim lights rise on her in a nightgown.)

ALICE: Hello.
JONES: It's Ollie, baby.
ALICE: Ollie? Whas wrong? Somethin' wrong, ain't it?
JONES: Are the childrens all right?
ALICE: They sleep, like I was. Whas done happen, Ollie?
JONES: Make sho' all da does locked, and don't let nobody in.

ALICE: The does? What . . . Ollie, whas wrong? You in trouble 'cause of that parade mess this morning? Ain't you? You hurt or anything?

JONES: Yeah, but I'm all right. Just a few bruises. My eyes still itchin' from the mace, but nothin' too bad.

ALICE: I saw all dat mess on TV and read 'bout it in da *Scimitar*. Day say ya'll attacked da police and started a riot. Turned over a squad car. Everything. Said somebody even pulled a gun on the police.

JONES: Well, das freedom of da press fah ya, I reckon. But it ain't got nothin' ta do with da truth. Police car run over some woman's foot. She went ta screaming and everything went outta control. They outright murdered Rev. Weatherford and beat the rest of us. Look, Alice Mae, we can't let the childrens go to school tomorrow. I'll be over dere in a few minutes and explain.

ALICE: They afta you, ain't they? You done gone and riled up white folks, ain't you? They wanna hurt my children too, don't they?

JONES: Naw, I ain't heard nothin' 'bout dat, but I figures it better ta play it safe 'til we see what they thinkin'. You cain't be too careful when it comes to wild crackers.

ALICE: *(trembling, near tears)* T.O., don't let them people hurt my childrens! Don't care what you have to do. Don't let them peepas hurt my childrens! They been hurt enough. Please Lawd!

JONES: Just lock da doors good and wait on me. Ya'll safe right now. All right, Alice Mae? *(Silence. JONES panics.)*

JONES: Alright, Alice Mae? Alice Mae! Alice!

ALICE: All right, Ollie.

(Lights out on ALICE. Someone pounds on JONES' door. HE jumps in fright, cocks his pistol. The pounding is insistent.)

VOICE: Jones, it's brothers in the struggle. Open the door. Jones!

JONES: Who is it!

VOICE: It's Swahili, man! Swahili!

(JONES cautiously lets them enter, points the gun at them initially. SWAHILI and CINNAMON, cum "revolutionary attire," dark glasses, check the place out. CINNAMON remains at attention by the door and always walks and stands at attention throughout scenes in which he appears. THEY each briefly remove glasses when introducing themselves by name; otherwise they'll wear them throughout the play.)

SWAHILI: Habari Gani, mzee. Sheikamu! We the Invaders formally greet you in solidarity and brotherly love.

BLUESMAN: You never met us, but I'm certain you heard of us in the local fascist press.

JONES: Yeah, I heard of ya. Ya'll got some kinda Black Panther gang goin'.

BLUESMAN: The wretched of the earth have been bathed in the perception of those who torture them.

SWAHILI: We captured Africans in America don't know nothin' about ourselves 'cept what we read in the two most racist newspapers in the South. We ain't got nothin' ta do with da Panthers. That's anotha story, but we wit dem in Black Solidarity. *(Unique salute)* Power to the People!

CINNAMON: *(returning salute)* Powa ta da Peepas!

SWAHILI: They call me Swahili. This is my podna, Brotha Cinnamon. He's the other half of the body guard contingent assigned to protect you by Commander Whisper. I know you heard about P.J. Whisper!

JONES: Yeah, I believe somebody tole me day read about him too.

SWAHILI: They lied! P.J. Whisper trying to bring knowledge and discipline to the community. He feels the community have the right to defend theyself against enemies by any means necessary. He don't mean no harm to nobody 'bout nothin', just so long as they don't mean no harm to captured Africans in America. That's his whole philosophy in a nutshell. And he got a social program go 'long wit dat.

JONES: What bring ya'll here tonight?

SWAHILI: You represent the only Black power move in this city. Everybody else talkin' and walkin' in step to whitey's brass band. You ˙ stepped forward and declared yo'self a Black man. You a runaway. That's dangerous in Babylon. These crackers fidden ta swoop down on you like a flock of ducks on a fat junebug. You need protection and the Invaders program say protect you at all costs, by any means necessary, even against yo' will if need be. You a asset to the poor, working people. We here to serve and protect you and yo' family from the people who say they're civilized but act like beasts, even toward one another. We got a squad stationed outside yo' wife home now. And me and Brotha Cinnamon, we stationed outside yo' door. That's it, Mzee. *(Saluting)* Power to the People.

CINNAMON: *(saluting Jones)* Powa ta da peepas!

JONES: You say you got somebody outside my wife doe right now?

SWAHILI: Back and front doe. Where you and yo' family go, we go too. Invaders are thorough.

JONES: How P.J. Whisper fine out I need protection?

SWAHILI: Whisper got ways of knowing everything happenin' in Memphis if it got anything ta do with capture Africans.

JONES: How long ya'll figure to give protection?

SWAHILI: For as long as the nation is endangered. Face up to it! You a leader, brotha, a righteous warrior. We at your command, my brotha! We give respect and praise to you. We prepared to give our lives to save yours.

JONES: Thank Gawd fah dat! Lawd knows I needs help now!

SWAHILI: We that help. Walk strong in righteousness. And don't forget: the lord you talkin' 'bout is a Black man. We won't disturb you anymore tonight. You needs yo' res' after the battle you fought today. But, just ta let you know we serious brothas in the revolution:

(*THEY open their jackets to reveal pistols and sawed-off doublebarrel shotguns. JONES is impressed.*)

JONES: I got me a army at las'!

SWAHILI: Power to the People!

CIN: Powa ta da peepas!

(*As lights fade quickly to black on them, a single light rises on the BLUESMAN. MLK's VOICE speaks. The BLUESMAN plays softly a refrain of "We Shall Not Be Moved" under his voice.*)

MLK's VOICE: ". . . recognize that he who is greatest among you shall be your servant . . . it means that everybody can be great. Because everybody can serve . . . You don't have to have a college degree to serve. You don't have to make your subject and verb agree to serve . . . You only need a heart full of grace. A soul generated by love. And you can be that servant."

(*As the BLUESMAN exits, he continues playing the refrain. Lights to black.*)

End of Act 1

Act 2

(*When Houselights are at half, MLK's VOICE speaks.*)

MLK's VOICE: ". . . I'm delighted to see each of you here tonight in spite of a storm warning. You reveal that you are determined to go on anyhow. Something is happening in Memphis, something is happening in our world . . ."

(*Lights and Images and SOUND suggest an airport lounge. It is the next day. The BLUESMAN, wearing a t-shirt that says "BEALE STREET BLUES," stands in a separate light playing softly, his cup available for donations. JOSH SOLOMON, white, CRAIG WILLINS, Black, both carrying bags, enter conversing heatedly with JONES. SOLOMON walks with a noticeable limp due to a foot deformation from childhood polio. Willins carries a copy of the* Commercial Appeal *newspaper. A PERSON enters and dumps garbage nearby and exits. For the remainder of the play, SOMEONE will enter and dump garbage in the playing areas, causing an accumulation that doesn't interfere with the playing too much. Sometimes specific dumping is indicated in the stage directions. The GARBAGE DUMPER will not be noticed by the OTHERS. Wherever possible the garbage itself should be used as props, as tables, as chairs, as food, as artifacts, as filing cabinets, etc. Items will actually be taken from garbage cans and piles of garbage by the actors.)*

SOLOMON: Why didn't ya notify us sooner, T.O.?

JONES: Things movin' so fast, wudden no time.

BLUESMAN: Man, would you stop that! Please? What happened to your union discipline?

WILLINS: Team? Remember? You're on a team. You can't just call a strike any ole time you please.

JONES: Why not? We a union, ain't we?

BLUESMAN: You're a union local affiliated with AFSCME. I'm the international representative and he's a top field assistant.

SOLOMON: *(railing)* We're your brothers in this struggle. How in hell do we, your brothers, end up being the last to hear about the strike? Some damn newspaper calls me up in New York and wants my comments. "Duhhh," what do I know from a strike in Memphis? I tell 'im, I'm in N.Y., in my office, spreading cream cheese. They print it!

JONES: *(angry at Willins)* And we was down here eatin' garbage! We went on strike! If you cain't support us, den . . .

(ANOTHER PERSON enters, dumps garbage nearby and exits.)

SOLOMON: Relax! We're in your corner. Forgive us. Jetlag, ya know? He dropped everything and came here on 12 hours notice. My wife is having a difficult pregnancy. Touch and go. Not your problems, of course. We're irritated agitators from New York is all. Look, let's drop it. Where are we headed first?

JONES: To yo' hotel, I reckon.

SOLOMON: Can we move out or what? I need to call my wife; we've got an appointment with the Mayor . . .

JONES: My escort be here d'rectly. Day a few minutes behine schedule.

WILLINS: How about a taxi? They have taxis in Memphis?

JONES: Da situation such we betta off wit my escort.

SOLOMON: What is this escort?

JONES: Some peepas done threaten my life and my family's. These brothas wanna make sho of safety. Das all. Just our safety.

WILLINS: I hope you kept a record of the threats. We could use that.

JONES: I remembas everything.

WILLINS: We could have a press conference on that alone this afternoon. Speaking of the press down here, they're giving you hell. What's your overall assessment of local press coverage?

JONES: Da press in the Mayor's pocket, so I don't botha wit 'em.

SOLOMON: The press has got to be spoonfed. You can't ignore them when you're conducting a public strike. They'll nail ya to the wall. Look, one question I have to ask. Why the hell did ya call a strike in February when garbage don't stink?

JONES: Garbage stink all da time when you got ta carry it on yo' head.

SOLOMON: Good answer.

WILLINS: Which has nothing to do with the question!

JONES: I answer the question! He axe me . . .

WILLINS: I heard what he asked you. You've called a strike with no preparation and no backing from the International, and you expect us to just come down here at your personal behest and jump right on in like we're only baking a blueberry pie or something. You're a paid AFSCME organizer, $1,000 a month, since 1964. All the training sessions you've been to, you can't remember to call us?

JONES: We called you in '66 when we wanted ta strike.

SOL: And we immediately sent someone to assist you.

JONES: And he tole us, say go back to wuck, obey da coat injunction. Hmph! I got more done dealin' wit the city den yo' man did wit all his runnin' 'roun' and press conferencin'.

SOL: And when our man got back to N.Y., I fired him for backing down from a mere injunction.

WILLINS: And, the fact is, injunction or no, you all were just as unprepared then as now. It was damned unwise and it jeopardized our plans for . . .

SOLOMON: Willya lay off, Willins. That's history. Whadda ya gonna do? We got a strike to win, and I got an appointment with your Mayor to which I'll be late if your "escorts" don't get here soon. As a matter of fact, I think I'll catch . . .

JONES: Here dey is now. I tole 'em all 'bout ya'll.

(SWAHILI AND CINNAMON enter in a fast lockstep type of walk. THEY are wary of SOLOMON because he is white, but they are stiffly polite.)

SWAHILI: *(formally to Solomon)* You must be Joshua Solomon and *(warmly)* you must be brotha Craig Willins, the great organizer of the people. Power to the people!

CINNAMON: Powa ta da peepas!

SOLOMON: *(subtlest sarcasm)* I feel utterly safe! What can I say? Very secure. Can we get to the hotel now?

JONES: *(sensing, uneasy)* Sho, we kin do dat.

SOLOMON: *(to JONES as they all exit)* On the way over fill us in on everything.

(Lights and images and sound cut to a "banquet hall" where suspended are three flags, confederate, U.S., and the state flag of Tennessee. We hear a

tremendous ovation and see the MAYOR graciously acknowledging the "au-
dience." He stands behind a "garbagecan podium." SOLOMON and WILLINS,
wary and bored, watch from the "back" of the hall. As the MAYOR speaks,
several times PEOPLE come out and empty kitchen garbage containers or
place a garbage can somewhere, adding to the piles. Flashbulbs go off as the
MAYOR speaks.)

MAYOR: I thank you for this most kind honor. I had only stopped in on
my way to a very important meeting and hadn't expected to be acknowledged at this gathering. After all, we're here today to honor
Frank, the highly esteemed publisher of what I consider to be the very
best newspaper in the South, the Memphis *Scimitar*. Under Frank the
Scimitar has stood for the very best values the South has to offer, and,
I might add, the nation has to offer. Stability, truth, justice, honesty,
hard work, solid family values. It is only fitting and proper that Frank
be honored by the Jewish and Christian Fellowship Society of Memphis. His newspaper has brought more inter-ethnic and inter-faith
understanding than any other institution I can think of in this town.
Frank and I go a long ways back. The same Alma Mater, same church,
same neighborhood, same watering spots. *(A ripple of polite chuckles
from the "audience.")* I won't dwell on that last reference. *(More polite
chuckles.)* And I won't take up anymore of your time. I would like to
acknowledge Joshua Solomon, the international representative of the
American Federation of State County and Municipal Employees, who's
come here to meet with me and help me solve an important labor
dispute that is occurring as I speak this very moment. Joshua, where
are you? *(SOLOMON half-heartedly raises his hand and accepts very luke-
warm applause.)* Thank you, ladies and gentlemen; I bid you adieu
and God bless each and every one of you.

*(Another rousing, long ovation and flashbulbs popping as the MAYOR leaves
the area and walks into his office where he meets SOLOMON. The BLUESMAN
pushes on a desk that is made of garbage cans. Lights and images shift.)*

SOLOMON: I'm here on behalf of Mr. Jones and his men who work in the
sanitation department.
MAYOR: Ah yes, the deranged Mr. Jones.
SOLOMON: You say deranged?
BLUESMAN: He came into my office, flashed me, and for no reason struck
me.
SOLOMON: Flashed ya? Whaddya mean?
MAYOR: He pulled off his clothes and struck me.
SOLOMON: I don't know what you're talking about. I came because they
are members of my union and they've declared a strike.

MAYOR: They are poor, uneducated colored men to whom the city extends an opportunity to earn a living that is on a level with their education, or lack of it.

SOLOMON: I can't believe what I'm hearing.

MAYOR: Those men were riled up by an irresponsible Mr. Jones who has some ignorant political agenda up his sleeve. I suggest you get your facts straight if you want to help me resolve the problem.

SOLOMON: Let's be frank, Mr. Mayor. I am not here to help *you* to do anything. I'm here to help a bunch of poor working men salvage a little dignity out of this whole mess.

MAYOR: In 1956 the distinguished novelist William Faulkner gave the Negroes some solid advice in an essay he called "If I Were a Negro." He said, "We must learn to deserve equality so that we can hold and keep it after we get it. We must learn responsibility, the responsibility of equality." (*Ebony* Magazine, 9/56, pp. 70–73)

SOLOMON: Hey, sounds great, but I'm not a Southern fiction man. I do know that Southern fiction and Southern reality get mixed up sometimes. But I never needed a book to tell me that. Maybe one day we'll do literary chitchat over tea. Right now I have another purpose.

MAYOR: I think I know your purpose, Mr. Solomon.

SOLOMON: And I think I know yours. I know why you dragged us through that syrupy Christian and Jewish . . .

MAYOR: Jewish and Christian . . .

SOLOMON: Right. Look, first I think: what is this "Take a Jew to Lunch" bit? I think it's useless. But anyway, that's another story. Then I realize you want me to witness what a great guy they think you are. You smile and preen before the cameras and then come into the lion's den with me.

MAYOR: I'm hardly what you'd call a lion, Mr. Solomon.

SOLOMON: Not you, me. Your banquets don't impress me, unless they can deliver formal recognition of the union, union dues checkoff, an immediate wage increase and vastly improved working conditions. That dues checkoff is paramount. We want city payroll to deduct dues directly from the paychecks and give the money to us.

MAYOR: That wage increase is worth discussing, but the other three are illegal and impossible. This whole thing is beginning to sound like a union ploy to get the men's money. This city has never dealt with unions and never will.

SOLOMON: Bullshit! Ever since Mayor Crump's administration back in 1909 and even before that—since the Civil War ended—there's been informal recognition of every white union in this town that does any business with the government.

MAYOR: Congratulations, you've done some homework.

SOLOMON: Yeah, I did a little homework on Memphis and you too.

MAYOR: Then surely you understand that the Crump administration set the precedent, which is that the city merely generates certain understandings with certain contractors who, in turn, deal with their workers. And if there are ever problems, they are handled through the open door policy that this administration follows. Why, I've done more personally for those men than any other administrator in this city; I . . .

SOLOMON: In other words, we can come to the big house on our knees and beg you for favors.

MAYOR: New Yorkers love the theater.

SOLOMON: And there's plenty of it here in Memphis. Mr. Mayor, this strike is not going to go away.

MAYOR: *(waving letters)* And neither is the opposition, Mr. Solomon. I've gotten hundreds of letters supporting my position. Memphis is known as America's cleanest city. We aim to keep it that way. Here's numerous letters from volunteers who've offered to help collect garbage: Jaycees, Boy Scouts, church groups, P.T.A.s, college professors, you name it, even a couple of Negro organizations. I shall not back down from my position!

SOLOMON: Position? You mean as in prize *geshmat*? Huh? Best little ole converted Jew this side of the West Bank.

MAYOR: *(angry, defensive)* I don't think you're making any sense now.

SOLOMON: I'm making all the sense in the world if ya had the sense to see what's really happening in this town. You lost your guts and converted to Episcopalianism.

MAYOR: That has nothing to do with . . .

SOLOMON: It has to do with everything. What are ya, crazy? Or some kind of perverted *shlemiel*? It's one thing for a Jew to convert to Christianity. It's something else for a Jew to convert to redneck posturing. You should know better! You're upholding a system that hates Jews too! You can't be a redneck *putz* without hating Jews, along with Negroes and anybody else who ain't redneck. You wanna get along down here, so you go along with whatever they tell ya. You're a goddam *putz* is what ya are!

BLUESMAN: You have no right to come here telling me how to live my life, what to believe and what to be!

MAYOR: If you were from Memphis, you'd understand some very basic things about this place. My family's been here four generations. One learns that there are regional traditions which you may not be astute enough to understand, but which have brought any kind of progress we do have. I was Mayor in 1963, you must have read.

SOLOMON: Yeah, I read, and I even read that your wife may be the next queen of the Cotton Festival or something. Great! I'm tickled pink for her. But if you're about to give me any crap about how you personally made everything better for the "uneducated, poor colored" sanitation men, or how your favorite chauffeur is a Negro, spare me.

MAYOR: I was about to say that when the question of union recognition came up, the temporarily misguided city council had passed a resolution to recognize the union. The public raised such an outcry that I publicly resigned from the mayor's office rather than sign that resolution. And when they changed the form of government to the Strong-Mayor/weak council system, I ran again for Mayor and won overwhelmingly. Just a few months ago, as a matter of fact. The people gave me a fresh mandate. I will uphold it. People here do things differently and no Yiddish-speaking, Jewish thug from New York is gonna come here and reorder our ways!

SOLOMON: I don't speak Yiddish, I use it when appropriate. I sure as hell ain't no thug, even though I'm from New York. And I am not *Jewish*! To be *Jewish* is to be Jew-*like*. I am not *like* a Jew, I am a Jew! And I ain't about to convert to some archaic "ways" of behavior that are an affront to human decency, and I don't mean the Episcopalians. You're a dud, man, a gauleiter at the loading pens. *(shouting)* For Chrissake, get it through your head that we consider Memphis our Armageddon of the South!

MAYOR: *(derisive laughter)* Your Armageddon, indeed! I've got a *putz* here with grandiose illusions. I should call you General Solomon perhaps?

SOLOMON: Listen to this, you smarmy, backwoods Pharaoh: Everyday. Everyday, we'll be out there marching and singing, maybe even dancing when we cross Beale Street—not me, of course. But we'll be out there until doomsday if we hafta. And those people who you think are with you, ain't gonna be so with you when Memphis has its spring awakening. Those magnolias ain't gonna do the trick. And I wanna say one more thing: You're a conceited, racist, *geshmat* sonuvabitch and your lying tongue is coated with redneck shit!

(The MAYOR leaps up, enraged as the BLUESMAN loudly hits a discordant chord. Lights and Images shift to the Lorraine Motel, night, where JONES, SWAHILI and CINNAMON heatedly converse. The BLUESMAN sits in a dark corner.)

SWAHILI: You da leader, not Solomon, not Willins, not the NAACP, not the ministers wit all that Jesus talk. We here to back up and protect you, not them.

CIN: Right on!

JONES: I unnastans dat. But we needs day hep too. You gotta figure dat in.

SWAHILI: Help, sure. "Help" is what they 'sposed ta do, not run things. They meeting and strategizing like they running things. We don't take no orders from no whitey. Stokely Carmichael got that straight. He said BLACK Power, not Negro Power.

CIN: Right on!

SWAHILI: Look, mzee, we ready to follow you into battle. We'll give our lives at yo' orders. But we need you to be a strong leader. To keep the Black man in control of the black man's destiny.

CIN: Right on!

JONES: You don't hafta worry 'bout dat. I know how to keep control.

(Lights and Images shift to NAACP FIRST SECRETARY's "office," where she talks excitedly with SOLOMON, WILLINS AND MOORE. Before we actually hear them speak MLK's VOICE speaks. As MLK speaks, the BLUESMAN wanders in and perches on a garbage can.)

MLK's VOICE: ". . . The masses of people are rising up. And wherever they are assembled today, whether they are in Johannesburg, South Africa; Nairobi, Kenya: Accra, Ghana; New York City; Atlanta, Georgia; Jackson, Mississippi; or Memphis, Tennessee—the cry is always the same—'We want to be free.' "

BLUESMAN: *(singing blues fashion)*
    FREE, FREE, FREE, OH LAWD, FREE
    BUT WHERE'S THE KEY TO UNLOCK THE CHAINS
    WHERE'S THE KEY THAT WILL SET US FREE

SECRETARY: *(as if answering him)* The NAACP is making plans to mount a boycott of downtown businesses which will further pressure the Mayor. We're also issuing a national press release so that we can avoid the local press.

WILLINS: That's it? What about funds to help the strikers' families?

SECRETARY: That they can't do, but they can ask others to solicit funds as soon as an account is set up.

WILLINS: What's wrong with our union accounts? Why are they delaying progress?

SECRETARY: We merely feel local agencies should handle relief funds. I wouldn't say we're "delaying progress." That's a real stretch, even for you.

WILLINS: Meaning?

SECRETARY: Meaning that your pushy condescension toward people down here is a bit much.

WILLINS: Pushy? We're the ones being pushed.

SOLOMON: Look, what about lawyers from the Defense Fund? Lots of people will be arrested before this is over.

SECRETARY: They've promised us three full time.

WILLINS: Three? Three? What are we supposed to do with 'em, crucify 'em or something?

SOLOMON: We'll work with the three and, Craig, make a note, have the international send us some additional ones. And, by the way, where's Jones? Wasn't he supposed to be here an hour ago?

WILLINS: Maybe he's out declaring another strike.

MOORE: Did he call?

SECRETARY: No.

SOLOMON: This is a heck of way to plan a strike. Alright, let's talk about ministerial support. Rev. Moore, what's the scoop there?

MOORE: I've got seven big Negro churches lined up so far. They promise good singing, good preaching and plenty of good fried chicken. Lawd ham'mercy!

WILLINS: Amen to that!

MOORE: Much as I hate to say it, that mace they sprayed on us at the parade opened up a lot of eyes. A group of ministers formed a group called Community on the Move for Equality, or, COME, for short. I hate that name, but they based it on Isaiah, Chapter One, Verse 18, so I couldn't say anything. Anyway, they've offered to negotiate with the Mayor.

SOL. AND WILLINS: No way!

WILLINS: No group negotiates for the union! We are a striking union, not a civil rights demonstration or a religious revival!

SECRETARY: It was an offer, not a demand!

SOLOMON: Rev. Moore, you think they'll help us plan strike strategy? Mobilize bodies?

MOORE: I'm sure. They said "negotiate" because that's usually a role that Negro clergy play down here.

WILLINS: Well, there's no more "down here" or "up there." Some methods just won't do anymore.

MOORE: Those COME people have the power to raise lots of money for a strike fund.

SOLOMON: Of course, and we welcome whatever they raise. Meanwhile, Craig, take a note: ask all the Federation locals to donate money and food. And ask George Meany to tap the National AFL-CIO. Tell 'im we estimate $15,000 weekly to pull this off. And, by the way, the Sanitation workers are eligible to get food stamps. Put somebody on that.

MOORE: You know, there's a chance we could get King down here to help out, maybe lead a march.

SECRETARY: I don't think that's a good idea. We could lose our focus on the issues.

WILLINS: We could also get national attention focused on Memphis.

SOLOMON: As long as the strike remains the central focus, I have no objection to King's coming.

MOORE: Well, some of the ministers in that COME group know King personally.

WILLINS: Could you specifically ask them if they'd look into getting King?

MOORE: Sure. Any objection to that, Miss Secretary?

MISS SECRETARY: No, I'll go along with the group. Let's get King.

(JONES, SWAHILI, and CINNAMON enter. JONES noticeably swaggers. SWAHILI and CIN. act like menacing bodyguards. WILLINS is obviously disgusted with them.)

SOLOMON: I don't understand; did I give you the wrong time for the meeting?

JONES: No, you gived da right time, but dere was impo'tent union work had ta be done.

SOLOMON: We thought we were doing important union work. What were you doing?

JONES: *(rapidly speaking)* We got us a strike on. Peepas don't get no paydays. Day got to eat. Bertha Wilson over on Hernando got six chilrens not one speck of cornmeal in the house, no milk, no rice or potatoes. Her husband was sick las' week, ain't got but one day's pay. And now he on strike. Day needed food. We collect some money and food and carry it to 'em. But while I'm takin' care of Miss Wilson, long come Shiloh Rankin live over on Grant Street and his son still in jail from the march. Cain't make bail and he gittin' sick 'cause he got da sickle cell, but da police say he fakin'. I hada fine some money and send a few of my mens ta run see about dat. Alright, now we meet back at Retail Clerks Hall and fidden to come here, den the phone ring. One of our union men had a fight with some scabs over on Handy Square at Beale Street. He hurt two a dem and got cut up fah his troubles and day taken him to the hospital 'mergency. Hospital 'mergency say he got ta pay foe day treat 'im. He ain't got two quartas ta rub tagetha. I run 'round and got what donations I could and run over to the hospital. Den we stop by here.

SOLOMON: I can't say that ya wasted your time. Everything ya did was necessary. Okay? But . . .

WILLINS: Since you collected all that money, and I hope you kept receipts, couldn't you have used one dime of it to call here and alert us?

JONES: Wudden no time and I didn't know da numba nohow.

WILLINS: *(mimicking Southern accent)* No phonebooks in Memphis, eh?

JONES: *(exploding)* I ain't got no time ta stop and be studyin' some phone-book or hustlin' receipts while mah mens is sufferin' and need my help!

SWAHILI: We showed what we been doing. What about ya'll? Sittin' up here havin' tea?

MOORE: Now, hold on, young man. Everybody been . . .

WILLINS: We've been organizing an intelligent response to the events. That's all!

SWAHILI: While the people perish in the streets!

WILLINS: Not nearly as much as your brain seems to perish when confronted with sound reason.

SWAHILI: Just 'cause you bring your tired, bourgeois ass from *UPSOUTH* to Memphis, you think . . .

WILLINS: Popcorn, man! Damn Popcorn! That's all you talk!

SOLOMON: Goddamit, Willins! Look what you're doin!

MOORE: Gentlemen, we have a lady present. Lawd ha'mercy!

SOLOMON: *(trying to make peace)* I apologize for the language, Miss Secretary, Reverend, but not for the sentiment. I was trying to say, our signals got a little crossed, but we all seem to be doing something useful. Bury the hatchet or the Mayor's gonna take a giant, aristocratic crap on all of us!

SECRETARY: *(taking Solomon's signal)* Now that makes sense. T.O., you guys are doing a great job. You just taught me something about what it takes to keep a strike going. I sympathize with Mrs. Wilson.

MOORE: *(a friend)* Brotha Jones always been just like that. He can't help himself when he sees his men in need.

SWAHILI: *(blindly)* Dig dat!

CIN: Right on!

SOLOMON: Okay, that's all understood. Now, we can go on with this meeting. You guys pull up a seat. With your knowledge of what's happening on the streets, we can make even better plans for this . . .

SWAHILI: The Invaders don't share no knowledge unless we're sure of who we sharing it with. The pig got ghetto listening posts everywhere. It's a sure bet they got the NAACP wired up.

SECRETARY: I can assure you that my office is . . .

WILLINS: Good God!

MOORE: Perhaps we can share with you what's already been decided.

SWAHILI: How can you make any decisions without the leader? Jones is the leader, understand. This strike is being led by a black warrior. Ya'll have a difficult time accepting that, but that's what happenin'.

SOLOMON: This strike is being led by the workers. We are here to serve them in various capacities, and in an organized fashion. Let's get that straight now!

SWAHILI: Well, let's do that! That's what Brotha Jones and the rest of us been doing, serving in various capacities. That's elementary! Che Guevera teaches us that . . .

WILLINS: If Jones is the leader, why are you doing all the talking?

SWAHILI: I only sought to defend him.

WILLINS: Well, he looks capable enough of defending himself. After all, he is the "warrior leader." Mr. Jones, can we go on with the meeting?

JONES: We can, but not now.

SOLOMON: What's wrong with now? We're trying to get caught up with . . .

JONES: Tomorrow is grocery shopping day. Whole lotta folks out dere ain't gon' have nothin' ta shop wit. Right now, I got to make some runs and collect donations, and den I got ta . . .

WILLINS: What are you saying?

JONES: I'm 'fficially adjournin' da meetin' 'till foe' o'clock tomorrow when I can be h . . .

WILLINS: Wait!

SOLOMON: *(to Willins)* No! Don't start.

SECRETARY: T.O., we can't let that much time elapse with nothing done.

MOORE: Brotha Jones, let me explain; we . . .

JONES: Ain't no 'splainin', Brotha Moe. Cain't be done no otha way. I got too much on my plate now. Let me take care of those otha mattas first, den I kin tell mah plan. Ya'll kin help me work out da mechanics.

SWAHILI: *(subtle threat)* For the record, the Invaders completely back Mzee Jones on this decision to adjourn.

SOLOMON: Fine! Meeting adjourned. Why don't you guys run along now?

JONES: Thank you, fah dat respeck. Brotha Moe, would you like to come along wit us and help collect donations?

MOORE: Uh, not tonight, but, uh, I got collection plates goin' 'round my congregation on Sunday.

SOLOMON: I'll check in with you early in the morning, okay?

JONES: Fine wit me. Let's move out.

(JONES exits, followed by SWAHILI and CINNAMON who salute at the "door" as they leave.)

SWAHILI: Power to the People!

CINNAMON: Powa ta da Peepas!

SOLOMON: Reverend Moore, you know T.O. better than any of us. What's going on?

MOORE: Jones is basically a good man with a big dream. Sometimes a person's dream is the highest achievement in his life. You get my drift?

SOLOMON: *(to Willins)* I think I do. But Jones seems like he's in the grip of a potential nightmare. Neo-Stalinists. It's like the Stalinists have returned in a different guise. I used to have regular fistfights with Stalinists all over Brooklyn. In the 40s. I can't go through that again.

WILLINS: The age of fists is over. But we still have to fight them, and we have to win, some kinda way, and I think we will. *(commanding tone)* Let me handle this problem, Josh, okay?

BLUESMAN: *(singing as before while lights fade)*
FREE FREE FREE, OH LAWD FREE
BUT WHERE'S THE KEY TO UNLOCK THE CHAINS
WHERE'S THE KEY THAT WILL SET US FREE

(Lights and Images shift to a "meeting room" in City Hall. The MAYOR, POLICE CHIEF, SOLICITOR, and the COLLABORATOR in shadows. It is several days later.)

MLK's VOICE: "... It is no longer a choice between violence and non-violence in this world; it's nonviolence or nonexistence ..."

COLL: We don't see the Invaders as much of a problem; we have several infiltrators keeping an eye on them. FBI says they're Communist inspired.

SOLICITOR: How did the FBI get involved in this?

CHIEF: I called them for background information. Among other things that Solomon guy was a member of the Young Peoples Socialist League. And Mr. Jones is merely an ex-poolhall hustler, an eighth grade drop-out, a rakish buffoon who possesses a crude shrewdness. We may be able to use all that.

SOLICITOR: For what?

MAYOR: For the wellbeing of our city, of course!

SOLICITOR: How about just negotiating a settlement of the strike? Did the FBI tell you how to do that?

MAYOR: Continue.

POLICE CHIEF: Is there any chance they'll try to get King down here?

COLL: A good chance. They want King to lead one of their daily marches.

MAYOR: Mr. Solicitor, you will prepare an injunction against that march.

SOLICITOR: The whole thing is escalating because we're not facing some facts. All of us know that those men deserve some kinda raise, some kinda simple consideration, which could ...

MAYOR: I'd rather have our meeting after the agent has finished.

SOLICITOR: Bunk the formalities!

MAYOR: This is the *Mayor's* Advisory Board.

SOLICITOR: I don't give a damn whose advisory board it is.

(The MAYOR nods to the CHIEF who quietly dismisses the COLLABORATOR. The SOLICITOR talks through it all.)

SOLICITOR: I'm on it by law, and I'm an elected representative of all the people like you. I have the responsibility to advise the Mayor, even if he's too bullheaded to accept honest advice! Injunctions past and present are virtually useless in these kinds of situations. Might as well get an injunction to stop the Mississippi River from flooding. Fact: the union is not going to go away. Fact: They're mobilizing much of this town and galvanizing national support. Fact: In sixty and sixty-one boycotters managed to practically close down the main shopping districts. Why this confrontation? Let's be flexible and save ourselves a lot of headache.

MAYOR: So, you'd get rid of a headache by chopping off your head? This city cannot appear to cave in to demands from any union. We'd be bankrupt in three years. We'd look like New York or Detroit.

SOLICITOR: You exaggerate! Look, Negroes have been here ever since there was a Memphis and it behooves us to . . .

MAYOR: To placate Jones and his ilk without outside influence. Memphis belongs to Memphians. We can resolve our own problems without carpetbagging agitators. I have a plan in process now. But it takes time.

(Lights and Images shift to the MAYOR's office where JONES awaits the MAYOR. The BLUESMAN leads in the MAYOR and POLICE CHIEF.)

MLK's VOICE: ". . . let us keep the issues where they are. The issue is injustice. The issue is the refusal of Memphis to be fair and honest in its dealings with its public servants, who happen to be sanitation workers . . ."

MAYOR: You're early, Mr. Jones.

JONES: Dat's 'cause I want to settle dis strike soon. And I hope dis ain't no tricknology wit da Pole-lease here and everything.

MAYOR: Absolutely not! I can assure you. The Chief is here officially as a member of my Advisory Board. You can walk out of here anytime you like.

JONES: I stay fah now. But let me be clear: I'm heah on da men's behalf. It ain't got ta do wit' no special favors fah me. It's da mens need hep like I tried ta tell ya in the fust place back in early February. Here it is, March fixin' to close off and we still scufflin'. If you took the time to listen to me, none of this mess woulda happen.

MAYOR: Fine. I'm ready to listen now, but are you? Last time we spoke you said you do the authorizing among your men, is that not so?

JONES: Dat's so.

MAYOR: Why, then, have others begun calling the shots?

JONES: Who you speakin' of?

MAYOR: No games, Jones. Solomon, Willins, the NAACP, the ministers. I thought I was dealing with one man, you. Now, I understand that Martin King is coming to lead a march.

JONES: *(standing)* King? Who said that?

CHIEF: That Willins fella got a police permit for a special parade on March 28. Says King is supposed to lead it.

JONES: Willins?

MAYOR: Didn't you help plan the march?

JONES: *(raging)* I don't know nothin' 'bout no King comin' here! I didn't authorize that.

MAYOR: Just as I suspected, which means that you don't control things anymore, or at least you won't when King gets here.

JONES: Bullshit! Dey can't do nothin' without da mens and dat's me. That damn Willins went behine mah back!

MAYOR: *(pressing his case)* Indeed he did. And that Solomon fellow strikes me as a man who would milk his neighbor's cow through the fence.

JONES: Maybe, at las' we agree on something.

MAYOR: Sit please. I'll speak plainly to you, because I can tell you're a man who appreciates the truth and who has an intelligent grasp on reality: I've reconsidered. I think we can sit down and balance things out, so no one loses everything, and everyone wins something. But I want to talk directly to the boss, and that's you, I think.

JONES: *(preening)* Oh, it's me all right. You can ask any of the mens about dat. I come to talk man to man, like in the old days. I'll settle this strike myself!

MAYOR: *(gleefully)* Good! Let's talk, man to man. You told me what you want, let me tell you what I want.

(The BLUESMAN frowns at JONES and turns his back and walks directly into the next scene where he sits scowling. Lights and Images shift to office of the SECRETARY where she talks animatedly with MOORE and WILLINS. It is now March 20. Projected headlines show that King is coming to lead the march.)

MOORE: The national guard, the sheriff, state highway patrol and every policeman in the city will be on duty the 28th. Lawd ham'mercy!

WILLINS: Don't fret. Memphis doesn't want bad press. It'll be a peaceful march.

(Enter a swaggering JONES, wearing dark glasses, SWAHILI and CINNAMON. The latter two stand "guard" behind T.O.)

JONES: *(to SWAHILI and CIN.)* At ease. *(to the OTHERS)* Sorry I'm late. I come here ta tell ya'll da march is cancelled.

WILLINS: *(laughing derisively, incredulously)* Oh yeah, who cancelled it?

JONES: Me! Things got outta hand. Ya'll got King comin' ta march, but afta King go away we got the same garbage lef'. I respeck King very much, he done a lot fah our peepas, but ya'll shoulda cleared bringin' in King with the local first. Ain't nobody listenin' to da sanitation mens.

WILLINS: The whole thing is about the sanitation men.

SECRETARY: T.O., we listened to the sanitation men; that's why we're here.

JONES: Brotha Moe here been wit me befoe any of ya'll. He know what I'm talkin' 'bout. 'Bout da onliest thing the sanitation men doin' now is providin' bodies fah da daily march.

MOORE: But, I honestly think that King's presence will do more good than harm for the strike.

JONES: It ain't 'bout that, Brotha Moe. Can't no Messiah hep us. If peepas cain't save theysef, ain't no savin' gon' happen. We don't need no civil rights march, much as we needs a strike settlement.

WILLINS: Man, are you cra . . .

MOORE: *(rapidly)* Brotha Jones, the sanitation men are poor and King is running a Poor People's Campaign, because if you're poor, you don't have any civil rights or labor rights that most people respect. That's why . . .

JONES: I knowed dat, Rev. Moore. But I'm talkin' 'bout leadership decisions. I made my decision. I'm givin' orders to cancel da march.

SECRETARY: That's stupid!

WILLINS: You can't stop the march!

JONES: I can if I declare da strike ova and tell da mens not ta march.

WILLINS: *Declare* the strike over? What a bumbling, inept, simple . . .

MOORE: *(desperate as a friend)* T.O., do you know something we don't know? Solomon's in the negotiating session with the mediation board now. Did they reach an agreement?

JONES: Not far as I know, but since the mens ain't present, any agreement is something we ain't agreed to.

SECRETARY: I think you better take stock of what you're saying. Think, T.O., think!

MOORE: Have you figured out some way to settle this thing without the march?

JONES: I have a way. I been talkin' to top peepas.

WILLINS: "Top peepas?" Is this a new race of human beings, these "top peepas?"

JONES: Da Mayor included.

WILLINS: You talked to the Mayor? When?

JONES: A while ago. Been talkin'. Dere are better ways ta settle dis strike and da impo'tent people involved need ta throw day ideas on the table.

WILLINS: You've been talking to the Mayor behind our backs. Making your own deals? Is that it?

JONES: It's our own strike, ain't it?

WILLINS: You ignorant damn fool!

SWAHILI: Don't disrespect our leader like that!

WILLINS: And you're just a simple-minded nigga!

MOORE: Maybe if we'd just listen to what he has to say, we could fix this.

JONES: Ain't no fixin', it's through. I'm calling my mens off the streets.

WILLINS: If you try to do something like that, . . . Can't you understand that if union labor loses in Memphis, it loses the South? I won't let you destroy us! You and these nappy nignogs can go to hell. You're through in this strike. I'll see that you're fired before nightfall.

SWAHILI: Little sucker ass oreo nigga. You the principal reason why black people been wallowing in America's pigslop. You went to some white man's school and learned two/three big words and think you can lead the people. You was sent here by Charley to cool the niggas out with marching and singing, to stop the people's revolution. You the enemy! My leader has declared the strike ended.

WILLINS: Leader? He couldn't lead ducks to a pond in the Sahara desert. Revolution? The only revolution you people ever made was with circular rhetoric. You can't even organize a strike, much less a revolution. Go organize your miserably ignorant life! *(Laughing sarcastically)* Revolutionaries!? What is that, a new TV talk show? I ain't got nothin' for a ignorant chittlin chewer.

SWAHILI: *(whipping out his sawed off shotgun)* What you got for this? Huh?

SECRETARY: Stop this! Please God!

MOORE: Ain't no need for that, Swahili.

JONES: *(also fearful)* At ease, Swa . . .

SWAHILI: *(beyond listening)* Shut up, alla ya'll. *(to WILLINS)* Oh, you quiet now, ain'tcha?

WILLINS: I'm quiet 'cause I'm amazed at how far a nigga will go to prove he's a revolutionary. You wanna kill me, Mr. Swahili. Here *(rips open his shirt and exposes his bare flesh)*. Show the world how a brave Black revolutionary can kill another Black man. Show what it took for a Black man to kill Malcom X! Kill me! Kill me! Go ahead! Maybe the crackers'll give you a medal for killing another nigga. Kill me, nigga!

JONES: *(clearly pleading)* We don't need no moe of dem, let's move out.

(A tense pause after which SWAHILI puts his gun away. Even CINNAMON breathes a sigh of relief. As the BLUESMAN plays a sorrowful sounding few notes, JONES, SWAHILI and CINNAMON depart. Lights and Images shift to the Lorraine Motel, JONES' room, late evening. JONES is having a drink. WILLINS enters. The BLUESMAN sits in a dark corner.)

WILLINS: I don't know why you asked me over, but I'm glad you did; I wanted to talk privately with you too.

JONES: Pull up a chair, have a drink.

WILLINS: Tennessee corn. That's illegal.

JONES: And good too!

WILLINS: I'll have one, thanks. Why'd you ask me over and, by the way, where's your dogs?

JONES: Day run off to a meetin'. I ask you ova to apologize for what happened this afternoon. I ain't neva intended fah none a dat.

WILLINS: *(sincerely)* I know. I know. And I apologize for what I said. Anger, man, just anger.

JONES: Day call dayself protectin' me 'cause I got threats on my life, quite a few. I'm scared. Das all. Just plain scared.

WILLINS: Well, so am I.

JONES: You didn't act scared!

WILLINS: I'm scared for the movement, the union, the strike, this whole damn country, things like that. What you said about calling off the strike scared me.

JONES: I didn't mean fah it ta do dat. It's how I truly feel; it's what I got ta do fah da wellbein' of da mens.

WILLINS: Well, I have to do something for the wellbeing of the movement.

JONES: Yeah?

WILLINS: *(pulling out papers with figures)* Jones, the records say you collected and disbursed something like seven thousand dollars over the last month. We don't have enough receipts to account for one tenth of that. The executive board is concerned about allegations of theft. What happened to that money?

JONES: I didn't steal no money!

WILLINS: These are the statements of institutional donors. Each one shows what they raised and have given to the relief fund through you. These are the receipts for some of that money, and this is the figure that shows the amount of money unaccounted for from you. It looks like stealing.

JONES: I didn't steal no money! Who said I stolt it?

WILLINS: No one, yet. But imagine what would happen if this got out. The IRS, the press, the courts—they'd all get involved. The strike fails, the union is busted and you get indicted and go to prison. And the press has the freedom to fan the flames. I've spoken to several lawyers about this and they all agree that such things could happen if this got out.

JONES: But I didn't steal no money is what I'm tryin' ta tell ya. Fact is I ain't never done nothin' like dat wit money dat belong ta da union.

WILLINS: I don't have a personal judgement in the matter; I think you're an honest man; I'm talking about others, especially the men. They'd be buried up under a mountain of public relations garbage. Nowadays, facts are irrelevant.

JONES: Fah da record I didn't steal no money, but I see yo' point. Is somebody tryin' ta put da word on da streets?

WILLINS: Not yet. I'll be frank. There's only a few of us who know. We don't want anything to happen to the movement or to you, but . . .

JONES: But what?

WILLINS: In America when you want someone to do something for you, it costs. When you want someone to do *nothing* for you, it costs. If you declare the strike over, you're gonna make some people mighty angry. So angry, I couldn't stop them from releasing that information to the national press.

JONES: "Oh, I see," said da blind man. You really wantin' me ta give up leadership of my union.

WILLINS: *(folding up his papers)* No, on the contrary, I want you to be a brave leader of your union. I want you to save it. The deal is this: You can still be president and keep your salary and come to all the meetings, but you have to follow the international's leadership. And no more private talks with the Mayor!

JONES: *(bitterly)* You been tryin' ta git me eva since you got here.

WILLINS: Me get you? You got yourself, my brother. You got yourself when you dumbly called a garbage strike in the winter without any preparation or backing, when you improvised a march that left many people injured and in jail, when you attached yourself to those Invaders from the Black Power Planet. They're great! They protect you by threatening to kill me, who came here to serve the union. We are not making you an offer, Jones.

JONES: Why you do this? Why you instead of me? I built a house witout yo' hep. And now heah you come movin' in.

WILLINS: You're building a plantation shanty; we're building a house. We have tools that you don't have.

JONES: Hmph! Ya'll ain't built nothin' in the South with dem tools. Da whole country heah now because me and my mens taken action. And dis happen 'foe ya'll come.

WILLINS: Even when I use your metaphors I can't make you understand.

JONES: Don't throw that metashit in my face! You da high and mighty. You use da white man's talk good as he do. But what do all dat talk mean? Huh? It mean you kin kill a man like me, kin kill a whole country fulla peeps, and all you got ta do is explain it real pretty, and turn it into whatever yo' words sound like. You talk shit, but you make it smell sweet.

WILLINS: You talk some pretty good dudu yourself. I've had my say. You can take it or leave it. What's the word, mzee?

JONES: "Take it or leave it." Dat's a lie! You a lie!

WILLINS: What? I'm a . . .

JONES: You a lie 'cause you ain't give no choice.

WILLINS: You can't understand what I'm saying, can you?

JONES: *(shouting)* I stood up for those mens when nobody else did!

WILLINS: *(shouting back)* Well now you gon' hafta sit down for them!
Cause that's what they need. Can you understand that?

(JONES sighs in heavy frustration, nods "yes," pours himself another drink, drinks it down, stares off into space. WILLINS smiles in victory.)

(Lights and Images shift to a late night street in Memphis. CINNAMON, wearing sandals, walks alone. Revolving red lights, as in a police car, suddenly flash across his body. TWO POLICEMEN, ONE WHITE AND ONE BLACK, step into CINNAMON's path.)

WHITE POLICEMAN (WP) *(Mimicking)*
"Powa ta da Peepas," Brother Cinnamon.

CIN: What ya'll want?

(THEY grab and disarm him.)

WP: Whatsamatter, havin' a spat with the wife?

CIN: What is dis about?

BP: *(holding up shotgun)* This heah is about life on the chaingang, boy.
But those sandals sure are pretty. They come from Africa?

WP: That's where you shoulda stayed, if you don't like the good ole USA.

(THEY begin beating him. He tries in vain to fight back. He is quickly beaten into semi-conciousness.)

WP: Hold him up straight. Chief of Police sent you this message:

(The WHITE POLICEMAN bangs the shotgun butt down repeatedly on CINNAMON's toes. CIN. screams in agony. Lights, Images, and Sound shift to scenes of violence and mayhem taken from photos and recordings of the March 28, 1968, march. WE SHOULD SEE examples of looting, beatings, brick throwing, cops shooting, cops arresting, national guardsmen, fearful looks, fires burning, smoke billowing, mob hysteria. SOUNDS are screams, gunshots, tear gas canisters exploding, shouts, running feet, breaking glass, sirens, grief-stricken cries, frenzied traffice and police whistles. Discordant blues sounds filter through it all. LOCAL NEWSPAPER HEADLINES from March 28 & 29, 1968, are projected, particularly those that say MLK ran because he was afraid. Lights and Images cut to the SEC'Y's office where SOLOMON, MOORE, WILLINS, and JONES meet. JONES is sullen, sulks in a corner. The OTHERS stand over him. The BLUESMAN sympathetically watches JONES.)

MLK's VOICE: "Now we're going to march again, and we've got to march again, in order to put the issue where it is supposed to be . . . Somehow, the preacher must say with Jesus, 'The spirit of the Lord is upon me, because he hath anointed me to deal with the problems of the poor . . .' "

SOL: Another march? Are you certain this is the best way?

SEC'Y: No choice.

WILLINS: King's people were humiliated. If he can't lead a nonviolent march in Memphis, his entire movement is dead.

MOORE: Not to mention his poor people's march on Washington next month.

SOLOMON: All true, but still another march in Memphis right now is suicidal.

JONES: Shouldna had no march in the first place!

SOLOMON: I realize you feel that way, but . . .

JONES: Whole lot moe den me feel dat way.

SEC'Y: But they marched nonetheless. Almost all of the sanitation men.

JONES: Day was tole day had ta.

SOLOMON: Okay, let's get back to business. When is the next march planned?

MOORE: April 8ᵗʰ. We got a commitment from King himself.

SOLOMON: *Oy vey!* Well, if it has to be, it has to be, but we need to . . .

SEC'Y: To assure the peace. T.O., you know the men best, and you know the street. Can you talk to those people?

JONES: What fah?

MOORE: The mayor's got a army parked outside Memphis. All they need is one excuse for butchery.

JONES: If nobody march, da army stay put.

WILLINS: Well, another march will happen, and, this time, we gotta make sure it works. None of us has a choice. You understand, T.O.?

SOLOMON: He's right, T.O. We need your help. You've got to spread the word to your men. No violence this time.

JONES: Mah mens didn't bring no violence, I'm tryin' ta tell ya! I don't know how violence come! Nobody seem to know just who started what and why! That's the word on the street.

SEC'Y: Yes, T.O., I understand, but maybe your men could help stem the violence this time. We'll need lots of parade marshalls.

MOORE: Right! Invaders could help set an example for peace by being parade marshalls. The ministers could train them in the techniques of nonviolence. Can you do that, T.O.?

WILLINS: *(a challenge)* You mean does T.O. have any more influence over the Invaders?

SOLOMON: It would save lives and it would keep the media's focus on the strike, not on violence. Will you do that, T.O.?

JONES: *(insecure behind this boast)* Dey still listen to me. All right, you want parade marshalls, you got parade marshalls!

(Lights and Images cut to JONES' *room at the Lorraine. We hear* SWAHILI *shout out as soon as the lights shift to him.)*

SWAHILI: Nigga, is you crazy? You want us to be what? Parade Marshalls?
(*JONES enters. The BLUESMAN sits in a corner.*)

JONES: Since ya'll protectin' me, I . . .

SWAHILI: Dig this, we thought was protectin' the leader. But lately something else happenin'. The ministers negotiating, organizing, giving
press conferences. That honky from New York and his number one
field nigga running the union, telling the men what to do and when,
and the men doing what they told. Ain't paying you no mind. The
NAACP and Boy Wilkins gettin' all the play in the national press
along with Martin Luther King. King shoulda been glad he was leading a army instead of a buncha lay-down-in-the-street-and-kick-me-
niggas! And he comin' back to try again! Why the niggas always got
to be the ones being peaceful? When whitey get mad at other whiteys,
or anybody else, he go to war. Look what he doin' right now in
Vietnam! But he pay the "knee-e-e-e-egro-o-o-oes" to let him roll
some tanks over them. The pigs making plans to kill Black people
right now! The FBI got prisons set up for the rest of us. With uniforms and everything ready. And you want us to march the people
right down to the slaughterhouse. Peacefully! No way! No way the
Invaders gon' lay down and die peacefully, you dig? Next week we
planning on roast pig! It's time to resist by any means necessary like
Malcolm X say.

JONES: Ya'll want to lead the Black race, but when I offer you responsible
leadership, you ton it down.

SWAHILI: Leading Black people to their slaughter is not responsible leadership! You be the Christian that get eat up in the stadium, not me!

JONES: You afraid.

SWAHILI: Afraid? You right. I'm afraid of being helpless in the face of
whitey's brutality. You oughtta see Brotha Cinnamon's feet, what left
of them.

JONES: You cain't stop dat kinda of brutality wit mo' brutality. You afraid
of the power of nunviolence.

SWAHILI: You ever try to stop a wild dog with nonviolence? Naw, nonviolence ain't got enough power to stop these barbaric crackers from
stomping your black ass in the ground, unnastan?

JONES: Ya'll oughtta 'least speak ta da ministers, see what they say.

SWAHILI: Hmmph! Another bunch of darky preachers officiating over the
Negro community! I ain't g . . .

JONES: They tryin' ta keep peepas from bein' hurt. Da onliest things my
men ever wanted was safety and moe pay, better conditions.

SWAHILI: I . . .

JONES: And ya'll fixin' ta take day safety away. Day garbage men, not
warriors. Day collects garbage, not guns. I don't want my mens hurt

behine no foolishness. You betta go talk to the ministers. I ain't 'llowin' my mens to go violent.

SWAHILI: Your "mens"? You ain't got no "mens" no more. They don't listen to you. You layed down and got run over. Matta of fact, the street sayin' somebody payin' you to keep quiet. You a useless pile of shit!

(JONES tries to grab SWAHILI who easily avoids him and whips out his gun which he points at JONES who stops.)

SWAHILI: Don't even think about it, mzee! Your life ain't even at risk anymore. Don't nobody need you! If you died tomorrow, it wouldn't make any difference to what's going on in Memphis; the strike, the union, nothing!

(The BLUESMAN strums a low, funky blues as the Lights and Images shift to a Beale St. Bar which he enters. JONES shortly stumbles in, now drunk he, bottle in hand, stands swaying before the BLUESMAN. He begins dancing, slowly, dancing out of sorrow. The song's refrain goes as follows:)

BLUESMAN: THE GRAVEDIGGER IS YO' VERY BEST FRIEND.
THE GRAVEDIGGER IS YO' VERY BEST FRIEND
HE ONLY LET YOU DOWN ONCE NO MATTER WHAT YOU BEEN

(JONES stops dancing, angrily hurls the bottle which breaks offstage. He speaks the following to no one in particular over the background instrumental accompaniment of the BLUESMAN:)

JONES: When I was toting garbage, I knowed every alcoholic in town, da ones live in da shacks and da ones what living high in the big houses. I knowed who was creepin' 'round some back doe on dey husband or wife. I knowed who was taking high price drugstore drugs and street drugs. I run to da back of da house ta git da garbage and I seed all kinda womens in the window. Naked! Not a stitch on! Justa lookin' down at ole stinkin', black, empty-face me, and smilin' real big. I seed big, impo'tent men in dis town beatin' on soft, little white womens in da back bedrooms. I heard dem womens scream and beg for mercy. I once seed a father touchin' his near 'bout growed up daughter, touchin' her where no fatha 'sposed ta touch his daughter. One time I pulled a dead baby from the garbage, a little white baby, just born, blood still fresh. Somebody throwed it in the garbage behine a big fine mansion. And peepas treat me like I stink. Nothin' stink worse den da garbage dat da garbage man leave behine everyday.

(JONES staggers out. The music continues for a short moment until it fades to silence as Lights and images shift to City Hall where the MAYOR, SOLICITOR

and CHIEF *watch the* COLLABORATORS *on the monitor. We see headlines that say the courts will allow the second march to happen.)*

COLL: King is staying in the Lorraine Motel, Room 306, overlooking Mulberry St. He'll be there through April 8th.

SOLICITOR: Why do we have to know what room?

CHIEF: Security. His security.

MAYOR: If someone's after him, it's better they don't get him in Memphis.

CHIEF: Anything new on those Invaders?

COLL: They bought guns in Arkansas and they robbed a gun store on the west side two nights ago. One of them bought every copy of the *New York Times* he could find. Looked suspicious to us. That's it.

CHIEF: You're dismissed. *(The monitor goes blank.)*

MAYOR: Mr. Solicitor, are you sure you've exhausted every legal means to stop another march?

SOL: Yes, but like I said weeks ago, injunction or no, they would march. Most judges know that Assembly and petition is a right. What's the p . . .

MAYOR: Misguided liberal judges could cost this city several millions in property damage and a few lives. Did they think of that?

SOL: Mr. Mayor, it's a new South. It's a new world, and we don't own it. You might as well know that my wife is going to march with them.

MAYOR: Well, I certainly hope she has proper protection.

SOL: She'll have proper protection. Me. I'll be there with her.

MAYOR: I see! Throwing away a good career in city government?

SOL: No, Mr. Mayor. I'm starting a good career in city government.

MAYOR: *(boiling)* Chief?

CHIEF: We interrogated that Cinnamon fella the other night, and we feel there's gonna be violence. I got six thousand national guard troops, 3,000 officers from all over the state, and five tanks on standby.

MAYOR: Fine. Order your men to shoot looters on sight.

(A clap of thunder resounds and we hear a rain storm raging as if outside. Lights, Sounds and Images shift to a collage of MLK activities. The projected images include those of his working amidst the poverty and despair among urban and rural Southern Blacks. The activities will highlight the span of his national career as an advocate of civil rights, world peace and poor people in 1 minute. Excerpts from his final speech are heard shortly after the images have begun. We should hear sounds from the audiences that listened to his speech on April 3, and we should hear the thunder and lightning crashes of the torrential storm that occurred that night as he spoke at the Masonic Temple.)

MLK's VOICE: "Well, I don't know what will happen now. We've got some difficult days ahead. But it doesn't matter with me now. Because

I've been to the mountaintop. And I don't mind. Like anybody, I would like to live a long life. Longevity has its place. But I'm not concerned about that now. I just want to do God's will. And He's allowed me to go up to the mountain. And I've looked over. And I've seen the promised land. I may not get there with you. But I want you to know tonight, that we, as a people will get to the promised land. And I'm happy, tonight. I'm not worried about anything. I'm not fearing any man. Mine eyes have seen the glory of the coming of the Lord."

(As the images fade, lights rise slowly on JONES alone in his hotel room. The Projected Image says: LATE AFTERNOON, APRIL 4. He holds a glass in one hand. Nearby is a bottle. Sounds from the street outside enter. We hear VOICES singing nearby. THEY are singing "Precious Lord, Take My Hand" It is the Operation Breadbasket Band and several ministers who were practicing upstairs at the Lorraine just before King's murder. The BLUESMAN randomly strums along with them. The phone rings in JONES' room. Lights fade up on ALICE MAE in another area. JONES answers. MUSIC continues LOW under the voices of JONES and ALICE MAE.)

JONES: Hello.

ALICE: Ollie?

JONES: None otha.

ALICE: I see you feelin' real good this evenin'. Did you catch King's speech?

JONES: On the radio. He talk so fine, he could talk the sweetness out a pecan pie. Reckon dat what it take nowadays. Pretty talk!

ALICE: Well, that oughtta make ya uplift or somethin'.

JONES: Alice Mae, why you callin' me?

ALICE: You should be callin' me. It's April fourth and I ain't seen one dime from you. You got paid on the first.

JONES: Yo money comin'; right now I'm just flusterated, okay? Call me tomorrow.

ALICE: You gon' be worse than flusterated if I have to march down to family court and git dat judge ta snatch yo' paycheck. Strike or no strike, yo' children hafta eat. Don't let me have ta do no marchin'. You betta take the time ta rememba dat!

(She hangs up. Lights to black on her. JONES slowly hangs up. FRIENDLY YELLING VOICES emanate from outside the windows. Images are photos of MLK taken at the Lorraine Motel just before his death.)

VOICE 1: Ya'll ain't ready yet? What kinda preachers come late for dinner?

VOICE 2: Hungry preachers.

VOICE 1: If ya'll don't get down here to the parking lot in five minutes, I'll have to flunk you. You know what that means.

VOICE 2: What it mean?

VOICE 1: No hot cornbread with the collard greens.

VOICE 3: Rev., you need to stop threatening us poor colored preachers. Yo' wife so pretty, I had to stop and put on some cologne.

VOICE 1: My wife ain't gonna act pretty ya'll mess up her dinner. She been cooking all day. Fried chicken, greens, candied yams, roast beef, slaw, potato salad, macaroni and cheese, ham, stringbeans, yellow squash, smothered turkey wings, custard pie . . .

VOICE 2: Lawd ha'mercy! Keep the motor running.

VOICE 3: Martin Luther King can't eat none of that; he too fat. Can't even button his shirt he bought last month. Call yo' wife and tell her, say make a lettuce salad for Rev. King.

VOICE 2: I am a *lamb* of the Lord, but I cain't eat like one. If he keep talking that way, this boy gon' lose his license to preach.

VOICE 1: Rev. King, better bring a coat; it's getting cool out here.

VOICE 2: Say what?

VOICE 1: I said, it's getting cold and . . .

(The explosion of rifle fire cuts short his remarks. JONES leaps up, alert. There is a moment of silence. Suddenly a cacophony of VOICES is heard. Screams, shouts, cries, running feet, etc.)

VOICE 1: Martin's been shot! They shot Martin!

VOICE 4: Everybody take cover.

VOICE 3: Get a ambulance. Call a ambulance.

(JONES drops his drink and starts to run to the door, but he stops short in fear. He barricades the "door" shut with any available garbage. He sits in stunned disbelief and fear as the sounds of mayhem continue and images of King's death and its immediate aftermath are projected. There are the headlines, the photos of the body—if available—, the riots, the fires burning, looting, glass breaking, the sound of more gunshots, and the general crowd hysteria that accompanied this event. The sounds fade to silence as the images continue for the duration of "Precious Lord" as sung by the BLUESMAN. As he sings, the surrounding images slowly change to those of the funeral in Atlanta, the general mourning throughout the country. This includes news headlines and photos. The last set of headlines and photos should be the announcement that the strike is settled. Time has passed during this scene and we understand that it is now April 16, evening, as the BLUESMAN finishes the song and retires to a corner. Images return to stills of the external Lorraine Motel. MOORE pushes the garbage aside and enters, a black ribbon pinned to his lapel. JONES barely acknowledges him.)

MOORE: It's over, T.O., it's over. *(silence)* Did you hear me? I said, it's over. *(pause)*

JONES: What's over?

MOORE: The strike, man! Lawd ham'mercy! The strike over. You won. You listening? You won!

JONES: Naw, Brotha Moe, I ain't won. I loss. If I coulda stopped King from coming, he'd be alive. I loss everything now.

MOORE: I been knowing you for over 20 years, and I ain't never heard you sound this sorry for yourself. It's time to celebrate now.

JONES: They got a eight cents a hour raise. I saw it on the tv. Martin Luther King died fah a eight cent raise? Celebrate? Dat's a damn shame!

MOORE: They got a memorandum of agreement. That means . . .

JONES: Hah! A memorandum. Dat ain't offisha recognition! What is it? A piece of paper dat say "we'll think about it later!"

MOORE: *(angry)* It's an agreement made with a public employees' union for the first time in the history of Memphis, in the history of the whole South! *(pause)* Look, T.O., everything that's happened over these last few weeks is more important than your personal rage. You can't control what happens in this world. Everything is bigger than us. It's a start, T.O. Next year, we renegotiate, after things cool down.

JONES: We? You mean you and Solomon and Willins and all dem?

MOORE: You're still president of the local.

JONES: I ain't nothin', rememba? Just a bundle of personal rage that got King killed.

MOORE: Lawd Ha'mercy! King's death is part of God's plan. You got to have faith and keep toiling. You lose your faith, you fall into an abyss of chaos; you lose everything that keeps you human.

JONES: *(sharply)* Brotha Moore, I don't feel like no sermon 'long through here.

MOORE: Well, brotha Jones, you need one! But I didn't come here to preach. Your men sent me up. Look outside.

JONES: *(irritated)* What fah?

MOORE: Lawd Ha'mercy, just look outside!

(JONES looks "outside" and is taken aback by what he sees. Crowd sounds emanate from the street when he appears at the "window.")

CROWD: *(off)* T.O.! T.O.! T.O.! T.O.! T.O.!

(JONES steps back from the "window." The sounds subside.)

MOORE: They've been ordered back to work starting tonight. They want you to conduct the final vote. They want to share their triumph with you.

JONES: Triumph! A eight cent triumph! They don't need me for dat.

MOORE: Brotha Jones, those men said they won't move one truck, empty one garbage can or pick up one tub unless you say so. They want to hear the word from you.

(JONES ponders this for a moment and then bursts into a rueful chuckle.)

JONES: Da Mayor done tricked all of us. All these workers of striking. All them peepas killed or hurt! All the marchin' and jailin' and beatin's! All that starvin' and prayin' and downright cryin'! King dead! Murdered! What we git in return? One piece of paper and eight bright, shiny pennies. Eight pennies and a maybe! Ain't a damn thing change! In twenty-five years, when things cool down, day gon' break every union in this country. Sanitation men was sold back inta slav'ry and dey come here axin' me if it's all right.

MOORE: Joy? Joy is all right. Always has been. Joy is a treasure. If you can't go out there and cheer and dance and laugh and sing and cry with those men . . . well . . . if you lost your faith, then you go tell them. I'm not going to be a messenger of despair and bitterness!

(There is a moment of silence as JONES ponders. The men outside are growing impatient as they sing or chant. Tears of resignation gather in JONES' eyes. MOORE silently prays. Wearily JONES goes to the "window" and shouts outside to the men.)

JONES: What the hell ya'll stannin' 'round looking at me fah? Ya'll think the buzzards gon' eat up all that garbage? I'm tired of lookin' at Memphis garbage! Clean it up. *(Cheers from the CROWD outside. JONES raises his arms in victory, manages a smile and then turns back to MOORE.)*

JONES: *(sighing heavily)* Let's go hep 'em.

(As THEY exit, the BLUESMAN strolls on and plays an appropriate, uptempo blues that segues into a curtain call.)

DA END

Medal of Honor Rag

Tom Cole

Tom Cole

Playwright, screenwriter and fiction writer, Tom Cole is best known in terms of his theater work for *Medal of Honor Rag,* based on the true story of Black Congressional Medal of Honor winner Dwight Johnson. The play focuses on Johnson's confrontation with his Jewish psychiatrist in a U.S. army hospital, shortly before the young veteran's release. Johnson was killed soon after that when he pulled a gun on a Detroit storeowner—whether to obtain cash or to obtain an honorable end to the agony of Vietnam, one can only speculate. In its two-person, seventy-minute, unbroken session, this drama manages to expose a double tragedy: that of Blacks in a city from which many middle-class Black and white people have fled and that of Vietnam veterans returning "home" with no celebration of their sacrifice and no justification for the deaths they inflicted or the deaths inflicted on their comrades in arms.

First produced in 1975 in Boston and then in 1976 in New York, *Medal of Honor Rag* had the distinction among Vietnam plays of focusing on the way the return of the Vietnam veterans, difficult at best, was exacerbated by conditions for Black veterans. Tom Cole's Black protagonist, D.J., becomes symbolic of the Black veteran in America, who wins medals for sacrifice and bravery and then is unable to acquire even the most basic recognition—a chance for a decent job, a place for his family in his own hometown. The play was telecast nationally on PBS "American Playhouse" in 1982 produced by Joyce Chopra, the writer's wife, and directed by Lloyd Richards, for many years director of the Eugene O'Neill Playwrights Center and the Yale School of Drama.[1]

The play has had numerous productions, including a number of 25-year anniversary presentations that occasion a comparison of the circumstances of African American men today and a quarter century ago. Conditions of conflict raging on the streets of urban ghettos, a paucity of opportunity, and the inability of the helping professions to reach veterans of urban wars—these elements are still akin to the ones in *Medal of Honor Rag*. The "rag"of the ironic title is still less a lively interaction and more a dance macabre in which society fails to rescue its Black heroes. As Lawrence Van Gelder stated in his review of the 25th anniversary New York production, Cole's play remains "absorbing theater and a bracing reminder of time past and distance yet to be traveled."[2]

Tom Cole deals with another kind of casualty in the 1985 film *Smooth Talk*, directed by Joyce Chopra and based on the Joyce Carol Oates short story "Where Are You Going, Where Have You Been?"[3] While acknowledging that some aspects of her story were "impossible to transfigure into film," Oates congratulates Cole and Chopra for the "filling in, expanding and inventing" necessary to change the short fiction into a complete film. "Connie's story becomes lavishly, and lovingly, textured; she is not an allegorical figure so much as a 'typical' teenaged girl...in a vivid and absolutely believable world. . . ."[4]

Cole has also written the plays *About Time, Fighting Bob,* and *Dead Souls,* adapted from Gogol. His short stories have been anthologized in the yearly O. Henry Prize collections for 1962, '66 and '70, and his novel, *An End to Chivalry,* won the Rosenthal Award of the American Academy of Arts and Letters. Whether working on plays, screenplays or fiction, Cole has been particularly effective at capturing the grim reality of ordinary heroes and victims.

Notes

1. Tom Cole, *Medal of Honor Rag* (New York: Samuel French, 1976), p. 3.

2. Lawrence Van Gelder, "The Tunnel And the Dark Didn't End In Vietnam (*The New York Times,* February 1, 2001).

3. http://www.suntimes.com/ebert/ebert . . . reviews/1986/o5/57590.html.

4. http://www.cocc.edu/humanities/HIR/Film/smoothtalk.htm) [Originally published in *The New York Times,* March 23, 1986. Rpt. In Eng 104 Textbook: Charters as *Smooth Talk:* Short Story into Film," pp. 913–916.]

Medal of Honor Rag

Cast of Characters

DOCTOR: A white man in his middle years, informal, hardworking (even overworked—the doctor with simultaneous commitments to hospital, private patients, writing, family, research, teaching, public health, public issues, committees, special projects). White shirt and bow tie, soft jacket, somewhat weary. He is of European background, but came to this country as a child. Possessor of a dry wit, which he is not averse to using, for therapeutic purposes.

DALE JACKSON: A black man two weeks before his 24th birthday, erect and even stiff in bearing, intelligent, handsome, restrained. An effect of power and great potential being held in for hidden reasons. Like the doctor, given to his own slants of humor as a way of dealing with people and, apparently, of holding them off.

HOSPITAL GUARD: A sergeant in uniform and on duty. White. An MP, on transitional assignment.

The Scene: *An office, but not the doctor's own office. No signs of personal adaptation—looks more like an institutional space used by many different people, which is what it is. Rather small. A desk, a folding metal chair for the patient, a more comfortable chair for the doctor. Wastebasket. Ashtray.*

Stage Directions: *With the lights still low, a squalid sound from a kazoo is heard, which flows into a rendition of the "Fixin-to-Die-Rag," by Country Joe and the Fish.*

A few verses: to bring back the mood of Vietnam.

While the music plays, door opens Stage Rear and the DOCTOR enters. Light pours in from the corridor, but the DOCTOR can't find the light switch in the room. He feels about in half-light, then steps outside again, to find the switch there. Fluorescent overhead light comes on, and the DOCTOR putters about, hurriedly, in the office. He re-arranges the patient's chair. Takes several folders and a notepad out of his briefcase.

He studies one of the dossiers and then, after a beat, looks at his wristwatch. Takes out a cigarette, filter-holder, and match; puts cigarettes into filter and filter in his mouth and lights the match. Holds the match and lets it burn without lighting the cigarette, while he looks into the folder again. Puts match down, picks up pencil to make hurried notes in the dossier. Takes a small cassette recorder out of his briefcase, rummages for a cassette, checks its title, and puts it into recorder. Lights another match and this time lights the cigarette. Puts briefcase on floor beside the desk. Looks at watch, starts to make another note, takes a drag on cigarette as—

Knock on door, and DALE JACKSON *enters, escorted by* HOSPITAL GUARD. JACKSON *wears "hospital blue denims" and slippers or soft shoes.* GUARD *places paper forms, in triplicate, on* DOCTOR'*s desk, points brusquely to place for signature. Holds out a ball-point pen to* DOCTOR. DOCTOR *signs, glancing at* DALE JACKSON. GUARD *tears off one sheet for* DOCTOR, *retains others, and holds out his hand to reclaim his pen.* DOCTOR *hands back pen, abstractedly, and* GUARD *[in full Sergeant's regalia] salutes him snappily. The* DOCTOR *looks at the* GUARD *as if he were crazy. The man still stands there, at attention.* DALE JACKSON *watches this. Finally, the* DOCTOR *gets up halfway from his chair—a funny, inappropriate gesture, and waves at the man.)*

DOC: You can leave us alone.

GUARD: *(Snappy salute.)* Yes, sir! I'll report back for Sergeant Jackson on the hour, sir! *(About face, marches off. The* DOCTOR *and* DALE JACKSON *look at each other.)*

DOC: Sergeant Jackson? *(*DALE JACKSON *nods.)* Well, they seem to be keeping a pretty close eye on you.

D.J.: Where's the other doctor?

DOC: *(Settling back in his chair.)* Sit down, please.

D.J.: They keep changing doctors.

DOC: Would you rather see the other doctor?

D.J.: No, man . . . it's just I have to keep telling the same story over and over again.

DOC: Sometimes that's the only way to set things straight.

D.J.: You're not in the Army, huh?

DOC: *(Twinkle.)* How can you tell?

D.J.: Your salute is not of the snappiest.

DOC: I came down from New York today. To see you.

D.J.: I must be a really bad case.

DOC: You're a complicated case.

D.J.: Like they say, a special case. I am a special case. Did you know that?

DOC: They keep a pretty close eye on you now.

D.J.: I went AWOL twice. From this hospital.

DOC: Oh?

D.J.: But they'll never do anything to me.

DOC: I understand.

D.J.: You understand, huh?

DOC: I understand your situation.

D.J.: Yeah, well, mind telling me what it is?

DOC: You don't need me to tell you that.

D.J.: So what *do* I need you for?

Doc: I don't know—maybe *I* need *you.*

D.J.: That's a new one. That's one they haven't tried yet.

Doc: Oh?

D.J.: Every doctor has his own tricks.

Doc: Oh?

D.J.: That's one of yours.

Doc: Oh? What's that?

D.J.: When it's your turn to talk, you get this look on your face—kind of like an old owl who's been constipated for about five hundred years, you know, and you say *(Imitation of Doc's face)*, "oh?" *(The* Doctor *laughs at this, a little, but he is watching D.J. very closely. Sudden anger.)* Man, this is a *farce!* *(D.J. turns away—as if to "go AWOL" or to charge to the door . . . but he gets immediate control of himself. He is depressed.)*

Doc: *(Calmly.)* What should we do about it?

D.J.: Who's this "we?"

Doc: Who else is there?

D.J.: We just going to keep asking each other questions?

Doc: I don't know—What do you think?

D.J.: What do *you* think, man? *Do* you think?

Doc: I listen.

D.J.: No, man, I mean, what do you think? You got that folder there. My life is in there. I'm getting near the end of the line with this stuff. I mean, sometimes I feel like there's not much time. You know? *(As D.J. talks, he has wandered over to the desk; where he proceeds to thumb through the folders on his case. He does this with a studied casualness.)*

Doc: I'm aware of that.

D.J.: You some big-time specialist? *(Suddenly suspicious.)*

Doc: In a manner of speaking.

D.J.: What are you a specialist in?

Doc: Among other things, Vietnam veterans and their problems.

D.J.: Well I can *see* that, man. But what do you *specialize* in?

Doc: I specialize in grief.

D.J.: *(Laughs, embarrassed.)* Shit. Come on.

Doc: *(As if taking a leap.)* Impacted grief. That's the . . . special area I work in.

D.J.: *(Disgusted.)* I'm going to spend another hour in jive and riddles and doubletalk. Only it's not even an hour, right? It's, like, impacted.

Doc: You know the word "impacted"?

D.J.: How dumb do you think I am?

Doc: I don't think you're dumb at all. Matter of fact, the reverse . . . *(While speaking these words, he has opened the dossier to a sheet, from which he reads aloud.)* "Subject is bright. His Army G.T. rating is equivalent of

128 I.Q. In first interviews does not volunteer information—" *(Smiles to D.J., who allows himself a small smile of recognition in return; then continues reading.)* "He related he grew up in a Detroit ghetto and never knew his natural father. He sort of laughed when he said he was a "good boy" and always did what was expected of him. Was an Explorer Scout and an altar boy..." *(The DOCTOR stares quietly at D.J. D.J. stares back. This goes on for a while. The DOCTOR shifts position. D.J. shifts his, too. They lean toward each other. Finally:)*

D.J.: The other doctor talked a lot about depression.

DOC: What did he say about it?

D.J.: He said I had it.

DOC: Oh? And?

D.J.: He thought I oughta get rid of it. You know? *(The DOCTOR reacts.)* Yeah, well he was the chief doctor here. The chief doctor for all the psychos in Valley Forge Army Hospital! See what I mean?

DOC: Valley Forge.

D.J.: Yeah ....

DOC: Why *don't* you get rid of it?

D.J.: *(Animated.)* Sometimes that's just what I want to do! Sometimes I want to throw it in their faces! *(Recollecting himself.)* Now ain't that stupid? Like, whose face?

DOC: *(He is keenly on the alert, but tries not to show it in the wrong way.)* What do you want to throw in their faces?

D.J.: What are we talking about?

DOC: What are you talking about? *(D.J. stares at him. He won't or can't say anything. DOC continues gently, precisely.)* I was talking about depression. You said your doctor said you should try to get rid of it. I asked, simply, why *don't* you get rid of it? *(D.J. stares at him, still. He is a man for whom it is painful to lose control. He is held in, impassive.)* You meant the medal, didn't you, when you said, "throw it in their faces"?

D.J.: Well. That's why you're here, right? Because of the medal?

DOC: *(Gentle, persistent.)* But I didn't bring it up. You did.

D.J.: You asked me why I don't get rid of it.

DOC: *(Repeating.)* I was talking about depression.

D.J.: No. You meant the medal.

DOC: *You* meant the medal. I never mentioned it ... Are you glad you have it?

D.J.: The depression?

DOC: No. The medal.

D.J.: *(Laughs.)* Oh, man ... Oh, my ... Suppose I didn't have that medal ... You wouldn't be here, right? You wouldn't know me from a hole in the wall. I mean, I would be invisible to you. Like a hundred thousand other dudes that got themselves sent over there to be shot at by a lot of little Chinamen hiding up in the trees. I mean, you're some famous doctor, right? Because, you know, I'm a special case! Well I am, I am one big tidbit. I am what you call a "hot property" in this man's Army. Yes, sir! I am an authentic hero, a showpiece. One look at me, enlistments go up 200% . . . I am a credit to my race. Did you know that? I am an honor to the city of Detroit, to say nothing of the state of Michigan, of which I am the only living Medal of Honor winner! I am a feather in the cap of the Army, a flower in the lapel of the military—I mean, I am *quoting* to you, man! That is what they say at banquets, given in *my* honor! Yes, sir! And look at me! *Look at me!! (Pointing to himself in the clothing of a sick man, in an office of an Army hospital.)*

DOC: I'm here because you're here.

D.J.: What?

DOC: You ask, would I be here if you hadn't been given that medal. Probably not, because if you hadn't been given that medal, you wouldn't be here, either. If my grandmother had wheels she'd be a trolley car. It's a big "if . . ."

D.J.: Yeah, but I'm saying a different "if." If a trolley car didn't have wheels it still wouldn't be nobody's grandmother. It would just be a trolley car that couldn't go nowhere. Am I right?

DOC: *(After a pause.)* You're right . . . *(Brisk, again.)* Do you still have stomach pains?

D.J.: Yup.

DOC: Nightmares?

D.J.: Yup.

DOC: Same one?

D.J.: Yup.

DOC: *(Reads from folder.)* "An anonymous soldier standing in front of him, the barrel of his AK-47 as big as a railroad tunnel, his finger on the trigger slowly pressing it."

D.J.: That's the one.

DOC: Who is that anonymous soldier?

D.J.: You know who that is.

DOC: No, I don't.

D.J.: Ain't you done your homework? *(Pointing to folder.)*

DOC: My memory is shaky . . . Please?

D.J.: That's the dude who should have killed me.

DOC: "Should have?"

D.J.: Would have.

DOC: What happened?

D.J.: He misfired.

Doc: And?

D.J.: And that's it.

Doc: That's what?

D.J.: That's it, man. What do you want—a flag that pops out of his rifle and says "Bang?"

Doc: They say you then beat him to death with the butt of your weapon . . . In combat, near—Dakto.

D.J.: That's what they say.

Doc: That is what they say.

D.J.: So I have heard.

Doc: What else have you heard?

D.J.: That I showed "conspicuous gallantry."

Doc: You're quoting to me?

D.J.: That is what they say, at banquets given in my honor.

Doc: It's part of the citation. Is it not?

D.J.: (Quoting; far-away look.) Con-spicuous gallantry, above and beyond the call of duty . . . (With Texas accent.) "Ouah hearts and ouah hopes are turned to peace . . . as we assemble heah . . . in the East Room . . . this morning . . ."

Doc: Lyndon B. Johnson?

D.J.: You got it.

Doc: What did you feel?

D.J.: Nothing.

Doc: But when he hung the medal around your neck, you were crying.

D.J.: See, you *done* your homework!

Doc: Are you going to poke fun at me for the whole hour?

D.J.: Anything wrong with fun?

Doc: Dale—

D.J.: People call me "D.J." That's in the folder, too.

Doc: D.J.

D.J.: Yes, Doctor?

Doc: Do you want to listen to me for a moment?

D.J.: You said *you* was the one to listen.

Doc: I can't listen if you won't tell me anything!

D.J.: I am *telling* you, man! If I knew what to tell to make me feel better, I woulda told myself a long time ago. I ain't the doctor, I can't cure myself . . . (Pause.) Except one way, maybe.

Doc: (gently, after a beat) What are you thinking of, right now?

D.J.: Nothing.

Doc: No image? Nothing in your head?

D.J.: It doesn't have nothing to do with me.

Doc: But *you* thought of it.

D.J.: It's about other guys, in The Nam. Stories we used to hear.
Doc: Yes?
D.J.: "Standing up in a firefight . . ." (*Doc waits*) We used to hear this . . . combat story. I wasn't in much combat, did you know that?
Doc: Except for Dakto.
D.J.: Yeah. These guys, in their tenth or eleventh month—you know, we had to be there for 365 days on the button, right? Like, we got fed into one end of the computer and if we stayed lucky the computer would shit us back out again, one year later. These grunts—that's what we called the infantry . . .
Doc: I know.
D.J.: I was in a tank, myself.
Doc: What happened to these grunts you heard about?
D.J.: Ten months in the jungle, their feet are rotting, they seen torture, burnings, people being skinned alive—stories they're never going to tell no doctor, believe me . . . Like, *you* never seen anything like that, right, so you can't comprehend this . . . (*The Doctor starts to say something in rebuttal, but then waits.*) You never seen your best friend's head blown right off his body so you can look right down in his neck-hole. You never seen somebody you loved, I'm telling you like I mean it, somebody you *loved* and you get there and it's nothing but a black lump, smells like a charcoal dinner, and that's your friend, right?—a black lump. You never seen anything like that, am I right?
Doc: (*Quietly.*) If you say so.
D.J.: Well, *look* at you, man! Look at you, sitting there in your . . . suit!
Doc: What's wrong with my suit?
D.J.: Ain't nothing wrong with your suit! . . . It's the man wearing the suit. That's what we are talking about!
Doc: You were telling me a story. *The Doctor seems to show some satisfaction here—that D.J.'s feelings are beginning to pour out, even if obliquely.*)
D.J.: A story?
Doc: (*Looking at words he has jotted down.*) About grunts . . . "standing up in a firefight."
D.J.: (*As if puzzled that he was recalling this.*) Oh. Yeah. So, they been through all these things, and they stayed alive so far, they kept their weapons clean, kept their heads down under cover, and then in the middle of a big firefight with 50-caliber rounds, tracers, all kinds of shit flying all over the place, they'll just stand up.
Doc: They stand up?
D.J.: Yes, start firing into the trees, screaming at the enemy to come out and fight . . . Maybe not screaming. Just standing straight up.

Doc: And? *(Writing.)*

D.J.: Get their heads blown off.

Doc: Every time?

D.J.: Oh, man—*guaranteed*! You know how long you last standing up
that way?

Doc: A few seconds?

D.J.: You're a bright fella.

Doc: So, why did they stand up?

D.J.: *(Retreating again.)* Yeah, why?

Doc: Why do you think they stand up?

D.J.: I don't know. You're the doctor. You tell me.

Doc: What made you think of it just now?

D.J.: I don't know.

Doc: What do you feel about it?

D.J.: Nothing.

Doc: Nothing . . . *(Silence, for a moment. The* Doctor *gets up, restless,
takes a step or two—looks at* Dale Jackson, *who sits, immobilize.)* D.J.,
I am going to tell you a few things. Right away.

D.J.: *(Perking up.)* You're breaking the rules here, ain't you, Doc?

Doc: So be it—sometimes there is nothing else to do.

D.J.: I mean, how do you know I won't report you to your superior?

Doc: *(Smiling.)* My superior?

D.J.: Don't shrinks have superiors? There must be a Shrink Headquarters
somewhere. Probably in New York.

Doc: Probably.

D.J.: So, I'll report that *you* did all the talking and made me—a psycho—
take notes on everything you said. Here, man—*(He sits down in* Doc's
place at desk, takes pad and pen, sets himself to write.) I'm ready. Tell
me, how do you feel now that you're going to get busted into the
ranks, emptying bedpans and suchlike? . . . Oh?

Doc: *(He leans forward, to make his words take hold.)* You see what's
happening: we are playing games with each other. Because that's easy
for you, and you are good at it. You could fill this hour, the week, the
month that way until it really *is* too late! Do you understand that?

D.J.: Do you?

Doc: How dumb do you think I am?

D.J.: *(Trace of a smile.)* I ain't decided yet. I don't have a folder on you
with your scores in it.

Doc: Yes. You're a very witty man, very quick—as long as the things we
touch on don't really matter to you. But when they do, you go numb.
You claim to feel nothing. Do you recognize what I'm saying?

D.J.: *(Dull.)* I don't know.

Doc: Even your voice goes flat. Can you hear the sound of your own
voice?

D.J.: *(Flat.)* I don't know.

Doc: Do you see that?

D.J.: What?

Doc: I merely *mentioned* the fact that you go numb—and you did! What do you think about that?

D.J.: Nothing.

Doc: Nothing! You think nothing about the fact that you just go one-hundred-percent numb, like a stone, in response to everything that matters most in your own life? *(The* Doctor *surreptitiously glances at his watch. They are well into the hour.)*

D.J.: Well, now I *am* going to tell you something, man! *(Breaks out, as if he had been cornered.)* I don't have to stay in this hospital! See? I don't even know why I'm here! I don't know why I'm in this room!

Doc: Then why don't you leave it? We're not getting anywhere.

D.J.: *(Mocking.)* You mean, I don't have to "reside" here till my hour's up?

Doc: No. I'm not your Commanding Officer. So, go.

(D.J. does start to go. But he stops on the way to the door, once again, to return to the Doctor's *desk. There he picks up the various folders and drops them into the wastebasket. He does the same thing, pointedly, with the doctor's pen. He stares at the* Doctor *for a moment, then walks to the door, opens it, and steps out into the corridor. The* Doctor *watches him, then heaves a sigh, and leans on the desk to think about what has happened. But D.J. appears again at the door.)*

D.J.: If I go out there, I'll be in the corridors, I hate the corridors. You ever walk the corridors of this place?

Doc: Never had that pleasure.

D.J.: There's seven miles of them. Lined with basket cases. And I've walked them all, man. I've walked them all . . .

Doc: So you're going to stay here with me just to keep out of the corridors for a while?

D.J.: That's right.

Doc: *(Not forcing the issue.)* Fine. Make yourself comfortable.

(D.J. smiles, goes to a chair, settles in, stretches, takes off his robe and/or slippers—wiggles his bare feet as if they were amusing animals. Begins to do a musical beat on the chair, ignoring the Doctor. *The* Doctor *calmly goes back to the wastebasket, extracts his folders and notebook, shakes the ashes off them. He takes out his pen, taps it against the side of the basket, in counter-rhythm to D.J.'s beat, and blows the dust off. Then the* Doctor *settles comfortably at his desk, lights a cigarette, whistles a bit of the Mozart G-minor Symphony, begins to look through the folder as if to do some work on his own.)*

Doc: Do you mind if I write for a while? To pass the time?

D.J.: *(Cool.)* Help yourself.

Doc: *(After a beat; musingly.)* Here's an interesting story . . . a case study I've been working on . . . trying to write it out for myself . . . about a certain man who was an unusual type for the world he came from . . . *(Reads from or refers to folder, as if in discussion of a neutral matter.)* Rather gentle, and decent in man . . . almost always easygoing and humorous. Noted for that. As a kid in a tough neighborhood, he had been trained by his mother to survive by combining the virtues of a Christian and a sprinter: he turned the other cheek and ran faster than anyone else. . . . *(D.J. is beginning to listen with interest.)* This man was sent by his country to fight in a war. A war unlike any war he might have imagined. Brutal, without glory, without meaning, without good wishes for those who were sent to fight and without gratitude for those who returned. He was trained to kill people of another world in their own homes, in order to help them. How this would help them we do not really know. He was assigned to a tank and grew close with the others in the crew, as men always do in a war. He and his friends in that tank were relatively fortunate—for almost a year they lived through insufferable heat, insects, boredom, but were never drawn into heavy combat. Then one night he was given orders assigning him to a different tank. For what reason?

D.J.: There was no reason.

Doc: There was no reason.

D.J.: It was the Army.

Doc: It was the Army. The next day, his platoon of four M-48 tanks were driving along a road toward a place called Dakto, which meant nothing to him. Suddenly they were ambushed. First, by enemy rockets, which destroyed two of the tanks. Then, enemy soldiers came out of the woods to attack the two tanks still in commission. This man we were speaking of was in one of those tanks. But the tank with his old friends, the tank he would have been in—

D.J.: Should have been in.

Doc:—the tank that he might have been in—that tank was on fire. It was about sixty feet away, and the crew he had spent eleven months and twenty-two days with in Vietnam was trapped inside it . . . *(D.J. looks away, in pain.)* He hoisted himself out and ran to the other tank. Speaking of standing up in a firefight . . . Why he wasn't hit by the heavy crossfire we'll never know. He pulled out the first man he came to in the turret. The body was blackened, charred, but still alive. That was one of his friends.

D.J.: He kept making a noise to me, over and over again. Just kept making the same noise, but I couldn't find where his mouth was. . . .

Doc: Then the tank's artillery shells exploded, killing everyone left inside. He saw the bodies of his other friends all burned and blasted, and then—for 30 minutes, armed first with a 45-caliber pistol and then with a submachine gun he hunted the Vietnamese on the ground, killing from ten to twenty enemy soldiers (no one knows for sure)— by himself. When he ran out of ammunition, he killed one with the stock of his submachine gun.

D.J.: He kept making this same noise to me . . . over and over.

Doc: *(After a pause.)* When it was over, it took three men and three shots of morphine to quiet him down. He was raving. He tried to kill the prisoners they had rounded up. They took him away to a hospital in Pleiku in a straitjacket. Twenty-four hours later he was released from that hospital, and within 48 hours he was home again in Detroit, with a medical discharge. . . .

D.J.: My mother didn't even know I was coming. . . .

Doc: Go on.

D.J.: *(Looking up.)* You go on.

Doc: That is the story.

D.J.: That's not the whole story.

Doc: What happened when you got back to his country?

D.J.: What do you mean, what happened?

Doc: One day you're in the jungle. These catastrophic things happen. Death, screaming, fire. Then suddenly you're sitting in a jet airplane, going home. No time even to tell your mother. What happened?

D.J.: They had *stewardesses* on that plane! D'you know that?

Doc: Oh?

D.J.: *Stewardesses,* for shit's sake, man! They kept smiling at us.

Doc: Did you smile back?

D.J.: *(Straightforward.)* I wanted to kill them.

Doc: White girls.

D.J.: That's not the point.

Doc: Are you sure?

D.J.: A white guy would have felt the same way I did. I . . . wanted to throw a hand grenade right in the middle of all those teeth.

Doc: Do you think that was a bad feeling?

D.J.: Blowing up a girl's face, because she's smiling at me? Well, I'll tell you, man, it wasn't the way my mother brought me up to be. Not exactly.

Doc: Neither was the war. Was it?

D.J.: Doc. Am I crazy?

Doc: Maybe a little bit. But it's temporary . . . It can be cured.

D.J.: *You* can cure me? *(Stares at him.)*

Doc: I didn't say that.

D.J.: Yeah, but you mean it, don't you?

Doc: What was it like, when you touched ground, in this country?

D.J.: You actually think that you can cure me!

Doc: Did they have a Victory Parade for you?

D.J.: *Victory Parade?!*

Doc: Soldiers always used to get parades, when they came home. Made them feel better.

D.J.: Victory parades! Man . . . *(Laughs at the insane wonder of the idea.)*

Doc: You mean there wasn't a band playing when you landed in the States?

D.J.: Man, let me tell you something—

Doc: You didn't march together, with your unit?

D.J.: Unit? What unit?

Doc: Well, the people you flew back with.

D.J.: I didn't know a soul in that plane, man! I didn't have no *unit.* Any unit I had, man, they're all burned to a crisp. How'm I supposed to march with that unit?—with a whiskbroom, pushing all these little black crumbs forward down the street, and everybody cheering, "There's Willie! See that little black crumb there? That's our Willie! No, no, that there crumb is my son, George! Hi, Georgie. Glad to have you home, boy!"? Huh?. . . . What are you talking about?! This wasn't World War Two, man, they sent us back one by one, when our number came up. I told you that!

Doc: People were burned to a crisp in World War Two.

D.J.: Yeah, well there was a difference, because I *heard* about that war! When people came back from that war they *felt* like somebody. They were made to feel *good,* at least for a while.

Doc: That's just what I was thinking.

D.J.: Then why didn't you just say it?

Doc: I'd rather that you said it.

D.J.: Were you in that war?

Doc: I remember it—very well.

D.J.: And you knew guys who had a parade with their unit?

Doc: I did. Banners. Ticker tape.

D.J.: *(Laughs at the thought.)* Oh, man. How long ago was that?

Doc: Where did you land?

D.J.: Seattle.

Doc: Daytime? Night?

D.J.: Night. *(A pause.)*

Doc: Nothing?

D.J.: Nothing, man. Nothing. *(Pause.)*

Doc: I had one patient who told me he got spat on, at the Seattle airport.

D.J.: Spat on?

Doc: For not winning the war. He said an American Legionnaire, with a red face, apparently used to wait right at the gate . . . so he could spit on soldiers coming back, the moment they arrived.

D.J.: What are you telling me this for?

Doc: Then, inside the terminal there was a group of young people screaming insults. White kids, with long hair. *(No reaction from D.J. The Doctor watches him carefully.)* Do you want to know why they were screaming insults?

D.J.: No, Doctor, I do not.

Doc: For burning babies.

D.J.: I didn't burn no babies! *(D.J. begins to pace. He is agitated. The Doctor watches, waits.)* The day I arrived, like, everything was disorganized. There was a smaller plane took us to the nearest landing strip, know what I mean?—and then you had to hitch a ride, or whatever, to find your own unit.

Doc: Are you talking about Seattle?

D.J.: No, man. In The Nam. Like, my first day over there. My *first day,* mind you! So, I hitched a ride on this truck. About six or seven guys in it, heading toward Danang. I was a F.N.G., so I kept my mouth shut.

Doc: F.N.G.?

D.J.: *(He pulls his chair up closer to the Doctor's desk, as if to confide in him, and he sits.)* A F.N.G. is a Fucking New Guy. See? They all pick on you over there, they hate you just because you're new. Like, nobody trusts you for the simple fact that you never been through the miseries they been having. At least, not yet . . . —Then you get friendly with your own little group, see, your own three or four friends—the guys in my tank—and they mean everything to you, they're like family—they're like everything you got in this world—I—see, that was the—thing about—that was the—. . .

(Dale Jackson suddenly can't go on. He buries his face in his hands and is attacked by a terrible grief—ambushed by it. He tries to pull his hands away to speak again, but it is impossible. He sobs, or weeps, into his hands. The Doctor hesitates, then goes around to the chair where D.J. sits, and stays there by him for a moment. He begins to lay a hand, lightly, on D.J.'s shoulder, so that D.J. will not be completely alone with his grief. But D.J. breaks away, violently. He heads away, as if to escape. The Doctor moves to block another impetuous exit, but D.J. had no clear intention. He is frozen, sobbing. If his face is visible, it is painful to see. The Doctor watches him intently, almost like a hunter. He seems to be gauging his moment, when D.J. will be just in control enough to hear what the Doctor is saying. But still vulnerable enough for a deep blow to be struck. Finally:)

Doc: Is it the tank? *(D.J. cannot really answer.)* Can you say it? *(D.J. almost begins to speak, but the catch in his throat is still there. He will break down again, if he speaks. He shakes his head.)* Do you want me to say it? *(D.J. cannot answer.)* You don't know why you are alive and they are dead. *(D.J. watches.)* You think you should be dead, too. *(D.J. listens, silent. At times he tries to run away from the words, but the Doctor stalks him.)* Sometimes you feel that you *are* really dead, already. You can't feel anything because it's too painful. You dream about the rifle that should have killed you, with the barrel right in your face. You don't know why it didn't kill you, why just that rifle should have misfired . . . *(D.J. hangs on these words.)* And what about those orders that transferred you out of their tank? Why just that night? Why you? Why did the ambush come the next day? . . . There must be something magical about this, like the AK-47 that misfired for no reason. Perhaps you made all these things happen, just to save yourself. Perhaps it is all your fault, that your friends are dead. If you hadn't been transferred from their tank, then somehow they wouldn't have died. So you should die, too.

D.J.: *(bellowing.)* I'm dead already!

Doc: *(quieter.)* Yes. You *feel*, sometimes, that you are dead already. You would like to die, to shut your eyes quietly on all this, and you don't know who you can tell about it. You keep it locked up like a terrible secret . . . *(D.J. remains silent. The Doctor's words have the power to cause great pain in him. After a pause.)* This is our work, D.J. This is what we have to do.

D.J.: I can't, man! I can't!

Doc: You can. I know you can.

D.J.: *(stares at him; then:)* How do you know all this? From a book?

Doc: I've been through it.

D.J.: *You* were in The Nam?

Doc: No. But I had my own case of survivor guilt.

D.J.: That's jive and doubletalk! Don't start that shit with me.

Doc: It's just shorthand to describe a complicated . . . sickness. It's the kind of thing that can make a man feel so bad that he thinks he wants to die.

D.J.: Where'd you get yours?

Doc: You think it will help you to know that?

D.J.: Man, I take off my skin, and you just piss all over me! And . . .

Doc: You want me to take my skin off, too. That's what you want?

D.J.: I want to get better! I don't want to be crazy!

Doc: Yes. That's why I'm here, to—

D.J.: *(cutting him off)* You're not here!

Doc: I'm not?

D.J.: There's something here. And it's wearing a bowtie. But I don't know *what* it is . . .

Doc: Well, in this treatment, that's the way it works. Normally, it's better that you *not* know about your doctor's personal—

D.J.: *Normally?!* Man, this ain't normally!

(The Doctor *considers this, as a serious proposition. Historically. The abnormal war. The desperation of this man. And he goes ahead, against his own reluctance.)*

Doc: All right. All right . . . I wasn't born here. I'm from Poland. I had a Jewish grandmother, but I was brought up as a regular kid. All right? . . . Life in Poland tends to get confusing. Either the Russians or Germans are always rolling in, flattening the villages and setting fire to people. You've got the picture? Anyway, World War II came, the Nazis, the SS troops, and this time the Jewish kids were supposed to be killed—sent to Camps, gassed, starved, worked to death, beaten to death. That was the program . . . I didn't think of myself as Jewish. We didn't burn candles on Friday night, none of that. I wasn't Jewish. But my mother's mother was. So, to the Nazis I was Jewish. So, I should be dead now. I shouldn't be here. You're looking at someone who "should" be dead, like you . . . See *(D.J. nods. He listens intensely.)* They sent me to one of those Camps. But I was saved, by an accident . . . You understand what I'm saying? Someone came along— a businessman—and he said he would buy some Jewish children, and the Nazis could use the money for armaments, or whatever. A deal. One gray morning—it was quite warm—they just lined us up, and started counting heads. When they got to the number the gentleman had paid for, they stopped. I got counted. The ones who didn't—my brother and sister and the others—they all died. But not me. For what reason? *There was no reason* . . . So, that's it. Eventually, I ended up over here, I lied about my age, got into the Army at the end of the War. I thought I wanted revenge. But now I know that I wanted to die, back over there. To get shot. But I failed. Came back, and I even marched in a Victory Parade, with my unit! So I was luckier than you, D.J . . . But still, I didn't know why I hadn't died when everyone else did. I thought it must have been magic, and that it was my fault the others were dead—a kind of trade-off, you see, where my survival accounted for their deaths. My parents, everybody. I became quite sick. Depressed, dead-feeling . . .

D.J.: How did you get better?

Doc: The same way you will.

D.J.: I thought you wasn't going to cure me.

Doc: No. Essentially, you are going to cure yourself.

D.J.: Wow. *(shakes his head)*

Doc: Others, men like you, have gone through such things, and they have gotten better. That might make you feel a little better, too, for a start.

D.J.: Yeah, misery loves company. Right?

Doc: Nothing magical happened, D.J. None of this was your fault. *(glances at his watch)*

D.J.: How much time we got left, Doc?

Doc: Don't worry about the time. We have all the time we'll need.

D.J.: You're the one is always stealing a look at your watch!

Doc: It's just a bad habit. Like picking my nose.

D.J.: I ain't seen you picking your nose.

Doc: You will. You will.

D.J.: I guess that gives me a little something to look forward to, in my hospital stay.

Doc: *(laughs)* I guess it does.

D.J.: A treat instead of a treatment. *(The Doctor is no longer amused. He stares at D.J., expectantly. D.J. grows uneasy.)* You want something from me.

Doc: Mm. The truck.

D.J.: The truck?

Doc: The story of the first—

D.J.: *(Interrupting.)* What truck?

Doc: There was a truck.

D.J.: A truck . . . ?

Doc: First day in Vietnam. F.N.G. You hitched a ride in a truck.

D.J.: Jesus.

Doc: Don't feel like talking about it?

D.J.: No. I don't.

Doc: That's as good a reason as any for telling me.

D.J.: *(Reacts to this notion, but then goes along with it. Sits down again, as he gets into the story.)* Well, uh . . . we were riding along, in the truck. Real hot, you know, and nobody much was around . . . and we see there's a bunch of kids, maybe three, four of them crossing the road up ahead . . . You know?

Doc: How old were they?

D.J.: Well, it's hard to tell. Those people are all so *small*, you know?— I mean, all dried-up, and tiny, man . . . Maybe ten years old, twelve, I don't know . . .

Doc: And?

D.J.: Well, we see they're being pretty slow getting out of the road, so we got to swerve a little bit to miss them . . . Not a lot, you know, but a little bit. This seems to make the guys in the back of the truck really mad. Like, somebody goes, "Little fuckers!" You know? . . . Then those kids, as soon as we pass, they start laughing at us, and give us the finger. Know what I mean? *(D.J. gives the DOCTOR the finger, to illustrate. The DOCTOR starts to laugh, but then puts his hand to his head, as if knowing what is to come.)* Yeah. So I'm thinking to myself, "Now where did they learn to do that? That ain't some old oriental custom. They musta learned it from our guys." . . . Suddenly the guys on the truck start screaming for the driver to back up. So he jams on the brakes, and in this big cloud of dust he's grinding this thing in reverse as if he means to run those kids down, backwards. The kids start running away, of course, but one of 'em, maybe two, I don't know, they stop, you see, and give us the finger again, from the side of the road. And they're laughing . . . So, uh . . . everybody on the truck opens fire. I mean, I couldn't believe it, they're like half a platoon, they got M-16's, automatic rifles, they're blasting away, it sounds like a pitched battle, they're pouring all this firepower into these kids. The kids are lying on the ground, they're dead about a hundred times over, and these guys are still firing rounds into their bodies, like they've gone crazy. And the kids' bodies are giving these little jumps into the air like rag dolls, and then they flop down again . . .

DOC: *(Very quiet.)* What happened then?

D.J.: They just sorta stopped, and me and these guys drove away. *(DOC waits.)* I'm thinking to myself, you know, what *is* going on here? I must be out of tune. *My first day in the country,* and we ain't even reached the Combat Zone! I'm thinking, like, this is the enemy? Kids who make our trucks give a little jog in the road and give us the finger? I mean, come on, man! . . . And one guy, he sees I'm sort of staring back down the road, so he gives me like this, you know— *(D.J. simulates a jab of the elbow.)* and he says, "See how we hose them li'l motherfuckers down, man?" Hose 'em down. You like that? . . . And they're all blowing smoke away from their muzzles and checking their weapons down, like they're a bunch of gunslingers, out of the Old West . . . *(D.J. shaking his head. He still has trouble believing he saw this.)*

DOC: *(Measured.)* Why do you think they did all that?

D.J.: I don't know . . . *(Pause.)* They went crazy, that's why!

DOC: Went crazy . . . Were all those soldiers white?

D.J.: I don't remember.

DOC: What do you think?

D.J.: *(a little dangerously)* I think some of them were white.

DOC: *(Waits. D.J. does not add anything.)* And what did you do?

D.J.: What do you mean, what did I do?

DOC: Well, did you report them to a superior officer?

D.J.: *(Explodes.) Superior officer?!* What superior officer? Their fucking lieutenant was *right there in the fucking truck,* he was the first one to open fire! I mean what are you talking about, man? Don't you know what is going on over there?

Doc: Why get mad at me? I didn't shoot those children.

D.J.: *(Confused, angry.)* God *damn . . .* ! *(Glaring at the DOCTOR.)* I mean, what are you accusing me of, man?

Doc: I'm not accusing you of anything.

D.J.: Well, I'm asking you! What would you have done? You think you're so much smarter and better than me? You weren't there, man! That's why you can sit here and be the judge! Right? *(No reaction from the DOCTOR, except for a tic of nervousness under the extreme tension that has been created.)* I mean, look at you sitting there in your suit, with that shit-eating grin on your face!

Doc: You're getting mad at my suit again! You think my suit has caused these problems? *(DALE JACKSON can't control his rage and frustration any longer. He blows up, grabs his chair—as the only object available— and swings it above his head as a weapon. The DOCTOR instinctively ducks away and shouts at him to stop; shouting—improvised.)* Wait a minute! Sergeant! Stop that! *(D.J. crashes the chair against the desk, or the floor. He cannot vent his physical aggression directly against the DOCTOR. After he has torn up the room, D.J. stands exhausted, confused, emptyhanded. While D.J. subsides:)* Are you all right? *(D.J. stares at the DOCTOR, panting. He moves away, into the silence of the room, then suddenly turns in a passion:)*

D.J.: *I didn't kill those kids, man!*

Doc: I didn't say you did! Did I? *(Waits. But a deep point has been made, and both men are aware of it. After a pause.)* Did you ever tell people at home about any of this? About Dakto, about the truck?

D.J.: No. I didn't.

Doc: Didn't they ask? Didn't anyone ever wonder why you came home early?

D.J.: Yeah, they asked.

Doc: Who asked?

D.J.: My mother. Little kids, sometimes. My girl, Bea. . . .

Doc: Sounds like everybody.

D.J.: No, not everybody. A lot of people didn't give a shit what happened.

Doc: And you pretended you didn't give a shit what happened.

D.J.: What do you want me to say, man?

Doc: But what did you say when your mother or your friends asked you?

D.J.: You guess. You're the specialist.

Doc: *(After a pause.)* All right, I will. You said, "Nothing happened. Nothing happened over there."

D.J.: Right on. Word for word.

Doc: It's in the folder.

D.J.: Yeah, sure.

Doc: *(Takes words from report in the folder.)* It also says you "lay up in your room a lot, staring at the ceiling . . ." *(The* Doctor *waits, to see if D.J. has anything to add.)*

D.J.: Read. Read, man. I'm tired.

Doc: Did you do that—did that happen to you right away?

D.J.: Right away . . . ? No. Well, at first I felt pretty good. Considering . . . *(Trails off.)* Considering, uh . . .

Doc: Considering that you had just been heavily narcotized, tied up in a straitjacket, and shipped home in a semi-coma. After surviving a hell of death and horror, which by all odds should have left you dead yourself.

D.J.: Yeah. Considering that.

Doc: You felt lucky that you had survived? At first?

D.J.: I just used to like going to bars with my cousin, William . . . my friends. I was glad to see my girl, Beatrice, and my mama. I joked around with them. I tried to be good to them . . . I shot baskets with the kids, down the block. Understand?

Doc: Of course. And then what happened?

D.J.: It didn't last.

Doc: And?

D.J.: I started laying up in my room. Staring at the ceiling.

Doc: But what happened? What changed you?

D.J.: I don't remember.

Doc: But you did go numb?

D.J.: You're talking me around in circles, Doc!

Doc: I'm sorry . . . You know, this terrible delayed reaction, after a kind of relief—it seems so mysterious, but it's the common pattern for men who went through your kind of combat trauma . . .

D.J.: *(With irony.)* Well, I'm glad to hear that. But I sometimes began to suspect that my girl, Bea, might just prefer a man that can see and hear and think and feel things. And *do* things! You follow my meaning? A man that can walk and talk, stuff like that?

Doc: Did you stop having sexual relations with her?

D.J.: Well, I have been trying to send you signals, man! You're none too quick on the pick-up.

Doc: Did she criticize you?

D.J.: Not about that . . . She wanted me to get a job, so we could get married.

Doc: Well. The job situation must have been difficult in Detroit.

D.J.: Especially if you lay up in your room all day, staring at the ceiling. Funny thing about the city of Detroit—not too many people come up through your bedroom offering you a job, on most days. Did you know that?

Doc: I've heard that, yes . . . Did you stop getting out of bed altogether?

D.J.: No, I put my feet to the floor once in a while. Used to go on down to the V.A. and stand in line for my check.

Doc: How did they treat you down there, at the Veteran's Office?

D.J.: Like shit.

Doc: Did you know why you got treated that way?

D.J.: It wasn't just me personally, man.

Doc: I know. But why?

D.J.: You know that a vet down the block from me flipped out last week—jumped up in the middle of his sleep and shot his woman in bed, because he thought she was the Vietcong laying there to ambush him? . . . *(The DOCTOR goes sharply on the alert at this, but waits for D.J. to continue. D.J. is profoundly uneasy about his own train of thought.)* Man, if I lose my cool again—just, freak out—what's to stop me from going up and down the streets of Detroit killing everything I see?

Doc: *(Concerned, quiet.)* Do you actually think you could do that?

D.J.: How can you ask me that?

Doc: I'm asking.

D.J.: *(Charging at him.)* Well, what did I *do*—what did I get that medal for, man? For my good manners and gentle ways? *(They stare at each other for a tense moment. The DOCTOR starts to fit up another cigarette and filter, but throws the filter away and lights up the cigarette. Begins to pace restlessly. DALE JACKSON watches him. Then the DOCTOR abruptly turns back to D.J.)*

Doc: Tell me when you actually got the medal.

D.J.: You're making me nervous!

Doc: *(Keeps pacing.)* As my grandmother used to say, "That should be the worst would ever happen to you."

D.J.: That's the grandmother, could have been a trolley car?

Doc: *If* she had wheels.

D.J.: If she had wheels. Right. *(During this colloquy—in which signs of an ease, a trust seems to be forming between them—the DOCTOR has restrained himself, but he is impatient now to pick up the thread.)*

Doc: Tell me when you actually got the medal! *(This story is relatively easy for DALE JACKSON to launch into; he settles into his old chair in the course of telling it.)*

D.J.: I been home eight, nine months. Then I get this call, they say it's some Army office. They want to know if I'm clean—if I had any arrests since I been back, you know. I tell them I'm clean and just leave me alone. Then two MP's come to the door, in uniform, scare the shit out of my mama. They just tell her they want to find out a few things about me—whether I've been a good boy—whether I've been taking any drugs. She makes me roll up my sleeves right there *(D.J. does so for the DOCTOR.)*, to show—no tracks, see? When they leave, she is sure I've done something terrible, that I shouldn't be afraid to tell her, that she'll forgive me anything. And all I can do is sit there in the kitchen and laugh at her, which makes her mad, and even more sure I done something weird. . . . Well, about fifteen minutes later a Colonel calls up from the Department of Defense in Washington, tells me they're going to give me the Congressional Medal of Honor, and could I come down to Washington right away, with my family, as President Lyndon B. Johnson himself wants to hang it around my neck, with his own hands. He'll pay for the ticket, he says.

DOC: So, another sudden ride on a jet plane.

D.J.: A goddamn *Honor Guard* meets us at the airport. Beatrice is peeing in her pants, my mother's with me, my cousin, William . . . They got a dress-blue uniform waiting for me, just my size. Shoes, socks, everything. Escort, sirens. Yesterday afternoon for all they knew I was a junkie on the streets, today the President of the United States can't wait to see me. . . . *(The DOCTOR has picked up his cassette recorder while D.J. was finishing the story, and now he clicks it on. The voice of Lyndon B. Johnson plays, from the award ceremony:)*

VOICE OF L.B.J.: ". . . Secretary Resor . . . General Westmoreland . . . Distinguished guests and members of the family . . . Our hearts and our hopes are turned to peace as we assemble here in the East Room this morning. All our efforts are being bent in its pursuit. But in this company—" *(DOCTOR points the recorder at D.J.)* "we hear again, in our minds, the sounds of distant battle . . ." *(The DOCTOR turns the volume down, and the voice of L.B.J. drones quietly in the background, as he waits for D.J.'s reaction.)*

D.J.: Ain't that a lot of shit?

DOC: You wept.

D.J.: I don't know, I kind of cracked up. The flashbulbs were popping in my eyes, my mother's hugging me, she's saying, "Honey, what are you crying about? You've made it back." It was *weird!* *(The DOCTOR has turned the volume up again to let a few more phrases from the presidential ceremony play, giving D.J. more time for re-living the moment.)*

VOICE OF L.B.J. FROM THE CEREMONY: "This room echoes once more to those words that describe the heights of bravery in war—above and beyond the call of duty. Five heroic sons of America come to us today from the tortured fields of Vietnam. They come to remind us that so long as that conflict continues our purpose and our hopes rest on the steadfast bravery of young men in battle. These five soldiers, in their separate moments of supreme testing, summoned a degree of courage that stirs wonder and respect and an overpowering pride in all of us. Through their spectacular courage they set themselves apart in a very select company . . ." (*The* DOCTOR *underlines these last words—"set themselves apart in a very select company"—with a gesture. Then he flicks off the cassette recorder.*)

D.J.: Weird, man.

DOC: Why was it weird?

D.J.: I . . . I don't know?

DOC: You *do* know!

D.J.: What are you driving at?

DOC: What did you get that medal for? (*repeating D.J.'s earlier words*) For your "good manners and gentle ways"?

D.J.: (*Stares at the* DOCTOR. *The* DOCTOR *stares back.*) I got that medal because I went totally out of my fucking skull and killed everything that crossed my sight! (*pause*) . . . They say I wanted to kill all the prisoners. *Me.*

DOC: *You don't remember?*

D.J.: Nothing . . . A few flashes, maybe. Those people are all so small . . .

DOC: (*He taps a finger on the cassette recorder, trying to re-capture the specific moment they have been talking about—in the White House—but he gradually gets caught up in the intense rush of his own thoughts*) So, your mother was hugging you, in the White House, for doing what she had trained you all your life not to do—for being a killer. And everybody was celebrating you for that . . . And your dead friends from the tank, whom you had tried so hard to bury, came back again, to haunt you. You had to re-live that story, that flash of combat when a man's life is changed forever, when he literally goes crazy, psychotic, in a world of no past and no future, compacted into a few seconds, a wild pounding of the heart, blinding light, explosions, terror, and his whole earlier life slides away from him through a . . . membrane as if lost forever, and all he can do is kill—all *that* was named, broadcast, printed on a banner and waved in your own face so you can never forget . . . And you wonder why you wept, why you were confused, why you are here in this hospital? You wept for your dead friends, you wept for your dead self, for your whole life that slid away in the first fifteen seconds of that ambush on the road to Dakto. You were choking on your grief, a grief you couldn't share with anyone, and you became paralyzed by your guilt, and you still are, and you're going to be, until *you* decide to make your own journey back through that membrane into some acceptable reality . . . Some real life, of your own . . . (*Both* DALE JACKSON *and the* DOCTOR *seem momentarily stunned by the latter's outpouring.*)

D.J.: I don't know how to do that, Doc.

Doc: I will tell you . . . *(glances at watch, as if recollecting himself)* D.J., do you intend to stay in this hospital for a while?

D.J.: Why do you ask?

Doc: *(reads from folder for an answer)* "Maalox and bland diet prescribed. G.I. series conducted. Results negative. Subject given 30-day convalescent leave 16 October 1970. Absent Without Leave until 12 January 1971, when subject returned to Army hospital on own volition. Subsequent hearing recommended dismissal of A.W.O.L. charge and back pay reinstated . . . in cognizance of subject's outstanding record in Vietnam."

D.J.: Well, yeah, they can't do anything to me.

Doc: Because of the medal?

D.J.: Because of the medal . . .

Doc: *(after a beat)* I'm afraid we have only a few more minutes today. *(scanning his appointment book)* I can come down the day after tomorrow, and I'd like to talk with you again. After that, if you want, I can see you three or four times a week.

D.J.: *(He automatically readies himself for the end of the hour.)* Busy man like you? *(light mockery)*

Doc: Mm-hm. But I'd like to have you transferred up to New York. I can do that, if you'll make the request . . . *(He looks questioningly at D.J. D.J. does not answer—nor does he necessarily imply a "No.")* Well?

D.J.: We'll see.

Doc: We'll see what?

D.J.: We'll see, when you come down again.

Doc: Can I be sure you'll be here?

D.J.: You're looking for too many guarantees in life, man.

Doc: No, I'm not. I'm looking for you to make a decision about yourself. *(A knock at the door, and the HOSPITAL GUARD [Military Police Sergeant] immediately enters.)* You *can* get better, you know. . . .

GUARD: Reporting in for Sergeant Jackson, sir. *(The DOCTOR and D.J. look at each other. D.J. gets up, automatically, to go.)*

Doc: *(to GUARD)* Will you wait outside for a moment? In the corridor?

GUARD: Will do, sir. May I ask, sir, how long?

Doc: Not long. Until the interview is concluded.

GUARD: May I ask, sir, is the interview almost concluded?

Doc: The interview is almost concluded. Just giving a summation.

GUARD: Will wait in corridor, sir, until conclusion of summation of interview. *(He snaps to, gives salute. The DOCTOR waves him off, with his own facsimile of a salute. The GUARD wheels into an about-face and exits to station himself outside the door, as.)*

D.J.: Attaboy.

DOC: So?

D.J.: So?

DOC: Do we have a deal?

D.J.: Hit me with the "summation."

DOC: *(He closes up his folder.)* There is nothing to say that you don't already know. The only question is what to do about it. *(D.J. laughs.)* It was a badly damaged self that you brought back to this country, and nothing has happened here, you see, to help you—

D.J.: *(cutting him off)* You're leaving a little something out, ain't you. Man, they gave me the Congressional Medal of Honor!

DOC: So they did. And what happened?

D.J.: Well . . . I became a big hero!

DOC: You became a big hero . . . You appear on TV. The head of General Motors shakes your hand. You get married. You re-enlist—re-enlist!— travel around the state making recruiting speeches. You get a new car, a house with a big mortgage. Everybody gives you credit . . . for a while.

D.J.: Rags to riches, man.

DOC: And then? *(D.J. makes a gesture of self-deprecation, meaning, more or less, "Here I am.")* Back to rags again.

D.J.: *(challenging)* But I got the medal! Didn't that medal save me from a lot of shit?

DOC: *(beginning to pack up)* Did it ever occur to you that the medal, in some ways, might have made things worse?

D.J.: *Worse?* What are you talking about, man?

DOC: Well, that's where we can begin our next session . . . If you will simply commit yourself to being here. That's all I'm asking, you know.

D.J.: *(opening up the DOCTOR's folder again)* No! I want to talk about it now. I mean, it sounds like you're just getting down to the nitty-gritty, am I right?

DOC: It's all nitty-gritty, D.J. It's one layer of nitty-gritty after another, until you feel like living again. But we can't just extend this hour arbitrarily—

D.J.: Why not? Just tell the cowboy out there to take a walk. You got the rank here . . .

DOC: That's not the issue. Look, for one thing I'm a little tired, too. I got up at five this morning, and—

D.J.: Yeah. Well that should be the worst would ever happen to you!

DOC: All right. Let's just say for now, that it's the rules of the game, by which we *both* can—

D.J.: *(pouncing on the word "game")* So we *are* playing games! You hear?

DOC: We're playing a game for your life!

D.J.: *(studies the DOCTOR)* What do you want from me, man?

Doc: I want you to get better.

D.J.: No, you said you were going to tell me what I had to do.

Doc: I said that?

D.J.: Yeah, you did—after a long speech about killing, when you got all excited. Probably, it slipped out, huh?

Doc: Well, that gives us something else to look into, next time.

D.J.: *(sullen)* No, man. You want something from me. I been getting used to that . . . I think you're a starfucker.

Doc: A what?

D.J.: A star-fucker. Like, in the Rock world, or in the movies, these chicks who hang around close to the stars. They get their kicks, their thrills out of that.

Doc: I'm not a "chick."

D.J.: But you're like one.

Doc: Meaning?

D.J.: You come down here, you sniff me out. Because in your world, I'm probably a famous case. Because of my medal. Am I right?

Doc: *(gets up, and starts to escort his patient to the door)* I think we're back to where we started the hour. None of this will be easy, D.J., but I will be here the day after tomorrow, and as you say, we'll see what happens . . .

D.J.: *(interrupting)* You want to take that medal away from me, don't you?

Doc: *(a little stunned)* No. Why do you say that?

D.J.: Now be honest with me, man. Otherwise, you're going to turn my head around backwards, for good . . . *(They look at each other for a long beat.)*

Doc: No, D.J., I don't want to take that medal, or anything else away from you. But when the time is ripe, when you are ready, you may not need it any more. That's why *you* spoke, early this hour, of wanting to get rid of it, sometimes, and of "throwing it in their faces." You see, part of you already wants to throw it away, while—

D.J.: *(pulling away)* Throw it away!? *(angrily)* You're the one who's crazy. You know what I'd be without that medal? I'd be just another invisible Nigger, waiting on line and getting shit on just for being there! I *told* you about that, man! You just don't *listen*!

Doc: That's one of the very things that's driving you crazy.

D.J.: What is?

Doc: That once again, in Detroit, you have been singled out from all the others.

D.J.: What are you talking about?

Doc: *(pursuing him)* You know what I'm talking about! It's the same story as the tank, all over again. Why are all the others suffering, on the streets, and only you have been spared? But you haven't been spared, and you *are* suffering . . .

D.J.: So what are *you* doing? You going around telling every dude who has the Congressional Medal of Honor to just throw it away? You just dropping out of the sky into every hospital and nut house in the country, scrambling up the brains of everybody who—

Doc: *(pouncing)* You think, then, that everybody with the Medal of Honor must be in some kind of hospital?

D.J.: Did I say that?

Doc: You did. You let it slip out . . . In some deep way, you agree with me.

D.J.: That what?

Doc: That the medal can make a man sick—drive him into a hospital.

D.J.: The whole damn thing makes a man sick! There's a lot of sick vets who didn't get no Medal of Honor! And they're mainlining and getting beat up in the streets and sucking on the gin bottle, and they didn't get no Bronze Star, no nothing except maybe a Purple Heart and a *"less than honorable discharge"*—bad paper, man, you can't get a job, you can't get benefits, you can't get nothing if you got bad paper. Now you tell me, what does my medal have to do with *that?* *(A knock on the door—on the words "bad paper, man"—and the GUARD immediately enters. Poker-faced, he listens to the end of D.J.'s tirade.)*

GUARD: Has the summation been concluded, sir?

D.J.: God *damn.*

Doc: Will you please wait just a minute?

GUARD: You'll have to contact chief of section, sir, about that.

D.J.: *(Heated.)* Didn't you hear the man? Now, fuck off!

Doc: D.J.—

GUARD: Look, Sergeant. To him you're an important case, but to me you're just another nut.

D.J.: *(He makes a threatening move at the GUARD.)* Just another nut. Okay . . . *(The Guard prepares to subdue D.J. with his club, if necessary. In no time, a serious scuffle is ready to break out.)*

Doc: *(Throwing himself between them.)* Will both of you stop this! That's an order!

GUARD: Sorry about that, sir. *(returns to parade rest; stares stonily ahead)*

D.J.: I'll bet you are.

Doc: *(He looks from one to the other of these near-combatants. D.J. is still simmering, with his back to him.)* D.J. Do you watch TV here?

D.J.: Some.

Doc: The news?

D.J.: Not if I can help it.

Doc: You didn't see it? The other night?

D.J.: What?

DOC: The medals . . . *(watching D.J. closely)* Vietnam vets. Heroes? In wheelchairs, some of them; on crutches? At the Capitol steps? Washington? Throwing their medals away? A kind of miracle-scene, like the old—

D.J.: *(breaking in)* And that's what you want me to do! Hop right on down there and toss it up—

DOC: You saw it?

D.J.: *I didn't see nothing!*

DOC: Some of those men . . . I happen to know some of those men . . .

D.J.: You cured them?

DOC: They're curing themselves. And they're a lot like you. *(D.J. watches, non-commital.)* . . . But they refuse to stay isolated. They meet, in therapy groups, which they started. Up in New York, "Rap sessions" . . . a new kind of unit, you might say . . . Everybody tells his story. You see? They're people who have been through the same fires you have, who were *there*, whom you can trust . . .

D.J.: *(after a pause)* Doc, those dudes on TV are all white.

DOC: You *have* been watching them.

D.J.: Yup, and I'm going to tell you something. You got your reasons for wanting to see no more war, right?—and no more warriors. I dig that, for your sake. But a lot of folks don't want the black veteran to throw down *his* weapons so soon. Know what I mean? Like, we are supposed to be preparing ourselves for another war, right back here. Vietnam was just our basic training, see? I'm telling this to both of you, y'see, so you won't be too surprised when it comes. *(The GUARD looks to the DOCTOR for instructions.)*

DOC: *(to D.J.)* Why are you saying this right now?

D.J.: I want you to have something to think about, for the next session. Give us a good starting point. . . .

DOC: Still poking fun at me?

D.J.: *(He waits a moment, then smiles and gives the DOCTOR a pat on the arm.)* Don't you worry, Doc. I'll be seeing you. You just sit down now, and write your notes. In the folder.

(D.J. walks to the door, where the GUARD momentarily blocks him, in order to give a last, official salute to the DOCTOR. The DOCTOR gives a half-despairing wave as D.J. watches. D.J. turns to the door, stops, and gives the GUARD an imperious cue to open the knob and make way for him. The GUARD does so, grudgingly. It is a minor, private triumph for D.J. The two exit. The DOCTOR reflects for a moment, at his desk. Then, showing his weariness, he packs up his belongings, gives the room a last look, and prepares to leave. Light on stage is reduced until he is alone in the light with darkness

around him. The feeling must be of a change in time. The DOCTOR steps forward out of the confines of the room, to the edge of the apron, and addresses the audience.)

DOC: When I drove down again from New York, two days later, Dale Jackson did not appear for his hour of therapy. He was in fact AWOL, back in Detroit. He intended to do something about his money troubles. His wife was in a hospital for minor surgery, and he had been unable to pay the deposit. There were numerous protectors he might have gone to in the city for help—people who would not have allowed a Medal of Honor winner to sink into scandalous debt. But he went to none of them, this time. His wife was disturbed about the bill. This was on the evening of April 30. He promised her that he would come back to the hospital that night with a check, and also with her hair curlers and bathrobe. As he was leaving, he said, "Ain't you going to give me a kiss good-bye?" And he put his thumb in his mouth like a little boy, which made her laugh. He asked some friends to drive him to a place where he claimed he could get some money, and asked them to park—in a white section of town. He walked down the block, entered a grocery story and told the manager he was holding it up. He took out a pistol, but never fired a shot while the manager emptied his own gun, at point-blank range, into D.J.'s body. Death came, a few hours later, in Detroit General Hospital, of five gunshot wounds. His body went on a last unexpected jet airplane ride to Arlington National Cemetery, where he was given a hero's burial with an eight-man Army Honor Guard. I wrote to his mother about him, about what a remarkable human being even I could see he was, in only sixty minutes with him. She wrote back: "Sometimes I wonder if Dale tired of this life and needed someone else to pull the trigger." In her living room, she keeps a large color photograph of him, in uniform, with the Congressional Medal of Honor around his neck. *(Lights slow fade down to darkness, as the DOCTOR walks off. Blackout; and then lights up as the DOCTOR, DALE JACKSON, and the GUARD converge, stand side-by-side, and bow to the audience.)*

Note

The continuous text of Lyndon B. Johnson's ceremonial address quoted in this play, is as follows:

"... Secretary Resor ... General Westmoreland ... Distinguished Members of Congress. Distinguished guests and members of the family ... Our hearts and our hopes are turned to peace as we assemble here in the East Room this morning. All our efforts are being bent in its pursuit. But in this company, we hear again, in our minds, the sounds of distant battle. . . . This room echoes once more to those words that describe the heights of bravery in war, above and beyond the call of duty. Five heroic sons of America come to us today from the tortured fields of Vietnam. They come to remind us that so long as that conflict continues, our purpose and our hopes rest on the steadfast bravery of young men in battle. These five soldiers, in their separate moments of supreme testing, summoned a degree of courage that stirs wonder and respect and an overpowering pride in all of us. Through their spectacular courage, they set themselves apart in a very select company. . ."

This text is an excerpt from remarks made by President Johnson at a Congressional Medal of Honor award ceremony at the White House on November 19, 1968.

The address was recorded, and the tapes of the President's voice are maintained at the Lyndon B. Johnson Library in Austin, Texas.

The Day the Bronx Died

Michael Henry Brown

Michael Henry Brown

M ichael Henry Brown does not pretend to be politically correct. He grew up in the Bronx during the late fifties and early sixties with a variety of ethnic groups including Blacks and Jews. Some of those Black people were admirable and some, as the protagonist of *The Day the Bronx Died* puts it, were "evil scum." Brown doesn't believe Black playwrights need to present mainly noble Black characters, or always have a noble Black character to balance out an ignoble one. "I write about my experience, and I am a Black guy born in the Bronx. So obviously it's a Black point of view. It's just dealing with who I am and the world around me. I'm not the great, noble Negro writer, and I don't want to be. I write about people—and sometimes they're very tough people with very tough words."

Brown's mother lives in a part of the Bronx that can still be called a pleasant neighborhood, but he understands why many white people fled. "Who wants to live where the crime is ridiculous and you're afraid to come home and afraid for your kids to go out? As an adult, you have a family and you have to protect your own."[1]

Yet Brown is saddened by the polarization that has taken place all over New York, leaving very few mixed neighborhoods and very few boyhood friendships between Blacks and Jews, such as the one depicted in his play. "Will our groups become the Palestinians and the Jews?" he wondered during a 1994 interview for a Jewish publication. "It ain't quite that bad, but there's something that needs to be addressed . . . People should walk away from the play thinking . . . that there's a long history between Blacks and Jews, and that shouldn't be forgotten."[2]

Since getting his MFA from Columbia University, Michael Henry Brown has had 15 plays produced. When *Generations of the Dead or Into the Abyss of Coney Island Madness* was produced at the Long Wharf Theater in New Haven, Connecticut, where several of his plays have premiered, it was called "daredevil playwriting, brimming with the dynamic stage language and swaggering confidence of a writer in control."[3]

Generations also involves a young man whose dream is slowly poisoned and eroded by the ghetto, corrupting the good kid and the dreams of generations of Black families. *Ascension Day* is a dramatization of the events that led to Nat Turner's slave revolt. *Borders of Loyalty* deals with anti-Semitism in the theater world. *King of Coons* is based on the life of Steppin Fetchit, the first Black movie star whose diffidence on screen projected a 1929 stereotype which later became anathema to African Americans.

Brown's nobility lies in confronting corruption and polarization within the Black community and between Blacks and other groups. He does so unflinchingly with a boldness and anger that has its genesis in a time of greater innocence and a vision of greater civility.

Notes

1. Robert Neuwirth, *New York Newsday*, "Interview with Michael Henry Brown, 'I'm Not the Great, Noble Negro Writer' " 4-01-1993, pp. 103.

2. Susan Josephs, " 'An Attempt at Healing': A black playwright and a Jewish director." *Jewish Week*, 03-24-1994; http://www.fb10.uni-bremen.de/anglistik/kerkhoff/ContempDrama/Brown.htm.

3. Jan Stuart, *Newsday*, quoted in http://www.fb10.uni-bremen.de/anglistik/kerkhoff/ ContempDrama/Brown.htm.

The Day the Bronx Died

Cast of Characters

BIG MICKEY: black, professional, in his late thirties to early forties.

MOTHER: black, hard working and domestic, forty years old.

YOUNG MICKEY: black, smart, and baseball loving. Athletic, given to introspection and thirteen years old.

ALEXANDER: black, fourteen, tough teenager with a gentle side. The Errol Flynn of the community, both in looks and rakishness.

THE PRINCE: black, street tough and fifteen. The Prince is the prototype for what was to come in the 1980s and '90s.

BILLY KORNBLUM: white, Jewish, with a quick wit and thinks he knows everything. Thirteen years old.

DANIEL: black, a gifted teenage musician, and Young Mickey's friend and piano teacher.

ODD JOB: black, fifteen, a bully, and physically imposing. Like most bullies, Odd Job, when not with the crowd is quite the coward.

OFFICER BREAM: black, late thirties.

MR. KORNBLUM: white, Billy's father, and coach of the little league team.

BUTTER: black, teenager, basketball player from Brooklyn.

SILK: black, teenager, basketball player from Brooklyn.

DOCTOR: black, mid thirties.

Act 1

Scene 1

In the dark, the sounds of a respirator and hospital intercom. Lights up on BIG MICKEY, a black man in his late thirties. He walks onstage as if he's just been told he can follow the patient being wheeled into the emergency operating room, not further. He is trying to make sense of the unbelievable . . .

BIG MICKEY: He's only thirteen years old . . . he never did anything vicious to anybody. They didn't even rob him . . . they just beat him for the joy of it . . . thirteen years old. And I don't know if my son will see fourteen. *[Pause.]*

It came out of nowhere. I was working in my office in our apartment when the phone rang. We live in one of those exclusive, doorman buildings in Manhattan. It's the kind of place my Mother toiled in as a domestic . . . a cook. She would find it most gratifying that my wife and I live comfortably in a building where not too long ago we would've only been able to enter through the "servants' entrance" . . . We have someone to clean . . . a nanny for our baby. I thought I was doing so well for a boy from the Bronx. Now . . . my life, or more accurately, my son's life, is spread across the tabloids and six o'clock news. *[Pause.]* He was attacked on the subway. *[Pause.]* The motive of the gang was unknown.

And I stand here waiting to hear the outcome of his operation. Waiting for him to tell me and the police who did this to him . . . if he's able. Now, as I wonder what we could have done to have prevented this from happening . . . my mind flashes back to the time when I was thirteen . . . My parents had bought a nice house in a working middle-class section of the Bronx. They thought they were protecting me from the things that were deteriorating in other parts of the city. *[Pause.]*

My father had just died. I had really admired him and I did not handle his death well at all. I thought I was handling it like a man.

MOTHER: You didn't even cry. How could you not cry? Ain't nobody studyin' you . . . How can you learn to be a man when you don't mourn your own father?

BIG MICKEY: My mother was the cook for the Rubenstein family. The Rubensteins of Sutton Place, that is.

[YOUNG MICKEY sees the gift is a book. He frowns.]

MOTHER: You like the gift Mrs. Rubenstein bought you, Mickey?

YOUNG MICKEY: It's uhh . . . uhh . . . .

MOTHER: Signed by James Baldwin. Mrs. Rubenstein is good friends with him. Ain't that something?

YOUNG MICKEY: Yeah, somethin' . . .

MOTHER: Somethin' wrong?

YOUNG MICKEY: I thought maybe it would be the latest James Bond book . . .

MOTHER: James Bond! Boy, that's James Baldwin. That's literature. You mean to tell me you prefer some make believe Superman?

YOUNG MICKEY: Secret Agent . . .

MOTHER: Boy, you better read the message Jimmy Baldwin got for all the people. I'll put it on your desk.

BIG MICKEY: Because I straddled two worlds, I had two best friends.

ALEXANDER: C'mon, Mickey!

[ALEXANDER runs on and joins YOUNG MICKEY. They dance.]

BIG MICKEY: *[With record.]* I know you wanna leave me . . .

ALEXANDER AND YOUNG MICKEY: . . . but I refuse to let you go . . .

[BIG MICKEY stops singing. He watches the two youngsters pretend they are the Temptations. He enjoys the music, and the memory before him. As the music plays, MICKEY'S MOTHER comes in as they dance and starts rooting them on. The boys turn and see her.]

MOTHER: How you doin', Alexander?

ALEXANDER: Hi, Ma'am.

MOTHER: You stayin' out of trouble?

ALEXANDER: Uh huh.

MOTHER: Are you?

ALEXANDER: Yeah.

[MOTHER watches the boys dance as another Temptations' song comes on.]

MOTHER: I'm off to work. The Rubinsteins are having Leonard Bernstein for dinner. *[MOTHER exits.]*

ALEXANDER: Who's that?

YOUNG MICKEY: He's that guy on the young people's concerts on TV.

ALEXANDER: Well, I didn't know.

YOUNG MICKEY: Well, now you know.

ALEXANDER: Come on, let's do another one. *[ALEXANDER begins to prepare to sing leads.]*

YOUNG MICKEY: You said it was my turn to sing leads.

ALEXANDER: I sing the David Ruffin leads . . . you've got the high voice like Eddie Kendricks . . . Now with this next record you be Eddie.

[The Temptations "The Way You Do the Things You Do" now begins to play. YOUNG MICKEY pretends he is singing into a microphone. ALEXANDER sings the background. They dance in a synchronized manner. They are having a ball. BIG MICKEY is smiling, having a good time with his memory. The song finally fades.]

YOUNG MICKEY: I'm gonna write my own songs one day.

ALEXANDER: You still writin' those lyrics? . . .

YOUNG MICKEY: Yeah, and when Daniel teaches me how to write music . . .

ALEXANDER: Man, we can get some other guys . . .

YOUNG MICKEY: Have a singing group . . .

ALEXANDER: That'll be boss . . .

[Music fades. Lights down on the boys. They exit.]

BIG MICKEY: The one with the bandanna wrapped around his head is Alexander . . . Alexander the Great to be exact. He was the toughest kid in the neighborhood. If you were a private house kid, and you

ventured toward guys from the projects, there were only three words
that could stop you from being stomped, stripped of your clothes, and
forced to walk home naked . . .

[Lights up on YOUNG MICKEY *and* THE PRINCE. YOUNG MICKEY *is holding
a baseball glove and is wearing a Pittsburgh Pirate cap.]*

THE PRINCE: Who do you know?
BIG MICKEY: And, those words were . . .
YOUNG MICKEY: Alexander the Great!
THE PRINCE: That sucker who swings through trees? You jivin' me?
YOUNG MICKEY: I'm not jivin' . . . I live around the corner from him.
THE PRINCE: Yeah, all right. You cool . . . If I find out you lyin' . . . yo'
ass is grass, and I'm a lawnmower.

*[*THE PRINCE *walks away.* YOUNG MICKEY *stays there.* ALEXANDER *swings in
with a Tarzan yell. Pushes* YOUNG MICKEY *aside.]*

ALEXANDER: *[To* PRINCE.*]* You got a problem?

*[*THE PRINCE *exits.* ALEXANDER *follows off after a laugh with* YOUNG MICKEY.*]*

BIG MICKEY: When I was thirteen years old, my greatest passions were
baseball, Roberto Clemente, baseball . . . Robert Clemente . . . baseball.
A few years earlier I discovered Clemente on a cool spring afternoon
in Shea Stadium . . . There was a fly ball hit deep to right . . . Clemente
glided back and made a graceful catch . . . the Mets had a man on
third, and it looked like an easy tag up for the score . . . and when
Clemente caught the ball the man at third started home. From deep
in right field, Roberto threw a perfect strike to home plate. It was
incredible . . . I've never seen anything like it, by the laws of baseball
he was supposed to be safe, but Roberto's arm broke the laws of
baseball . . . Between innings, I went to the souvenir stand and bought
a Pittsburgh Pirate cap . . . Roberto Clemente was always there for
me . . . And so was Billy Kornblum.

[Fade up. BILLY KORNBLUM, *a Jewish kid of twelve, joins* YOUNG MICKEY.
He wears a Baltimore Oriole cap. BILLY *goes to shortstop, and* YOUNG MICKEY
goes to third base.]

BILLY: You just gotta switch with me . . . you gotta let me play third . . .

*[They mime taking ground balls. The crack of the bat can be heard and they
react. Sometimes they catch the ball, at other times they react, they watch the
ball go somewhere else.]*

YOUNG MICKEY: What's in it for me?
BILLY: Why you gotta be a *schmuck*, Mickey?
YOUNG MICKEY: I'm a *schmuck* who' gonna play third base for the Bruins.

BILLY: But I've got the better arm.

YOUNG MICKEY: *[Laughs.]* You start shootin' dope or something? Talkin' like a dope addict ... Man, I've got an arm like Clemente. I can throw right field to home on one bounce ....

BILLY: That's what I mean ... your arm is too strong for third ... but mine is perfect for third ...

YOUNG MICKEY: But your father has Nolan Sokol in right ... my next best position is third ...

BILLY: I've got four Roberto Clemente's. *[Pause.]*

YOUNG MICKEY: How'd you get four Roberto Clemente's? I've been buying cards for weeks and I haven't got one yet ...

BILLY: You want 'em?

[Suddenly, YOUNG MICKEY dives for a ball, gets up, and fires to first.]

BILLY: Way to go ... So, what ya say?

YOUNG MICKEY: What about your father?

BILLY: He said it's okay if we make the switch.

YOUNG MICKEY: I want to play right field like Clemente.

BILLY: We need Nolan's power, and can you imagine His Fatness playing short?

YOUNG MICKEY: Okay, okay ... *[BILLY goes over to third.]*

YOUNG MICKEY: *[Cont'd.]* Not so fast ... where's the Clementes?

[BILLY goes into his back pocket and pulls out baseball cards and hands them to YOUNG MICKEY.]

YOUNG MICKEY: Wow, this is boss, Billy ...

BILLY: Wait a minute ... my uncle's in there ... gimme ...

YOUNG MICKEY: Take 'im. I have plenty of Brooks Robinson's ... Anyway, he's not your uncle ...

BILLY: Is too.

YOUNG MICKEY: He don't look Jewish ...

BILLY: Neither does Paul Newman ... I told you, he's my mother's brother. His real name's Robinski. But he changed his name so people would think he was a goy. My grandmother and mother disowned him ... If being a Jew was good enough for Koufax, then it was good enough for Robinski ... even on her death bed, my mother didn't want him at the funeral ... so the family disowned him ... and his Bar Mitzvah was revoked.

YOUNG MICKEY: Git outta here. How can you take back somethin' that was done when he was thirteen?

BILLY: The Rabbi says it ... and it's done.

YOUNG MICKEY: Yeah, right.

BILLY: I'm a Jew ... you're a Methodist ... I think I know about Jews. Hey, you comin' to my Bar Mitzvah?

YOUNG MICKEY: I don't know . . . is your grandmother gonna be there?

BILLY: She's my grandmother . . .

YOUNG MICKEY: Every time she sees me . . . "Ovey . . . the little *schwartzer oodsh kevah* . . ."

BILLY: That's a lousy imitation of Yiddish . . . Anyway, she's used to you now.

YOUNG MICKEY: She thinks I'm a vampire.

BILLY: Ya comin?

YOUNG MICKEY: Yeah, yeah, yeah . . .

BILLY: Good . . . bring a gift! *[BILLY dives for a line drive, catches it, gets up and fires to second.]* All right, that's two. It's mine.

[BILLY exits as he catches ball. MOTHER enters and crosses to YOUNG MICKEY.]

MOTHER: See, Mickey, these white people don't want to live with us . . . They too good for niggas . . . We move in, they move out. Like we poison or something. So they seek a haven in Larchmont or Pelham Manor . . . where they can get away from us . . . the racist bitches! . . . Now a Jew, he be a different kind of white animal . . . Fact, he not like white people at all. Not like them Irish potato pickers or nasty-ass Eye-talians . . . No, no, the Jew be a different breed all together . . . more . . . human . . . almost . . . colored . . . Yes, Sir, the Jew, he be alright. Like us he be a ancient people . . . A people that know the truth fo' these Europeans created a new truth . . .

[YOUNG MICKEY leaves.]

MOTHER: *[Cont'd.]* They like us . . . a truly mystic people that everybody else is scared shitless of.

ALEXANDER: We gonna war!

YOUNG MICKEY: With who?

ALEXANDER: If you had been at the war party, instead of with those white boys . . .

YOUNG MICKEY: We had practice.

ALEXANDER: So did we. Are you a Gladiator or what?

YOUNG MICKEY: We're getting too old for this.

ALEXANDER: War is for men.

YOUNG MICKEY: You're fourteen.

ALEXANDER: You gonna war or are you turnin' into a faggot?

YOUNG MICKEY: I ain't no faggot!

ALEXANDER: Is that it? Is that what it is? You got sugar behind your ears?

YOUNG MICKEY: I ain't no faggot.

ALEXANDER: Mickey is a sweet boy . . . Mickey is a sweet boy.

YOUNG MICKEY: I'm warning you.

ALEXANDER: You got some nuts . . . then you can warn . . . but you're a sweet boy.

YOUNG MICKEY: Alexander, shut up!

ALEXANDER: I see you going to that faggot's house . . . I see you going to Daniel's house.

YOUNG MICKEY: He's teaching me piano . . .

ALEXANDER: He's teachin' you how to take it up the booty. *[YOUNG MICKEY takes a step forward.]* The li'l sissy is going to try something that even the Prince won't do . . .

YOUNG MICKEY: I'm gonna kick your ass.

ALEXANDER: You're gonna kiss my ass? I knew you were a faggot.

[YOUNG MICKEY rushes ALEXANDER. ALEXANDER catches YOUNG MICKEY and gives him an expert Judo flip. YOUNG MICKEY gets up and goes after ALEXANDER again. This time ALEXANDER twists him around and wraps his arm around YOUNG MICKEY's neck. ALEXANDER is laughing all through this.]

YOUNG MICKEY: I'm not gonna say uncle . . . I'm not gonna . . .

ALEXANDER: Okay, okay . . . you've got nuts, Mickey.

YOUNG MICKEY: *[Still struggling.]* That's right, I got big nuts.

ALEXANDER: So don't waste 'em on a fellow Gladiator, save 'em for the Eagles.

[Pause. YOUNG MICKEY relaxes.]

ALEXANDER: *[Cont'd.]* Hangin' with that Jew-boy hasn't turned you into a chump yet.

[ALEXANDER lets him go.]

YOUNG MICKEY: He's a good guy.

ALEXANDER: Nah, they're all the same. His old man is just like the Jew my Pops works for . . . They got all the money you know?

YOUNG MICKEY: Who says?

ALEXANDER: My Pops. Rebekoff's filthy rich. You know why he's rich?

YOUNG MICKEY: 'Cause he works hard?

ALEXANDER: Works hard? Are you kiddin' me? My Pops, he works hard supervisin' . . . makin' sure Rebekoff's trucks are loaded. Rebekoff don't do nothin'.

YOUNG MICKEY: He had to do somethin', how else could he get rich?

ALEXANDER: Tha's what I'm tryin' to tell ya. He's rich 'cause he's cheap. They're all cheap. My Moms says they're like squirrels . . . they store away every penny like a squirrel do nuts. It's all a plot, man. That's why they don't believe in Christmas . . . so they don't have to buy presents.

YOUNG MICKEY: Get outta here.

ALEXANDER: Square bizness. My Pops says they're real slick because they own all the stores where everybody else shops for Christmas. You know . . . Abraham & Strauss, Klein's, Alexander's, Macy's, man, they're all Jews. Even E.J. Korvettes . . .

YOUNG MICKEY: Korvettes ain't no Jewish name.

ALEXANDER: See, that's how slick they are. My Pops says it's a code. E.J. Korvettes really stands for Eight Jewish Korean Veterans.

YOUNG MICKEY: How does your Pops know that?

ALEXANDER: He works for a Jew . . . he knows . . . .

YOUNG MICKEY: Yeah, well . . . all I know is Billy ain't rich . . .

ALEXANDER: You don' wanna believe me? Fine. We need to talk about the Eagles.

YOUNG MICKEY: There ain't gonna be no rules with those guys. Those project guys really want to hurt us. How we gonna fight 'em?

ALEXANDER: Hand to hand.

YOUNG MICKEY: Whoa!

ALEXANDER: Our Karate and Judo against their boxing.

YOUNG MICKEY: But you're the only Gladiator who really knows martial arts.

ALEXANDER: They don't know that.

YOUNG MICKEY: Yeah, but I'll let you in on a secret . . . don't ask me how . . . but even though they're from the projects, I think they'll figure it out. Those guys get up in the morning fighting.

ALEXANDER: I've been teaching you guys, and we've got time to train.

YOUNG MICKEY: Whew! Good . . . geez, now that makes sense.

ALEXANDER: We've got 'til Saturday. *[Pause.]*

YOUNG MICKEY: Saturday . . . as in the day after tomorrow?

ALEXANDER: Well, it ain't Saturday next week.

YOUNG MICKEY: Why couldn't it be Saturday next week?

ALEXANDER: Don't go getting faggoty on me again . . .

YOUNG MICKEY: Look, Alexander, my Mother's paying an awful lot for these piano lessons . . . and she wouldn't want me to go and break my fingers.

ALEXANDER: She wouldn't want me to break your nappy head either.

YOUNG MICKEY: Alex . . .

ALEXANDER: Weez bloodbrothers since we wuz l'il guys . . . I know we're getting' older now . . . but my blood is still your blood and your blood is still mine . . . These here Eagles have been snatchin' pocketbooks . . . You know how I hate those project kids . . .

YOUNG MICKEY: I don't hate project kids . . . they're just like us.

ALEXANDER: They ain't just like us . . . They eat welfare peanut butter which they also use for glue. If I lived in the projects, man, I don't even want to think about it! And stealin' from ladies who live in private houses. They don't give a shit what color you are. This is our honor. We've got to teach those bums. Your mother could be next. *[Pause.]* So ... you a Gladiator ... or you gonna play Jew-ball with the Jew-boy?

YOUNG MICKEY: Billy's cool.

ALEXANDER: He ain't a Gladiator, he ain't cool. We ain't prejudice, he can join if he can take the initiation.

YOUNG MICKEY: Alex, it's getting late ...

ALEXANDER: It ain't late ...

YOUNG MICKEY: I got piano practice. *[YOUNG MICKEY starts to leave.]*

ALEXANDER: Don't forget the Vaseline. *[ALEXANDER laughs. YOUNG MICKEY gives him the finger.]*

ALEXANDER: You down, huh? *[Long pause.]*

YOUNG MICKEY: You're my bloodbrother, ain't cha?

[YOUNG MICKEY walks off. ALEXANDER does a "Kata" and the Lights fade slowly on him. Lights up on MICKEY's MOTHER.]

MOTHER: Mickeeeey!!!

[Lights up on another part of the stage on DANIEL playing a Mozart piece on the piano. He is sixteen. He plays with great skill and love of the music. YOUNG MICKEY goes to his MOTHER.]

MOTHER: Where you been, boy? ...

YOUNG MICKEY AND BIG MICKEY: Out.

MOTHER: Rumblin' and bumblin' and swingin' the streets ...

YOUNG MICKEY AND BIG MICKEY: No, Ma! ...

MOTHER: Rumblin' and bumblin' and swingin' in the streets ... ain't got no time to mourn ... ain't got time to cry. No, you too busy runnin' and gunnin' and lingerin' in the streets. You are going to pull yourself together and stop running in the streets.

YOUNG MICKEY: Aw, Ma ...

MOTHER: Sunday morning ... after church ... don't you make any plans ... 'cause we are going to the Metropolitan Museum ...

YOUNG MICKEY: I went there with my class last year ...

MOTHER: Yeah, well, you're going with me this year. Then I got tickets to see *Hello Dolly!* You need some culture.

YOUNG MICKEY: I got practice on Sunday.

MOTHER: Well, you're going to miss it. See, I ain't gonna raise no little ignorant hoodlum ... There's another world out there and I'm gonna make sure you know it.

YOUNG MICKEY: I don't wanna go. I'm not a baby. Why should I go someplace I don't want to go? *[YOUNG MICKEY starts to leave.]*

MOTHER: Mickey, get over here! Do you think you're grown or something?

YOUNG MICKEY: Daddy didn't make me do anything I didn't want to do. Even at his funeral.

MOTHER: Hush! Go on, you're late for your piano lesson.

[MOTHER walks off. YOUNG MICKEY goes to the piano and begins to play . . .]

BIG MICKEY: I enjoyed going to Daniel's . . . there was a solace in this music that I didn't quite understand . . .

[As YOUNG MICKEY begins playing, DANIEL puts his arm around him.]

BIG MICKEY: *[Cont'd.]* Daniel Van Drake was the first . . . the only genius I have ever known. His real name wasn't really Van. He adopted it from his favorite musician, Van Cliburn. Daniel was in love with Van Cliburn.

[YOUNG MICKEY notices DANIEL'S hand on his shoulder. He is uncomfortable, but continues to play.

DANIEL'S hand moves down YOUNG MICKEY'S back. YOUNG MICKEY abruptly gets up.]

DANIEL: What's the matter?

YOUNG MICKEY: What's the matter? *[Light pause.]*

DANIEL: Oh . . . I was just encouraging you.

YOUNG MICKEY: Yeah, well . . . encourage me with a little less . . . you know . . .

DANIEL: It didn't bother you before.

YOUNG MICKEY: Yeah, well, it bothers me now.

DANIEL: I can't touch you?

YOUNG MICKEY: You ain't a girl.

DANIEL: You touch girls!

YOUNG MICKEY: Not yet . . . Never thought about it . . . but it's starting to get interesting. I feel like touching them. I mean, sex and all the stuff is confusing.

DANIEL: I don't find it confusing.

YOUNG MICKEY: Like, you know, I found baseball . . . and I thought that was life. What else could a guy want? Now I want to touch girls . . . Guys touchin' guys . . . that seems creepy to me.

DANIEL: I'm not creepy. I see guys touch you all the time . . . you don't get the creeps . . .

YOUNG MICKEY: Don't no guys touch me . . .

DANIEL: On the ass.

YOUNG MICKEY: Git outta here!

DANIEL: Every time I go to one of your baseball games and you get a hit, or make a great play, I see your teammates . . . they pat you on the butt. Your little Jewish friend is always doing it . . . Mickey makes a great catch, Billy pats him on the butt . . . Mickey gets a hit . . . Billy pats him on the butt . . . And when you guys play football, and he's the quarterback, and you're . . .

YOUNG MICKEY: All right! Okay. Drop it.

DANIEL: But why do you let them pat your . . .

YOUNG MICKEY: It's tradition!

DANIEL: Well, it's a tradition I'm totally behind. *[Pause.]* Sit, okay?

YOUNG MICKEY: No hands . . .

DANIEL: No hands. Continue. *[YOUNG MICKEY begins to play a shaky Mozart Piece.]*

DANIEL: *[Cont'd.]* I've got a competition coming.

YOUNG MICKEY: You'll win.

DANIEL: You sound so sure . . .

YOUNG MICKEY: You can play this weirdo stuff better than anyone I know. *[Slight pause.]*

DANIEL: You've been getting really good at reading music . . . and I was thinking . . .

YOUNG MICKEY: Yeah? . . .

DANIEL: Will you be my page turner?

YOUNG MICKEY: For what?

DANIEL: Because I asked you. Maybe you'll bring me luck.

YOUNG MICKEY: I don't know. I . . . I . . . *[YOUNG MICKEY continues to play. Then he stops playing.]* Can't I play something else?

DANIEL: When you learn to play this perfectly.

YOUNG MICKEY: This is boring.

DANIEL: Well, Mickey . . . think of your boredom as an obstacle, which has been put in your way so that you can overcome it . . .

YOUNG MICKEY: I've been playing this dumb song for three weeks . . .

DANIEL: Perhaps if you would concentrate a little . . .

YOUNG MICKEY: I'd concentrate a whole lot better if it was something hip.

DANIEL: Oh, like rock 'n roll? For six months I've been trying to impart to you the beauty of playing piano . . . Your mother wants me to cultivate you. She knows the music can make you see the world totally different. You listen to that junk and that's what your mind becomes. But I give you Van Cliburn records and what do I hear coming from your house? The Beatles.

YOUNG MICKEY: Jimi Hendrix! I haven't played a Beatles record in months.

DANIEL: *[Throws up his hands.]* What am I going to do with you?

YOUNG MICKEY: Teach me to write songs.

DANIEL: Compose? Chile, first you've got to get the basics down. Then we can talk. Anyway, are you going to compose like Mozart? No! You're going to pollute the world with Jimi Hendrix and the Beatles . . .

YOUNG MICKEY: I'll be your page turner at the concert. *[Pause.]*
DANIEL: You will?
YOUNG MICKEY: But I want you to do me a favor . . . Seein' as I ain't
ready to write my own music . . . *[YOUNG MICKEY pulls out a crumpled
sheet of paper and gives it to DANIEL. DANIEL looks at it.]*
DANIEL: What's this supposed to be? Lyrics?
YOUNG MICKEY: Right now it's a poem . . .
DANIEL: Okay, it's a poem. So?
YOUNG MICKEY: Write music to it.
DANIEL: Van Cliburn would disown me . . . Mozart would roll over in his
grave . . .
YOUNG MICKEY: Daniel . . . please . . .
DANIEL: Well . . . I suppose it wouldn't hurt to give it a little Rodgers and
Hammerstein treatment.
YOUNG MICKEY: I was thinking more Lennon/McCartney . . . or at least
Smokey Robinson.
DANIEL: I will not write trash. I mean, it's been the classics since I was
five, chile. I was a genius at conception, and I am a genius now at
fifteen. No niggity be bop, boop boop dee doo for me! *[Lights down
on YOUNG MICKEY and DANIEL.]*

Scene 2

Lights up on Big Mickey.

BIG MICKEY: Saturday came . . . I did not sleep the night before in antici-
pation of the pain that was sure to come . . . Those project guys did
not play around. While we hung out in the woods pretending to learn
karate, the Eagles were learning to be full time hoods. They were
ripping off people for money . . . bustin' up kids who stepped on their
sneakers . . . even beating up teachers in our junior high school. The
Eagles were getting a reputation. *[Lights up on YOUNG MICKEY as he
jumps into the air, screaming as he executes a flying kick. ALEXANDER
enters. He watches YOUNG MICKEY throw a kick.]*
ALEXANDER: Get that leg up higher. Higher! *[YOUNG MICKEY kicks again.]*
ALEXANDER: *[Cont'd.]* That's the way Kato does it on the Green Hornet.
That's a number one kick.
YOUNG MICKEY: Thanks . . . where's everybody at?
ALEXANDER: Thought you didn't want to fight?
YOUNG MICKEY: I'm here, ain't I?
ALEXANDER: Thought you wuz scared.
YOUNG MICKEY: Yeah . . . I'm scared.

ALEXANDER: But youse here. Why?

YOUNG MICKEY: 'Cause we been bloodbrothers since we wuz little. 'Cause I owe ya for savin' me from guys like the Prince. You know, it's gonna be worse if we beat 'em. They gonna get us alone, man. They gonna take it out on our houses . . . come over from the projects . . . and throw rocks at our windows. But I'm here see . . . Where's the other guys? Skip, Greenie-boy, Grey-man and Pablo? *[Pause.]*

ALEXANDER: They're not comin'.

YOUNG MICKEY: Not comin'? Whatcha mean?

ALEXANDER: There ain't gonna be no fight today.

YOUNG MICKEY: When we gonna fight 'em?

ALEXANDER: We ain't never gonna fight 'em . . . *[Pause.]*

YOUNG MICKEY: What are you talkin' about?

ALEXANDER: I'm moving to the projects.

YOUNG MICKEY: *[Laughing]* Who you tryin' to psyche on? Got to do better than that.

ALEXANDER: I ain't kiddin', man. My Pops got into it with that Jew he works for. He worked for him for ten years. He just up and fired my Pops.

YOUNG MICKEY: You don't gotta move to the projects . . . Your Pops just got fired, he'll find another job.

ALEXANDER: Naw, man, it ain't like that. My Pops has been outta work for months. . . . him and my Moms just didn't tell me. They was barely payin' the mortgage when he was workin' . . . They shoulda told me . . .

YOUNG MICKEY: They didn't want to worry you.

ALEXANDER: Yeah, well, I'm worried now.

YOUNG MICKEY: You're movin' to the projects?

ALEXANDER: Square bizness. My Moms says that if things don't get better we might have to get on welfare . . .

YOUNG MICKEY: Dag . . .

ALEXANDER: Yap . . . Anyways, we can't fight the Eagles.

YOUNG MICKEY: Sure we can. I know you're feelin' down now . . . but when you're feeling better, we'll get the fellas together . . .

ALEXANDER: There ain't gonna be no gettin' the fellas together. There ain't gonna be no more Gladiators.

YOUNG MICKEY: Why not?

ALEXANDER: C'mon, Mickey, I'm a project kid now . . .

YOUNG MICKEY: I don't care if you're a project kid . . . you're my bloodbrother.

ALEXANDER: Listen to me. I'm making a deal with the Prince.

YOUNG MICKEY: You don't gotta make no deal with the Prince. You can just square off on him and beat him.

ALEXANDER: It ain't that easy. Man, you know even if I get in a fight with him it ain't gonna be fair . . . One of the guys in his gang will jump in if I get the best of him. They ain't gonna let him lose no fight . . . So don't you start believin' that. Now I'm gonna make a deal with them so that you guys will . . .

YOUNG MICKEY: What kinda deal you makin' with those creeps? *[ALEXANDER see THE PRINCE coming. THE PRINCE enters with one of his boys, ODD JOB. YOUNG MICKEY breaks into a Karate stance. ODD JOB laughs. He makes his finger like a gun and shoots. He laughs.]*

ODD JOB: That's what I got for that Karate shit. Just wait, dufus . . . 'cause your shit is weak. And this here's a new click. Oh yeah . . .

THE PRINCE: Odd Job, step back and shut up.

ALEXANDER: Back off, Mickey.

THE PRINCE: Alexander ever tell you about the time I wuz visitin' his house, and I had to go to the bathroom . . . so I asked his momma how to get there . . . and she hand me a flashlight and a bat, and said, "that way, and good luck!"

ODD JOB: Sound . . . sound . . . He sounded you down.

ALEXANDER: The Prince ever tell you about the time I went to his house for dinner . . . and I asked his momma what he was eatin' . . . and she gimme a fork and say, "First one who fall asleep!"

THE PRINCE: *[Laughs.]* Now that's a cold sound. *[Pause.]* So . . . what's my War Counselor ran down to me . . .

ODD JOB: Yeah, yeah, Alexander the Great on his knees . . . Make 'im kiss your ass, Prince . . . make 'im kiss yo' ass.

YOUNG MICKEY: No!!!

[YOUNG MICKEY rushes toward them, but ALEXANDER grabs him before he can get to the THE PRINCE. He wrestles YOUNG MICKEY to the ground. ODD JOB and THE PRINCE come over.]

ODD JOB: Hold his li'l ass down.

ALEXANDER: What?

THE PRINCE: Nobody touches The Prince in anger.

ALEXANDER: What's the debt?

ODD JOB: Six shots in the chest. Now hold him down so I can slam him. *[Pause.]*

ALEXANDER: I'll do it.

THE PRINCE: I thought he was your man?

ODD JOB: Whoa, whoa, I'm the executioner . . . you don't come out into the Eagles giving orders.

THE PRINCE: Okay, do it. And since he wuz your main man, and I feel merciful, make it one shot.

ODD JOB: One shot? Aw, Boss, one shot . . . you lettin' this guy come in and . . .

THE PRINCE: The sight of his blood would make me happy, and it would convince me of your loyalty. *[ALEXANDER looks at YOUNG MICKEY.]*

The Prince: Hold 'im up, Odd Job. *[ODD JOB does.]*

THE PRINCE: Do it. *[ALEXANDER does. YOUNG MICKEY crumples. ODD JOB lets him fall to the ground.]* If the faggot is crying, give him another, Odd Job.

ALEXANDER: But you said . . .

THE PRINCE: Shut the fuck up. *[ODD JOB checks YOUNG MICKEY.]*

THE PRINCE: *[Cont'd.]* Is he crying?

ODD JOB: *[Laughing.]* He ain't cryin' . . . But he sure is bleeding like his momma on her period. His eye is swellin' but he ain't cryin' . . . Want me to make him cry?

THE PRINCE: Yo' man got heart.

ALEXANDER: Mickey don't cry for nothin' . . . not even when we wuz li'l guys. Mickey don't cry for nobody. His Pops died last month . . . Not a tear, not a tear.

THE PRINCE: I thought all little private house kids cried.

[ALEXANDER goes over to YOUNG MICKEY who is still on the ground. ALEXANDER takes the bandanna from his head. He gives it to YOUNG MICKEY and wipes his nose. YOUNG MICKEY slowly gets up. Then leaves, pushing at THE PRINCE as he goes.]

THE PRINCE: Yeah, li'l man got heart.

ALEXANDER: Yeah, he got plenty of heart.

ODD JOB: Yeah, well, what we wanna know is, do you?

ALEXANDER: Why? You lookin' to find out?

THE PRINCE: The both of youse cool it. Then . . . you one of us, right?

ALEXANDER: Yeah, I'm down.

THE PRINCE: You say that like a pussy . . . Oh, your eyes got big when I said that shit . . . like you were gonna kick some ass or somethin' . . . *[THE PRINCE pulls a pistol from his jacket and puts it to ALEXANDER's head.]*

ODD JOB: Oh, shit, Prince, where'd you get the gun? Huh? Huh? Where'd you get the gun?

THE PRINCE: Yo' momma's ass. *[ALEXANDER does not move.]*

THE PRINCE: *[Cont'd.]* Now. Let's get this straight. You movin' to my project, Motherfucker. My project. Now either you with us or you ain't. And if you ain't, you be the first punk I kill . . . It don't make no difference . . . I got to start somewhere.

ODD JOB: Blow his noodle out. Let's see his noodle on the ground.

THE PRINCE: You with us?

ALEXANDER: I kissed your ring. What else I got to do?

THE PRINCE: *[Puts the gun to his side.]* I don't know, but I'll think of somethin'.

ALEXANDER: Where'd you get the gun, Prince?

THE PRINCE: Tomorrow's my birthday. I'll be fifteen years old. My brother called me from jail this morning and tell me he got a present for me . . . He tell me to go to this hidin' place he got in the closet . . . away from my Moms . . . So I go to it and there this be. And when I get back to the phone he say, "Happy Birthday you short-stuff-young-blood motherfucker! You a man now. The world is changin' and you gotta be ready for the shit that's gonna come down." He tell me to don't let nobody fuck with me and mine. Now if y'all are mine you ain't got nothin' to worry about, 'cause I'll go down for ya. *[Pause.]* Now they ain't gonna be no more Gladiators, and they ain't gonna be no more Eagles either.

ODD JOB: Whatcha mean no more Eagles?

THE PRINCE: It's time to grow up. It's time that there's some meanin' to what we're doin'.

ALEXANDER: I don't understand.

THE PRINCE: It's time we get in the shit. *[ALEXANDER, THE PRINCE, and ODD JOB exit. Lights up on the MOTHER and OFFICER BREAM.]*

MOTHER: It's them project kids. It ain't none of our kids. They mommas don't do nuthin' but lay up in the bed all day and make babies . . . Collecting welfare while the rest of us work our fingers to the bone. Don't give they children no discipline. It's them project kids that's running this neighborhood.

OFFICER BREAM: You're absolutely right. And we're letting them.

MOTHER: They need to drop an atom bomb on them projects. Then build some nice private homes . . . or, even better, a nice park where everybody, black and white, can have picnics together . . . But it ain't our kids. It's them project kids I tell you.

OFFICER BREAM: You're absolutely right. I wish more mothers and fathers were like you. You're raising a fine boy, can hit a ball left-handed or right. You're doing a better job than some two-parent families.

[MOTHER looks at OFFICER BREAM a beat.]

MOTHER: I do the best I can.

OFFICER BREAM: I know you work all the time with those folks in mid-Manhattan . . . and when you're not working you're taking care of the boy . . . I know that. *[They look at each other a beat.]*

OFFICER BREAM: *[Cont'd.]* I was thinkin' . . . maybe the next time I umpire one of Mickey's games . . . uhh . . . uhh *[Pause.]*

MOTHER: Yes? . . .

OFFICER BREAM: Maybe next time you come to a game . . . I really like Mickey. He like seafood? You like seafood?

MOTHER: Mickey loves it . . . so do I.

OFFICER BREAM: Great. Maybe . . . after the game . . . we could drive out to City Island. Whatcha think? *[YOUNG MICKEY enters.]*

MOTHER: I . . . uhhh . . . oh, hi, Mickey.

YOUNG MICKEY: Hi, mom. Hello, Officer Bream. Hey, aren't you umping the game? *[OFFICER BREAM, looking at his watch.]*

OFFICER BREAM: Oh, yeah, I better get down there. Mickey, you better hurry up, too. Game starts in a few minutes.

YOUNG MICKEY: Bye, mom. *[Lights up on YOUNG MICKEY, MOTHER, and BILLY. YOUNG MICKEY and BILLY playing baseball.]*

MOTHER: Where'd you get that black eye, boy? *[Pause.]* Who beat your ass, boy?

YOUNG MICKEY: No, it was Karate practice . . .

MOTHER: Karate, my ass . . . Boy, who are you kiddin'?

YOUNG MICKEY: It was an accident.

MOTHER: I told you to stay out of them streets. You play your baseball with that nice Jewish boy . . . you do your music with Daniel . . . but you stay away from them hoodlums. You stay out of trouble or I'll put you away.

YOUNG MICKEY: Ma, I'm gonna be late.

MOTHER: Actin' up now that your father's dead. They could have put your eyes out.

YOUNG MICKEY: No problem.

[MOTHER leaves. BILLY goes to third, YOUNG MICKEY to short. The crack of a bat. YOUNG MICKEY dives for a ball as BILLY backs him up. YOUNG MICKEY gets up and throws the ball.]

BREAM'S VOICE: You're out!

[YOUNG MICKEY wipes off his uniform pants. BILLY comes over and pats YOUNG MICKEY on the butt. YOUNG MICKEY leaps like he's been stung by a cattle prod.]

YOUNG MICKEY: Stop it!

BILLY: What's the matter with you?

YOUNG MICKEY: Nothin' . . . *[BILLY and YOUNG MICKEY trot in. They both pick up bats. BILLY is in the On Deck Circle swinging his bat. YOUNG MICKEY is kneeling behind him.]*

BREAM'S VOICE: Strike one!

BILLY: Why are you going weird on me?

YOUNG MICKEY: Nothin' . . . I told you. Just drop it.

BILLY: This guy got a real good fast ball.

YOUNG MICKEY: Yeah, hey, he's only no hit us for six innings. It could be worse. Mercifully it ends with this inning.

BREAM'S VOICE: Strike two!

BILLY: Damn right . . . I'm gonna break up the no hitter . . .

YOUNG MICKEY: Sure . . .

BILLY: That's right . . . and you're gonna knock us both in with a homer . . . C'mon, I'll be Brooks. You be Clemente, and we win two to one.

BREAM'S VOICE: Strike three, you're out!

YOUNG MICKEY: Looks real promising.

BILLY: Valencia couldn't hit a fast ball if you paid him.

YOUNG MICKEY: Like we can.

BILLY: Watch my dust. *[BILLY goes off to bat. ALEXANDER enters.]*

ALEXANDER: Mickey . . . Mickey! *[YOUNG MICKEY takes notice of him, then turns away.]*

ALEXANDER: *[Cont'd.]* Are you okay? *[YOUNG MICKEY continues to ignore him. Pause.]*

ALEXANDER: *[Cont'd.]* How's the eye?

BREAM'S VOICE: Ball one.

YOUNG MICKEY: Way to go, Billy, take what he gives you . . .

ALEXANDER: It was the only way.

YOUNG MICKEY: Take you time, Billy baby, he's tired . . .

ALEXANDER: If I didn't do it, they'da busted you up good. *[YOUNG MICKEY turns and looks at ALEXANDER, then turns back to the game.]*

BREAM'S VOICE: Ball.

YOUNG MICKEY: Two and O, baby . . . good lookin' it over . . .

ALEXANDER: We moved in today. I can't believe this . . . the projects. I haven't seen my Pops for a week. He didn't help us move. When he does come, he won't be sleepin' with my Moms . . . he sleeps on the couch . . . I hate the projects.

BREAM'S VOICE: Strike one.

ALEXANDER: But I've got some good news, man. The Prince likes you. He wants you to join the new clique . . . Sez you can't fight . . . but you got heart.

YOUNG MICKEY: *[Still faced toward the game.]* You think I wanna be a Eagle . . .

ALEXANDER: Eagles are dead . . .

YOUNG MICKEY: You got that right.

ALEXANDER: I'm tellin' ya there ain't no Eagles . . .

BREAM'S VOICE: Strike two.

ALEXANDER: We gotta new name S.P.E.C.T.R.E. . . . Like in James Bond. *[YOUNG MICKEY gets up and goes over to ALEXANDER.]*

YOUNG MICKEY: I don't believe you. Odd Job's a punk . . . and the Prince is scared of you. And now you're kissin' his butt. Not me, man. I'm gonna be somebody.

ALEXANDER: Whata ya mean be somebody? You tryin' to be white or somethin?

YOUNG MICKEY: You don't get it . . . That's why we're marchin' in the South with Dr. King. To let people know you don't gotta be white to be somebody.

ALEXANDER: Get over it. You're watchin' too much TV. You gonna join Spectre or what? *[ODD JOB enters.]*

ODD JOB: He better join Spectre. *[YOUNG MICKEY goes back to the On Deck Circle.]*

ALEXANDER: Well, are you? . . .

ODD JOB: Bust his ass . . . Let's rearrange his dooty chords after the game. *[The crack of the bat is heard.]*

YOUNG MICKEY: Way to go, Billy.

ODD JOB: I hate white ball . . . Whitey Ford and shit . . .

ALEXANDER: Come on, Mickey, you gonna join, right?

YOUNG MICKEY: I thought we wuz gonna try to have a singin' group.

ALEXANDER: I ain't got time for no kiddie shit.

YOUNG MICKEY: Yeah, I just wanna play baseball.

ALEXANDER: You wanna be a faggot like your Jew-boy friend?

ODD JOB: He wants to be a motzah-ball eatin', spooka-Jew. *[YOUNG MICKEY walks away.]*

ALEXANDER: Why don't you wear a yarmulke, nigger-Jew boy?

ODD JOB: Rag his ass, the chittlin' and lox eatin' motherfucker!!!

ALEXANDER: You ain't my bloodbrother, Faggott!!! Little pussy . . . Li'l blackeyed-bloody-nosed pussy. Mickey is a pussy. Mickey is a pussy.

BREAM'S VOICE: Hey, kid, you wanna cut it? *[ALEXANDER gives him the "finger."]*

ODD JOB: Suck my dick!!! *[OFFICER BREAM enters. He takes off his catcher's mask. He is followed by MR. KORNBLUM, who is wearing the same baseball cap as YOUNG MICKEY and BILLY.]*

OFFICER BREAM: Is there a problem here?

ODD JOB: Suppose there is?

ALEXANDER: Yeah, what you gonna do about it? *[ALEXANDER and ODD JOB laugh. OFFICER BREAM laughs with them.]*

OFFICER BREAM: Take you to the forty-seventh precinct and wash your mouths out with clorox. *[ALEXANDER backs away, but ODD JOB stands his ground.]*

MR. KORNBLUM: Okay, Okay, Officer Bream . . . the boys were just foolin' around. Right, boys?

ODD JOB: Man, shut the fuck up! *[OFFICER BREAM slaps ODD JOB.]*

ODD JOB: What ya hit me for? *[ALEXANDER pulls ODD JOB away.]*

ODD JOB: *[Cont'd.]* Don't you know I could get one of those bats and . . .

ALEXANDER: Nah, man . . . he's a pig.

ODD JOB: A fuckin' cop?

MR. KORNBLUM: You didn't have to do that, Bream.

OFFICER BREAM: It's what he understands.

MR. KORNBLUM: What do you want? They're just kids . . .

OFFICER BREAM: What? Look . . . I'm not gonna stand here while some kids disrupt the game, and are disrespectful to adults.

MR. KORNBLUM: But you don't have to get violent.

OFFICER BREAM: With that type of kid, you have to get violent. It's their language. PLAY BALL! *[As OFFICER BREAM goes back to the game, MR. KORNBLUM stands there bewildered. DANIEL enters and sees YOUNG MICKEY at bat.]*

DANIEL: Do it, Mickey! *[The crack of the bat is heard. ALEXANDER looks. Sounds of kids, parents.]*

DANIEL: Homerun! Homerun! *[ALEXANDER smiles. BILLY runs in, followed by YOUNG MICKEY. DANIEL is jumping up and down in excitement.]*

DANIEL: Go, Mickey! *[BILLY attempts to pat YOUNG MICKEY on the butt, but YOUNG MICKEY avoids him.]*

BILLY: You're actin' weird today.

YOUNG MICKEY: From now on, pat me on the back.

BILLY: What's the matter with you?

DANIEL: Nice hit, Mickey. *[DANIEL pats YOUNG MICKEY on the butt.]*

ALEXANDER AND ODD JOB: *[Imitating DANIEL.]* Nice hit, Mickey. *[They laugh.]*

BILLY: C'mon, let's go to Sal and Amel's . . . I'm buying the chocolate egg creams.

DANIEL: No, let me buy sodas. You're the heroes.

ALEXANDER AND ODD JOB: You're the heroes!

DANIEL: So how 'bout it, guys?

BILLY: Sure. *[YOUNG MICKEY, BILLY, and DANIEL start to leave.]*

ALEXANDER: Mickey . . . *[YOUNG MICKEY keeps walking.]*

ODD JOB: Bust his ass.

ALEXANDER: Who do you think you are?

YOUNG MICKEY: You guys go ahead. I'll catch up. *[BILLY and DANIEL exit.]*

ALEXANDER: What's the matter with you? *[Pause.]* You walkin' away from me? . . . You forgot I've been whipping your ass since you could remember?

YOUNG MICKEY: So what? You're gonna bully me now? Look, I gotta go.

ALEXANDER: You think you're better than me or something? You'd rather be with your faggot friends?

YOUNG MICKEY: You'd rather be with the Prince and this dumbo than with me. *[ODD JOB goes at YOUNG MICKEY. YOUNG MICKEY steps back in a Karate stance. ODD JOB stops.]*

ODD JOB: You don't know no Karate.

YOUNG MICKEY: Then you should be able to wipe up this ballfield with me.

ODD JOB: Tha's right . . . let's bust him up, Alexander.

YOUNG MICKEY: You don't need Alexander.

ALEXANDER: Nah, you don't need me.

ODD JOB: He don't know no Karate.

ALEXANDER: Tha's right, he only knows what I taught him. *[Pause.]*

ODD JOB: Just wait, uh huh, just wait and I'm gonna do ya. Just wait.

[ODD JOB backs off. YOUNG MICKEY comes out of his Karate stance. ODD JOB feints like he's coming at him. YOUNG MICKEY swings but misses. ODD JOB laughs and backs away.]

ODD JOB: *[Cont'd.]* Yep, I'm gonna do ya . . . do ya . . . good, good, good.

ALEXANDER: *[Laughs.]* You wuz right when you said I wuz getting too old to swing through trees . . . Spectre is no kiddy gang, it's . . .

YOUNG MICKEY: I don't wanna hear about no Spectre . . .

ALEXANDER: But it's . . .

YOUNG MICKEY: I don't care.

ALEXANDER: Fuck you, man. *[ALEXANDER pushes YOUNG MICKEY.]*

ODD JOB: Bust his ass!

ALEXANDER: Git outta my face . . .

[YOUNG MICKEY begins to walk away.]

ALEXANDER: Chump! Momma's boy! *[YOUNG MICKEY is gone.]*

ODD JOB: Whatcha let 'im walk away for? Huh, whatcha let 'im . . .

ALEXANDER: Don't worry, he'll get his . . . he's a traitor.

Scene 3

Lights up on BIG MICKEY.

BIG MICKEY: Josh Kornblum, Billy's father, loved kids. Loved being involved with kids. Josh was not only the coach of our baseball team, he was also the leader of our Boy Scout troop, as well as coach of a girl's softball team, and he was also . . . well . . . I think you get the idea. Josh was a *mensch.*

[Lights up on MR. KORNBLUM and YOUNG MICKEY.]

BIG MICKEY: *[Cont'd.]* When my father died, Josh was the only grownup who didn't treat me like a kid.

MR. KORNBLUM: I guess you're tired of everybody tellin' you they're sorry about your father.

YOUNG MICKEY: Every time someone says it, it makes it worse.

MR. KORNBLUM: I know . . .

YOUNG MICKEY: And then you get the really stupid grownups . . .

MR. KORNBLUM: There's plenty of them around . . .

YOUNG MICKEY: They tell you it's all right to cry. What's the big thing about cryin', Mr. Kornblum? . . .

MR. KORNBLUM: Absolutely nothin' . . .

YOUNG MICKEY: I mean, dag, it's like they think I'm a little kid or somethin' . . . I'm thirteen years old . . .

MR. KORNBLUM: See, if you converted to Judaism, you'd have had a Bar Mitzvah at thirteen, and you would have been a man . . . and nobody would treat you like a little kid because your dad died.

YOUNG MICKEY: Gee, that's boss.

MR. KORNBLUM: Yeah, it's pretty neat. On the other hand, if you should want to cry . . . even if you're a man . . . there's nothin' wrong with that . . .

YOUNG MICKEY: I don't feel like cryin' . . .

MR. KORNBLUM: That's been established. All I'm saying is . . . When my Doris died, Billy was just a little baby, I cried. And you know, I needed to cry . . . It was a good cry. I mean, it was definitely up there with the great rain storms . . . with Noah and the forty days forty nights bit. *[Chuckles.]* So . . . who are they to tell you when you should cry? It's totally up to you.

[Lights down on MR. KORNBLUM and YOUNG MICKEY.]

BIG MICKEY: Josh Kornblum was one of the few truly sane adults in my life. At Billy's Bar Mitzvah, he gushed all over his son. He bragged about him to everyone.

[Lights up on BILLY, YOUNG MICKEY, and MR. KORNBLUM. They all wear yarmulkes. YOUNG MICKEY holds a gift in his hand.]

MR. KORNBLUM: I'm really proud of you . . . you know that, William?

BILLY: I know, Pop . . . you've told me that fifty times . . . ever since I got outta bed this morning.

MR. KORNBLUM: You're prone to exaggeration. I've told you only forty-nine times. *[Chuckling.]* And why shouldn't I? Face it, you're great. You're doomed to be great. *[He grabs BILLY and kisses him.]*

BILLY: Aw, Pop.

MR. KORNBLUM: Get outta here with your "Aw, Pop," you may be a man today, but you'll always be my boy. Hey, I'm gonna leave you alone, but I think its appropriate, now that you're a man, that I give you some manly advice. And I want you should listen, too, Mickey . . . Lotta guys, they walk the streets . . . they live their lives as men, and they don't know the secret to manhood. Can there really be such a thing?

And if there is, what is this secret? Lotta guys . . . they think if they can squeeze a girl on the tusch . . .

[The boys giggle. MR. KORNBLUM looks heavenward.]

MR. KORNBLUM: *[Cont'd.]* Sorry, Doris, but he's growing up . . .
[Back to the boys.] Lotta guys think if they squeeze that girl's tusch that makes him a man. It don't make him nothin', 'cause that's not how you treat a lady. Real men don't do that. Lotta guys think . . . 'cause they're big and strong, that it makes them a man if you beat up everybody on the block. Don't you believe it. If you're a man, and you happen to be strong, then you protect those you love. This is good. But you don't be a bully . . .

BILLY: Pop?

MR. KORNBLUM: Yeah?

BILLY: Could you like get to the secret of manhood? *[BILLY looks around as if this is a secret he doesn't want anyone else to hear.]*

MR. KORNBLUM: The secret to manhood is . . . truth.

YOUNG MICKEY: Truth?

MR. KORNBLUM: It will never fail you. Be true to yourself. Be true to what you believe in. Stand up when you know you're right. Tell the truth against injustice.

BILLY: That's all?

MR. KORNBLUM: That's all? Okay, I know it sounds simple, but to live your life with truth is not an easy thing. The older you get, the more difficult it becomes to tell the truth . . . to be true to yourself. Hey, maybe it doesn't sink in now . . . and what do I know? I'm still grappling with this myself. Take this as an observation from someone who has been a man for a while. *[He hugs BILLY.]*

MR. KORNBLUM: *[Cont'd.]* Mazeltov.

[He kisses BILLY. Then he goes to hug YOUNG MICKEY. BILLY wipes off the kiss.]

MR. KORNBLUM: *[Cont'd.]* Mazeltov on your Bar Mitzvah, Billy . . . *Mazeltov*, Mickey. *[MR. KORNBLUM leaves.]*

BILLY: Geeesh! Sorry about that.

YOUNG MICKEY: That's alright. It was actually kinda neat. Your Dad's really cool . . .

BILLY: Yeah, well, you don't have to live with him every day.

YOUNG MICKEY: You don't know how lucky you are.

BILLY: C'mon.

YOUNG MICKEY: I used to be like you. I didn't know I had it so good.

[BILLY hasn't really been paying attention. He's eyeing the gift that YOUNG MICKEY is holding.]

BILLY: So . . . are you holdin' that for me?

YOUNG MICKEY: Oh, yeah . . .

BILLY: Then let me relieve you of your burden.

[BILLY takes it away from YOUNG MICKEY.]

YOUNG MICKEY: I'm really lousy at picking gifts out . . .

BILLY: I'll let you know if that's an accurate assessment in about three seconds . . . *[BILLY opens the present. It is a framed photograph of Brooks Robinson. It is autographed. BILLY is truly blown away by this.]*

BILLY: Wow! An autographed picture of Brooks Robinson . . .

YOUNG MICKEY: I knew you wouldn't have one.

BILLY: Because he's been thrown out of the family . . .

YOUNG MICKEY: That's right . . . and I thought, what better present than an autographed picture of your uncle . . . So I sent it to Baltimore . . . I didn't really think I'd get it back in time. Heck, I didn't even know that he'd sign it. But he did, and there it is.

BILLY: This is boss, Mickey. This is the best present I've ever got.

YOUNG MICKEY: Really?

BILLY: Nothing I ever got touches this. You're the best!

[BILLY looks at the photo admiringly. Then he puts his arm around YOUNG MICKEY's shoulder and they walk off together.]

BIG MICKEY: Billy and I were like brothers. We were not that uncommon back then in what was called the melting pot of the world. But as time passes, as the ugliness swells around us each day, I have to wonder if the warm moments with Billy and his father are memories I've distorted over the years. Whatever is true, what came afterward I buried deeply. Very deeply. Their names were Butter and Silk . . . that's how smooth they were on a basketball court and with the girls. They came from Brooklyn by the way of the Iron Horse. They were undefeated and suave in the Big Park tournament. Every weekend they'd come, and with skill they'd destroy any team that was in their way. It was half-time . . . Brooklyn Boyz 50, Projects 43.

[BUTTER and SILK stop dribbling. They go downstage to the trophies.]

BUTTER: Another half and these trophies belong to us.

SILK: Butter, they already do.

BUTTER: And some of these fly mommies too . . .

SILK: Brooklyn Boyz done conquered the Bronx . . . kicked Bronx ass big time.

[They slap "fives."]

THE PRINCE: What's that?

BUTTER: Oh, he wasn't talkin' to you, Bro' . . .

THE PRINCE: 'Scuse me? . . .

BUTTER: Bro' he was rappin' with me . . .

THE PRINCE: He said somethin' 'bout Bronx ass . . .

SILK: Wasn't 'bout you, my man . . .

THE PRINCE: Oh, it wuz about my woman . . .

SILK: Hey, hey, hey . . . we was rappin' about the game.

THE PRINCE: You're wearin' an attitude.

SILK: Naw, dude, I'm wearin' a basketball uniform.

[SILK and BUTTER laugh. THE PRINCE smiles. ODD JOB and ALEXANDER move in closer.]

THE PRINCE: Listen, you dufus-assed-faggot-faced-in-the-wrong-borough-jive-assed-Brooklyn Pussies.

BUTTER: Whoa . . . What's . . .

[ALEXANDER slaps BUTTER.]

ODD JOB: Silence when the Prince is talkin'.

THE PRINCE: Dig this, I ain't cha Bro', I ain't cha man . . . and I ain't cha dude . . . I'm the Prince.

[BUTTER and SILK look around the park.]

ALEXANDER: Your teammates have been sent home courtesy of fellow comrades in Spectre. Just count the cashmere coats. This is our park.

THE PRINCE: Who am I?

SILK AND BUTTER: The Prince.

THE PRINCE: Whoa, whoa, I don't like you . . . You look like one of them brave motherfuckers . . .

SILK: Not as brave as you and the twenty dudes surrounding this park . . .

THE PRINCE: The Prince must have his court . . . Say it.

SILK AND BUTTER: The Prince must have his court.

THE PRINCE: *[Offering his hand.]* Kiss my ring . . .

BUTTER: I ain't kissin' no dude's ring . . .

[ODD JOB kicks BUTTER in the back. BUTTER falls to the ground. YOUNG MICKEY, DANIEL, and BILLY watch. BIG MICKEY turns away from the action, then sees the audience and is embarrassed. He puts his head down.]

THE PRINCE: You right, man, you can't reach high enough to kiss my ring . . . So kiss my shoes . . . the bottoms.

[ALEXANDER and ODD JOB raise their canes.]

ALEXANDER: Get on your stomachs.

[SILK and BUTTER do so. ODD JOB stands over them.]

ODD JOB: Hey, Prince, they lay there so nice, 'cause Brooklyn Boyz like to take it in the hiney . . .

THE PRINCE: *[Laughing.]* Nah, man, that ain't true.
ODD JOB: Oh, yeah, they do . . .

[ODD JOB puts his cane at SILK's behind and turns the cane.]

ODD JOB: Hiney, hiney!

[SILK moves. THE PRINCE kicks him.]

THE PRINCE: Be still.
ODD JOB: You know what they call it in the joint? Round eye. See a candy-ass Brooklyn boy . . . and then pop his round eye! *[ODD JOB touches BUTTER's behind with his cane. BUTTER does not move.]*
ODD JOB: He likes it.

[ALEXANDER returns with SILK and BUTTER's shoes and trousers.]

ALEXANDER: Y'all dig these vines?
BUTTER: Hey . . .

[ODD JOB hits BUTTER with the cane.]

ODD JOB: Shad up.
ALEXANDER: Suede playboys . . . alligator shoes . . . Shadow-striped pants.
THE PRINCE: Y'all rich Brooklyn boys. Well, we gonna donate 'em to the church for ya boys.

[ALEXANDER tosses the clothes off.]

THE PRINCE: Them uniforms are smellin' up my park.
ODD JOB: Get up and take them fuckin' uniforms off. What the fuck you lookin' at?

[ALEXANDER gestures with his cane. They strip off their uniforms. BUTTER and SILK stand there in their underwear. THE PRINCE, ODD JOB, and ALEXANDER laugh.]

ALEXANDER: That's cold, Man. Tha's cold . . .

[BUTTER and SILK try to cover themselves with their hands.]

ODD JOB: Take their panties so we can see some hiney . . .

[BUTTER and SILK cover more.]

THE PRINCE: Out with your balls.

[Long pause. Then BUTTER lets out a gut-wrenching howl. He goes after THE PRINCE. BUTTER is thrown down, as is SILK. THE PRINCE, ODD JOB, and ALEXANDER circle them. BUTTER and SILK are on their knees, crouched and covering their heads with their hands. They are struck with the canes in unison. Then they are beaten in a frenzy. DANIEL covers his eyes. YOUNG MICKEY tries to pull BILLY out of the park but BILLY does not allow it. The

gang stops caning BUTTER *and* SILK. *A siren is heard and a police beacon is seen reflected on the back wall. All scatter.]*

THE PRINCE: Now ain't nobody seen nothin' . . . and there will be no evil upon you.

*[*OFFICER BREAM *enters. The gang has spread apart, and away from* BUTTER *and* SILK. OFFICER BREAM *bends down to* BUTTER *and* SILK *who are dazed.]*

OFFICER BREAM: You guys alright? You need an ambulance or anything?
SILK AND BUTTER: We're fine.
OFFICER BREAM: Can somebody tell me what happened?
ODD JOB: Looks like two sweet boys havin' a orgy.

[Laughter. OFFICER BREAM *goes to* ODD JOB.*]*

OFFICER BREAM: This your idea of comedy . . . Did you do this?
ODD JOB: Officer . . . *[*ODD JOB *crosses his heart.]* I just got here . . . Cross my heart and hope to die.
OFFICER BREAM: I'm thinking a lot of people hope you die . . . including your Momma.
ALEXANDER: Ooooh he sounded you down.
THE PRINCE: Oinks ain't suppose to sound on nobody . . .
OFFICER BREAM: What did you say?
THE PRINCE: Nuthin'
OFFICER BREAM: Yeah, you're the Prince . . . *[THE PRINCE smiles.]* . . . Prince of pimple-faced, pre-pimp, pre-penitentiary-punks . . . Don't suppose you . . .
THE PRINCE: Had my back turned, Officer . . .
OFFICER BREAM: And nobody's foot found its way up your ass?
THE PRINCE: Now, officer . . . I look nuthin' like you from behind.

[Laughter all around the park. OFFICER BREAM *goes to* ALEXANDER.*]*

OFFICER BREAM: What about you?
ALEXANDER: I ain't seen nuthin' . . .
OFFICER BREAM: You used to be a good kid . . .
ALEXANDER: I ain't seen nuthin' . . .
ODD JOB: Tha's right.
OFFICER BREAM: I know that . . .
ALEXANDER: How you know that?
OFFICER BREAM: 'Cause you're blind . . .
ALEXANDER: Tha's right . . . blind as a bat, Officer.
OFFICER BREAM: And ignorant enough to be proud of it. *[*OFFICER BREAM *goes to* DANIEL.]*
OFFICER BREAM: *[Cont'd.]* You a member of the gang? *[There is laughter from everyone in the gang.]*
ODD JOB: Ain't no faggots in Spectre . . .

OFFICER BREAM: Just wait 'til they get a hold of your ass in lock-up. What you see, son?

[DANIEL looks around. THE PRINCE, ODD JOB, and ALEXANDER strike their canes on the ground at the same time.]

OFFICER BREAM: You want to tell me something?

[Canes strike the ground again.]

DANIEL: I . . . I . . . nothin' . . . I was just passing by . . . I didn't see a thing . . .

[OFFICER BREAM goes over to YOUNG MICKEY and BILLY.]

OFFICER BREAM: Hey, I know you guys . . . You guys did a great job of breaking up that no hitter . . .

BILLY: Gee, thanks . . .

YOUNG MICKEY: Thanks. Officer Bream . . .

OFFICER BREAM: You guys play so well together . . . Anyway, can you fill me in on what happened here?

BILLY: Well, Officer . . .

YOUNG MICKEY: We were just passing by to go to baseball practice . . .

OFFICER BREAM: Oh, yeah, practice today . . .

BILLY: Officer, those kids were . . .

YOUNG MICKEY: You have the time?

OFFICER BREAM: 3:30.

YOUNG MICKEY: We're gonna be late for practice, Billy.

BUTTER: No man, no . . .

OFFICER BREAM: God damn it, get away from him.

ODD JOB: I was just helping him out . . .

OFFICER BREAM: Tell me, they did it, right?

SILK: Nobody did nothing, it wasn't these guys.

[ODD JOB goes to BUTTER and threatens him with cane. OFFICER BREAM runs to them. YOUNG MICKEY tries to pull BILLY away. OFFICER BREAM helps BUTTER. BILLY pulls away and goes back towards OFFICER BREAM. The canes strike the ground again.]

YOUNG MICKEY: Billy! Billy!

BILLY: What?

YOUNG MICKEY: They'll get me, too.

BILLY: Not if they're in jail.

YOUNG MICKEY: What are you tryin' to do?

BILLY: Exercise my duty as a citizen.

YOUNG MICKEY: Exercise your what? You think this here is Dragnet or somethin'?

[THE PRINCE, ODD JOB, and ALEXANDER point their canes at BUTTER and SILK. OFFICER BREAM does not see this.]

OFFICER BREAM: Tell me, so I can lock the hoodlum sons of bitches up! *[BUTTER and SILK look at the canes pointing at them.]*
OFFICER BREAM: Don't you want to lock up the guys who did that? . . .
SILK: I don't remember . . .
OFFICER BREAM: I've got a witness right over there who will back you up . . . Talk to me. *[Sees THE PRINCE's cane.]* You stupid lowlife punk! *[Slowly they put their canes down. OFFICER BREAM goes to THE PRINCE. He snatches the cane and breaks it over his thigh and throws it off. He shoves THE PRINCE.]*
OFFICER BREAM: *[Cont'd.]* Look at that, he don't even bite back. *[OFFICER BREAM goes to BUTTER and SILK. THE PRINCE reaches into his coat.]*
OFFICER BREAM: *[Cont'd.]* Talk to me! Talk to me! *[THE PRINCE draws his pistol. BILLY starts to say something, but YOUNG MICKEY grabs him from behind and pulls him to the ground.]*
BILLY: Officer! *[YOUNG MICKEY pulls BILLY out of danger. THE PRINCE shoots OFFICER BREAM six times in the back. Everyone but THE PRINCE, ALEXANDER, and ODD JOB run off.]*
THE PRINCE: You broke my cane . . . My cane! . . . You gonna come in here, in my park . . . my kingdom . . . sell some wolf tickets? I'm 'sposed to 'low this? . . . I'm a man. Respect me or die. My boy's standin' here . . . all the fly mommies . . . and you gonna fuck with me? . . . You know why you dead? 'Cause it's like my Moms say . . . A Nigga cop treat his own kind worse than a white paddie cop . . . So, see, you supposed to be dead . . . 'Cause a nigga who think like a white man . . . he a roach, and I'm Raid, mother fucker! It bees the way sometime . . . When you invade another man's turf . . . kingdom . . . death come fast, natural, like a hard on. *[ALEXANDER runs off.]*
THE PRINCE: *[Cont'd.]* Where the fuck you going? *[ODD JOB and THE PRINCE run off. YOUNG MICKEY and BILLY run on to YOUNG MICKEY's house. ALEXANDER runs in to join them.]*
MOTHER: I thought y'all was supposed to be at practice . . . What's wrong? *[They look at her. Lights down.*

BIG MICKEY goes over to dead OFFICER BREAM's body and looks at it. YOUNG MICKEY rises from tableau and goes to OFFICER BREAM's body. BIG and YOUNG MICKEY look at each other.
Blackout.]

Act 2

Scene 1

Lights up on BIG MICKEY who has a bandage on his arm from the I.V. He rolls down his sleeve.

BIG MICKEY: About a year ago, an old friend of mine asked me if I was interested in joining the Republican Party. *[Laughs.]* I was appalled. I was indignant. He said to me, "Hey, Brother, you and the Mrs. are doing fabulous. Isn't it time you protect your assets and join the Grand Old Party?" And he told me, quite seriously, that by remaining a Democrat I was not looking out for the best interests of my family . . . and, finances. I told him that I was not going to forget who I was and where I came from. He looked me in the eye, and said, "You better remember who you've become, and where you want to be." *[Pause.]*
It actually reminds me of something my Father might say.

[Lights up on the MOTHER. *She has* YOUNG MICKEY, BILLY, *and* ALEXANDER *sitting in front of a television set.]*

MOTHER: Y'all weren't near the park, were you? . . .
YOUNG MICKEY: No, Ma . . .
MOTHER: You weren't near that shooting . . .
YOUNG MICKEY: No, Ma . . .
MOTHER: You ran in here looking scared of something.
YOUNG MICKEY: Scared . . . No. We were just fooling around.
MOTHER: Since ya'll ain't got nuthin' to do . . .
YOUNG MICKEY: But, Ma . . . we got to get to practice . . .
MOTHER: Y'all sit and watch Dr. King. It won't take but a few minutes. You may not appreciate it now, but twenty years from now you'll understand. *[*MOTHER *turns TV up and Martin Luther King begins to speak. The lights go down on the kids. She and* BIG MICKEY *look at each other. Then they leave the stage as the lights come up on the boys.* YOUNG MICKEY *gets up and turns the TV down.]*
YOUNG MICKEY: Where do you think Officer Bream is now?
BILLY: Dead.
YOUNG MICKEY: You think he's somewhere?
BILLY: Wherever he's at, he ain't here.
YOUNG MICKEY: Maybe he's happier . . . Him, my father . . .
ALEXANDER: I think they're happier . . .
BILLY: You killed the cop.
ALEXANDER: I didn't kill that cop, Jew-boy.
YOUNG MICKEY: Alex!
BILLY: That's right, I am a Jew-boy.
ALEXANDER: Motzaball-motzah-cracker-eatin' cracker.
BILLY: You want to offend me, call me a kike.
ALEXANDER: I'm gonna fly you like one.
BILLY: Killer . . .
ALEXANDER: I didn't kill anyone . . . Say it again and I'll kick your ass . . .
YOUNG MICKEY: Not in my house you won't.

ALEXANDER: What are you, Jewish now, Mickey?
YOUNG MICKEY: It's better than being the Prince's flunky.
ALEXANDER: Weez bloodbrothers. Ain't nothin' change that since six.
YOUNG MICKEY: Yeah, I took a blood oath with somebody . . . but I don't
think it was you.
ALEXANDER: It was me. When I whip you 'til your dooty chords hurt
you'll remember it was me . . .
YOUNG MICKEY: Alexander the Great . . . that was a name everybody around
here respected . . . but that was somebody else. Private house or
project . . . didn't make no difference, you still coulda been Alexander
the Great . . .
BILLY: Now he's only great at one thing—killin'.
ALEXANDER: You keep your mouth shut . . . this here is between brothers . . .
YOUNG MICKEY: Billy's just as much my brother as you . . .
ALEXANDER: He's a Jew.
YOUNG MICKEY: Martin Luther King says we're all brothers on this Earth.
ALEXANDER: My pops says King's one too.
YOUNG MICKEY: What?
ALEXANDER: A Jew lover.
YOUNG MICKEY: At least, I ain't no murderer.
ALEXANDER: Man, I didn't know the Prince would do something like
that . . .
YOUNG MICKEY: You messed with those guys over a stupid basketball
game . . .
ALEXANDER: We wuz just foolin' around . . . it got outta hand.
BILLY: My grandmother . . . she told me that's what the Nazis said when
they got caught.
ALEXANDER: Shut him up, or I'm gonna fuck him up!
YOUNG MICKEY: Why are you here?
ALEXANDER: Just like you guys . . . I wuz scared. I didn't know what to do.
YOUNG MICKEY: They're your gang now. You shoulda stuck with them.
ALEXANDER: Mickey . . . I didn't want to hurt nobody . . . *[Pause.]*
BILLY: Then we gotta tell what happened.
YOUNG MICKEY: What?
BILLY: We gotta make sure this Prince guy don't get away with this.
ALEXANDER: You are a fucking Dudley-do-right-dufus. This Jew-boy is
gonna get you crucified, Mickey.
BILLY: My dad'll drive us to the police . . .
ALEXANDER: Jewish kids s'posed to be so smart, what the hell happened
to you?
BILLY: You want to be a mensch again, Alexander?
ALEXANDER: I don't speak that shit, all right? . . . I don't even speak
Spanish . . .

BILLY: Come with us to the police . . .

YOUNG MICKEY: Us? *[ALEXANDER begins to laugh.]*

BILLY: We'll be witnesses . . .

ALEXANDER: Maybe Mickey wants to die along with you, but I don't. Look, Mickey, I need to talk to you. You're lettin' him come between us? We mixed our blood. We took an oath.

YOUNG MICKEY: You broke that oath when you became one of them.

ALEXANDER: I never broke no oath to you. Square bizness. We was supposed to be forever. Ace boons . . . But no, you act this way? Treat me like a pussy that's been gang-fucked? You let the likes of him come between us, Nigga?

YOUNG MICKEY: Ain't nobody afraid of you.

ALEXANDER: You ain't supposed to be afraid of me . . . you're supposed to be my main man you stupid Uncle Tom-aintcha-mama-on-the-pancake-box, motherfucker. What you learn from that faggot Daniel so you can poke your friend here up his Kosher ass?

YOUNG MICKEY: Go home.

ALEXANDER: Fuck you. *[Pause.]* Look, man I wanna rap to you about . . .

YOUNG MICKEY: I don't care . . . just go.

ALEXANDER: My friend! Yo' ass is mine. *[ALEXANDER leaves. Pause.]*

BILLY: Forget him.

YOUNG MICKEY: What???

BILLY: He's trash.

YOUNG MICKEY: Billy, you don't know him well enough . . .

BILLY: He's a creep, and . . .

YOUNG MICKEY: Shut your mouth. Sometimes it's like you think you know everything. The two of yous are like that . . . think you know everything . . .

BILLY: I ain't like him . . .

YOUNG MICKEY: Don't you understand, he was scared . . .

BILLY: He was spying on us for that scumbag Prince.

YOUNG MICKEY: He was scared, man!

BILLY: Then if he was scared . . . why'd you make him go?

YOUNG MICKEY: 'Cause I wasn't sure 'til he went away.

BILLY: C'mon.

YOUNG MICKEY: Where?

BILLY: To get my father, we're going to the police.

YOUNG MICKEY: Billy, I'm not going to . . .

BILLY: The neighborhood will finally be rid of these guys.

YOUNG MICKEY: You rat on the Prince and you'll choke on the cheese . . .

BILLY: You gotta be true, Mickey . . . like my Dad says . . .

YOUNG MICKEY: He's not talking about something like this.

BILLY: He's talkin' about life.

YOUNG MICKEY: Well, if you want to lose yours, rat on the Prince. *[BILLY starts to leave.]*

BILLY: I ain't afraid. Maybe you're not behind me, but my dad will be. *[BILLY leaves. YOUNG MICKEY looks after him. Lights fade.]*

Scene 2

Lights up on BILLY and MR. KORNBLUM.

MR. KORNBLUM: No, no . . . no way. Forget it! You hear me, William?

BILLY: Then just tell me I'm wrong.

MR. KORNBLUM: You want me to say you're wrong. *[Pause.]* You're wrong.

BILLY: What about the truth, Pop?

MR. KORNBLUM: You listen to me, mister . . . I want the truth . . .

BILLY: You're always talking about being true . . . whether it's hitting a baseball or life . . .

MR. KORNBLUM: William, there's nothing to discuss.

BILLY: Pop, we're talking about a cop . . .

MR. KORNBLUM: Look, someone probably already told the cops what happened.

BILLY: That's what Mickey said.

MR. KORNBLUM: See . . . he should know. He understands the *schwartzer* mentality . . .

BILLY: What? *[Pause.]*

MR. KORNBLUM: Uhh . . . You know what I mean . . .

BILLY: No, Pop . . . I don't know what you mean.

MR. KORNBLUM: I mean . . . he knows that someone in the park . . . some grownup will get involved . . .

BILLY: But what if they don't, Pop? Huh? There was only kids there . . . white ones, too, for your information. So what if they don't?

MR. KORNBLUM: Then . . . they don't . . .

BILLY: Pop, you and Grandma . . . you always taught me that all life is sacred . . .

MR. KORNBLUM: That's right . . . and nothing is more sacred to me than your life, William . . . I've lost a wife, I'm not going to lose a son . . . Do you understand? Don't you understand that I don't want you hurt by those neanderthal hoodlums? They'll be out of jail in a day. They'll put a bullet in you. And there's the end of my world. I'm a dead man. Do you understand? I mean, when your mother was dying . . .

BILLY: I understand, Pop . . .

MR. KORNBLUM: Do ya? . . .

BILLY: Yeah . . . and it ain't good enough, Pop. *[MR. KORNBLUM slaps his son. Pause.]*

BILLY: Gee, Pop, you should join Spectre . . . you'd fit right in.

MR. KORNBLUM: You requested that, young man.

BILLY: I thought you treasured the truth. Always talking about how the Jews in Europe took too much crap, and here you are . . .

MR. KORNBLUM: This isn't Germany, William . . .

BILLY: Thank God it isn't, Pop . . . 'cause if you're afraid of a bunch of bullies . . . then I'm scared to think what kind of coward you'da been over there.

[MR. KORNBLUM draws closer.]

BILLY: *[Cont'd.]* Slap me again, Pop. It ain't gonna change a thing. You slap my face a hundred times . . . you're still a blowhard. You're still a coward. You preach the truth without even believing in it . . . My Pop, my Pop, my swell truth-sayer Pop . . . with a spine of a shrimp . . . which ain't Kosher.

MR. KORNBLUM: William . . . Billy . . .

[BILLY walks away. Lights fade slowly on MR. KORNBLUM.]

MR. KORNBLUM: *[Cont'd.]* Billy . . . son, let's talk about this . . . BILLY!

[Blackout.]

Scene 3

Lights up on THE PRINCE.

THE PRINCE: James Bond movies are fly 'cause the dudes he be fightin' . . . mainly the Spectre gang, well, they the baddest of the bad . . . and I dig 'em 'cause they know it don't matter. See, I believe that Spectre could kick James Bond, that faggoty talkin' Englishman, I believe they could kick his ass, and do . . . but they change the story . . . the Dude with the cat . . . he treats his people right . . . but they fuck up and gotta pay the price.

[Lights up on ALEXANDER with the noose around his neck. The rope is tossed over a branch. ODD JOB pulls the other end of the rope while ALEXANDER dangles hanging.]

THE PRINCE: Why you run?

[ALEXANDER struggles.]

THE PRINCE: *[Cont'd.]* Nobody in Spectre runs . . . Why you run?

[THE PRINCE signals for ODD JOB to let ALEXANDER down. ODD JOB does.]

THE PRINCE: *[Cont'd.]* I say, why you run?
ALEXANDER: I . . . I . . . I . . .

[ALEXANDER coughs. THE PRINCE signals and ODD JOB pulls the rope leaving ALEXANDER dangling once again.]

THE PRINCE: I wish I had one of them trap doors like Blofeld . . . with an alligator waitin' to chomp your ass up. I'd say #1 stand over there.

[THE PRINCE signals for ODD JOB to give the rope some slack.]

THE PRINCE: *[Cont'd.]* I'm only fifteen and nobody messes with me. What's it gonna be like when I'm twenty? . . . Why'd you run? *[Pause.]* String his ass again.
ALEXANDER: No, wait . . . wait . . .
THE PRINCE: What it be like? Why you run when you know Spectre don't gotta run?
ALEXANDER: I . . . I . . . I was spyin'.
THE PRINCE: Spyin'? Do I look like Laurel and Hardy and shit. Hang 'im. Hang 'im high!
ALEXANDER: No, no . . . square bizness . . . on the up and up . . .
THE PRINCE: What you rappin'?
ALEXANDER: When you offed that pig . . .
ODD JOB: He's jivin', he's jivin'. Let's just hang his ass.
ALEXANDER: That's my job as your #1 . . . to look out. I followed them . . .
ODD JOB: That little rat Mickey . . .
ALEXANDER: No, no, Mickey's cool . . . real cool . . . if we can get him away from that Jew-boy. It's the Jew-boy . . . he wants to go to the cops.
THE PRINCE: Let him down.

[ODD JOB does.]

THE PRINCE: *[Cont'd.]* That's a dead Jew. He been to the cops yet?
ALEXANDER: No, but he's tryin to push Mickey to go with him.
THE PRINCE: What Mickey say?
ALEXANDER: No way.
ODD JOB: What about the fag?
THE PRINCE: Don't worry about him. I've got something to gag him up. Believe me. *[Pause.]*
All right then. I'll spare you . . . and Mickey too . . . and if he keeps his mouth shut . . .
ODD JOB: What about the Jew, Your Grace?
THE PRINCE: Death!

[THE PRINCE exits.]

ODD JOB: Death! Death!

[ODD JOB exits. ALEXANDER watches as they leave. Lights fade.]

Scene 4

The woods. DANIEL is dressed in a suit. He carries several music books with him. He is humming a classical tune. THE PRINCE remains hidden, as ODD JOB comes forward.

ODD JOB: Hey . . .

DANIEL: Yes?

ODD JOB: What the fuck is that . . ."yes" . . . say it like you from the Bronx . . . say "yeah" . . . only faggots from Queens and Staten Island say "yes" 'cause they ain't got no balls.

DANIEL: Yes . . .

ODD JOB: I'll call you my little Queenie . . . You wanna be my little Queenie?

[THE PRINCE walks up. He blows kisses at DANIEL. He and ODD JOB draw closer to DANIEL.]

DANIEL: What do you want?

THE PRINCE: What do you want?

DANIEL: Look, I'm going to be late for my concert.

THE PRINCE: How'd you like to play my flute?

[ODD JOB starts to laugh. THE PRINCE viciously pushes DANIEL to his knees. Now ODD JOB unzips his pants in front of DANIEL's face.]

ODD JOB: Play me a song . . .

THE PRINCE: Blow, punk, blow.

DANIEL: Why are you doing this to me?

THE PRINCE: You supposed to like this. You a punk! C'mon, let's run a train on this bitch.

[THE PRINCE unzips his pants. He starts to try to undo DANIEL's pants. DANIEL turns, THE PRINCE slaps him.]

THE PRINCE: Don't worry about what I'm doin' back here . . . just start smokin' Odd Job's pole.

[As THE PRINCE starts to unbuckle DANIEL's pants, ODD JOB brings his crotch closer to DANIEL's face. Suddenly, DANIEL punches ODD JOB in the balls. ODD JOB falls to the ground. DANIEL hits THE PRINCE with an elbow to the stomach. DANIEL then gets up and tries to run. THE PRINCE is not hurt, in fact, he seems to enjoy this. He chases after DANIEL and corners him.]

THE PRINCE: You got balls, huh, sweetboy?

DANIEL: I just want to go to my concert . . .

THE PRINCE: You're a wild one. Like to fight before you give it up.

[DANIEL tries to hit THE PRINCE, but THE PRINCE knocks him down.]

THE PRINCE: You want some more? . . . Damn, you got some balls. I give you that. You actually tried to punch out the Prince.

[ODD JOB is up now.]

DANIEL: Why are you picking on me? I didn't do anything to you.
THE PRINCE: What are you yip yappin' about?
DANIEL: I'm not the enemy. We don't have time to hurt each other no more.
THE PRINCE: Ain't that some shit? Then you don't know nothin' 'bout that cop, do ya?
DANIEL: No, no, no.
THE PRINCE: Then I don't wanna hear a motherfucking thing but you screamin' with delight when I lay my pipe on you.
ODD JOB: That li'l punk motherfucker.

[ODD JOB kicks DANIEL.]

THE PRINCE: Come on, let's give 'im what he likes.

[DANIEL tries to fight, but they beat him to the ground. Then, as ODD JOB holds him, THE PRINCE pulls DANIEL's pants down. Blackout.]

Scene 5

The concert hall. YOUNG MICKEY sits at the edge of the stage. DANIEL comes in. His clothes are in disarray.

YOUNG MICKEY: I told you I'd be here.
DANIEL: First we'll go with the Mozart piece . . . Just in case you have trouble reading the music, I'll nod my head at the end of each page . . .
YOUNG MICKEY: Like we practiced . . .
DANIEL: Right.

[YOUNG MICKEY looks at DANIEL.]

YOUNG MICKEY: What happened to your clothes?
DANIEL: I tripped when I cut through the woods. *[Pause.]*
YOUNG MICKEY: You sure you're all right?

[YOUNG MICKEY begins to dust the dirt from DANIEL's shirt.]

DANIEL: Don't touch me!
YOUNG MICKEY: What's eatin' you?
DANIEL: I'm sorry, I . . .
YOUNG MICKEY: What happened to you? You didn't trip in the woods?
DANIEL: Yeah . . . I tripped all right. Over the Prince and Odd Job.

YOUNG MICKEY: They beat you up?

DANIEL: They did something worse...

YOUNG MICKEY: What? They what?

DANIEL: I tease you sometimes... I know. And I act like I know it all. But the only thing I really know is my music. I would never hurt you...

YOUNG MICKEY: I know that, Daniel.

DANIEL: I can't go on tonight.

YOUNG MICKEY: What do you mean you can't go on? The audience is just comin' back from intermission.

DANIEL: I can't...

YOUNG MICKEY: You're always tellin' me about overcoming obstacles... Well, you just gotta do that...

DANIEL: Why?

YOUNG MICKEY: 'Cause I heard these others play, and they suck, you're the best, Daniel, and...

DANIEL: Just leave it alone, Mickey!

VOICE ON THE M.C: The next contestant is sixteen-year-old Daniel Van Drake.

YOUNG MICKEY: Daniel, let 'em know how you feel.

[YOUNG MICKEY goes to the piano with DANIEL. There is applause. DANIEL is still a bit shaken and unsure as the applause dies down. YOUNG MICKEY sits next to him and turns the first page of the composition.

Long pause.

DANIEL begins playing a Mozart piece. First shakily, but, by the time YOUNG MICKEY turns the page for him, he is confident. The lights fade slowly on this.]

Scene 6

Lights up on YOUNG MICKEY and BILLY. YOUNG MICKEY has a stickball bat in hand and BILLY is pitching a Spaldeen that is invisible to the audience. They silently mime the stickball game "Strikeout" as BIG MICKEY enters. YOUNG MICKEY wears his Pirate cap, while BILLY wears an Oriole cap.

BIG MICKEY: Strikeout was a stickball game with the fast pitching of a Spaldeen... All the guys who loved baseball... when they couldn't play hard ball or softball played Strikeout. Now in Brooklyn they called it fast pitch, and in Manhattan it was Pitch in, but everybody knows they don't know anything about baseball. I guess that's why the Dodgers and the Giants left. Anyway, for 69 cents you could get a stickball bat in various colors with the end taped, and you could get a genuine Spaldeen for about 35 cents . . . The big strikeout courts were behind P.S. 112. There were about seven or eight chalked boxes. If you pitched in the box it was a strike . . . outside the box it was a ball and . . .

[BILLY pitches. YOUNG MICKEY swings and hits.]

YOUNG MICKEY: There's a line drive by Clemente! . . . *[BILLY dives for the ball.]*

YOUNG MICKEY: *[Cont'd.]* It gets between Belanger and Robinson . . . Base hit!!! *[YOUNG MICKEY makes the sound of the crowd.]*
The bases are loaded . . . it's the bottom of the ninth . . . and out of the on-deck circle comes that man . . . Willie Stargell . . .

BILLY: You gotta bat left handed . . .

YOUNG MICKEY: I know that . . . Stargel's left handed . . .

BILLY: Robinson comes over to talk to McNally . . .

YOUNG MICKEY: Who's in the bullpen?

BILLY: Nobody . . . McNally's still pitching a shutout, folks . . .

YOUNG MICKEY: Not for long, folks . . . the bases are loaded . . .

BILLY: It's three nothin' Orioles . . .

YOUNG MICKEY: With Clemente on first, Alley and Alou on second and third . . .

BILLY: Robinson pats McNally on the tusch . . . and McNally steps on the mound.

YOUNG MICKEY: Stargell steps into the batter's box . . .

BILLY: Left handed . . . left handed . . .

YOUNG MICKEY: I know . . . I know . . .

[YOUNG MICKEY bats left handed.]

BILLY: McNally winds and the pitch . . .

[YOUNG MICKEY swings.]

BILLY: *[Cont'd.]* Stargell swings and misses . . . Strike one . . . as Stargell shakes his head in disbelief . . . now McNally goes into the stretch position . . . He looks over to first . . . he winds, rocks and deals . . .

[BILLY pitches. YOUNG MICKEY does not swing.]

BILLY: *[Cont'd.]* Strike two on the outside corner.

[BILLY catches the ball as it bounces back off the wall.]

YOUNG MICKEY: Git outta here . . . that was a ball.

BILLY: You kiddin' me? Didn't you see that chalk explode when the ball hit the wall . . .

[BILLY looks at the ball and smiles.]

BILLY: *[Cont'd.]* There's chalk all over . . .

YOUNG MICKEY: Throw it and let me see.

[BILLY brings it to him instead.]

YOUNG MICKEY: *[Cont'd.]* That's old chalk.

BILLY: It's not.

YOUNG MICKEY: You wipe that ball off.

BILLY: Always do . . .

YOUNG MICKEY: Not in this life you don't . . .

[BILLY walks back to the mound.]

BILLY: You're just a sore loser . . .

YOUNG MICKEY: You put it in the box, you little twerp . . . have some balls . . . Pirates are a National League team . . . we like fastballs. The pitchers challenge you in the N.L. . . . instead of throwing that slick stuff . . . Gimme a fastball and it's ovah . . .

BILLY: Give you my slow-sinking-double-clutch-knuckle-curve and it's ovah!

YOUNG MICKEY: A faggot pitch for a faggot league.

BILLY: Yeah, the faggot league of Mickey Mantle, Brooks Robinson, Harmon Killebrew, Al Kaline, Carl Yastremski . . .

YOUNG MICKEY: That's right . . . against the challenge league of Willie Mays, Roberto Clemente, Willie McCovey, Juan Marichal . . .

BILLY: Denny McClain!

YOUNG MICKEY: Bob Gibson!

BILLY: The National League sucks!

YOUNG MICKEY: American League is a puff league . . .

BILLY: Get up to bat and I'll show you puff league . . .

YOUNG MICKEY: Only way you get me out . . . you throw me one of them American League puff balls . . . you give me a man's pitch.

BILLY: Shut up and get to bat . . .

YOUNG MICKEY: Who you tellin' to shut up? I'm gonna hit a line drive right in your mouth . . .

BILLY: Good, and it'll be an out . . . I take 'em as I get 'em . . .

[YOUNG MICKEY waits for the pitch.]

BILLY: *[Cont'd.]* McNally looks for the signal from Andy Echebarren, he shakes off the sign.

YOUNG MICKEY: That's right, ladies and gentlemen, it was a signal for fastball, but McNally shook it off. After the game, McNally and Robinson will go have cream puffs and tea. Stargell and Clemente? Why, of course, they'll have a Schlitz.

BILLY: And run over some little ol' lady from Pasadena because they were driving drunk.

YOUNG MICKEY: Roberto Clemente don't drive drunk!!! Brooks Robinson takes it up the ass!!!

BILLY: The Pirate bench is yelling profanities that we cannot repeat . . . But the Baltimore team are cool professionals who are unflappable . . . McNally goes into the stretch . . . he rocks . . . he deals . . .

[BILLY pitches. YOUNG MICKEY swings. He hits the ball and watches as it ascends a majestic height. BILLY turns and watches the ball.]

YOUNG MICKEY: That ball is deep, deep . . .

BILLY: But it's curvin' foul . . . foul . . .

YOUNG MICKEY: But deep . . . deep . . . still fair . . . and high . . . The ball is outta here!!!! On the roof!!!! Fourteen freakin' stories . . . A grand slam for Willie Stargel!!!

[YOUNG MICKEY starts to run imaginary bases in a homerun trot.]

YOUNG MICKEY: *[Cont'd.]* Stargell suckered McNally into throwing a fastball and the ball game is over. The Pirates win 4 to 3. What a shot!

BILLY: Stop showing off, hot dog . . .

YOUNG MICKEY: You show off all the time.

BILLY: You're a hot dogger like all those National Leaguers. Mays and Clemente with their basket catches . . . they're not in the jungle . . . they don't need baskets . . .

YOUNG MICKEY: The jungle? Tell you what, I'd like to see Mantle or Robinson in the N.L . . . .they'd never make it. American League's a prejudiced league . . .

BILLY: Yeah, yeah, yeah . . . All I know is, as good as the Pirates are, they can't even make it to the World Series.

YOUNG MICKEY: All I know is, I just beat your ass . . .

BILLY: I beat you three days in a row last week . . .

YOUNG MICKEY: But this is this week.

BILLY: Yeah, yeah, yeah . . . good shot . . . better get to the roof and get my ball . . .

YOUNG MICKEY: Hey . . . your Dad take you to the precinct?

BILLY: No.

YOUNG MICKEY: I knew he wasn't gonna let you go to the cops.

BILLY: The hell with the truth.

YOUNG MICKEY: Billy, he don't care about the truth . . .

BILLY: Damn right . . .

YOUNG MICKEY: He just don't wanna see you hurt. Can't you see that, you jerk? If my father were still alive, I'd obey him even if I thought he was wrong.

BILLY: Yeah, screw the truth. The truth is, you're both scared of a bunch of bullies. The whole neighborhood is. Nobody cares about the cop. I keep seein' it over and over . . . in the back . . . that looney tunes wacko didn't even give him a chance. My father . . . my best friend . . . tell me I'm wrong when I know I'm right . . . People you count on the most . . . One's a scared little Jew, and the other's a nigger.

[BIG MICKEY cringes. YOUNG MICKEY belts BILLY who falls to the ground. Pause.]

BILLY: It don't mean nothin' if you can beat me. Can you beat the Prince? Can you walk through the doors of the 47th Precinct with me and beat the Prince? . . .

YOUNG MICKEY: Why should I walk in with you? Who wants to talk with you anyway? You know, Alexander's right. I'm just a nigger to you . . . Jew-boy . . .

[BILLY starts to get up, but YOUNG MICKEY pushes him back down. He hovers over BILLY as if he's about to hit him again. Then he leaves.

BILLY sits there alone as the lights fade.]

Scene 7

Lights up on BIG MICKEY.

BIG MICKEY: Billy and I didn't see each other for the next few days. I didn't speak to him in class . . . And I missed two days of baseball practice just to avoid him. I thought he was wrong . . . that he should keep his mouth shut, listen to his father. That's what I thought . . . until it all went down . . . None of us would ever be the same again.

[Lights down.

Martin Luther King's last speech, the "Mountain Top" begins to play. MOTHER enters.]

MOTHER: Mickey! Mickey! Where are you? I know you hear me, boy. Get down here and witness history and watch Dr. King work his mojo on America. Listen to him weave his words . . . strut his stuff . . . James Brown is bad, but Martin is baaad. He got soul and he superbad. Get down here, boy. Get down here. Mickey, come live history. Hear Reverend King in Memphis. Watch us rise!

[Blackout. Shots are heard in the dark. Lights up on BIG MICKEY.]

BIG MICKEY: That very next day . . . the Bronx died . . . it never has recovered from this day. It was not the beginning of the end, but the end. You see . . . a disciple of peace dies in Memphis and it leads to rage in the Bronx. Come 3 o'clock, if you were white, your ass was grass. Nobody black stood up when Spectre Gestapo'd the neighborhood supermarket. They destroyed it. Nobody black said a damn

thing when Milton Friedman got the shit beat out of him as he
opened his bakery one morning. No one black, of good conscience,
said a fucking word . . . And in the end, when we had no neighborhood supermarket . . . or bakery of fine pastries . . . they only moaned
that familiar, sick, sorry, blame everybody but-your-fuckin'-self whine!

*[Lights up on BILLY carrying his books. Yelling and screaming is heard.
General riot using all company members.*

*Billy runs to the other side of the stage and runs into YOUNG MICKEY. BILLY
backs away. He is afraid YOUNG MICKEY is going to strike him.]*

YOUNG MICKEY: Hey, Billy, I . . .
BILLY: Get away from me!!!

*[BILLY drops his books and runs to the other side of the stage where he bumps
into THE PRINCE. He bolts again and runs into ODD JOB. He runs again
and runs into ALEXANDER.]*

THE PRINCE: Jesus . . . then Malcolm . . . now King . . . and, of course,
    me. The Prince.
ODD JOB: Let's roast this little Jew pigette.
THE PRINCE: Yeah, I'm in the mood for the kill . . .
ODD JOB: The kill . . .
ALEXANDER: Beat his ass so he'll remember not to go to the cops.
THE PRINCE: Hey, this ain't about no beating. This is about shuttin' up
    a squealin' pig.

*[THE PRINCE pulls out his gun. THE PRINCE and ODD JOB draw closer to
BILLY. ALEXANDER stands there, not quite sure what to do. YOUNG MICKEY
drops his books and runs across the stage.]*

YOUNG MICKEY: Nooooooo!!!

*[BILLY sees YOUNG MICKEY coming at him. He covers himself up as if expect-
ing to be hit by YOUNG MICKEY. YOUNG MICKEY knocks the gun from THE
PRINCE's hand.]*

THE PRINCE: You touched the Prince. I'm gonna off you first.

*[ODD JOB picks up the gun and hits YOUNG MICKEY in the back of the head.
YOUNG MICKEY slumps to the ground. THE PRINCE takes the gun from ODD
JOB.]*

ALEXANDER: You said you wasn't gonna hurt Mickey.
THE PRINCE: He got in my way.

[BILLY bends down to take care of YOUNG MICKEY.]

ALEXANDER: Okay, man . . . he's learned his lesson.
THE PRINCE: Yeah, but this little yarmulke wearing son of a bitch ain't.

ALEXANDER: You ain't gonna say nothin' about what happened in the park, are you, Billy?

BILLY: I don't wanna die . . . I don't want Mickey to die . . . I just wanna get Mickey home. I won't say nothin'.

[THE PRINCE aims at BILLY.]

ALEXANDER: You don't have to do this. We can let him go.

THE PRINCE: When the fuck you start wearin' the balls around here?

ALEXANDER: I just don't want you to go off . . . like you did with that cop.

THE PRINCE: Just hope I don't go off on you. Now 'cause I feel in a good mood, I'll let Mickey go . . . but Jew-boy . . .

[THE PRINCE is still aiming at BILLY.

BILLY places YOUNG MICKEY's head gently down. He rises and backs away.]

BILLY: You just don't give a shit . . . You're a fucking animal.

ALEXANDER: Hey, man . . . Prince . . . don't do this. Like, I know the cop and all . . . You lost your temper. But this is cold-blooded.

THE PRINCE: He's a fuckin' Jew-boy.

ALEXANDER: He's just a kid, man.

THE PRINCE: Fuck around here and you next, bitch!

[ALEXANDER looks at BILLY. He smiles.]

ALEXANDER: I guess you right, Jew-boy.

BILLY: *[Backing away slowly, nervously.]* Huh?

ALEXANDER: The motherfucker is an animal.

[Suddenly, ALEXANDER grabs THE PRINCE by the head, he brings his own knee up and smashes THE PRINCE's head into it. THE PRINCE collapses to the ground. Severely dazed, he drops the gun.

ALEXANDER goes to THE PRINCE.]

ALEXANDER: You know what we gonna do?

BILLY: What?

ALEXANDER: We're gonna get Mickey home, and then you and me are gonna go to the 47th Precinct. We're gonna tell 'em what happened in the park . . . We ain't gotta be afraid of these guys . . .

YOUNG MICKEY: Help me up . . .

ALEXANDER: Are you okay?

[ODD JOB goes after the gun. BIG MICKEY is frantic. ALEXANDER sees ODD JOB going for the gun. ALEXANDER turns and sees ODD JOB. They race for the gun, but ODD JOB is closer. ODD JOB points the gun at ALEXANDER.]

BIG MICKEY and YOUNG MICKEY: No!!!!

[*YOUNG MICKEY tries to go to* ALEXANDER, *but* BILLY *pulls him down to the ground.* ODD JOB *fires.* BIG MICKEY *turns and sees* ALEXANDER *stand for a few beats.*]

ALEXANDER: Mickey . . .

[ALEXANDER *falls.*]

YOUNG MICKEY: Alexander.

[ODD JOB *grabs* THE PRINCE *and helps him off.*

YOUNG MICKEY and BILLY *go to the fallen* ALEXANDER. *YOUNG MICKEY holds him in his arms.*

YOUNG MICKEY begins rocking ALEXANDER *in his arms.*]

YOUNG MICKEY: Alexander . . . Alexander . . . you're going to be OK. It's gonna be OK. Stay with me. Somebody get some help!!

[BILLY *runs for help.*]

YOUNG MICKEY: Help's coming. It's gonna be OK. You're gonna be OK, Alex . . .

[ALEXANDER *lies dead. Church bells toll. Lights.*]

Scene 8

Lights up on BIG MICKEY.

BIG MICKEY: Billy and I were pallbearers at the funeral. For the first thirteen years of my life, death was something very vague. An obscure stranger who was not a part of my reality. I lost my father, then Alexander, in a period of four months. Death had established an unwanted intimacy with me.

[*Lights up on the* MOTHER *and* MR. KORNBLUM. *They are dressed in black.*]

MOTHER: Feel like everything's dead . . .
MR. KORNBLUM: He was just a baby . . . babies with guns.
MOTHER: I didn't know I had such a well of tears in me. Mickey's daddy . . . well, he was an old man, but I flooded the house. This time I can't stop at all.

[MR. KORNBLUM *gives her a handkerchief.*]

MOTHER: [*Cont'd.*] In less than a day . . . King and Alexander . . . when I'm not cryin' for one I'm cryin' for the other.
MR. KORNBLUM: They gotta do something to get this neighborhood back together.

[They go off together.

BILLY *and* YOUNG MICKEY *enter. They are wearing black suits.]*

BILLY: I always thought a casket would be heavy. But six of us . . . six kids . . . we lifted it like it was nothing.

YOUNG MICKEY: I thought it was kind of heavy.

BILLY: It wasn't heavy.

YOUNG MICKEY: To me it was. I couldn't wait to put it down. I was thinkin', "gosh, Alexander, you sure are heavy."

BILLY: I'm moving.

[Pause.]

YOUNG MICKEY: You're just trying to psych my mind.

BILLY: I ain't psyching you.

[Pause.]

YOUNG MICKEY: Where you moving to?

BILLY: Larchmont.

YOUNG MICKEY: It's your Dad, huh?

BILLY: He says it's not like it used to be around here. He says the whole city is turning into a dump. He's scared of what might happen next.

[Pause.] So am I. Kids aren't supposed to have bullets in them. Their friends shouldn't have to carry their coffins.

YOUNG MICKEY: Well, I'm gonna get out of here too one day . . . away from all this. Like when my mother takes me to the shows and the museums . . . Those buildings with doormen. I'm gonna have one of them apartments. And if I have kids . . . they ain't never gonna have to deal with something like this.

BILLY: How you gonna do that?

YOUNG MICKEY: I'm gonna be somebody. I ain't gonna stay here forever.

[Lights up on DANIEL. *He begins to play his piano. An R. Nathaniel Dett piece, "The Place Where the Rainbow Ends." He plays it low.]*

YOUNG MICKEY: *[Cont'd.]* Baseball ain't gonna be fun anymore without Brooks Robinson's nephew beside me.

BILLY: He ain't my uncle.

YOUNG MICKEY: Yes he is.

BILLY: You know he isn't.

[Pause.]

YOUNG MICKEY: Yeah . . . I know . . . but it was fun pretending.

BILLY: We're too old to pretend.

*[*BILLY *walks away. The* MOTHER *enters. She goes to* YOUNG MICKEY.*]*

MOTHER: You're just the opposite of me, Mickey. Nothing touches you. It's a sin for someone to be so cold. Or is it that there's a drought in your well of tears? You're all I've got in the world. They're going to have to hire people to cry at my funeral 'cause my child surely won't.

[YOUNG MICKEY begins to cry. DANIEL puts his arm around him.]

DANIEL: It's okay. Go ahead and let it run.

[The lights lower on YOUNG MICKEY and DANIEL.

THE DOCTOR enters. BIG MICKEY turns and sees him. Their eyes meet for a beat.]

BIG MICKEY: Is it over?
DOCTOR: He's in recovery.
BIG MICKEY: Will he make it?
DOCTOR: I'm not sure. I don't have the answer to that at this point . . . It's too early to tell. But he has a chance.
BIG MICKEY: A good chance?
DOCTOR: He has a chance.

[Pause. THE DOCTOR leaves.]

BIG MICKEY: He's going to be all right. That's what my heart tells me. We'll play catch in the park again. He'll let me win at chess . . . And I'll yell at him for any number of things that a parent yells at a child for . . . I'm going to find a safe place. Now I know some of you think there is no such place. You probably think I'm naïve. But I've got to believe such a place exists. You see, my wife could be next, my baby . . . me. Let's face it . . . the melting pot has faded into antiquity with the sixty-nine cent stickball bat. *[Pause.]*
I lived high above it all. I took pity upon them. Upon them. As if they were helpless victims. Well, the tables have turned, and I, you . . . we're the victims . . . of ourselves . . . because we don't have the guts to take back our civilization. *[Pause.]*
I don't want to bury my children. I want it as it was meant to be . . . That when they are in middle-age, my children will stand over the graves of their parents.

END OF PLAY

Driving Miss Daisy

Alfred Uhry

Alfred Uhry

"**W**hen I wrote this play I never dreamed I would be writing an introduction to it because I never thought it would get this far. The original schedule was a five-week run at Playwrights Horizons, a New York nonprofit theatre, in the spring of 1987, and I made sure various family members from Atlanta would get to town during that period." A year and a half later, *Driving Miss Daisy* had won the Pulitzer Prize and Alfred Uhry was working on the screenplay which went on to win an Academy Award, as well as winning the Oscar for Best Picture of 1989.

"When I wonder how all this happened (which I do a lot!)," says Uhry, still surprised that his little play is being printed and lionized, "I can come up with only one answer. I wrote what I knew to be the truth and people have recognized it as such."[1]

The model for Miss Daisy was a friend of Uhry's grandmother in Atlanta back in the forties when he was growing up there in a German Jewish family. Hoke is based on the chauffeur of Uhry's grandmother, but also on other black chauffeurs he knew in that period. Though the model for Miss Daisy was unmarried, the Miss Daisy of the play has a son, Boolie, a composite of many men the young Alfred encountered in Atlanta, including a piece of himself. As Uhry mentioned in a recent interview, "When I write about the past, if I get myself quiet enough I can still hear the voices. I'm just kind of the secretary."[2] Others have used their childhood as the basis for a play or two—few with the success of Uhry and this particular play.

Uhry, beginning his career as a lyric writer working for Frank Loesser, made his Broadway debut with "Here's Where I Belong" in 1968. Uhry's book and lyrics for *The Robber Bridegroom* were nominated for a Tony Award. A series of re-created musicals followed, but twenty years elapsed before *Daisy* brought the relatively unknown Uhry into the spotlight. His second play, 1997 Tony winner, *The Last Night of Ballyhoo*, deals more directly with Uhry's immediate family and the conflict between a strong desire for assimilation in southern German Jewish homes, whose Christmas trees are only mentioned in *Daisy*, and the forces of anti-Semitism brewing in the world of the thirties, forces which would ultimately destroy most of European Jewry and unify American Jewry.

Uhry returned to the musical form to write the book for *Parade*, about the early twentieth-century Leo Frank case which resulted in an innocent Jewish man being lynched by the resurgent Ku Klux Klan after he was pardoned for the murder of a young girl. With Jason Robert Brown's excellent music and lyrics, this true story made for a stirring musical.

Uhry remains a bit surprised at the recognition he has received and is most appreciative of his wife and three daughters who supported him through the lean years. He is also very grateful to the original chauffeur in the play, Morgan Freeman, who played him in the film with co-star Jessica Tandy. Enthusiastic about the thrilling developments from a Jewish boyhood in Atlanta, Uhry exclaims: "This has been one helluva ride!"[3]

Notes

1. Alfred Uhry, "Introduction," *Driving Miss Daisy*, New York: Theatre Communications Group, 1987), p. ix.
2. Sandee Brawarsky, "Telling Stories That Haven't Been Told Before: Alfred Uhry as a Writer, http://members.tripod.com/OldRedHills/uhrywriter.html. http://members.tripod.com/OldRedHills/uhrywriter.html.
3. Alfred Uhry, op. cit., p. ix.

Driving Miss Daisy

Cast of Characters

DAISY WERTHAN, a widow (age 72–97)

HOKE COLEBURN, her chauffeur (age 60–85)

BOOLIE WERTHAN, her son (age 40–65)

Time and Place: *This play takes place from 1948 to 1973, mostly in Atlanta, Georgia. There are many locales. The scenery is meant to be simple and evocative. The action shifts frequently and, I hope, fluidly.*

In the dark we hear Daisy call from offstage: "Idella, I'm gone to market." A car ignition is turned on; then we hear a horrible crash, followed by bangs and booms and wood splintering. The very loud noise stops suddenly and the lights come up on Daisy Werthan's living room. Daisy, age seventy-two, is wearing a summer dress and high-heeled shoes. Her hair, her clothes, her walk, everything about her suggests bristle and feistiness and high energy. She appears to be in excellent health. Her son, Boolie Werthan, forty, is a businessman, Junior Chamber of Commerce style. He has a strong, capable air. The Werthans are Jewish, but they have strong Atlanta accents.

DAISY: No!

BOOLIE: Mama!

DAISY: No!

BOOLIE: Mama!

DAISY: I said no, Boolie, and that's the end of it.

BOOLIE: It's a miracle you're not laying in Emory Hospital—or decked out at the funeral home. Look at you! You didn't even break your glasses.

DAISY: It was the car's fault.

BOOLIE: Mama, the car didn't just back over the driveway and land on the Pollard's garage all by itself. You had it in the wrong gear.

DAISY: I did not!

BOOLIE: You put it in reverse instead of drive. The police report shows that.

DAISY: You should have let me keep my La Salle.

BOOLIE: Your La Salle was eight years old.

DAISY: I don't care. It never would have behaved this way. And you know it.

BOOLIE: Mama, cars don't behave. They are behaved upon. The fact is you, all by yourself, demolished that Packard.

DAISY: Think what you want. I know the truth.

374

BOOLIE: The truth is you shouldn't be allowed to drive a car anymore.
DAISY: No.
BOOLIE: Mama, we are just going to have to hire somebody to drive you.
DAISY: No *we* are not. This is my business.
BOOLIE: Your insurance policy is written so that they are going to have to give you a brand-new car.
DAISY: Not another Packard, I hope.
BOOLIE: Lord Almighty! Don't you see what I'm saying?
DAISY: Quit talking so ugly to your mother.
BOOLIE: Mama, you are seventy-two years old and you just cost the insurance company twenty-seven hundred dollars. You are a terrible risk. Nobody is going to issue you a policy after this.
DAISY: You're just saying that to be hateful.
BOOLIE: Okay. Yes. Yes I am. I'm making it all up. Every insurance company in America is lined up in the driveway waving their fountain pens and falling all over themselves to get you to sign on. Everybody wants Daisy Werthan, the only woman in the history of driving to demolish a three-week-old Packard, a two-car garage and a freestanding tool shed in one fell swoop!
DAISY: You talk so foolish sometimes, Boolie.
BOOLIE: And even if you could get a policy somewhere, it wouldn't be safe. I'd worry all the time. Look at how many of your friends have men to drive them. Miss Ida Jacobs, Miss Ethel Hess, Aunt Nonie—
DAISY: They're all rich.
BOOLIE: Daddy left you plenty enough for this. I'll do the interviewing at the plant. Oscar in the freight elevator knows every colored man in Atlanta worth talking about. I'm sure in two weeks' time I can find you somebody perfectly—
DAISY: No!
BOOLIE: You won't even have to do anything, Mama. I told you. I'll do all the interviewing, all the reference checking, all the—
DAISY: No. Now stop running your mouth! I am seventy-two years old as you so gallantly reminded me and I am a widow, but unless they rewrote the Constitution and didn't tell me, I still have rights. And one of my rights is the right to invite who I want—not who you want—into my house. You do accept the fact that this is my house? What I do not want—and absolutely will not have is some—*(She gropes for a bad-enough word)* some chauffeur sitting in my kitchen, gobbling my food, running up my phone bill. Oh, I hate all that in my house!
BOOLIE: You have Idella.
DAISY: Idella is different. She's been coming to me three times a week since you were in the eighth grade and we know how to stay out of

each other's way. And even so there are nicks and chips in most of my wedding china and I've seen her throw silver forks in the garbage more than once.

BOOLIE: Do you think Idella has a vendetta against your silverware?

DAISY: Stop being sassy. You know what I mean. I was brought up to do for myself. On Forsyth Street we couldn't afford them and we did for ourselves. That's still the best way, if you ask me.

BOOLIE: Them! You sound like Governor Talmadge.

DAISY: Why, Boolie! What a thing to say! I'm not prejudiced! Aren't you ashamed?

BOOLIE: I've got to go home. Florine'll be having a fit.

DAISY: Y'all must have plans tonight.

BOOLIE: Going to the Ansleys for a dinner party.

DAISY: I see.

BOOLIE: You see what?

DAISY: The Ansleys. I'm sure Florine bought another new dress. This is her idea of heaven on earth, isn't it?

BOOLIE: What?

DAISY: Socializing with Episcopalians.

BOOLIE: You're a doodle, Mama. I guess Aunt Nonie can run you anywhere you need to go for the time being.

DAISY: I'll be fine.

BOOLIE: I'll stop by tomorrow evening.

DAISY: How do you know I'll be here? I'm certainly not dependent on you for company.

BOOLIE: Fine. I'll call first. And I still intend to interview colored men.

DAISY: No!

BOOLIE: Mama!

DAISY: *(Singing to end discussion):*
After the ball is over
After the break of morn
After the dancers leaving
After the stars are gone
Many a heart is aching
If you could read them all—

Lights fade on Daisy as she sings and come up on Boolie at the Werthan Company. He sits at a desk piled with papers, and speaks into an intercom.

BOOLIE: Okay, Miss McClatchey. Send him on in.

Boolie continues working at his desk. Hoke Coleburn enters, a black man of about sixty, dressed in a somewhat shiny suit and carrying a fedora, a man clearly down on his luck but anxious to keep up appearances.

Yes, Hoke isn't it?

HOKE: Yassuh. Hoke Coleburn.

BOOLIE: Have a seat there. I've got to sign these letters. I don't want Miss McClatchey fussing at me.

HOKE: Keep right on with it. I got all the time in the worl'.

BOOLIE: I see. How long you been out of work?

HOKE: Since back befo' las' November.

BOOLIE: Long time.

HOKE: Well, Mist' Werthan, you try bein' me and looking for work. They hirin' young if they hirin' colored, an' they ain' even hirin' much young, seems like. *(Boolie is involved with his paperwork)* Mist' Werthan? Y'all people Jewish, ain' you?

BOOLIE: Yes we are. Why do you ask?

HOKE: I'd druther drive for Jews. People always talkin' 'bout they stingy and they cheap, but doan' say none of that roun' me.

BOOLIE: Good to know you feel that way. Now, tell me where you worked before.

HOKE: Yassuh. That what I'm getting' at. One time I workin' for this woman over near Little Five Points. What was that woman's name? I forget. Anyway, she president of the Ladies Auxiliary over yonder to the Ponce De Leon Baptist Church and seem like she always bringing up God and Jesus and do unto others. You know what I'm talkin' 'bout?

BOOLIE: I'm not sure. Go on.

HOKE: Well, one day, Mist' Werthan, one day that woman say to me, she say "Hoke, come on back in the back wid me. I got something for you." And we go on back yonder and, Lawd have mercy, she have all these old shirts and collars be on the bed, yellow, you know, and nasty like they been stuck off in a chifferobe and forgot about. Thass right. And she say "Ain' they nice? They b'long to my daddy befo' he pass and we fixin' to sell 'em to you for twenty-five cent apiece."

BOOLIE: What was her name?

HOKE: Thass what I'm thinkin'. What *was* that woman's name? Anyway, as I was goin' on to say, any fool see the whole bunch of them collars and shirts together ain' worth a nickel! Them's the people das callin' Jews cheap! So I say "Yassum, I think about it" and I get me another job fas' as I can.

BOOLIE: Where was that?

HOKE: Mist' Harold Stone, Jewish gentleman jes' like you. Judge, live over yonder on Lullwater Road.

BOOLIE: I knew Judge Stone.

HOKE: You doan' say! He done give me this suit when he finish wid it. An' this necktie too.

BOOLIE: You drove for Judge Stone?

HOKE: Seven years to the day nearabout. An' I be there still if he din' die, and Miz Stone decide to close up the house and move to her people in Savannah. And she say "Come on down to Savannah wid me, Hoke." 'Cause my wife dead by then and I say "No thank you." I didn't want to leave my grandbabies and I doan' get along with that Geechee trash they got down there.

BOOLIE: Judge Stone was a friend of my father's.

HOKE: You doan' mean! Oscar say you need a driver for yo' family. What I be doin'? Runnin' yo' children to school and yo' wife to the beauty parlor and like dat?

BOOLIE: I don't have any children. But tell me—

HOKE: Thass a shame! My daughter bes' thing ever happen to me. But you young yet. I wouldn't worry none.

BOOLIE: I won't. Thank you. Did you have a job after Judge Stone?

HOKE: I drove a milk truck for the Avondale Dairy through the whole war—the one jes' was.

BOOLIE: Hoke, what I'm looking for is somebody to drive my mother around.

HOKE: Excuse me for askin', but how come she ain' hire fo' herself?

BOOLIE: Well, it's a delicate situation.

HOKE: Mmmm-hmm. She done gone roun' the bend a little? That'll happen when they get on.

BOOLIE: Oh no. Nothing like that. She's all there. Too much there is the problem. It just isn't safe for her to drive anymore. She knows it, but she won't admit it. I'll be frank with you. I'm a little desperate.

HOKE: I know what you mean 'bout dat. Once I was outta work my wife said to me "Oooooh, Hoke, you ain' gon get now nother job." And I say "What you talkin' 'bout, woman?" And the very next week I go to work for that woman in Little Five Points. Cahill! Miz Frances Cahill. And then I got to Judge Stone and they the reason I happy to hear you Jews.

BOOLIE: Hoke, I want you to understand, my mother is a little high-strung. She doesn't want anybody driving her. But the fact is you'd be working for me. She can say anything she likes but she can't fire you. You understand?

HOKE: Sho I do. Don't worry none about it. I hold on no matter what way she run me. When I nothin' but a little boy down there on the farm above Macon, I use to wrastle hogs to the ground at killin' time, and ain' no hog get away from me yet.

BOOLIE: How does twenty dollars a week sound?

HOKE: Soun' like you got yo' mama a chauffeur.

Lights fade on them and come up on Daisy, who enters her living room with the morning paper. She reads with interest. Hoke enters the living room.

*He carries a chauffeur's cap instead of his hat. Daisy's concentration on
the paper becomes fierce when she senses Hoke's presence.* Mornin', Miz
Daisy.

DAISY: Good morning.

HOKE: Right cool in the night, wadn't it?

DAISY: I wouldn't know. I was asleep.

HOKE: Yassum. What yo' plans today?

DAISY: That's my business.

HOKE: You right about dat. Idella say we runnin' outta coffee and Dutch
Cleanser.

DAISY: We?

HOKE: She say we low on silver polish too.

DAISY: Thank you. I will go to the Piggly Wiggly on the trolley this
afternoon.

HOKE: Now, Miz Daisy, how come you doan' let me carry you?

DAISY: No, thank you.

HOKE: Ain't that what Mist' Werthan hire me for?

DAISY: That's his problem.

HOKE: All right den. I find something to do. I tend yo' zinnias.

DAISY: Leave my flower bed alone.

HOKE: Yassum. You got a nice place back beyond the garage ain' doin'
nothin' but sittin' there. I could put you in some butter beans and
some tomatoes and even some Irish potatoes could we get some ones
with good eyes.

DAISY: If I want a vegetable garden, I'll plant it for myself.

HOKE: Well, I go out and set in the kitchen then, like I been doin' all
week.

DAISY: Don't talk to Idella. She has work to do.

HOKE: Nome. I jes' sit there till five o'clock.

DAISY: That's your affair.

HOKE: Seem a shame, do. That fine Oldsmobile settin' out there in the
garage. Ain't move a inch from when Mist' Werthan rode it over here
from Mitchell Motors. Only got nineteen miles on it. Seem like that
insurance company give you a whole new car for nothin'.

DAISY: That's your opinion.

HOKE: Yassum. And my other opinion is a fine rich Jewish lady like you
doan' b'long draggin' up the steps of no bus, luggin' no grocery-store
bags. I come along and carry them fo' you.

DAISY: I don't need you. I don't want you. And I don't like you saying
I'm rich.

HOKE: I won' say it then.

DAISY: Is that what you and Idella talk about in the kitchen? Oh, I hate
this! I hate being discussed behind my back in my own house! I was

born on Forsyth Street and, believe you me, I knew the value of a penny. My brother Manny brought home a white cat one day and Papa said we couldn't keep it because we couldn't afford to feed it. My sisters saved up money so I could go to school and be a teacher. We didn't have anything!

HOKE: Yassum, but look like you doin' all right now.

DAISY: And I've ridden the trolley with groceries plenty of times!

HOKE: Yassum, but I feel bad takin' Mist' Werthan's money for doin' nothin'. You understand?

DAISY: How much does he pay you?

HOKE: That between me and him, Miz Daisy.

DAISY: Anything over seven dollars a week is robbery. Highway robbery!

HOKE: Specially when I doan' do nothin' but set on a stool in the kitchen all day long. Tell you what, while you goin' on the trolley to the Piggly Wiggly, I hose down yo' front steps.

Daisy is putting on her hat.

DAISY: All right.

HOKE: All right I hose yo' steps?

DAISY: All right the Piggly Wiggly. And then home. Nowhere else.

HOKE: Yassum.

DAISY: Wait. You don't know how to run the Oldsmobile!

HOKE: Miz Daisy, a gearshift like a third arm to me. Anyway, thissun automatic. Any fool can run it.

DAISY: Any fool but me, apparently.

HOKE: Ain't no need to be so hard on yo'seff now. You cain' drive but you probably do alotta things I cain' do.

DAISY: The idea!

HOKE: It all work out.

DAISY: *(Calling offstage):* I'm gone to the market, Idella.

HOKE: *(Also calling):* And I right behind her!

Hoke puts on his cap and helps Daisy into the car. He sits at the wheel and backs the car down the driveway. Daisy, in the rear, is in full bristle.

I love a new car smell. Doan' you?

Daisy slides over to the other side of the seat.

DAISY: I'm nobody's fool, Hoke.

HOKE: Nome.

DAISY: I can see the speedometer as well as you can.

HOKE: I see dat.

DAISY: My husband taught me how to run a car.

HOKE: Yassum.

DAISY: I still remember everything he said. So don't you even think for a second that you can—wait! You're speeding! I see it!

HOKE: We ain't goin' but nineteen miles an hour.

DAISY: I like to go under the speed limit.

HOKE: Speed limit thirty-five here.

DAISY: The slower you go, the more you save on gas. My husband told me that.

HOKE: We barely movin'. Might as well walk to the Piggly Wiggly.

DAISY: Is this your car?

HOKE: Nome.

DAISY: Do you pay for the gas?

HOKE: Nome.

DAISY: All right then. My fine son may think I'm losing my abilities, but I am still in control of what goes on in my car. Where are you going?

HOKE: To the grocery store.

DAISY: Then why didn't you turn on Highland Avenue?

HOKE: Piggly Wiggly ain' on Highland Avenue. It on Euclid, down there near—

DAISY: I know where it is and I want to go to it the way I always go. On Highland Avenue.

HOKE: That three blocks out of the way, Miz Daisy.

DAISY: Go back! Go back this minute!

HOKE: We in the wrong lane! I cain' jes'—

DAISY: Go back I said! If you don't, I'll get out of this car and walk!

HOKE: We movin'! You cain' open the do'!

DAISY: This is wrong! Where are you taking me?

HOKE: The sto'.

DAISY: This is wrong. You have to go back to Highland Avenue!

HOKE: Mmmm-hmmmm.

DAISY: I've been driving to the Piggly Wiggly since the day they put it up and opened it for business. This isn't the way! Go back! Go back this minute!

HOKE: Yonder the Piggly Wiggly.

DAISY: Get ready to turn now.

HOKE: Yassum.

DAISY: Look out! There's a little boy behind that shopping cart!

HOKE: I see dat.

DAISY: Pull in next to the blue car.

HOKE: We closer to the do' right here.

DAISY: Next to the blue car! I don't park in the sun! It fades the uphol-stery.

HOKE: Yassum.

He pulls in, and gets out as Daisy springs out of the back seat.

DAISY: Wait a minute. Give me the car keys.

HOKE: Yassum.

DAISY: Stay right here by the car. And you don't have to tell everybody my business.

HOKE: Nome. Doan' forget the Dutch Cleanser now.

Daisy fixes him with a look meant to kill and exits. Hoke waits by the car for a minute, then hurries to the phone booth at the corner.

Hello? Miz McClatchey? Hoke Coleburn here. Can I speak to him? *(Pause)* Mornin' sir, Mist' Werthan. Guess where I'm at? I'm at dishere phone booth on Euclid Avenue right next to the Piggly Wiggly. I jes' drove yo' mama to the market. *(Pause)* She flap around some on the way. But she all right. She in the store. Uh-oh. Miz Daisy look out the store window and doan' see me, she liable to throw a fit right there by the checkout. *(Pause)* Yassuh, only took six days. Same time it take the Lawd to make the worl'.

Lights out on Hoke. We hear a choir singing.

CHOIR: May the words of my mouth
    And the meditations of my heart
    Be acceptable in Thy sight, O Lord
    My strength and my redeemer. Amen.

Light up on Hoke waiting by the car, looking at a newspaper. Daisy enters in a different hat and a fur piece.

HOKE: How yo' temple this mornin', Miz Daisy?

DAISY: Why are you here?

HOKE: *(Helping her into the car)* I bring you to de temple like you tell me.

DAISY: I can get myself in. Just go. *(She makes a tight little social smile and a wave out the window)* Hurry up out of here!

Hoke starts up the car.

HOKE: Yassum.

DAISY: I didn't say speed. I said get me away from here.

HOKE: Somethin' wrong back yonder?

DAISY: No.

HOKE: Somethin' I done?

DAISY: No. *(A beat)* Yes.

HOKE: I ain' done nothin'!

DAISY: You had the car right in front of the front door of the temple! Like I was Queen of Romania! Everybody saw you! Didn't I tell you to wait for me in the back?

HOKE: I jes' tryin' to be nice. They two other chauffeurs right behind me.

DAISY: You made me look like a fool. A g.d. fool!

HOKE: Lawd knows you ain' no fool, Miz Daisy.

DAISY: Slow down. Miriam and Beulah and them, I could see what they were thinking when we came out of services.

HOKE: What that?

DAISY: That I'm trying to pretend I'm rich.

HOKE: You is rich, Miz Daisy!

DAISY: No I'm not! And nobody can ever say I put on airs. On Forsyth Street we only had meat once a week. We made a meal off of grits and gravy. I taught the fifth grade at the Crew Street School! I did without plenty of times, I can tell you.

HOKE: And now you doin' with. What so terrible in that?

DAISY: You! Why do I talk to you? You don't understand me.

HOKE: Nome, I don't. I truly don't. 'Cause if I ever was to get a hold of what you got I be shakin' it around for everybody in the world to see.

DAISY: That's vulgar. Don't talk to me!

Hoke mutters something under his breath.

What? What did you say? I heard that!

HOKE: Miz Daisy, you needs a chauffeur and Lawd know, I needs a job. Let's jes' leave it at dat.

Light out on them and up on Boolie, in his shirtsleeves. He has a phone to his ear.

BOOLIE: Good morning, Mama. What's the matter? *(Pause)* What? Mama, you're talking so fast I . . . What? All right. All right. I'll come by on my way to work. I'll be there as soon as I can.

Light out on him and up on Daisy, pacing around her house in a winter bathrobe. Boolie enters in a topcoat and scarf.

I didn't expect to find you in one piece.

DAISY: I wanted you to be here when he comes. I wanted you to hear it for yourself.

BOOLIE: Hear what? What is going on?

DAISY: He's stealing from me!

BOOLIE: Hoke? Are you sure?

DAISY: I don't make empty accusations. I have proof!

BOOLIE: What proof?

DAISY: This! *(She triumphantly pulls an empty can of salmon out of her robe pocket)* I caught him red-handed! I found this hidden in the garbage pail under some coffee grounds.

BOOLIE: You mean he stole a can of salmon?

DAISY: Here it is! Oh I knew. I knew something was funny. They all take things, you know. So I counted.

BOOLIE: You counted?

DAISY: The silverware first and the linen dinner napkins and then I went into the pantry. I turned on the light and the first thing that caught my eye was a hole behind the corned beef. And I knew right away. There were only eight cans of salmon. I had nine. Three for a dollar on sale.

BOOLIE: Very clever, Mama. You made me miss my breakfast and be late for a meeting at the bank for a thirty-three-cent can of salmon. *(He jams his hand in his pocket and pulls out some bills)* Here! You want thirty-three cents? Here's a dollar! Here's ten dollars! Buy a pantry full of salmon!

DAISY: Why, Boolie! The idea! Waving money at me like I don't know what! I don't know what! I don't want the money. I want my things!

BOOLIE: One can of salmon?

DAISY: It was mine. I bought it and I put it there and he went into my pantry and took it and he never said a word. I leave him plenty of food every day and I always tell him exactly what it is. They are like having little children in the house. They want something so they just take it. Not a smidgin of manners. No conscience. He'll never admit this. "Nome," he'll say. "I doan' know nothin' 'bout that." And I don't like it! I don't like living this way! I have no privacy.

BOOLIE: Mama!

DAISY: Go ahead. Defend him. You always do.

BOOLIE: All right. I give up. You want to drive yourself again, you just go ahead and arrange it with the insurance company. Take your blessed trolley. Buy yourself a taxicab. Anything you want. Just leave me out of it.

DAISY: Boolie . . .

Hoke enters in an overcoat.

HOKE: Mornin', Miz Daisy. I b'lieve it fixin' to clear up. S'cuse me, I didn't know you was here Mist' Werthan.

BOOLIE: Hoke, I think we have to have a talk.

HOKE: Jes' a minute. Lemme put my coat away. I be right back. *(He pulls a brown paper bag out of his overcoat)* Oh, Miz Daisy. Yestiddy when you out with yo' sister I ate a can o' your salmon. I know you say eat the left-over pork chops, but they stiff. Here, I done buy you another can. You want me to put it in the pantry fo' you?

DAISY: Yes. Thank you, Hoke.

HOKE: I'll be right wit' you Mist' Werthan.

Hoke exits. Daisy looks at the empty can in her hand.

DAISY: *(Trying for dignity):* I've got to get dressed now. Goodbye, son.

She pecks his cheek and exits. Lights out on Boolie. We hear sounds of birds twittering. Lights come up brightly, indicating hot sun. Daisy, in a light dress, is kneeling, a trowel in her hand, working by a gravestone. Hoke, jacket in hand, sleeves rolled up, stands nearby.

HOKE: I jes' thinkin', Miz Daisy. We bin out heah to the cemetery three times dis mont' already and ain' even the twentieth yet.

DAISY: It's good to come in nice weather.

HOKE: Yassum. Mist' Sig's grave mighty well tended. I b'lieve you the best widow in the state of Georgia.

DAISY: Boolie's always pestering me to let the staff out here tend to this plot. Perpetual care they call it.

HOKE: Doan' you do it. It right to have somebody from the family lookin' after you.

DAISY: I'll certainly never have that. Boolie will have me in perpetual care before I'm cold.

HOKE: Come on now, Miz Daisy.

DAISY: Hoke, run back to the car and get that pot of azaleas for me and set it on Leo Bauer's grave.

HOKE: Miz Rose Bauer's husband?

DAISY: That's right. She asked me to bring it out here for her. She's not very good about coming. And I believe today would've been Leo's birthday.

HOKE: Yassum. Where the grave at?

DAISY: I'm not exactly sure. But I know it's over that way on the other side of the weeping cherry. You'll see the headstone. Bauer.

HOKE: Yassum.

DAISY: What's the matter?

HOKE: Nothin' the matter.

He exits. She works with her trowel. In a moment Hoke returns with flowers.

Miz Daisy . . .

DAISY: I told you it's over on the other side of the weeping cherry. It says Bauer on the headstone.

HOKE: How'd that look?

DAISY: What are you talking about?

HOKE: *(Deeply embarrassed):* I'm talkin' 'bout I cain' read.

DAISY: What?

HOKE: I cain' read.

DAISY: That's ridiculous. Anybody can read.

HOKE: Nome. Not me.

DAISY: Then how come I see you looking at the paper all the time?

HOKE: That's it. Jes' lookin'. I dope out what's happening from the pictures.

DAISY: You know your letters, don't you?

HOKE: My ABCs. Yassum, pretty good. I jes' cain' read.

DAISY: Stop saying that. It's making me mad. If you know your letters then you can read. You just don't know you can read. I taught some of the stupidest children God ever put on the face of this earth and all of them could read enough to find a name on a tombstone. The name is Bauer. Buh buh buh buh Bauer. What does that buh letter sound like?

HOKE: Sound like a B.

DAISY: Of course. Buh Bauer. Er er er er er. Bau-*er*. That's the last part. What letter sounds like er?

HOKE: R?

DAISY: So the first letter is a—

HOKE: B.

DAISY: And the last letter is an—

HOKE: R.

DAISY: B-R. B-R. B-R. Brr. Brr. Brr. It even sounds like Bauer, doesn't it?

HOKE: Sho' do Miz Daisy. Thass it?

DAISY: That's it. Now go over there like I told you in the first place and look for a headstone with a B at the beginning and an R at the end and that will be Bauer.

HOKE: We ain' gon worry 'bout what come in the middle?

DAISY: Not right now. This will be enough for you to find it. Go on now.

HOKE: Yassum.

DAISY: And don't come back here telling me you can't do it. You can.

HOKE: Miz Daisy . . .

DAISY: What now?

HOKE: I 'preciate this, Miz Daisy.

DAISY: Don't be ridiculous! I didn't do anything. Now, would you please hurry up? I'm burning up out here.

Light goes out on them and in the dark we hear Eartha Kitt singing "Santa Baby." Light up on Boolie. He wears a tweed jacket, red vest, holly in his lapel. He is on the phone.

BOOLIE: Mama? Merry Christmas. Listen, do Florine a favor, all right? She's having a fit and the grocery store is closed today. You got a package of coconut in your pantry? Would you bring it when you come? (*He calls offstage*) Hey, honey! Your ambrosia's saved! Mama's got the coconut! (*Back into the phone*) Many thanks. See you anon, Mama. Ho ho ho.

Lights out on Boolie and up on Daisy and Hoke in the car. Daisy is not in a festive mood.

HOKE: Ooooooh at them lit-up decorations!

DAISY: Everybody's giving the Georgia Power Company a Merry Christmas.

HOKE: Miz Florine's got 'em all beat with the lights.

DAISY: She makes an ass out of herself every year.

HOKE: *(Loving it):* Yassum.

DAISY: She always has to go and stick a wreath in every window she's got.

HOKE: Mmm-hmmm.

DAISY: And that silly Santa Claus winking on the front door!

Hoke: I bet she have the biggest tree in Atlanta. Where she get 'em so large?

DAISY: Absurd. If I had a nose like Florine I wouldn't go around saying Merry Christmas to anybody.

HOKE: I enjoy Christmas at they house.

DAISY: I don't wonder. You're the only Christian in the place!

HOKE: 'Cept they got that new cook.

DAISY: Florine never could keep help. Of course it's none of my affair.

HOKE: Nome.

DAISY: Too much running around. The Garden Club this and the Junior League that! As if any one of them would ever give her the time of day! But she'd die before she'd fix a glass of ice tea for the Temple Sisterhood!

HOKE: Yassum. You right.

DAISY: I just hope she doesn't take it in her head to sing this year. *(She imitates)* Glo-o-o-o-o-o-o-o-o-o-o-o-o-oriaaaa! She sounds like she has a bone stuck in her throat.

HOKE: You done say a mouthful, Miz Daisy.

DAISY: You didn't have to come. Boolie would've run me out.

HOKE: I know that.

DAISY: Then why did you?

HOKE: That my business, Miz Daisy. *(He turns into a driveway and stops the car)* Well, looka there! Miz Florine done put a Rudolph Reindeer in the dogwood tree.

DAISY: Oh my Lord! If her grandfather, old man Freitag, could see this! What is it you say? I bet he'd jump up out of his grave and snatch her baldheaded!

Hoke opens the door for Daisy.

Wait a minute. *(She takes a small package wrapped in brown paper from her purse)* This isn't a Christmas present.

HOKE: Nome.

DAISY: You know I don't give Christmas presents.

HOKE: I sho' do.

DAISY: I just happened to run across it this morning. Open it up.

HOKE: (*Unwrapping package*) Ain't nobody ever give me a book. *(Laboriously reads the cover)* Handwriting Copy Book-Grade Five.

DAISY: I always taught out of these. I saved a few.

HOKE: Yassum.

DAISY: It's faded but it works. If you practice, you'll write nicely.

HOKE: (*Trying not to show emotion*) Yassum.

DAISY: But you have to practice. I taught Mayor Hartsfield out of this same book.

HOKE: Thank you, Miz Daisy.

DAISY: It's not a Christmas present.

HOKE: Nome.

DAISY: Jews don't have any business giving Christmas presents. And you don't need to go yapping about this to Boolie and Florine.

HOKE: This strictly between you and me.

We hear a record of "Rudolph the Red-Nosed Reindeer."

They seen us. Mist' Werthan done turn up the hi-fi.

DAISY: I hope I don't spit up.

Hoke takes her arm and they walk off together as the light fades on them. Light up on Boolie, wearing madras Bermuda shorts and Lacoste shirt. He is in his late forties, waiting by the car.

BOOLIE: *(Calling):* Come on, Hoke! Get a wiggle on! I'm supposed to tee off at the club at 11:30.

Hoke enters.

HOKE: Jes' emptyin' the trash. Sad'dy garbage day, you know.

BOOLIE: Where's Mama?

HOKE: She back in her room and she say go on widdout her. I think she takin' on 'bout dis.

They have gotten in the car, both in the front seat. Hoke is driving.

BOOLIE: That's crazy. A car is a car.

HOKE: Yassuh, but she done watch over dis machine like a chicken hawk. One day we park in front of de dry cleaner up yonder at the Plaza and dis white man—look like some kind of lawyer, banker, dress up real fine—he done lay this satchel up on our hood while he open up his trunk, you know, and Lawd what he do that for, fore I could stop her, yo' mama jump out de back do' and run that man every which way. She wicked 'bout her paint job.

BOOLIE: Did she tell you this new car has air conditioning?

HOKE: She say she doan' like no air-cool. Say it give her the neckache.

BOOLIE: Well, you know how Mama fought me, but it's time for a trade. She's losing equity on this car. I bet both of you will miss this old thing.

HOKE: Not me. Unh-unh.

BOOLIE: Oh come on. You're the only one that's driven it all this time. Aren't you just a little sorry to see it go?

HOKE: It ain' goin' nowhere. I done bought it.

BOOLIE: You didn't!

HOKE: I already made the deal with Mist' Red Mitchell at the car place.

BOOLIE: For how much?

HOKE: Dat for him and me to know.

BOOLIE: For God's sake! Why didn't you just buy it right from Mama? You'd have saved money.

HOKE: Yo' mama in my business enough as it is. I ain' studyin' makin' no monthly car payments to her. Dis mine the regular way.

BOOLIE: It's a good car, all right. I guess nobody knows that better than you.

HOKE: Best ever come off the line. And dis new one, Miz Daisy doan' take to it, I let her ride in disheah now an' again.

BOOLIE: Mighty nice of you.

HOKE: Well, we all doin' what we can. Keep them ashes off my 'polstry.

Light out on them and up on Daisy's driveway. Daisy, wearing traveling clothes and a hat, enters lugging a big heavy suitcase. She looks around anxiously, checks her watch and exits again. In a moment she returns with a full dress bag and a picnic basket. She sets them by the suitcase, looks around, becoming more agitated, and exits again. Now she returns with a large elaborately wrapped package. Hoke enters, carrying a small suitcase.

DAISY: It's three after seven.

HOKE: Yassum. You say we leavin' at fifteen to eight.

DAISY: At the latest, I said.

HOKE: Now what bizness you got draggin' disheah out de house by yo'seff?

DAISY: Who was here to help me?

HOKE: Miz Daisy, it doan' take mo'n five minutes to load up de trunk. You fixin' to break both yo' arms and yo' legs too fo' we even get outta Atlanta. You takin' on too much.

DAISY: I hate doing things at the last minute.

HOKE: What you talkin' 'bout? You ready to go fo' de las' week and half! *(He picks up the present)*

DAISY: Don't touch that.

HOKE: Ain' it wrap pretty. Dat Mist' Walter's present?

DAISY: Yes. It's fragile. I'll hold it on the seat with me.

Boolie enters carrying his briefcase and a small wrapped package.

Well, you nearly missed us!

BOOLIE: I thought you were leaving at quarter of.

HOKE: She takin' on.

DAISY: Be still.

BOOLIE: Florine sent this for Uncle Walter.

(Daisy recoils from it) Well, it's not a snake, Mama. I think it's notepaper.

DAISY: How appropriate. Uncle Walter can't see!

BOOLIE: Maybe it's soap.

DAISY: How nice that you show such an interest in your uncle's ninetieth birthday.

BOOLIE: Don't start up, Mama. I cannot go to Mobile with you. I have to go to New York tonight for the convention. You know that.

DAISY: The convention starts Monday. And I know what else I know.

BOOLIE: Just leave Florine out of it. She wrote away for those tickets eight months ago.

DAISY: I'm sure *My Fair Lady* is more important than your own flesh and blood.

BOOLIE: Mama!

DAISY: Those Christians will be mighty impressed!

BOOLIE: I can't talk to you when you're like this.

Daisy has climbed into the car. Boolie draws Hoke aside.

I've got to talk to Hoke.

DAISY: They expect us for a late supper in Mobile.

BOOLIE: You'll be there.

DAISY: I know they'll fix crab. All that trouble!

BOOLIE: *(To Hoke):* I don't know how you're going to stand all day in the car.

HOKE: She doan mean nothin'. She jes' worked up.

BOOLIE: Here's fifty dollars in case you run into trouble. Don't show it to Mama. You've got your map?

HOKE: She got it in wid her. Study every inch of the way.

BOOLIE: I'll be at the Ambassador Hotel in New York. On Park Avenue.

DAISY: It's seven sixteen.

BOOLIE: You should have a job on the radio announcing the time.

DAISY: I want to miss rush hour.

BOOLIE: Congratulate Uncle Walter for me. And kiss everybody in Mobile.

DAISY: *(To Hoke):* Did you have the air condition checked? I told you to have the air condition checked!

HOKE: Yassum. I got the air condition checked but I doan' know what for. You doan' never 'low me to turn it on.

DAISY: Hush up.

BOOLIE: Good-bye! Good luck! *(Light out on the car)* Good God!

Light out on Boolie and back up on the car. It's lunchtime. Daisy and Hoke are both eating. Hoke eats while he drives.

HOKE: Idella stuff eggs good.

DAISY: You stuff yourself good. I'm going to save the rest of this for later.

HOKE: Yassum.

DAISY: I was thinking about the first time I ever went to Mobile. It was Walter's wedding, 1888.

HOKE: 1888! You weren't nothin' but a little child.

DAISY: I was twelve. We went on the train. And I was so excited. I'd never been on a train, I'd never been in a wedding party and I'd never seen the ocean. Papa said it was the Gulf of Mexico and not the ocean, but it was all the same to me. I remember we were at a picnic somewhere—somebody must have taken us all bathing—and I asked Papa if it was all right to dip my hand in the water. He laughed because I was so timid. And then I tasted the salt water on my fingers. Isn't it silly to remember that?

HOKE: No sillier than most of what folks remember. You talkin' 'bout first time. I tell you 'bout the first time I ever leave the state of Georgia?

DAISY: When was that?

HOKE: 'Bout twenty-five minutes back.

DAISY: Go on!

HOKE: Thass right. First time. My daughter, she married to Pullman porter on the N.C. & St. L., you know, and she all time goin'—Detroit, New York, St. Louis—talkin' 'bout snow up aroun' her waist and ridin' in de subway car and I say, "Well, that very nice Tommie Lee, but I jes' doan' feel the need." So dis it, Miz Daisy, and I got to tell you, Alabama ain' lookin' like much so far.

DAISY: It's nicer the other side of Montgomery.

HOKE: If you say so. Pass me up one of them peaches, please ma'am.

She looks out the window. Suddenly she starts.

DAISY: Oh my God!

HOKE: What happen?

DAISY: That sign said Phoenix City—thirty miles. We're not supposed to go to Phoenix City. We're going the wrong way. Oh my God!

HOKE: Maybe you done read it wrong.

DAISY: I didn't. Stop the car! Stop the car! *(Very agitated, she wrestles with the map on her lap)* Here! Here! You took the wrong turn at Opelika!

HOKE: You took it with me. And you readin' the map.

DAISY: I was getting the lunch. Go on back! Oh my God!

HOKE: It ain't been thirty minutes since we turn.

DAISY: I'm such a fool! I didn't have any business coming in the car by myself with just you. Boolie made me! I should have come on the train. I'd be safe there. I just should have come on the train.

HOKE: Yassum. You should have.

Lights dim to suggest passage of time and come right back up again. It is night now. Daisy and Hoke are somewhat slumped on the seats. Hoke driving wearily.

DAISY: They fixed crab for me. Minnie always fixes crab. They go to so much trouble! It's all ruined by now! Oh Lord!

HOKE: We got to pull over, Miz Daisy.

DAISY: Is something wrong with the car?

HOKE: Nome. I got to bixcused.

DAISY: What?

HOKE: I got to make water.

DAISY: You should have thought of that back at the Standard Oil Station.

HOKE: Colored cain' use the toilet at no Standard Oil . . . You know dat.

DAISY: Well there's no time to stop. We'll be in Mobile soon. You can wait.

HOKE: Yassum. *(He drives a minute then stops the car)* Nome.

DAISY: I told you to wait!

HOKE: Yassum. I hear you. How you think I feel havin' to ax you when can I make my water like I some damn dog?

DAISY: Why, Hoke! I'd be ashamed!

HOKE: I ain't no dog and I ain' no chile and I ain' jes' a back of the neck you look at while you goin' wherever you want to go. I a man nearly seventy-two years old and I know when my bladder full and I getting' out dis car and goin' off down de road like I got to do. And I'm takin' de car key dis time. And that's de end of it.

He leaves the car, slamming his door, and exits. Daisy sits very still in the back seat. It's a dark country night. Crickets chirp, a dog barks.

DAISY: *(Angry)*: Hoke! *(She waits. No sound. Then, less angry)* Hoke! *(Silence. Darkness. Country sounds. Now she is frightened)* Hoke?

No answer. Light fades on her slowly and comes up on Boolie, in his office. He speaks into his phone in answer to an intercom buzz.

BOOLIE: Well, hell yes! Send him right on in here!

Hoke enters.

Isn't it your day off? To what do I owe this honor?

HOKE: We got to talk.

BOOLIE: What is it?

HOKE: It Mist' Sinclair Harris.

BOOLIE: My cousin Sinclair?
HOKE: His wife.
BOOLIE: Jeanette?
HOKE: The one talk funny.
BOOLIE: She's from Canton, Ohio.
HOKE: Yassuh. She tryin' to hire me.
BOOLIE: What?
HOKE: She phone when she know Miz Daisy be out and she say "How are they treating you, Hoke?" You know how she soun' like her nose stuff up. And I say "Fine" and she say "Well, if you looking for a change you know where to call."
BOOLIE: I'll be damned!
HOKE: I thought you want to know 'bout it.
BOOLIE: I'll be goddamned!
HOKE: Ain't she a mess?
   (A beat) She say name yo' sal'ry.
BOOLIE: I see. And did you?
HOKE: Did I what?
BOOLIE: Name your salary?
HOKE: Now what you think I am? I ain' studyin' workin' for no trashy somethin' like her.
BOOLIE: But she got you to thinking, didn't she?
HOKE: You might could say dat.
BOOLIE: Name your salary?
HOKE: Dat what she say.
BOOLIE: Well, how does sixty-five dollars a week sound?
HOKE: Sounds pretty good. Seventy-five sounds better.
BOOLIE: So it does. Beginning this week.
HOKE: Das mighty nice of you Mist' Werthan. I 'preciate it. Mist' Werthan, you ever had people fightin' over you?
BOOLIE: No.
HOKE: Well, I tell you. It feel good.

Light out on them. We hear a phone ringing. Light up on Daisy's house. It's a dark, winter morning and there is no light on in the house. Daisy enters, wearing her coat over her bathrobe and carrying a lit candle in a candle-stick. She is up in her eighties now and walks more carefully, but she is by no means decrepit.

DAISY: Hello?

Light up on Boolie at home, also dressed warmly.

BOOLIE: Mama, thank goodness! I was afraid your phone would be out.
DAISY: No, but I don't have any power.
BOOLIE: Nobody does. That's why I called.

Daisy: I found some candles. It reminds me of gaslight back on Forsyth Street. Seems like we had ice storms all the time back then.

Boolie: I can't come after you because my driveway is a sheet of ice. I'm sure yours is too.

Daisy: I'm all right, Boolie.

Boolie: I imagine they're working on the lines now. I'll go listen to my car radio and call you back. Don't go anywhere.

Daisy: Really? I thought I'd take a jog around the neighborhood.

Boolie: You're a doodle, Mama.

Daisy: Love to Florine.

Boolie: Uh-huh.

Light out on Boolie. Daisy talks to herself.

Daisy: Well, I guess that's the biggest lie I'll tell today.

She tries to read by the candlelight without much success. She hears the door to outside open and close and then footsteps. She stands alarmed.

Who is it?

Hoke enters carrying a paper bag and wearing an overcoat and galoshes.

Hoke: Mornin' Miz Daisy.

Daisy: Hoke. What in the world?

Hoke: I learn to drive on ice when I deliver milk for Avondale Dairy. Ain' much to it. I slip around a little comin' down Briarcliff, but nothin' happen. Other folks bangin' into each other like they in the funny papers, though. Oh, I stop at the 7-11. I figure yo' stove out and Lawd knows you got to have yo' coffee in the mornin'.

Daisy: *(Touched):* How sweet of you, Hoke.

He sips his own coffee.

Hoke: We ain' had good coffee roun' heah since Idella pass.

Daisy: You're right. I can fix her biscuits and you can fry her chicken, but nobody can make Idella's coffee. I wonder how she did it.

Hoke: I doan' nome. Every time the Hit Parade come on TV, it put me in mind of Idella.

Daisy: Yes.

Hoke: Sittin' up in de chair, her daughter say, spry as de flowers in springtime, watchin' the Hit Parade like she done ev'ry Sad'dy the Lawd sent and then, durin' the Lucky Strike Extra all of sudden, she belch and she gone.

Daisy: Idella was lucky.

Hoke: Yassum. I 'spec she was. *(He starts to exit)*

Daisy: Where are you going?

Hoke: Put deseheah things up. Take off my overshoes.

DAISY: I didn't think you'd come today.

HOKE: What you mean? It ain' my day off, is it?

DAISY: Well, I don't know what you can do around here except keep me company.

HOKE: I see can I light us a fire.

DAISY: Eat anything you want out of the icebox. It's all going to spoil anyway.

HOKE: Yassum.

DAISY: And wipe up what you tracked onto my kitchen floor.

HOKE: Now Miz Daisy, what you think I am? A mess? *(This is an old routine between them and not without affection)*

DAISY: Yes. That's exactly what I think you are.

HOKE: All right, then. All right.

He exits. She sits contented in her chair. The phone rings.

DAISY: Hello?

Light on Boolie.

BOOLIE: It'll all be melted by this afternoon. They said so on the radio. I'll be out after you as soon as I can get down the driveway.

DAISY: Stay where you are, Boolie. Hoke is here with me.

BOOLIE: How in the hell did he manage that?

DAISY: He's very handy. I'm fine. I don't need a thing in the world.

BOOLIE: Hello? Have I got the right number? I never heard you say loving things about Hoke before.

DAISY: I didn't say I love him. I said he was handy.

BOOLIE: Uh-huh.

DAISY: Honestly, Boolie. Are you trying to irritate me in the middle of an ice storm?

She hangs up the phone. Light out on her. Boolie stands a moment in wonder. Light out on him. In the dark we hear the sounds of horns blaring. A serious traffice jam. When the lights come up, Daisy is in the car, wearing a hat. She is anxious, twisting in her seat, looking out the window. Hoke enters.

Well what is it? You took so long!

HOKE: Couldn't help it. Big mess up yonder.

DAISY: What's the matter? I might as well not go to temple at all now!

HOKE: You cain' go to temple today, Miz Daisy.

DAISY: Why not? What in the world is the matter with you?

HOKE: Somebody done bomb the temple.

DAISY: What? Bomb the temple!

HOKE: Yassum. Dat why we stuck here so long.

DAISY: I don't believe it.

HOKE: That what the policeman tell me up yonder. Say it happen about a half hour ago.

DAISY: Oh no. Oh my God! Well, was anybody there? Were people hurt?

HOKE: Din' say.

DAISY: Who would do that?

HOKE: You know as good as me. Always be the same ones.

DAISY: Well, it's a mistake. I'm sure they meant to bomb one of the Conservative synagogues or the Orthodox one. The temple is Reform. Everybody knows that.

HOKE: It doan' matter to them people. A Jew is a Jew to them folks. Jes' like light or dark we all the same nigger.

DAISY: I can't believe it!

HOKE: I know jes' how you feel, Miz Daisy. Back down there above Macon on the farm—I 'bout ten or 'leven years old and one day my frien' Porter, his daddy hangin' from a tree. And the day befo', he laughin' and pitchin' horseshoes wid us. Talkin' 'bout Porter and me gon have strong good right arms like him and den he hangin' up yonder wid his hands tie behind his back an' the flies all over him. And I seed it with my own eyes and I throw up right where I standin'. You go on and cry.

DAISY: I'm not crying.

HOKE: Yassum.

DAISY: The idea! Why did you tell me that?

HOKE: I doan' know. Seem like disheah mess put me in mind of it.

DAISY: Ridiculous! The temple has nothing to do with that!

HOKE: So you say.

DAISY: We don't even know what happened. How do you know that policeman was telling the truth?

HOKE: Now why would that policeman go and lie 'bout a thing like that?

DAISY: You never get things right anyway.

HOKE: Miz Daisy, somebody done bomb that place and you know it too.

DAISY: Go on. Just go on now I don't want to hear any more about it.

HOKE: I see if I can get us outta here and take you home. You feel better at home.

DAISY: I don't feel bad.

HOKE: You de boss.

DAISY: Stop talking to me!

Lights fade on them. We hear the sound of applause. Boolie enters in a fine three-piece suit, holding a large silver bowl. He is very distinguished, in his late fifties.

BOOLIE: Thank you, Red. And thank you all. I am deeply grateful to be chosen man of the year by the Atlanta Business Council, an honor I've seen bestowed on some mightly fine fellas and which I certainly never expected to come to me. I'm afraid the loss here *(He touches his hair)*, and the gain here *(He touches his belly)*, have given me an air of competence I don't possess. But I'll tell you, I sure wish my father and my grandfather could see this. Seventy-two years ago they opened a little hole-in-the-wall shop on Whitehall Street with one printing press. They managed to grow with Atlanta and to this day, the Werthan Company believes we want what Atlanta wants. This award proves we must be right. Thank you. *(Applause)* One more thing. If the Jackets whup the Dawgs up in Athens Saturday afternoon, I'll be a completely happy man.

Light out on him. Daisy enters her living room and dials the phone. She dials with some difficulty. Things have become harder for her to do.

DAISY: Hidey, Miss McClatchey. You always recognize my voice. What a shame a wonderful girl like you never married. Miss McClatchey? Is my son in? Oh no. Please don't call him out of a sales meeting. Just give him a message. Tell him I bought the tickets for the UJA banquet. Yes, UJA banquet honoring Martin Luther King on the seventeenth. Well, you're a sweet thing to say so. And don't you worry. My cousin Tillie in Chattanooga married for the first time at fifty-seven.

Light dims and comes right back. Boolie has joined Daisy.

BOOLIE: How do you feel, Mama?
DAISY: Not a good question to ask somebody nearly ninety.
BOOLIE: Well you look fine.
DAISY: It's my ageless appeal.
BOOLIE: Miss McClatchey gave me your message.
DAISY: Florine is invited too.
BOOLIE: Thank you very much.
DAISY: I guess Hoke should drive us. There'll be a crowd.
BOOLIE: Mama, we have to talk about this.
DAISY: Talk about what?
BOOLIE: The feasibility of all this.
DAISY: Fine. You drive. I thought I was being helpful.
BOOLIE: You know I believe Martin Luther King has done some mighty fine things.
DAISY: Boolie, if you don't want to go, why don't you just come right out and say so?
BOOLIE: I want to go. You know how I feel about him.
DAISY: Of course, but Florine—
BOOLIE: Florine has nothing to do with it. I still have to conduct business in this town.
DAISY: I see. The Werthan Company will go out of business if you attend the King dinner?

BOOLIE: Not exactly. But a lot of the men I do business with wouldn't like it. They wouldn't come right out and say so. They'd just snicker and call me Martin Luther Werthan behind my back—something like that. And I'd begin to notice that my banking business wasn't being handled by the top dogs. Maybe I'd start to miss out on a few special favors, a few tips. I wouldn't hear about certain lunch meetings at the Commerce Club. Little things you can't quite put your finger on. And Jack Raphael over at Ideal Press, he's a New York Jew instead of a Georgia Jew and as long as you got to deal with Jews, the really smart ones come from New York, don't they? So some of the boys might start throwing business to Jack instead of old Martin Luther Werthan. I don't know. Maybe it wouldn't happen, but that's the way it works. If we don't use those seats, somebody else will and the good Doctor King will never know the difference, will he?

DAISY: If we don't use the seats? I'm not supposed to go either?

Boolie: Mama, you can do whatever you want.

DAISY: Thanks for your permission.

BOOLIE: Can I ask you something? When did you get so fired up about Martin Luther King? Time was, I'd have heard a different story.

DAISY: Why, Boolie! I've never been prejudiced and you know it!

BOOLIE: Okay. Why don't you ask Hoke to go to the dinner with you?

DAISY: Hoke? Don't be ridiculous. He wouldn't go.

BOOLIE: Ask him and see.

Boolie exits. Daisy puts on an evening wrap and a chiffon scarf over her hair. This is not done quickly. She moves slowly. When she is ready, Hoke enters and helps her into the car. They ride in silence for a moment.

DAISY: I don' know why you still drive. You can't see.

HOKE: Yassum I can.

DAISY: You didn't see that mailbox.

HOKE: How you know what I didn't see?

DAISY: It nearly poked through my window. This car is all scratched up.

HOKE: Ain' no sucha thing.

DAISY: How would you know? You can't see. What a shame. It's a bran' new car, too.

HOKE: You got this car two years come March.

DAISY: You forgot to turn.

HOKE: Ain' this dinner at the Biltmo'?

DAISY: You know it is.

HOKE: Biltmo' straight thissaway.

DAISY: You know so much.

HOKE: Yassum. I do.

DAISY: I've lived in Atlanta all my life.

HOKE: And ain' run a car in onto twenty years.

A beat.

DAISY: Boolie said the silliest thing the other day.

HOKE: Tha' right?

DAISY: He's too ole to be so foolish.

HOKE: Yassum. What did he say?

DAISY: Oh, he was talking about Martin Luther King. *(A beat)* I guess you know him, don't you?

HOKE: Martin Luther King? Nome.

DAISY: I was sure you did. But you've heard him preach?

HOKE: Same way as you—over the TV.

DAISY: I think he's wonderful.

HOKE: Yassum.

DAISY: You know, you could go see him in person anytime you wanted. *(No response)* All you'd have to do is go over there to the—what is it?

HOKE: Ebeneezer.

DAISY: Ebeneezer Baptist Church some Sunday and there he'll be.

HOKE: What you gettin' at, Miz Daisy?

DAISY: Well, it's so silly. Boolie said you wanted to go to this dinner with me tonight. Did you tell him that?

HOKE: Nome.

DAISY: I didn't think so. What would be the point? You can hear him anytime—whenever you want.

HOKE: You want the front do' or the side do' to the Biltmore?

DAISY: I think the side. Isn't it wonderful the way things are changing?

HOKE: What you think I am, Miz Daisy?

DAISY: What do you mean?

HOKE: You think I some somethin' sittin' up here doan' know nothin' 'bout how to do?

DAISY: I don't know what you're talking about.

HOKE: Invitation to disheah dinner come in the mail a mont' ago. Did be you want me go wid you, how come you wait till we in the car on the way to ask me?

DAISY: What? All I said was that Boolie said you wanted to go.

HOKE: *(Sulking):* Mmm-hmmm.

DAISY: You know you're welcome to come, Hoke.

HOKE: Mmmm-hmmm.

DAISY: Oh my stars. Well, aren't you a great big baby!

HOKE: Nevermind baby, next time you ask me someplace, ask me regular.

DAISY: You don't have to carry on so much!

HOKE: Das all. Less drop it.

DAISY: Honestly!

HOKE: Things changin', but they ain' change all dat much. *(They are at the door)* I hep you to the do'.

DAISY: Thank you, Hoke. I can help myself.

Daisy gets herself out of the car, which takes some effort. Hoke sits still in his seat. Daisy looks at him when she is out of the car, but thinks better of what she was going to say and walks slowly towards the door. Lights out on them and up on Boolie at his house.

BOOLIE: *(On the phone)*: Hello, Hoke? How are you?

HOKE: I'm tolerable, Mist' Werthan.

BOOLIE: What can I do for you this morning?

HOKE: It yo' mama.

BOOLIE: What's the matter?

HOKE: She worked up.

BOOLIE: Why should today be different from any other day?

HOKE: No, this ain' the same.

DAISY: *(Offstage)*: Hoke?

HOKE: Yassum? *(Back to phone)* She think she teachin' school. I'm real worried 'bout her. She ain' makin' sense.

BOOLIE: I'll be right there.

Lights out on Boolie. He exits. Daisy enters. She is in disarray. Her hair is not combed and her housecoat is open, the slip showing underneath.

DAISY: Hoke? Hoke?

HOKE: Yassum?

DAISY: Where did you put my papers?

HOKE: Ain' no papers, Miz Daisy.

DAISY: My papers! I had them all corrected last night and I put them in the front so I wouldn't forget them on my way to school. What did you do with them?

HOKE: You talkin' outta yo' head.

DAISY: The children will be so disappointed if I don't give them their homework back. I always give it back the next day. That's why they like me. Why aren't you helping me?

HOKE: What you want me to do, Miz Daisy?

DAISY: Give me the papers. I told you. It's all right if you moved them. I won't be mad with you. But I've got to get to school now. I'll be late and who will take care of my class? They'll be all alone. Oh God! Oh Goddy! I do everything wrong.

HOKE: Set down. You about to fall and hurt yo'seff.

DAISY: It doesn't matter. I'm sorry. It's all my fault. I didn't do right. It's so awful! Oh God!

HOKE: Now you lissen heah. Ain' nothing awful 'cep the way you carryin' on.

DAISY: I'm so sorry. It's all my fault. I can't find the papers and the children are waiting.
HOKE: No they ain'. You ain' no teacher no mo'.
DAISY: It doesn't make any difference.
HOKE: Miz Daisy, ain' nothin' the matter wit' you.
DAISY: You don't know. You don't know. What's the difference?
HOKE: Your mind done took a turn this mornin' thass all.
DAISY: Go on. Just go on now.
HOKE: You snap right back if you jes' let yo'seff.
DAISY: I can't! I can't!
HOKE: You a lucky ole woman, you know dat?
DAISY: No! No! It's all a mess now. And I can't do anything about it!
HOKE: You rich, you well for your time and you got people care about what happen to you.
DAISY: I'm being trouble. Oh God, I don't want to be trouble to anybody.
HOKE: You want something to cry about, I take you to the state home, show you what layin' out dere in de halls.
DAISY: Oh my God!
HOKE: An' I bet none of them take on bad as you doin'.
DAISY: I'm sorry. I'm so sorry. Those poor children in my class.
HOKE: You keep dis up, I promise, Mist' Werthan call the doctor on you and just as sho' as you born, that doctor gon have you in de insane asylum fore you know what hit you. Dat de way you want it to be?

Daisy looks at him. She speaks in her normal voice.

DAISY: Hoke, do you still have that Oldsmobile?
HOKE: From when I firs' come here? Go on, Miz Daisy, that thing been in the junkyard fifteen years or more. I drivin' yo' next-to-las' car now, '63 Cadillac, runnin' fine as wine.
DAISY: You ought not to be driving anything, the way you see.
HOKE: How you know the way I see, 'less you lookin' outta my eyes?
DAISY: Hoke?
HOKE: Yassum?
DAISY: You're my best friend.
HOKE: Come on, Miz Daisy. You jes'—
DAISY: No. Really. You are. You are. *(She takes his hand)*
HOKE: Yassum.

The lights fades on them. Boolie enters. He is sixty-five now. He walks slowly around Daisy's living room, picking up a book here and there, examining an ashtray. He leafs through his mother's little leather phone book and puts it in his pocket. Hoke enters. He is eighty-five. He shuffles a bit and his glasses are very thick.

HOKE: Mornin' Mist' Werthan.

BOOLIE: Well Hoke, good to see you. You didn't drive yourself out here?

HOKE: Nawsuh. I doan' drive now. My granddaughter run me out.

BOOLIE: My Lord, is she old enough to drive?

HOKE: Michelle thirty-seven. Teach biology at Spelman College.

BOOLIE: I never knew that.

HOKE: Yassuh.

BOOLIE: I've taken most of what I want out of the house. Is there anything you'd like before the Goodwill comes?

HOKE: My place full to burstin' now.

BOOLIE: It feels funny to sell the house while Mama's still alive.

HOKE: I 'gree.

BOOLIE: But she hasn't even been inside the door for two years. I know I'm doing the right thing.

HOKE: Doan' get me into it.

BOOLIE: I'm not going to say anything to her about it.

HOKE: You right there.

BOOLIE: By the way, Hoke, your check is going to keep coming every week—as long as you're there to get it.

HOKE: I 'preciate that, Mist' Werthan.

BOOLIE: You can rest easy about it. I suppose you don't get out to see Mama very much.

HOKE: It hard, not drivin'. Dat place ain' on no bus line. I goes in a taxicab sometime.

BOOLIE: I'm sure she appreciates it.

HOKE: Some days she better than others. Who ain't?

BOOLIE: Well, we'd better get on out there. I guess you have a turkey dinner to get to and so do I. Why don't we call your granddaughter and tell her I'll run you home?

They exit and the light comes up on Daisy, ninety-seven, slowly moving forward with a walker. She seems fragile and diminished, but still vital. A hospital chair and a table are nearby. Boolie and Hoke join her.

Happy Thanksgiving, Mama. Look who I brought.

Boolie helps Daisy from her walker into her chair.

HOKE: Mornin', Miz Daisy. *(She nods)* You keepin' yo'seff busy?

Silence.

BOOLIE: She certainly is. She goes to jewelry making—how many times a week is it, Mama? She makes all kinds of things. Pins and bracelets. She's a regular Tiffanys.

HOKE: Ain't that something.

Daisy seems far away.

BOOLIE: *(Keeping things going):* Hoke, you know I thought of you the other morning on the Expressway. I saw an Avondale milk truck.

HOKE: You doan' say.

BOOLIE: A big monster of a thing, must've had sixteen wheels. I wonder how you'd have liked driving that around.

DAISY: *(Suddenly)* Hoke came to see me, not you.

HOKE: This one of her good days.

BOOLIE: Florine says to wish you a Happy Thanksgiving. She's in Washington, you know. *(No response)* You remember, Mama. She's a Republican National Committeewoman now.

DAISY: Good God! *(Hoke laughs, Boolie grins)* Boolie!

BOOLIE: What is it, Mama?

DAISY: Go charm the nurses.

BOOLIE: *(To Hoke):* She wants you all to herself. *(To Daisy)* You're a doodle, Mama.

Boolie exits. Daisy dozes for a minute in her chair. Then she looks at Hoke.

DAISY: Boolie payin' you still?

HOKE: Every week.

DAISY: How much?

HOKE: That between me an' him, Miz Daisy.

DAISY: Highway robbery. *(She closes her eyes again. Then opens them)* How are you?

HOKE: Doin' the bes' I can.

DAISY: Me too.

HOKE: Well, thass all there is to it, then.

She nods, smiles. Silence. He sees the piece of pie on the table.

Looka here. You ain' eat yo' Thanksgiving pie.

She tries to pick up her fork. Hoke takes the plate and fork from her.

Lemme hep you wid this.

He cuts a small piece of pie with the fork and gently feeds it to her. Then another as the lights fade slowly out.

END OF PLAY

The Left Hand Singing

Barbara Lebow

Barbara Lebow

B arbara Lebow, born in Brooklyn and graduated from Vassar College, moved to Atlanta during the early sixties, forming an affiliation with the Academy Theatre where many of her twenty plays originated, including *Shayna Maidel, Little Joe Monaghan, The Keepers, Tiny Tim Is Dead* and, in 1997, *The Left Hand Singing.*

As head of the Academy's human service program, and more recently in her role as Alabama Shakespeare Festival playwright-in-residence, she has also directed the group development of plays with disenfranchised populations: the homeless, *People of the Brick;* the addicted, *On the Edge;* the developmentally disabled, *I Want to Be,* and the imprisoned, *Transformations: Reality by Degrees.*[1] "I get a great deal of pleasure from watching people who doubt their own value, watching them light up and discover that they've got something to say that others respond to—that an audience responds to . . . The energy that is released by working with people in this way also feeds my own creative energy."[2]

The Left Hand Singing, focusing on the surviving parents of three young people murdered while trying to register Black voters in the South, invites comparisons to the real individuals who were among those murdered during the civil rights struggle: James Chaney, Andrew Goodman and Michael Schwerner. With the help of a Fellowship from the John Simon Guggenheim Foundation, Lebow researched the period conscientiously, studying biographies, newspaper articles, watching videotapes and newsreel footage. She also interviewed living people who remembered the voter registration drives and could express feelings about the sacrifices made during the fifties and sixties by African Americans, and by Jewish and Christian whites who risked their lives to help them. She spoke to those who could comment on the progress recorded over the decades and on the decline in idealism and hopefulness during the nineties. When asked whether she was concerned how audiences would receive her depiction of a real person for her play *Lurleen,* based on Lurleen Wallace, Lebow revealed a significant aspect of the playwright's connection to characters or situations rooted in real events.

> I am always concerned about how an audience is going to receive any play that I write. I know there will be people who love it and those who don't because we are all very different. There's always an element of me in my writing; this carries the fear and excitement of self-exposure. I don't think I could have written this without finding parts of myself in Lurleen. I identify with her as a mother and with her struggle to become herself. I always write out of a core of emotion and figure that if I feel something, at least a portion of the audience will feel the same.[3]

The core of emotion which forms the wellspring for Lebow's plays runs deep and includes a rare combination of compassion and toughness that won't brook sentimentality. Thus the friendship and easy interaction of the three students in *The Left Hand Singing,* an African American young woman, a Jewish young woman and a Protestant young man, who embark hopefully on a journey to register voters in the South, is not duplicated in the nineties in the relationship of their surviving parents. Lebow will not allow us to bask in past advances, but challenges us to deal with present inter-group conflict. Whether as the catalyst for new plays created by the previously disenfranchised, or the creator of her own plays, Lebow demands that we hear authentic voices that transport us beyond stereotypes, a little closer to the truth.

Notes

1. Sarah Blacher Cohen, *Making a Scene: The Contemporary Drama of Jewish-American Women* (Syracuse, NY: Syracuse University Press, 1997), p. 73.

2. http://home.adelphia.net/~dgeisen/lebow.htm.

3. Ibid.

The Left Hand Singing

Cast of Characters

LINDA WINNNICK: 20, a college sophomore, Jewish, from New York City. Her innocence is covered by a veneer of toughness.

HONEY JOHNSON: 20, a college sophomore, African American, from Opelika, Alabama. Her cover is humor and sarcasm.

WESLEY PARTRIDGE: 21, a college junior, white, Methodist, from Charlotte, NC. Unsure, self-deprecating, and wanting to please, he hasn't quite caught up with himself.

BEA WINNICK: changes from 40 upward, LINDA's mother. She is compact, with a ready, nervous energy.

MADDY JOHNSON: changes from 52 upward, HONEY's mother. Outwardly calm. She is secure, stubborn.

REV. JOHN PARTRIDGE: changes from 50 upward, WES's father. He tries to contain his emotions, take care of others first. His idealism, hopefulness, and innocence are like his son's.

CLAIRE PARTRIDGE: changes from 46 upward, WES's mother. Outwardly, a classic southern lady. She is always surprising.

All characters speak with regional rhythms and pronunciation. There are recognizably similar physical, vocal, and emotional patterns within each family.

The action of the play takes place between the end of May, 1964, and the beginning of June, 1994, in a college in upstate New York and various locations in Mississippi, NYC, North Carolina, and Alabama.

One stage area, a realistic college dormitory room, is used only for the students' scenes together. A wall clock in the room reads 10:12 as the play begins. At the start of each successive scene, the clock continues from the moment the previous scene ends.

The other stage areas are flexible. Specific locations are indicated by suggestion. The characters' movements among them define changes in time and place. Depending on technical capabilities, these settings can use actual pieces, built-ins, or "floating" benches and to represent required furniture.

Music not otherwise indicated can be found in Ravel's *Concerto for the Left Hand* and *Concerto in G major*, Gershwin's *Concerto in F* and the *1812 Overture* by P.I. Tchaikovsky. There are various adaptations of *I'm On My Way*, a traditional song. Suggested is a recording by Barbara

Dane, in a 2 CD collection, *Freedom Is a Constant Struggle: Songs of the Mississippi Civil Rights Movement,* Folk Era Productions. Her cut is listed as "Used by permission of Dreadnaught Music, BMI." The CD is produced by Susie Erenrich, Cultural Center for Social Change, Washington, D.C. (© 1994).

Walls in the dorm room and floors in all areas are dark, muted, non-reflective, to help with the isolation in the lighting and with the students exiting and entering invisibility for the crossfades at the beginning and end of the parents' scenes.

Act 1

Scene 1: *A small college, upstate N.Y., late May, 1964, around 10:15 PM. A women's dormitory room. There are muted posters featuring JFK, MLK Jr., Che, the Beatles. A football jersey reading "BUBBA," pink cheerleading pom-poms, and other bits of memorabilia adorn the walls. The two beds (one unmade), desks, floor pillows, and spool table hold assorted books, clothing, LP albums from library, food.*

Ravel's Concerto for the Left Hand is heard, a clear piano section. As lights rise, the music lowers and shifts to a small phonograph. LINDA and HONEY are barefoot, in the midst of books, papers, notes, shoes, LPs. They are each reading and making notes. During these scenes, the students sit on floor, beds, and, sometimes, chairs. The door is ajar.

LINDA yawns, plays with her pencil, eats a potato chip, finishes a Coke. Finally, with a show of exhaustion, she falls on the unmade bed, putting her open book over her face.

HONEY: *(Amused familiarity)* What are you doing now?
LINDA: *(Lifting book bottom)* I'm listening.
HONEY: No, you're not. Any second, you're going to start that awful snoring again.
LINDA: I told you, I never snore!
HONEY: You snore like a horse. With adenoids! Mouth all open and drooling.
LINDA: Liar!
HONEY: It kept me up half the night! Now you're gonna keep me from studying.
LINDA: It just so happens, I'm wide awake. Memorizing the music.
HONEY: And the Nietzsche by osmosis, I suppose. A brilliant way to study! Ravel, accompanied by *(Snorts loudly)*.
LINDA: All right, already!

She slams the book onto the floor. HONEY *answers with a loud chair adjustment,* LINDA *stomps her foot as she stands. She moves to the book and begins repeated rises on it.*

LINDA: *(cont.)* *(Pleased, in exercise rhythm)* Osmosis my *foot*... of Nietzsche ... And if Professor Dahlberg ... plays the Ravel ... for the exam ... I'll remember it ... Plus build my muscles.

HONEY: So you can chase after Wes on one of his endless hikes.

LINDA: So I can wear shorts.

HONEY: Nothing you do is gonna put any shape in those legs.

LINDA: Thanks a lot, pal!

HONEY: Heck! You're not going to study! You aim to slide past like always. Maybe you can afford that, but us po' scholarships can't get by with no C's. *(She lifts the arm off the record.)*

LINDA: *(Stopping the rises)* I never got a C in my life! Besides, whatever you accomplish here is nothing compared to what we're gonna be doing in Mississippi.

HONEY: *(After a beat)* There's something I better tell you. You might not like this, but—*(Pause)* I got a letter today. Curtis wants me to help him sell cars all summer instead.

LINDA: You're kidding!

HONEY: What's wrong with that? With him down at Morehouse and me up here the rest of the year. We both need the money. If he's going to law school and I'm gonna teach—

LINDA: *(Outraged)* Talk of someone chasing after someone! I can't believe—after convincing me about how bad things are down there—I can't believe you'd consider some half-baked scheme of—

HONEY: It so happens his uncle's got an empty lot where we can put up banners like at the big places. And we'll be working together, building for the future.

LINDA: "Building for the future?" A quote from Curtis, I'll bet. He just wants to keep an eye on you. Also, he thinks Mississippi is a waste of time. You should find a boyfriend who's socially conscious, at least.

HONEY: Like Wes, who's so "socially conscious" he won't even try to hold your hand? Looks like you'll have to help him along, po' thing.

LINDA: *(Flustered)* I keep telling you he's happy just being friends! *(She hurries to put the arm down on the record again.)* And so am I.

HONEY: Now give me some peace and quiet and let me get back to work.

LINDA: You want me to turn it off?

HONEY: Please!

LINDA: But killer Music 101! Followed by killer Philosophy 210! How are we ever gonna pass both of them?

HONEY: By doing one thing at a time. Or I can go over to the library.

LINDA: But Wes might come by.

HONEY: *(Looking at the clock)* No men in the dorm past eleven. He doesn't have much time. Anyway, I don't have to be here.

LINDA: Yes, you do.

HONEY: So you can use me for a cover? I think Wesley Partridge is half the reason you're going to Mississippi.

LINDA: And Curtis Andrews is why you might not go! I'd be there even without Wes. I'm committed to the Movement.

HONEY: And I'm committed to getting my work done. *(She jumps up, grabs her books, ready to leave.* LINDA *lifts the arm from the record.)* Blessed silence. Thank you.

LINDA: How are we supposed to tell Ravel from Debussy, anyway? And Nietzsche from what's-his-name? This is gonna help me in government studies?

HONEY: "Government studies?" What happened to pre-law?

LINDA: Too narrow.

HONEY: So it's gone the way of pre-med and anthropology and Greco-Roman whatever it was and—?

LINDA: They take too long. The bomb'll probably blow us up first anyway. Hiroshima . . . BOOM! Besides, we won't remember any of this stuff when we're forty!

HONEY: It's not supposed to be easy all the time, Lin. You're spoiled. Comes from being an only child, po' thing.

LINDA: What's with this "po' thing" every minute?

HONEY: Something my mama says.

LINDA: She doesn't talk like that.

HONEY: How do you know? You ever been down south?

LINDA: Florida.

HONEY: *Flahrida* doesn't count. Just wait till you get to Mississippi, Miss Subways. You and them speak a different tongue, 'specially the white ones.

LINDA: Not Wes. Not every white southerner belongs to the Klan, you know.

HONEY: Wes doesn't count. He's from *North* Carolina. Kind of eccentric anyway. Like you.

LINDA: Look how she picks on me! And I was glad when I got you for a roommate!

HONEY: So you could show off how open-minded you are. The minute I saw you I knew you were a knee-jerk.

LINDA: I only stuck with you because of your yellow sweater.

HONEY: Your purple socks. "Damn if the girl ain't just my size," I thought, "Let me see what I can take advantage of."

LINDA: Of course, if I had your coloring I'd look much better in it.

HONEY: And if I had your hair I could toss my head around like a Breck commercial.

LINDA: The dean said, *(Nasally)* "We'll stick the *colored* one and the *Jewish* one together so—"

HONEY: Look, shut up for ten minutes, then you can put Ravel back on and we'll trade your thin little Nietzsche for my big fat Descartes. *(Lifting a much thicker book)* He'll be better for our legs.

LINDA: Deal.

WES rushes in, carrying three mugs of coffee and a canvas briefcase. LINDA quickly removes her eyeglasses.

WES: I'm only here for a minute. Things are definitely not going well!

LINDA: What things?

WES: *(Giving a mug to each before his dire announcement)* Harvey Weintraub is dropping out.

LINDA: Who?

WES: Tall guy, skinny, bad complexion, glasses? I figured you knew him.

LINDA: Because he's Jewish?

WES: *(After a moment of embarrassment)* Of course not! Because he comes from New York. *(Quick laughter from LINDA and HONEY)* It's just that Weintraub came to me! He knew I was recruiting for the summer and he came to me! I thought he was interested. Now he says he's going to be a camp counselor in Vermont!

HONEY: A right smart fella', that Weintraub.

WES: I said I'd have six volunteers by the end of exams. If Weintraub drops out, I'll only have four.

HONEY: How do you get that?

WES: The freshman from Indiana and us.

HONEY: Wait a minute. I never said I was definite.

WES: But you're the one got me interested in the first place!

HONEY: Maybe I was wrong.

LINDA: Curtis is giving her trouble about going.

HONEY: Not to mention my whole family.

WES: Same with mine. *(To HONEY)* Listen here. This is the biggest thing I've ever been involved in. The most important. You know that, even if most of the creeps around here don't. You can't let me—us—the project—down.

HONEY: I swear I never saw someone in such a hurry to go where they're not wanted.

LINDA: Now, that sounds like your big brother. Of course we're not wanted. By the rednecks. That's the whole point.

HONEY: Or by the law. Sedrick knows what he's talking about. Got a good wash down with a fire hose in Birmingham. Of course, Mississippi might not be as bad as Alabama.

WES: Spare us your sarcasm, please, Miss Honey.

HONEY: Listen, you two. If you're determined to save Negroes this summer, then my advice is *(WES)* you go and corral that Harvey what's-his-name and *(LINDA)* you quit batting your eyes and pay some attention to Nietzsche. Or you'll find yourself in summer school till September and the whole thing'll be moot.

WES: You're right. I'm going after Weintraub. Then I'll come back and see to you. *(On his way out, he quickly grabs some papers from his case, gives one to each of the women)* Here. Look at these. I wrote out some basic things about schedule, housing, orientation and all. You can use it on your mothers. *(Grabbing a flyer for Weintraub)* Like the song says, I'm on my way.

HONEY: What would you know about that song?

LINDA: We sing it at meetings. *(Starts to sing, an example)* I'M ON MY WAY/AND I WON'T BE BACK/I'M ON MY—

HONEY: *(Hands over ears)* Spare me! I know that song and you don't. *(To WES)* And I don't want to hear you try, either.

WES: *(Leaving again)* Nothing you say, none of your cruel words, shall deter the invincible Partridge!

HONEY laughs. WES stops again, looks at her.

HONEY: Pardon. "The Invincible Partridge." Sounds like a cartoon. Something like the Roadrunner.

WES, still leaving, stops at the record player.

WES: I see you're on the twentieth century. *(Picking up the record)* Concerto for the Left Hand. Depressing. Written for a guy whose right hand got cut off.

HONEY: Cut off? Why?

WES: For making fun of people's names. *(LINDA giggles)*

HONEY: I said, pardon. How do you know so much, anyway?

LINDA: He got a B+ from Dahlberg last year.

WES: *(Mockingly, playing the piano in the air with his free hand)* Lady Claire used to play it. Endlessly.

HONEY: Your mother.

WES: *(Picking another record)* This one's better.

He puts it on the player, puts the needle down well into the piece, exits.

LINDA: *(Calling after WES)* Good luck!

Pause. They listen for a moment.

HONEY: Concerto in G major.

LINDA: Show off!

HONEY: Poor Weintraub! He's about to be attacked by the Invincible Partridge! *(She beeps like the Roadrunner)*

LINDA: Don't make fun of him!

HONEY: *(Victorious)* Aha! Told you.

LINDA: *(Flustered)* It's just that he means well. Like a little kid. *(She hurries to pick up her book, hides behind it.)*

HONEY: *(Going to* LINDA, *tipping the book away from her face.)* Why, Miss Linda, you're blushing.

LINDA *and* HONEY *giggle,* LINDA *embarrassed. Quick blackout when—*

Scene 2.—*the Ravel is cut off by two sudden, amplified rings of a telephone. It is late August, 1964. A tight spot rises on* BEA, *away from the students' area.*

BEA: The phone was ringing, but I couldn't answer it! I couldn't pull myself out of my dream, like I was stuck in mud. *(Terrified, as if waking from a nightmare)* Those boys! Those three murdered boys!

A tight spot up on MADDY JOHNSON, *coming in instantly. Each parent picks up, without pause, from the previous speaker.*

MADDY: I have faith in the Lord. I know He wouldn't let nothing happen to Honey and her friends, except for them getting lost or something like that.

A tight light rises on JOHN, *quiet, intense.*

JOHN: The phone rang at three AM, but Claire didn't move. We're used to bells. Telephones, doorbells, church bells. Calling the faithful. Marking time. Marking events. It was Miss Hightower calling from Clemens, Mississippi, asking if I was Reverend Partridge. *(Light out)*

MADDY: Miss Hightower called Sedrick in the middle of the night and told how Honey and the other two came up missing, so he stopped by in the morning to tell me. His face was set and hard, like a wood carving. *(Light out)*

BEA: Linda wrote me. "Miss Hightower's a classic, Mom—could be Ethel Barrymore's twin. And it's the safest place in the whole state to stay because no one, not even the Klan, would bother her. They just think she's senile, putting all us volunteers up and they respect her 'impeccable heritage.'"

As JOHN *speaks, the lights widen. The parents are in a small waiting area of the sheriff's office in Clemens, Mississippi.* BEA *is pacing,* MADDY *is seated,* JOHN *standing, speaking to both women. The scene continues without interruption.*

JOHN: She wanted me to know that the three of them were so close, like family, with Wes the big brother, but they should have been back hours ago. She asked if Wes is a careful driver.

BEA: Miss Hightower. Miss Hightower said they were—

MADDY: *(Concerned, but deferential, maintaining her "place" with strangers)* Miz Winnick, you're shaking something awful. Why don't you sit down for a while?

BEA: I can't! How can I? You know what she said? Miss Hightower? Before they even called the FBI? "Our people are already searching." Not looking for them, but searching, she said. That's so much worse! To search, rather than look!

JOHN: All we know is they went to some little dirt road village to help folks study for the votin' test. Right away, I thought of the other three, just the same as you. Those three murdered boys in the mud. The burnt-out station wagon. God forgive me, but it gives me hope— that the same thing could not happen again.

BEA: Even before those boys were found, I begged her to come home. I begged! I know she was scared—Don't tell me all those kids weren't scared—but she wouldn't hear of it.

MADDY: Same with Honey. Told me they'd be safer than before, with the FBI finally down here.

JOHN: Well, it makes sense, don't you think? Wesley said the same thing. FBI all over. No one would try anything now. It makes sense.

BEA: *(To JOHN)* What time is it, Reverend? The sheriff's supposed to see us at three—

JOHN: It's not even five after, Mrs. Winnick.

BEA: Have you met him? Sheriff Mack?

JOHN: Not yet.

BEA: I'll bet he's fat and stupid and spits tobacco.

JOHN: Like in the movies? No, he was rather quick and terse on the phone, like he was doing me a favor.

MADDY: *(Quietly)* Was just plain rude to me.

BEA: Condescending S.O.B.! I couldn't even get through to him!

JOHN: All he told me was he was too busy to go through this three times. So, here we are together.

BEA: *(To MADDY)* Are you cold? My hands are like ice. They won't warm up.

MADDY: Feels kind of warm to me in here. But you're such a jittery little thing . . .

JOHN: We'll have some answers soon. Why don't you sit down, Mrs. Winnick?

BEA looks at him, sits, making an attempt to compose herself.

BEA: *(To JOHN)* Linda speaks highly of Wesley. Wes.

JOHN: I know. Her friendship means a lot to him, Mrs. Winnick.

BEA: I only met him once, but I could tell he's a nice boy. And call me Bea. Please.

JOHN: John.

They look at MADDY, who hesitates.

BEA: Mrs. Johnson?

MADDY: Madeline. Everyone calls me Maddy.

BEA: They said the kids would probably show up so why waste a trip all the way down from New York. But how could I wait?

MADDY: Honey's boyfriend—that's Curtis, a fine young man—and Sedrick, my boy, wanted to come before me, but I talked them out of it.

JOHN: Sedrick—is he older than Honey?

MADDY: Yes, sir. He's the one started callin' her "Honey," when I named her "Harriet" for Harriet Tubman. Thought she belonged to him since she the one come next. Now he's mad at everything 'round her, even mad at Curtis.

JOHN: He just wants to protect his little sister. Jack—Wesley's big brother— was a fighter like that. Wes used to shut down tight and cover his ears when they teased him at school every Christmas with that "partridge in a pear tree," while Jack would come out swinging.

MADDY: That's Sedrick all right! Your Wesley seems more peaceable.

BEA: That's one of the things Linda likes so much about him. And she's always been a good child herself. Always tells the truth. She said she'd be safe with Miss Hightower and at school!

MADDY: I told Sedrick they were better off staying with a white lady in town, 'stead of in the country in a colored farmer's house like the others, but—

BEA: *(Pacing again)* I should have forbidden her to go. Just plain said no, but I couldn't. She wanted it so much! And I thought by some of the parents going to Washington to ask—*beg*—for protection, they'd at least—

MADDY: All that didn't do no good.

BEA: Till after the three boys. *(Abruptly panicked again)* How can they go on—their parents? With something so horrible. Unspeakable. With their children gone forever! How can they wake up each day knowing what happened? How can they survive it?

JOHN: *(Going to BEA, the counselor)* Because . . . because if they don't, if they don't survive, it would be like . . . like their children never lived.

Pause. BEA sits again, breathes deeply, trying to gain control of herself.

MADDY: *(After a while, to JOHN)* Is Mrs. Partridge coming?

JOHN: Mrs. Partridge is ill, at home.

MADDY: *(With BEA)* I'm sorry to hear that.

BEA: *(With MADDY)* I'm sorry.

JOHN: Thank you both for your concern.

Pause.

MADDY: *(To BEA)* Your girl favors you.

BEA: You've met Linda?

MADDY: Honey told me. And I saw that picture they took together. The funny one.

BEA: From Stunt Night?

JOHN: Their skit?

MADDY: Honey said they sang like the Supremes. "Baby Love," with some new words—

JOHN: "Bubba Love."

They all chuckle.

BEA: The girls dressed up like football players!

MADDY: Chawin' and spittin'—

They all laugh disproportionately.

JOHN: My son made quite a cheer leader.

BEA: With pink pom-poms—

JOHN: And hairy legs!

MADDY: The girls had shoulders out to here—

BEA: And five-o'clock shadow! *(To MADDY, hardly able to speak)* And you saw the resemblance from that?

MADDY nods midst near hysterical laughter.

BEA: *(Cont.)* Thanks a lot!

The two women burst out again. They fall silent, look at each other for a moment.

BEA: *(Cont.)* I'm glad you're here. *(Pause.)* What's taking so long?

They sit in silence.

JOHN: *(After a while)* Wesley is a careful driver. A good driver.

BEA: The deputy said they knew he drove fast. He was caught speeding more than once. That's what was implied.

MADDY: I wouldn't believe what no deputy says. Or no sheriff. No, sir. That's why I'm here now, instead of Sedrick. He would tell them to their face and wind up in more trouble.

Pause.

JOHN: Have either of you met Miss Hightower?

MADDY: No, sir. I came here straight from the bus station.

BEA: *(Shaking her head)* The airport. But I intend to go over there.

JOHN: I have my car. I'll be happy to take you both to the house after they speak with us.

BEA: What's it like? The house?

JOHN: Filled with young people packing up to go home. Five and six to a room. Mattresses on the floor. *(He hesitates.)* There are also mattresses pushed up against the walls. And across the windows. *(Quickly)* Now, don't get the wrong idea—I'm sure it's only a precaution—just in case. They haven't had the slightest bit of trouble.

BEA: But Linda said—

MADDY: Your girl don't want you to worry. Mine either. Same with my other children. Y'all know how that is.

BEA: Linda's an only child.

JOHN: *(After a beat)* Wesley's brother died in Korea. *(Pause)* That's why I'm inclined to be so concerned over Claire—Mrs. Partridge. But just because she—we—lost Jack, doesn't mean we're going to lose Wes. Just the opposite. It couldn't happen. Not twice.

MADDY: That's right. You're a man of God, a good man. You already had your grief. No way the Lord's going to give you and your wife no more to suffer. Now, with respects, if the boy was colored and the girls white, then there could be some real trouble. But this here's going to turn out fine.

JOHN: Miss Hightower believes they will play it down, encourage us to keep it quiet. So if it's nothing, we won't be embarrassed.

BEA: And if they *are* in danger? Linda's not the type to go running off to Mexico on a whim. Without telling me.

MADDY: Neither is Honey. But maybe that's just what they did for once. Said, "The whole thing's almost over. Freedom Summer's almost over. We've done our work. Now let's have us a little freedom summer of our own for a change, before school begins again."

BEA: Yeah. Why would anyone threaten them when they're all getting ready to leave, anyhow? The three boys . . . that was to scare off everyone else. But at this late date—

JOHN: That's what I told Claire. They're all good kids, serious kids, our three. Individually, they'd never do anything rash. But together—

MADDY: Sure! They're having themselves a good time somewhere. Up north! Gonna send us a postcard. Had to get away from this heat for a bit is all.

They sit silently.

OFFSTAGE VOICE: Reverend Partridge? Miz Winnick? If ya'll 'll follow me now, Sheriff Mack is waitin' for you.

The three stand, look at each other quickly, and begin walking in to see the sheriff as lights fade on them and the interrupted Ravel from Scene 1 is heard.

Scene 3. *Lights rise on HONEY and LINDA, who are giggling, continued from the end of Scene 1. HONEY picks up WES's flyer, reads it to herself as LINDA puts on her glasses and returns to her book.*

HONEY: *(Reading pointedly from the flyer)* "In answer to some of your questions: There is no expectation that the Federal government will protect us in any way." *(Turning off the music)* This is your dreamboat's brilliant information that's supposed to help me with Curtis? And mama?

LINDA: He's laying out the facts the way you should in any movement, any revolution. If you sugar coat the message, the troops get suspicious.

HONEY: Well, he ain't no Che Guevara, I'll tell you that. *(Reading)* "The orientation will include training on how to deal with local police and hostile mobs. You will be well schooled in the principles of non-violence."

LINDA: He's being realistic.

HONEY: Fat lot of good that does! You know what happened in Birmingham. You ready to get your head bashed in? What about *your* mother, for goodness' sake? (*NY accent*) I'm so worried about my little princess! My Linda!

LINDA: As I've already explained to the queen of Jewish Motherhood, there's a big difference between demonstrating and working quietly, helping people pass a test.

HONEY: If you want to go teach some poor colored sharecroppers how to appreciate Ravel—

LINDA: Very funny.

HONEY:—maybe no one will care, but teaching them how to get past that voting test will not go unnoticed. It's worse than demonstrating. Mississippi's a foreign country. People who've tried to change things down there have been getting killed—*killed*, hear?—for years.

LINDA: I'm going to do this. We've got to set an example, even if some of us do get hurt.

HONEY: You've got a Joan of Arc complex.

LINDA: So what if I do? It happens she accomplished something.

HONEY: On second thought, maybe it's a Little Red Ridinghood complex. You're skipping merrily through the woods with your basket of do-goodies, and the Klan is just drooling, licking its chops.

LINDA: Yeah? Well, I'm tougher than you think, Miss Freud.

They resume studying. WES rushes in.

WES: Weintraub's wallowing in guilt, but he's not going to give up Vermont! *(To HONEY)* And we have to talk. About you coming.

HONEY: I'm trying to study.

WES: What if I told you I've decided to take my car?

HONEY: You'd get Mississippi mud all over that little bug of yours? Your folks didn't even want you driving it up here.

WES: Unlike you two, I'm twenty-one and no one can stop me. So you'd be riding in comfort. Well, relative comfort. Better than the bus.

HONEY: Just the three of us? *(WES nods.)* That might make a difference.

WES: *(Relieved)* I thought so.

HONEY: If I come with y'all—*if,* that is—then maybe we could circle 'round and see your folks in Charlotte.

LINDA: She's pulling your leg.

WES: I appreciate the warning, but she doesn't scare me. North Carolina is more enlightened than you think, Honey Johnson. My father's preached on it. Lost half of his congregation at first, but stuck to his guns and lots of 'em came 'round.

HONEY: And your mother?

WES: She came 'round too. In the end, the pastor's wife always acquiesces. If you want to see for yourself, we can stop off down home.

HONEY: We'll give 'em the old one-two. Me and Linda. *(Pulling WES to sit down and watch)* This'll be better than "Bubba Love."

She hurries to LINDA, whispers to her. With LINDA following HONEY's lead, both stand atop a bed, using it as a stage. A fanfare, ta-dum! Melodrama style, HONEY becomes a southern white lady, fanning herself with one of WES's flyers. WES watches, amused.

HONEY: *(Cont.) (To LINDA)* Come on in, darlin'. You must be Wesley's little Jewish friend. Ah can tell bah yoah nose.

LINDA: *(Stereotype, laughing, they've done this before.)* Oy, vey! I thawt I could pass!

HONEY: Ah hope you don't mind, sweetie pumpkin, weah havn' pawk chops faw dinnuh?

LINDA: Oy, vey! I'd radduh have *kishke* and *schmalz.*

HONEY: What is that, sugah dumplin'—some kind of mixed drink?

LINDA: *(Hitting her cheek)* Oy, vey!

HONEY: And who's this with you, candy drops, the maid? *(Becoming another stereotype, handing LINDA the "fan")* No, ma'am. I'se Honey. I'se betrobed to yo' boy. *(LINDA trembles in shock)* Nebbah you mind. You soon be mah mama.

LINDA screams, faints. She and HONEY laugh.

LINDA: *(To WES)* Sorry.

WES: I'm used to you girls conspiring against me.

HONEY: *(Scarlett, to WES)* Fiddle de dee, sugar! It's us who are compatriots and we have to instruct Miss Yankee here 'bout the south. *(To*

LINDA, *pulling* WES *along with her)* We'll go on to Opelika and mama'll fix you some real southern cooking. Might even get her to do some barbecue.

WES: *(Enthusiastic longing)* Barbecue!

LINDA: Barbecued what?

HONEY: *(Dropping the accent)* Exhibit A, "Barbecued what?" I rest my case. *(To* LINDA*)* You know as much about ol' Dixie as an Eskimo!

WES: *(To* HONEY*, warming up)* We could do a *Pygmalion* on her.

HONEY: It'd take a lot of work.

WES: *(To* LINDA*)* Repeat after me. "Y'all."

LINDA: C'mon, Wes. I said I was sorry.

WES: *(Smiling at her)* Your turn.

LINDA: Okay. Have your fun, *(Emphasizing the separate words)* you all.

HONEY: Hopeless. "Y'all come back, now."

LINDA: You all come back now. You all.

WES: "Ah'd lak me a heap o' them ham hocks and greens."

LINDA: Ham hocks and greens. You all. My grandfather—

HONEY: Granddaddy—

LINDA: My *zayde's* toinin' ovuh in his grave! You awl.

HONEY: *(High voice)* "Ah doan know nuthin' 'bout birthin' no babies!"

WES: *(Hand over heart)* Bull Run, Chickamauga, Stonewall Jackson, grits—

HONEY *is humming Dixie, marching.*

LINDA: That's enough.

WES: Jefferson Davis, General Robert E. Lee, Ty Cobb—

LINDA: *(Not joking)* Enough, already!

WES: *(Outraged)* "Enough, already?" "Enough, already?" Just where are you from, ma'am? *(To* HONEY*)* Sounds like Yankee talk to me.

HONEY: New York Yankee, if you know what ah mean. *(Dropping accent)* That's what I've been trying to tell her. They'll eat her up alive. She ain't never gon' pass.

LINDA *balls up a piece of paper and throws it at* HONEY.

LINDA: Cornpone!

*A north-south paper snowball fight ensues [*HONEY *and* WES *vs.* LINDA*].*

HONEY: Carpetbagger! Marxist!

LINDA: Cracker!

WES: Pointy-headed liberal!

This is becoming fun. Laughter begins, grows as they continue.

LINDA: Redneck! Handkerchief-head!

HONEY: Egghead! Beatnik!

WES: Scalawag! Commie!

HONEY: Foreigner!
LINDA: Right wing bigot!
WES: Agitator!

Crossfade with the sounds of a small crowd and a few camera shutters clicking while . . .

Scene 4 . . . *immediate lights up on* MADDY, JOHN, *and* BEA, *standing together, facing the audience, holding large photographs of their children's faces.*

JOHN *gives the photo of* WES *to one of the women, who stand at his side, holding the pictures.* JOHN *speaks as to a small group, trying to keep his emotions in check.*

JOHN: Thank you . . . those of you members of the press who've seen fit to be here. I . . . we . . . are grateful for your attention. I have a brief statement on behalf of the families involved. First of all, this is not a hoax. Our children are responsible young adults who simply believe in equal rights for all people. Believe me, this is *not* a hoax. No more than the bomb that killed those four little girls in Birmingham was a hoax. *(A sudden, uncontrolled outburst)* Perpetrated by Black Muslims, you printed! For sympathy! *(Outrage growing)* And now this too? For publicity the politicians say, and you print it! False witness! *(Pause. With great effort, he regains control, speaks quietly)* I apologize for . . . it's only that this is hard . . . especially coming after the three boys were found . . . murdered . . . just a few weeks ago. We understand that both law enforcement and the populace might become inured to such terrible events. But we want you to know that Wesley and Harriet and Linda are somebody's children. *(His voice wavers.)* How can I tell Mrs. Winnick and Mrs. Johnson—and my own wife—that the never ending tears spilling from their eyes make you suspicious? No one vanishes from the face of the earth without a trace. What happened before could be happening again. Right now. And we need your help in getting out the word! So we can find them . . . before . . . *(He has difficulty speaking)* So we can . . . tell . . . see . . . see them . . . again.

Sound of the small crowd as lights fade and cross with . . .

Scene 5. . . . *a tight light rising on* CLAIRE *in the Partridge house in Charlotte, North Carolina. She wears a bathrobe; is seated, looking at a large, framed photograph. She speaks her thoughts.*

CLAIRE: When the phone rang, I knew right away. I expected it from the moment Wesley left to go to this so-called "Freedom Summer," so-called "Summer of Love." *(Bitterly)* Whose freedom? What kind of love? *(Pause)* From the day he left, I waited for the call to come, as it came about Jack, as it was bound to come again. *(Pause)* Wesley wanted only to please me, to see me smile, to make up for Jack dying. He was so little then. He'd curl up like a kitten under the piano, listening to me play. Listening to me tell him with the music. *(Pause. She holds the photograph out, looking at it)* Now it's over. At last. When that phone call came from Mississippi, it was a relief. No more waiting.

JOHN *enters as the light widens, dimly. He speaks gently, as to a child.*

JOHN: Claire? *(She does not move.)* I'm home. *(He looks over her shoulder at the picture.)* It's my favorite, too. I remember how the photographer made faces at the boys till he got it.

CLAIRE *holds the frame against herself and turns away from* JOHN.

JOHN: *(cont.)* I've spoken with the senator—

She looks at him abruptly.

JOHN: *(cont.)* Nothing. Yet.

She turns away again, continues twisting her body further as he speaks, showing no sign of hearing him. When he touches her, she flinches. He is variously soothing, hopeful, impatient, angry, desperate.

JOHN: *(cont.)* But it's only been a few days. Mrs. Johnson and Mrs. Winnick haven't given up hope. Neither should we. *(Pause)* May I open a window? A curtain? Let some light in here? *(Pause)* We think it's possible they've been taken by some group. For brainwashing. *(Pause)* Did you say something? Do you have anything to say? *(Pause)* I know you blame my political sympathies. But maybe if you hadn't been so—No. I apologize. It's my fault. His disappearance. Whatever has happened to him. A man is responsible for the actions of his sons. *(Pause)* If you'd just turn to me! Speak to me. *(He falls to his knees)* Pray with me. "Escape for thy life," Lot was warned, "Look not behind thee."

CLAIRE *twists further away from him.*

JOHN: *(cont.)* Whatever happened, Claire, you mustn't keep looking back. Don't leave me again!

CLAIRE *turns away until she is a contortion.*

JOHN: *(cont.)* I see. It's already come to pass. You are the pillar of salt.

As the light on CLAIRE *and* JOHN *begins to fade, the [echo] sounds of the students' voices are heard—*

WES: "Commie!"—HONEY: "Foreigner!" LINDA: "Right wing bigot!" Then LINDA's laughter as another light rises on . . .

Scene 6 *A room in the Hightower house, Clemens, a few days later. A bare mattress, on which are scattered belongings.* MADDY *and* BEA *are separating*

them into two boxes; folding articles of clothing, looking through papers.
BEA, holding a book, is not moving.

BEA: Do you hear that?
MADDY: What?
BEA: Laughter. Like an echo.
MADDY: No.
BEA: It's too quiet here.
MADDY: Didn't used to be, I bet.
BEA: Sometimes, when I called up, Linda'd have to shout over the noise and music. *(She slams the book shut, looks about.)* I don't think I can do this. I can't, Maddy. It feels like I'm abandoning her, like I'm giving up. I can't do it!
MADDY: You want Miss Hightower to pack up her things?
BEA: No! Why can't we just leave it all? In case they come back.
MADDY: 'Cause no one knows when that might be.
BEA: No one knows anything, damn it!
MADDY: Ain't no need to cuss. You done heard for yourself.
BEA: That little pipsqueak of a sheriff? Playing dumb, but he's sly. Reminds me of a mole.
MADDY: None of their friends know what happened either. And you checked every inch of that road yourself. Many times as you had Reverend Partridge driving back and forth. Covered every inch of ground between here and the school.
BEA: I didn't know what else to do. At least I'm not crying. Why did he say that about never ending tears? It's not true.
MADDY: He's a good man. Made sure Honey's picture was in the papers with the other two. Not like when those three boys disappeared and they only gave the white boys' names. So never mind what he says about your tears. A preacher's way of taking is all. Here—*(Giving BEA one end of a bed sheet.)*—Help me with this.

They fold the sheet as they talk. Again, BEA's nervous energy thinly covers her fear.

BEA: I swore I wouldn't cry till there was something real to cry about. But my condition's rather precarious—*(Seeing MADDY's quick question.)*—I mean, I'm so shaky. And you're so calm.
MADDY: I've put it in God's hands. *(She puts the sheet in her box as BEA returns to the clothes.)*
BEA: I didn't like you riding in the back of the car.
MADDY: The maid sits in back. You see how no one bothered with us. *(BEA picks up a yellow sweater.)* No. That one is Honey's. I gave it to her last Christmas. *(As BEA hands it to her.)* Thanks. *(To herself)* Now, why do you think a smart girl like that would bring a sweater to Mississippi in the summer?

BEA: *(Reading from a piece of paper)* "The problem is that you want to be me. You want to change more than your pigmentation; you want to change the very essence of your being. You want to exchange your birth for mine—your childhood, your experience, for mine. We'll have to talk some more."

MADDY: *(Quickly offended)* She's saying that to my girl? That Honey wants to be white?

BEA: *(Handing the letter to MADDY)* No, no. Look. There's no handwriting. It's typewritten. And it doesn't sound like Linda.

MADDY: It's not Honey's kind of words neither.

BEA: Well, who then?

MADDY: Someone else they work with. All their things are so mixed up together, the way the sheriff and the FBI's been through them.

BEA: *(Laying the paper aside)* So we'll save it and they can tell us when they get back.

MADDY: All this "pigmentation" business. Foolish as the rest of it.

BEA nods, holds up a pack of Camels.

BEA: Honey's?

MADDY: Never took the first puff. I wouldn't have no cigarettes in *my* house.

BEA: *(Putting the cigarettes aside)* Let's look once more. On the road. On foot. To make sure.

MADDY: All right. First thing in the morning. *(Picking up a blouse)* I believe this one's Linda's.

BEA: They share everything.

BEA holds the blouse for a long time while they speak before she packs it. MADDY continues with other items.

BEA: *(Cont.)* Linda always jokes about how they got put together. Two minorities in one fell swoop.

MADDY: I reckon that dean of housing figured there'd be no complaints from either one of them. Or us.

BEA: And it's worked out, hasn't it? They're like sisters.

MADDY: *(With some irony)* Not exactly. Honey told me 'bout New York, when she visited you all. How she almost had to ride up the service elevator in your apartment house.

BEA: I don't—

MADDY: But one of you was always with her to go past the doorman and up in the front elevator.

BEA: We just happened to—

MADDY: "Happened to," nothing. You were afraid they'd make her go up the back way if she was by herself.

BEA: Oh, god—were her feelings hurt?

MADDY: Maybe so, but it wasn't *your* rules. I believe you have a good heart. Anyway, it ain't nothing to cry over. She's used to it.
BEA: Do you, Maddy? Cry? When you're alone? When no one's looking?
MADDY: I'm never alone. When no people are around, I pray.
BEA: Do you forget about it for even an instant?
MADDY: It's one of those things rides with you, but it's bound to be over soon.
BEA: Linda used to have nightmares when she was little, that scared her so much. But I could always comfort her. What if she's frightened now? I couldn't live . . . I don't want to live if—
MADDY: *(Suddenly angry, affronted)* Don't you talk that way! No matter what happens, never refuse the life God gave you.
BEA: But she's all I have.
MADDY: *(Bristling)* Five other children don't make up for Honey being missing.
BEA: I didn't mean—
MADDY: Each one's special in they own way. But Honey—she's my baby. And my gift from God and William, I always say. From William right before he took sick. And he's at God's right hand, watching out for all of us. He won't let nothing happen to those children.

BEA is silent, looks away.

MADDY: *(Cont.)* Call on your faith. It'll help you.
BEA: *(A bit condescending—yet envious)* I don't have that kind of faith.
MADDY: That's too bad, poor thing. Your mama and daddy should of seen to it.
BEA: *(Apologetic)* They were very religious. Papa beat it into us. I guess that's what made me pull away. Plus what happened to the Jews in Europe.
MADDY: Well, I can tell you, the Lord's in everything . . . Here *(A brassiere)* This one's got to be Linda's. Honey takes after me in that department.

BEA takes the bra, delicate and lacy. She looks at it, folds it carefully, then holds it to her face. She is still, then suddenly moans. Her knees weaken and she sinks to the floor. The sounds that come are from deep within her, a primal sobbing.

MADDY holds her as the light on them fades . . .

Scene 7 . . . *and* LINDA's *echoing laughter, then the others', fades in.*

LINDA: *Right wing bigot!*
WES: Agitator!

Their laughter becomes present, real, as lights rise on the dorm room "snowball fight." A loud pounding from the other side of the wall.

LINDA: Bumpkin!

HONEY: Good shot!

The pounding stops them.

HONEY: I guess some folks 'round here are actually trying to study. *(Calling)* Sorry!

WES: *(Calling)* Sorry!

LINDA: Hey, you two! Don't apologize!

WES goes to get his bag. HONEY picks up a book, sits at the spool table, opens a book.

LINDA: *(Gently)* So, what about it—kidding aside—if Wes takes his car?

HONEY: To Mississippi? Listen, y'all. Mama agrees with everything Curtis says.

WES: *(Joining from a distance at first)* Same with my folks. The grounds being that my mother's too fragile, but—

HONEY: The grounds being that Negroes get killed too often. Especially in Mississippi.

LINDA: But this'll be different. Safety in numbers. There'll be hundreds of us. The rednecks won't have a chance.

HONEY: *Your* mother's having a fit, too.

LINDA: Tough. She's stuck. She belongs to the NAACP. She volunteers in Harlem.

HONEY: A well-known hotbed of Klan activity.

LINDA: So she dabbles. She's still stuck with her own philosophy.

WES: My father's the same. Talks a good game, sermonizing infinitely on the egalitarian nature of God. But what has he ever done? I simply called his bluff.

HONEY: That's a good reason to put your life on the line. To prove something to your parents. This has nothing to do with helping colored folks to vote. What you call "rednecks" is nothing but a big joke to y'all.

LINDA: I didn't mean—

HONEY: Well, it's not a joke! You two just don't know!

LINDA: I do know. I know how you feel. They're your Nazis.

HONEY: *(Quieter, after a beat)* Yours too, girl. You're only a half-step behind me on their list.

WES: *(To HONEY)* I know how careful we have to be. I don't intend to let any of us end up in jail or in the hospital.

HONEY: I understand. You're sincere, you have ideals. But you're in love. *(Responding to WES and LINDA's quick embarrassment)* It's *like* you're in love. And that's making you blind to the danger. You romanticize us. Negroes, I mean. Everything we do is wonderful just because we're black. *(To LINDA)* You've got that one too. *(Back to WES)* But you've got a double case, po' thing. You ain't got you no slavery or no Holocaust—

WES: And that's what you think I'm doing here?

LINDA: *(Angry)* Wait a minute. What did you mean—that I had that one too? What one?

HONEY: Being romantic about black folks. Like that time your mama took you to hear Dr. King.

LINDA: Well, it had an effect on me! Made me want to annihilate bigots.

HONEY: So much for nonviolence. All you have to do is open your mouth and some sorry fool is gonna peg you for trouble. Miss New York Big-mouth is gonna walk right into it.

LINDA: You think I'm an idiot?

HONEY: In a pinch, even I could blend in, disappear among the natives. But you two will stick out like cornstalks in a bean field. *(To LINDA)* Especially you.

WES: If anyone questions her—or me, we'll be deferential, the essence of nonviolence. It's part of the training.

HONEY: Nonviolence just frustrates them, makes them want to hurt you.

LINDA: Me? They wouldn't dare. I'd just smile and turn my back on them.

HONEY: Medgar Evers was a peaceable man who got shot in the back.

LINDA: But this summer will be different. Lots of publicity. The world will be watching. We have to prove that some of us won't be silent witnesses to oppression! *(WES signals her to lighten up. She does, changing to an offhand tone, smiling)* Anyway, the worst your mean white folks'll do is dress up like ghosts and try to scare us.

HONEY: *(Softly)* Agitator.

LINDA smiles, turns her back, ready for this new role-playing. HONEY becomes a swaggering redneck stereotype, moving toward LINDA. WES sits, anticipating their fun.

HONEY: Hey you! Li'l Yankee gal! *(LINDA continues smiling, her back to HONEY, who moves in on her.)* Where you think you're goin', girl? Whyn't you go back where you come from? *(Shoving LINDA)* Whyn't you mind your own damn business?

LINDA: *(Sitting down at the table)* Okay, Honey, that's enough.

HONEY becomes serious as the character, leaning over LINDA. WES gets up, concerned.

HONEY: Don't you tell *me* what's enough or when to stop, girl! Race mixer like you. Commie bitch! Nigger-lover! Jew!

LINDA: *(Covering her ears, screams)* Stop it!

The pounding on the wall begins again as WES goes over to LINDA and HONEY.

WES: Whoa, Honey! Show's over.

HONEY: *(Pushing past WES)* The Klan is not a show! You shouldn't go! And the more I think about it, neither should I! I'm going to help Curtis. In Alabama.

WES: You'll regret it for the rest of your life if you're not part of this.

HONEY: I'm part of it every day, just living. Curtis says it's our own future comes first. And I've just decided that's my thinking now, too.

LINDA: And your mother's.

HONEY: Sure. Maybe she's right for once. You want a personal guide into the colored world? You'll find plenty in Mississippi.

As they continue, HONEY takes a cigarette from a pack of Camels, lights it, and starts smoking.

WES: A guide? I was thinking more of a friend.

LINDA: I can't believe you and your mother would let Curtis dictate what you should think! My mom would never let anyone—

HONEY: Your mom's a pushover. But she's cute. Earnest, yet perky. You favor her.

LINDA: Perky? Thanks a lot! So my mother is a cross between Mahatama Gandhi and Debbie Reynolds. But it doesn't mean I'd want to spend the whole summer in her divine presence, schlepping between her and a used car salesman, being their slave.

HONEY: *(Abruptly, quietly)* What was that?

LINDA: *(Embarrassed, grabbing the cigarette)* Come on, Honey. You know you'd rather be with us. *(Puffs, coughs, stubs out the cigarette)*

HONEY: Would I?

WES: Sure you would!

HONEY: Pardon, but I've got to study.

WES: What are you so mad about?

HONEY: Nothing. How could I be when you think we're a poster for tolerance? The three of us, gazing at the horizon, bathed in golden sunlight, our faces full of brotherly love. "The Dawn of Democracy."

LINDA: *(Near tears)* It may seem corny to you, but it's true.

HONEY: It's a lie. Life's not like us. We're not even like us. The three of us together is some ideal picture of this country. Admit it, Wes, you'd love to show up at the orientation with a Negro and a Jew. Women, no less. Three feathers in your hat.

WES: How can you even think that? What's bothering you?

HONEY: You are! *(In a fury)* You two just keep coming at me like you can't survive without me, like your life depends on *me!* I don't get enough of that at home. *(While putting on her shoes)* Curtis can't sell his cars without me! Mama'll die if I'm not on the dean's list. Honey's the one going to college! Honey's the one gonna make good! Honey's the living incarnation of her poor dead daddy's dreams on earth!

Every single one of them breathing down my neck to be something for *them*. Well, I'm not here to make up for whatever's missing in you two either. You damn well better learn to do without me! *(She grabs some books as the pounding on the wall is heard again. She screams at it.)* Shut up!

She stomps out of the room, slamming the door. She moves downstage in the "hall" to a corner of the students' platform. Lights in the room fade quickly. The light on HONEY remains.

Scene 8. *Sound of birds, which are heard occasionally during the scene. Late March, 1965, Opelika, Alabama. Light up on MADDY in a porch rocker. She is looking over at HONEY who stands still, holding her books.*

The light on MADDY widens as BEA enters behind her, wearing a shirt recognizable as one of LINDA's. She walks over to MADDY carrying two cups of tea.

BEA: *(Cheerfully)* Got the refills.

MADDY stares at HONEY. No response to BEA.

BEA: *(cont.)* You seem absolutely determined to spoil me. *(Holding out a cup to MADDY. When MADDY doesn't turn, BEA continues as if MADDY had responded.)* But you've done plenty already. You're kind enough to put me up for a few days, I'm not gonna let you wait on me. I refuse to be a nuisance. I hardly did anything, while you helped to fix all that food and serve it up for the marchers. I think they really liked it, don't you? *(Still no response. She tries to maintain a normal tone.)* I had a great ride to Selma. A whole bus load from your church and me the only white face in the bunch. I hope I didn't embarrass you too much. *(Holding out the cup to MADDY again)* Here, Maddy, it's good. It'll make you feel better, whatever's bothering you. Everything went fine, didn't it? This isn't like you. Please, Maddy, say something!

MADDY: *(Very softly)* I'm ashamed. Ashamed 'cause I can't understand what the Lord was up to with Honey.

She turns slowly to BEA. As she does, the light on HONEY fades to black.

MADDY: *(cont.)* I told you I wanted to go help out the Movement. *(Pause)* But when we was in that crowd 'round the Capitol, I kept on expecting to see our girls. The two of them together, wearing each other's clothes. And that boy right with them.

BEA: Me, too.

MADDY: I did think I saw them. More than once. Honey by herself more than once. But it never was her.

BEA: I know.

MADDY: Now, that's the end of it. It told me for sure she's gone. And I'm sitting here wondering what's the use. What's the use of me trying to do anything in this world? Someone good as Honey, with her whole life ahead. With a fine young man like Curtis, who don't know what to do with hisself now. And the children they would have. *(Pause)* She wasn't going to Mississippi. She was decided on that. Now, what made her change her mind? I'll never understand it. What was it made her decide to go? *(She wipes her eyes, pats her nose; no other sign of tears)* I put too much on her. We all did. So she had to go her own way faster. *(Wipes her eyes, puts the handkerchief away)*

BEA: Maddy, you and John Partridge just about saved my life. You know, he couldn't come down and help out like he wanted to because his poor wife is sick again. But you are a strong woman.

MADDY: Reckon I'm tired of that.

BEA: *(Amused)* You can't help it. It's in your nature.

MADDY: I know you're trying to pull me up, telling me I've got important things to do when all I ever done before was cook over at the restaurant. Or help out at white folks' parties. I wonder am I good for anything else.

BEA: You're good for being a teacher, like Honey. Real good. Look at all the practice you've had with your own kids. With the kids in the Movement, too. And you're good for me. I need you, Maddy. We need each other. *(Holding the tea out again)* Here. Before it gets cold.

MADDY: *(Taking the cup)* Thank you.

BEA sits in another chair. They sip and rock.

MADDY: *(Cont.)* Two widow ladies, all alone, sipping their tea on the porch.

BEA: You've got your children. *(Forcing a mood change)* The girls are lovely. And your grandchildren.

MADDY: *(Making an effort)* Sometime, maybe you can meet Sedrick. George and Hugh—my other boys—are up north.

They rock and sip. As their talk continues, it gradually becomes more natural and animated; a relief to both of them.

BEA: I really love your house.

MADDY: William built it with his own two hands.

BEA: And this porch—it's fantastic!

MADDY: This here is what William called the "piece de resistance" [*English pronunciation*]. Wouldn't put it on till we had a whole house to come out from. We would sit out here like we was keep watch. Like we was in the front of some kind of ship floating on the ocean, and the children all safe and sound behind us.

BEA: I'll bet you still miss him.

MADDY: *(Nodding)* You miss your husband?

BEA: Myron? I hardly remember him. We were only married a year when he enlisted. Didn't even wait to be drafted. I was mad, to start with.

I was pregnant. We were kids. He couldn't wait to kill Germans. I mean, he didn't just get sick and die, like your William. He chose to leave us. But his family's been generous.

MADDY: Young as you were then, you never found you no one else?

BEA: I never looked. Linda was enough. Maybe I'm an anomaly, *(An-swering MADDY's look)*—an exception—but my mother and my sisters haven't given up on me yet.

Pause.

MADDY: You were a real help in Selma. They ain't—there aren't—many white folks would fit in like you.

BEA: Thank you. I can't believe how you put up with it, all of you, them beating up your people.

MADDY: Martin Luther King says no matter how hard it is, to turn the other cheek and to love our enemy into understanding.

BEA: I noticed his picture inside, right between Jesus and JFK.

MADDY: William had Franklin Roosevelt in the president's place, but I took him down for John Kennedy. Now, *his* mother, there's a woman lost more than anyone. A son killed in the war, another one shot dead in Texas, a daughter in a plane crash or something, and another one not right in the head.

BEA: She *is* an example. How she manages to go on.

MADDY: Sometimes the good comes out of the bad. People like you padding on down here to join in. *(Pause, ironically)* Now we're getting integrated killing.

BEA: But things have started to change.

MADDY: And your people keep coming anyway. Maybe that's why you're God's chosen.

BEA: "My people?" I'm on my own. I do very little.

MADDY: You're the one taught Linda, ain't you?

BEA: *(Very softly)* And that's what made her go to Mississippi.

MADDY: Don't be getting yourself into trouble, now, like I did. We best just hold to what our girls were doing, believing in the "beloved community" what Martin Luther King calls it.

BEA: I heard him give a sermon once. In a synagogue.

MADDY: In person? *(BEA nods)* I didn't know he did no Jewish preaching. Up north?

BEA: About eight or nine years ago, I took Linda for Friday night services. Because he was guest preacher.

MADDY: And you not the praying kind.

BEA: This was different. I was curious.

MADDY: Our Dr. King is like y'all's Moses.

BEA nods. She begins speaking, her emotion building as she relives the event.

BEA: Half the congregation was Negro that day. All around, the faces were dark and white mixed together. I never even imagined anything like it before! Linda was squeezed between me and a woman who was with her kids, two little boys. It was right around the time of the bus boycott in Montgomery. I can't really tell you what Dr. King said— I was so caught up in the atmosphere. What I do remember was the benediction. How they did it was, first the rabbi said it in Hebrew, then Dr. King said it in English. *(Stumbling a bit)* "Y'va-reh-" It's been a while—"Y'va-reh-" You know, the first part—"May God bless you and keep you . . ." *(MADDY nods)* And everyone was standing and it was crowded so we were touching, all connected. And, on top of that, there were beams of sunlight coming through the stained glass windows. I swear it, Maddy! *"Ya'air Adonai panav*—May God's face shine on you—"

MADDY: *(Overlapping)* "—lift up His countenance unto you and be gracious unto you."

BEA: *(With MADDY)* *"Yi'sah Adonai panav ay-lecha v-ya-same l'cha shalom."*

MADDY: *(With BEA)* "May the Lord cause the light of His countenance to shine upon you and grant you peace." *(Alone)* Amen.

BEA: *(After a moment)* When it was over, I started to cry; why, I still don't know. And I never felt so safe and happy. *(Pause)* So that's it. I'd like to feel that way again. *(She waits, looks into her tea cup)* It's cold. *(Reaching for MADDY's cup)* Here. Give me that.

MADDY hands her the cup. As BEA exits the lit area, MADDY calls after her.

MADDY: Bring the whole pot this time, sugar? We can sit out here all day!

BEA exits. MADDY's light narrows.

MADDY: *(cont.)* Guess it's time I give Honey's things away, now the Selma march is over. But you'll keep everything, Bea. Linda's room like she left it, same as you wear her clothes to make you feel better, like you were just borrowing them. But our girls ain't coming home. And it's time to stop waiting.

Her light fades as . . .

Scene 9 . . . a tight light rises on JOHN, at home. His thoughts are reflective, troubled.

JOHN: After a year or so, I gave their things, what was still any good— furniture and blue jeans and footballs and the like—to the church flea market. I left the rooms empty. With the doctor's agreement. *(Pause)* Claire has been in and out of hospitals. She would be almost all right for a time each visit home. She sat upright and ate and walked up or down the stairs when she was called in either direction.

Upstage of JOHN, CLAIRE moves silently. In dim light, she wears a white nightgown, anticipating and echoing fragments of what he describes.

JOHN: *(cont.)* She floated through the house like a ghost, never really touching anything, causing only the slightest shifting of air where she moved, with no footfall, no breath, no sound to announce her coming and going. *(Pause)* Then a morning would come when even her slight presence was missing. I'd find her curled on her side, asleep in one of the boys' rooms, on his bed, under the covers, her cheeks rosy, maybe even snoring a little. And she'd scream and carry on if I tried to get her out of that bed—holding on to the mattress as if it were a life preserver and she was lost at sea. Finally the doctor would come and give her a shot so she'd quiet down. Then we'd carry her on back to the hospital.

CLAIRE exits. The dim light remains where she was.

JOHN: *(cont.)* But now the rooms are empty. So, when she came home yesterday, I took her up and showed her and said let's plan how to fix these rooms so we can use them. She did not respond. But late last night I heard a terrible pounding and crashing. There she was in the boys' empty rooms, running like a caged rabbit, banging into the walls, bleeding, unaware of her bruises. Running into one wall, then another, blindly, but with great force.

The light on JOHN crossfades as pounding starts slowly . . .

Scene 10 . . . *then speeds up with full lights rising on WES and LINDA in the dorm.*

LINDA: *(Hitting the wall, shouting to it)* All right! *(The pounding stops)*
WES: I've never seen her so angry.
LINDA: I have.
WES: I shouldn't go after her?
LINDA: She needs to be by herself for a while. She's under a lot of pressure. You heard her.
WES: Family looking at her like some kind of guiding light, boyfriend putting it on thick, then we start hacking at her, too.
LINDA: She'll cool off.
WES: You're sure?
LINDA: When you're upset, you run away on one of your hikes. She explodes.
WES: And you?
LINDA: I don't get upset. Except when Honey teases me. Sometimes.
WES: *(Glancing at the clock)* I hope she comes back before I have to go. No one's ever yelled at me like that.
LINDA: No one?

WES: Jack maybe, when I was being a pest. But he was my brother. I expected it.

LINDA: So Honey's like my sister. The nearest I've ever had to one. I guess she's entitled to yell.

WES: You don't believe that "feather in my hat" business, do you?

LINDA: *(Shaking her head)* I know you're committed to the Movement.

WES: I wouldn't risk our friendship.

LINDA: I know.

WES: I mean, I wouldn't risk it by doing anything. Anything even to change it and take the chance of messing it up.

LINDA: *(Uncomfortable)* I know. Honey teases me—about us—but I told her she's wrong.

WES: *(He hesitates, starts to speak, hesitates again)* For now, anyway.

LINDA: *(Lifting a stack of records, looking through them)* Yeah.

WES moves to her. The tension of mutual attraction draws them closer, face to face, as they continue.

WES: First things first. The summer. Us working together is the most important thing.

LINDA: For us *and* the country.

WES: Since Kennedy was killed, the priorities have changed.

LINDA: Yeah. I know.

WES: I mean, you could jump right into eat, drink, and be merry, or you could get suicidal or you could try to balance it out by doing something.

LINDA: I still miss him. Johnson makes my ears ache. I can't wait till we're down there—everything that this can lead to.

WES: So we'll see what we can do this summer. With you and me trusting each other. Taking no chances with that. *(LINDA nods)* You think Honey'll come 'round?

LINDA: If we leave her alone. Take off the pressure.

They are still for a moment, very close. Abruptly WES takes the stack of records from her.

WES: Let me help you with this for a minute. Make up for interrupting.

He heads for the phonograph, mad at himself for the missed opportunity.

LINDA: Honey'll be jealous if she misses something.

WES: *(Selecting a record)* But we don't have much time. You can explain it to her. You sure she'll be all right?

LINDA nods. WES puts the needle down carefully, looks at her; a question.

LINDA: I have no idea what that is.

WES smiles, changes the record, looks at LINDA again.

LINDA: I know they've Ravel, but I can't tell which—
WES: One is Ravel and one is George Gershwin.
LINDA: Then I'm in big trouble.
WES: They're both Jewish, you know.
LINDA: Ravel is Jewish? How do you know that kind of thing?
WES: *(Shrugging)* You've got a lot of brilliant composers.
LINDA: Me?
WES: Dahlberg's going to ask about them. He always does. Which one influenced the other? A chicken and egg question. I believe he asks it every year.
LINDA: And you got a B+? I'm impressed.
WES: Actually, I should have done better.
LINDA: So, which is which?
WES: I can't tell you that if I'm going to teach you anything. You've got to hear it for yourself.

She takes his hand and pulls him to sit with her on the floor. After a moment, unsure of himself, he drops her hand.

WES: *(cont.)* Just listen a bit.
LINDA: It's not fair. You've got a trained ear. From sitting under your mother's piano.
WES: I told you about that? *(She nods)* Well, she played a lot of these things. The last one was Gershwin, this one's Ravel. Nice, don't you think?
LINDA: I thought you didn't like him. Something you said before.
WES: Only the piece for the left hand. There was a time when that's all she would play. Like her other hand was tied behind her. Pieces for the left hand. Ravel, and something from Scriabin—and one by Prokofiev.
LINDA: I see.

Again she takes his hand. Awkwardly, he pulls away.

LINDA: *(cont.)* What? What is it?
WES: *(Softly)* There's more.

Pause.

LINDA: It's okay. You don't have to explain.

Pause. Just the music playing. WES takes her hand, looks at her straight on, even as his emotions color what he says.

WES: Listen. It's just that after Jack got killed in Korea, my mother quit talking. For quite a long time. She just played that piece. The Ravel. For the left hand. She played it on the piano, over and over. It was like a code. I kept trying to figure it out. I thought it was for him, a song about her grieving. Then I realized it was for me. I was all that remained. She was telling me that with the music. Again and again. She was telling me I was everything to her. That left hand singing was me.

They look at each other. LINDA smiles. Tentatively, he does the same. The music continues and rises while lights fade to black.

END OF ACT 1

Act 2

Scene 1. *September, 1968, near Clemens. A loud police car siren, cutting off while red and white lights flash. A tight light on each of the three parents, separated. The red-and-whites fade. The parents pick up rhythmically from each other, as if speaking with one voice.*

BEA: *(Amazed)* All this time, they were in the river!

MADDY: Right by the road, in the river!

JOHN: The fisherman snagged his line. The car—and the bones—for *four* years—they were here all the time!

BEA: It never came, Linda—the flying saucer that picked you up and would return you; all three of you, like the lost boys in Never-Never Land—

MADDY: So much has happened, baby! In just four years. Martin Luther King was shot dead. Sedrick changed his name and moved his family up north. And I'm teaching first grade now. All this, while you've been here!

JOHN: All this time, while your mother kept her silence, you kept yours, too.

MADDY: I wanted you to be proud of me working *steady*, not like Bea, with her hair all wild like a heathen hippie, sitting in one day and marching for the Vietnam war the next! I put it in God's hands, same as finding you.

BEA: Everything goes in God's hands for Maddy! So why didn't he tell her you were here?

JOHN: "At least she knows where *her* children are buried." Your mother said that about Rose Kennedy. Right after Bobby Kennedy was killed. She's quite taken with the Kennedys...

As MADDY speaks, her light broadens to include JOHN and BEA, who is pacing back and forth, apart from the others.

MADDY: Reverend! Would you please come on over here for a minute? You've got to talk to her! She's walking back and forth like a wind-up soldier toy, mumbling and carrying on something fierce, and I'm ready to go home!

JOHN: She's trying to get some more information from Sheriff Mack.

MADDY: With respect, Reverend, he's not going to tell you or her anything new, no matter what kind of polite act he's putting on. *(Calling)* Watch it, Bea, before you fall in the river!

BEA: I walked around here. I walked right by here, I don't know how many times. Every year when I went down to you in Opelika—every year, with the books, the supplies—we came to Clemens and stayed with Miss Hightower.

MADDY: I know what we did!

BEA: We always walked from the school, along the river here. We never found anything! You were with me, Maddy. Didn't we pass this very spot?

MADDY: Yes. We passed it.

BEA: From the very first day when we all tried to trace their path, they must have been here. But I didn't feel it. I had no idea.

JOHN: None of us did. Why don't you rest for a minute, Bea?

BEA: I don't understand! I should have felt something.

MADDY: *(Impatient)* Why? What makes you more perceptive than anyone else?

JOHN: *(To MADDY)* She didn't mean—

BEA: That's all right, John. We're all upset.

MADDY: *(Softening)* I'm sorry, Bea. But I've got to get back home.

BEA: *(Going to MADDY)* I know. I know. But I want to finish this. Sheriff Mack says there's no telling when the car went in. He says it could have been weeks after they disappeared. *(Hopefully)* Maybe nothing violent. Maybe them just returning from Mexico.

MADDY: *(Challenging, like a lawyer; this grows)* You believe that? You satisfied with the sheriff's explanation, Reverend Partridge?

JOHN: It's been four years. If there were skid marks, they're long gone. Or tracks in the grass. Or footprints. Or anything else. The explanation doesn't matter anymore. They say they're not even sure who was driving.

MADDY: *(Overtly angry)* They say! That fisherman—how did he happen to throw his line in right on the spot and no one got snagged on that car for all this time?

BEA: They said the water's lower than usual.

MADDY: Or someone with a guilty conscience finally *decided* to find them.

BEA: *(Indicating the sheriff)* He'll hear you.

MADDY: *(Loudly)* So what? We're not the ones with something to hide!

JOHN: But all this time, in the silt, in the mud.

With no pause in their lines, they begin to separate themselves, the lights gradually isolating them again. Their words, spoken matter-of-factly, in natural rhythm, sometimes overlap. They shift subtly from interactive to internal as the lighting changes.

JOHN: *(Cont.)* No dials left, no indicators. Nothing but—

BEA: There's no evidence except their—

JOHN:—bones. Evidence of trauma to their skulls. But it could have been—

MADDY: An accident? You really believe that?

JOHN: Hitting the dash, the steering wheel—

MADDY: *Being* hit—by a shovel, a club—

BEA: We may never know what happened.

MADDY: The windows were closed. But it's hot here in August. Too hot—

BEA: Too hot to keep the windows closed, but the sheriff suggested—

JOHN: It was raining that night, and he said—

MADDY: Had the *nerve* to say maybe they didn't want to get wet!

JOHN: But, because the windows were closed, the bones were saved. Tangled. Shifting four years in the river mud. They asked for dental records.

BEA: I wanted the girls to be buried together, in Alabama, near Maddy's house. They were best friends.

JOHN: For the second time, I officiated at one of my son's funerals.

MADDY: She wanted them to be together, like when they were alive—

BEA: Not where I finally buried her, in New York, one of those gray places in Queens, near the expressway, with soot on the tombstones.

MADDY: Too bad about Bea, what she wanted for Linda, but in Alabama—

BEA: Even cemeteries are segregated. Still, their bones—

JOHN: The skulls were easy, they said. And Wesley's bones were very different—

BEA: But the girls were almost the same size, the way they wore each other's clothes—

MADDY: So, in spite of cracker law, there's no telling how—

BEA: How much of Linda is resting in that churchyard in Opelika, Alabama—

MADDY: How much of my Harriet is far away, in a Jewish cemetery in the cold, gray, ugliness in Queens, New York.

JOHN: *(With open prayer book, as at a funeral, while the lights on MADDY and BEA fade.)* "May the Lord bless and keep you. May the Lord lift up His countenance unto you and be gracious unto you. May the Lord cause the light of His countenance to shine upon you and grant you peace. Amen."

Crossfade to . . .

Scene 2 . . . *a sanitarium.* CLAIRE *is alone. Her words are carefully enunciated, polite in tone.*

CLAIRE: Rose Kennedy. Rose Kennedy, I hate you. Your noble suffering. You have buried three sons to my two. And a daughter, I believe. How bravely you bear it! Standing in fashionable black at one grave after another after another after another. Here, in this place, they tell me about you frequently. Perhaps they think you will be an inspiration for my recovery. Perhaps I don't wish to recover. Some of the photographs, they tape up in my room. On occasion, I am led to a television set and placed before it to watch yet another documentary about your cursed, courageous family; you at the center, the tiny, intrepid matriarch, your dyed hair, your frozen face. *(Screaming)* Why don't you tear your hair out, Rose? *(Pause. Quietly again)* You glide through your grief like a dancer born for the role. Like you accept your destiny without question, showing up to mourn as required. *(Screaming)* Why don't you wail like a colored woman, Rose? And throw yourself on the grave? *(Pause. Quietly)* My oldest son, Jack, had nightmares as a child, when his daddy was overseas in the war. Did your boy? I held him tight and let him sleep with me. Did you comfort your children in your bed, too? Did they comfort you? *(Screaming)* Did they? *(Quietly)* You have gotten used to losing your children, Rose. I have not. I will not. I choose not to. I chose not to attend the service for Wesley. Not to see his father drop what's left of him in the ground, next to what's left of his brother.

The Ravel eases in. Crossfade . . .

Scene 3. . . . *with lights rising on the dorm room,* LINDA *and* WES *looking at each other, still holding hands. The music ends while they are speaking, but they do not notice.*

LINDA: I know what you mean about your mother. Mine's the same way—wrapping her life around me—except without a tragedy like your brother.
WES: What about your father dying?
LINDA: Not tragic for me. It was before I was born. I guess it was tough for my mother, though. He was just a little older than you.
WES: Pretty sad, huh?
LINDA: Sure. I wish I knew him. I wish he was around to keep my mother off my back. And all his relatives. My grandparents are even worse than she is.
WES: You're all that's left of their son. *(Pause.* LINDA *lets go of his hand)* It's a lot to carry around, isn't it?
LINDA: But your mother's problems aren't your responsibility. You feel things so much. Too much.
WES: Sometimes, maybe.
LINDA: Like after Kennedy.

WES: I was pretty bad, wasn't I?

LINDA: A ghost, a zombie. For days. Pale and kind of vacant. We were worried about you.

WES: I was pretty scared.

LINDA: So was everyone. But you took it even harder.

WES: It wasn't just that he was dead. It was something else. You know Chet Rower?

LINDA: The idiot football player?

WES: Who used to do a sports column featuring himself. Well, I was setting up galleys for the paper when he came running in like his team just won the Rose Bowl, shouting . . .

HONEY opens the door softly, holding her books, stopping when she sees LINDA and WES. She backs out, leaving the door open.

WES: *(Cont.)* ". . . They got him! They shot Kennedy! We're rid of him!"

LINDA: You're kidding!

WES: No one knew what to think. Maybe it was a sick joke or something. But the guy was out of his mind delirious with joy. Someone finally put on the radio so we could hear for ourselves. And that's what started me on the road to Mississippi.

LINDA: It is?

WES: Some of the others who knew Rower hushed him up. Everybody but old Chet was kind of stunned. Me, I could hardly breathe. And before I knew it, I picked up the print tray, all those letters, that heavy wood, and I threw it down on the floor, right next to Chet. The whole thing crashed and smashed all over in little pieces. He jumped about ten feet straight up. Then I walked out. And I felt scared. *(LINDA takes his hand again)* At the power of my feelings. And at what I had done.

HONEY abruptly moves to the phonograph and lifts the scratching needle from the record. LINDA and WES quickly drop their hands.

WES: *(Jumping up)* Welcome back.

LINDA: *(Jumping up)* You all right?

HONEY: *(Polite and formal)* Caffeine and nerves. I had no call to wash my family linen in front of—

WES: That's okay. We were concerned.

HONEY: I can see that.

LINDA: I was getting a music lesson.

HONEY: Obviously. Well, I'm going on to the library. I just came back to tell you what—

LINDA: You can stay, you know.

WES: *(Checking the clock)* I've got to get out of here soon anyway.

HONEY: I didn't mean to intrude on your discussion about our late President. How his death moved you to action.

WES: Well, it did.

HONEY: Whatever Kennedy did for civil rights, he came to it slowly, like pulling teeth. He was forced into being a hero.

WES: He would have accomplished much more if—

LINDA: When it happened, it was like the whole future was over. *(To HONEY)* You even felt that way.

HONEY: Okay. Sure I did. Because he was young. And smart. Who could imagine him dying? *Everybody* was shook up. 'Specially mama, which is rare. Cried like he was her own.

LINDA: My mother, too.

WES: My folks called that night, and my mother tried to talk about Thanksgiving break like nothing was wrong, but Reverend Partridge could barely talk at all for once.

HONEY: Yeah. JFK does well as a martyr. *(To WES, kindly)* But if that's part of Mississippi for you—to try and balance out all the Chet Rowers down there—to make something out of Kennedy's death—

WES: We have to, or he might as well not have lived at all.

HONEY removes her shoes, gets ready to start studying again.

WES: *(Cont.) (To HONEY)* This summer's just the first step. After I graduate, I'm thinking I'll join the Peace Corps.

HONEY: *(To LINDA, accepting)* You too, I suppose. Go off and have exotic adventures. Fix all the problems out there.

LINDA: Why not?

HONEY: Guess I'll just have me my own little Peace Corps with the babies down home in Opelika. *(Pause. To both)* You gonna let me work now or do I have to throw another fit to shut you up?

LINDA grabs a book, opens it.

HONEY: *(cont.)* Y'all can put back that music if you want.

WES puts the needle back on the record, goes to the table and his flyers. "Bluesy" music.

HONEY: *(cont.)* George Gershwin, right?

A triumphant smile from LINDA as crossfade to . . .

Scene 4 . . . *New York City, early winter, 1978. A hotel room. The bluesy music fades as MADDY and BEA enter, MADDY with a suitcase. They are wearing coats, are older in appearance. They are uncomfortable, awkward together, remain standing. MADDY is aloof, with a veneer of politeness. BEA forces cheeriness. As she takes off her gloves, she assesses the room.*

BEA: Pretty nice.

MADDY: Sure is chilly in New York.

BEA: You can turn up the heat, you know. You'll get used to it.

MADDY: Won't be here long enough to where I have to.

BEA: I still wish you would have stayed with me. In my place. I have a perfectly good sofa bed.

MADDY: Thank you, but this is where they sent me and this is where I'll stay.

BEA: Very plush. Wait'll you see the towels.

MADDY: The district's paying for it. And I'll be assigned a roommate.

BEA: I wasn't accusing you of junketing. All the times you put me up— or should I say, put up with me? Even though it's been a while, I'd like to return the favor. Show you around. You know.

MADDY: Reckon I'll be too busy to go sightseeing.

BEA: So, what exactly is all this about? *(Reading a button on* MADDY'S *coat)* "BCHC, '78."

MADDY: Black Children's Heritage Council. Lots of us teachers. On our own. And this is the year for change. We want some textbooks improved, for one thing.

BEA: Good. It's about time. I'm glad you got political before you have to retire. You can keep your finger in.

MADDY: I look to you like I'm ready to retire?

BEA: You look great. I just meant, I thought there was mandatory—

MADDY: They can extend who they want.

BEA: I'm sure they don't want to lose you.

MADDY: Even three days off for me like this is hard on my children, black and white.

BEA: I'm sure.

MADDY: So I intend to bring back some good news. We'll be better organized after this, too. *(Dismissing* BEA*)* Well, I've got to go downstairs in a few minutes.

BEA starts to put on her gloves, stops.

BEA: If you didn't want us to spend any time together, why'd you let me know you were coming?

MADDY: It was only about finding the cemetery. I didn't mean for you to meet me at the train.

BEA: I wanted to. When you called from Philly, it was a good surprise. How's Sedrick?

MADDY: Hakim. He's fine.

BEA: Any more children?

MADDY: Hanan. She's a year old.

BEA: That makes an even half-dozen, like you. *(MADDY nods)* You didn't let me know when she was born.

MADDY: Guess I forgot.

BEA: It's the first time you have. So, what's going on?

MADDY: I was hoping you'd tell me how to get out to that cemetery. I can't pronounce the name.

BEA: I can take you there.

MADDY: I'd rather go by myself.

BEA: I meant, what's going on between us? From you to me? What's happened?

MADDY: Not everything has to do with you and me.

BEA: Is it that I didn't come down last year?

MADDY: Some people *honor* their commitments.

BEA: I know it was important to you. To me, too. I sent the supplies, anyway. And the books. I'm sorry if—

MADDY: *(Her sarcasm measured)* I can understand you being too busy to spend the time. Opelika's hardly as exciting as Buenos Aires.

BEA: *(In kind)* The world really does exist beyond Alabama.

MADDY: I'm sure it does, even though there's plenty to do there.

BEA: I had to go. You've heard of *los Desaparecidos,* the Disappeared. You know what the mothers are going through. How they want to find their children. How they care about their children.

MADDY: So do the mothers in Opelika.

BEA: I told you, I couldn't come. *(Pause. Impulsively; the martyr attacking MADDY's hostility)* There was something that happened. Before Argentina.

MADDY: Oh?

BEA: It happens pretty often in New York. No big deal. I wasn't even going to tell you. *(Pause)* I was mugged.

MADDY: *(Quickly, concerned)* Were you hurt?

BEA: I lost my balance when he grabbed my purse. I fell. I got a few bruises.

MADDY: I'm sorry, Bea. Really.

BEA: You would have noticed. *(Ending the topic)* That's why I didn't come down.

MADDY: You should have told me. You know I've seen worse. *(Pause)* So why didn't you?

BEA: I . . . I couldn't.

MADDY: Much as you like to talk?

BEA looks away with no attempt to speak.

MADDY: *(cont.)* What? What is it?

Pause.

BEA: He was black. It was a black man.

Pause.

MADDY: If he was white—then would you have told me?

BEA: I . . . I don't know. But he wasn't.

MADDY: What does it mean—that this criminal was black? *(Pause)* We all look the same to you?

BEA: Don't be ridiculous!

MADDY: Think about it.

BEA: I have. I know he was just one individual. But it shouldn't have happened to me!

MADDY: After all you've done?

BEA: Of course not. Only—

MADDY: Why didn't you tell him 'bout your good work among black folk? Maybe that would have stopped him.

BEA turns away, silent.

MADDY: *(Cont.) (After a while, softly)* You did, didn't you?

BEA: I don't remember.

MADDY: That's just what you did! No wonder you ran off to Argentina.

BEA: I thought he was going to kill me. I said whatever came into—

MADDY: You tell him how you were best friends with a black woman? *(She laughs)* I'm sure that made a difference! *(She laughs harder)*

BEA: *(Stricken)* You think it's funny?

MADDY: I bet he laughed at you too. *(Suddenly not laughing)* You tell him 'bout Linda and Honey? You use our girls to try and—

BEA: You don't understand!

MADDY: *(Sarcasm and anger building)* Not everyone understands about your good works. When they're hungry, they might not hear your do-good credentials. You tell him 'bout how you marched into Montgomery and got his people the vote? How you marched to end the Vietnam War? And you don't understand why he laughed in your face?

BEA: No!

MADDY: You want him to say he's sorry he needs your money and sorry he tore up the streets in Watts and Detroit and sorry he doesn't appreciate all you've been trying to do for him?

BEA: This is just why I didn't tell you! *(Headed out)* Forget it! It's none of your damn business, anyway!

They are shouting, cutting into each other's words.

MADDY: You're the one should stay out of people's business! Gallivanting all over, sticking your nose in—

BEA: Trying to help!

MADDY: Playing like you're Eleanor Roosevelt.

BEA: I'm not playing!

MADDY: That kind of help got Honey to change her mind and go to Mississippi.

BEA: Why didn't you take her out of school then? Away from my Linda, who was used by people like you!

MADDY: Who was using who? It was you and your kind kept the attention on black folk so the crackers wouldn't pick on you!

Pause. BEA is barely under control.

BEA: Me and my kind?

MADDY: Yes!

BEA: *(Taking a card from her pocket)* Here's the cemetery. Someone will tell you how to get there. *(Slapping the card into MADDY's hand)* Whether you can pronounce it or not!

BEA exits quickly. MADDY turns furiously from her as the chords of the Ravel are heard. Lights out quickly . . .

Scene 5 . . . *and up on the students. As LINDA and HONEY speak, WES starts folding some flyers.*

LINDA: *(To HONEY)* Gershwin? No. This one's Ravel. I've almost got him down. *(Grabbing a pillow and moving to the record player)* Is it really okay to leave it on? Real soft? I want to keep listening till I can tell the difference.

HONEY shrugs. LINDA turns down the volume, lies on the floor near the record player.

HONEY: You're going to fall asleep is what you're going to do.

LINDA: Am not.

HONEY: *(To WES)* I give her about half a minute till the snoring starts.

LINDA: *(Settling comfortably)* I don't snore.

She closes her eyes. WES keeps folding, HONEY writes in her notebook for a while, then eyes LINDA carefully.

HONEY: Out like a light. I know the signs.

She tests LINDA, then, satisfied, goes to WES, looks over his shoulder.

WES: *(Softly)* Last ditch stuffing of mailboxes. Ignore me.

HONEY: I can't. You're the one I want to talk to.

WES: *(Smiling, relaxing)* No kidding!

HONEY motions him to come further from LINDA, who remains asleep.

HONEY: *(As WES joins her)* I look like somebody's "mammy" or something?

WES: What?

HONEY: 'Cause I don't want to play chaperone to you and Linda, here or anywhere else.

WES: Of course not. I wouldn't think of—

HONEY: You want me to ride down south with you so your folks won't raise a fuss or to keep you from temptation or whatever—

WES: I do not!

HONEY:—same as her wanting me to stay with you all in here. She denies it, like you, but you two are such babies, I can read you like a book.

WES: Can you really?

HONEY: Sure. Both of you.

WES: I . . . There's no one else I can talk to . . . about her, I mean. If . . . that is, maybe, if you—

HONEY: I can listen if you need me to.

WES: Like a sister?

HONEY: I've had plenty of practice.

WES: And you've got Curtis. I've never had . . . that is . . . I'm not exactly Don Juan, you know.

HONEY: Only because the girls 'round here think you're kind of strange—

WES: Thanks.

HONEY:—and naïve. Which you are. But they don't realize that's one of your charms. You and Sleeping Beauty over there are a good match in that department. You two feel exactly the same way about things. Including each other.

WES: How can you tell?

HONEY: It's obvious. The balance. Sometimes I even wish Curtis and I . . .

WES: I don't think it's a good idea to mix up anything—well, you know— anything romantic with the summer. Do you?

HONEY: It can muddy up your thinking. Everyone thrown in together, singing the songs, fighting the fight, proving their independence.

WES: That's what I mean. *(Pause)* Don't make fun of me, okay?

HONEY: I wouldn't. Not now.

WES: Sometimes I think I'm just scared. I mean, about Linda.

HONEY: I know.

WES: And the stuff about the summer is an excuse. *(HONEY nods)* So what should I do?

HONEY: Follow your instincts, son.

WES: What instincts? I'm too scared to have instincts. What if I go too far and she laughs at me?

HONEY: She won't. *(Suddenly moved)* Sometimes you're a right sweet boy, Partridge. *(She abruptly calls out)* Hey, Linda! Had enough yet? *(No response. She goes over to LINDA)* Heck! The child's done gone and fell really asleep!

WES: *(Following, with a tentative smile)* I could wake her with a kiss.

HONEY: Go on, boy. Surprise yourself.

He kneels by LINDA, then smiles up helplessly at HONEY. She selects another record, laughing when she shows it to WES. As she replaces the old record, he nervously joins in. Their laughter grows while crossfade begins . . .

*Scene 6 . . . to MADDY and JOHN laughing. Spring, 1979, Opelika. MADDY
is seated, showing some children's paintings to JOHN.*

MADDY: . . . and she said, *(Like a child)* "No, Mrs. Johnson, I'm the
doctor and my brother's the nurse!"
JOHN: Smart girl. I love what you're doing here, Maddy.
MADDY: So do I.
JOHN: It's like you've kept a promise to Honey. Carrying on. Finishing
school. Running this place. You've kept a promise.
MADDY: Thank you.
JOHN: What would you say if I told you I want to follow in your foot-
steps? I'm thinking of changing my line of work.
MADDY: *(Surprised)* To what?
JOHN: Something real. Far away from what's familiar. Someplace where
I get dirt under my fingernails. Building things, maybe. Just not
talking so much. Speechifying. Trying to convince people. Words.
Gestures. Nothing. It's all so empty, it scares me.
MADDY: That's a sad thing, Reverend John, if the work of the Lord scares
you.
JOHN: I think He'd accept something else from me after all these years.
He's probably tired of my sermons, too.
MADDY: What about Mrs. Partridge? I was thinking she'd come down
with you this time.
JOHN: She doesn't like to travel.
MADDY: It was quite a crowd for the funeral over in Clemens.
JOHN: Miss Hightower had a lot of friends.
MADDY: And a lot of enemies in that town. Who cut her off. But plenty
came from the old days.
JOHN: It was like a reunion.
MADDY: Lots of funerals are that way. Folks who haven't seen each other
for a long spell.
JOHN: Those young people are approaching middle age, some of them.
Hardly seems possible. You ever wonder what—
MADDY: Anytime I catch myself wondering, I just stop. There's no re-
ward in "what if."
JOHN: It's nice they remember our children, though.

*Lights rise in another area, NYC, summer, 1979, where BEA is bringing in
two mugs of coffee.*

BEA: So, what's the matter? You ate like a bird.

The lights on MADDY dim.

JOHN: I apologize. Thanks for the dinner, Bea. It was good.
BEA: You're not leaving already! I have dessert.

JOHN: No. I'm just nervous. I want to ask you something. I have a request.

BEA: Go ahead.

JOHN: I feel honor bound to tell you, Maddy already turned me down.

BEA: I didn't know you two were in the habit of getting together.

JOHN: I saw her a few months ago. At Miss Hightower's funeral. Then back in Opelika. Like you used to. I brought up your friendship.

BEA: Former friendship.

JOHN: She told me it was none of my business.

BEA: Can I kindly ask you to stay out of it, too? No offense?

JOHN: I want to say something, though, before I pop my big question.

BEA: I really don't—

JOHN: No preaching, I promise. It's something personal.

BEA: Okay.

JOHN: The first time I saw you, in Sheriff Mack's waiting room, I thought you'd never survive. But you've surprised me, Bea, and I admire you. Your strength. You've built a life out of your love for Linda.

BEA: Thanks. It's surprising to me, too. So what's wrong? What's so hard to ask me?

JOHN: I've been feeling like everything has broken down. What our children were trying to do. "Black power," "white supremacy," riots, people like you and Maddy, who were working together, turning on each other. Nothing holding together, nothing working anymore.

BEA: Everyone gets disillusioned when things don't happen fast enough. They get impatient. And they push the pendulum all the way over. Maybe they just need a rest from each other.

JOHN: I wish the cure were that simple. You and Maddy are the worst of it.

BEA: We're only two people. Two individuals.

JOHN: But you were friends.

MADDY's light rises and BEA's light dims.

MADDY: It *was* a good turnout for Miss Hightower, though.

JOHN: *(Carefully, as he enters MADDY's area)* I thought Bea would come.

MADDY: You don't know where she is?

JOHN: I haven't heard from her for months.

MADDY: Gone on another one of her fool trips to Argentina, I expect.

JOHN: She wrote after she saw you in New York. She was sad. And hurt.

MADDY: Can't be helped. We see things differently now.

JOHN: Then there was nothing you said that was, at least according to Bea, that she seemed to think might be—

MADDY: Anti-Semitic? That's her excuse for a lot of things. Bea can only see one side is the problem. If she came upon you and me talking here right now, she'd say we Christians were ganging up on her.

JOHN: I don't think that's fair.

MADDY: Let me ask you, Reverend John—Did I ever even imply to you that *she's* a racist? She put you up to talking to me, trying to mend fences?

JOHN: No. It was my idea. I guess I made a mistake.

BEA: Not every friendship is forever.

JOHN: *(Making the transition, with the lights, to BEA's area)* You both are so important to me, what happened between you made me want to give up for a time. But at least you're each doing great things on your own. And me? I haven't taken on Wes's challenge yet. Maybe you're sick of each other, but I'm sixty-five years old and sick of myself!

BEA: *(The analyst)* A crisis of faith!

JOHN: No. Job had it worse, and he stuck it out. Rather a crisis of leadership, of purpose. I'm not very good at those.

BEA: Don't be so hard on the good Reverend Partridge.

JOHN: It's him I've got to get away from.

BEA: And find your "real" self? The motto of the seventies. I think you're just suffering the symptoms of the decade.

JOHN: I want to start over. In a new place, where no one knows me or thinks they know who I am!

BEA: If you reject the past, wouldn't you be turning your back on our kids?

JOHN: You two blaming each other is harder on their memory.

MADDY: Worst of all would be me not teaching, like Honey was going to do.

JOHN: *(Moving to MADDY)* She'd be proud of you. You're good at it.

MADDY: I'll be better when we get the annex done at the church.

JOHN: I could come and work on that for you. I'm a pretty decent carpenter, and—

MADDY: Mostly, it's brick.

JOHN: I can learn, can't I? *(Excited)* It's just what I was talking about!

MADDY: We're trying to help ourselves now, set an example for the youngsters.

As BEA speaks, her light rises. Now MADDY remains lit. Although JOHN is with each woman separately, the rhythm of the scene continues as if the three were together.

BEA: *(Still skeptical)* The next line usually has to do with finding yourself.

JOHN: So it does. Could you find a place for me in one of your projects? Argentina would be fine. *(Excitement building steam. He is between them, could be speaking to either one)* Not as a pastor, I mean, but as a worker. Doing something tangible. So, what do you think?

BEA: On your own?

JOHN: Claire's fine now. She'll be agreeable.

MADDY: Mrs. Partridge wouldn't mind moving down here for a time?
JOHN: I wouldn't ask her to do that. I'll take a leave of absence, enough time to do this one project, and then—
MADDY: I'm sure there's a poor white church you can help with up in Charlotte.
BEA: I'm sure there are people in need you can work with down in Charlotte.

JOHN bursts out laughing.

BEA: *(With MADDY)* What's so funny?
MADDY: *(With BEA)* Did I say something funny?
JOHN: No. Sorry.

The lights on both women fade to black as JOHN continues alone.

JOHN: *(cont.)* It's just that being away from everything I know, everyone who knows me, is what would make it perfect! It's what Wes would want—me *doing* something for once. All you have to do is point me in the right direction. I'm ready!

At the height of enthusiasm, JOHN stands isolated as . . .

Scene 7 . . . *Lights rise on* CLAIRE, *at home, one month later, doing needlepoint. She rarely addresses* JOHN *directly, speaks with genteel politeness. A small bag is on the floor nearby.*

JOHN: *(Entering her area with boyish excitement)* I'm ready, Claire.
CLAIRE: You got everything in one bag.
JOHN: Easily. I'm traveling light.
CLAIRE: The winters in Atlanta are cold.
JOHN: Thank you for being concerned, but I want to go like any poor laborer. I almost feel like walking there. Straight into the inner city. Starting anew. *(He moves closer to her)* Thank you for letting me go, for understanding.
CLAIRE: It's not for me to let you go. It's not for me to keep you here. I control nothing, John, and I make no attempt to understand.
JOHN: If you wanted me to stay—if it made a difference to you . . .
CLAIRE: Nothing makes a difference. I am as I am, John.
JOHN: If you need me, I can fly home in an hour. If you miss me . . . *(Pause)* If you weren't well now, I wouldn't go. You're a survivor, Claire. You've managed to survive, in spite of—
CLAIRE: In spite of nothing. In spite of everything. "Survival." A word. I simply live.
JOHN: I'll write every day. And I packed the camera. I can send pictures of the houses I work on. And of me, hitting my thumb with a hammer, no doubt.
CLAIRE: As you wish.

JOHN: I expect a new man will come home to you. With calluses on his hands. John Partridge reborn. As if I were my own child. *(No response. CLAIRE keeps sewing)* When I get back, things will be different. Maybe we can travel together! Or even stay right here. But I'll be a better person, a better husband. And a better pastor. I'm sure of it!

A car horn sounds discreetly.

CLAIRE: There's Henry, to take you to the station.

JOHN: You won't be lonely. Mrs. Eubanks will come by every day. And your schedule is full.

CLAIRE: Mondays, volunteer at the hospital. Tuesdays, the auxiliary tea. Wednesdays, the bridge club. Thursdays—

The horn sounds again.

JOHN: I know. It's splendid! You're busier than Rosalynn *[pron. "Rose Lynn"]* Carter. You'll manage to squeeze in some time to write to me, won't you? *(No response)* Won't you, Claire? Like the old days, when I was in the army? Promise?

JOHN leans over and kisses CLAIRE's cheek. For the moment, her needle does not move.

JOHN: *(cont.)* Well, I'm on my way. Bless you, Claire.

The horn again.

CLAIRE: Henry is waiting.

JOHN: *(On his way out)* There'll be a lot to tell. I'll write every day!

He exits. CLAIRE looks up from her sewing, speaks quietly.

CLAIRE: Goodbye, John.

Lights fade on CLAIRE as the approach to the finale of the 1812 Overture is heard, as if a comment on JOHN's coming adventure. The music grows as crossfade . . .

Scene 8 . . . *to the students. The music blasts loudly as lights rise on them. HONEY and WES still laughing. Cannons boom! LINDA sits abruptly, breathing hard, terrified. Pounding on the wall from next door. LINDA looks up at the others, then covers her face with her hands. HONEY quickly lifts the arm off the record. The pounding stops.*

HONEY: Lin? *(No response)* I'm sorry. *(Touching LINDA's shoulder)* You okay?

LINDA, not looking up, flails out with one arm, pushing HONEY away.

LINDA: Leave me alone! *(She flings herself flat on her stomach, her arms still protecting her face from view)*

WES: *(Stricken)* She didn't mean to.

LINDA: *(Muffled, through tears)* Go away! Leave me alone!

WES *looks helplessly at* HONEY, *indicating his intention to leave.* HONEY *stops him, signing for him to go back to the flyers. He does. She reads. They both watch* LINDA, *who is unsuccessfully trying not to cry.*

After a few moments, LINDA *speaks indecipherably, her head still buried.* WES *remains distraught.* LINDA *reaches out toward* HONEY, *who gives her a tissue.*

LINDA: *(Turning her head a little, so she can be understood)* The whole thing was probably just a few seconds. A really bad dream. To go with the music.

She wipes her face, blows her nose. She sits up, disoriented for a while as she speaks, trying to reconstruct her dream.

LINDA: Central Park. Lots of children. I was watching them. Playing in the meadow. Dancing around Maypoles, weaving patterns with colored ribbons. Then a cloud came over and the air, the sky, turned kind of green. Maybe a tornado coming, someone said, the air gets green before a tornado. Not in New York! I said, not in the park. There has never been in history, a tornado. But I knew it was dangerous where the children were dancing. Then I saw a street sign. It was Japanese. And all at once there was a rushing—like the wind—and I couldn't walk against it to get to the children. Then the explosion. Lots of explosions. *(Pause)* I saw the children. In the sky somehow, frozen in their dancing. Now they were ash! And their ashes started falling. Like snow. Like the trail from fireworks. It wouldn't stop. *(She blows her nose hard)* And that's what happened from your stupid Tchaikovsky!

WES: I wish we could take it back.

LINDA: I couldn't do anything to help. Nothing.

HONEY: You all right now?

LINDA: I guess. Embarrassed. *(To* WES*)* That you saw me like this. I'm not usually like this.

HONEY: He might as well know it now, how tender you are. Me, I don't have any dreams.

WES: *(Quickly)* I do. Don't worry. I have nightmares, too. Sometimes I put myself in my brother's airplane when it was shot down. Sometimes in a dream, but sometimes awake, just thinking about it, trying to imagine how he felt. I go through the hit, the loss of control, spinning down, falling through emptiness, the water coming closer. I make myself go through it over and over, so I won't be scared anymore. I think of my father, how I don't want him to see me frightened, how I've got to show him I'm fine, the way he has to show my mother he is. I try hard not to be scared. But I still am.

Crossfade, with somber organ music.

Scene 9 . . . *March, 1980. A tight spot on* BEA.

BEA: *(To herself)* I read it in *The Times* obits. March seventeenth, nineteen-eighty. Five days ago. "Reverend John Partridge, Civil Rights Advocate." I discovered it with my morning coffee.

A tight spot on MADDY, *apart from* BEA.

MADDY: *(To herself)* It was a surprise. The news and hearing Bea's voice on the phone after more than a year. I always thought the reverend would be around at least as long as I was.

BEA: You and I hadn't talked for over a year, but I didn't want you to find out about it the way I did. I was sure you'd want to know. Besides, at that moment, I wanted to hear your voice.

MADDY: I didn't say anything about going up to the funeral, things were too starchy between us.

BEA: I didn't tell you I intended to go down for the funeral. I wasn't sure you'd want to see me.

MADDY: Soon as I hung up the phone, I packed my bag and reserved a seat on the train from Birmingham.

They turn towards each other across the chasm of darkness between them, still speaking thoughts; briefly reliving.

MADDY: *(cont.)* Look at you, over in that crowd. You look mighty small. And older. But still the same.

BEA: It's an old comfort to see you in the midst of the congregation. Hey! Why'd you turn away from me?

MADDY: You could have waved, at least.

Pause. They are turned from each other. The organ music fades.

BEA: It was beautiful at the cemetery; a perfect, spring day. I saw Claire for the first time, seated at the grave site, perfectly dressed in black, set off beautifully among the flowers. Her hands, folded in her lap in their black lace gloves, never moved. She was a portrait of grief in good taste. She's holding up well, I thought. She's acquitting herself well.

MADDY: After the service, someone came to me with a letter—

BEA: —a hand-written note on blue-embossed paper.

MADDY: The writing was so neat, it looked like a machine did it. "According to the wishes of my late husband—"

BEA: "—I request your presence for tea this afternoon at four o'clock." When I arrived, the house was full of people. Someone asked my name and guided me down a hallway. Only then did I see—

MADDY: You came down the hall behind the maid, and didn't lay eyes on me until the doors at the end slid open and—

The lights widen to include CLAIRE, *waiting behind the central of three chairs complimenting a tea table.* BEA *and* MADDY *arrive there, glance at each other, then away again.*

CLAIRE: Please sit down. *(All three sit)* I've asked that we be left alone.

She begins pouring tea from a silver service. MADDY *and* BEA *sit on either side of her. During what follows,* CLAIRE *serves the tea smoothly, perfectly, no matter what is being discussed. She passes the cups on their saucers, the spoons, the sandwiches, without a hitch. Her guests settle on the edges of their seats, not looking at each other. They focus their attentions on* CLAIRE, *the smiling, patrician hostess.*

MADDY: Mrs. Partridge, I'd like to express my condolences. Your husband was a good man.

BEA: He was a great comfort to me over the years and if there's any way in which I can be of help to you now, I would—

CLAIRE: Sugar?

The other respond to such questions with nods or shakes of their heads.

MADDY: "From the fruit of his words a man has his fill of good things, and the work of his hands comes back to reward him." Reverend Partridge is sure to be receiving his reward now.

BEA: I'm glad to find you in good health, Mrs. Partridge, Claire, if I may. I know you feel the loss tremendously.

CLAIRE: No less than you, I'm certain, Mrs. Winnick. Lemon?

BEA: I didn't mean—

CLAIRE: The sandwiches are cucumber or watercress. It was my husband's written wish that the three of us sit down for tea after his death.

BEA: He wanted us to be friends, like our children.

CLAIRE: I have no children, Mrs. Winnick. It's my understanding that you are childless as well.

BEA: I never think of it that way, even though—

CLAIRE: I'm not certain of my husband's intentions, but I am following his wishes.

MADDY: He often spoke of your accomplishments, carried on something fierce about how you could play the piano.

CLAIRE: I gave the piano to the Salvation Army years ago.

Pause.

BEA: He thought we'd have something to say to each other. I imagine he thought of us all as survivors.

MADDY: And he wanted it to be right, what we were doing in life. Living up to our potential, as they say.

BEA: I think that's what drove him the last few months. He was so pleased about going to build in the inner city! At least he was happy when—

CLAIRE: My husband committed suicide.

A shocked silence. MADDY and BEA look at each other for the first time.

CLAIRE: *(cont.)* What he used to fear I would do.

BEA: What?

MADDY: I can't believe he'd do such a thing.

CLAIRE: Perhaps he would not want me to tell you, but since you were his closest friends—More tea?

BEA: It can't be! The newspaper said—

CLAIRE: As usual, they know very little of the truth.

BEA: But the last I heard was, he was—Are you curious as to the means? That's often the first question.

MADDY: All that matters to me is that he's gone.

CLAIRE: The cause of death was "myocardial infarction."

BEA: A heart attack?

MADDY: But you said—

CLAIRE: My husband's heart needed mending, according to Dr. Hodgekiss. No, I am not speaking metaphorically. The doctor recommended aggressive treatment. And rest. Perhaps even surgery. No travel whatsoever. *(To MADDY)* But my husband visited you in Alabama.

MADDY: He never said a word.

CLAIRE: *(To BEA)* And you in New York.

BEA: He was filled with ideas for the future! He seemed healthy.

CLAIRE: My husband was advised against excitement, against activity. He chose not to share this information with me.

MADDY: I had no idea.

BEA: He wanted to work.

CLAIRE: And so he did. Lifting cinder blocks. Digging trenches. In impossible conditions. I'd call that suicide, wouldn't you?

BEA: I prefer thinking he was doing what gave him joy.

MADDY: Getting plenty of dirt under his fingernails!

CLAIRE: I'm not blaming either of you. John was a grown man, was he not? But I believe you to be complicit.

BEA: I think I speak for both of us when I say—that we loved John like a brother.

MADDY: *(With BEA)*—I loved Reverend Partridge like a brother—

CLAIRE: My husband sacrificed his life for the ideals he shared with you both. *(To BEA)* He left me once before, forty years ago, to serve in a war in the interests of your people. *(Looking at her tea cup, as she carefully puts it down)* Jack emulated him by going to Korea. *(To MADDY)* My husband joined in your war, too, and Wesley followed his misguided example. I believe that's why John killed himself; because he could not create a meaning for Wesley's death. And, indeed, there is none.

CLAIRE *pats her mouth delicately with a napkin and puts it on the table. She smiles a polite, rigid smile.*

CLAIRE: *(cont.)* *(To both)* Reverend Partridge expressed his wish that we meet, and now we have done so. You may show yourselves out.

MADDY *and* BEA *leave* CLAIRE's *area, stopping for a moment. They want to, and almost do, speak; decide against it. They walk into separate, isolated light as the lights on* CLAIRE *fade. The organ music again. They speak their thoughts over it.*

BEA: I can't say a word to you. At least we both had enough control to keep our mouths shut in there. *(Turning towards* MADDY*)* In the old days you'd make some crack about Claire Partridge being nutty as a fruitcake. Then you'd scold me for laughing. But now—

MADDY: I wanted to slap that crazy woman, Lord forgive me, I did! Would have, too, if it wouldn't show disrespect for Reverend Partridge. *(Turning towards* BEA*)* I could say that to you and maybe it would break the ice between us, and you would laugh, but how do I know? *(Turning away)* I reckon I've got nothing to say to you.

BEA: *(Turning away)* There's no point. I mean, am I supposed to apologize for Claire Partridge just because we're both white?

Quick blackout as . . .

Scene 10. *Lights rise in the dorm room.*

WES: *(Continuing, to* LINDA*)* I can't go around scared for the rest of my life! *(To* HONEY*)* Jack wasn't.

HONEY: Maybe he'd still be alive if he was.

WES: But how alive? What kind of life? Going half way, like my father?

HONEY: Maybe your daddy's right to play it safe. He's got obligations, real ones.

LINDA: *(To* WES*)* But you don't.

HONEY: What do you want to prove, boy? That you're the same as your brother?

WES: I don't know. I just don't want it all hanging 'round *my* neck. *(Pause)* Harvey Weintraub told me his parents lost a whole other family—their first children—in the war. In a concentration camp. Now they'll hardly let him and his sister out of their sight. How can you blame them, considering? But it's not fair to him, either.

LINDA: No, it's not.

HONEY: Nothing's fair.

WES: I have to get out on my own. Further than ever before. I can't be everything to—what my mother wants—what she's afraid of—I can't!

He looks at the women, a plea. The light on them fades and remains on WES . . .

Scene 11 . . . as tight light rises on CLAIRE. *They see each other across time. As* CLAIRE *begins to read a letter she has just written, the light on* WES *fades to a dim glow, now including* HONEY *and* LINDA. *They are frozen in time.*

CLAIRE: June 1, 1994. To the Memorial Committee and Trustees of the College: I am in receipt of your invitation to the dedication of the memorial to my son, Wesley Partridge, and two other civil rights volunteers. I do not approve of either the sculpture or the scholarships bearing the name of my son and the others. Your memorial is misguided. Both of my sons have been sacrificed, one of them while enrolled in your college. I see no reason to celebrate the sacrifice of young lives to futile causes. I will not be attending the ceremony in conjunction with graduation on June 10. Sincerely yours, Mrs. John Partridge.

Lights on students out. Crossfade from CLAIRE *to . . .*

Scene 12 . . . the college, update, New York. June 10, 1994. Distant sounds of a college choral group, which finishes while MADDY *speaks. A conference room.* MADDY *sits alone, a furled umbrella planted on the floor in front of her. Her posture is erect, her hands rest on the umbrella's handle. She wears a dress and head wrap in African style. A thermos of iced tea and some paper cups rest on the table.*

MADDY: *(To the room; she's used to talking to herself)* Thirty years. Almost to the day. The day those children left this college and thought they were coming back in the fall. It's just how I pictured it from when they sent Honey the brochures and that application. I should have said, "Now, Honey, it looks like the place for you," then she never would have come up here. Uh, oh. Listen to me. I'm the one tells everyone to stay away from "should of" and "what if." *(Pause)* It's a fine honor, now, isn't it? Something good for the three children. In a way, today, it'll be like I'm graduating for her. *(Pause)* Best get up and take a look out that window.

She pulls herself up, using the umbrella like a cane.

MADDY: *(cont.)* Sit too long and your bones harden like cement.

She stands raises the umbrella horizontally overhead with both hands, stretches with a slight knee bend.

MADDY: *(cont.)* That's better.

She walks to look out of the [downstage] window.

MADDY: *(cont.)* Look at them sashaying along out there. At their age, they think they've got forever. *(Looking out in another direction)* What am I looking out there for? She'll be here, all right. Her name is on the program. *(Pause)* I have nothing to say to her. Honey would tell me, "How 'bout 'Hello, Bea?'" *(Pause, she waves the thought off)* Anyhow, maybe she won't get here in time. *(She poses, just in case. Tries a condescending tone)* "Hello, Bea." *(She shakes her head, tries forced warmth)* "Hello, Bea." *(She shakes her head again, brushes the idea away)* No way.

She sits regally, facing away from the entrance. After a while, BEA enters quietly, remaining at a distance, behind MADDY.

BEA: *(Quietly)* Hello, Maddy.

MADDY does not respond in any way, as if unaware of BEA.

BEA: *(cont.)* They sent me in here.

MADDY: *(Looking at BEA, flatly)* Hello, Bea.

She turns away, facing front again.

BEA: *(Coolly)* How are you?

MADDY: *(Her tone judgmental)* Seems you don't change, except for the hair.

BEA: Well, I've lost some body parts since I saw you, but nothing I can't do without. *(She hesitates)* May I come in? All the way, I mean. I don't think it'll be much longer till they're ready to begin.

MADDY nods. BEA comes further into the light, but remains standing, keeping her distance.

BEA: *(cont.)* *(Still uncomfortable)* I guess I've got good genes. My mother made it to a hundred and three.

MADDY: It's nice you had her so long. *(BEA nods)* They left us some ice tea. I won't vouch for it.

BEA: I am thirsty. I drove up from the city.

As she continues speaking, her familiar nervous energy returns. Running on, she pours the tea and offers some to MADDY, who refuses it.

BEA: *(cont.)* They were nice enough to offer me a limo, but I wanted to drive myself. So I could have time to think, you know. My car's a mess, twelve years old, and I have to park it on the street and move it every day, so it's quite a nuisance, but at least I don't have to depend on anyone else this way. The last time I drove up was thirty-one years ago, before freshman year, to help Linda bring all her things. I never thought I'd want to come back here for anything, but the memorial was such a grand idea, and the scholarships to go with it! I think the children would be proud, don't you? *(She gulps some tea)*

MADDY: You always do go on when you're nervous.

BEA: You're right. I am nervous. Not about the memorial. About you. I didn't know what to expect. I figured you might be here.

MADDY: I'm here, all right.

BEA: We're only missing John. *(Looking about)* Is she—

MADDY: Her name is not on the program.

BEA: Thank goodness! *(She sits. Pause)* How are your children?

MADDY: *(She considers this step, then speaks)* I have seventeen grandchildren, eleven greats, and two great-greats.

BEA: That's wonderful, Maddy!

MADDY: Hugh passed on some years ago. Same thing that took William.

BEA: Oh! I'm so sorry!

MADDY: The others are all just fine.

BEA: I'm glad of that. *(She gets up, goes to the window)* Linda and Honey— well I think they'd like today, not all the attention, I mean, but such a pretty day, us being here, you know, kind of graduating for them.

Surprised, MADDY *looks hard at* BEA.

BEA: *(cont.)* They'd be older than we were when we first met down in Clemens. The young women out there remind me of them. *(Pause)* I still miss Linda. After all these years.

MADDY: *(Amused irritation)* And you still think you're special, don't you? *(With feeling, wanting* BEA *to understand)* But everybody loses their children. I've lost all of mine. Two are with the Lord—the others I've lost just to time, just to them growing up. It feels good to have them healthy, but if I set to wondering, I'd miss them, too, when they were children. Those children, all of them, are gone for good. And nothing will take them back to being my babies again and won't make Honey get any older, ever, than just turned twenty.

BEA: But it's not the same. You've had—

MADDY: *(A barbed reminder)* Been to Argentina lately?

BEA: You want a confession? *(Slamming down the cup)* All right! I've been to lots of places. I work with groups who call attention. In Columbia and Bosnia. Africa, too. And next week I'm driving all the way to Mexico. Juarez. Across the border from El Paso. There are American factories there, you know. The Mexican girls work for next to nothing, and sometimes they're raped, and killed—their lives are considered cheap, too, and—

MADDY: You do get around.

BEA: And you? *(Condescension)* Are you still teaching?

MADDY: Not in the system anymore, but the Annex, the place John wanted to help out with. I'm in charge there. Only now we call it day care. They don't bring up their own like we did.

BEA: *(Sitting again)* Lots of things have changed since we used to sit on your porch. *(Pause)* I still care, even if you don't want me to. And I still regret what happened between us.

MADDY: *(Grudging amusement)* Two grown ladies yelling at each other.

BEA: Sometimes I forget what about. And my memory's pretty sharp.

MADDY: About who caused the most grief.

BEA: John would have enjoyed today. Seeing us together.

MADDY: Most of all, he'd be glad we're still breathing. So we can do something out in the world.

BEA: How's Hakim?

MADDY: He's so mad, he's going to get an ulcer one of these days.

BEA: There's been a lot for him to be mad about. Me too.

MADDY: Why are you looking at me like that?

BEA: Like what?

MADDY: Like you thought I was going to chop off your head with a hatchet.

BEA: Or at least poke me with that umbrella, huh?

MADDY: That's the look.

BEA: Because I still believe in affirmative action, for god's sake!

MADDY: And you think *I* might believe the best way to help is not to help at all.

BEA: You might. And you still might not trust me. I might not trust you. But I'm not asking what you believe. And I don't want to know. Not today, anyway. *(Pause)* God, Maddy, where's an old liberal to go? Don't tell anyone, but I still believe in nonviolence, too. I know it's passé nowadays—

MADDY: I thought we were skipping politics.

BEA: No matter what, it'll never be like it was between us.

MADDY: Those days are gone.

BEA: *(Moving to the window again)* Still, we'll be sitting up on the stage together in a few minutes. Sitting in for the three of them.

Pause.

MADDY: Doesn't I-85 through Opelika eventually take up with the road to El Paso?

BEA: I guess so. Why?

MADDY: I'm considering something.

BEA: You want me to stop off?

MADDY: Maybe. Just for an hour or two. See if we can talk without insulting one another. Make a list beforehand, each of us, so we don't get off the track. Depending on the weather, I'll make us some kind of tea.

BEA: I'm afraid of you, Maddy.

MADDY: I know. You're pretty scary yourself. You let me know, then.

BEA *nods. "Pomp and Circumstances" in the distance.*

STUDENT'S VOICE: *(Off stage)* Mrs. Johnson? Mrs. Winnick? The ceremony's about to begin.

MADDY: We'll be right along.

She has some difficulty pulling herself up with her umbrella-cane. BEA moves to help her. MADDY waves her off emphatically.

MADDY: *(cont.)* Stay out of my way, Bea. I'm perfectly able to get up on my own two feet!

BEA throws up her hands. She waits, aside. As the light on them tightens, MADDY stands slowly, triumphantly. She throws a final book at BEA. Lights remain on them . . .

Scene 13 . . . *as lights begin to rise on the students . . .*

HONEY: *(Answering WES)* Mothers aren't always right. Mine isn't, and neither is Linda's.

The lights on BEA and MADDY hold briefly as HONEY continues, then fade to black.

HONEY: *(cont.)* So don't worry 'bout your money for a change. Go on and break aloose. I understand why you have to go to Mississippi. Honest. What else can I say?

WES: Nothing. Not even that you'll come along. I mean, I could just go off into the wilds, show my independence, but so what, if that's all it is? This summer is the first time I have the chance to do anything worth a damn.

LINDA: Me, too. You were right. Till now it's been small and personal. Because of Wes. And you. And how mad I was to think someone would want to hurt *you*, to pick on *you*. But now I realize that even with you not going, I have to. Even without Wes, I'd go alone.

WES: I wanted you to be part of it, but I'm not going to ask you anymore. It's not fair to you. And your reasons not to go are none of my business.

LINDA: You know what my mother's like. She's given me some sense of being responsible for what goes on around me. But always from a distance, always how I should send in my dimes or volunteer for an afternoon like she does. As long as it's safe. Never, never, have I put myself, my very body, on the line. But this time I'm going to. I believe in this so much, I can't stand the thought anymore of living in the world like it is!

HONEY: *(To WES)* What about your reputation as an organizer?

WES: Not as important as us staying friends.

LINDA: Nothing is. So, no matter what, I'm on my way.

HONEY: *(After a moment)* Thanks. Both of you. It's a relief I don't have to baby-sit you, after all. You'll really be on your own for once.

WES: Look at that clock. *(On his way out)* I'm 'bout to turn into a pumpkin.

HONEY: Just a second. *(WES waits)* Who's going in my place? If you take your car?

WES: I don't know. The fella' from Indiana, maybe.

HONEY: You see, there was no way. I'd have had to go see Curtis first, and mama, to tell them my mind. In person.

LINDA: That's what I'm doing. Going down to the city for a few days to drop off some of my stuff.

WES: I'm camping out for a while. Along the Appalachian Trail, matter of fact. Then I'll swoop on down in the buggy and fetch Linda.

HONEY: *(To WES)* You're not going home?

WES: I'll see them on the way back. After the summer.

HONEY: You two wouldn't have wanted a third, anyway.

LINDA: Not if it was some jerk from Indiana.

HONEY: I would have missed the orientation.

WES: We'd have told you about it when we picked you up. Opelika's right on the way down.

HONEY: No. I'd have met you in Birmingham.

LINDA: *(To WES)* Sedrick wouldn't approve of us.

HONEY: Damn right he wouldn't! But it's up to *me*. Not him, not Curtis, not mama. *(To LINDA)* You really going to study the boring Constitution and Mississippi history so you can teach it to the locals?

LINDA: More relevant than Nietzsche, don't you think?

HONEY: Who's gonna translate for you two? *(They shrug, wait carefully)* I guess . . . *(She mumbles something, turning away)*

WES: What?

HONEY: *(A firm realization)* I guess I don't really want to have old Curtis for my boss. *(Pause)* I've got to set that man straight. Maybe after I get you started off—

LINDA: That means—

HONEY: Yeah. That you've got a *shoonk* for a roommate.

LINDA: *(Laughing)* A schnook. *(Jumping up and down, hugging HONEY, while WES whoops and pounds on the wall)* She's in!

WES: Sounds like our reverse psychology ploy—

LINDA: And our honesty act—

WES: Won her over.

HONEY: *(New York)* Don't press your luck, buddy.

LINDA: *(Grabbing HONEY's hand)* Thank y'all evah so much, Honey Johnson. Y'all.

WES: *(Taking HONEY's other hand)* Me too.

The three stand, hands joined. HONEY, between LINDA and WES, pulls them close together.

HONEY: Now do we sing "We Shall Overcome"?

LINDA and WES laugh, drop hands.

LINDA: *(To HONEY)* How can you make fun of that song?
HONEY: How can you be such a knee-jerk?
LINDA: How can you be such a—
WES: How 'bout us making a toast.

He grabs a coffee cup, as do the others.

HONEY: All right. *(Starting big, a joke)* Here's to—*(Suddenly quiet)* . . . to
   the summer of '64.
LINDA: *(Quietly)* To changing the future.

Pause. They look at each other happily.

ALL THREE: The future!

They raise their arms in a toast as lights fade to black.

*At the last edge of the fade, a full-throated, high-spirited version of "I'm On
My Way," begins playing into and through the blackout.*

END OF PLAY

Fires in the Mirror

Anna Deavere Smith

Anna Deavere Smith

Anna Deavere Smith "has created a new form of theater, a blend of theatrical art, social commentary, journalism and intimate reverie," noted the MacArthur Foundation in 1996 when presenting her with one of their prestigious fellowships. The best known plays emerging from Smith's unique blend of interview, playwriting and performance are *Fires in the Mirror*, produced in 1992, and *Twilight: Los Angeles, 1992*, produced in 1993.

Fires in the Mirror is based on individuals involved in and reacting to the 1991 rioting in the Crown Heights neighborhood of Brooklyn, New York, following the accidental death of a seven-year-old Black boy killed by a white Hasidic driver and the murder of a Jewish student by Black teenagers in the aftermath of that accident. *Twilight: Los Angeles, 1992* again uses a variety of individuals to examine the rioting which followed the Rodney King verdict acquitting police despite videotaped evidence in the beating of African American King. Though both plays were eventually performed by other actors, they were launched as one-person plays in which the playwright transformed herself into a variety of Jewish, African American, Asian American and white characters. In the case of *Fires in the Mirror*, Smith so thoroughly expresses the words of twenty-six characters, one forgets she is a light-skinned, Baltimore-born Black woman of a particular age. One hears only the individual voices, one by one.

While the actual people depicted in these plays are often in conflict, the fact that they are all enacted by one person tends to undercut emotions of alienation, animosity and hatred. In productions of these plays which do not feature Smith as the single, all-purpose performer, multiple roles are usually played by just a few actors to continue the effect of lines being crossed between men and women, old and young, African American, Jewish American and white Christian characters. And so, without a forced message of brotherhood, each audience member is encouraged to make a personal leap of empathy with all these varied characters.

Smith has told live audiences, "I think we all have immense potential for compassion as individuals. But that gets stopped when we take on fixed positions."[1]

Early in her career, Smith convinced individuals to participate in her playmaking by saying: "If you give me an hour of your time, I'll invite you to see yourself performed." Though some of those she portrays are recognizable personalities, most of her subjects are part of the anonymous crowd. Her works, much like the oral histories of Studs Terkel, provide a cure for invisibility. In the introduction to the published version of *Fires in the Mirror*, Smith observes that "everyone, in a given amount of time, will say something that is like poetry. The process of getting to that poetic moment is where 'character' lives."[2]

> My sense is that American character lives not in one place or the other, but in the gaps between the places, and in our struggle to be together in our differences. It lives not in what has been fully articulated, but in what is in the process of being articulated, not in the smooth-sounding words, but in the very moment that the smooth-sounding words fail us. It is alive right now. We might not like what we see, but in order to change it, we have to see it clearly.[3]

To the academic world, Anna Deavere Smith is a pioneer using playwriting and theater to illuminate significant social upheavals. She is a Professor at New York University's Tisch School of the Arts and founder of the Institute on the Arts & Civil Dialogue based at Harvard, where she works with the Ford Foundation to explore the role of the arts in relation to vital social issues. Actors, writers, and other artists know her as the author of *Talk to me: Listening between the lines* and the dispenser of advice from her own varied career, *Letters to a Young Artist*.

To the public, she is a television actress, memorable on *The West Wing* and *The Practice*, a featured performer in movies including *Dave, Phila-delphia, The Human Stain,* and *The American President.* Those who have witnessed her performing her plays know her as the woman of a thousand faces and voices. But the greatest compliment to Smith would be not knowing her, just knowing the individuals whose words she has culled and delivered with utter authenticity.

Notes

1. http://www.salon.com/bc/1998/12/cov...08bc.html.
2. Anna Deavere Smith, "Introduction," *Fires in the Mirror* (New York: Anchor Books/Doubleday, 1993), p. xxxi.
3. Ibid, p. xli.

Fires in the Mirror

Cast of Characters

NTOZAKE SHANGE: Playwright, poet, novelist.

ANONYMOUS LUBAVITCHER WOMAN: Preschool teacher.

GEORGE C. WOLFE: Playwright, director, producing director of the New York Shakespeare Festival.

AARON M. BERNSTEIN: Physicist at Massachusetts Institute of Technology.

ANONYMOUS GIRL: Junior high school black girl of Haitian descent. Lives in Brooklyn near Crown Heights.

THE REVEREND AL SHARPTON: Well-known New York activist, minister.

RIVKAH SIEGAL: Lubavitcher woman, graphic designer.

ANGELA DAVIS: Author, orator, activist, scholar. Professor in the History of Consciousness Department at the University of California, Santa Cruz.

MONIQUE "BIG MO" MATTHEWS: Los Angeles rapper.

LEONARD JEFFRIES: Professor of African American Studies at City University of New York, former head of the department.

LETTY COTTIN POGREBIN: Author *Deborah, Golda, and Me*. One of the founding editors of *Ms.* magazine.

MINISTER CONRAD MOHAMMED: New York minister for the Honorable Louis Farrakhan.

ROBERT SHERMAN: Director, Mayor of the City of New York's Increase the Peace Corps.

RABBI JOSEPH SPIELMAN: Spokesperson in the Lubavitch community.

THE REVEREND CANON DOCTOR HERON SAM: Pastor, St. Mark's, Crown Heights Church.

ANONYMOUS YOUNG MAN #1: Crown Heights resident.

MICHAEL S. MILLER: Executive Directory at the Jewish Community Relations Council.

HENRY RICE: Crown Heights resident.

NORMAN ROSENBAUM: Brother of Yankel Rosenbaum. A barrister from Australia.

ANONYMOUS YOUNG MAN #2: African American young man, late teens, early twenties. Resident of Crown Heights.

Sᴏɴɴʏ Cᴀʀsᴏɴ: Activist.

Rᴀʙʙɪ Sʜᴇᴀ Hᴇᴄʜᴛ: Lubavitcher rabbi, spokesperson.

Rɪᴄʜᴀʀᴅ Gʀᴇᴇɴ: Director, Crown Heights Youth Collective. Co-director Project CURE, a Black-Hasidic basketball team that developed after the riots.

Rᴏsʟʏɴ Mᴀʟᴀᴍᴜᴅ: Lubavitcher resident of Crown Heights.

Rᴇᴜᴠᴇɴ Osᴛʀᴏᴠ: Lubavitcher youth, member, project CURE; at the time of the riot, was seventeen years old. Worked as assistant chaplain at Kings County Hospital.

Cᴀʀᴍᴇʟ Cᴀᴛᴏ: Father of Gavin Cato. Crown Heights resident, originally from Guyana.

Ntozake Shange

The Desert

(This interview was done on the phone at about 4:00 p.m. Philadelphia time. The only cue Ntozake gave about her physical appearance was that she took one earring off to talk on the phone. On stage we placed her upstage center in an arm chair, smoking. Then we placed her standing, downstage.)

Hummmmm.

Identity—

it, is, uh . . . in a way it's, um . . . it's sort of, it's uh . . .

it's a psychic sense of place

it's a way of knowing I'm not a rock or that tree?

I'm this other living creature over here?

And it's a way of knowing that no matter where I put

myself

that I am not necessarily

what's around me.

I am part of my surroundings

and I become separate from them

and it's being able to make those differentiations clearly

that lets us have an identity

and what's inside our identity

is everything that's ever happened to us.

Everything that's ever happened

to us as well as our responses to it

'cause we might be alone in a trance state,

someplace like the desert

and we begin to feel as though
we are part of the desert—
which we are right at that minute—
but we are not the desert,
uh . . .
we are part of the desert,
and when we go home
we take with us that part of the desert that the desert gave us,
but we're still not the desert.
It's an important differentiation to make because you
    don't know
what you're giving if you don't know what you have and
    you don't
know what you're taking if you don't know what's yours
    and what's
somebody else's.

Anonymous

Lubavitcher Woman

Static

(This interview was actually done on the phone. Based on what she told me
she was doing, and on the three visits I had made to her home for other
interviews, I devised this physical scene. A Lubavitcher woman, in a wig, and
loose-fitting clothes. She is in her mid-thirties. She is folding clothes. There are
several children around. Three boys of different ages are lying together on the
couch. The oldest is reading to the younger two. A teen-age girl with long hair,
a button-down-collar shirt, and skirt is sweeping the floor.)

Well,
it was um,
getting toward the end of Shabbas,
like around five in the afternoon,
and it was summertime
and sunset isn't until about eight, nine o'clock,
so there were still quite a few hours left to go
and my baby had been playing with the knobs on the
    stereo system
then all of a sudden he pushed the button—
the *on* button—
and all of a sudden came blaring out,

at full volume,
sort of like a half station
of polka music.
But just like with the static,
it was blaring, blaring
and we can't turn off,
we can't turn off electrical,
you know electricity, on Shabbas.
So um,
uh . . .
there was—
we just were trying to ignore it,
but a young boy that was visiting us,
he was going nuts already, he said
it was giving him such a headache could we do something
    about it,
couldn't we get a baby
to turn it off;
we can't make the baby turn it off but if the baby,
but if a child under three
turns something on or turns something off it's not
    considered against the Torah,
so we put the baby by it and tried to get the baby to turn it off,
he just probably made it worse,
so the guest was so uncomfortable that I said I would go
    outside
and see if I can find someone who's not Jewish and see if
    they would
like to—
see if they could turn it off,
so you can have somebody who's not Jewish do a simple
    act like
turning on the light or turning off the light,
and I hope I have the law correct,
but you can't ask them to do it directly.
If they wanna do it of their own free will—
and hopefully they would get some benefit from it too,
so I went outside
and I saw
a little
boy in the neighborhood
who I didn't know and didn't know me—
not Jewish, he was black and he wasn't wearing a
    yarmulke because you can't—

so I went up to him and I said to him
that my radio is on really loud and I can't turn it off,
could he help me,
so he looked at me a little crazy like,
Well?
And I said I don't know what to do,
so he said okay,
so he followed me into the house
and he hears this music on so loud
and so unpleasant
and so
he goes over to the
stereo
and he says, "You see this little button here
that says on and off?
Push that in
and that turns it off."
And I just sort of stood there looking kind of dumb
and then he went and pushed it,
and we laughed that he probably thought:
And people say Jewish people are really smart and they
     don't know
how to turn off their radios.

George C. Wolfe

101 Dalmatians

(The Mondrian Hotel in Los Angeles. Morning, Sunny. A very nice room. George is wearing denim jeans, a light blue denim shirt, and white leather tennis shoes. His hair is in a ponytail. He wears tortoise/wire spectacles. He is drinking tea with milk. The tea is served on a tray, the cups and teapot are delicate porcelain. George is sitting on a sofa, with his feet up on the coffee table.)

I mean I grew up on a black—
a one-block street—
that was black.
My grandmother lived on that street
my cousins lived around the corner.
I went to this
Black—Black—
private Black grade school
where

I was extraordinary.
Everybody there was extraordinary.
You were told you were extraordinary.
It was very clear
that I could not go to see *101 Dalmatians* at the Capital
    Theatre
because it was segregated.
And at the same time
I was treated like I was the most extraordinary creature
    that had
been born.
So I'm on my street in my house,
at my school—
and I was very spoiled too—
so I was treated like I was this special special creature.
And then I would go beyond a certain point
I was treated like I was insignificant.
Nobody was
hosing me down or calling me nigger.
It was just that I was insignificant.

(Slight pause)

You know what I mean so it was very clear of

(Teacup on saucer strike twice on "very clear")

where my extraordinariness lived.
You know what I mean.
That I was extraordinary as long as I was Black.
But I am—not—going—to place myself

(Pause)

in relationship to your whiteness.
I will talk about your whiteness if we want to talk about that.
But I,
but what,
that which,
what I—
what am I saying?
My blackness does not resis—ex- re-
exist in relationship to your whiteness.

(Pause)

You know

(Not really a question, more like a hum)

(Slight pause)
it does not exist in relationship to—
it *exists*
it *exists.*
I come—
you know what I mean—
like I said, I, I, I,
I come from—
it's a very *complex,*
confused,
*neu-*rotic,
at times destructive
reality, but it is completely
and totally a reality
contained and, and,
and full unto itself.
It's complex.
It's demonic.
It's ridiculous.
It's absurd.
It's evolved.
It's all the stuff.
That's the way I grew up.

(Slight pause)

So that *therefore*—
and then you're White—

(Quick beat)

And then there's a point when,
and then these two things come into contact.

Aaron M. Bernstein

Mirrors and Distortions

(Evening, Cambridge, Massachusetts. Fall. He is a man in his fifties, wearing a sweater and a shirt with a pen guard. He is seated at a round wooden table with a low-hanging lamp.)

Okay, so a mirror is something that reflects light.
It's the simplest instrument to understand,
okay?

So a simple mirror is just a flat
reflecting
substance, like,
for example,
it's a piece of glass which is silvered on the back,
okay?
Now the notion of distortion also goes back into literature,
okay?
I'm trying to remember from art—
You probably know better than I.
You know you have a pretty young woman and she looks
    in a mirror
and she's a witch

(He laughs)

because she's evil on the inside.
That's not a real mirror,
as everyone knows—
where
you see the inner thing.
Now that really goes back in literature.
So everyone understood that mirrors don't distort,
so that was a play
not on words
but a concept.
But physicists do
talk about distortion.
It's a big
subject, distortions.
I'll give you an example—
if you wanna see the
stars
you make a big
reflecting mirror—
that's one of the ways—
you make a big telescope
so you can gather in a lot of light
and then it focuses at a point
and then there's always something called the circle of
    confusion.
So if ya don't make the thing perfectly spherical or
    perfectly
parabolic

then,
then, uh, if there are errors in the construction
which you can see, it's easy, if it's huge,
then you're gonna have a circle of confusion,
you see?
So that's the reason for making the
telescope as large as you can,
because you want that circle
to seem smaller,
and you want to easily see errors in the construction.
So, you see, in physics it's very practical—
if you wanna look up in the heavens
and see the stars as well as you can
without distortion.
If you're counting stars, for example,
and two look like one,
you've blown it.

Anonymous Girl

Look in the Mirror

(Morning. Spring. A teen-age Black girl of Haitian descent. She has hair which is straightened, and is wearing a navy blue jumper and a white shirt. She is seated in a stairwell at her junior high school in Brooklyn.)

When I look in the mirror . . .
I don't know.
How did I find out I was Black . . .

(Tongue sound)

When I grew up and I look in the mirror and saw I was
 Black.
When I look at my parents,
That's how I knew I was Black.
Look at my skin.
You Black?
Black is beautiful.
I don't know.
That's what I always say.
I think White is beautiful too.
But I think Black is beautiful too.
In my class nobody is White, everybody's Black,

and some of them is Hispanic.
In my class
you can't call any of them Puerto Ricans.
They despise Puerto Ricans, I don't know why.
They think that Puerto Ricans are stuck up and
    everything.
They say, Oh my Gosh my nail broke, look at the cute
    guy and everything.
But they act like that themselves.
They act just like White girls.
Black girls is not like that.
Please, you should be in my class.
Like they say that Puerto Ricans act like that
and they don't see that they act like that themselves.
Black girls, they do bite off the Spanish girls,
they bite off of your clothes.
You don't know what that means? biting off?
Like biting off somebody's clothes.
Like cop, following,
and last year they used to have a lot of girls like that.
They come to school with a style, right?
And if they see another girl with that style?
Oh my gosh look at her.
What she think she is,
she tryin' to bite off of me in some way
no don't be bitin' off of my sneakers
or like that.
Or doin' a hairstyle
I mean Black people are into hairstyles.
So they come to school, see somebody with a certain style,
they say uh-huh I'm gonna get me one just like that uh-huh,
that's the way Black people are.
Yea-ah!
They don't like people doing that to them
and they do that to other people,
so the Black girls will follow the Spanish girls.
The Spanish girls don't bite off of us.
Some of the Black girls follow them.
But they don't mind
They don't care.
They follow each other.
Like there's three girls in my class,
they from the Dominican Republic.
They all stick together like glue.

They all three best friends.
They don't follow nobody,
like there's none of them lead or anything.
They don't hang around us either.
They're
by themselves.

The Reverend Al Sharpton

Me and James's Thing

(Early afternoon. Fall. A small room that is a part of a suite of offices in a building on West Fifty-seventh Street and Seventh Avenue in New York. A very large man, Black man with straightened hair. Reverend Sharpton's hair is in the style of James Brown's hair. He is wearing a suit, colorful tie, and a gold medallion that was given to him by Martin Luther King, Jr. Reverend Sharpton has a pinky ring, a very resonant voice even in this small room. There is a very built, very tall man who sits behind me during the interview. Reverend Sharpton's face is much younger, and more innocent than it appears to be in the media. His humor is in his face. He is very direct. The interview only lasts fifteen minutes because he had been called out of a meeting in progress to do the interview.)

James Brown raised me.
Uh . . .
I never had a father.
My father left when I was ten.
James Brown took me to the beauty parlor one day
and made my hair like his.
And made me promise
to wear it like that
'til I die.
It's a personal family thing
between me and James Brown.
I always wanted a father
and he filled that void.
And the strength that he's demonstrated—
I don't know anybody that reached his heights,
and then had to go as low as he did and come back.
And I think that if anybody I met in life deserved that type of
tribute from
somebody
that he wanted a kid

to look like him
and be like his son . . .
I just came home from spending a weekend with him now,
uh, uh,
I think James deserved that.
And just like
he was the father I never had,
his kids never even visited him when he went to jail.
So I was like the kid he never had.
And if I had to choose between arguing with people about my
hairstyle
or giving him that one tribute
he axed,
I'd rather give him that tribute
because he filled a void for me.
And I really don't give a damn
who doesn't understand it.
Oh, I know not you, not you.
The press and everybody do
their thing on that.
It's a personal thing between me and James Brown.
And just like
in other communities
people do their cultural thing
with who they wanna look like,
uh,
there's nothing wrong with me doing
that with James.
It's, it's, *us.*
I mean in the fifties it was a slick.
It was acting like White folks.
But today
people don't wear their hair like that.
James and I the only ones out there doing that.
So it's certainlih not
a reaction to Whites.
It's me and James's thing.

Rivkah Siegal

Wigs

*(Early afternoon. Spring. The kitchen of an apartment in Crown Heights.
A very pretty Lubavitcher woman, with clear eyes and a direct gaze, wear-*

ing a wig and a knit sweater, that looks as though it might be hand knit.
A round wooden table. Coffee mug. Sounds of children playing in the street
are outside. A neighbor, a Lubavitcher woman with light blond hair who no
longer wears the wig, observes the interview at the table.)

Your hair—
It only has to be—
there's different,
u h m,
customs in different
Hasidic groups.
Lubavitch
the system is
it should be two inches
long.
It's—
some groups
have
the custom
to shave their
heads.
There's—
the reason is,
when you go to the mikvah [bath]
you may, maybe,
it's better if it's short
because of what you—
the preparation
that's involved
and that
you have to go under the water.
The hair has a tendency to float
and you have to be completely submerged
including your hair.
So . . .
And I got married
when I was a little older,
and I really wanted to be married
and I really wanted to, um . . .
In some ways I was eager to cover my head.
Now if I had grown up in a Lubavitch household
and then had to cut it,
I don't know what that would be like.
I really don't.

But now that I'm wearing the wig,
you see,
with my hair I can keep it very simple
and I can change it all the time.
So with a wig you have to have like five wigs if you want to
    do that.
But I, uh,
I feel somehow like it's fake,
I feel like it's not me.
I try to be as much myself as I can,
and it just
bothers me
that I'm kind of fooling the world.
I used to go to work.
People . . .
and I would wear a different wig,
and they'd say I like your new haircut
and I'd say it's not mine!
You know,
and it was very hard for me to say it
and
it became very difficult.
I mean, I've gone through a lot with wearing wigs and not
    wearing
wigs.
It's been a big issue for me.

Angela Davis

Rope

*(Morning. Spring. Oakland, California. In reality this interview was done
on the phone, with myself and Thulani Davis. Thulani and I were calling
from an office at the Public Theatre. We do not know exactly what Angela
was doing or wearing. I believe, from things she said, that she was sitting
on her deck in her home, which overlooks a beautiful panorama of trees.)*

Race, um—
of course
for many years in the history
of African Americans in this country—
was synonymous with community.
As a matter of fact

we were race women and race men.
Billie Holiday for example
called herself a race woman
because she supported the community
and as a child growing up in the South
my assumptions were
that if anybody in the race
came under attack
then I had to be there
to support that person,
to support the race.
I was saying to my students just the other day,
I said,
if in 1970,
when I was
in jail,
someone had told me
that in 1991,
a Black man
who
said that his, um . . .
hero—

(Increased volume, speed, and energy)

one of his heroes
was Malcolm X—
would be nominated to the Supreme Court
I would have celebrated
and I don't think it would have been possible at that time
to convince me
that I would
be absolutely opposed,
a Black candidate—
I mean like absolutely—

(A new attack, more energy)

or that if anyone would have told me that
a *woman* would
finally be elected to the Supreme Court,
it would have been very difficult,
as critical as I am with respect to feminism,
as critical as I have always been with what I used to call,
you know, narrow nationalism?
I don't think

it would have been possible to convince me that things
    would have so absolutely
shifted that
someone could have evoked
the specter of lynching
on national television
and that specter of lynching would be used to violate our
    history.
And I still feel that
we have to point out the racism involved
in the razing of a Black man
and a Black woman
in that way.
I mean [Ted] Kennedy was sitting right there
and it had never occurred to anyone to bring him up
before
the world,
which is not to say that I don't think it should happen.
And it is actually a sign of how we,
in our various oppressed
marginalized communities,
have been able to turn
terrible acts of racism directed against us
into victory . . .
And therefore I think
Anita Hill did that,
and so it's very complicated,
but I have no problems aligning myself politically
against Clarence Thomas in a real passionate way,
but at the same time I can talk about the racism that led
to the possibility
of constructing those kinds of hearings
and
the same thing with Mike Tyson.
So I guess that would be,
um . . .
the way in which I would begin to look at community,
and would therefore think
that race has become, uh,
an increasingly obsolete way
of constructing community
because it is based on unchangeable

immutable biological
facts
in a very pseudo-scientific way,
alright?
Now
racism is entirely different
because see *racism*,
uh,
actually I think
is
at the origins of this concept of race.
It's not—
it's not the other way around,
that there were racists,
and then the racists—
one race came to dominate
the others.
As a matter of fact
in order for a European colonialist
to attempt
to conquer the world,
to colonize the world,
they had to construct this notion
of,
uh,
the populations of the earth being divided into certain,
uh,
firm biological, uh,
communities,
and that's what I think we have to go back and look at.
So when I use the word race now I put it in quotations.
Because if we don't transform
this . . . this intransigent
rigid
notion of race,
we will be caught up in this cycle
of genocidal
violence
that, um,
is at the origins of our history.
So I think—
and I'm

convinced—
and this is what I'm working on in my political practice
    right now—
is that we have to find ways of coming together in a
    different way,
not the old notion of coalition in which we anchor ourselves very solidly
in our,
um,
communities,
and simply voice
our
solidarity with other people.
I'm not suggesting that we do not anchor ourselves in our
    communities;
I feel very anchored in,
um,
my various communities,
but I think that,
you know,
to use a metaphor, the rope
attached to that anchor should be long enough to allow us
    to move
into other communities
to understand and learn.
I've been thinking a lot about the need to make more
    intimate
these connections and associations and to really take on
    the responsibility
of learning.
So I think that we need to—
in order to find ways of working with
and understanding
the vastness
of our many cultural heritages
and ways of coming together without
rendering invisible all of that heterogeneity—
I don't have the answer,
you know
I don't know.
What I'm interested in is communities
that are not static,
that
can change, that can respond to new historical needs.
So I think it's a very exciting moment.

Monique "Big Mo" Matthews

Rhythm and Poetry

(In reality this interview was done on an afternoon in the spring of 1989, while I was in residence at the University of California, Los Angeles, as a fellow at the Center for Afro-American Studies. Mo was a student of mine. We were sitting in my office, which was a narrow office, with sunlight. I performed Mo in many shows, and in the course of performing her, I changed the setting to a performance setting, with microphone. I was inspired by a performance that I saw of Queen Latifah in San Francisco, and by Mo's behavior in my class, which was performance behavior, to change the setting to one that was more theatrical, since Mo's everyday speech was as theatrical as Latifah's performance speech. Speaking directly to the audience, pacing the stage.)

And she say, "This is for the fellas,"
and she took off all her clothes and she had on a leotard
that had all cuts and stuff in it,
and she started doin' it on the floor.
They were like
"Go, girl!"
People like, "That look really stink."
But that's what a lot of female rappers do—
like to try to get off,
they sell they body or pimp they body
to, um, get play.
And you have people like Latifah who doesn't, you know, she talks
   intelligent.
You have Lyte who's just hard and people are scared by her
hardness,
her strength of her words.
She encompasses that whole, New York—street sound.
It's like, you know, she'll like . . .
what's a line?
What's a line
like "Paper Thin,"
"IN ONE EAR AND RIGHT OUT THE OTHUH."
It's like,
"I don't care what you have to say,
I'm gittin' done what's gotta be done.
Man can't come across me.
A female she can't stand against me.
I'm just the toughest, I'm just the hardest/You just can't
   come up
against me/if you do you get waxed!"

It's like a lot of my songs,
I don't know if I'm gonna get blacklisted for it.
The image that I want is a strong strong African strong
    Black woman
and I'm not down with what's going on, like Big Daddy
    Kane had a song
out called "Pimpin Ain't Easy," and he sat there and he
    talk for the
whole song, and I sit there I wanna slap him, I wanna slap
    him so
hard, and he talks about, it's one point he goes, yeah
u m,
"Puerto Rican girls Puerto Rican girls call me Papi and
White girls say
even White girls say I'm a hunk!"
I'm like,
"What you mean 'even'?
Oh! Black girls ain't good enough for you huh?"
And one of my songs has a line that's like
"PIMPIN' AIN'T EASY BUT WHORIN' AIN'T
    PROPER. RESPECT AND
CHERISH THE ORIGINAL MOTHER."
And a couple of my friends were like,
"Aww, Mo, you good but I can't listen to you 'cause you be Men
bashin'."
I say,
"It ain't men bashin', it's female assertin'."
Shit.
I'm tired of it.
I'm tired of my friends just acceptin'
that they just considered to be a ho.
You got a song,
"Everybody's a Hotty."
A "hotty" means you a freak, you a ho,
and it's like Too Short
gets up there and he goes,
"B I AYYYYYYYYYYYYYE."
Like he stretches "bitch" out for as long as possible,
like you just a ho and you can't be saved,
and 2 Live Crew. . . . "we want some pussy," and the
    girls! "La le la le la le la,"
it's like my friends say,
"Mo, if you so bad how come you don't never say nothing
    about Two

Live Crew?"
When I talk about rap,
and I talk about people demeaning rap,
I don't even mention them
because they don't understand the fundamentals of rap.
Rap, rap
is basically
broken down
Rhythm
and Poetry.
And poetry is expression.
It's just like poetry; you release so much through poetry
    you get
angry, you get it?
Poetry is like
intelligence.
You just release it all and if you don't have a complex
    rhyme
it's like,
"I'm goin to the store."
What rhymes with store?
More store for more bore
"I'm going to the store I hope I don't get bored,"
it's like,
"WHAT YOU SAYIN', MAN? WHO CARES?"
You have to have something that flows.
You have to be def,
D-E-F.
I guess I have to think of something for you that ain't slang.
Def is dope, def is live
when you say somethin's dope
it means it is the epitome of the experience
and you have to be def by your very presence
because you have to make people happy.
And we are living in a society where people are not happy
    with their everyday lives.

Leonard Jeffries

Roots

*(3:00 p.m. Wednesday, November 20, 1991. A very large conference room
in the African American Studies Department at CUNY. Drawn venetian*

blinds, fluorescent lighting. Dr. Jeffries wears a light, multicolored African top, and a multicolored African hat. His shoes are black functional shoes, like the shoes to a uniform. He sits facing the table, and often sits back with the chair back from the table, often touches the table, and often sits back with the chair on its back legs only. Sometimes he scratches his head by throwing his hat forward on his head with great ease and authority. There is a bodyguard, a large heavy-set African American man, present.)

People are asking who is this guy Jeffries?
When they find out my background they're gonna be
    surprised.
They are gonna find out that I was even related to Alex Haley.
In fact I was a major consultant for *Roots.*
In fact there might not have been a *Roots* without me.
Now when I say that,
that's my own personal in-group joke wit' Alex.
He was in Philadelphia
getting his ticket to go down to Jamaica
and
Roots was lost.
He had it in a duffle bag,
a big duffle bag like this,
the whole manuscript.
It was lost in the airport of Philadelphia.
I got on my horse and ran around the airport of
    Philadelphia
and found *Roots.*
So that's my joke.
He had this manuscript,
Alex didn't have anything else but this manuscript.
Now if he had lost that, that would have been it.
He didn't have any photocopies.
Alex did everything on a shoestring.
u h m
so for him to deny me now . . .
He never even acknowledged
Pat
Alexander
his girlfriend/secretary who he had paid with affection and
    not with
resources.
So I didn't expect him to acknowledge me.
He called me to come down.
I called my wife who was working on her Ph.D. at Yale.

I said, "Rosalind, Alex wants us to come down to
    Brunswick, Georgia,
they're filming *Roots*."
She said yes she'd come down and we'd go, then she called
    me back.
She said, "I got too much work," so I went down to
    Brunswick, Georgia.
He introduced me to Margulies,
who was the, um, director
of *Roots*,
as the leading expert in America on Africa, and I said,
    "Wow," to
myself, "that's kind of high."
When Margulies said,
"That makes me number two," then I realized what Alex
    was doing to keep *Roots* honest.
So for two weeks I tried to change *Roots*.
Alex would say, "Wait a
minute, let's consult the experts."
After two weeks they got tired of me, sat me down
and said, "Dr. Jeffries," at lunch,
"we are very happy to have you here
but we just bought the rights to the book *Roots*
and we are under no obligation to maintain the integrity of
    the book
and we certainly don't have to deal with the truth of Black
    history."
Now,
this was a wipeout for me
I
I, there's been very few *traumatic*
moments

(Longest pause in his text)

uh, just to think.
Now I wasn't even prepared for this
but Pat had called me before and said,
"Len, I'm looking at this document and I don't know what
    to make of it."
I said, "What is it, Pat, what is it?"
and I knew she was nervous, she said,
"I'm reading a contract that says
"*Roots* has been sold to David Wolper and their heirs for
    ever and
ever

(He is thumping his hand on table)
and their heirs for ever and ever."
Alex had signed the contract for fifty thousand dollars.
(He is thumping his hand on table)
Fifty thousand dollars for paperback *Roots*.
Something that made how much?
Three hundred million dollars?
He was suing them for years.
The millions he made on TV *Roots* he spent a lot of it to
    sue
Doubleday to get a better deal—I don't know if he ever got
    it.
Roots was a devastation.
The tens of millions and hundreds of millions made on
    Roots
went to produce,
not to make more Black series,
like *Roots*,
but they went to produce a *series*
maybe a dozen mini-series on *Jewish* history
as opposed to Black history.
You can document what was produced in terms of Black
    history
compared to what was produced of Jewish history.
It's a devastation.
But the *one* thing that came out of this for me,
was that when these people told me, you know,
"We bought your research.
We bought your history.
You really have no . . . "
I was thrown off.
I had to get out of there.
I stayed for another couple of days.
I told Alex I had to make a pilgrimage to my grandfather's
    grave.
Never saw my grandfather.
Then I watched one more scene in the Alex Haley thing
and that finished it for me.
A cutaway of a slave ship
that was so real that they had to bring in these high school
    kids,
and once these high school kids played the enslaved
    Africans greased

down in simulated vomit
and feces
they couldn't come back,
so they had to continue to get,
go take these youngsters,
and some little White woman
who was there sleeping with one of those guys,
they told her, "You cannot take these kids without
    authorization."
But she would drive a bus
up to the schoolyard,
put the kids in it, and bring them to the set.
And it almost produced a riot
there.
But anyway this slave scene
was so realistic
the trainer's up on a lower deck
and Kunta Kinte's on a bottom deck
and they call down to each other,
and the trainer says,
"Kunta Kinte,
Be strong! Be strong!
We may have to fight.
Kill the White man and return to Mother Africa."
This was high drama.
All of us grown men over hiding in the shadows in *tears*.
Then
Green rushes out and said, "Break! Break!"
He said he didn't want the scene.
We said, "What?"
Even Lou Gossett and them were ready to *fight*!
You know 'cause they had—
a movie script is just
a skeleton,
you have to put your soul in a movie script,
and they put their heart and soul into what would have
    been . . .
And with the African—
because the "earth is mother" all over Africa.
So to say to go back to Mother Africa is a very meaningful
    phrase.
But this
Englishman refused
to accept it,

and they almost had a physical fight on the set.
They compromised and said,
"We—are—all—from—one—village,"
(Hitting his hand rhythmically on the desk)
which is not the same thing.
After that I said, "I have to go."
I said I have to go,
and I rented a—
I flew out with Lorne Greene of all people.
He saw me and we had known each other for a couple of
     weeks from
the set,
and he's sitting there drinking this little drink
talking about "Isn't *Roots* wonderful.
It's everybody's history,"
and I'm dying.

(Pause)

Get to Atlanta.
Rent a car. Cut across the Georgia countryside.
Came to a fork in the road,
made the right turn,
and there
on a bluff
was a clapboard church
made by my grandfather
and
four
other trustees.
Then when
I went across the cemetery
to see, uh,
the gravesite where he was—
the tallest tombstone in the graveyard was his.
Uhm,
It was an obelisk.
On it was a Masonic symbol.
He was the master of the lodge.
On it was his vital statistics:
"Born August the tenth 1868."
At the birth of the Fourteenth Amendment.
I later learned that his brother Sam was born
1865 at the birth of the Thirteenth Amendment!

And this is why people say,
"Who is he?
What is he?
Why is he?"
If they only know
I've had one of the best educations on the planet.
Yeah.
So . . .
When I went to Albany
in July,
I went knowing that you might not have
much time,
just like my wife said on the radio today:
"When we speak
we speak as though it is the last speech we're gonna make."
But I knew what was at stake
ever since they branded me a conspiracy theorist,
February 12, 1990,
two-column editorial in the *New York Times*.
That was,
in the concept of Jewish thinking,
the kiss of death.
I knew I had been targeted.
Arthur Schlesinger went and wrote a book
called *The Disuniting of America*.
He has everybody in the margin
except a half-page photo of myself
which said to us,
"This is the one they got to kill."
We knew that Schlesinger
and his people had sent out a thousand letters
to CEOs around the country
and foundation heads
not to have anything to do with
all of us involved in these studies
for multicultural curriculum
so, uh . . .
Knowing that I had taken this beating for two and a half
    years
it was my chance to strike out,
but people don't understand
that that was my way of saying,
"You bastids! . . .

for starting this process
of destroying *me*."
That was my striking out.
But people don't know the context.
They don't know that for two and a half years
I bore this burden
by myself
and I bore it well.
And now they've got a problem.
'Cause after they destroyed me,
here he's resurrected!!!!!
I spoke at Columbia, I spoke at Queens College. . . .

Letty Cottin Pogrebin

Near Enough to Reach

(Evening. The day before Thanksgiving, 1991. On the phone. Direct, passionate, confident, lots of volume. She is in a study with a rolltop desk and a lot of books.)

I think it's about rank frustration and the old story
that you pick a scapegoat
that's much more, I mean Jews and Blacks,
that's manageable,
because we're near,
we're still near enough to each other to reach!
I mean, what can you do about the people who voted for
    David Duke?
Are Blacks going to go there and deal with that?
No, it's much easier to deal with Jews who are also panicky.
We're the only ones that pay any attention

(Her voice makes an upward inflection)

Do you hear?
Well, Jeffries did speak about the Mafia being, um,
Mafia,
and the Jews in Hollywood.
I didn't see
this tremendous outpouring of Italian
reaction.
Only *Jews* listen,
only *Jews* take Blacks seriously,

only *Jews* view Blacks as full human beings that you
should *address*
in their rage
and, um,
people don't seem to notice that.
But Blacks, it's like a little child kicking up against Arnold Schwarzenegger
when they,
when they have anything to say about the dominant culture
nobody listens! Nobody reacts!
To get a headline,
to get on the evening news,
you have to attack a Jew.
Otherwise you're ignored.
And it's a shame.
We all play into it.

Minister Conrad Mohammed

Seven Verses

(April 1992, morning. A café/restaurant. Roosevelt Island, New York. We are sitting in the back, in an area that is surrounded by glass floor-to-ceiling windows. Mr. Mohammed is impeccably dressed in a suit of an elegant fabric. He wears a blue shirt and a bow tie. He has on fine shoes, designer socks, and a large fancy watch and wedding ring. His hair is closely cropped. He drinks black coffee, and uses a few packs of sugar. He is traveling with another man, also a Muslim, in the clothing of a Muslim, impeccable, who sits at another table and watches us.)

The condition of the Black man in America today is part
    and parcel,
through the devlishment
that permitted Caucasian people
to rob us of our humanity,
and put us in the throes of slavery...
The fact that our—our Black
parents
were actually taken
as cattle
and as, as
animals
and packed into
slave ships

like sardines
amid feces
and urine—
and the suffering of our people,
for months,
in the middle passage—
Our women,
raped
before our own eyes,
so that today
some look like you,
some look like me,
some look like brother . . .

(Indicating his companion)

This is a crime of tremendous proportion.
In fact,
no crime in the history of humanity
has before or since
equaled that crime.
The Holocaust did not equal it
Oh, absolutely not.
First of all,
that was a horrible crime
and that is something that is a disgrace in the eyes of civilized
people.
That, uh, crime also stinks
in the nostrils of God.
But it in no way compares with the slavery of our people
because we lost over a hundred
and some say two hundred and fifty,
million
in the middle passage
coming from Africa
to America.
We were so thoroughly robbed.
We didn't just lose six million.
We didn't just
endure this
for, for
five or six years
or from '38 to '45 or '39 to—
We endured this for over three hundred years—
the total subjugation of the Black man.

You can go into Bangladesh today,
Calcutta,

(He strikes the table with a sugar packet three or four times)

New Delhi,
Nigeria,
some really
so-called underdeveloped nation,
and I don't care how low that person's humanity is

(He opens the sugar packet)

whether they never
had running water,
if they'd never seen a television or anything.
They are in better condition than the Black man and woman
in America today
right now.
Even at Harvard.
They have a contextual understanding of what identity is.

(He strikes the table with another sugar packet three or four times and opens it)

But the Black man has no knowledge of that;
he's an amnesia victim

(Starts stirring his coffee)

He has lost knowledge of himself

(Stirring his coffee)

and he's living a beast life.

(Stirring his coffee)

So this proves that it was the greatest crime.
Because we were cut off from our past.
Not only were we killed and murdered,
not only were our women raped
in front of their own children.
Not only did the slave master stick

(The spoon drops onto saucer)

at times,
daggers into a pregnant woman's stomach,
slice the stomach open
push the baby out on the ground and crush the head of the
     baby
to instill fear in the Massas of the plantation.

(Stirring again)

Not only were these things done,
not only were our thumbs

(Spoon drops)

put in, in devices
that would just
slowly torture the slave
and tear the thumb off from the root.
Not only were we sold on the auction block
like cattle,
not permitted to marry.
See these are the crimes
of slavery that nobody wants to talk about.
But the most significant crime—
because we could have recovered from all of that—
but the fact that they cut off all knowledge from us,
told us that we were animals,
told us that we were subhuman,
took from us our names,
gave us names like
Smith
and Jones
and today we wear those names
with dignity
and pride,
yet these were the names given to us in one of the greatest
     crimes
ever committed on the face of the earth.
So this kind of thing,
Sister,
is what qualifies slavery
as the greatest
crime
ever committed.
They have stolen
our garment.
Stolen our identity.
The Honorable Louis Farrakhan
teaches us
that *we* are the chosen of God.
We are those people
that almighty God Allah

has selected as his chosen,
and they are masquerading in our garment—
the Jews.
We don't have an identity today.
Because we are the people . . .
There are seven verses
in the Bible,
seven verses,
I believe it is in Deuteronomy,
that the Jews base their chosen people, uh, uh,
claim the theology,
the whole theological exegesis
with respect
of being the chosen
is based upon seven verses
in the Scripture that talk
about a covenant
with Abraham.

Letty Cottin Pogrebin

Isaac

(Morning. Spring. On the phone. She is in her office in her home on West 67th Street and Central Park West in Manhattan. Her office has an old-fashioned wooden rolltop desk and bookcases filled with books. She says she was wearing leggings and a loose shirt.)

Well,
it's hard for me to do that
because
I think there's a tendency to make hay
with the Holocaust,
to push
all the buttons.
And I mean this story about my uncle Isaac—makes *me* cry
and it's going to make your audience cry
and I'm beginning to worry
that
we're trotting out our Holocaust stories
too regularly and that we're going to inure each other to
    the truth of
them.

But
I think
maybe if you let me read it,
I would prefer to read it:

(Reading from Deborah, Golda, and Me*)*

"I remember my mother's cousin
Isaac who came to New York
immediately after the war and lived with us for several
    months.
Isaac is my connection to dozens of other family members who
were murdered in the concentration camps.
Because he was blond and blue-eyed he had been
chosen as the designated survivor of his town.
That is the Jewish councils had instructed him to do
    anything
to stay alive and tell the story.
For Isaac
anything turned out to mean this.
The Germans suspected his forged Aryan papers and
    decided that he
would have to prove by his actions that he was not a Jew.
They put him on a transport train with the Jews of his town
and then gave him the task of herding into the gas chambers
everyone in his train load.
After he had fulfilled that assignment
with patriotic
German efficiency,
the Nazis accepted the authenticity of his identity papers
and let him go.
Among those whom Isaac packed into the gas chambers
    that day
dispassionately as if shoving a few more items into an
    overstuffed
closet
were his wife
and
two children.
The designated survivor
arrived in America
at about age forty

(Breathes in)

with prematurely white hair and a dead gaze within the
    sky blue

eyes that'd helped save his life.
As promised he told his story to dozens of Jewish agencies
and community leaders and to groups of families and
    friends which
is how I heard the account
translated from his Yiddish
by my mother.
For months he talked,
speaking the unspeakable.
Describing a horror
that American Jews had suspected but could not conceive.
A monstrous tale
that dwarfed the demonology of legend
and gave me the nightmare I still dream to this day.
And as he talked
Isaac seemed to grow older and older
until one night
a few months later
when he finished telling everything he knew
he died."

Robert Sherman

Lousy Language

(11:00 a.m. Wednesday, November 13, 1991. A very sunny and large, elegant living room in a large apartment near the Brooklyn Museum. Mr. Sherman is sitting in an armchair near an enormous bouquet of flowers for the birth of his first child. He wears sweats, and a bright orange long-sleeved tee shirt. Smiles frequently, upbeat, impassioned. Fingers his wedding ring. Each phrase builds on the next, pauses are all sustained intensity, never lets up. Full. Lots of volume, clear enunciation, teeth, and tongue very involved in his speech. Good-humored, seems to like the act of speech.)

Do you have demographic information on Crown Heights?
The important thing to remember is that—
and I will check these numbers when I get back to the
    office—
I think the
Hasidim
comprise only ten percent
of the population
of the neighborhood.
The Crown Heights conflict has been brewing on and off
    for twenty years

since the Hasidic community
developed some serious numbers
and some strength in Crown Heights and as African
    Americans and
Caribbean Americans came to make up the dominant
    culture in
Crown Heights.
Very important to remember that
those things that are expressed really as
bias,
those things
that we at the Human Rights Commission
would consider to be bias,
have the same trappings of bias,
which is complaints based on a characteristic, not on
    a knowledge of a
specific person.
There sort of is a soup
of bias—
prejudice, racism, and discrimination.
I think bias really does relate to
feelings with a valence,
feelings with a, uhm,

(Breathing in)

feelings that can go in a direction positive or negative
although we usually use bias to mean a negative.
What it means usually
is negative attitudes
that can lead to negative behaviors:
biased
acts, biased incidents,
or biased crimes.
Racism is hatred based on race.
Discrimination refers to
acts against somebody . . .
so that the words
actually tangle up.
I think in part
because vocabulary
follows general awareness . . . .
I think you know
the Eskimos have seventy words for snow?

We probably have seventy different kinds of bias,
  prejudice, racism, and
discrimination,
but it's not in our mind-set to be clear about it,
so I think that we have
sort of lousy language
on the subject
and that
is a reflection
of our unwillingness
to deal with it honestly
and to sort it out.
I think we have very, very bad language.

Rabbi Joseph Spielman

No Blood in His Feet

(9:30 a.m. Tuesday, November 12, 1991. A large home on President Street in Crown Heights. Only natural light, not very much light. Dark wood. A darkish dining room with an enormous table, could seat twenty. The rabbi sits at the head of the table. Lots of stuff on the table. He wears Hasidic clothing, a black fedora, black jacket, and reading glasses. As he talks, he slightly slides around the tape-recorder microphone, which is in front of him at the table. The furniture in the dining room including his chair is, for the most part, very old, solid wood. There are children playing quietly in another room, and people come in and out frequently, but always whispering and walking carefully not to make noise, unless they speak to him directly. The children at one point came over and stared at me.)

Many people were on the sidewalk,
talking, playing,
drinking
beer or whatever—
being that type of neighborhood.
A car
driven by an individual—
a Hasidic individual—
went through the intersection,
was hit by another car,
thereby causing it to go onto the sidewalk.
The driver on seeing

himself in such a position that he felt he was going to
    definitely hit
someone,
because of the amount of people on the sidewalk,
he steered at the building,
so as to get out of the way of the people.
Obviously, for the most part,
he was successful.
But regrettably,
one child was killed
and another child
was wounded.
Um,
seeing what happened,
he jumped out of the car
and, realizing
there may be a child under the car,
he tried to physically lift
the car
from the child.
Well, as he was doing this
the Afro-Americans were beating him already.
He was beaten so much he needed stitches in the scalp and
    the face,
fifteen and sixteen stitches
and also
there were three other passengers in the car
that were being beaten too.
One of the passengers was calling 911
on the cellular phone.
A Black person
pulled the phone out of his hand and ran.
Just stole the—stole the telephone.
The Jewish community
has a volunteer
ambulance corps
which is funded totally from the nations—
there is not one penny of government funds—
and manned by volunteers—
who many times at their expense—
supplied the equipment that they carry in order to save
    lives.
As one of the EMS ambulances were coming,

one of the Hasidic ambulances or the Jewish ambulances
    came
on the scene.
The EMS responded with three ambulances on the scene.
They were there before
the Jewish ambulance came.
Two or three police cars were already on the scene.
The police saw the potential for violence
and saw that the occupants of the car
were being beaten and were afraid for their safety.
At the same time the EMS asked
the Hasidic ambulances for certain pieces of equipment
    that they
were out of,
that they needed to take care of the Cato kid,
and,
um,
in fact, I was . . .
The Hasidic ambulance left, leaving behind one of the
    passengers.
That passenger had a walkie-talkie and he requested that I
come down to pick him up.
And at that time there was a lot of screaming and shouting
and it was a mixed crowd, Hasidic and Afro-American.
The police said, "Rabbi get your people out of here."
I told them to leave and I left.
Now,
a few hours later,
two and a half hours later,
in a different part of Crown Heights,
a scholar
from Australia,
Yankel Rosenbaum,
who, urr,
I think he had a doctorate or he was working on his
    doctorate,
was walking on the street
on his own—
I mean he was totally oblivious—
and he was accosted by a group of young Blacks
about twenty of them strong
which was being egged on by a Black
male approximately

forty years old and balding,
telling them,
"Kill all Jews—
look what they did to the kid,
kill all Jews,"
and all the epithets that go along with it,
"Heil Hitler" and all of it.
They stabbed him,
which later on the stab wounds were fatal
and he passed away in the hospital.
The Mayor,
hearing about the Cato kid,
came to the Kings County Hospital
to give condolences to the family of the child who had
  regrettably been killed.
At the meantime they had already wheeled in
Mr. Rosenbaum.
He was in the emergency room
and I was at the hospital at the same time,
and the Mayor, seeing me there,
expressed his concern
that a child,
uh, innocent child, had been killed.
Where I explained to him
the fact
that,
whereas the child was killed from an unfortunate accident
where there was no malicious intent,
here
there was an individual lying in the emergency room
who had been stabbed with malicious intent
and for the sole reason—
not that he did anything to anyone—
just from the fact that he happened to be Jewish.
And the mayor went with me to the emergency room
to visit Mr. Rosenbaum.
This was approximately one and a half hours before he
  passed away.
I noticed at the time that his feet
were
completely white.
And I complained to the doctor
on the scene,

"He's having a problem with blood circulation
because there's no blood in his feet."
And she gave me some asinine answer.
And the mayor asked her what his condition is:
"Serious but stable."
In the meantime he was screaming and in pain
and they weren't doing anything.
Subsequently they, um,
they started giving him anesthesia in a time that
they weren't allowed to give him anesthesia
and while he was under anesthesia,
he passed away.
So there was totally mismanagement in his case.
So whereas the Mayor,
had been fed . . .
his people got
whatever information he got out of the Black community was
that
the driver had run a red light
and also,
and that the ambulance,
the Hasidic ambulance,
refused to take care of the Black child that was dying and
rather took care of their own.
Nenh?
And this is what was fed amongst the Black community.
And it was false,
it was totally false
and it was done maliciously
only with the intent to get the riots,
to start up the resulting riots.

The Reverend Canon Doctor Heron Sam

Mexican Standoff

*(November 12, 1991, 4:00 p.m. The rectory office at St. Mark's Church in
Crown Heights. A small, short office. Lived in but impeccably ordered. Some
light from lamps, some from overhead. Plaques and awards everywhere. The
reverend is wearing a yellow shirt, priest's collar, tan summer jacket. He wears
spectacles. There are clocks that make noise and sound the hour in his office
and outside church bells sound during the interview, loud. Throughout the*

talk he is trying to get the corner of a calendar to stay down, but it continues
to stick up. Finally he uses a paperweight to keep it down.)

You can't have that kind of accident
if people are observing the speed limits.
People knew it was the Grand Rebbe.
People have seen the Grand Rebbe
charging through the community.
He is worried
about a threat on his life
from the Satmars.
These Lubavitcher people
are really very,
uh, enigmatic people.
They move so easily between
simplicity and sophistication.
Because
they fear for his life,   ·
because the Satmars
who are their sworn enemies

(He laughs/chuckles)

have threatened to *kill*
the Rebbe.
So whenever he comes out
he's gotta be *whisked!*
You know like a President
or even better than a President.
He says he's an intuhnational figuh
like a Pope!
I say
then, "Why don't you get the Swiss guards
to escort you
rather than using the police
and taxpayers' money?"
He's gotta be
whisked!
Quickly through the neighborhood.
Can't walk around.
He used to walk.
When I first came here.
Now he doesn't walk at all.
They drive him.
And when he walked
you could tell he was in front

because there was,
he was protected all around
and they spilled out onto the streets
and buses had to stop
because this BIG BAND
had to escort
the Rebbe from his house over there
to the synagogue.
So the Rebbe goes to the cemetery.
Every time the Rebbe goes to the cemetery,
which is once a week
to visit his wife—dead wife—
and father-in-law,
the police
lead him in escort
charging down the street
at seventy miles an hour in a metropolis—
what do you want?

(Swift increase in volume and suddenly businesslike)

It happened that on this occasion that as they were coming
   back,
uh,
the police car
with its siren,
had gone over a main
intersection with the light
in favor
of the police car.
The Rebbe's Cadillac had passed
when the lights had become amber
and nobody expected the bodyguard van,
uh,
station wagon
to deliberately go through the red light.
So the traffic
that had the right of way kept coming and
BANG!
came the collision and the careening
onto the sidewalk
had to damage whoever was there
and then, um, they were more concerned about licking
   their own

wounds.
Rather than pick
the car off the boy
who died as a result.
And then the ambulance that came—
the Jewish ambulance—
was concerned about the people in the van
while some boy lay dead,
a black boy lay dead on the street.
The people showed their anger,

(Increase in volume)

they burned and whatever else,
upturned
police cars
and looted,
and as a result,
I think in retaliation, murdered one of the Hasidics.
But that was just the match that lit the powder keg.
It's gonna happen again and again.
There's a Mexican standoff right now.
But it's gonna happen again.

Anonymous Man #1

Wa Wa Wa

*(7:00 or 8:00 p.m. Spring. A recreation room at Ebbets Field apartments.
A very handsome young Caribbean American man with dreadlocks, in his
late teens or early twenties, wearing a bright, loose-fitting shirt. The room
is ill equipped. There are a few pieces of broken furniture. It is poorly lit. A
woman, Kym, with dreadlocks and shells in her hair, is at the interview. It
was originally scheduled to be her interview. The Anonymous Young Man
#1 and the other Anonymous Young Man, #2, started by watching the
interview from the side of the room but soon approached me and began to
join in. Anonymous Young Man #1 was the most vocal. Anonymous Young
Man #2 stood lurking in the shadows. A third young man, younger than
both of them, wearing wire spectacles and a blue Windbreaker, who looks
quite like a young Spike Lee, sat silent with his hands and head on the table
the entire time. There is a very bad radio or tape recorder playing music in
the background.)*

What I saw was
she was pushin'
her brother on the bike like
this,
right?
She was pushin'
him
and he kept dippin' around
like he didn't know how
to ride the bike.
So she kept runnin'
and pushin' him to the side.
So she was already runnin'
when the car was comin'.
So I don't know if she was runnin' towards him
because we was watchin' the car
weavin',
and we was goin'
"Oh, yo
it's a Jew man.
He broke the stop light, they never get arrested."
At first we was laughin', man, we was like
you see they do anything
and get away with it,
and then
we saw that he was out of control,
and den
we started regrettin' laughin',
because then
we saw where he was goin'.
First he hit a car, right,
he tore a whole front fender off a car,
and then we was like
Oh
my god,
man, look at the kids,
you know,
so we was already runnin' over there
by the time the accident happened.
That's how we know he was drinkin'
cause he was like
Wa Wa Wa Wa

and I was like
"Yo, man, he's drunk.
Grab him,
grab him.
Don't let him go anywhere."
I said,
"Grab him."
I didn't want him to limp off
in some apartment somewhere
and come back in a different black jacket.
So I was like,
"Grab him,"
and then I was like,
"Is the ambulance comin' for the kids?"
'Cause I been in a lot of confrontations with Jews before
and I know that when they said an ambulance
is comin'
it most likely meant for them.
And they was like,
"oh, oh."
Jews right?
"Ambulance comin', ambulance comin',
calm down, calm down,
God will help them,
God will help them if you believe."
And he was actin' like he was dyin'.
"Wa Aww,
me too,
I'm hurt, I'm hurt, I'm hurt too."
Wan nothin wrong with him,
wan nothin wrong with him.
They say that we beat up on that man
that he had to have stitches because of us.
You don't come out of an accident like that unmarked,
without a scratch.
The most he got from us was slapped
by a little kid.
And here come the ambulance
and I was like, "That's not a city ambulance,"
not like this I was upset right
and I was like,
"YO,
the man is drunk!

He ran a red light!
Y'all ain't gonna do nothin'."
Everybody started comin' around, right,
'cause I was talkin' about
these kids is dyin' man!
I'm talkin' about the skull of the baby is on the ground man!
and he's walkin'!
I was like, "Don't let him get into that ambulance!"
And the Jews,
the Jews
was like private, private ambulance
I was like, "Grab him,"
but my buddies was like,
"We can't touch them."
Nobody wanted to grab him,
nobody wanted to touch him,
An' I was breakin' fool, man,
I was goin' mad,
I couldn't believe it.
Everybody just stood
there,
and that made me cry.
I was cryin'
so I left, I went home and watched the rest of it on TV,
it was too lackadazee
so it was like me, man, instigatin' the whole thing.
I got arrested for it
long after
in Queens.
Can't tell you no more about that,
you know.
Hey, wait a minute,
they got eyes and ears everywhere.
What color is the Israeli flag?
And what color are the police cars?
The man was *drunk*,
I open up his car door,
I was like, when—
I was like, he'd been drinkin'
I know our words don't have no meanin',
as Black people in Crown Heights.
You realize, man,
ain't no justice,

ain't never been no justice,
ain't never gonna be no justice.

Michael S. Miller

"Heil Hitler"

(A large airy office in Manhattan on Lexington in the fifties. Mr. Miller sits behind a big desk in a high-backed swivel chair drinking coffee. He's wearing a yarmulke. Plays with the swizzle stick throughout. There is an intercom in the office, so that when the receptionist calls him, you can hear it, and when she calls others in other offices, you can hear it, like a page in a public place, faintly.)

I was at Gavin Cato's funeral,
at nearly every public event
that was conducted by the Lubavitcher community and
    the Jewish
community as a whole
words of comfort
were offered to the family of Gavin Cato.
I can show you a letter that we sent
to the Cato family expressing, uh,
our sorrow over the loss,
unnecessary loss, of their son.
I am not aware of a word
that was spoken at that funeral.
I am not aware of a—
and I was taking notes—
of a word that was uttered
of comfort to the family of Yankele Rosenbaum.
Frankly this was a political rally rather than a funeral.
The individuals you mentioned—
and again,
I am not going to participate in verbal acrimony,
not only
were there cries of, "Kill the Jews"
or,
"Kill the Jew,"
there were cries of, "Heil Hitler."
There were cries of, "Hitler didn't finish the job."
There were cries of,
"Throw them back into the ovens again."

To hear in *Crown Heights*—
and Hitler was no lover of Blacks—
"Heil Hitler"?
"Hitler didn't finish the job"?
"We should heat up the ovens"?
From *Blacks?*
Is more inexplicable
or unexplainable
or any other word that I cannot fathom.
The hatred is so
deep seated
and the hatred
knows no boundaries.
There is no boundary
to anti-Judaism.
The anti-*Judaism*—
if people don't want me
to use,
hear me use the word anti-Semitism.
And I'll be damned if,
if preferential treatment is gonna
be the excuse
for every bottle,
rock,
or pellet that's, uh, directed
toward a Jew
or the window of a Jewish home
or a Jewish store.
And, frankly,
I think the response of the Lubavitcher community was
  relatively
passive.

Henry Rice

Knew How to Use Certain Words

*(Thursday, November 21, 1991. The Jackson Hole restaurant on Lexington
Avenue in the thirties in Manhattan. Lunchtime, dimly lit, a reddish haze
on everything, perhaps from a neon light. Mr. Rice, very neatly dressed, is
eating a large, messy hamburger and horizontally chopped pickles. Drinking
a Miller Lite. Beer is in a bottle next to a red plastic glass. He's wearing*

a baseball cap over very closely cut hair and a bright, multicolored, expen-
sive-looking colored nylon jacket. Heavy new Timberland boots. Struggling
to eat without making a mess of the food. At some point sits up from food
and has his right hand or fist on his hip—a very unaffected but truly
authoritative stance. Good-natured, handsome, healthy. Patsy Cline's "Crazy"
is very loud on the jukebox.)

I went back home and got my bike
because I knew I would have to be
illusive.
I was there in body and in spirit
but I didn't participate in any of the violence
because basically I have a lot to lose.
But I was there
and I would have defended myself if it was necessary,
most definitely.
I weaved around trouble.
When something broke out, I moved back,
when it calmed down, I would move back in on the front line.
I was always there.
And Richard Green heard me saying something to a bunch of kids
about *voting*
about the power of *vote*
the power of *numbers*
and he said,
uh,
I said, "Get away from me, you're an Uncle Tom,
get away from me.
Get back in your Mercedes-Benz!"
No! I said that to Clarence Norman
and to Richard Green,
both of them.
I was tearing them apart.
Richard Green was very persistent.
He said,
"Look, Mr. Rice,
I like the way you speak.
I need you.
Please help me.
I'm a community activist . . . .
ba, ba, ba, ba, ba."

(He drops some food on his clothes, or so it seems, he looks and grins)

It didn't get on me.
"I'm a community activist.

I need your help,
please help me,"
and so forth.
Again,
I didn't pay him no mind
but we spoke
some
the next day after that,
after the incidents that took place on that corner
of Albany Avenue.
A brother was beat up—
cops rushing into the Black crowd
didn't rush into the Jewish crowd,
cops rushed into the Black crowd
started beatin' up
Black people.
But the next day Richard came by in a yellow van,
a New York City Department of Transportation van,
with a megaphone,
yellow light flashing,

*(Music segues from Patsy Cline's "Crazy" to Public Enemy's
"Can't Truss It," or Naughty by Nature's "O.P.P.")*

the whole works
and, um,
he said,
"Henry, I need you in this van.
Drive around with me.
Let's keep some of these kids off the street tonight."
I said, "Okay."
He said,
"The blood
of Black men are on your hands tonight!"
I said, "Okay."
We drive around in the van,
"Young people stay in the house!
Mothers keep your children in the house,
please."
So I began fillin'
I began feeling like
I had to do it
after he told me that,
"the blood of the Black man"
were on my hands,

you know.
Richard Green sure know how to use certain words.

(He giggles)

I remember reaching Albany Avenue—
kids were being chased by the police.
I jump out with a portable megaphone,
I tell them, "Stop running!
The cops won't chase you!
And they won't hit you!"
The next thing I know,
cop grabs my megaphone hits me in the head with a stick,
handcuffs me,
and takes the megaphone out of my hand.
So I'm like,
"Wait a minute
I'm doing a community service for the mayor's office."
They don't want to hear it.
Matter of fact,
they still have the megaphone 'til this day.
I'm like,
"Richard Green get me
out of this police car, please!"
So a Black captain came by,
thank God,
and he says, "What's goin' on?"
Richard Green explained it to him.
He said, "Let him go."
Get back in the van,
there's another Brother in the van,
starts saying,
"Non violence!"
to the young Brothers.
They begin throwing bottles at the, uh,
at the van.
One guy got so upset
he had a nine-millimeter
fully loaded.
He said, "Get the hell out of this neighborhood!"
I told Richard Green, "Take me on home. Shit!"
The next day
more violence:
fires,

cars being burnt,
stores being broken into,
a perception that Black youth
are going crazy in Crown Heights
like we were angry over
nothing,
understand?

Norman Rosenbaum

My Brother's Blood:

(A Sunday afternoon. Spring. Crisp, clear, and windy. Across from City Hall in New York City. Crowds of people, predominantly Lubavitcher, with placards. A rally that was organized by Lubavitcher women. All of the speakers were men, but the women stand close to the stage. Mr. Rosenbaum, an Australian, with a beard, hat, and wearing a pinstripe suit, speaks passionately and loudly from the microphone on a stage with a podium. Behind him is a man in an Australian bush hat with a very large Australian flag which blows dramatically in the wind. It is so windy that Mr. Rosenbaum has to hold his hat to keep it on his head.)

Al do lay achee so achee aylay alo dalmo
My brother's blood cries out from the ground.
Let me make it clear
why I'm here.
In August of 1991,
as you all have heard before today,
my brother was killed in the streets of Crown Heights
for no other reason
than that he was a Jew!
The only miracle was
that my brother was the only victim
who paid for being a Jew with his life.
When my brother was surrounded,
each and every American was surrounded.
When my brother was stabbed four times,
each and every American was stabbed four times
and as my brother bled to death in this city,
while the medicos stood by
and let him bleed
to death, it was the gravest of indictments against this
country.

One person out of twenty gutless individuals
who attacked my brother has been arrested.
I for one am not convinced that it is beyond the ability of
   the New York police
to arrest others.
Let me tell you, Mayor Dinkins,
let me tell you, Commissioner Brown:
I'm here,
I'm not going home,
until there is justice.

Norman Rosenbaum

Sixteen Hours Difference

(7:00 a.m. Spring. Newark Airport, Departure Gate, Continental Airlines. Mr. Rosenbaum is moments before his flight to LA and then back to Australia. Wearing a pinstripe suit with an Australian fit. Hat. Suitcase. He has sparkling blue eyes with a twinkle, rosy cheeks, and a large smile throughout the interview.)

There's sixteen hours difference between New York and
   Melbourne
and I had just gotten back to my office
and I had a phone call from my wife,
and she said she wanted me to come home straight away
and I sensed the urgency in her voice.
I said, "are you all right?" She said, "Yeah."
I said, "are the children all right, you know the kids?" She
   says, "yeah."
So I'm driving home and I'm thinking, I wonder what's
   the problem now, you know?
We had some carpenters doing some work, I wonder if
   there has been a disaster,
some sort of domestic problem,
and I thought, oh my God, you know, my parents,
I didn't even ask after them,
how insensitive not to even ask after my parents,
and I've got a grandmother eighty-five years old, same
   sort of thing.
So I get home,
I walk to the door,
and a friend of mine was standing there,

close friend,
does the same sort of work as me, he's a barrister and an
    academic,
and he sees me and he says,
"There's got a pro-
uh,
we've got a problem.
There's a problem."
I thought he was talking about a case we were working on
    together,
he says, "'Z come,
come and sit down."
He goes to me,
"There's been a riot in New York,
been a riot in Crown Heights,
Yankel's been stabbed and he's dead."
And
my brother was the last in the world,
I hadn't even given him a thought.
I mean the fact that my brother
could be attacked
or die,
it just hadn't even entered my mind.
At first I appeared all cool, calm and collected.
I then
started asking questions
like who told you,
how do you know,
are you sure?
I just asked the question,
you know,
are you sure?

Anonymous Young Man #2

Bad Boy

*(Evening. Spring. The same recreation room as interview with Anonymous
Young Man #1. Young Man #2 is wearing a black jacket over his clothes.
He has a gold tooth. He has some dreadlocks, and a very odd-shaped multicolored hat. He is soft-spoken, and has a direct gaze. He seems to be very
patient with his explanation.)*

That youth,
that sixteen-year-old
didn't murder that Jew.

(Pause)

For one thing,
he played baseball, right?
He was a atha-lete,
right?
A bad boy
does
bad things.
Only a bad boy coulda stabbed the man.
Somebody who
does those type of things,
or who sees
those types a things.
A atha-lete
sees people,
is interested in athletics,
stretchin',
exercisin',
goin' to his football games,
or his baseball games.
He's not interested
in stabbin'
people.
So
it's not in his mind
to stab,
to just jump into somethin',
that he has no idea about
and
sta-
and kill a man.
A bad boy,
somebody who's groomed in badness,
or did badness
before,
stabbed the man.
Because I used to be a atha-lete
and I used to be a bad boy,
and when I was a atha-lete,
I was a atha-lete.

All I thought about was atha-lete.
I'm not gonna jeopardize my athleticism
or my career to do anything
that bad people do.
And when I became a bad boy
I'm not a athalete no more.
I'm a bad boy,
and I'm groomin' myself in things that is bad.
You understand, so
he's a athalete,
he's not a bad boy.
It's a big difference.
Like,
mostly the Black youth in Crown Heights have two things
    to do—
either DJ or be a bad boy, right?
You either
DJ, be a MC, a rapper
or Jamaican rapper,
ragamuffin,
or you be a bad boy,
you sell drugs or you rob people.
What do you do?
I sell drugs.
What do you do?
I rap.
That's how it is in Crown Heights.
I been livin' in Crown Heights mosta my life.
I know for a fact that that youth, that sixteen-year-old,
didn't kill that Jew.
That's between me and my Creator.

Sonny Carson

Chords

(Lunchtime. Spring. A fancy restaurant in Brooklyn. Sonny tells me it's where all the judges come for lunch. White linen tablecloths. Light wood walls, lamplight next to the table. Tile floor. He is eating crab cakes. He is dressed in a black turtleneck and a gray jacket. He has on a mud cloth hat. He has an authority stick with him, and it lays on the table. His bodyguard, wearing a black leather jacket, enters in the middle of the interview. Sonny chides him for being late.)

It's going to be a long hot summer.
I'm connected up with the young people all over the country
and there's a thread
leading to an eruption
and Crown Heights began the whole thing.
And the Jews come second to the police
when it comes to feelings of dislike among Black folks.
The police,
the police,
believe me, the police—
I know the police and the police know me
and they turned that whole place into an occupied camp
with the Seventy-first Precinct as the overseers.
And don't think that everything is OK within that precinct
    among those officers
either.
Don't think that,
don't think that.
You know the media has always painted me as the bad
    guy—
that's OK!
I'm a good guy to pick on.
Their viewers don't like me either,
they really don't like me because I *am* the bad guy,
I am the ultimate bad guy
because of my relationship to the young people in the city.
I understand their language.
I respect them as the future.
I speak their language. They don't even engage in long
    dialogue
anymore
just short.
"Words."
It always amazes me
how the city fathers,
the power brokers,
just continue to deny what's happening.
And it is just getting intolerable for me to continue to watch
this small
arrogant
group of people continue to get this kind of preferential
    treatment.
They sit on the school board.
A board of nine

and they have
four members, and their kids don't even go to public
   school.
So that's the kind of arrogance I'm talking about.
I have no reason to be eagerly awaiting the coming
   together of our
people.
They owe me first.
I'm not givin' in just like that,
I don't want it.
You can have it.
Like my grandmother said,
"Help the bear!
If you see me and the bear in a fight,
help the bear—
don't help me,
help the bear."
I don't need any of it from them!
And I'm not gonna advocate any coming together and
   healing of
America
and all that shit.
You kiddin'?
You kiddin'?
Just 'cause I can have the fortune of walking in here
and sitting and talking
and having a drink,
it appear that I have all the same kinds of abilities
of other folks in here.
No, it's not that way.
'Cause tonight
by nighttime it could all change for me.
So I'm always aware of that, and that's what keeps me goin'
today
and each day!

(He eats)

I have
this idea
about a film.
See,
these kids, they got
another kinda rhythm now,
there's a whole new kinda

step that they do.
When I first heard rap
I was sittin' in a huge open kinda stadium,
boys and girls high school field,
and I heard these kids come out and start rappin',
and I'm listening
but it's not really clickin',
but I was mesmerized though.
But it was simultaneous
all around the country
and I said, "Oh shit,"
and everybody I knew who was young was listenin' to it
and I said, "Wow."
Because I have always been involved with young people
and all of a sudden I got it,
I really heard the rhythm,
the chords,
the discord.
There's a whole new sound
that the crackers are tryin' to get, but they can't get it.
I heard it on a television commercial.
One of the most beautiful pieces of art
that I ever witnessed
was a play
called
um,
um,
um,
'bout, 'bout the Puerto Rican gang—
no, no, no, no, no—
the Puerto Rican gang,
the musical
that was on Broad—
yeah,
West Side Story—
the answer should be
a musical.

Rabbi Shea Hecht

Ovens

(Morning. Spring. A building on Eastern Parkway. A large room with a very long conference table. There are pictures of Lubavitcher men on the

walls. Rabbi Hecht is wearing a shirt, open at the neck. He has several crisp one-dollar bills in his shirt pocket. These are, apparently, dollar bills that the Rebbe has given him. It is the custom that the Rebbe gives out one-dollar bills on Sunday. Rabbi Hecht has a beard. He wears glasses, traditional Hasidic garb, including tsitses (ceremonial fringes that hang over his belt) and a red yarmulke with gold trim which is ripped. His daughter comes in frequently to get money from him. He keeps telling her to wait until he is finished. She becomes more and more agitated. His brother also enters frequently to ask him questions, and to tell him he's late.)

What is my goal?
My goal is not
to give anybody a message
that we plan on working things out
by integrating
our two
things.
By a person understanding more of their own religion
they will automatically respect another person.
The respect that my religion teaches me has nothing to do
with understanding you.
See, there's a problem.
If
the only way I'm going to respect you
is based on how much I understand you,
no matter what it is
in certain circles you're gonna run into problems.
Number one,
we are different,
and we think we should and can be different.
When the Rebbe said to the Mayor
that we were all
one people,
I think
what the Rebbe is talking about is that,
that common denominator that we're all children of God,
   and the
respect we all have to give each other under that banner.
But that does not mean that I have to invite you to my
   house for
dinner,
because I cannot go back to your home for dinner,
because you're not gonna give me kosher food.
And I said,
so, like one Black said,

I'll bring in kosher food.
I said eh-eh.
We can't use your ovens,
we can't use your dishes,
it's, it—
it's not just a question of buying certain food,
it's buying the food,
preparing it a certain way.
We can't use your dishes, we can't use your oven.
The—the higher you go
the more common denominator.
And what the Rebbe was saying,
you as the Mayor
don't get caught up in the differences,
you're—
from your position is—
you have to look at it as one city
and one
human race.
We are all New Yorkers
and therefore I will protect all New Yorkers.
You see
preferential treatment
suggests
that you're giving the person
the police car
not because they need the police car
but because
they are who they are.
You're not gonna
give them the housing
because they
need the housing—
you're giving it because of who they are.
But
just because I'm a Jew
therefore I
shouldn't get the police car.
The question is
a synagogue
that has five thousand Jews
leave
the synagogue
at the same time,

do they have a police car to stop the traffic?
The answer is every-single—synagogue,
temple,
mosque,
in
the
world
stops traffic
when five thousand people have to walk out
at the same time.

The Reverend Al Sharpton

Rain

(*As before.*)
The D.A.
came back with no indictment.
Uh, so then our only course
was to ask for a special prosecutor
which is appointed by the Governor,
who's been hostile,
and to sue civilly.
When we went into civil court
we went to get an order to show cause.
The judge signed it and gave me a deadline of three days.
The driver left the country. . . .
No one even said, "Why would he run?
If he did no wrong."
If you and I were in an accident we'd have to go to civil court.
Why is this man
above the law?
So they said, "He's in Israel."
So I said,
"Well, I'll go to Israel to show best effits."
And the deadline
was,
I had to serve him by Tuesday,
which was Yom Kippur—
that was the judge's decision not mine.
So we went.
Alton Maddox and I
got on a plane,
left Monday night,

landed Tuesday morning,
went and served the American embassy, uh,
so that
if this man had any decency at all
he could come to the American embassy and receive service,
which he has not done to this day.
Come back,
went to court
and showed the judge the receipts,
and the judge said, "You made best effits,
therefore you are now permitted,
by default,
to go ahead
and sue the rabbi or whomever
because you cannot do the driver."
So it wasn't just a media grandstand.
We wanted to show the world
one, this man *ran*
and was *allowed* to run, and, two, we wanted to be able to
    legally go
around him,
to sue the people he was working for so that we can bring
    them into
court and establish *why* and what happened.
And it came out in the paper the other day
that the driver in the other car didn't even have a driver's
    license.
So we're dealing with a *complete* outrage here,
we're dealing with a double standard,
we're dealing with uh, uh, a, a
situation where
Blacks do not have equal protection under the law
and the media is used to castigate us
that merely asked for justice
rather than castigate those that would hit a kid
and walk away like he just stepped on a roach!
Uh,
there also is the media
contention of the young Jewish scholar
that was stabbed that night
and they've even distorted
saying *my words at the funeral.*
I *preached* the funeral.
Uh, [the newspaper said I]

helped to, to, uh, uh,
spark or, or, or, or, or *inspire* or *incite* people to kill him
   [Yankel Rosenbaum]
when he was dead the day before
I came out there.
He was killed the night
that the young man
was killed with the car accident.
I didn't even get a call
from the family
'til eighteen hours later.
So there's a whole media distortion
to protect them [the Lubavitchers].
Nobody is talking about,
"Why
is this guy
in flight?"
If I was a rabbi
(I am a ministuh)
and my driver hit a kid,
I would not let the driver *leave*
and I certainlih would give my condolences,
or anything else I could,
to the family,
I don't care what race they are.
To this minute the Rebbe has never even uttered a word of
sympathy
to the family,
not even sent 'em a *card*
a *flower* or *nothing*!
And he's supposed to be a religious leader.
So it's treating us with absolute contempt
and I don't care how controversial it makes us.
I *won't* tolerate being insulted.
If you piss in my face I'm gonna call it *piss*.
I'm not gonna call it rain.

Richard Green

Rage

*(2:00 p.m. in a big red van. Green is in the front. He has a driver. I am
in the back. Green wears a large knit hat with reggae colors over long*

dreadlocks. Driving from Crown Heights to Brooklyn College. He turns
sideways to face me in the back, and bends down, talking with his elbow on
his knee.)

Sharpton, Carson, and Reverend Herbert Daughtry
didn't have any power out there really.
The media gave them power.
But they weren't turning those youfs on and off.
Nobody knew who controlled the switch out there.
Those young people had rage like an oil-well fire
that has to burn out.
All they were doin' was sort of orchestratin' it.
Uh, they were not really the ones that were saying, "Well
stop, go, don't go, stop, turn around, go up."
It wasn't like that.
Those young people had rage out there,
that didn't matter who was in control of that—
that rage had to get out
and that rage
has been building up.
When all those guys have come and gone,
that rage is still out here.
I can show you that rage every day
right up and down this avenue.
We see, sometimes in one month, we see three bodies
in one month. That's rage,
and that's something that nobody has control of.
And I don't know who told you that it was preferential
    treatment for
Blacks that the Mayor kept the cops back. . . .
If the Mayor had turned those cops on?
We would still be in a middle of a battle.
And
I pray on both sides of the fence,
and I tell the people in the Jewish community the same thing.
"This is not something that force will hold."
Those youfs were running on cops without nothing in their hands,
seven- and eight- and nine- and ten-year-old boys were running at
those cops
with nothing,
just running at 'em.
That's rage.
Those young people out there are angry
and that anger has to be vented,

it has to be negotiated.
And they're not angry at the Lubavitcher community
they're just as angry at you and me,
if it comes to that.
They have no
role models,
no guidance
so they're just out there growin' up on their own,
their peers are their role models,
their peers is who teach them how to move
so when they see the Lubavitchers
they don't know the difference between "Heil Hitler"
and, uh, and uh, whatever else.
They don't know the difference.
When you ask 'em to say who Hitler was they wouldn't even be able
to tell you.
Half of them don't even know.
Three quarters of them don't even know.

(Phone rings, Richard picks it up, it's a mobile phone)

"Richard Green, can I help?
Aw, man I tol' you I want some color
up on that wall. Give me some colors.
Look, I'm in the middle of somethin'."

(He returns to the conversation)

Half them don't even know three quarters of 'em.
Just as much as they don't know who Frederick Douglass was.
They know Malcolm
because Malcolm has been played up to such an extent now
that they know Malcolm.
But ask who Nat Turner was or Mary McCleod Bethune or
    Booker T.
Because the system has given 'em
Malcolm is convenient and
Spike is goin' to give 'em Malcolm even more.
It's convenient.

Roslyn Malamud

The Coup

(Spring. Midafternoon. The sunny kitchen of a huge, beautiful house on Eastern Parkway in Crown Heights. It's a large, very well-equipped kitchen.

We are sitting at a table in a breakfast nook area, which is separated by shelves from the cooking area. There is a window to the side. There are newspapers on the chair at the far side of the table. Mrs. Malamud offers me food at the beginning of the interview. We are drinking coffee. She is wearing a sweatshirt with a large sequined cat. Her tennis shoes have matching sequined cats. She has on a black skirt and is wearing a wig. Her nails are manicured. She has beautiful eyes that sparkle, are very warm, and a very resonant voice. There is a lot of humor in her face.)

Do you know what happened in August here?
You see when you read the newspapers.
I mean my son filmed what was going on,
but when you read the newspapers . . .
Of course I was here
I couldn't leave my house.
I only would go out early during the day.
The police were barricading here.
You see,
I wish
I could just like
go on television.
I wanna scream to the whole world.
They said
that the Blacks were rioting against the Jews in Crown Heights
and that the Jews were fighting back.
Do you know that the Blacks who came here to riot were not my neighbors?
I don't love my neighbors.
I don't know my Black neighbors.
There's one lady on President Street—
Claire—
I adore her.
She's my girl friend's next-door neighbor.
I've had a manicure
done in her house and we sit and kibbitz
and stuff
but I don't know them.
I told you we don't mingle socially
because of the difference
of food
and religion
and what have you here.
But
the people in this community

want exactly
what I want out of life.
They want to live
in nice homes.
They all go to work.
They couldn't possibly
have houses here
if they didn't
generally—They have
two,
um,
incomes
that come in.
They want to send their kids to college.
They wanna live a nice quiet life.
They wanna shop for their groceries and cook their meals and go to
their Sunday picnics!
They just want to have decent homes and decent lives!
The people who came to riot here
were brought here
by this famous
Reverend Al Sharpton,
which I'd like to know who ordained him?
He brought in a bunch of kids
who didn't have jobs in
the summertime.
I wish you could see *The New York Times,*
unfortunately it was on page twenty,
I mean, they interviewed
one of the Black girls on Utica Avenue.
She said,
"The guys will make you pregnant
at night
and in the morning not know who you are."

(Almost whispering)

And if you're sitting on a front stoop and it's very, very hot
and you have no money
and you have nothing to do with your time
and someone says, "Come on, you wanna riot?"
You know how kids are.
The fault lies with the police department.
The police department did nothing to stop them.
I was sitting here in the front of the house

when bottles were being thrown
and the sergeant tells five hundred policemen
with clubs and helmets and guns
to duck.
And I said to him,
"You're telling them to duck?
What should I do?
I don't have a club and a gun."
Had they put it—
stopped it on the first night
this kid who came from Australia . . .

(She sucks her teeth)

You know,
his parents were Holocaust survivors, he didn't have to die.
He worked,
did a lot of research in Holocaust studies.
He didn't have to die.
What happened on Utica Avenue
was an accident.
JEWISH PEOPLE
DO NOT DRIVE VANS INTO SEVEN-YEAR-OLD BOYS.
YOU WANT TO KNOW SOMETHING? BLACK PEOPLE
    DO NOT DRIVE
VANS INTO SEVEN-YEAR-OLD BOYS.
HISPANIC PEOPLE DON'T DRIVE VANS INTO
    SEVEN-YEAR OLD BOYS.
IT'S JUST NOT DONE.
PEOPLE LIKE JEFFREY DAHMER MAYBE THEY DO IT.
BUT AVERAGE CITIZENS DO NOT GO OUT AND TRY
    TO KILL.

(Sounds like a laugh but it's just a sound)

SEVEN-YEAR-OLD BOYS.
It was an accident!
But it was allowed to fester and to steam and all that.
When you come here do you see anything that's going on, riots?
No.
But Al Sharpton and the likes of him like *Dowerty,*
who by the way has been in prison
and all of a sudden he became Reverend *Dowerty*—
they once did an exposé on him—
but
these guys live off of this,

you understand?
People are not gonna give them money,
contribute to their causes
unless they're out there rabble-rousing.
My Black neighbors?
I mean I spoke to them.
They were hiding in their houses just like I was.
We were scared.
I was scared!
I was really frightened.
I had five hundred policemen standing in front of my house
every day
I had mounted police,
but I couldn't leave my block,
because when it got dark I couldn't come back in.
I couldn't meet anyone for dinner.
Thank God, I told you my children were all out of town.
My son was in Russia.
The coup
was exactly the same day as the riot
and I was very upset about it.
He was in Russia running a summer camp
and I was very concerned when I had heard about that.
I hadn't heard from him
that night the riot started.
When I did hear from him I told him to stay in Russia,
     he'd be safer
there than here.
And he was.

Reuven Ostrov

Pogrom

(9:00 p.m. November 1991. In a basement of a Crown Heights house. Mr. Ostrov wears a yarmulke. Eating popcorn and sliced apples. Very low, gentle-sounding nigunim music plays in the background, it almost sounds like New Age music, perhaps because traditional music is played on a modern electronic keyboard instrument. In the show, I wore a basketball jacket with project CURE's insignia, which Mr. Ostrov did not do at this interview, but previously had at a basketball game. He is clean-shaven, which is unusual for a Lubavitcher man his age. He had chosen to shave his beard. He has a very rich, deep voice.)

I was working in a hospital.
I work as an assistant chaplain at
Down State Kings County Hospital.
I heard that Yankel Rosenbaum was stabbed and, um, they
were gonna give him an *aurtopsy*
and they asked if he had an
aurtopsy
or not because in the Jewish religion a person is not
allowed to have
an aurtopsy
and I found out later that he did have one
a few days later.
I found a Jewish man in a room,
a Russian man.
His mother committed suicide
because she was, uhm, she was terrified.
She jumped out of the third floor of her apartment building,
committed suicide.
The mother originally came from Russia.
I was speaking to her son
in one of the rooms near the morgue
trying to get his mother not to have an aurtopsy
and he was telling me that the mother
came from Russia eleven years ago
and the mother left Russia eleven years ago
because of the hardships that they had over there,
and when they came to America
and when this thing started to happen in Crown Heights.
It became painful
and it felt like, like there was no place to go.
It's like you're trapped,
everywhere you go there's Jew haters.
And then he told me she commit suicide,
told me the next morning he woke up
he heard the doorbell ring.
He wasn't,
she wasn't there.
He noticed that the window was open,
which is never open
because she was afraid of the cold
even in the summertime.
And he saw his mother
with blood all over her

landed head first
on the concrete side of the apartment building.
After that we already knew this was getting serious,
because we had,
we had Sonny Carson come down
and we had, um,
Reverend Al Sharpton come down
start making pogroms.

Carmel Cato

Lingering

(7:00 p.m. The corner where the accident occurred in Crown Heights. An altar to Gavin is against the wall where the car crashed. Many pieces of cloth are draped. Some writing in color is on the wall. Candle wax is everywhere. There is a rope around the area. Cato is wearing a trench coat, pulled around him. He stands very close to me. Dark outside. Reggae music is in the background. Lights come from stores on each corner. Busy intersection. Sounds from outside. Traffic. Stores open. People in and out of shops. Sounds from inside apartments, televisions, voices, cooking, etc. He speaks in a pronounced West Indian accent.)

In the meanwhile
it was two.
Angela was on the ground
but she was trying to move. Gavin was still.
They was trying to pound him.
I was the father.
I was 'it, chucked, and pushed,
and a lot of
sarcastic words were passed towards me
from the police
while I was trying to explain: It was my kid!
These are my children.
The child was hit you know.
I saw everything, everything,
the guy radiator burst
all the hoses,
the steam,
all the garbage buckets goin' along the building.
And it was very loud,

everything burst.
It's like an atomic bomb.
That's why all these people
comin' round
wanna know what's happening.
Oh it was very outrageous.
Numerous numbers.
All the time the police sayin'
you can't get in,
you can't pass,
and the children laying on the ground.
He was hit at exactly eight-thirty.
Why?
I was standing over there.
There was a little child—
a friend of mine
came up with a little child—
and I lift the child up
and she look at her watch at the same time
and she say it was eight-thirty.
I gave the child back to her.
And then it happen.
Um, um . . .
My child, these are the things I never dream about.
I take care of my children.
You know it's a funny thing,
if a child get sick and he dies
it won't hurt me so bad,
or if a child run out into the street and get hit down,
it wouldn't hurt me.
That's what's hurtin' me.
The whole week
before Gavin died
my body was changing,
I was having different feelings.
I stop eating,
I didn't et nothin',
only drink water,
for two weeks;
and I was very touchy—
any least thing that drop
or any song I hear
it would effect me.

Every time I try to do something
I would have to stop.
I was
lingering, lingering, lingering, lingering,
all the time.
But I can do things,
I can see things,
I know that for a fact.
I was telling myself,
"Something is wrong somewhere,"
but I didn't want to see,
I didn't want to accept,
and it was inside of me,
and even when I go home I tell my friends,
"Something coming I could feel it
but I didn't want to see,"
and all the time I just deny deny deny,
and I never thought it was Gavin,
but I didn't have a clue.
I thought it was one of the other children—
the bigger boys
or the girl,
because she worry me,
she won't et—
but Gavin 'ee was 'ealtee,
and he don't cause no trouble.
That's what's devastating me now.
Sometime it make me feel like it's no justice,
like, uh,
the Jewish people,
they are very high up,
it's a very big thing,
they runnin' the whole show
from the judge right down.
And something I don't understand:
The Jewish people, they told me
there are certain people I cannot be seen with
and certain things I can not say
and certain people I can not talk to.
They made that very clear to me—the Jewish people—
they can throw the case out
unless
I go to them with pity.

I don't know what they talkin' about.
So I don't know what kind of crap is that.
And make me say things I don't wanna say
and make me do things I don't wanna do.
I am a special person.
I was born different.
I'm a man born by my foot.
I born by my foot.
Anytime a baby comin' by the foot
they either cut the mother
or the baby dies.
But I was born with my foot.
I'm one of the special.
There's no way they can overpower me.
No there's nothing to hide,
you can repeat every word I say.